MICROSOFT® OFFICE®
AND BEYOND

MICROSOFT OFFICE AND BEYOND
Computer Concepts and Applications

Theodor Richardson

Charles Thies

MERCURY LEARNING AND INFORMATION
Dulles, Virginia
Boston, Massachusetts

Publisher: David Pallai

MERCURY LEARNING AND INFORMATION
22841 Quicksilver Drive
Dulles, VA 20166
info@merclearning.com
www.merclearning.com
1-800-758-3756

This book is printed on acid-free paper.

Theodor Richardson and Charles Thies.
MICROSOFT OFFICE AND BEYOND: *Computer Concepts and Applications.*
ISBN: 978-1-9364202-9-2

The publisher recognizes and respects all marks used by companies, manufacturers, and developers as a means to distinguish their products. All brand names and product names mentioned in this book are trademarks or service marks of their respective companies. Any omission or misuse (of any kind) of service marks or trademarks, etc. is not an attempt to infringe on the property of others.

Library of Congress Control Number: 2011932079

111213321

Printed in Canada

Our titles are available for adoption, license, or bulk purchase by institutions, corporations, etc. For additional information, please contact the Customer Service Dept. at 1-800-758-3756 (toll free).

To my mother, Deborah Richardson; she is my calm voice of reason and one of the strongest people I have ever known. I am blessed to have you as my mother, and I love you very much.

— Theodor Richardson

To Nestor Garcia, my uncle and friend, who always encouraged me to work hard and to pursue my dreams. You are missed by all who knew you, and we will not forget your courage and perseverance to the end.

— Charles Thies

Contents

Introduction   xix

Acknowledgments   xxiii

Section I: The Computer Environment

1. Introduction to Computer Concepts   1

In This Chapter

1.1 What is a Computer?   2

    1.1.1 Computer Software   2

    1.1.2 Computer Hardware   3

1.2 History and Background of Computing Technology   4

1.3 Purchasing a New Computer System   4

1.4 Windows Personal Computer Basics   7

1.5 Macintosh Computer Basics   9

1.6 How the Computer Works   11

    1.6.1 Input Hardware Devices   12

    1.6.2 Output Hardware Devices   13

    1.6.3 Processing Hardware Devices   14

    1.6.4 Data Storage   14

    1.6.5 What Computers Can and Cannot Do   15

1.7 An Introduction to the Windows Operating System   16

1.8 An Introduction to Mac OS X   17

Chapter Summary   20

Chapter Exercises   20

Chapter Knowledge Check   21

2. Navigating the Computer Environment 23

   In This Chapter

   2.1 Navigating the Desktop 24

      2.1.1 The Windows 7 Desktop 24

         2.1.1.1 The Control Panel 25

         2.1.1.2 Desktop Gadgets 26

         2.1.1.3 Jump Lists 27

         2.1.1.4 Task Manager 27

         2.1.1.5 Libraries Feature 27

      2.1.2 The Macintosh OS X Desktop 28

         2.1.2.1 The Finder 29

         2.1.2.2 The Dock 30

         2.1.2.3 The Dashboard, Exposé, and Spaces 31

         2.1.2.4 Force Quit 32

   2.2 Organizing Files and Folders 33

      2.2.1 Files and Folders in Windows 33

      2.2.2 Files and Folders on a Mac 35

   2.3 Working with Files on Your Computer 37

      2.3.1 WordPad on Windows 37

      2.3.2 Text Edit for Macintosh 40

   Chapter Summary 42

   Chapter Exercises 42

   Chapter Knowledge Check 43

3. Working with the Web 45

   In This Chapter

   3.1 Background and Historical Context of the Web 46

      3.1.1 How the Web Works 48

      3.1.2 Connecting to the Internet 51

   3.2 Using a Web Browser to Surf the Web 52

      3.2.1 Microsoft Internet Explorer 52

      3.2.2 Mozilla Firefox 56

      3.2.3 Apple Safari 58

   3.3 Using Search Engines to Find Information on the Web 60

   3.4 Using Web Browser Plug-Ins 62

   3.5 The Web and Fair Use 62

   Chapter Summary 64

   Chapter Exercises 64

   Chapter Knowledge Check 65

4. Microsoft Outlook and E-mail Clients   67

In This Chapter

4.1 Introduction to Electronic Mail   68

4.2 E-mail Structure   68

4.3 E-mail Addresses   70

4.4 Creating a Personal E-mail Account   71

   4.4.1 E-mail Account Types   71

   4.4.2 Microsoft Windows Live Hotmail   72

      4.4.2.1 Creating an Account   72

      4.4.2.2 Navigating and Opening E-mail   74

      4.4.2.3 Composing an E-mail   76

      4.4.2.4 Logging Out and Logging In   77

   4.4.3 Gmail by Google   78

      4.4.3.1 Creating an Account   78

      4.4.3.2 Navigating and Opening E-mail   79

      4.4.3.3 Composing an E-mail   80

      4.4.3.4 Logging Out and Logging In   81

   4.4.4 Creating a Microsoft Windows Live ID   82

4.5 E-mail Clients   83

   4.5.1 Microsoft Windows Live Mail   84

   4.5.2 Macintosh Mail   85

   4.5.3 Mozilla Thunderbird   87

   4.5.4 Connecting to Your E-mail Remotely   90

4.6 Microsoft Outlook   90

   4.6.1 Anatomy of Microsoft Outlook 2010   91

   4.6.2 Anatomy of Microsoft Outlook 2011   92

   4.6.3 Managing E-mail   93

   4.6.4 Managing Calendars   94

   4.6.5 Managing Contacts   96

   4.6.6 Tasks and Notes   97

4.7 E-mail Etiquette   97

Chapter Summary   100

Chapter Exercises   100

Chapter Knowledge Check   101

Section II: Word Processing and Microsoft Word

5. Introduction to Word and Word Processing   103

In This Chapter

5.1 Introduction to Productivity Software   104

5.1.1 The File Menu 105

5.1.2 Document Management 107

5.1.3 Help Files 108

5.1.4 Productivity Shortcuts 108

5.1.5 The System Clipboard 109

5.2 Introduction to Word Processing Software 110

5.3 Anatomy of Microsoft Word 111

5.3.1 Microsoft Word 2010 113

5.3.2 Microsoft Word 2011 115

5.4 Diving into Word Processing 118

5.4.1 Writing a Cover Letter 119

5.4.2 Formatting Text 120

5.4.2.1 The Font Panel 121

5.4.2.2 The Paragraph Panel 124

5.4.2.3 Format Painter 125

5.4.3 Bullets and Numbering 125

5.4.4 Document Review 126

5.4.4.1 Spelling and Grammar 126

5.4.4.2 Thesaurus 128

5.4.4.3 Find and Replace 128

5.4.5 Using Document Templates 129

5.4.6 Writing a Resume 132

5.4.7 Using Headers and Footers 134

5.4.8 Document Types 134

5.5 OpenOffice.org Writer 135

5.5.1 Anatomy of Writer 135

5.5.2 Completing the Cover Letter in Writer 136

5.5.3 Completing the Resume in Writer 138

Chapter Summary 141

Chapter Exercises 141

Chapter Knowledge Check 142

6. Developing and Editing Documents 145

In This Chapter

6.1 Writing a Research Article 146

6.1.1 Outlining the Document 147

6.1.2 Using and Managing Styles 148

6.1.3 Using the Navigation Pane and Document Map Pane 150

6.2 Managing Citations 151

   6.2.1 Footnotes and Endnotes 153

   6.2.2 Creating a Bibliography 155

6.3 Setting a Page Layout 156

   6.3.1 Formatting Columns 158

   6.3.2 Adding Graphic Elements and Captions 158

6.4 Additional Document Elements 160

   6.4.1 Adding a Cover Page 161

   6.4.2 Adding a Table of Contents 162

Chapter Summary 165

Chapter Exercises 165

Chapter Knowledge Check 166

7. Advanced Features of Word Processing   169

In This Chapter

7.1 Mail Merge 170

   7.1.1 Mail Merge in Microsoft Word 2010 171

   7.1.2 Mail Merge in Microsoft Word 2011 174

   7.1.3 Mail Merge in OpenOffice.org Writer 175

7.2 Additional Document Elements 178

   7.2.1 Adding Symbols 179

   7.2.2 Editing Equations 180

   7.2.3 Adding Tables 182

   7.2.4 Adding Shapes 183

7.3 Editing Existing Documents 184

   7.3.1 Document Comparison 184

   7.3.2 Track Changes 185

   7.3.3 Comments 187

Chapter Summary 189

Chapter Exercises 189

Chapter Knowledge Check 190

Section III: Presentation Software and Microsoft PowerPoint

8. Introduction to PowerPoint and Presentation Software   193

In This Chapter

8.1 Introduction to Presentation Software 194

8.2 Anatomy of Microsoft PowerPoint 194

   8.2.1 Microsoft PowerPoint 2010 195

   8.2.2 Microsoft PowerPoint 2011 199

8.3 Diving into Presentations   201

    8.3.1. Text Formatting   201

    8.3.2. Inserting and Formatting Shapes   203

    8.3.3 Inserting, Manipulating, and Cropping Images   206

    8.3.4 Arranging, Linking, and Grouping Elements   209

    8.3.5 Adding Text and Hyperlinks   212

    8.3.6 Clip Art and Screenshots   216

       8.3.6.1   Clip Art in Office 2010   217

       8.3.6.2 Clip Art in Office 2011   217

       8.3.6.3 Getting Clip Art from Office.com   219

       8.3.6.4 Handling Clip Art   219

    8.3.7 Sorting Slides   221

    8.3.8 Inserting Screenshots   222

    8.3.9 Transitions   223

8.4 OpenOffice.org Impress   224

    8.4.1 Anatomy of OpenOffice.org Impress   225

    8.4.2 Completing the Project in Impress   227

Chapter Summary   231

Chapter Exercises   231

Chapter Knowledge Check   232

9. Creating Effective Presentations   235

In This Chapter

9.1 Writing Your Value Proposition   236

9.2 Establishing a Visual Style   236

    9.2.1 Modifying the Slide Master   237

    9.2.2 Planning Your Design   238

    9.2.3 Assigning a Theme   239

    9.2.4 Colors, Fonts, and Effects   239

    9.2.5 Bullets and Numbering   242

    9.2.6 Adding and Formatting Slide Footers   243

    9.2.7 Formatting Text on the Slide Master   244

    9.2.8 Branding Your Slides   246

9.3 Constructing an Effective Presentation   249

    9.3.1 Outlining   250

       9.3.1.1 Adding Slide Notes   250

       9.3.1.2 Best Practices for Outlining   251

    9.3.2 Grabbing Attention in Your First Slide   252

    9.3.3 Build the Need for Your Presentation   253

9.3.4 Present Your Main Contribution 255

    9.3.4.1 Effective Visualization 255

    9.3.4.2 Modifying Layouts 256

    9.3.4.3 Tips for Success 256

9.3.5 Summarize and Conclude 257

9.4 Presenting Your Masterpiece 258

9.4.1. Live Presentations 258

9.4.2. Recording Narration 260

9.4.3. Sharing Your Presentation 261

Chapter Summary 264

Chapter Exercises 264

Chapter Knowledge Check 265

10. Advanced Features of Presentation Software 267

In This Chapter

10.1 Creating Handouts 268

10.1.1 Modifying the Handout Master 269

10.1.2 Modifying the Notes Master 270

10.2 Adding Advanced Media 272

10.2.1 Sound and Video 272

10.2.2 Tables 276

10.2.3 Charts 278

10.2.4 SmartArt 281

10.2.5 Animations 284

10.3 Editing Presentations 287

10.3.1 Opening and Editing Existing Presentations 287

10.3.2 Slide Setup and Slide Orientation 288

10.3.3 Creating a Custom Layout 289

10.3.4 Hiding and Showing Slides 290

10.3.5 Optimizing and Exporting Images from Slides 291

Chapter Summary 292

Chapter Exercises 292

Chapter Knowledge Check 293

Section IV: Spreadsheet Software and Microsoft Excel

11. Introduction to Excel and Spreadsheet Software 295

In This Chapter

11.1 Introduction to Spreadsheet Software 296

11.2 Anatomy of Excel   296

     11.2.1 Microsoft Excel 2010   297

     11.2.2 Microsoft Excel 2011   300

11.3 Diving into Spreadsheets   302

     11.3.1 Adding and Formatting Text   302

     11.3.2 Formatting Values   304

     11.3.3 Using Sequences   305

     11.3.4 Formatting Cells   306

     11.3.5 Freezing Panes   307

     11.3.6 Adding Basic Formulas   309

         11.3.6.1 Mathematical Calculations   309

         11.3.6.2 Freezing Cells in Formulas   310

         11.3.6.3 The SUM Function   310

     11.3.7 Using Directional Fill   311

     11.3.8 Navigating the Spreadsheet   312

11.4 Adding Charts   313

     11.4.1 Chart Data   314

     11.4.2 Formatting Charts   315

11.5 OpenOffice.org Calc   316

     11.5.1 Anatomy of OpenOffice.org Calc   316

     11.5.2 Creating a Budget in Calc   318

     11.5.3 Adding Charts in Calc   320

Chapter Summary   323

Chapter Exercises   323

Chapter Knowledge Check   324

12. Developing Worksheets and Graphic Representations   327

In This Chapter

12.1 Constructing a Worksheet   328

     12.1.1 Merging and Splitting Cells   328

     12.1.2 Adding and Deleting Rows and Columns   329

     12.1.3 Hiding Rows and Columns   330

     12.1.4 Advanced Cell Referencing   330

12.2 List Management   331

     12.2.1 Using Sorting and Filters   332

     12.2.2 Removing Duplicates   334

     12.2.3 Text to Columns   334

     12.2.4 Table Formatting   336

12.3 Additional Formatting Elements 337

    12.3.1 Conditional Formatting 337

    12.3.2 Tab Color 338

    12.3.3 Comments 339

    12.3.4 Text Boxes 340

12.4 Chart Types 340

    12.4.1 Column 341

    12.4.2 Line 342

    12.4.3 Pie 342

    12.4.4 Bar 342

    12.4.5 Area 342

    12.4.6 Scatter 343

Chapter Summary 344

Chapter Exercises 344

Chapter Knowledge Check 345

13. Advanced Features of Spreadsheet Software 347

In This Chapter

13.1 Business Applications 348

13.2 Using Formulas 349

    13.2.1 Common Functions 349

    13.2.2 Text Functions 351

    13.2.3 Value Lookup 352

    13.2.4 IF Statements and Logic 355

    13.2.5 Function Wizard 356

    13.2.6 Calculation Options 357

    13.2.7 Tracing Variables 357

    13.2.8 Data Validation 359

13.3 Subtotals 359

    13.3.1 Grouping Cells 360

    13.3.2 Constructing Subtotals 360

13.4 Pivot Tables 362

    13.4.1 Constructing a Pivot Table 362

    13.4.2 Using Pivot Table Values in Formulas 363

13.5 What If Analysis 365

13.6 External Data Management 366

    13.6.1 External Data Sources 366

    13.6.2 Exporting Data 367

13.7 Arranging the Workspace 367

Chapter Summary 368

Chapter Exercises 368

Chapter Knowledge Check 369

Section V: Database Software and Microsoft Access

14. Introduction to Access and Database Software 371

In This Chapter 371

14.1 Introduction to Access 372

14.2 Working with the Interface 373

  14.2.1 Creating a Database 374

  14.2.2 Creating a Database Table 376

  14.2.3 Working with Design View 378

  14.2.4 Primary Keys 379

  14.2.5 More on Data Types 380

14.3 Data Integrity, Validation, and Good Design Practices 382

  14.3.1 Database Backups 385

  14.3.2 Compressing and Repairing the Database 385

14.4 Building Tables in OpenOffice.org Base 386

Chapter Summary 392

Chapter Exercises 392

Chapter Knowledge Check 393

15. Developing Relationships, Queries, and Reports 395

In This Chapter 395

15.1 Working with Relationships in Microsoft Access 398

  15.1.1 Defining Relationships 398

15.2 Data Manipulation Using Queries 404

  15.2.1 Basic Queries 404

  15.2.2 Using Query Design to Develop Queries 405

  15.2.3 Working with SQL View 407

  15.2.4 Implementing Inner and Outer Joins 407

15.3 Learning to Develop Reports 410

15.4 Understanding OpenOffice.org Base Relationships 411

  15.4.1 Developing Queries in Base 413

  15.4.2 Developing Reports in Base 413

Chapter Summary 414

Chapter Exercises 414

Chapter Knowledge Check 415

16. Developing the User Interface and Sharing Your Database   417

  In This Chapter   417

  16.1 Developing a Simple Form   418

      16.1.1 Using Forms to Add, Delete, and Print Records   419

  16.2 Using OpenOffice.org Base Forms   423

  16.3 Sharing Your Access Database with Others   428

  Chapter Summary   431

  Chapter Exercises   431

  Chapter Knowledge Check   432

Appendices

A. Additional Productivity Software   435

  A.1 Adobe® Reader®   435

      A.1.1 Portable Document Format (PDF)   435

      A.1.2 Adobe Reader Tools   436

          A.1.2.1 Adobe Reader X for Windows   437

          A1.2.2 Adobe Reader 9 for Macintosh   438

  A.2 Microsoft OneNote for Windows   439

      A.2.1 Anatomy of Microsoft OneNote 2010   439

      A.2.2 Adding and Organizing Media and Notes   441

      A.2.3 Linked Notes   441

      A.2.4 Printing to OneNote   442

      A.2.5 Saving and Sharing Notebooks   443

  A.3 Microsoft Word Notebook Layout View for Macintosh   444

      A.3.1 Notebook Layout View   444

      A.3.2 Adding and Organizing Media and Notes   445

B. Online Document Creation and Collaboration   447

  B.1 Windows Live SkyDrive   447

      B.1.1 Microsoft Word Web App   447

      B.1.2 Microsoft PowerPoint Web App   449

      B.1.3 Microsoft Excel Web App   450

      B.1.4 Microsoft OneNote Web App   450

      B.1.5 Sharing and Saving Documents   450

      B.1.6 Microsoft Office 2011 Document Connection   452

  B.2 Google Docs   452

      B.2.1 Document   453

      B.2.2 Presentation   454

      B.2.3 Spreadsheet   454

      B.2.4 Sharing and Saving Documents   455

C. Excel Functions   457

D. Answers to Odd-Numbered Exercises
      Chapter Knowledge Check Questions   459

Index   461

Introduction

If you have ever wanted to learn about using either the Microsoft operating system or the Mac operating system, along with productivity tools necessary for the modern business world, then this book is for you. You might be a new student who has little to no experience with this type of software or maybe you are a novice computer user wanting to learn to use an alternative platform; in either case, you should find this book to be a helpful and constructive companion on your journey.

When we first started looking at developing an introductory textbook, we noticed that a variety of schools offered intro courses that focused on the Microsoft environment, yet many students seemed to be showing up to class with Apple computers or an alternative to the Microsoft Office suite of tools such as OpenOffice.org. Through the years, we have noticed that students come to class with both Microsoft and Apple products.

We have yet to find an introductory textbook that offers the range of alternatives that this book offers. *Microsoft Office and Beyond: Computer Concepts and Applications* is divided into five sections with 16 chapters that progressively introduce you to computer concepts from the moment you hit the power button all the way through to using a variety of productivity software applications available in Microsoft Office 2010, Microsoft Office for Mac 2011, and the OpenOffice.org suite.

Section I is composed of four chapters that introduce you to the computer environment. In Section I, you will learn about hardware and software, including everything from turning on your computer to identifying its major hardware components, no matter which platform you are using. Here you will also learn about using the Web and E-mail functionality on a variety of platforms.

Section II is composed of three chapters and introduces you to word processing software that includes Microsoft Word for both the Mac and Microsoft environments. Here you will learn to develop basic word processing documents, as well as add advanced functionality. As an alternative, you are introduced to OpenOffice.org Writer, in which you can create documents using features similar to those of the Microsoft product line.

Section III is composed of three chapters and introduces you to presentation software that includes Microsoft PowerPoint 2010, Microsoft PowerPoint for Mac 2011, and OpenOffice.org Impress. In this section, you will learn how to plan your presentation as well as how to build advanced presentations that incorporate a variety of media elements.

Section IV is composed of three chapters that introduce you to spreadsheet software. Just about any type of organization uses spreadsheet software to transform data into useful information that adds value to the organization. In this section, you will learn how to manipulate data by developing useful spreadsheets and to present data visually using graphics and charts.

Section V is composed of three chapters and introduces you to the world of databases using Microsoft Access 2010 (which is only available for the Microsoft operating system) and the OpenOffice.org Base. Databases are much different than spreadsheets, although at first you might think they are similar. By using Access or Base, you can establish complex relationships between data sets, populate a database with data, and develop powerful queries that produce useful information.

The appendices of the textbook have information on other common computer applications, including Adobe Reader (for reading PDF files) and Microsoft OneNote for Windows (for managing files). Online collaboration software such as Windows Live SkyDrive and Google Docs, are also available. These Web applications can be leveraged for a variety of situations where collaboration is needed or when documents too large for E-mail can be uploaded.

Chapter Structure

Each chapter is structured to provide an overview of the key concepts in order for you to demonstrate mastery at the completion of the chapter project. The sections on productivity software include a project for each chapter with detailed descriptions of how to use the various tools, functions, and commands in the respective software packages. In addition, we include the theory and history of how these applications have evolved and information on how these applications can be used to accomplish multiple tasks. Finally, chapter exercises and "Knowledge Checks" are provided to test your comprehension of the chapters. Answers to the odd-numbered questions are provided at the back of the book.

Student Resource DVD

The textbook provides a DVD inside the back cover that includes resources and sample video tutorials for the student. This DVD includes all of the files needed to complete the chapter exercises within the text. You will also find a repository of high-resolution images from the chapters and companion Excel template documents for using common functions effectively.

There are also student resources with additional project samples and videos for each chapter, as well as video tutorials, on the companion Web site for the book.

Instructor Resource DVD

The instructor DVD contains the solutions for all of the exercises and knowledge checks, along with PowerPoint presentations for each chapter.

Acknowledgments

I am so pleased to have been involved with this book. I have never seen anything like it on the market, and I want to thank David Pallai for taking the chance on publishing a book like this; his experience and guidance have shaped this into the book you hold in your hands. I want to thank my coauthor and friend, Charles Thies, for burning the midnight oil right along with me to see this through to completion. I also want to thank Katie Kennedy for her support, patience, and valuable assistance with the content of the spreadsheet chapters; she is a master of Excel, and her experience and expertise has allowed these chapters to be as user-friendly as possible for otherwise daunting software. I also want to thank my grandparents, Leonard and Sylvia Ullom, and my parents, Dan and Deborah Richardson, for giving me such a wonderful upbringing and helping me to capitalize on the opportunities that have led to my lifelong dream of seeing a book of my own creation in print. Thank you to everyone who worked on this project to meet the tight deadlines, and thank you to the readers who chose this book over others.

— Theodor Richardson

This book has been an amazing endeavor and would not have been possible without the help of many people. I would like to extend my sincere appreciation to everyone involved in this work. Thank you to my beautiful wife, Lea, who patiently waited each night for me to finish writing another section and provided her words of encouragement; my sons, Matt and Will, for their patience and support throughout this process; and Ted, my co-author and friend, for all of his guidance and support throughout the project. We certainly could not have completed this work without David Pallai, who worked tirelessly into the night to publish our book on schedule and provided the leadership to guide our project to the finish line; Beth Kohler, our editor, who did an absolutely amazing job finalizing our project; and Tim Anderson, who recommended our project to Mercury Learning and Information. Finally, a very special thank you to all of the people—some of whom we have never met—who worked to make this textbook possible.

— Charles Thies

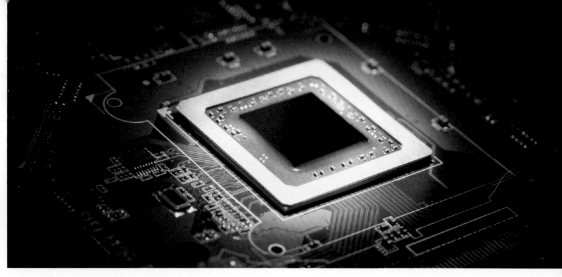

Introduction to •
Computer Concepts

This chapter is an introduction to foundational computer concepts. You will learn how to perform basic tasks on a computer and identify hardware interfaces on your machine. You will also learn about the essential components that allow a computer to function. Once you have completed the chapter, you will be able to:

- Discuss modern computer systems

- Choose and identify an adequate computer specific to your needs based on software requirements

- Explain how a computer works

- Identify input and output devices

- Identify modern operating systems

- Demonstrate basic tasks on commonly used operating systems

WHAT IS A COMPUTER?

Computers are widespread throughout today's world, whether for home or business use or in a handheld device. All of these devices are centered on the fundamental need to manage, store, and use information. On a personal level, you probably have information that is important to you and that you need to access on a regular basis. This can range from phone numbers and addresses of family and friends to account information for a variety of services.

Organizations have the same needs when it comes to information, as they must constantly innovate to maintain a competitive edge. Organizations have two very important assets that contribute to research and development, which in turn leads to increased profitability. The first important asset is the intellectual capital the organization maintains. Intellectual capital is the knowledge derived from ideas and innovation from its personnel. As a result, organizations develop large amounts of data that must be processed into useful information. To do this, they use the organization's information systems infrastructure, which is the second important asset an organization maintains. In this chapter, you will learn about the foundational component that helps to create, process, and store the information we need to operate as businesses or individuals in the world today: the modern computer.

A **COMPUTER** *is an electronic programmable device used to store, process, and manipulate data.*

Computers are used to convert data into useful information. They are absolutely everywhere in our daily life, and they come in many forms, such as desktop computers and laptops, and in cars, boats, airplanes, and phones. The desktop computer found in our homes and schools uses powerful applications that enable you to send email, develop professionally formatted documents, and process financial data for either personal or business applications.

If you are just getting started with computers, the actual thought of turning on the computer can be overwhelming, but there is no need to panic. This text will guide you to proficiency in both basic computer operations and productivity tasks. A computer system works with two elements: software and hardware devices. The following sections introduce you to these terms so you can get a better understanding of how your computer operates.

Computer Software

A software program is also referred to as an *application*. Applications are developed by computer programmers and are used to perform a series of tasks that process data in some way. One of the most important software programs on your computer is the Operating System (OS). The OS can be viewed as the manager of the other software on your machine; this program takes the commands you input and translates them into actions in the computer, such as running other applications or storing information. Some other software programs you may recognize are the Microsoft® Office suite or the

OpenOffice.org™ suite; these are examples of productivity software, which contains word processing, spreadsheet, and presentation applications.

> An **APPLICATION**, *or software program, is an executable piece of code that runs on computer hardware to perform a specified task. Applications can be automated to run without user interaction or they can be interactive, requiring input from the user to perform some task.*

There are two types of common software applications with which you should become familiar. The first type is the client-based program. These programs are installed with a disk or downloaded from the World Wide Web (or Web) and installed on the computer. These types of applications assist a user in performing common tasks. Microsoft Office and OpenOffice.org are examples of client-based software programs and are covered extensively in this text.

The second type of application is the Web-based application, and it is accessed via the Web. Examples of Web-based applications are a Web portal, such as the one you use to access your bank checking account balance, and an online store, such as *www.amazon.com*, where you can safely shop and conduct secure financial transactions. As connections among computers have become more common and more robust, the number of applications that are available on the Web has increased dramatically.

Computer Hardware

Hardware is any physical device that is attached to the computer. Hardware devices come in many forms, such as input, processing, data storage, and output devices. Common input devices are the keyboard, mouse, and video camera (or Webcam). An input device is any physical interface that accepts information from the user and translates it for use inside the machine. For instance, you press a key on the keyboard and the code for the key you pressed is translated for the computer to understand.

> **HARDWARE** *is a physical device that performs some function in allowing the computer system to run. Common types of hardware are input devices, processing devices, data storage devices, and output devices.*

Processing of input data happens through a microprocessor. The microprocessor that controls the overall operation of the computer is called the *Central Processing Unit* (*CPU*). Computers can have one processor or multiple processors that comprise the CPU. Other devices, such as video cards and sound cards, that provide enhancements to the computer system may also contain their own processors.

In addition to processing information for use, the computer needs somewhere to store the information. A data storage device is a hardware device that saves data and information to a location where it can be accessed later. A common example is a hard drive (also called a hard disk). There are also attachable devices such as flash drives or external drives that can be added for additional storage space.

Output devices translate information back to the user. The most common example of an output device is the computer monitor; this translates the internal information of the machine into a viewable output signal that you can understand. Additional examples of output devices include printers and speakers.

HISTORY AND BACKGROUND OF COMPUTING TECHNOLOGY

Now that you have some understanding of the different elements of a computer, you may be wondering where and how computer technology came about and how we know it works. It is important to note that the principles that drive a computer system have been around for a very long time. Ancient civilizations as long ago as 4000 B.C. in Sumer began to try to organize data into useful information on clay tablets. The abacus, one of the earliest forms of a calculating device, was developed in Babylonia in approximately 3000 B.C.

These early computing tools were not electronic but rather were mechanical instruments that assisted in computation. It was not until 1943, after much research on the theory of digital circuits and other developments in computing, that Colossus, a British computer, became operational. Because this was a wartime project, it remained classified for a number of years.

Colossus was used by the British military to successfully break the famous German Enigma cipher. For its time, this was a massive achievement that was partially responsible for the defeat of Germany in World War II. The development of Colossus and the construction of the vacuum tube computer ENIAC in the United States around the same time were important stepping-stones toward the modern computing model. While these early computers were big enough to fill an entire room, they could only perform limited calculations.

In the 1970s, silicon chips, the foundation for today's high-speed computing devices, were developed. These chips allowed computers to become faster, smaller, and less expensive, leading to the computing devices we see today. Today's mobile devices, such as smartphones, have millions of times more capability than early computers because of the advent of silicon-based chips. The advancement in computing technology continues. For the foreseeable future, computing devices will continue to get smaller, faster, and more powerful with increased processing and data storage capabilities.

PURCHASING A NEW COMPUTER SYSTEM

Now that you have learned about some aspects of a computer system, how do you know which system to buy? You may have gone to the local computer store and been tempted to purchase the most expensive system, but that may not be the best solution for your needs. Purchasing a computer can be accomplished most effectively by knowing what to look for and by conducting a little research. A computer purchase must be made based primarily on the requirements of its use. If you were to buy the most expensive system, you might just be spending money on processing power and storage space you will never need.

The first question to ask is: What tasks do you need to perform on the computer? You may simply want to surf the Web and perform basic functions like word processing and email. Or you could require the much heavier processing power associated with computer gaming applications. The next question is: What system requirements does the software have? One way to begin your research is to simply take a look at the processing requirements of the applications you intend to use. For example, you can find the system requirements for Microsoft Office on the outside of the packaging for the application or look for the information on the Web at the Microsoft TechNet site (*http://technet.microsoft.com/en-us/library/ee624351.aspx*). Finding the correct hardware requirements for the software you intend to use and taking the largest value in each category will give you a good idea of the minimum requirements for your system.

There are many other questions to answer. For example, what size and type of monitor do you need? Smaller monitors can be strenuous on the eyes, so a bigger monitor is usually better; in a laptop environment, however, a larger monitor means a heavier machine. Memory is another factor to consider. There are two types of computer memory: Random-Access Memory (RAM) and Read-Only Memory (ROM). RAM is volatile memory; this means it is temporary. Anything stored in RAM is lost once the computer is turned off. You can run multiple applications more smoothly when you have more RAM, as an increase in RAM can improve performance. ROM, on the other hand, is not volatile. This means that when you shut down your computer, the last set of instructions and the data you have saved to ROM are not lost.

Other options to examine include data storage capability such as hard drive space. The growth of technology in data storage solutions has made hard drive technology affordable to most users. Hard drives have two aspects to consider: storage space and speed. The faster the hard drive speed, the faster data travels. Normally faster and higher performance applications benefit from the increased speeds, however, these speeds are not generally required for the average user.

Storage space allows you to keep more data in your hard drive, such as pictures and video. If you take lots of digital pictures and video, then a larger hard drive is essential. Most computers today have hard drives in the range of 500 GB (gigabytes) to 1 TB (terabyte) of storage space.

Figure 1.1 shows the inside of a Personal Computer (PC). Note that this is an older model and could be classified as a midrange system. The layout is similar to many of the systems you find today. Notice the motherboard in the background of the picture; this in essence is the heart of the computer chassis in every system out there today, as it provides the connections between the various

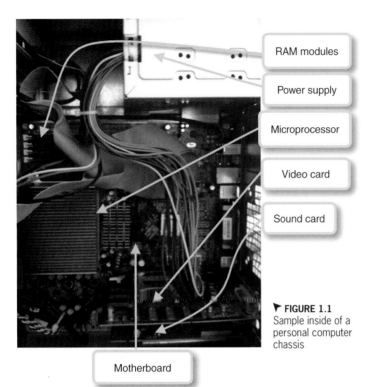

RAM modules

Power supply

Microprocessor

Video card

Sound card

▼ **FIGURE 1.1**
Sample inside of a
personal computer
chassis

Motherboard

hardware components and disseminates electrical power. The item in Figure 1.1 labeled "Microprocessor" has a silver slotted appearance; this is the heat sink that keeps the small CPU cool enough to operate safely.

You can also see the power supply that powers the motherboard and the memory modules. This entire environment should be kept free of dust to enable a long life for the system. Dust is one of the biggest enemies of electronic components. Note that this particular motherboard has a video card and a sound card that fit into its expansion slots.

Sound and video options can also be a factor in your selection of a new system. Many computer systems include an integrated sound card. These sound cards are more than adequate for the average user. Video cards also come integrated to deliver information to the computer monitor but

can be upgraded to much higher quality cards that improve video output. If you are the average user running office applications and email, you may not need a very high-quality video card. If you like to edit video or play performance-intensive computer games, then a more expensive and capable video card is most likely necessary.

Other factors to consider include operating system. We discuss some of these more advanced topics in the next sections, but it is important to realize that there is a difference between operating systems and how they perform. While the Windows® 7 Operating System is more widely used, there are other operating systems to consider, such as the Apple® Mac® OS X® and Linux®. Macintosh® Operating Systems are generally considered to be more secure than some other brands of OS.

Ergonomics are also a consideration when deciding on a computer purchase. Ergonomics include your posture, how you sit, and how your hands rest on the keyboard. Keyboards and computer mice, along with special office furniture, are sometimes included with a computer purchase. Ergonomically correct computer equipment can be helpful, but you should always test any products under consideration to be sure you have the right product for you.

Additionally, there are a number of options for purchasing a computer. You can find equivalent value on a new system either online or in a physical (brick and mortar) store. Whether you purchase a Mac or PC, there are several steps to take before getting started.

Most systems provide quick-start guides that guide you through the process of unpacking and installing your new system. One of the first steps after connecting the external hardware as instructed is pressing the power button. If you have purchased a new system, you will be guided through system setup when you first start the machine.

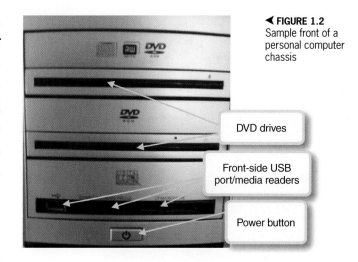

◀ FIGURE 1.2
Sample front of a personal computer chassis

DVD drives

Front-side USB port/media readers

Power button

1.4 WINDOWS PERSONAL COMPUTER BASICS

You will notice that the Windows PC shown in Figure 1.2 has several ports on the front: the power button, Digital Versatile/Video Disc (DVD) drives, a Universal Serial Bus (USB) slot, and a media slot that accepts different media cards. It should be noted that most Windows and Linux PCs have similar front ports and power buttons.

Figure 1.3 shows several additional ports at the back of the PC chassis. The back of the PC is where you connect many of the external hardware devices. The sound card jack is where you install your

speakers, microphones, and headset if needed (these are not mandatory items). Your monitor plugs into the Video Graphics Array (VGA) port, and the Ethernet port provides Internet access if you do not use wireless service. There are additional USB ports for the keyboard and mouse as well as for other accessories on the back of the chassis. Figure 1.3 also shows the vent for the system fan. Some PCs have more than one vent and it is important that you keep this vent clean and clear of any debris. Although it is not visible in the figure, the back of the computer is also where you plug in the power cord that transfers electrical power to the PC.

It is important not to treat the power button as a light switch; it does not simply shut down the computer. Although holding down the power button for immediate shutdown might be your only option in some cases, it should be avoided whenever possible. There are several shutdown options available to you depending on which system you purchase. It is important to follow the proper shutdown procedure

The power button is located in different places depending on which system you purchase, but it is usually at the front of the computer as shown in Figure 1.2. It looks like a *1* character inside of a *0* character. This was originally two separate characters signifying on and off, respectively. However, as technology evolved, it became easier to use the same pushbutton switch for both powering up and powering down a computer. Finding the power button should be your first task on any computer system.

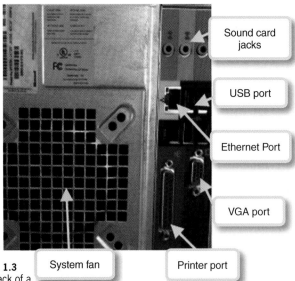

▼ FIGURE 1.3
Sample back of a personal computer chassis

Sound card jacks

USB port

Ethernet Port

VGA port

System fan

Printer port

available to you such as powering down your system. *Sleep* is a power-saving measure that places your computer in a state in which you can save energy, yet quickly bring your computer back up to where you left off so you can resume any activities you were performing.

Hibernate is primarily used in laptops. During hibernation, your laptop can be brought back up for use much more rapidly than from a completely powered-down state but slower than when in sleep mode. Hibernation mode is the setting that draws the least amount of power of all the power-saving modes available. Hibernation actually places your open documents and files on the hard drive and then shuts down; this enables your laptop battery to last longer.

The *Shut down* menu offers additional options, including locking your computer. During computer setup you will be asked to create a username and password for your system. Many people mistakenly leave the password blank, making their

to prevent problems with your computer, such as data loss or corruption. Failing to properly shut down your computer can create issues with your system, which include the following:

• Systems with system restore software can fail during restoration if the system was in the process of saving important files supporting a restoration point.

• Losing files not saved due to improper shutdown.

• Damage to hardware (on a Macintosh).

You can see an example *Start* menu (accessed through the icon in the lower-left corner of the computer screen) for a Windows machine in Figure 1.4; choosing *Shut down* will close all applications and then terminate power to the machine. A closer look at Figure 1.4 reveals that there are a few other options

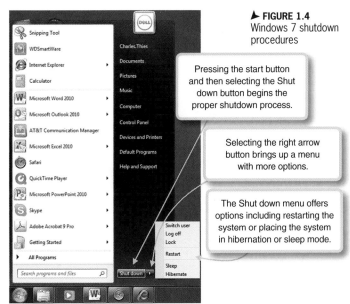

▶ FIGURE 1.4
Windows 7 shutdown procedures

Pressing the start button and then selecting the Shut down button begins the proper shutdown process.

Selecting the right arrow button brings up a menu with more options.

The Shut down menu offers options including restarting the system or placing the system in hibernation or sleep mode.

computer vulnerable to security threats by unauthorized users. Always be sure to set up a strong password that uses a combination of letters, numbers, and special characters. It is also important that you avoid using static passwords. A *static password* is a password you use for many systems. For example, some people will use the same password to log into their bank checking account system, school portal, and favorite shopping site. It is important that you develop unique passwords (known as *dynamic passwords*) for each system.

1.5 MACINTOSH COMPUTER BASICS

Powering up your Macintosh computer can be done by pressing the power button shown in Figure 1.5. The power button on the iMac® desktop system is located on the back of the monitor (at the opposite end of the panel from the input ports shown in Figure 1.6). The ports at the back of the iMac (Figure 1.6) are used to install external hardware devices such as headsets, microphones, and external hard drives.

Powering down your Mac by selecting *Shut Down* from the *Apple* menu (accessed by clicking the apple icon at the upper-left corner of the computer screen as shown in Figure 1.7) is the safest way to shut down your computer to avoid causing hardware damage. Sometimes you cannot avoid improper shutdown, such as during a power outage. You can avoid this problem by using an *Uninterruptable Power Supply* (UPS). A UPS is basically a system that plugs into the wall and keeps a battery inside charged; it

▲ **FIGURE 1.5** iMac power button

contains a power strip that not only protects the power source, but also stabilizes the power level to keep your electronic equipment from being damaged during a power surge caused by lightning or some other event. In most cases, UPS systems will detect the power outage and automatically shut down your computer in a predetermined amount of time.

The default Macintosh OS X Leopard® operating system version uses energy saver preference features that place your Mac in sleep or idle mode when it detects a lack of activity; this applies to Mac OS X 10.3, Mac OS X 10.4, and Mac OS X 10.5 editions as well. If you are using a Mac laptop, your computer will

▼ **FIGURE 1.6** Sample input ports for an iMac

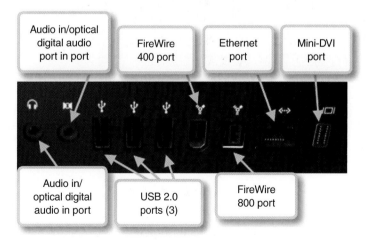

Audio in/optical digital audio port in port

FireWire 400 port

Ethernet port

Mini-DVI port

Audio in/ optical digital audio in port

USB 2.0 ports (3)

FireWire 800 port

➤ **FIGURE 1.7**
Mac OS X Leopard
Apple menu

enter sleep mode automatically when you close the lid to your laptop. When a Mac is in sleep mode, three things will transpire:

- The computer microprocessor reduces the amount of power consumption.

- The video card turns off.

- The hard disks turn off.

To place your Mac into sleep mode, select *Sleep* from the *Apple* menu, as shown

▼ **FIGURE 1.8** Mac OS X Leopard System Preferences dialog box

in Figure 1.7. You will notice that the *Apple* menu contains several other options aside from *Shut Down* and *Sleep*.

The *About This Mac* selection provides information about system specifics such as operating system version and basic capability. Choosing *Restart* gives you the ability to restart your system, which is often necessary after system updates or software installation. It is important to save all of your important files prior to restarting your system to avoid losing important information.

The *System Preferences* selection in the *Apple* menu allows you to adjust your sleep mode settings. Choose the *Energy Saver* selection from the System Preferences dialog box in Figure 1.8. You can then adjust your sleep settings as shown in Figure 1.9.

The Energy Saver dialog box shown in Figure 1.9 offers several options to properly adjust your sleep settings. The *Sleep* tab, which is highlighted in blue on the left, lets you force your computer into sleep mode after it has been inactive for a certain predefined time that you set. You also have the option to set your computer display (or displays) to sleep mode after a predetermined amount of time.

The *Options* tab, highlighted in blue on the right of Figure 1.9, lets you set your *Wake Options*; when selected, this allows a system administrator of a computer network to remotely access your computer while it is in sleep mode. There are three additional settings available under *Other Options*.

You will notice that in this particular instance the *Allow power button to sleep the computer* is selected, which allows the

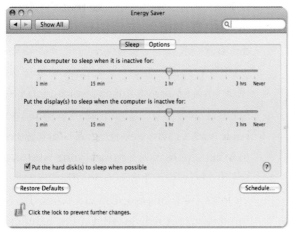
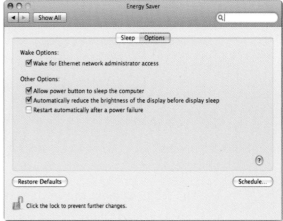

▲ **FIGURE 1.9** Mac OS X Energy Saver dialog box

user to automatically place the computer in sleep mode by pressing the power button. The next selection, *Automatically reduce the brightness of the display before display sleep*, forces the display to decrease its brightness just before entering sleep mode. The final option, which is not selected in the figure, is *Restart automatically after a power failure*; this forces the computer to restart after a power outage. It is important to emphasize that a UPS system should always be used to prevent issues with power outages from damaging your Mac.

1.6 HOW THE COMPUTER WORKS

So far you have learned that a computer can accept data, process data, store data, and output data. There are several hardware components and software that help modern computers complete this series of tasks. At the center of the modern desktop computer is the CPU that is attached to the motherboard. The motherboard is the interface that allows the user to connect physically attached hardware devices to the computer. When the power button is turned on, the computer power supply converts the 120 volts of electricity it receives from the outlet to 12 volts, which moves into the motherboard at the speed of light.

This process happens practically instantly as the electrons travel at approximately 186,000 miles per second. The instant power enters the motherboard, it powers up the *BIOS*. The BIOS, or the Basic Input/Output System, is the *firmware* (or software built into the computer) of the machine and is the first software that loads from the ROM (which as you might remember is nonvolatile, meaning that it does not go away when the computer is turned off). The BIOS handles all input into

With most systems, you can usually hit one of the function keys at the top of your keyboard, such as *F8* or *F11*, to enter the BIOS system menu. Through this menu you can check such things as the microprocessor temperature (either one or multiple processors if equipped) and system fan operation. Computer operations produce a great deal of heat and require the use of fans to keep the system cool.

the computer when it is first turned on and handles all of the hardware attached to the motherboard, including everything from the keyboard to external disk drives.

A **DRIVER** *is software code written by a hardware manufacturer that tells the hardware device how to communicate with the operating system.*

The BIOS signals the hard drive to spin up and load the operating system, which is the user interface you see when you turn on the computer, such as the Windows 7 operating system. The BIOS also manages the boot order; this is the order in which the hard drive or disk drive loads up during the power-up operations. The process of initial startup where the motherboard is powered up, hard drives spin, and the operating system loads is known as the *booting process*.

Once the computer has booted up, it continues to load any required default

Always keep in mind that the motherboard contains capacitors that can discharge dangerous or even potentially deadly voltage several minutes after the computer has been shut down. It is imperative that you not open the cover of the computer until the capacitor has discharged after the computer has been shut down and unplugged from the power supply. The time frame of discharge and the danger level of the capacitors will vary by computer; generally, the smaller the machine the less time it will take and the less you need to worry about the capacitor voltage. You can assure your safety by wearing an anti-static wrist strap and keeping the computer and its components off of external metal surfaces when working with the internal components of the machine. Always check the system documentation to determine how to open your computer chassis cover for maintenance and how long you should wait for the capacitors on the machine to discharge.

applications and hardware. Another important hardware device that starts up during boot up is the video card. The video card transmits data to your monitor so that you can see the user interface or the operating system screen. The BIOS also runs initial system checks such as verifying that the memory chips are all working and functional.

The BIOS is also responsible for loading up system drivers that allow compatibility between the motherboard and the hardware. For example, you may have purchased both a computer and a printer. Proper installation of the printer requires installation of the system drivers. Each individual computer platform (whether Mac or Windows) requires system drivers for effective compatibility with associated hardware devices.

Proper care and safety procedures are important for any computer. It is important to understand the basic operation of hardware and basic maintenance activities, especially if you ever want to open your machine chassis. It is also important to routinely use an air can, available at computer stores, to blow dust out of the inside of the computer chassis. Dust should be blown from all components, the power supply, and system fans.

Input Hardware Devices

1.6.1

Input hardware devices are responsible for providing input to the computer system. For example, a mouse, a keyboard, a video camera, and a microphone are all considered input devices. In order to use all of these hardware devices, the computer must have the proper drivers installed so that the devices all work correctly.

The keyboard is the most common type of input device and is used to type instructions to the computer. The keyboard plugs into the desktop computer using a USB port and transmits a signal for further processing. The keyboard can also be used to execute shortcut key instructions such as *Ctrl-C* (which is a shortcut for copying text or an object from a document).

The mouse is also a very common device and is used to move the cursor (which by default looks like an arrow) along the screen. The mouse also has two buttons (a *left-click* button and a *right-click* button) and an optional scroll button. You can use the mouse to point at an application and then *double-left-click* to execute the application. You can examine the properties of a file or folder by pointing and selecting the *right-click* button on the mouse. The scroll button can be used to scroll through pages in a document that contains a scrollbar.

A microphone is another example of an input device that can be used for many purposes when properly installed with the assigned drivers on the computer. The microphone is generally plugged into the back of the desktop in the sound card audio input jack or one of the USB ports. This signal can then be used in many ways. For example, the signal can simply be stored on the hard drive and the file can then be processed using some other application, or you might create a Power-Point® presentation and want to add narration so that a viewer can listen and view slides simultaneously.

Video cameras are used extensively for Web conferences and to record video. Companies can use them to monitor security and provide training events. The data stream for a video camera can be saved in a digital format on the computer's main hard drive or even an external hard drive.

Output Hardware Devices

1.6.2

Output devices are used to process output data feeds from the computer. This is usually done as a result of data that has been processed through the computer in some fashion. The most common output device is the computer monitor screen; this provides a visual interface between the user and the computer. Most monitors today are Liquid Crystal Displays (LCDs), which provide a sharp image and transmit video data streams to the user. Additionally, there are overhead projectors that can display your computer screen directly on a wall; this is useful for showing multimedia presentations to large crowds.

Another example of an output device is a printer. A printer produces printed pages that contain output from an application. Some printers can also be used as input devices; for example, you may have seen printers that are referred to as all-in-one devices that have built-in fax machines (which can both send and receive faxes) and scanners (which convert an object or text into a digital image). Some printers have document feeders that allow you to make copies of important documents.

Your computer's speakers are another common output device. The speakers are integrated devices within a laptop but are externally attached to the desktop computer. On an iMac, the speakers are integrated output devices. External speakers are connected directly to the sound card toward the rear of the desktop computer via the output sound jack that connects to the computer's sound card. Other output devices include headphones that allow you to hear sound privately rather than through the speakers. Most sound cards have an output jack for headphones.

1.6.3 ## Processing Hardware Devices

The main functions of the CPU are to process instructions, manage the flow of information, and perform calculations. The CPU is considered the brain of the computer and communicates with the output, input, and storage devices via the BIOS firmware that resides in the ROM. The motherboard is the circuit board where the CPU and memory attach.

All of these devices help to process and produce results based on the instructions received from the input devices. The CPU receives data transmissions as you have already learned, but what does the computer actually see? It is actually simpler than you might think. When you type a letter or number into your computer, the computer does not actually read or understand the character you typed.

What the computer is really processing are ones and zeros. In the world of mathematics, we refer to this number scheme as the *binary* system. For example, the decimal number 1 is interpreted as the 4-bit binary number 0001. Each digit in a binary number system refers to a power of two based on its position (beginning with 2^0 for the rightmost binary digit); each binary digit is called a *bit*.

The binary system is a base two system in which each bit is double the value of the previous bit, following the pattern of 1, 2, 4, 8, 16, 32, 64, and so on. The pure mathematics are beyond the scope of this text, but a 1 in any of the positions for the bit indicates that particular power of two should be included in the sum of the value to convert it to the decimal system with which you are familiar. An example of this is the binary number *0101*, which converts to the decimal value 5. Even if you do not fully follow the logic of this, you should understand that the computer processes information using this binary system, which equates everything to a yes or no value (or equivalently an on or off value).

Data Storage
1.6.4

You have already learned about computer memory that stores nonvolatile and volatile memory on your computer. In order to store large amounts of data, though, you must have a hard drive. This is typically located inside your computer. The hard drive has a disk inside that can be rewritten repeatedly to store documents, video, multimedia presentations, and photographs. This internal hard drive is also where your operating system resides, along with all of your system settings and preferences.

Data on a hard drive is stored in a binary format of ones and zeros using a magnetic storage technique. Hard disk data can last a very long time and information is rarely completely erased. Most people mistakenly assume that pressing the Delete button or emptying the Recycle Bin or Trash folder on your machine automatically deletes information forever, but this is not the case; while the information is removed from the operating system's repository, the data still exists on the drive until something else overwrites it. It is important to note that although sometimes hard drives fail or become damaged, much, if not all, of the data can be recovered using special techniques.

You may have heard someone mention their computer breaking and losing their information. There are two important things to remember here. First, all of the data can probably be recovered by a data recovery technician, even in cases of fire or water damage. Secondly, you should always use a secondary storage device, such as an external hard drive, to back up all of your important files and photographs so you do not lose them. External hard drives are readily available and can be used to store or back up all of your system files and preferences. External hard drives usually come with either USB or FireWire® connections. Most hard drives come formatted to be used in either a Windows or Mac computer.

Disk formatting is the process of preparing a disk or hard drive for use with a particular operating system. This process installs the filesystem or structure compatible with the particular operating system. The Windows OS uses the NTFS filesystem and is configured on your hard drive or disk at the time of formatting. On a Mac, you would need either a Mac OS (Journaled) partition if the disk is to be used for booting purposes or a Mac OS Extended (No Journaling) partition if you will just be using the partition to store files, pictures, and video.

A *partition* is a block of storage in a particular file structure that allows it to be accessed by the chosen operating system. You can set up multiple partitions on your hard drive at the time of formatting to allow for multiple purposes. For example, if you want to use an external hard drive on both a Mac and a Windows PC, you would create a Mac partition and an NTFS partition.

There are other types of data storage devices that you can use to store either backup copies or important files. Flash drives (commonly called thumb drives), DVDs, and CD-ROMs are all commonly used for data storage. In any case, all data storage devices must be formatted for the correct operating system or media format desired. Figure 1.10 shows an example of a USB attached Western Digital® My Passport® 1 TB external hard drive.

What Computers Can and Cannot Do

1.6.5

Computers are not devices that can actually think or make decisions unless

▲ FIGURE 1.10
Western Digital My Passport 1 TB external hard drive

you program them to give you specific facts based on predetermined rules. In other words, computers are not self-aware. Despite the fact that they contain lots of processing power, computers are not able to make their own decisions nor do they have any feelings or morals. Computers must be programmed to complete every single task they perform.

Some technologies specific to the decision support field use advanced algorithms to help humans make the right decisions based on data that has been collected over time. Although these types of decision support systems continue to improve, they are far from being able to think or act like humans without human direction. All computers, no matter how advanced they are, must be programmed to complete their assigned tasks.

This also means that the results a computer provides are only as good as the data put into the system. You have probably called a bank, the human resources department at your employer, or a utility company, only to find they have incorrect information about you. This is an example of where a human enters incorrect data in the system and the computer system provides that same incorrect data back to the user. The computer lacks the ability to correct mistakes made by humans. There is no telling what the future holds as far as technology goes, but for now, computer output is only as good as the input provided by its user.

AN INTRODUCTION TO THE WINDOWS OPERATING SYSTEM

1.7

The Microsoft Windows 7 OS is a graphical interface used to interact with the computer and applications that reside on the hard disk. The new OS comes with many features that make working in the environment easy and convenient. There are a few new features that are immediately apparent if you are familiar with prior versions of Windows; some of these are identified in Figure 1.11. You can see the layout is similar to previous versions of Windows, but there are some differences that increase the ease of use.

The taskbar at the bottom of the screen has a new *Aero Peek* feature that lets you view thumbnails (preview images) of running applications. You can place your mouse over the icon for the application to see a larger image as shown in Figure 1.12; this action displays a grouped image with a preview of all of the open windows for that application. By using the *Aero Peek* feature you can also close files from the thumbnails themselves by holding your mouse over the

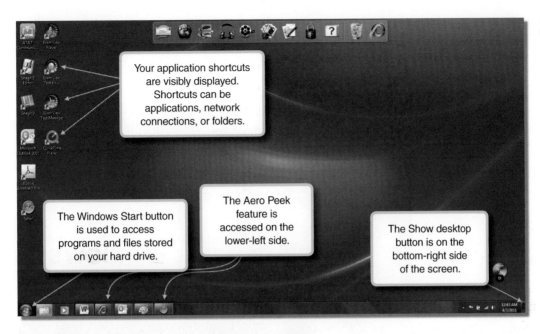

Your application shortcuts are visibly displayed. Shortcuts can be applications, network connections, or folders.

The Windows Start button is used to access programs and files stored on your hard drive.

The Aero Peek feature is accessed on the lower-left side.

The Show desktop button is on the bottom-right side of the screen.

▲ FIGURE 1.12 Using the Aero Peek feature

application group and selecting the *Close* icon (which looks like an *X*).

The *Show desktop* button on the bottom-right corner of the taskbar (shown in Figure 1.11) can be used to quickly alternate between the applications that are open by minimizing them with one click (of the left mouse button) and maximizing them with a second click.

By clicking on the Windows *Start* button in the lower-left corner you will see the menu shown in Figure 1.13. You have several options here, including customizing the way listed applications appear. You can add programs to this initial menu list by right-clicking the mouse on the application you

want to add and selecting *Add to start menu*. If you hold your mouse cursor (which looks like an arrow) over one of the applications, you will see all of the most recent files used within that particular application. In Chapter 2, "Navigating the Computer Environment," we will continue to discuss more of the features available with Windows 7 and how to perform additional tasks with the operating system that will help you to refine your skills and become proficient with the Windows 7 OS.

AN INTRODUCTION TO MAC OS X

1.8

This section is an introduction to the elements of the Macintosh OS X desktop. The Mac OS X platform is a graphical interface used to interact with the computer and applications that reside on the hard disk and works in a

The Mac platform is credited with being one of the most user-friendly operating systems, as well as an operating system that faces far fewer security threats than the Windows platform. If you are new to the Apple platform and are used to Microsoft's products, there is a significant learning curve involved.

The Mac platform can perform the same tasks that a Windows machine can, although sometimes different procedures are necessary to achieve equivalent functionality. The iMac desktop shown in Figure 1.14 contains display features you might not recognize, but you must learn about these as a first step toward building proficiency with the Mac OS X platform.

Along the right side of the screen you will find the *Macintosh HD* icon. It is important to note that Apple prefers users to keep their desktops clear of any icons. If you are using the Leopard version, you should not have anything on the desktop at all unless you upgraded from a previous version and you kept those icons on your desktop.

The *Dock* is the launcher for all of your programs and files; it is located along the bottom of the interface. The *Dock* has a *divider* line designed to keep applications on the left side and files and folders on the right side. You can easily drag new programs to the Dock or remove them by dragging them off of the Dock. The *Apple* menu, shown earlier in the chapter, is used to shut down the computer or put it in sleep mode. You are also able to initiate software updates and adjust system preferences here.

▲ **FIGURE 1.13** The Windows 7 Start menu

manner similar to the Windows 7 platform. When you first log into your computer, you are in the *Finder* window as displayed in Figure 1.14; this is the equivalent of a PC desktop or workspace.

Menu extras are located on the top right hand portion of the Mac OS window and let you control system volume or manage your Internet connections as illustrated in Figure 1.14.

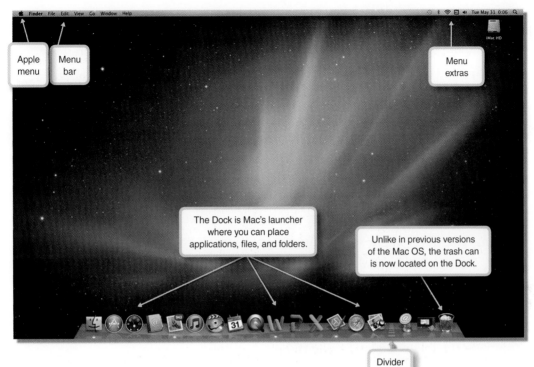

Apple menu

Menu bar

Menu extras

The Dock is Mac's launcher where you can place applications, files, and folders.

Unlike in previous versions of the Mac OS, the trash can is now located on the Dock.

Divider

The *Sidebar* (shown in Figure 1.15) is located on the left-side pane of every Finder window. The sidebar has four sections: Devices, Shared, Places, and Search For. A double left-click (hereafter referred to simply as a double-click) on an application's icon opens that application. Minimizing applications is a matter of clicking on the yellow button at the top left of any application window; the application minimizes to the right side of the Dock. Chapter 2 will continue the exploration and use of the Macintosh OS X interface.

Sidebar

▲ FIGURE 1.15 The Mac OS X sidebar in the Finder window

CHAPTER SUMMARY

This chapter provided an introduction to computer concepts and covered the hardware and software components used in modern personal computers. Additionally, we provided a brief historical basis for computer systems and pointed out the basic elements of both the Windows and the Mac platforms. This text is designed so that both Mac and Windows users are able to acquire enough knowledge to successfully start their computer and navigate the desktop. In the next chapter, we will cover how to successfully manage files and folders. Users will develop proficiency in all of the basic tasks needed to successfully manage a personal computer at the operating system level.

CHAPTER EXERCISES

Complete the following labs using the platform of your choice:

1. This exercise requires you to conduct some basic research using the World Wide Web to learn about various aspects required to select and purchase the right personal computer to meet your needs. Since we still have yet to cover the Web, complete this assignment by visiting your local library and working with the librarian. (Optionally, if you do have some computing experience you may use the Web on your own to complete this assignment.) Begin by thinking about which category of user you fall under, such as student or gamer. The student user usually needs a computer that is able to run Microsoft Office applications or some variant. A gamer or high-performance computer user requires more memory, faster processors, and a high-performance graphics card. Using the Web, find additional research supporting facts required to purchase the right system. For this exercise, research the minimum system requirements for the software you will be using or would like to use. Once you have the system requirements, go to the Web and use three online shopping sites to find the three best prices for a PC that meets your specific needs. List the system requirements and the PCs you chose and provide a substantive explanation for your decision. You do not have to use any computer applications to write this assignment.

2. Go to the local library and research sites to develop a historical time line that explains the development of computing technology. Optionally, if you have some computer skills you may use the Web on your own to complete the assignment. Write out a time line on paper that explains important milestones and lists the contributors responsible for each achievement.

CHAPTER KNOWLEDGE CHECK

1

What was the earliest device used for mathematical calculations?

○ **A.** Abacus

○ **B.** Clay tablet

○ **C.** Bean counter

○ **D.** Both a & b

2

The Colossus was the first vacuum tube-based computer used to crack the Enigma code.

○ True

○ False

3

_____ options can also be a factor in selecting your new system.

○ **A.** Sound and video

○ **B.** Video and battery

○ **C.** Monitor and video card

○ **D.** Hard drive and ROM

4

The power button on the iMac desktop system is located on the back of the monitor.

○ True

○ False

5

A _____ is a system that plugs into the wall and keeps a battery inside charged. It contains a power strip that not only protects the power source, but also stabilizes the power source to keep your electronic equipment from being damaged during a power surge.

○ **A.** Power outage

○ **B.** Brown out

○ **C.** UPS

○ **D.** Lightning

6 Computers are devices that can actually think and make decisions without you having to set any predetermined rules.

- ○ True
- ○ False

7 The _____ feature lets you view thumbnails of applications that are running.

- ○ **A.** Aero Peek
- ○ **B.** PC Peek
- ○ **C.** Finder View
- ○ **D.** Presentation View

8 The Mac platform can perform all of the same tasks that a Windows machine can.

- ○ True
- ○ False

9 The _____ is located on the left side of every Finder window.

- ○ **A.** Sidebar
- ○ **B.** Dock
- ○ **C.** Color icon
- ○ **D.** None of the above

10 The_____ is the launcher for all of your programs and files on the Mac platform.

- ○ **A.** Menulet
- ○ **B.** Dock
- ○ **C.** Finder window
- ○ **D.** Both a & b

Navigating •— *the Computer Environment*

This chapter will teach you how to navigate and use the computer desktop environment. You will learn how to work in the computer environment using files and folders you develop from client applications available on your computer. You will also learn about navigating the environment by searching for files and folders as well as by using keyboard shortcuts to traverse the desktop environment. Once you have completed the chapter, you will be able to:

- Describe and identify elements of the user interface

- Navigate the desktop and locate applications, files, and folders

- Demonstrate the use of folders to organize files on your computer

- Construct and save files from basic applications

2.1 NAVIGATING THE DESKTOP

Whether you are using a Mac or a Windows-based computer while working your way through this text, navigation is done by interacting with the computer's *Graphical User Interface* (*GUI*). The user interface is the visual (graphical) display provided by the computer's operating system that allows the user to visually interact and issue tasking commands into the BIOS. By interacting with the user interface, software applications can be started, closed, installed, and uninstalled.

2.1.1 The Windows 7 Desktop

In the previous chapter, you were introduced to the Windows 7 desktop

---

A **MENU** *is a selection of commands and options that are similar enough to form a group; the title of the menu is generally indicative of the type of commands it contains. Common examples of a menu are the File menu and Help menu.*

A **TOOLBAR** *is a collection of icons that acts like the visual equivalent of a text menu, typically providing shortcuts to common commands and actions.*

A **PANE** *is a section of a window with a specific purpose.*

A **DIALOG BOX** *is an encapsulated version of a user interface that is typically used for minor data entry or configuration. In most applications, an open dialog box has to be closed or otherwise dealt with to perform other tasks in the application.*

The **GRAPHICAL USER INTERFACE** *(or GUI) is the graphical display that allows the computer user to see the computer output and interact with the core components of the computer in a visual manner.*

The **DESKTOP** *is the primary workspace for a graphical user interface; it is the digital equivalent of a physical desk. It typically contains menus to perform system functions and icons that represent applications or files on the computer system.*

An **ICON** *is a small graphical representation of a program or command; clicking it usually starts a program or performs an action, depending on what the icon represents.*

A **WINDOW** *is an area of the screen acting as a standalone user interface to an application. A single application may use multiple windows (commonly one window per open file).*

---

environment, which is the computer's user interface. One of the primary functions of a user interface is to help humans visually interact with the computer and utilize the software programs available for various activities. Accessing the software programs on your computer can be done in one of two ways: by using the *Start* button shown in Figure 2.1 or by *double-clicking* on a particular shortcut icon on the desktop (double-clicking is two rapid clicks using the left button on your mouse) or in he folder in which the application is installed.

◄ FIGURE 2.1
Windows 7
Start Button

The *mouse* is the hardware device you use to move the cursor on the computer screen over the desktop to interact with programs and files. You can begin your exploration by moving your cursor (by moving the mouse) to the *Start* button and pressing the left button on the mouse one time. Performing this action will activate the Start menu, shown in Figure 2.2.

The Start menu in Figure 2.2 is divided into two areas. The section on the left lists programs that have recently been opened and *pinned* programs. Recently used programs are listed at the top-left side of the Start menu, and pinned programs are closer to the bottom-left side. *Pinning* is a new feature available in Windows 7 that allows you to create a shortcut to an application by retaining (or pinning) the program icon in the Start menu. The pinned program will then appear in the Start menu until it is unpinned. To remove the program from the Start menu, right-click the program name and then select *Unpin from the Start Menu*. You can also drag the icons to change the order of appearance of the list of pinned programs in your Start menu.

2.1.1.1 *The Control Panel*

The right side of the Start menu has several fixed options, one of which is the Control Panel option. The Control Panel (shown in Figure 2.3) gives the user the ability to make system setting changes. This includes hardware and software installations and uninstallations (uninstalls).

It is important to note we will not cover every setting available in this text, but discussing some of them will help you

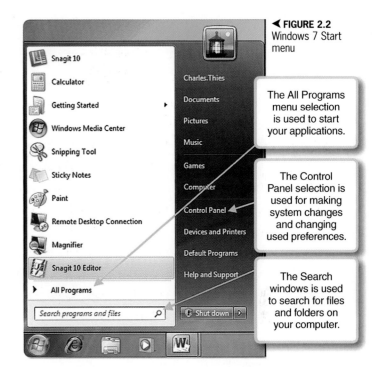

◄ FIGURE 2.2
Windows 7 Start menu

The All Programs menu selection is used to start your applications.

The Control Panel selection is used for making system changes and changing used preferences.

The Search windows is used to search for files and folders on your computer.

develop proficiency so you can navigate the desktop environment successfully and efficiently.

We now examine how you can further customize the Start menu. Notice the Appearance and Personalization submenu in the Control Panel. Selecting this option brings up several options available to customize your desktop environment, as shown in Figure 2.4.

When you select the *Task Bar and Start Menu* submenu, you are immediately brought to the dialog box (a window requesting user interaction) shown in Figure 2.5. This is the Task Bar and Start Menu Properties dialog box and it allows you to change everything from the picture and icon display on your Start menu to the way your computer shuts down.

Notice in the *Appearance and Personalization* submenu in Figure 2.4 that you

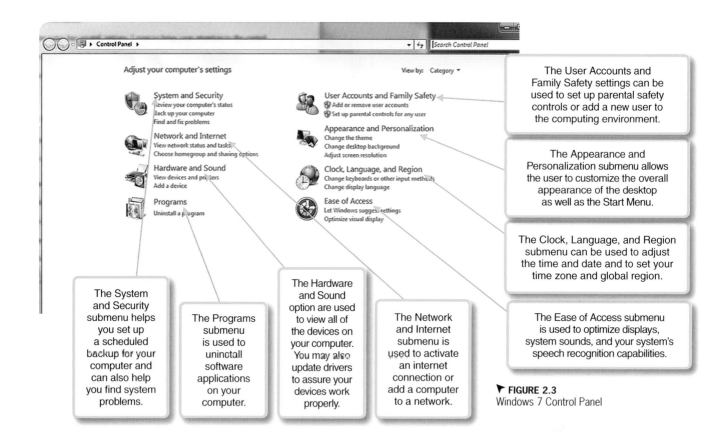

The User Accounts and Family Safety settings can be used to set up parental safety controls or add a new user to the computing environment.

The Appearance and Personalization submenu allows the user to customize the overall appearance of the desktop as well as the Start Menu.

The Clock, Language, and Region submenu can be used to adjust the time and date and to set your time zone and global region.

The System and Security submenu helps you set up a scheduled backup for your computer and can also help you find system problems.

The Programs submenu is used to uninstall software applications on your computer.

The Hardware and Sound option are used to view all of the devices on your computer. You may also update drivers to assure your devices work properly.

The Network and Internet submenu is used to activate an internet connection or add a computer to a network.

The Ease of Access submenu is used to optimize displays, system sounds, and your system's speech recognition capabilities.

▼ **FIGURE 2.3**
Windows 7 Control Panel

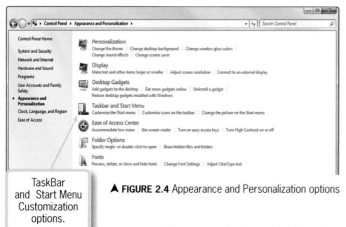

TaskBar and Start Menu Customization options.

▲ **FIGURE 2.4** Appearance and Personalization options

can personalize your desktop by changing the desktop theme, colors, and background. This submenu is also where you will find the display properties where you can adjust your graphics card's properties such as its screen resolution and whether you use one screen or two screens.

Desktop Gadgets   2.1.1.2

One interesting option available to Windows 7 users is the ability to add gadgets to the desktop. When you select *Desktop Gadgets* in the *Appearance and Personalization* submenu (shown in Figure 2.4), you will see the Desktop Gadgets window appear as shown in Figure 2.6.

This window allows you to add everything from a calendar to live RSS (Really Simple Syndication) feeds to the desktop. You will learn more about RSS feeds and

RSS (REALLY SIMPLE SYNDICATION) *is a Web feed commonly used to publish regularly updated electronic publications such as the news or weather.*

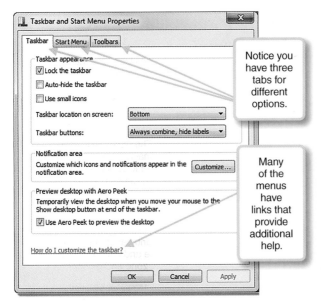

Notice you have three tabs for different options.

Many of the menus have links that provide additional help.

▲ **FIGURE 2.5** Taskbar and Start Menu Properties dialog box

the Internet in Chapter 3, "Working with the Web."

2.1.1.3 *Jump Lists*

Another feature to help you navigate the desktop more efficiently is a Jump List. *Jump Lists* allow a user to quickly open a recent file from an application on the taskbar or a pinned application on the Start menu, as shown in Figure 2.7. You can also pin items to Jump Lists on the taskBar.

2.1.1.4 *Task Manager*

Sometimes a program on your computer may lock up and cease to function. Most of the time Windows 7 will automatically send you a warning and either restart the program or close it completely. If for some reason the program does not close, you can open the *Task Manager* and end a process that has stopped working by pressing the *End Task* button at the bottom of the window shown in Figure 2.8.

A **KEYBOARD SHORTCUT** *is a particular combination of keys pressed at the same time and is used to access menus or other services efficiently without the use of the mouse.*

You can open the Task Manager in two ways. First, you can simply move the pointer to the task bar, right-click, and select *Task Manager* from the menu that appears. The second way to get to the Task Manager is to use the keyboard shortcut by pressing *Ctrl-Shif-Esc*. The Task Manager displays programs and services that are running on your computer at the time you open the window. You can also use the Task Manager to view network processes or users logged into your system.

Libraries Feature   2.1.1.5

Over time you may accumulate a large number of files and folders on your desktop, which can make navigating the desktop difficult. Libraries are a feature in Windows 7 that can help you find and organize your files in one consolidated location. This allows you to save time by having one place where all of your files and folders can easily be located. To access

▼ **FIGURE 2.6** Desktop Gadgets window

the Libraries feature, click the *Libraries* icon on the lower-left side of the taskbar. A visual reference of the Libraries icon can be seen in Figure 2.9. The Libraries window has a search box that allows the user to search for files and folders using options such as Kind, Date modified, Type, and Name as search criteria.

You can see by looking at Figure 2.9 that there are four standard libraries: Documents, Music, Pictures, and Videos. You can also create new libraries to help you organize your collections of files and folders. To create a new library, highlight the *Libraries* selection at the left side of the window, as shown in Figure 2.9, and right-click. This will produce a new menu; select *New,* then *Library* and name the new library folder. For example, this might be a library for all of your schoolwork. You might name the library *Undergraduate* or give it the name of the school you are attending and then

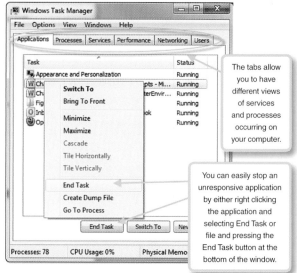

▲ **FIGURE 2.8** Task Manager

have subfolders in the library for each course that you are taking.

The Macintosh OS X Desktop

2.1.2

Although the Mac has a similar appearance, it is different from a Windows-based PC. Unlike the Windows 7 platform, many of the desktop settings on the Mac can be found in the *Apple* menu. As you might remember from Chapter 1, "Introduction to Computer Concepts," the Apple menu is accessed by clicking the apple icon (shown in Figure 2.10) at the top-left side of the menu bar.

Starting an application also works much differently than on a Windows machine. In a Windows environment, you may have used the Start button to access all of your settings and applications. On a Mac, all of the applications you use regularly reside on the *Dock* near the bottom of the interface (as shown in Figure 2.11).

To access applications on a Mac, you can start them either from the Dock

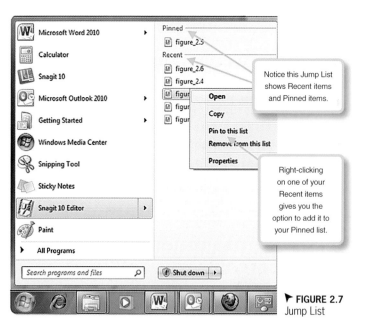

▶ **FIGURE 2.7** Jump List

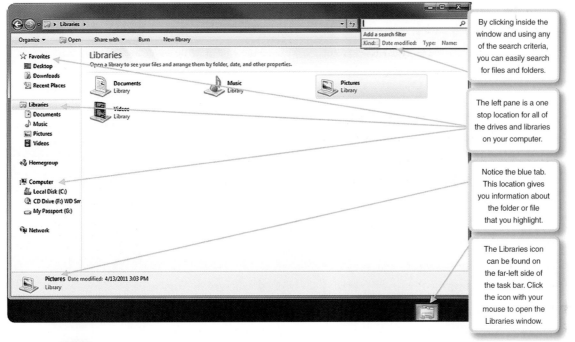

Libraries window

By clicking inside the window and using any of the search criteria, you can easily search for files and folders.

The left pane is a one stop location for all of the drives and libraries on your computer.

Notice the blue tab. This location gives you information about the folder or file that you highlight.

The Libraries icon can be found on the far-left side of the task bar. Click the icon with your mouse to open the Libraries window.

◄ **FIGURE** 2.10 Apple icon to access the Apple menu

or from the application's icon in the *Applications* folder. It is easy to add or remove applications from the Dock. You can simply click on a program icon and drag it away from the Dock to remove the application. To add an application to the Dock, you simply click on the application you want in the Applications folder and drag it to the left side of the divider (the dotted white vertical line) on the Dock. You can click and drag icons on the Dock to reorder them.

The **DOCK** *is the collection of program icons at the bottom of the Mac desktop screen used to quickly access the applications you use most frequently.*

The Finder

If you are using a new implementation of the Leopard OSX system, there is nothing on your desktop and you might be wondering how you access applications because there is so much more available than what you see on the Dock. The applications on your computer are found in the *Applications* folder. You can use the Finder window to access the Applications folder by clicking on the *Finder* program icon on the Dock (see Figure 2.12).

If you do not have any applications running, you will notice that the Finder menu is available at the top of your screen. You can alternatively click on the background of the screen and the active application menu will

2.1.2.1

◄ **FIGURE** 2.11
The Dock

Chapter 2 — Navigating the Computer Environment — **29**

► FIGURE 2.12
Finder program icon

be the Finder application. If a Finder window does not appear, you can select the *Go* option on the *Finder* menu, as shown in Figure 2.13.

The Go menu gives you the ability to navigate to different areas on your computer system. You will notice that to the right of the options are your shortcut keys. Mac has a wide selection of shortcut keys you can use to quickly navigate to areas within your system and perform common tasks.

The Dock   2.1.2.2

If the Dock is too small or too large for your personal preference, you can quickly and easily adjust its size by selecting the *Apple* menu, then the *Dock* selection, and finally *Dock Preferences* to open the window shown in Figure 2.14. Now you can simply move the Size slider to increase or decrease the size of the Dock.

One final feature on the Dock that you may need is the ability to view hidden menus. If you are simply taking a look at your program icons, it is not immediately apparent that there are more options available to the user. Simultaneously pressing the *Ctrl* button and clicking on a particular program's icon (the Mail icon in

► FIGURE 2.13
The Finder menu
Go selection

◄ FIGURE 2.14
Dock Preferences
window

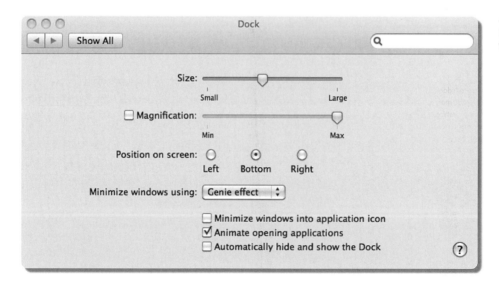

▲ **FIGURE 2.15** Hidden menu for the Mail application

In Windows 7 you have gadgets for your desktop; similarly, in the OS X environment you have widgets available in the *Dashboard*. When you activate the Dashboard (which will then appear to float over your desktop), you will see that it contains a clock, calendar, calculator, and the weather. You can use the Dashboard's hidden menu (see Figure 2.16) to change your Dashboard settings or add new widgets you find online. You can also change your Dashboard settings by accessing the *Apple* menu and selecting *System Preferences*. System Preferences is also where you can adjust settings for Exposé and Spaces.

Figure 2.15) displays the hidden menu for that program.

You can clearly see there are additional options in the hidden menu. At the top of the menu in Figure 2.15, you can see that there is an open associated file. Clicking on the open file labeled *TOC* brings up an email window. You can perform this action with any of your applications on the Dock or the OS X desktop to view hidden menus.

Exposé and Spaces are features within the Mac OS X environment that make desktop navigation and organization a breeze. Exposé is similar to the Aero Peek feature in Windows 7; both of these give you a preview of the applications you have open and let you open one by moving your cursor to it and clicking. With most keyboards, you simply press

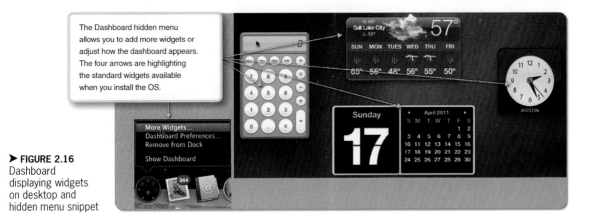

The Dashboard hidden menu allows you to add more widgets or adjust how the dashboard appears. The four arrows are highlighting the standard widgets available when you install the OS.

▶ **FIGURE 2.16** Dashboard displaying widgets on desktop and hidden menu snippet the *F3* key to view the Exposé of active applications.

Rather than placing a preview at the bottom of the taskbar for minimized applications, Exposé places your open and minimized application windows in small preview windows laid out so that you can see every application you have open at once as shown in Figure 2.17. Clicking on one of the application windows maximizes the window and brings you to the desired application.

Spaces is the other tab on the Exposé & Spaces configuration window. The Spaces feature lets you organize the applications on your desktop in a way that is efficient to the way you work. This feature allows you to assign applications to one of four spaces on your desktop. In Figure 2.18, you can see that if you select the + symbol you can add desired applications to a particular quadrant. This way, each time you open an application on the Dock, it appears in the quadrant you have selected.

Force Quit

2.1.2.4

If you want to stop an unresponsive application when using the Macintosh OS, you must use the *Force Quit* option. It is important that you only use the Force Quit option if you are absolutely unable to work with the application and it is unresponsive. Using this option will cause the application to close without saving any work. You can Force Quit out of an application by selecting the *Force Quit* option from the *Apple* menu. As an alternative, you can press the *Command-Option-Esc* keys simultaneously. You must then select the unresponsive application from the menu that appears.

> **FIGURE 2.17**
Active Exposé view

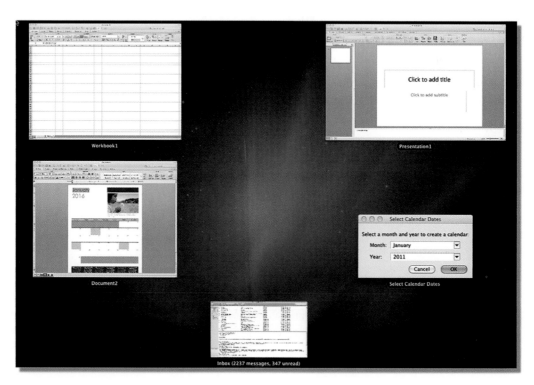

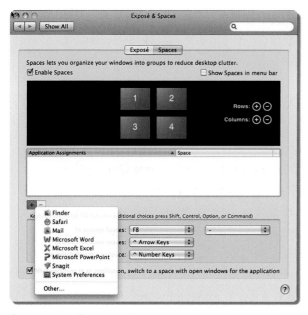

▲ **FIGURE 2.18** Spaces configuration settings

2.2 ORGANIZING FILES AND FOLDERS

Organizing files and folders is an essential task on a computer. By organizing your files effectively, you can quickly find documents you need. Part of this organization process is the use of folders to group similar content. These work just like real folders that you can use to organize paper documents. The fundamental principles are the same, regardless of the operating system you use. Each folder can contain subfolders in a hierarchical arrangement. Ultimately, all of your folders will stem from one source, such as your hard drive (typically labeled C on a Windows machine); the folders within that are subfolders, and each of those can contain subfolders. Even your desktop is a subfolder of the hard drive on which your operating system is stored.

Files and Folders in Windows

2.2.1

Organizing files and folders on Windows 7 is a common task, and there are many features that can be quite helpful if used properly. One of the first things to start off with is storing files in appropriate folders. Think of organizing files and folders on your computer as similar to organizing a filing cabinet at your home or office. Assume you wanted to use your filing cabinet to store all of your homework assignments for your first semester of undergraduate education. If you are taking four courses, you might make four folders. For this example, pretend you are taking Biology, Math, Sociology, and Business Ethics.

Creating your folders with categories is the first step to help you sort all of the documents you will quickly begin to accumulate during the semester. If your courses are eight weeks long, you might want eight subfolders to store assignments by week. This might require that you now create 8 subfolders for each course category for a total of 32 subfolders.

You can create a folder anywhere on your hard drive, external media, or desktop. Windows contains a default folder you can use for this purpose called *My Documents*. The problem, though, is that if you just drop all of your documents in there, overtime it can become a mess. Imagine having to scroll through 75 files. It is not as hard as you might think to accumulate that many files in a short amount of time. A great place to start the project of organizing your documents is to create your folders in the My Documents folder for each category of organization you want to have, such as folders for Home, Work, and School.

Once you have your filing cabinet categorized with folders and subfolders, you can begin to populate them with assignments, tests, and quizzes for each week of the semester. Each one of these documents you collect is part of the set of files that will populate your filing cabinet.

To translate this to the environment of the computer, the filing cabinet on the computer is located in the chosen storage location on the media you select. Recall from the previous chapter that media can be the computer's internal hard drive, an external hard drive, or a thumb drive that you use to store all of your important data. In the following example, you will use the *My Documents* folder (accessible via the Libraries functionality) to create a file structure to store your school documents.

You can see in Figure 2.19 that the Libraries and Documents selections on the left have been expanded and the My Documents folder is highlighted. The My Documents folder shown here does not have any files in it. Highlighting the My Documents folder opens the folder for you to view its contents. In this case, the folder simply has a title at the top of the window indicating the *Documents library* in green letters and *My Documents* in black letters. Now simply right-click with your mouse pointer in the window and a menu appears with New as an option near the bottom. Selecting *New* gives you many options, as shown in the menu at the right; one of them is the creation of a new folder.

Selecting *Folder* creates a new folder as shown in Figure 2.20 with the title *New folder* highlighted in blue. This indicates

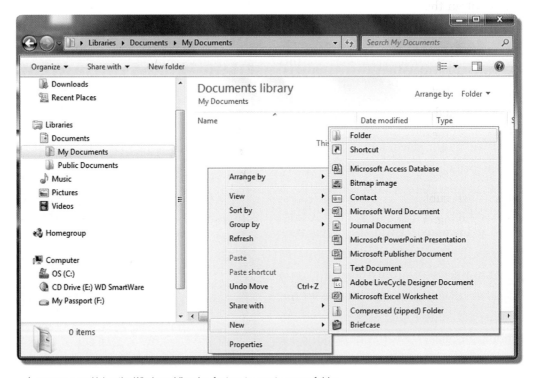

▲ FIGURE 2.19 Using the Windows Libraries feature to create a new folder

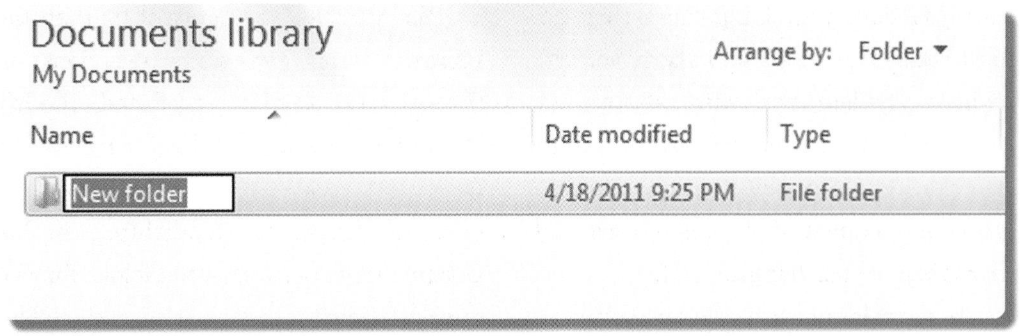

▲ **FIGURE 2.20** A new folder in the My Documents folder

you can proceed to type a desired name for the new folder. You should always take care to title your folders immediately, or you may forget what they contain or what their original purpose was supposed to be.

Now take a look at Figure 2.21 where the newly created *School* folder resides in the My Documents location of your computer; you can think of this as your School category. Now you can add subfolders that reside within this School folder. For example, you might create a subfolder within the School folder titled Biology, indicating a storage location for all of the work you complete and collect for the science course you are taking, and you can create a subfolder within that for each week during the term.

In Figure 2.22, you can see there are now four subfolders within the main School folder. Each subfolder represents a course you are taking. You could further develop

each subfolder by adding subfolders representing each week in your school term.

Files and Folders on a Mac

2.2.2

Organizing files and folders on a Mac is essential. If you have read the previous sections relating to the Mac environment, then you have already been introduced to the place where you will start. Your starting point is the Finder window, where you can access all of the applications and folders on your computer. You can actually create folders anywhere on the Mac including the desktop, but the current Mac culture encourages users to keep the desktop clean. For this example, you will begin by creating a filing system for your school documents in the *Documents* folder, as shown in Figure 2.23.

To create the main folder titled *School*, double-click on the *Documents* folder to

▲ **FIGURE 2.21** The new School folder in the My Documents folder

open it. The Documents folder in this instance contains only a Microsoft User Data folder that stores the preference settings for the Microsoft Office 2011 suite of applications. (The Snagit folder stores images for a screen capture application.) The School folder will be used to file schoolwork. Notice in Figure 2.23 how the button with a gear and a drop-down arrow is activated. A new menu has appeared beneath it. Select *New Folder* to create a folder.

Once the new folder appears on the desktop, you have the option to name the folder. In this case, name it *School*. Now if you were to dump all of your assignments in the School folder without any further organization, the folder would quickly become very cluttered and disorganized. The next step is to create subfolders for each subject that will reside in the School folder.

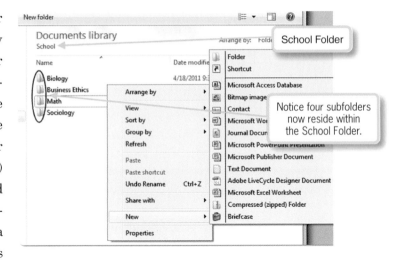

▲ **FIGURE 2.22** School folder with new subfolders

Open the *School* folder and create four subfolders, as shown in Figure 2.24. Subfolders are created in the same way you created the School folder.

Since you do not want clutter in your subfolders, you can create additional subfolders within your course subject for the weeks of the course as shown in Figure 2.25. You can name these new subfolders by week

➤ **FIGURE 2.23**
Finder window

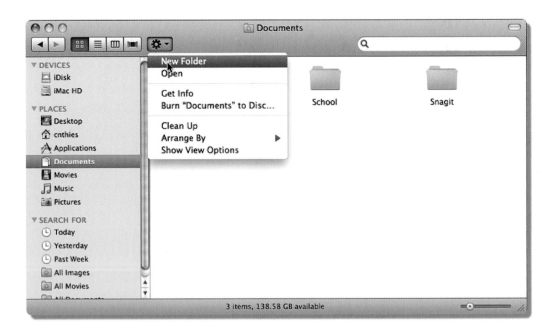

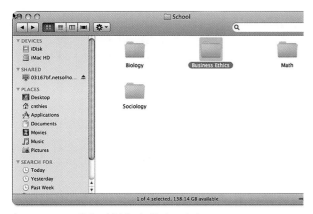

▲ FIGURE 2.24 School folder in Finder window

◀ FIGURE 2.25
Subfolders broken down into weeks

so that you can categorize and store each week's assignments in an organized fashion. Once you have finished creating this new structure, you will notice that this filing method matches a hierarchical structure. Following a similar format for data storage of all types will help you stay organized as you work with your computer.

2.3 WORKING WITH FILES ON YOUR COMPUTER

Now that you have learned about getting around on your system and developing a filing structure to organize application files, you can begin learning about files. A *file* can be an application document or image that can be stored on digital media, either externally or internally (such as on your computer hard drive). You have already learned about applications on your computer system, so it is time to put them to use.

You are probably reading this text to learn to use productivity software to construct professional presentations, databases, and other professional documents. Before you approach that task, you should get started with one of the basic applications that came with your personal computer to introduce you to the concept of a file. There are a couple of things you need to know about files. You may recall an earlier discussion on the concept of storage space on your computer in both the forms of available space on your hard drive and other media devices you use to store files. Before saving a file, you need to know where you will save it and the type of file it will be saved as. All files are associated with a file extension, which is usually a period (or decimal point) followed by three letters. For example, the name *my text.txt* is a valid filename. You get to define the part to the left of the period, but the part to the right should come from a list of existing file types so your machine can recognize it and know how to process the information.

WordPad on Windows

2.3.1

WordPad is a basic word-processing application on the Windows platform. To start WordPad, click with your pointer on the *Start* menu and select *All Programs* and then the *Accessories* folder. Within the *Accessories* folder, you will find the Word Padicon. Click on the *WordPad* icon to start the application and enter the

► FIGURE 2.26
WordPad
document sample

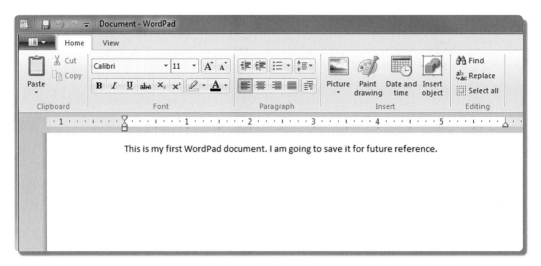

following message in the WordPad interface: *This is my first WordPad document. I am going to save it for future reference* (See Figure 2.26). If you are following along with your own version of WordPad, then congratulations, you have just created your first WordPad document.

We will not go into a lot of the functionality of WordPad here because you will be learning about more advanced Office applications in the next several chapters; just keep in mind that there is a lot you can do with it. If you have no other alternative, you can use WordPad to type documents and then open them later in the Microsoft Word application by using a file extension that Word understands.

Every application file needs to be saved with a file extension. Every application opens files based on the file extension with which it was saved. Now that you have created your first WordPad document, you must save it to avoid losing the information. Saving the document will allow you to reopen it at a future date.

To save your new WordPad file, select the *WordPad* button shown at the top left of Figure 2.27, and then select *Save as* and *Rich Text document*.

The file extension associates your new file with the applications that can open your file. It is important to keep in mind that sometimes more than one application may have the capability to open your file but may not be set as the primary application. In such cases, you should open the application you wish to use and open the file manually from within that application.

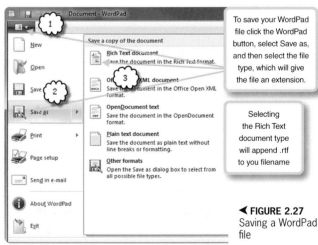

To save your WordPad file click the WordPad button, select Save as, and then select the file type, which will give the file an extension.

Selecting the Rich Text document type will append .rtf to you filename

◄ FIGURE 2.27
Saving a WordPad file

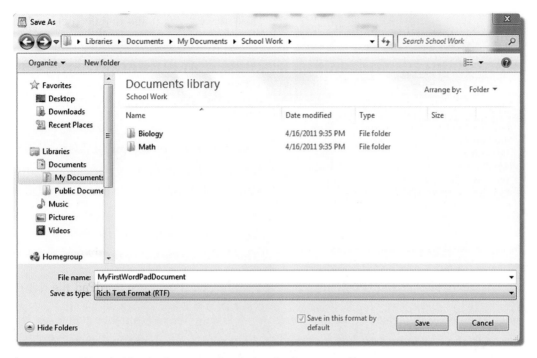

▲ **FIGURE 2.28** Using the Libraries feature to select the location for your new file

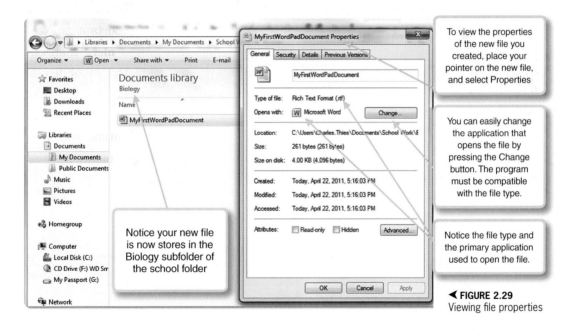

To view the properties of the new file you created, place your pointer on the new file, and select Properties

You can easily change the application that opens the file by pressing the Change button. The program must be compatible with the file type.

Notice the file type and the primary application used to open the file.

Notice your new file is now stores in the Biology subfolder of the school folder

◀ **FIGURE 2.29**
Viewing file properties

Now that you have selected to save your new WordPad file as a Rich Text Format (RTF) file, the Libraries menu comes up on your desktop. You may remember that earlier you created the folder structure for your school folders, which you developed inside your My Documents folder.

In the *Libraries* dialog that appears on the desktop, as shown in Figure 2.28, expand the *Documents* library and open

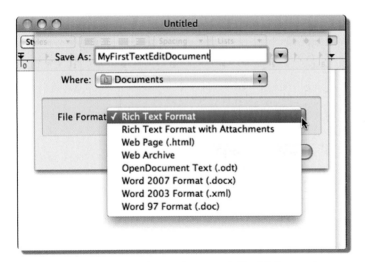

▲ FIGURE 2.30 Choosing the file type for a sample TextEditdocument

the *School* folder you created. Once you have the location selected, place your cursor in the *File name* text box and type the name for your new file, which in this case is *MyFirstWordPadDocument*. Be sure the correct file type extension, *Rich Text Format (RTF)* in this case, is selected in the *Save as type* text box. Finally, press the *Save* button to save your new WordPad file to your chosen location. You can view the properties of the file you create by following the example in Figure 2.29.

Text Edit for Macintosh

It is important to note that with any operating system you will use file extensions. Every time you save a new file, you have the opportunity to select the file type, which gives the file a new extension to associate it with an application that is able to open it. On the Macintosh, you have an application similar to WordPad called Text Edit. The Text Edit application also enables you to develop documents and even save the file as a Microsoft Word document. Notice in Figure 2.30 that the File Format options include some of the older Microsoft Word formats.

The TextEdit application can be found in the Applications folder on your Macintosh computer and can be located using the Finder applicationin the Dock on your desktop. Once you have the application open, type the following in the main document pane: *This is my first TextEdit document. I am going to save it for future reference.*

Locate the Documents folder in the Finder view, as shown in Figure 2.31, and save the file to the *School* folder you created earlier when you developed a file structure for all of your school work. Notice the *Untitled Save as* window gives you the option to save the file with a name that you choose, which in this case is *MyFirstText-EditDocument*.

After selecting where to save the file (the *Documents* folder) and the file format (*Rich Text Format*), it's time to save the file by pressing the *Save*

▼ FIGURE 2.31 Sample Documents view

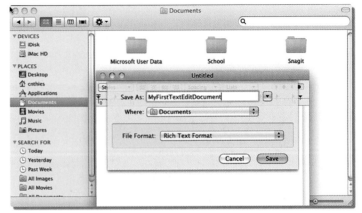

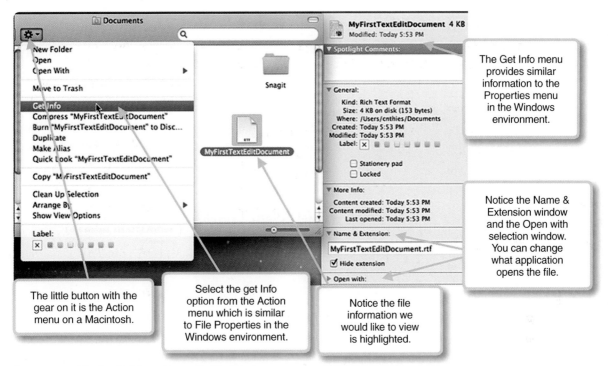

The Get Info menu provides similar information to the Properties menu in the Windows environment.

Notice the Name & Extension window and the Open with selection window. You can change what application opens the file.

The little button with the gear on it is the Action menu on a Macintosh.

Select the get Info option from the Action menu which is similar to File Properties in the Windows environment.

Notice the file information we would like to view is highlighted.

▲ **FIGURE 2.32** Viewing file information on the Macintosh

button. To examine the properties of the file you created in TextEdit, simply return to the folder where you stored it in the *Documents* folder, as shown in Figure 2.32.

Click on the file named *MyFirstTextEditDocument* and click on the Action menu. From the Action menu, you can select *Get Info*; the menu appears very similar to what you would see in the Windows environment showing the file properties. From this menu, you can change the file extension type and even the program that opens the file.

CHAPTER SUMMARY

This chapter provided an introduction to navigating the Windows and Macintosh desktops in an efficient manner. It covered the user interface on both operating systems and gave users an introduction to modifying system preferences and managing documents. Managing files and folders are an important part of using any computer system. You should now be able to create folders and subfolders to effectively organize your personal computing filing system. The next chapter focuses on the use of the Internet as a productivity tool; this will help you tremendously as you learn to use the different productivity software applications covered in this text.

CHAPTER EXERCISES

1. Think about a category of files you would like to organize on your computer's hard drive or an external media device. It could be any set of files on your computer, such as digital images or documents. Plan and develop a filing system to help you organize these files. Write a short document that describes the folder and subfolder setup you would develop to organize files stored on your computer system. You can complete this assignment in either the Macintosh or Windows 7 environment.

2. Use the Appearance and Personalization selection within the Control Panel to change your Windows 7 desktop theme, and use the Gadgets menu selection to add one widget of your choice. If you're using the Mac use the System Preferences to modify your desktop and customize your Widgets and Expose.

CHAPTER KNOWLEDGE CHECK

1. The _____ is the graphical display provided by the computer's operating system that allows the user to visually interact with and issue tasking commands to the Basic Input/Output System.

- ○ **A.** User interface
- ○ **B.** iPad2
- ○ **C.** Visual display
- ○ **D.** Both a and b

2. The mouse is the hardware device you use to move the pointer over the desktop to access programs and files.

- ○ True
- ○ False

3. To remove a program from the Start menu, simply right-click and then click _____ from the Start menu.

- ○ **A.** Delete
- ○ **B.** Unpin
- ○ **C.** Rename
- ○ **D.** None of the above

4. RSS (Really Simple Syndication) is a Web feed commonly used to publish regularly updated electronic publications such as the news or weather.

- ○ True
- ○ False

5. The Spaces feature allows you to assign applications to one of four a reason your desktop.

- ○ True
- ○ False

6. Exposé places your open and minimized application windows in a small window laid out so that you can see every application you have open.

- ○ True
- ○ False

7 _____ are a feature in Windows 7 that can help you find and organize your files in one consolidated location.

○ **A.** Libraries
○ **B.** Shelves
○ **C.** Folders
○ **D.** My Documents

8 The Mac platform can perform all of the same tasks that a Windows machine can complete.

○ True
○ False

9 Most keyboards allow you to simply press the F3 key to view your Exposé of active applications.

○ True
○ False

10 The _____ has a number of widgets available to be viewed in the desktop environment.

○ **A.** Dashboard
○ **B.** Finder window
○ **C.** Exposé window
○ **D.** Hidden menu

Working with the Web

This chapter will teach you how to navigate the World Wide Web (often referred to simply as the Web). You will learn about the various aspects of the Web, including the differences between the Web and the Internet. You will also learn about navigating the environment using a Web browser and conducting effective searches on the Web, along with the legal aspects and concepts of fair use. Once you have completed the chapter, you will be able to:

- Describe and identify the background and historical context of the Internet and the Web

- Discuss how the Internet and Web operate

- Describe the types of available Internet connections

- Demonstrate the use of different Web browsers to navigate the Web

BACKGROUND AND HISTORICAL CONTEXT OF THE WEB

Whether you are using a Mac or a Windows-based computer, you have the ability to access real-time information from a variety of sources. You need nothing more than an Internet connection and your computer to access a world full of possibilities. This is because Internet technologies open up a vast and global library full of information for anyone to use to access the Web. The Web is a powerful and evolving tool that can be used for the exchange of data and information.

DATA *is simply a collection of unprocessed facts (such as the number 10 or the letter A or the number 3.2756).*

INFORMATION *is the association of data with the context of its meaning; it is typically in a form that has been processed to a level where it becomes useful to an individual or organization. An example of information is: The ratio of the length to width of a particular rectangle is 3.2756.*

Before going any further it is important to give you some background and historical information about the Web and Internet. You may have heard your friends or colleagues use these terms synonymously, yet the two entities actually have different roles. First, the *Internet*, also known as the information superhighway, was developed during the 1950s by an organization known as the Advanced Research Projects Agency (ARPA), which was created by the U.S. government to conduct research and development in hopes of countering threats from the former Soviet Union. This endeavor was triggered by the Soviet Union's launch of the first satellite into space, called *Sputnik*.

It was soon after, on April 23, 1963, that Dr. Joseph Carl Robnett Licklider, a computer scientist working on a command and control research project at ARPA, first proposed the idea of a network interconnected by hosts. Dr. Licklider did not develop the actual Internet (an abbreviation of interconnected network) that connected computers across the globe, but his ideas led to the development of ARPANET, which later led to the development of what today we call the Internet. ARPANET in those early days had been developed as a way to interconnect computers so that they could be used to support military command and control operations in defense against what was seen as an emerging threat to national security at the time, specifically in the event of nuclear war.

NETWORK *is the term used to identify a situation where two or more computers connect to share resources.*

The **INTERNET** *is a global interconnection of networks made up of hardware devices, such as your personal computer, that supports communication between different computing devices using an addressing scheme known as Internet Protocol (IP).*

The **WORLD WIDE WEB** (*or* **WEB**) *is a service that runs on the Internet to provide access to documents, audio, and video and allows for the interconnection of these documents through the use of hyperlinks.*

For the purposes of this text, what you should know is that the development of ARPANET led to the development of the Internet, which is the fundamental infrastructure used to support the Web. It was in the late 1980s that research support from ARPA (now known as DARPA, or the Defense Advanced Research Projects Agency) ended and the Internet became available to the public for the first time. The Internet then was nothing more than a high-tech superhighway used to transfer data between universities and research centers by using complex techniques leveraging a unique addressing system known as Transfer Control Protocol and Internet Protocol, or TCP/IP.

The Internet was not known to the average computer user at the time and those that did know about it needed significant skills to conduct any type of data transfer. In 1989, Tim Berners-Lee, a physicist working as a contractor at CERN (Conseil Européen pour la Recherche Nucléaire, which translated from French means European Organization for Nuclear Research), developed what today we call the World Wide Web.

Berners-Lee had a grand vision for a system that could link information through a web of interconnections between computers using hyperlinks as a way of managing and sharing information between individual nodes or machines. Berners-Lee used a NeXT™ computer (which was the foundation for the modern-day Macintosh) running a computer programming language called Objective-C® (which the Macintosh still

uses to this day under the name Cocoa®). He developed the Hypertext Transfer Protocol (HTTP) that would essentially allow a user to click on hyperlinks to easily navigate from one Web site to the next using a Web browser; the early Web browser that he wrote was called *World Wide Web*. Essentially this required Web sites to reside on a Web server to work properly. A *Web server* is a computer that manages HTTP connections to allow the hosting of files, Web applications, and Web sites.

Not long after Tim Berners-Lee's efforts at CERN, when the Web had essentially been operational for sometime within the confines of the organization, Web servers began to emerge at research facilities and universities. This interconnected network of Web servers that hosted Web sites gave users the ability to quickly navigate from one Web site to the next by simply clicking on a hyperlink using any of the available Web browsers.

Popular Web browsers today include Microsoft Internet Explorer® (IE),

A **WEB SITE** *is a collection of Web pages, documents, audio, and video that is stored in a location such as a Web server and can be accessed by a unique address determined by a Uniform Resource Locator (URL) value.*

A **WEB SERVER** *is a repository that contains all of the files and folders for a Web site and provides remote access to them via various protocols such as HTTP and File Transfer Protocol (FTP) over the Internet.*

A **WEB BROWSER** *is a software application used to search, navigate, and retrieve information and data from the Web.*

AppleSafari®, and Mozilla® Firefox®; the shortcut icons for these programs are shown in Figure 3.1. Web browsers can be used to search the Web for information relating to nearly any subject, access Web applications such as those used in banking, and purchase products from a variety of vendors. One of the earliest companies providing user access to the Web was Netscape®; its most popular browser was Netscape Navigator®. Netscape was purchased by AOL® in 1998, the same year Communicator was released as an open source product as part of a new Mozilla project.

An **OPEN SOURCE** *product is one where the creator freely distributes the source code to the public, allowing changes for improvement and customization.*

This source code has evolved into Firefox. Firefox is a popular, free Web browser available from Mozilla, which manages changes to this open standards-based browser. Mozilla is the open standards group that emerged when the browser technology was released to the public. Firefox is one of the browsers whose icons is shown in Figure 3.1.

Figure 3.1 shows three icons representing the three most common Web browsers in existence. Windows Internet Explorer is in its ninth version and is available for use on the line of operating systems available from Microsoft. Both Apple Safari and Mozilla Firefox can be installed on a variety of operating systems.

How the Web Works

Now that you have a basic understanding of the differences between the Web and the Internet, you are in a better position to understand how it all works. Recall that a Web site is a collection of files and Web pages that span across the globe; each of these Web sites is stored on Web servers as a collection of documents called Web pages, along with the supporting media files that enrich the user experience. All of these documents are linked and transported using the HTTP protocol.

A *Web page* is a plain text document formatted using Hypertext Markup Language (HTML) and can be part of a larger Web site. *HTML* is a formatting language that is used to organize and present text and multimedia files for presentation in a Web browser (note that this is not a traditional programming language that issues logic arguments). A Web page can include embedded images, video, and audio to enhance the look and feel of the overall site. Now you might be wondering how the computer gets you to a Web site or Web page on the Internet.

Recall that the Internet works using an addressing scheme called TCP/IP. Every hardware device on the Internet has an IP address. Your computer uses a network adapter (called a Network Interface Card) to connect to the Internet using your IP

◀ FIGURE 3.1
Icons for common Web browsers

address to manage data traffic. The network adapter on your computer can be either wireless or wired; both options typically come standard on modern machines. You can find the IP address on a Windows machine by simply clicking the *Start* menu and then typing the command *cmd* in the search window, as shown in Figure 3.2.

Once you have typed the *cmd* command in the search window, the Command Prompt window appears. In the Command Prompt window, you can type the command *IPCONFIG/ALL* to view all of your network adapter properties. In the Command Prompt window shown in Figure 3.3, take specific notice of the IPv4 (Internet Protocol version 4) address; the example here is 192.168.1.2. The address listed here is what your home network will use to keep track of your

▲ FIGURE 3.2 Accessing the Command Prompt window

computer on the network and provide you with access to the Internet. The second setting you should notice is the DNS Servers address. A *Domain Name Server* (DNS) address is used for name resolution on the Internet.

Every single computer on the Internet uses an IP address, but this simple numerical address makes it difficult to immediately recognize a Web site you might want to visit. DNS servers help your computer translate humanly readable domain names used to identify Web sites on the Web. A *domain name* (also known as a hostname) is used to

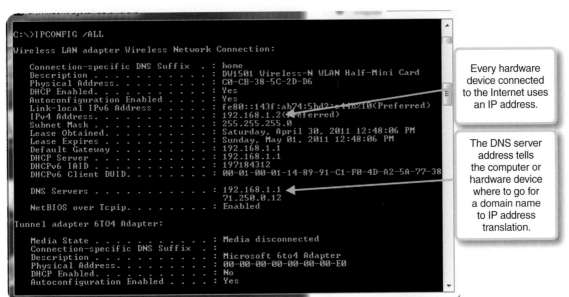

Every hardware device connected to the Internet uses an IP address.

The DNS server address tells the computer or hardware device where to go for a domain name to IP address translation.

◄ FIGURE 3.3 Computer network adapter properties

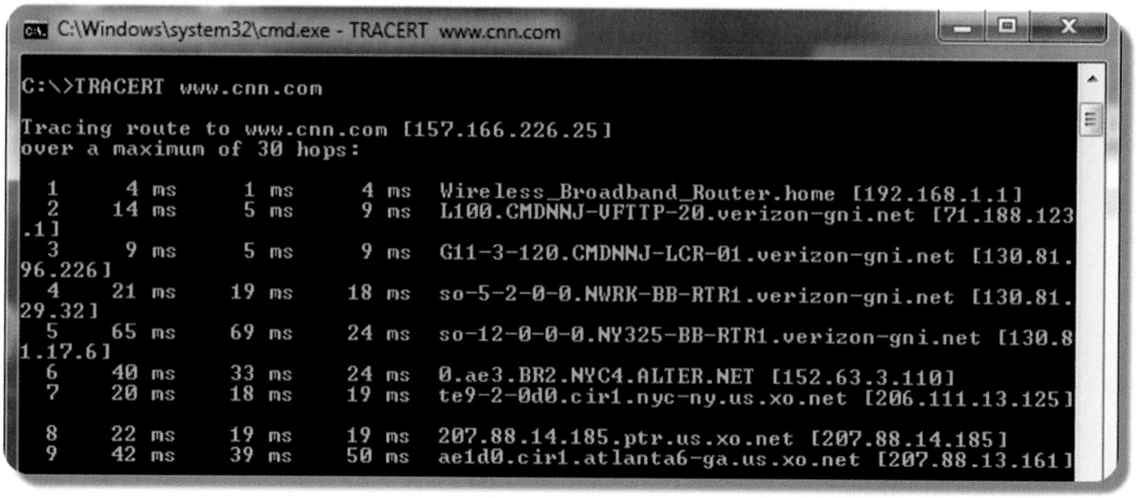

> FIGURE 3.4
Domain name translation

```
C:\Windows\system32\cmd.exe - TRACERT www.cnn.com

C:\>TRACERT www.cnn.com

Tracing route to www.cnn.com [157.166.226.25]
over a maximum of 30 hops:

  1     4 ms      1 ms      4 ms   Wireless_Broadband_Router.home [192.168.1.1]
  2    14 ms      5 ms      9 ms   L100.CMDNNJ-VFTTP-20.verizon-gni.net [71.188.123
.1]
  3     9 ms      5 ms      9 ms   G11-3-120.CMDNNJ-LCR-01.verizon-gni.net [130.81.
96.226]
  4    21 ms     19 ms     18 ms   so-5-2-0-0.NWRK-BB-RTR1.verizon-gni.net [130.81.
29.32]
  5    65 ms     69 ms     24 ms   so-12-0-0-0.NY325-BB-RTR1.verizon-gni.net [130.8
1.17.6]
  6    40 ms     33 ms     24 ms   0.ae3.BR2.NYC4.ALTER.NET [152.63.3.110]
  7    20 ms     18 ms     19 ms   te9-2-0d0.cir1.nyc-ny.us.xo.net [206.111.13.125]

  8    22 ms     19 ms     19 ms   207.88.14.185.ptr.us.xo.net [207.88.14.185]
  9    42 ms     39 ms     50 ms   ae1d0.cir1.atlanta6-ga.us.xo.net [207.88.13.161]
```

identify a Web site, such as *www.CNN.com* or *www.401k.com*. The Command Prompt in Figure 3.4 display show this domain name to IP address translation actually occurs.

If you were to type the Web site address *www.CNN.com* into your Web browser, the actions shown listed in Figure 3.4 are what really happens on your computer. The *TRACERT* command is used to see what route your computer is taking to reach the Web site *www.CNN.com*. Every line in the figure represents a hardware device used for routing (called a *router*) that helps direct you to the CNN Web site servers where the documents for the Web site reside. In this instance, by using the TRACERT command you can see that the Web server address for the CNN site is actually 157.166.226.25.

It is important to realize that there are many types of networks (such as LAN and WAN) that can include business networks and home networks. The important point to remember is that all of these networks can connect to the Internet to share and disseminate information using the Internet as the superhighway for navigation.

The Web provides the service on top of this infrastructure to enable you to view and navigate documents and media on the Web sites you want to visit.

Uniform Resource Locaters (URLs) are the addresses you type into your browser to

A **LOCAL AREA NETWORK** (*LAN*) *is a local network limited to a small geographical area. Your home network or the network at your workplace can be considered a LAN.*

A **WIDE AREA NETWORK** (*WAN*) *is a network that can span to global proportions. For example, an international shipper could use a WAN to manage shipments in multiple countries.*

connect and navigate to the Web site you want to see. For example, *www.Amazon.com* is the domain name that is registered with the Internet Corporation for Assigned Names and Numbers (ICANN), but to actually navigate to that Web site, you would type *www.Amazon.com* (which is equivalent to the full address *http://www.Amazon.com*

that includes the name of the protocol). This is the site's URL, which brings you to the site's home page. The *home page* of a Web site is the very first page you come to when you type the URL into your Web browser (the filename for this is typically *index.htm* or *index.html*). The prefix of the URL is the protocol that is used to access the site; in this instance it is the HTTP protocol.

If you want to acquire a domain name for your own purposes, you can do so by registering the name with ICANN. However, you never directly contact ICANN; you must register your domain name by using a third-party organization called an *Internet Service Provider* (ISP). ISPs are companies that lease service lines used to access the Internet to residential and business customers. ISPs also can also register domain names for customers and can determine whether your chosen domain name is available for lease.

Connecting to the Internet

ISPs are used to connect to the Internet. One of the first things you'll want to do when you acquire your computer is connect to the Internet so you can utilize the Web. Your local ISP is usually the same company that provides access to cable TV or phone services in your local area.

If you decide you would like to connect to the Internet, you need to know about the different services available. Most ISPs have service offerings that are significantly different from each other, so it is important to shop around to be sure you sign up for a service that provides the features you desire. Some ISPs simply provide a cable router that provides high-speed access to the Web. Comcast and Verizon are the typical service companies available in the United States. Sometimes your service provider can also be your cell phone company.

The specifics to understand as a user are the speed of the services provided versus the cost of the service; a higher connection speed is typically a more desirable scenario, but it also costs more. There are several types of services offered by ISPs with which you should be familiar before signing any long-term agreements. Most ISPs will require a service agreement for a period of time, usually from 12 to 18 months. Research is essential since all of these factors can vary with time requirements and price of the connection. When you are investigating options, you should also consider the connection speed, which includes a download speed and an upload speed.

Digital phone service is usually in the form of VoIP (or Voice over IP), which is basically a communication service accessed using Internet infrastructure. VoIP uses servers and computer systems to manage phone calls between users. The disadvantage to VoIP services is that they are susceptible to power outages and other types of computer system downtime issues. Analog telephone lines through your phone company are usually considered more reliable than VoIP lines.

The **CONNECTION SPEED** *is the rate at which information is transmitted between your computer and the network. Connection speeds are measured in the number of bits transmitted per second, particularly kilo bits per second (thousands of bits per second) or megabits per second (millions of bits per second). This is determined by two rates: download speed and upload speed.*

The **DOWNLOAD SPEED** *is the speed of data reaching your computer from the network.*

The **UPLOAD SPEED** *is the speed of information reaching the network from your computer.*

The following are the different types of Internet connections:

- Dial-up—This type of connection is an old technology that has been around for many years and uses an analog telephone connection to connect to the Internet. This connection operates at 56 Kbps (kilobits per second), is extremely slow, and requires that the user dial a phone number to access the Internet.

- Cable High-Speed Internet—In most instances, your cable TV company also can provide you with an Internet connection. The speed range depends on the price you are willing to pay. Some ISPs can provide speeds that promise 12 Mb (megabits per second) of download speed and 1.5 Mb of upload speed. These speeds can be higher or lower, depending on the plans that are available for your area. Cable high-speed Internet is significantly faster than dial-up.

- DSL—Also known as a Digital Subscriber Line, these connections use copper wire provided by the phone company

and are capable of speeds up to 128 Kbps; they can transmit voice and video at a relatively fast speed. They are considered slower than cable modem connections, yet faster than dial-up services.

- Wireless 3G networks—Your cell phone company can provide relatively fast service that enables a speed around 800 Kbps for uploads and 600 Kbps for downloads, depending on your geographical location. These speeds are faster than dial-up and DSL but significantly slower than cable modems. Figure 3.5 shows a common portable 3G device that plugs into your laptop using one of its USB ports. With this device, you can surf the Web on your laptop from any location.

USING A WEB BROWSER TO SURF THE WEB

3.2

Now that you understand how the Web and Internet work and how to acquire a connection that suits your needs, it is time to go back to the topic of navigating the Web. You already know that you can navigate the Web by using a Web browser. The following sections will teach you the anatomy of a Web browser and expose you to three of the most common Web browsers available.

Microsoft Internet Explorer

3.2.1

Microsoft provides Internet Explorer with all of the Windows operating systems it offers. In its ninth version, IE is very

▲ FIGURE 3.5
3G USB connection mini-modem

transaction is using the HTTP protocol with an encryption standard called Secure Sockets Layer (SSL) to protect your password and personal data while transmitting to and from your computer. *Encryption* is the use of an algorithm to change the text of your message to a code that is unreadable without the use of a special key to unlock the code.

Notice the little lock that is highlighted in yellow at the top left of Figure 3.6. Clicking on the lock brings up a small window that provides further Web site identification,

> *Digital certificates* are used in the information technology field specifically to identify the identity of the transaction or e-mail message. Digital certificates must be purchased from a trusted Certificate Authority (CA). A CA can be a private or public organization. One you may have heard of is VeriSign; you can read more about VeriSign at *https://www.Verisign.com*.

common and rather easy to use with some practice. The Web browser is what helps the user download files from the Web and navigate to Web sites to access information or conduct secure e-commerce transactions.

Safe e-commerce transactions are conducted using HTTPS. The easiest way to check to see if you are conducting a secure shopping transaction over the Web is to look at your Web browser URL window. If the URL is preceded by "https," your

such as any information about digital certificates and the valid dates for the certificates. The Web site identification window also tells you whether the information transferred on the site is encrypted.

The Web browser itself has a significant amount of functionality. One basic function you should learn to use is the ability to organize and save the addresses of the sites you visit on the Web. There are two common terms used to refer to this type of activity. On Internet Explorer, your favorite sites are referred to as *favorites*, and on Safari and Firefox Web browsers, these are called *bookmarks*.

> **E-COMMERCE** *(short for electronic commerce) is the act of purchasing and selling products using electronic transaction technologies over the Internet. There are a wide range of technologies available to safely conduct e-commerce transactions.*

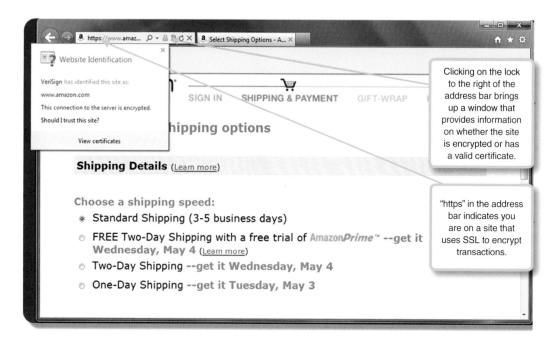

► **FIGURE 3.6**
Using Secure Sockets Layer for an encrypted transaction in Internet Explorer

Internet Explorer provides you with the ability to make all sorts of changes to the browser to meet your needs. In older versions, the toolbar was part of the browser. In IE9, the default view only shows you the Tools button, Favorites button, and Home button on the top-right side of the browser, as shown in Figure 3.7. If you prefer the old-style menu bar view, you can simply right-click the *Tools* button on the right side of the screen and select *Menu bar* from the menu, causing the menu bar to appear on the top-left side of the Web browser window, as shown in Figure 3.7.

Internet Explorer also gives you the ability to monitor and manage downloads with the Download Manager. This helps you control the types of applications that are downloaded and whether a download is installed or saved. You can easily view the Download Manager by either using the shortcut key (*Ctrl-J*) or pressing the

Tools button and selecting *Download Manager*, as shown in Figure 3.8. You may also use the (Alt) key as a shortcut to display the IE toolbar on the top-left side of the browser.

Selecting the *Tools* button and then *Internet Options* lets you adjust a series of settings including deleting your browsing history and changing default options for deleting history automatically. You can also change your default search settings and how Web pages appear in your browser, as demonstrated in Figure 3.9. The Internet Options dialog box gives you the ability to change many more settings related to security, privacy, and other areas; these are accessed by using the tabs at the top of window. Advanced settings are not covered here, as the goal is to expose you to the basic settings that will help you search and navigate the Web at an introductory level.

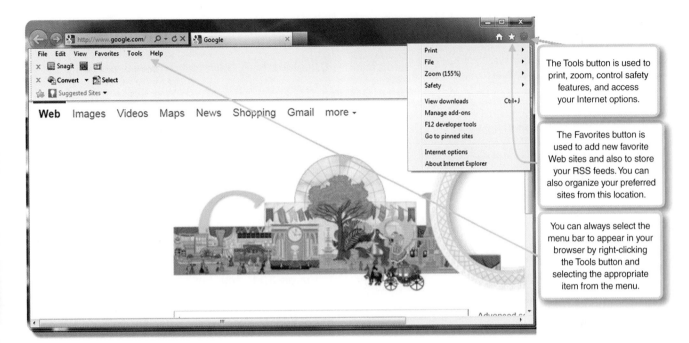

The Tools button is used to print, zoom, control safety features, and access your Internet options.

The Favorites button is used to add new favorite Web sites and also to store your RSS feeds. You can also organize your preferred sites from this location.

You can always select the menu bar to appear in your browser by right-clicking the Tools button and selecting the appropriate item from the menu.

▲ **FIGURE 3.7** Accessing toolbars and menus in IE9

▼ **FIGURE 3.8**
Accessing
the Download
Manager in IE9

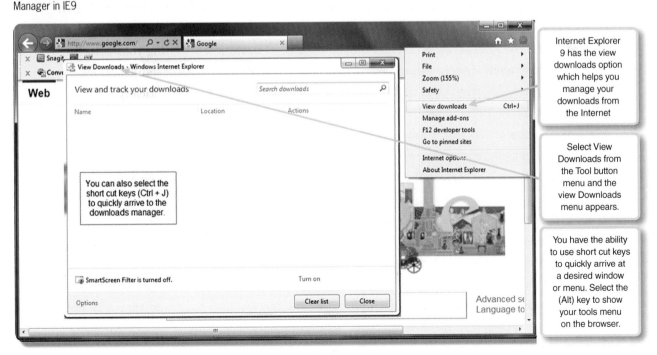

Internet Explorer 9 has the view downloads option which helps you manage your downloads from the Internet

Select View Downloads from the Tool button menu and the view Downloads menu appears.

You have the ability to use short cut keys to quickly arrive at a desired window or menu. Select the (Alt) key to show your tools menu on the browser.

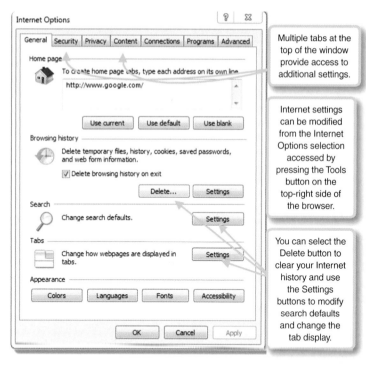

Multiple tabs at the top of the window provide access to additional settings.

Internet settings can be modified from the Internet Options selection accessed by pressing the Tools button on the top-right side of the browser.

You can select the Delete button to clear your Internet history and use the Settings buttons to modify search defaults and change the tab display.

▲ **FIGURE 3.9** Internet Options windows in IE9

3.2.2 Mozilla Firefox

The next browser you will learn about is Mozilla Firefox. Recall from earlier in this chapter that the Firefox browser originated from the early Netscape Navigator browser technology in the early 1990s. Firefox is a very popular browser that can be downloaded for free on either the Macintosh or Microsoft operating systems.

Notice the Firefox browser window pictured in Figure 3.10. Specifically, you should notice a star icon on the right side of the address window; this is quite similar to the Microsoft Internet Explorer icon used to save

a preferred site as a favorite's location. In Firefox, the star icon is used to save a bookmark. A *bookmark* is a site you like to revisit frequently; setting such a site as a bookmark simply requires pressing the star icon to save it in your Bookmarks folder. In Figure 3.10, notice the Bookmarks menu and all of the settings available to you, including the ability to categorize your bookmarked sites.

Setting your home page on Firefox is really quite easy to do. As shown in Figure 3.11, you can just click and drag the icon for the site you want to be your home page over to the Home button—and that is it. Once you have performed this action, anytime you are in Firefox and need your home page, just click on the

▼ **FIGURE 3.10** Firefox browser application

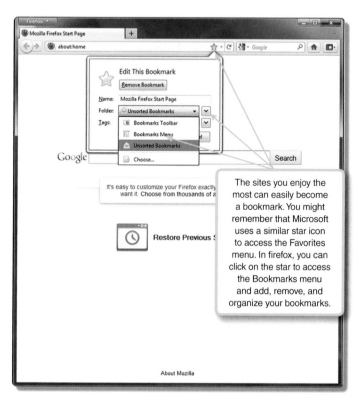

The sites you enjoy the most can easily become a bookmark. You might remember that Microsoft uses a similar star icon to access the Favorites menu. In firefox, you can click on the star to access the Bookmarks menu and add, remove, and organize your bookmarks.

▲ **FIGURE 3.11** Setting your home page in the Firefox browser

Home button and you will immediately be redirected to your home page.

All of the options for your Firefox browser are easily accessed by clicking on the Firefox button, as shown in Figure 3.12. With the Options selection, you can make many changes to your browser settings, such as managing add-ons (which are also known as plug-ins and are covered later in the chapter), changing your privacy settings so that you can decide whether you want the browser to save your browser history, or blocking pop-up ads.

Determining whether the Web site you are visiting is safe is easy to do in the Firefox Web browser. Figure 3.13 shows

three passport officer icons that provide information on Web sites and notify the user whether a particular site is encrypted or unencrypted and whether it has a valid digital certificate.

There are three color codes to help you identify the level of authenticity of a Web site:

- *Green*—The Web site is completely verified and uses an Extended Validation (EV) key. An EV is a new type of digital certificate that requires the Web site to go through a more rigorous process for identification.

- *Blue*—The Web site is identified and the connection is encrypted;

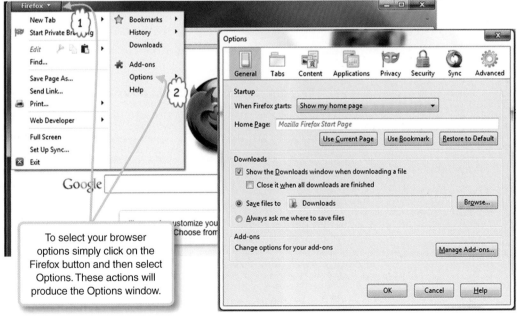

◀ **FIGURE 3.12** Accessing Firefox browser options

To select your browser options simply click on the Firefox button and then select Options. These actions will produce the Options window.

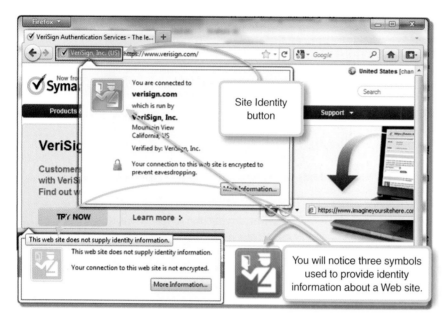

▲ **FIGURE 3.13** Determining whether a Web site is secure

Apple Safari

The final browser covered here is the Apple Safari Web browser. The Safari browser, shown in Figure 3.15, comes pre installed on all new Macintosh computers or can be downloaded from the Apple Web site at *www.Apple.com*.

Notice that there are similarities between the browsers covered in previous sections of this chapter and the Safari Web browser. Take a look at the Smart Address (URL) field, which is where you enter the address you would like to navigate to. To the right of this field is the RSS Feed button; by pressing this button, you can view your RSS feeds if you have any.

There are default RSS feeds that are delivered from Apple News to your browser. By cycling through the RSS button one more time, your screen will switch views and return to the Web content as displayed in Figure 3.15. You can manage your bookmarks as in other Web browsers by pressing the Add Bookmark button. You can also access your Safari settings by clicking the button on the top-right side of your browser which looks like a gear.

You may have determined by now that most Web sites use a lock symbol to indicate whether the site is using encryption. There are three elements in Figure 3.16 that immediately let you

it is safe from eavesdroppers who could be trying to intercept privacy information.

- *Gray*—The Web site is not verified, not encrypted, and does not have a valid digital certificate.

Finally, to manage your downloads, Firefox has a Downloads window that you can access at any time by either using the Ctrl-J keyboard shortcut or simply selecting the Firefox button and then Downloads from the menu. The Downloads window, shown in Figure 3.14, helps you determine the status of any file you download to your computer.

In addition to keeping track of application and file downloads, you can pause or cancel any of your downloads at any time. You can also open files or folders and save files to specific locations from the Downloads window. Once you have downloaded your file, you can remove the file from the list or retry a download from the Downloads window.

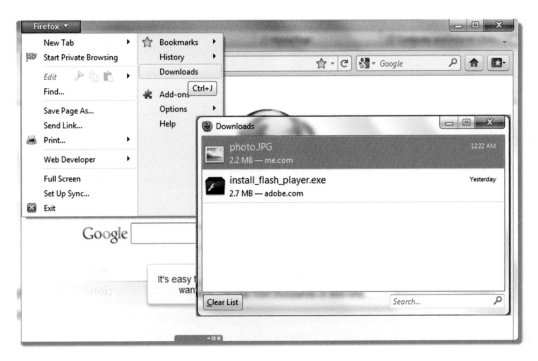

◀ FIGURE 3.14
Firefox Downloads
window

▼ FIGURE 3.15
Safari Web
browser window

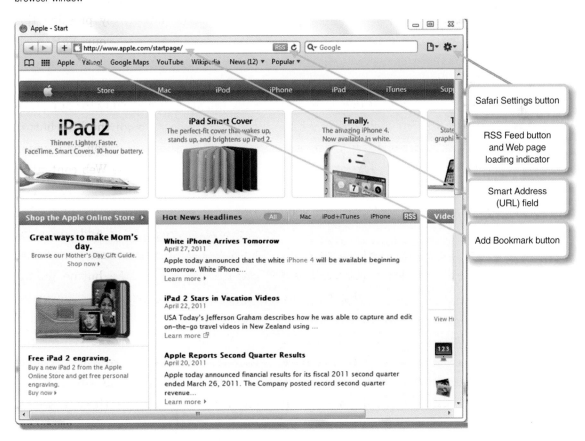

Safari Settings button

RSS Feed button
and Web page
loading indicator

Smart Address
(URL) field

Add Bookmark button

know that the Web site you are viewing is secure:

- The site uses HTTPS.

- There is a green VeriSign symbol in the Smart Address (URL) field. Clicking on either this symbol or the lock lets you view the digital certificate that verifies the site.

- There is a lock at the right side of the Smart Address (URL) field.

To modify settings on your Safari browser, you use the Safari settings button, which looks like a little gear and is located at the top-right side of the

A *search engine* is a software program that uses the text you enter into a search field to find matching keywords. The information on the Web is not a database but rather a repository of semi structured data that does not have any real organization such as what you might find in a database. Most Web sites are categorized by using a *Web crawler* service. A Web crawler service ranks Web sites based on the frequency of searches and indexes the sites for future searches. If you want your Web site to appear on search engine results, you would need to register your site with a service.

window. Pressing this button allows you to change various options.

Notice in Figure 3.17 the menu that appears when you press the settings button in Safari. The available options include showing your menu bar on the browser, reviewing Web surfing history, using the

Downloads window, and electing to browse the Internet privately, among others.

Selecting an option from the Safari Settings menu brings up a new window, as shown in Figure 3.18, giving you the ability to change the home page and download settings, among other options. You'll notice that there are tabs at the top of the window with additional settings that allow you to make additional changes to your browser in order to improve your browsing experience.

USING SEARCH ENGINES TO FIND INFORMATION ON THE WEB

3.3

Searching the Internet can be an enjoyable experience, but it also can present some challenges if you do not carefully watch what you are doing. You should never just click on a Web site simply because the link looks interesting on the search engine you are using.

Common search engines include Google™, Yahoo!®, and Bing™. When reviewing the results provided by the search engine, it is important to be sure that the site you are opening is a safe site or even the intended site. Even if you recognize the site, be sure you are going to the correct address. There are hackers who will create fraudulent Web sites with names similar to well-known companies and products to

▶ FIGURE 3.16
Determining whether the Web site is secure

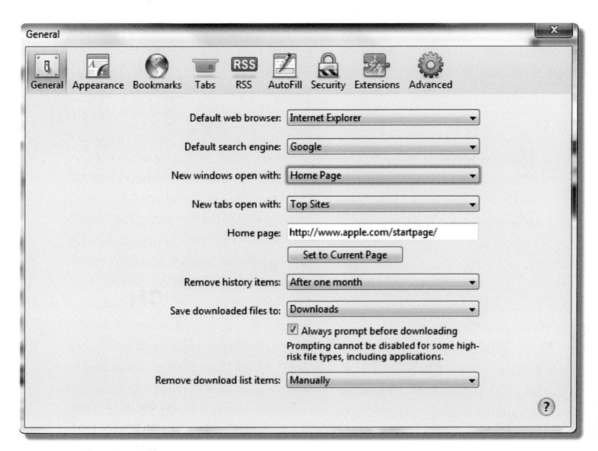

◀ FIGURE 3.17
Safari Settings
menu

◀ FIGURE 3.18
Safari preferences
window

entice unsuspecting computer users to quickly navigate to the site without realizing it is not valid.

One thing to remember is that all browsers will warn you if you are going to a Web site that is not a trusted source. Never ignore the warnings issued by your browser. Many times the warnings are valid, and proceeding to an untrusted site could bring you to a site loaded with *malware*.

Always search the Web for information that might give you warnings about a potential threat. It is important that you never give your privacy information to anyone. For example, many hackers use a scam in which they send you an e-mail purporting to be from your bank that asks for personal information. Remember that no one in a banking institution will ever ask you for your passwords or other personal information via an e-mail message.

3.4 USING WEB BROWSER PLUG-INS

A Web browser *plug-in* (sometimes called an add-on) is a special software program that attaches to a Web browser and enhances its functionality; plug-ins are required to access certain content on the Web. For example, some sites include video clips. Many times these sites will ask you to install a plug-in, such as Adobe® Flash® Player. Flash Player (available from *www.Adobe.com*) is a browser plug-in that allows the browser to run dynamic video, image rendering, and quicker graphics while accessing Web

> **MALWARE** *is malicious code or scripts that can be used to acquire privacy information from your computer and make it available to a computer hacker who may use the information inappropriately or resell it to someone who will.*

content that is only obtainable through the use of this plug-in.

It is important to realize that there is a difference between plug-ins and media players. Media players can run specific video formats and work independently from the browser. Some examples of media players include Microsoft Media® Player, RealNetworks® RealPlayer®, and Apple QuickTime®. All of these can be used to play back video or music as long as the player supports the file format that the file was created and stored in.

3.5 THE WEB AND FAIR USE

It is exceedingly important that you understand how to handle information you acquire from the Web while conducting academic research. Section II, "Word Processing and Microsoft Word," will teach you how to determine the value of a source for research. Here, we want to specifically address how to handle information legally without violating copyright laws. You cannot under any circumstances simply copy and paste material from the Web to use for your own work without providing the source from which you acquired the material.

In some cases, you should acquire permission from the owner of a publication prior to using it for your own work. In the academic field, you have some protections that are referred to as the Fair Use doctrine. Title 17 of the U.S. Code, Section 107 sets the following conditions for which a published work may be considered fair use and used as part of your work as long as you cite the source appropriately:

- Teaching
- Scholarship
- Research
- News media
- Criticism

It is also important that you find out what the proper writing style is for your school and acquire a good writing style manual that will help you to properly use and cite sources in your papers. Common publication manuals include:

- *Publication Manual of the American Psychological Association*, 6th ed.
- *The Chicago Manual of Style*, 16th ed.
- *MLA Style Manual and Guide to Scholarly Publishing*, 3rd ed.

When you begin using sources for research, you will likely find the prospect challenging. The most important part of all of this is to always remember to cite all of your sources properly by using the latest edition of a writing manual approved by your educational institution.

CHAPTER SUMMARY

The chapter provided an introduction to navigating the Web using the Internet to get you from one Web site to the next. It covered the use of Web browsers, how to connect to the Internet, and how to conduct searches on the Web. You should also consider safety and security in your navigation of the Web. The next chapter will introduce you to the use of e-mail and e-mail clients, which are part of a group of applications known as productivity software.

CHAPTER EXERCISES

1. Use your preferred Web browser to locate a Web browser plug-in and follow the instructions on the site to install the browser. Document your findings and steps you took to complete the assignment in a written format.

2. Use a Web search engine such as Google, Bing, or Yahoo! to find three Web sites of your choice. Using the skills you learned in this chapter, determine whether a site is using encryption or a digital certificate and the type of Web site involved. Describe all of the steps used to determine your findings in a written format.

CHAPTER KNOWLEDGE CHECK

1   Data is truly everywhere and can be identified most clearly as _____.

- ○ **A.** Unprocessed facts
- ○ **B.** Information
- ○ **C.** Query result
- ○ **D.** Both a and b

2   Information can be most clearly defined as data that has been _____.

- ○ **A.** Processed
- ○ **B.** Unprocessed
- ○ **C.** Improved
- ○ **D.** Deleted

3   A Web site is a collection of :

- ○ **A.** Web pages
- ○ **B.** Documents
- ○ **C.** Folders
- ○ **D.** None of the above

4   The Internet is a global interconnection of hardware devices, such as your personal computer, that supports communication between different computing devices using an addressing scheme known as Internet Protocol version 4 (IPv4) .

- ○ True
- ○ False

5   The Web browser is the software application used to search, navigate, and retrieve information and data from the Web.

- ○ True
- ○ False

6   A Domain Name Server (DNS) address is used for name design on the Internet.

- ○ True
- ○ False

7

A _____ is the term used to identify a situation where two or more computers connect to share resources.

- ⚪ **A.** Network
- ⚪ **B.** Router
- ⚪ **C.** Password
- ⚪ **D.** My Documents

8

The TRACERT command is used to see what route your computer is taking to reach the host.

- ⚪ True
- ⚪ False

9

E-commerce is the act of purchasing and selling products using nonelectronic transaction technologies.

- ⚪ True
- ⚪ False

10

Digital certificates must be purchased from a trusted _____.

- ⚪ **A.** Corporate authority
- ⚪ **B.** Certificate Authority
- ⚪ **C.** Retail outlet
- ⚪ **D.** None of the above

Microsoft Outlook® *and E-mail Clients*

Electronic mail, commonly referred to as e-mail, is one of the most essential tools for communication in the modern business environment. Learning to write e-mail effectively is an essential skill for success in any organization. This involves the use of an e-mail client to manage the incoming and outgoing mail for your account. Establishing a personal e-mail account may also be necessary for communication outside of a business setting, such as with friends or family. Once you complete this chapter, you will be able to:

- Describe how e-mail clients are used to read and organize electronic mail

- Setup and use a personal e-mail account

- Navigate and use Microsoft Outlook and other e-mail clients

- Assess whether a message you write conforms to e-mail etiquette practices

INTRODUCTION TO ELECTRONIC MAIL

E-mail is the digital equivalent of a letter or postcard and has become a preferred method for sharing information and resources in businesses and organizations. It is a fast and convenient form of communication that allows for quick transmission of information from one party to another. The benefits of e-mail are its fast transmission speed, the ability to attach electronic files to a message, and the asynchronous nature of the communication.

Asynchronous communication means that both parties do not have to be online at the same time. Instead, the sending party connects at one time and the receiving party can connect at any time after the transmission has been sent to retrieve the message.

This is also called the store-and-forward model of information transmission because the message is saved on an e-mail server for the recipient and can be retrieved at a later time.

E-MAIL STRUCTURE

Each e-mail message that is written (such as the one shown in Figure 4.1) is housed inside an electronic structure called the *envelope*. This envelope is typically used by the Simple Mail Transfer Protocol (SMTP) to direct the delivery of the message to the intended recipient. Like any other transmission over a network connection, it may experience multiple stops in the routing between the sender and the recipient (or recipients); these are handled by an initial Mail Submission Agent (MSA) and passed through Mail Transfer Agents (MTAs) until

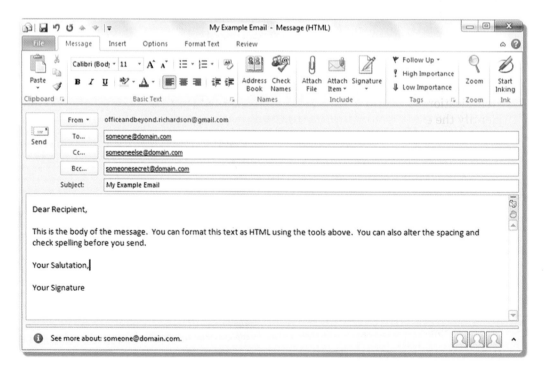

▲ **FIGURE 4.1** An example e-mail message

it reaches the Mail Delivery Agent (MDA) of the recipient. The destination is controlled by the envelope as opposed to the contents, just as it would be with a letter that is sent through the postal service. The various agents in the system can be compared to the postal workers that deliver standard mail.

Within the envelope, an e-mail has two components: the *header* and the *body*. The header contains the subject and addressing information for both the sender and the recipients of the message. Unlike a real letter, a single e-mail can be sent to multiple recipients with ease; this is controlled by the information added to the header. The header commonly contains the following fields:

- *From*—This is the address of the sender. In most e-mail clients, this is not an editable field.

- *Date*—This is the send date of the message. In most e-mail clients, this is not an editable field and may not even be visible.

- *Message-ID*—This is an automatically generated identification value that is used to identify the e-mail message.

- *To*—This field identifies the primary recipient or recipients of the e-mail message; this field is composed of e-mail addresses separated by a comma or semicolon.

- *CC*—This stands for Carbon Copy; this field is used to send e-mail to someone who is impacted by the circumstances described in the message body but who is not directly involved or does not need to take direct action.

- *BCC*—This stands for Blind Carbon Copy; this will (in most e-mail clients) hide the addresses of the person or persons listed in this field from other recipients. This option should be used for large groups to help protect e-mail addresses and keep the message header size small.

- *Subject*—This is a short description of the contents of the message; it should be a preview of what is contained in the message body.

The header may also optionally contain the following fields: In-Reply-To, Content-Type, Received, References, and Reply-To.

The body of the message is where the relevant content is placed in an e-mail message. In the actual e-mail message format, the body is separated from the header by a blank line. Most e-mail clients separate these two items entirely when viewing the message. The body contains the actual information that you want to send to the recipients. E-mail was once limited to plain text input, but most e-mail clients now allow you to enter HTML tags and formatting into the body of messages, meaning you can perform most of the operations of word processing in an e-mail message.

You can also add attachments to an e-mail message. These are external files that are enclosed in the envelope of the message along with the header and the body. There is no intrinsic size limitation

An **E-MAIL CLIENT** *is a software program on an end user's machine that is used primarily to read and compose electronic mail messages. This is also called a Mail User Agent (MUA) in relation to the transmission of e-mail messages to e-mail servers that accept outgoing messages and deliver incoming messages.*

on an e-mail message, but the standard cutoff for most e-mail clients is 25 MB per message including the header, body, and attachments. This is actually a high limit considering the amount of traffic and documents that are passed via e-mail in most organizations. Attachments are governed by the defined Multipurpose Internet Mail Extensions, commonly called MIME types. The *MIME type* is the format of the content that gives the information stored in the message context for interpretation just like file formats in an operating system.

E-mail is considered a *push technology*, which means the sender controls the flow of information rather than the recipient. When you are using e-mail, you are therefore subject to any messages that anyone wishes to send you. This is why unwanted messages (termed *spam*) are such an inconvenience; your Inbox can be filled with these messages

You should never open an e-mail message from a source you do not trust. If you have not requested the e-mail and you do not know the sender from prior contact, you should not open the e-mail message, no matter what the subject line states. There are professional scammers and attackers that excel at crafting subject lines to entice you to open harmful or deceitful messages. Any attachment that is contained in an untrustworthy e-mail should be deleted; attachments can contain malicious software that could compromise or destroy your machine. This is particularly true when the attachment is an executable file(one that has the extension. exe on a Windows machine); you should never open an executable file from an e-mail message unless you have verified by outside contact with the sender that the file is legitimate. It is possible to send e-mail falsely from another person's account, so knowing the person from whom you received the e-mail is not a guarantee that it is safe.

without your permission, and the range of possible e-mail addresses preclude blocking them all. It is therefore up to the spam filter of your e-mail client to try to determine which messages are legitimate and wanted and which messages are unwanted.

E-MAIL ADDRESSES　4.3

Each individual e-mail is routed via an e-mail address. This is a unique identifier for a single account. An example of an e-mail address is *officeandbeyond.richardson@gmail. com*. The information following the "@" symbol is the domain information; in this example, the host domain is *gmail* and the top-level domain name is *com*. The domain name in an e-mail address must conform to the same rules as a hostname in a URL. The domain part of the e-mail address is typically established by the organization hosting the e-mail account and operating the MSA. Note that there can be only one @ symbol in an e-mail address. The full stop character (also called a period or a dot) is used only to separate host domains in the domain part of an e-mail address, but it can be used as a standard character (with or without repetition) in the left side of the address (which is the local part).

The local part of the e-mail address is defined either by the user creating the account or the business establishing the account on the user's behalf, such as a work e-mail account. The local part of the example e-mail address is *officeandbeyond. richardson*. There are restrictions on the local part of the e-mail address; this is particularly relevant if you are creating a new e-mail account for your personal use. The local part of an e-mail address is limited to 64 characters; the combined length of the local part of the address and the domain part cannot exceed 253 characters. Additionally, the local part can only contain the following:

- Letters from the English alphabet (both uppercase and lowercase letters are permitted)
- Numbers from zero (0) to nine (9)
- The full stop (.) character (also called the dot or the period)
- The following special characters: ! # $ % & ' * + - / = ? ^ _ ` { | } ~

The local part of the address is case sensitive, but the use of different cases to distinguish different accounts is discouraged. Most e-mail providers disable this option by default. Some e-mail providers restrict the special characters allowed as well. For example, Microsoft Windows Live® Hotmail® only allows alphanumeric characters (uppercase English letters, lowercase English letters, and numbers), the underscore (_), the hyphen (-), and the dot (.).

4.4 ## CREATING A PERSONAL E-MAIL ACCOUNT

Whether or not you have a professional e-mail address, it is a good idea to have a separate personal e-mail address for communications outside of the professional environment. There are a number of e-mail account providers that allow you to create a free account with a fixed amount of storage space. While there are a number of providers that offer such services, like AOL (*www.aol.com*) and Yahoo! (*www.yahoo.com*), two popular options that are discussed in this chapter are Microsoft Windows Live Hotmail (*www.hotmail.com*) and Gmail™ by Google (*www.gmail.com*).

In most circumstances, you will have the option of defining your own local part of the e-mail address. While you can be creative with this choice, it is best to keep your e-mail address at least semiprofessional in case you ever need to use it for professional opportunities or include it in a resume. Your e-mail address is an identifier that tells someone information about you, so you should consider what the e-mail address will tell them when they read it. You also need to keep the ease of remembering the address in mind in case you need to share it verbally. A good solution for both instances (though you do not have to do this) is to use your first name, then a dot or underscore character, and then your last name as the local part of an e-mail address.

E-mail Account Types

4.4.1

There are different types of e-mail accounts that vary based on storage and delivery. The common types of e-mail accounts are POP (or POP3), IMAP, Web mail, and Microsoft Exchange accounts. POP3 is the Post Office Protocol version three. With a POP3 account, your messages are stored on the e-mail server of your domain until you access them. Once they are downloaded to your local machine, they are deleted from the server. This has the advantage of allowing you to read your mail when you are not connected to the e-mail server. Some Web mail clients use the POP3 protocol to retrieve the messages but do not subsequently delete them; it is up to the individual ISP to determine this option. SMTP is used to send messages; the SMTP and POP3 servers are usually the same.

> Port 25 is the standard port used for e-mail traffic outside of custom applications and services.

The Internet Message Access Protocol (IMAP) uses folders to store e-mail on the e-mail server and allows the user to access them on multiple machines. The typical means of accessing IMAP allows the user to view the header information for each e-mail and then select the ones for which the content should be displayed. The drawback of this protocol is that it requires you to be connected to the mail server to read your e-mail.

Web mail accounts may use either POP3 or IMAP to provide you with access to your messages. Web mail service is typically provided by your e-mail account provider and functions as a rudimentary client for reading and writing e-mail, allowing you the convenience of performing these tasks online without additional software beyond a web browser. Web mail is typically limited in

> Microsoft Exchange accounts require a special server (a version of the Microsoft Exchange Server) and are typically only used by businesses. Exchange accounts specialize in collaborative communications across an organization.

storage space and provides you with advertisements in exchange for using the account services free of charge.

Microsoft Windows Live Hotmail

4.4.2

Microsoft Windows Live Hotmail is one alternative for creating a free personal e-mail account. For Windows users, it is also a convenient way to integrate with your system in terms of online access to Office documents and native Windows services. The home page of Hotmail is *www.hotmail.com*. When you enter this address in your browser, the screen shown in Figure 4.2 appears. From here, you can either login to an existing account or create a new account. To create a new account, click the *Sign Up* button.

Creating an Account

4.4.2.1

To create a new account with Hotmail, you will need to complete the registration form shown in Figure 4.3. The first thing you need to determine is the local part of the e-mail address. Once you have entered it, you can click the *Check Availability* button; this step will let you know whether the name is available. You can also select whether you want the domain to be *live.com* or *hotmail.com*. Both are accessed from the same portal; this choice only affects your resulting e-mail address.

You need to create a password for your e-mail account as well. The combination of the e-mail address and the password you choose will be the information you need to access your account. Since your e-mail address is public, you must carefully guard

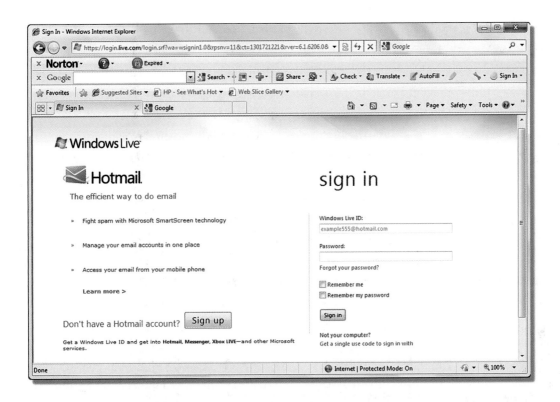

▲ **FIGURE 4.2** Hotmail login portal

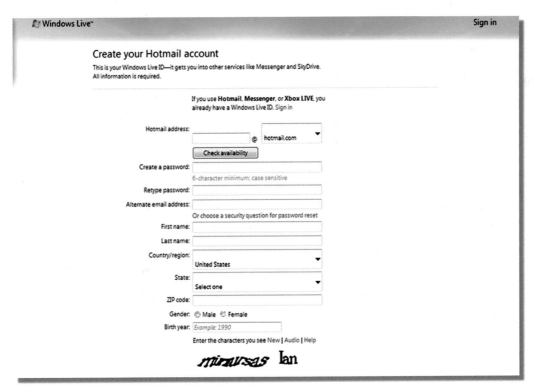

◀ **FIGURE 4.3**
Hotmail
registration form

your password and with whom you share it. The registration form requires you to reenter your password for verification. You will also need to either enter an existing e-mail address (which should not be your work e-mail address) or select a security question in case you forget your password and need to have it reset.

CREATING A PASSWORD

Choosing a password that is difficult to guess is incredibly important to the security of your e-mail account or any account that uses passwords as authentication mechanisms. Your password should not be too short (many sites require a six-character password) and it should contain a mix of lowercase and uppercase letters, numbers, and symbols. Any password that is easy to remember is likely easy to guess. To get around this, it is suggested you use a short sentence (called a *passphrase*) as a password. An example of this would be "Charlie is 2 awesome!" which is easy to remember and meets all of the criteria for a strong password.

The next few entries in the form are for your personal information including your first name, last name, country, state, and postal code. The first and last name you enter will be used as your display name in both the account and e-mail correspondence. You must then select a gender and enter a birth year. The registration form requires you to enter information in these fields, but you are not required to provide your full name in conjunction with the account if you are concerned about privacy. The system will verify that the postal code is valid within the country and state you select.

The final text entry is for a *captcha*, which is an altered set of letters that can be read by a human but cannot be reasonably parsed by a computer. This is to prevent automated scripts from registering active e-mail accounts within the system. You simply type the letters that are displayed in the image into the text box beneath it. The *I Accept* button at the bottom of the page will create the account; clicking this button means you agree to abide by the terms and conditions of use for Hotmail. You can read these terms and conditions by clicking on the links provided. Once you click this button, your account will be verified and created if there are no issues with the data you entered. If there are any errors, you will be prompted to correct them. If there are no errors, you will be taken to the dashboard interface for your account.

Navigating and Opening E-mail　　　4.4.2.2

When you are logged into your account, you will be taken to your account's dashboard by default. You can see how this looks in Figure 4.4. To get to your message Inbox, you can click either the *Go to Inbox* link or the *Inbox* link.

With your Inbox open, you should see your e-mail in the center of the window, as shown in Figure 4.5. Your folders are listed onthe left hand side. To add a new folder to help you organize your e-mails, click the *New Folder* link and enter the required information. When you sign into Hotmail, you are automatically connected to the Microsoft Messenger service, a synchronous instant messaging service. You can choose to stay signed into the service or logout using the *Sign out of Messenger* link. Your service links are across the top of the window where you can view your calendar or check news

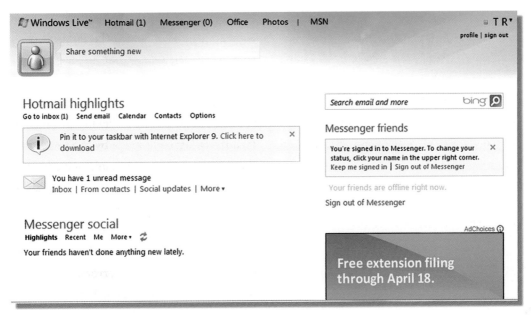

◀ FIGURE 4.4
Hotmail example
dashboard

categories on MSN®. Your message options are beneath the service links. Here you can delete, move, or print the selected messages. You can also arrange your e-mail by date, subject, size, or sender using the *Arrange by* drop-down menu.

You can open an e-mail message by clicking on either the name of the sender or the

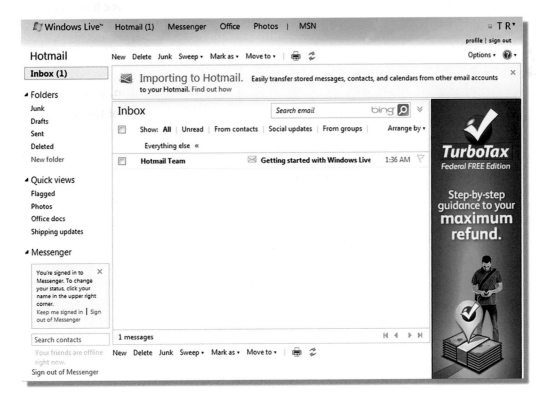

◀ FIGURE 4.5
Hotmail example
Inbox

subject of the message. If you have just created the account, you should see a welcome message from Microsoft with getting started hints. The message view, accessed by clicking on the subject, offers a list of options, including sending a reply to the message. At the left side of the window are links to take you to your Inbox or let you access any folders you want to check.

You have the same options for navigation and e-mail messages in each of your folders. When you delete an e-mail message, it will be moved to the Deleted folder. To permanently remove the e-mail, you must delete the message (a second time) from the Deleted folder itself. Clicking the *Junk* link with a message (or messages) selected will delete whatever is selected and block the sender, meaning you will not receive any future emails from that sender.

You can click the *profile* link to open your profile settings, which allow you to change your account privacy settings and your contact information using the *profile* menu. Clicking the *Options* link and then selecting *More options* opens the Hotmail Options menu. Using this menu, you can select *Safe and blocked senders* under *Preventing junk e-mail* to add senders you want to block or remove senders you previously blocked. You can change most of the account settings (other than your e-mail address) using the Hotmail Options menu.

The *Drafts* folder holds e-mail messages that you have written but have not yet sent. The drafts are stored on the e-mail server and will remain with the account until they are sent. The *Sent* folder stores messages that were sent from your account. The sent items will remain with the account on the e-mail server until they are deleted.

Composing an E-mail 4.4.2.3

You can create a new e-mail message from within any folder in your Inbox by clicking the *New* link at the top of the e-mail window. The new message editor will then appear in your browser window, as shown in Figure 4.6.

This window is where you enter the information in the header and compose your message. You should start with the header information. Your e-mail address appears at the top; this is the *From* field. The *To* field is below your e-mail address; you can type any address you want here and Hotmail will validate that it is in the correct format (this does not validate whether it is a legitimate recipient). Clicking on the To button open a pop-up menu showing recent contacts and stored contacts so you can select them directly. As you type e-mail addresses, if Hotmail recognizes a string of characters from your address book, it will provide a small pop-up menu that allows you to click the name to enter the rest of the address for

The added benefit of using Hotmail is the access to an online-only version of Microsoft Office. You can create and edit documents online using the Web-based interface (called Microsoft SkyDrive®). You can access these documents via a link that you can send to others for collaborative effort or for them to view what you have created. You must have an installed version of Microsoft Office to save these documents to your local machine.

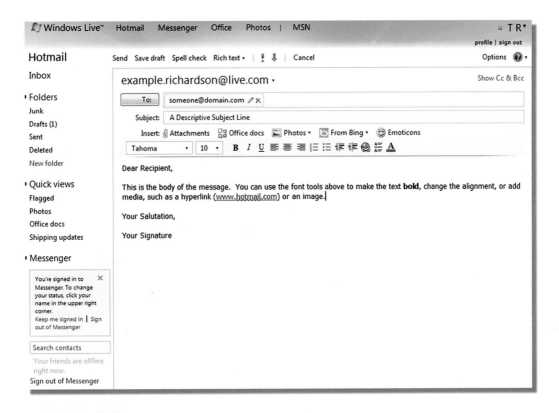

▲ **FIGURE 4.6** Hotmail new message editor

you. There is a *Show Cc & Bcc* link at the right side of the window that will make the CC and BCC header fields visible and usable.

You should always enter a subject line, and it should be descriptive of what the message contains. The body of the message is an HTML-enabled text editor, meaning that the toolbar across the top can be used to format your text by changing the font, font size, style, color, and alignment. You can add attachments and images using the toolbar

as well. Clicking the *Attachments* link opens a text box and activates a *Browse* button. The Browse button will open a File Upload dialog box in the native Web browser, allowing you to select the file that you want to include in the e-mail.

Logging Out and Logging In

4.4.2.4

Whenever you are using a Web-based service, you should always log out when you are done with the tasks you needed to perform. To log out of Hotmail, use the *sign out* link on the right side of the browser; you will then be automatically redirected to the MSN home page. Logging out will protect your account by preventing anyone else using the machine from artificially extending your session and accessing your e-mail.

Some files, such as Microsoft Office files, must be closed before they can be attached to an e-mail message. If a file is open in another program when you try to attach it, you will receive an error message and the file will not attach.

When you want to log back in to read your e-mail, you can go directly to the Hotmail Web site (*www.hotmail.com*) and enter your username and password to access your account. If you forget your password, you can use the *Forgot your password?* link, which will either prompt you to enter the answer to your security question or send a password recovery e-mail to an alternate account you specified when you registered.

4.4.3 Gmail by Google

Google offers its own free e-mail service in the form of Gmail by Google. You can access Gmail from either the Google home page (*www.google.com*) or the Gmail home page (*www.gmail.com*). From the Gmail home page, shown in Figure 4.7, you can either login using an existing account or create a new Gmail account.

Creating an Account

4.4.3.1

To create a new Gmail account, click on the *Create an account* button at the lower-right section of the Gmail home page. This will open the account creation form shown in Figure 4.8. First, you must enter information in the first name and last name fields and determine the local part of the e-mail account name. Again, you should keep the use of this account in mind when creating it. An easy way to create an e-mail address is to use your first name followed by a dot or an underscore and then your last name; this creates a professional, memorable address. You can determine if the account is available by clicking the button labeled *check availability!*

You must then create a password and retype it for verification. There is also a list

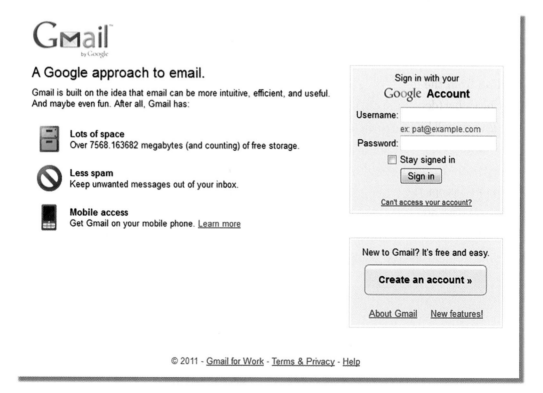

➤ **FIGURE 4.7**
Gmail home page

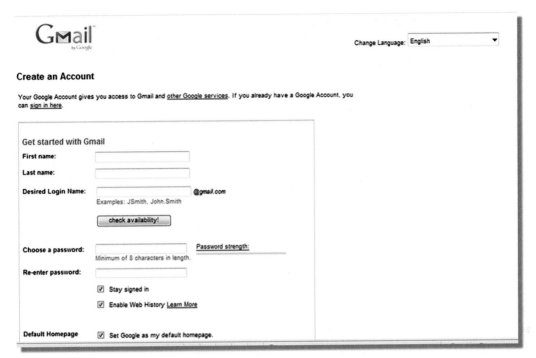

of options with checkboxes that you can enable or disable. Next, you should enter a security question to assist you in recovering a lost password and a backup e-mail account to which a link to reset your password can be sent; you must also select your location from the drop-down list and enter your birthday (depending on your location). Finally, you will be prompted to enter a verification captcha (discussed in the earlier section on Microsoft Windows Live Hotmail) and accept the terms and conditions of use for the account. You will be logged in to your new account once the form is error free and you click *I accept. Create my account.*

4.4.3.2 *Navigating and Opening E-mail*

When you log into your Gmail account, you will see a screen similar to Figure 4.9. This window contains a navigation menu of Gmail account services across the top. The left-side navigation menu contains a view of your Inbox folders, your connection to Google's instant messenger service, and a connection to the embedded VoIP service that allows you to make phone calls from your Gmail account. Note that this service requires additional software installation and charges for phone use may apply.

Above the list of e-mail messages in your Inbox is a set of options for organizing and managing your e-mail. You can move or delete messages that are selected and you can refresh your Inbox, downloading any new messages that have reached your account.

Gmail also provides a task manager, which provides a simple interface allowing you to create a to-do list of items, a connection to Google Docs™ (online

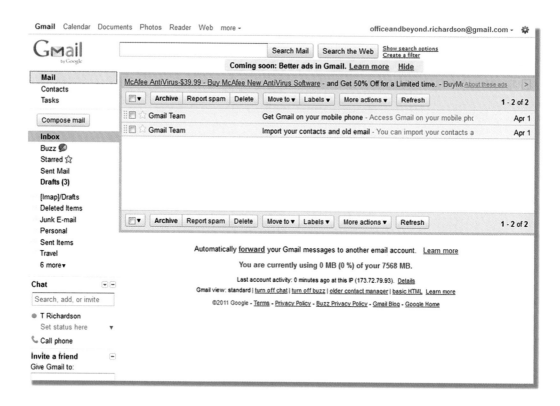

➤ **FIGURE 4.9**
Gmail example
Inbox

document management and creation software), and a link to your personal calendar (which is part of the larger Google account) that you can use to keep track of appointments.

To open an e-mail message in Gmail, you can click anywhere in the row displaying the message information. Messages that are displayed in bold are unread, and messages that display in standard text have already been opened. When you click on an e-mail message, the message will open in place of the Inbox display, allowing you to read the contents of the message, delete it, or archive it. The options to reply to the message, forward the message, and invite the sender to chat are found beneath the message content. You can return to your Inbox by selecting either the *Return to Inbox* link above

the message or the *Mail* link on the left side of the window.

Composing an E-mail

4.4.3.3

To create a new e-mail message in Gmail, click the *Compose mail* link. This opens the e-mail message editing window, as shown in Figure 4.10. The options presented here are similar to those in other Web mail clients. The header information is entered at the top of the message window. The *To* field and the *Subject* field are the two header fields that are initially visible. Click the *Add Cc* and *Add Bcc* links to add the respective header fields. Remember that your subject should be meaningful regarding the content of the e-mail. As you type an e-mail address in any of the recipient fields, Gmail will attempt to match it to your existing contacts; if it finds a match, you can click the address that appears beneath the address entry box to auto-fill the rest of the address. To the far right of the window is an expansion icon; clicking this will open the message in a new window and return the current window to the view of your Inbox.

The body is where you enter the content of your e-mail message; this is presented as a text area in the central part of the window. You can use HTML formatting in the content, but Gmail also presents you with a limited set of fonts and sizes from which you can choose. You can add bold, italic, and underline to the text as well as set the text alignment and add any bullets and numbering.

You can attach files to your e-mail message by clicking the *Attach a file* link. This will open an Upload File dialog box

in the native browser in which the e-mail account is open. When you are finished composing your e-mail, click the *Send* button to send it, the *Save Now* button to save it as a draft, or the *Discard* button to delete it.

Logging Out and Logging In

4.4.3.4

As with any account, you should always make sure you log out when you are finished. This helps to prevent unauthorized access and use of your account. To sign out of Gmail, click the down arrow beside your account name at the top of the window; this opens a pop-up menu containing the *Sign out* link at the bottom. You will be returned to the Gmail home page. Anytime you wish to sign back into your account, you can visit the home page for Gmail and enter your e-mail account and password. Since these

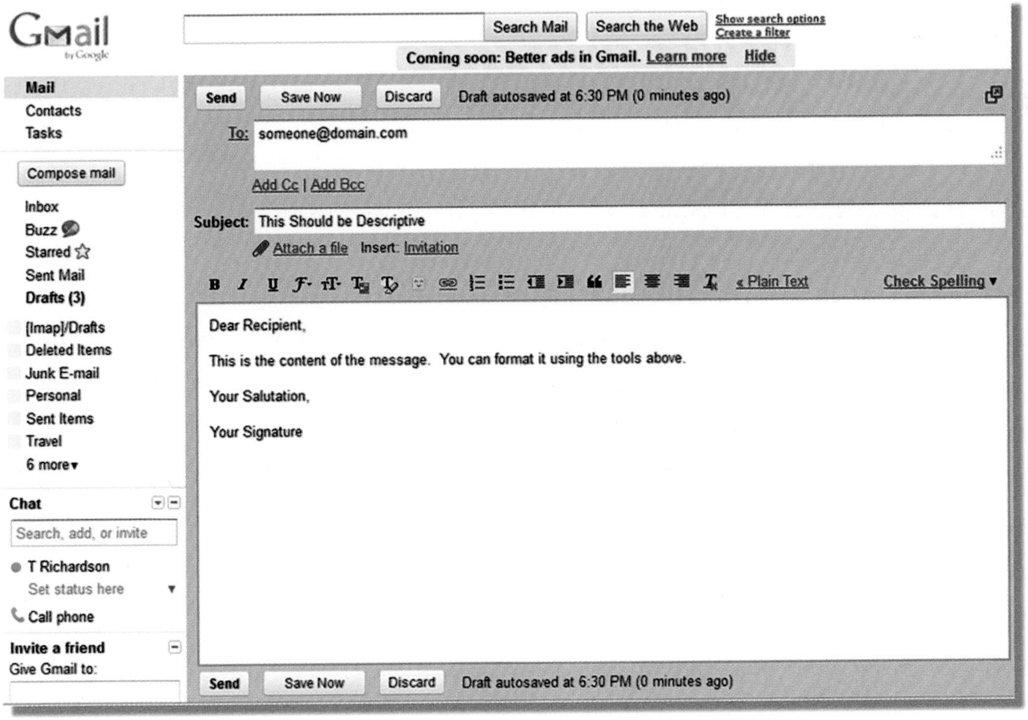

◀ **FIGURE 4.10**
Gmail message editing window

are the only credentials needed to access your account, you should keep your password carefully guarded.

<table><tr><td>4.4.4</td></tr></table>

Creating a Microsoft Windows Live ID

If you use Microsoft Windows as your operating system or use Microsoft products on your machine (including Microsoft Office), you may find it very helpful to create a Windows Live ID, which is the equivalent of a digital passport. A Windows Live ID allows you to access services and provide authentication credentials with an e-mail address and a password. Some features of Microsoft Office, such as broadcasting a Microsoft Office PowerPoint presentation, require you to have a Windows Live ID.

To create a new Windows Live ID, go to *www.passport.net* in a browser window. The interface for the Windows Live ID site is shown in Figure 4.11.

If you are already using Hotmail as your e-mail account provider, you can use that account information wherever the Windows Live ID is requested. If you are using another e-mail provider, you can create a new Windows Live ID by clicking the *Get started now* link under the *Use an e-mail address you already have* heading. You will then see the account creation form shown in Figure 4.12.

You only need to enter an existing e-mail address, a password for the Windows Live ID (which will be rated by the password strength indicator), a security question, and

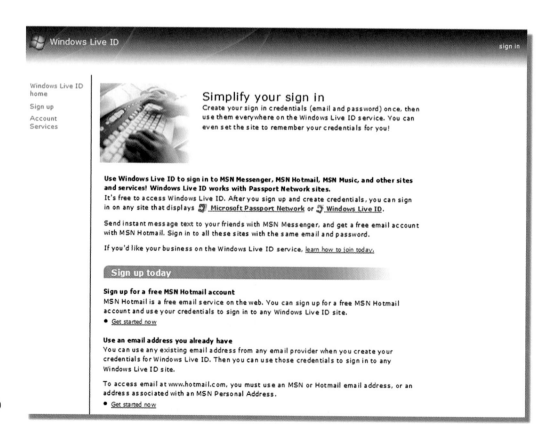

> ► **FIGURE 4.11**
> Windows Live ID home page

◄ **FIGURE 4.12**
Windows Live ID account creation page

the answer to the security question. Enter the characters in the verification *captcha* and then click *Continue*. An e-mail will be sent to the address you used to create the Windows Live ID account; open this e-mail and click the link contained within it to verify and activate the account. You can access or change your account settings at any time by using the login information at the Windows Live ID home page.

4.5 E-MAIL CLIENTS

Web mail functions as a limited e-mail client. Some incarnations of Web mail are closer to the standalone e-mail client applications than others. E-mail clients typically do not allow you to create an e-mail account but instead serve to manage an existing e-mail account through a range of supplemental services to manage tasks and promote productivity. The main advantage of e-mail clients over Web mail is the ability to save e-mail messages externally on the local machine; this option is typically not available in Web mail.

Microsoft Outlook is a professional e-mail client that includes a calendar, task manager, and robust e-mail capabilities and is widely used in businesses and organizations as a primary means of communication.

The full features of this product are covered in the section titled "Microsoft Outlook." Most operating systems come installed with a small e-mail client that allows for basic e-mail creation and management. One of the free alternatives to the more robust Outlook is Mozilla Thunderbird®, a companion program to Firefox that allows for simple account configuration, management, and use. This can be a good alternative to the preinstalled options if you are looking for an e-mail client to manage accounts on a home computer.

Microsoft Windows Live Mail

The installed e-mail client on a Windows machine is Microsoft Windows Live Mail; the

The **RIBBON INTERFACE** (*also called the* **RIBBON USER INTERFACE**) *is a productivity-oriented GUI that contains larger icons than standard toolbars and emphasizes organizing related tasks into the same subset (a ribbon), which remains open and visible when selected, unlike a traditional menu.*

2011 update to this software is part of the free Windows Live Essentials software package (available from *explore.live.com*) for Windows machines. This is a small application that allows for the management of multiple e-mail accounts. It configures most accounts using just the e-mail account name and password. The interface (shown in Figure 4.13) allows you to manage your e-mail accounts,

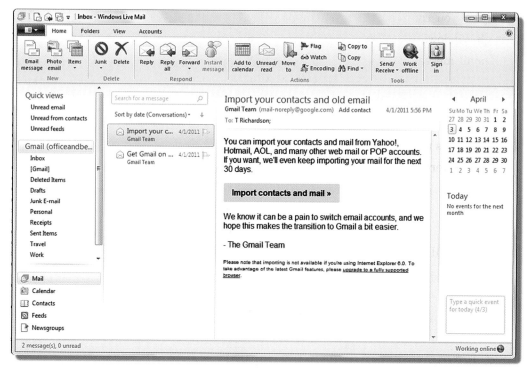

▶ FIGURE 4.13
Windows Live Mail 2011 interface and Accounts ribbon

calendar, contacts, and newsfeeds. Windows Live Mail 2011 uses the ribbon interface that Microsoft has implemented in the Microsoft Office suite.

You can add an account using the *E-mail* icon on the *Accounts ribbon*. To change account settings, select the *Properties* icon from the *Accounts ribbon*. To remove an account, right-click the account name and select *Remove account*, this procedure applies regardless of the current ribbon that is active.

Windows Live Mail allows you to manage your calendar and contacts as well as your e-mail. You can sign into a Windows Live ID account from the calendar or the contacts Home ribbon. From the contacts Home ribbon, you can e-mail your contacts directly or you can instant message them through Windows Messenger.

E-mail message creation in Windows Live Mail is similar to other Web mail clients with similar formatting options. The ribbon interface is slightly different, but it contains the same options; they are just in a different format. The message creation window has its own ribbons. You can create a new e-mail message by selecting the *E-mail Message* icon on the *Home ribbon* for mail. The e-mail creation window and its associated ribbons are shown in Figure 4.14.

The message header information and the message body are located beneath the ribbon interface. The *Message ribbon* allows you to format your e-mail content using the Font panel and the Paragraph panel; these create the message using HTML enhancements. To add attachments, images, hyperlinks, and emoticons, use either the Insert panel of the Message ribbon or the Insert ribbon. You can check the spelling for your message using the *Editing* menu and selecting *Spelling*. Delivery options can be set using the *Delivery* menu, but you should only use these options (like High Importance and Read Receipt) when it is absolutely necessary. The *Options* ribbon allows you to perform advanced tasks like encrypting the message, digitally signing the message, or delaying delivery.

A message can be saved as a draft using the *Save* icon in the quick links at the top of the interface. You can send the message using the *Send* icon next to the header information for the message itself. To save an e-mail as a file, select the message you want to save, click the *Windows Live Mail* menu (the blue menu on the far left), select *Save*, and then select *Save as file*. The file can be saved as an e-mail or text document or as HTML.

Macintosh Mail

4.5.2

The default e-mail client installed on a Macintosh computer is Macintosh Mail. Similar to Windows Live Mail, it provides a simple interface that allows you to manage multiple e-mail accounts. When you initially start the program, it will prompt you to enter a primary e-mail account; Mail will automatically configure most accounts using just the e-mail account and the password. The interface for Mail is shown in Figure 4.15.

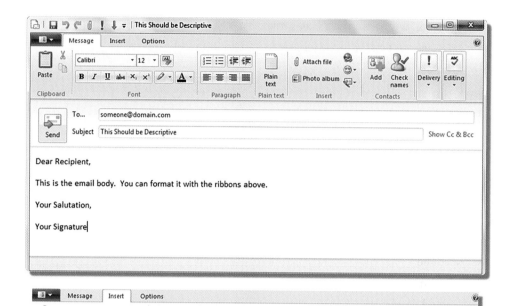

► FIGURE 4.14
Windows Live Mail
e-mail creation
window and
ribbons

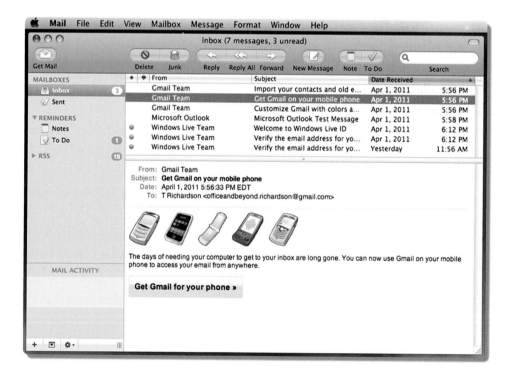

► FIGURE 4.15
Mail interface

Once you have configured an account, you can manage the account settings by selecting the *Mail* menu and then selecting *Preferences*. When the Preferences window opens, click *Accounts* to alter your settings and add or remove accounts. The Accounts interface is shown in Figure 4.16.

To save an e-mail as a file in Mail, select the message you want to save, click the *File* menu, and then choose *Save*. You can save a message as a raw e-mail file, a text file, or an RTF file. The interface for creating new messages is limited because the messages are constructed as rich text (which is simple text with some formatting information) instead of HTML (which provides a richer formatting and media environment); in short, this means you are limited to changing the font and color settings of the text of the message. Other options let you add attachments and photos to your e-mail message and save it as a draft.

4.5.3 Mozilla Thunderbird

The Mozilla Foundation, the makers of the Firefox Web browser, offers a free e-mail client for multiple platforms including Windows and Macintosh computers; this e-mail client is called Mozilla Thunderbird. You can download Thunderbird from *www.mozillamessaging.com/thunderbird*. Thunderbird allows you to setup multiple e-mail accounts and will configure most with just the e-mail account and password. You will be prompted to add an account when you first start the software and will then be taken to the main Thunderbird interface, shown in Figure 4.17.

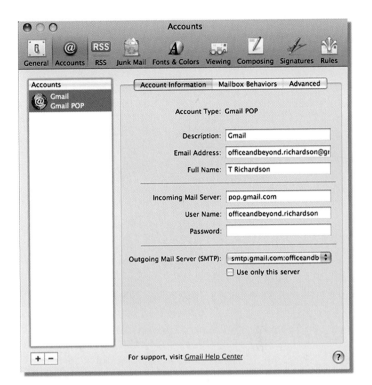

▲ FIGURE 4.16
Mail accounts preferences

Thunderbird provides a significant advantage over Web mail access with the ability to save e-mail to a file on your local machine. To do this, select a message, then select the *File* menu, *Save As*, and *File* (you can also do this with the *Ctrl-S* shortcut on a Windows machine and the *Command-S* shortcut on a Macintosh machine). You can choose whether to save the message as a mail document, HTML, or simple text file.

AUTHOR'S NOTE
While the basic tasks of e-mail creation and management can be accomplished with the limited e-mail clients that are installed with some operating systems, more robust features give a higher level of convenience for performing daily tasks and managing a large volume of e-mail. The Mozilla Thunderbird option is preferable to the more limited preinstalled clients in terms of productivity.

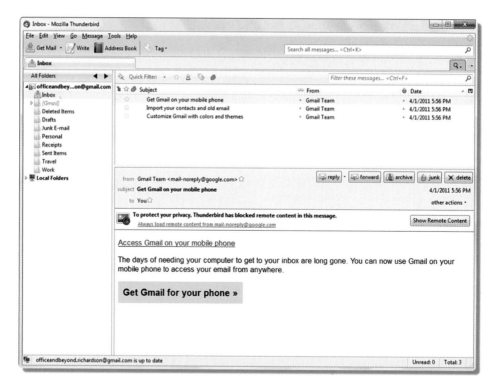

To add more accounts or change account settings after you have configured your initial account, choose the *Account Settings* option under the *Tools* menu. From here, you can select the *Account Actions* menu to add or remove e-mail accounts, as shown in Figure 4.18.

E-mail messages in any of your folders can be sorted by clicking the icons across the top that represent the field by which you want to sort (such as From or Subject). You can also switch to a threaded view, which will organize the messages by the inherent pattern of replies that they follow. To help organize and filter your e-mails, you can mark them with symbols like a star or a junk icon. The search box at the top of the interface can help you search your e-mail for a particular keyword or phrase.

There are several icons in the toolbar at the top of the interface. *Get Mail* lets you checks your account or accounts for any new mail that has been received, *Address Book* opens a new window that allows you to manage your contacts, and *Tag* places a color band on the selected message to draw attention to it and allow for easy sorting. Clicking the *Write* icon opens a new window (shown in Figure 4.19) where you can compose a new e-mail message.

You can choose which fields from the header you want to include and format your text with a range of HTML commands. The normal options of setting the font, size, and color are available, along with the ability to change the text alignment and add images, hyperlinks, and emoticons to the body of the text. You can add attachments, save the message as a draft, and send the e-mail message directly from this window.

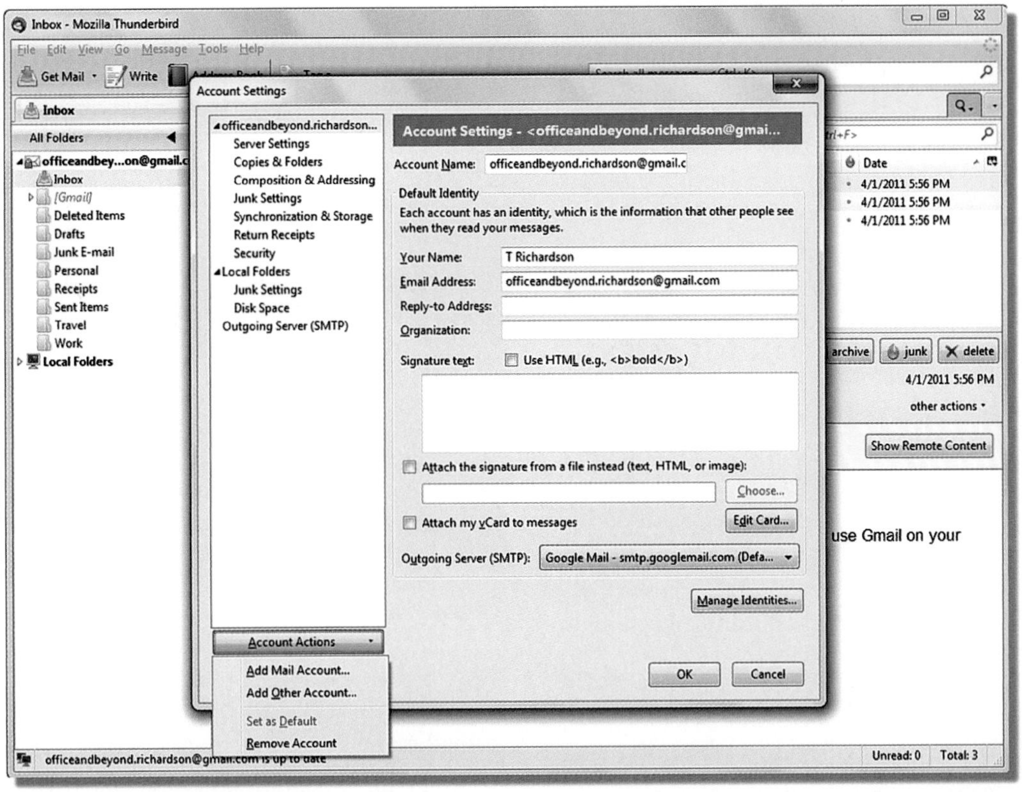

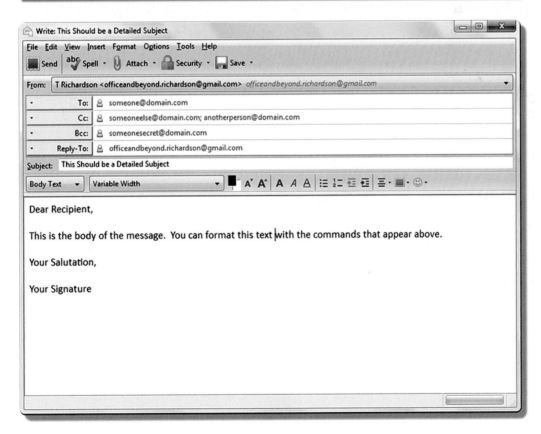

► FIGURE 4.18
Thunderbird
account settings

► FIGURE 4.19
Thunderbird
e-mail message
composition
window

One item worth noting is the Security feature in the message composition window of Thunderbird. This allows you to setup and use encryption to encrypt and decrypt messages; e-mail is typically sent over the networks in plain text, so any information you send in an e-mail message can be read by anyone who receives even a temporary copy of the packet on its way from the sender to the receiver. Windows Live Mail 2011 offers the ability to encrypt messages as well.

4.5.4

Connecting to Your E-mail Remotely

Most mobile phones with Web access can receive e-mail messages from existing accounts. Smartphones, like the iPhone® and Android™ phones, have utilities to configure your e-mail. You can setup remote access to your e-mail with either POP3 or IMAP and SMTP. Most mobile devices have their own version of an e-mail client (or a small mobile application called an *app*) that can configure a variety of accounts with the username and password for the e-mail account. Microsoft Windows Live Hotmail and Gmail by Google both have a mobile version available from the browser on your Web-enabled phone (regardless of the phone brand). Your e-mail account provider can also give you the manual configuration details to setup remote e-mail access on a mobile device. To setup a remote connection, you generally need the following information in addition to your e-mail address and password:

- *Incoming mail server*—This is typically a POP3 or IMAP server hostname.

- *Incoming mail port number*—This is the port number on which the incoming mail is received.

- *Incoming mail security settings*—This can be set to no security, SSL, or TLS (Transport Layer Security); you may also have to set it to accept certificates for the connection.

- *Outgoing mail server*—This is usually an SMTP server hostname.

- *Outgoing mail port number*—This is the outgoing mail port, which is typically port 25.

- *Outgoing mail security settings*—These are the outgoing settings and may or may not be the same as the incoming security settings; options include SSL and TLS.

MICROSOFT OUTLOOK

4.6

Microsoft Outlook is a professional e-mail manager and productivity tool; it is a commercial version of an e-mail client that adds functionality beyond just writing and managing e-mail. Outlook allows you to not only manage your e-mail (from one or multiple accounts) but also use a personalized calendar to keep track of events and meetings, manage your contact list, keep track of your tasks (which functions just like a to-do list), and manage notes (which are the digital equivalent of sticky notes). Outlook is part of the Microsoft Office program suite and is included with both Microsoft Office 2010 for Windows machines and Microsoft Office 2011 for Macintosh machines.

Outlook 2010 utilizes the ribbon interface structure. When you first start the program, it will prompt you to enter your e-mail address and the password for that e-mail account. Outlook will then attempt to automatically configure the account, determining the servers and settings associated with the incoming and outgoing messages. Your account provider can give you this information so you can enter it manually if Outlook cannot perform the configuration automatically. You are then taken to the main interface of the Outlook software. While the functionality of the software is consistent, the appearance of Outlook 2010 and Outlook 2011 are different. Both of these versions use the ribbon interface.

4.6.1 Anatomy of Microsoft Outlook 2010

The main interface of Microsoft Outlook 2010 is shown in Figure 4.20. The ribbons along the top allow you to perform tasks specific to each of the elements with which you are working. These ribbons change to match the context of whatever you select as active on the left side of the window (called the Navigation pane), whether it is Mail, Calendar, Contacts, Tasks, or Notes. The second icon at the top left of the interface is Send/Receive All Folders; this option is also accessible from the *Send/Receive ribbon* or by pressing the *F9* key. The Help icon is located the far right of the interface and it is also accessible by pressing the *F1* key.

The Send/Receive ribbon is constant, allowing you to get new mail for your connected accounts and send mail that was written offline. You can also switch from working offline to working online by

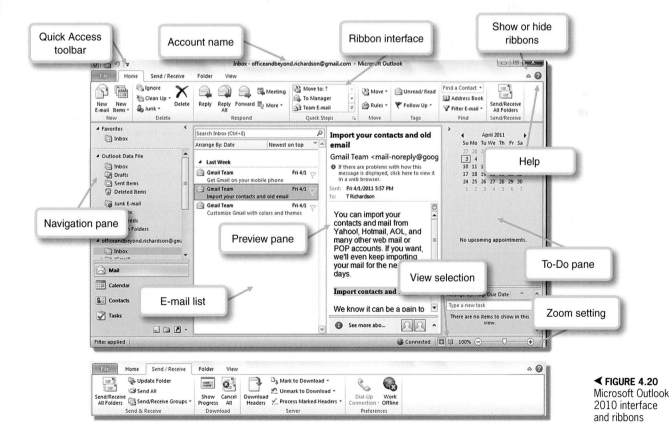

◄ FIGURE 4.20
Microsoft Outlook 2010 interface and ribbons

clicking the *Work Offline* icon (the state is determined by whether the icon is highlighted). When Mail is active in the Navigation pane, there are a few additional options on the Server panel in the Send/Receive ribbon that allow you to determine how you want to download information for the current e-mail message or the current folder of e-mail messages.

The File menu, located to the left of the ribbons, is shown in Figure 4.21. This is the menu you will use to adjust the settings on the default account that was setup when you started the software. To change any of the configured settings, click on *Info* in the left hand menu and select the *Account Settings* icon; this opens the Account Settings dialog box, which you can use to manage all of your connected accounts, contacts, and calendars. You can remove an account using the Account Settings dialog box by selecting

that account in the *E-mail* tab and then clicking the *Remove* icon above the accounts listed. To add new accounts using the File menu, simply click on *Info* in the left hand menu and then select *Add Account* under the Account Information display. You can save e-mail to the local machine by using the *File* menu and selecting *Save As*; e-mail can be saved as a text file, as a message, or in HTML format. To save a message to the local machine, click on the message and drag it to either the desktop or a folder.

Anatomy of Microsoft Outlook 2011

4.6.2

Microsoft Outlook 2011 is very similar in functionality to Outlook 2010, although it has a different appearance, as you can see in Figure 4.22. The Macintosh version of the software uses a combined menu and ribbon interface. The menu bar is located along

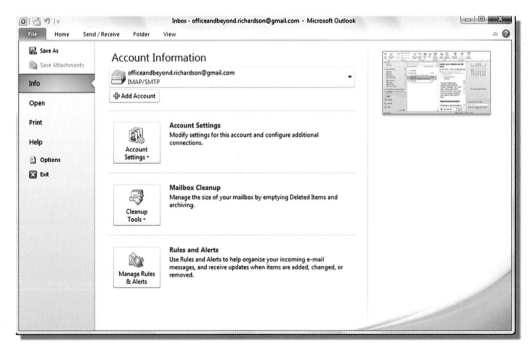

➤ **FIGURE 4.21**
Outlook 2010 File menu

the top of the computer screen next to the Apple icon. The ribbon is located along the top of the application window, with quick link icons above it. These icons allow you to send and receive messages and access the help files.

The *Tools ribbon* allows you to import or export information from Outlook and set whether you want to work online or offline. You can adjust the mode by moving the slider icon for *Online Mode* from Online to Offline (or Offline to Online). The *Schedules* icon in this ribbon can be used to send and receive mail, send mail only, or empty the Deleted Items folder.

You can manage your e-mail accounts by selecting the *Tools* menu and choosing *Accounts*. This will open the Accounts dialog box where you can use the + or - icons to add or remove accounts. You can also select an account from the list to edit the account's settings and save files to the local machine by clicking on the message and dragging it to the desktop or a folder.

Managing E-mail

4.6.3

Outlook allows you to perform all of the necessary tasks to create and manage e-mail. The Home ribbons for both Outlook 2010 and Outlook 2011 are shown

▼ FIGURE 4.22
Outlook 2011 interface and ribbons

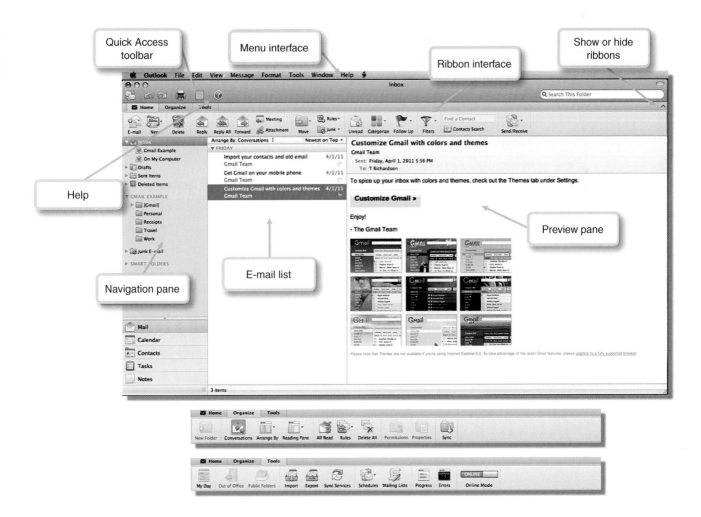

in Figure 4.23. This ribbon allows you to select a message and use Reply, Reply All, or Forward to respond. You can also choose advanced options such as Reply with Meeting, which will create a calendar instance in response to an e-mail. The *Move* icon lets you move your messages to another folder, and the *Rules* icon defines custom rules that determine automatic responses when you receive messages meeting specific criteria.

It is a good idea to clean out any unwanted messages so they do not clutter your e-mail folders. You should also setup folders to house important e-mail messages that you need to keep on the server. Any messages that you want to save but do not need to be kept active on the server should be archived to your local machine. To setup your e-mail archive in Outlook 2010 on the local machine, click *Auto Archive Settings* in the *Folder ribbon* with Mail active in the Navigation pane. To archive items to your local machine in Outlook 2011, click the *Export* icon on the *Tools ribbon*. To create custom folders, select *New Folder* from the *Folder ribbon* in Outlook 2010, or select *New* and then *New Folder* from the *Home ribbon* in Outlook 2011.

You can create a new e-mail message from the Home ribbon by selecting *New E-mail* (or *E-mail*). This opens a new window with its own ribbon interface.

The options presented in Outlook 2010 are organized into multiple ribbons, while Outlook 2011 offers only two ribbons, as shown in Figure 4.24.

Most of the necessary e-mail message editing options are available in the Message ribbon. These include icons to change the font, color, size, and alignment of the text; you can also attach files and a signature from the Message ribbon. Images and hyperlinks can be added in Outlook 2010 using the Insert ribbon; these options are available from the Message ribbon in Outlook 2011. The Options ribbon allows you to add the BCC field. To check spelling, select the *Spelling & Grammar* icon under the *Review ribbon* in Outlook 2010 or the *Spelling* icon in the *Options ribbon* in Outlook 2011.

Managing Calendars

4.6.4

An electronic calendar allows you to keep track of your schedule. Most e-mail account providers, including Gmail and Hotmail, have some form of calendar. These calendars allow the creation of events, which are simply the details needed for you to be present for a certain occurrence at a certain time. For instance, if you needed to call your parents at 3:00 p.m. next Tuesday, you would need the phone number you are calling, the time zone for the phone call, and the

▶ **FIGURE 4.23**
Home ribbon for e-mail in Outlook 2010 (top) and 2011 (bottom)

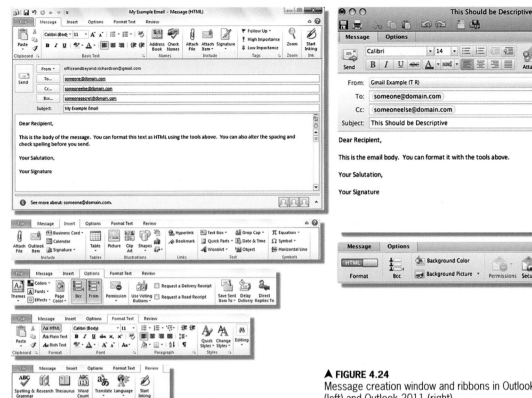
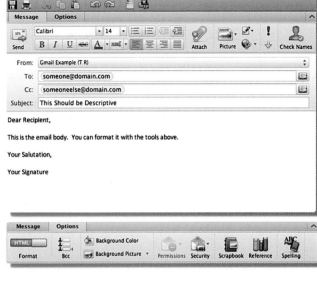

▲ FIGURE 4.24
Message creation window and ribbons in Outlook 2010 (left) and Outlook 2011 (right)

calendar date for next Tuesday. This is sufficient information to include in the event details. Most events also have a time period associated with them, so if it is going to be a brief 15-minute call, you would schedule the event from 3:00 p.m. to 3:15 p.m.

Microsoft Outlook provides you with an internal calendar and the ability to include additional calendars (such as personal and professional calendars). Unlike most general calendars that allow you to create everything as an event, Outlook differentiates between appointments and meetings. You can create either an appointment or a meeting from the Home ribbon of Outlook with the calendar active in the Navigation pane. The Home ribbon for the calendar is shown in Figure 4.25.

You should use an appointment for a personal event that involves you as the primary focus; you can still invite others to attend, such as an appointment to have coffee with a friend. If you are using a calendar on a work computer that is connected to others, you should set your appointments to private so others cannot see the details associated with the event; instead, the calendar will just show you as busy during that time. To set an appointment as private, click the *Private* icon on the *Appointment ribbon*.

A meeting should be used for professional events. Meeting details may or may not remain public. You should include any resources in your meeting request that will be used in the meeting. Since meeting notices are sent via e-mail, they will arrive

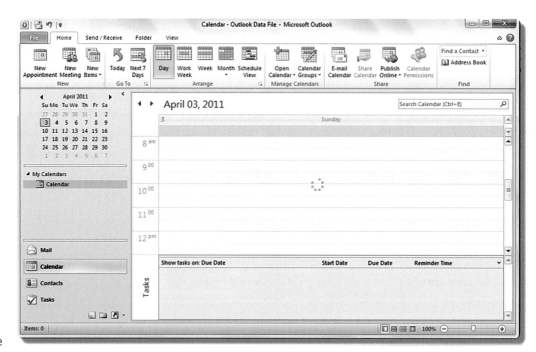

► FIGURE 4.25
Outlook 2010
Calendar interface

in the same Inbox with other e-mail messages (though some e-mail clients may not have the ability to transfer the meeting request to the recipient's calendar). Meeting details should include any call-in numbers for remote attendees, the location for local attendees, and any Web resources (such as a Cisco® WebEx® meeting) the attendee needs to utilize.

You can set how often meetings or appointments recur using the *Recurrence* icon when creating the initial event. Selecting the *All Day Event* check box clears your calendar for the day. The Scheduling Assistant will attempt to load calendars for any additional attendees that you have included in the meeting or appointment request. This will load your calendar in a row above the rest of the attendees so you can find a time when everyone is free. To access the Scheduling Assistant in Outlook 2010, select the

Scheduling icon; in Outlook 2011, *Scheduling Assistant* is a tab beside the Message tab beneath the header containing the scheduling details.

Managing Contacts

4.6.5

Your contacts are people you interact with on a personal or professional level. Outlook allows you to manage individual contacts and groups easily and stores them in an Address Book that you can use to look them up later. To create a new individual contact, simply click the *New Contact* icon on the *Home ribbon* with Contacts active in the Navigation pane; for an individual, you can store address, phone number, and personal information. If you store an address, you can use the *Map It* icon to load a new Web browser window that will locate the address using the Bing search engine. You can also set the contact to private by selecting the *Private* icon; this hides the information from others connected to your account, such as in an office or professional network environment.

For a group contact, you can store names and e-mail addresses as a list. To create a new group contact, click the *New Contact Group* icon in the *Home ribbon* with Contacts active in the Navigation pane. In Outlook 2011, you can type the names and e-mail addresses for the group directly and select the option for whether you want the addresses always included in the BCC header field to keep the addresses private. In Outlook 2010, you need to add the group members to your contacts before you can add them to a group.

When you have saved your contacts, Outlook allows you to look them up in your address book (or books if you have multiple accounts) rather than typing their e-mail addresses. Outlook will also attempt to automatically complete any address that you start to type that matches the address of someone in your contact list. Click the *Address Book* icon in Outlook 2010 whenever you are creating a new e-mail message or meeting to look up your contacts using a keyword search and choose the e-mail header field in which you want the e-mail address for your contact included. The address book is accessible in Outlook 2011 by selecting the icon that looks like an open address book (next to the address entry field).

4.6.6 Tasks and Notes

Outlook also allows you to use tasks and notes. Tasks are the digital equivalent of to-do lists that you would traditionally write by hand. You can create a task and give it a priority and a due date, and set reminders for when you need to follow up on it. A task entry is created using the *New Task* icon of the *Home ribbon*. When you are done with a task, you can select *Mark Complete*; this will remove the task from your active task list, but it will remain in Outlook so you can view your completed tasks later.

Notes are the digital equivalent of sticky paper notes that you would use to quickly jot down information. You can create notes and view existing notes by selecting *Notes* in the Navigation pane. Notes in Outlook just allow simple text entry, so you can write and save them quickly without any formatting. To create a note, click the *New Note* icon in the *Home ribbon* (or simply double-click inside the viewing pane in Outlook 2010).

> You can remove e-mail messages, tasks, contacts, and notes in Outlook by clicking on the individual item you want to remove and hitting the *Delete* key.

E-MAIL ETIQUETTE   4.7

There are a multitude of thoughts on the Web about what constitutes proper e-mail etiquette. You can conduct your own search to investigate this further, but there is a general consensus on some common tactics and practices that should be used in composing e-mail messages. The following 10 rules provide you with a suitable foundation for using e-mail effectively and professionally:

1. *Always include a subject line and make sure it relates to the message contents.* The subject line is a

preview of the message contents; therefore, it should explain in brief to the recipient what is contained in the message or what the message is about. A subject line should be short but descriptive.

2. *Only include recipients to whom the message is significant.* It is easy to get overburdened with the number of e-mail messages that enter your account. You should consider this when you are sending an e-mail and address it only to those individuals who are affected or would benefit from the message. If an individual is not involved in a situation, they should be left off of the communication. You should always avoid sending junk mail and you should never forward spam.

3. *Use To, CC, BCC, Forward, and Reply All properly.* You should use the *To* field for individuals who need to read the message to gain information or take some action in response. The *CC* field should be used for individuals who are impacted by the situation but who do not need to take direct action; this may include a supervisor in a situation where he needs to be kept informed. The *BCC* field should be used when you are sending information to a group; this is typically a hidden field so recipients will not see the e-mail addresses of everyone in the group and they will not be bothered with a long list of recipients in the header of the message. You should only use the *Forward* function to send messages in which you have something to contribute or if a recipient was necessary but left off of the original distribution; the latter case will still require some explanation to the recipient. The *Reply All* function should only be used when you have

a significant contribution to share with the entire group; if this is not the case, individual replies are a much better alternative.

4. *Keep your messages short and to the point.* E-mail messages should not be used for lengthy explanations; those are better suited to phone calls or in-person meetings. E-mail messages are most effective when they are short and clear. If the recipient needs to take some action as a result of the e-mail, it should be apparent. The recipient should never have to guess at the intention of your message or the next steps required.

5. *Make sure you address all questions in your response and curtail further discussion.* One approach to writing and responding to e-mail is to have the goal of stopping the discussion with the current message. This means you should make sure any questions are addressed and any predictable questions are answered before you send the message. Failure to do this will slow down the communication and delay any outcome that is necessary from the communication.

6. *Use clear writing and a neutral tone in your message.* Your e-mail messages should be clear; this means you should use proper sentence structure at all times and standard sentence casing. Changing the case in words makes the message more difficult to read. Because there is no tone in e-mail, you should avoid irony and sarcasm; the context of the message and the tone with which you wrote it are lost, so your message should be neutral in tone with proper grammar and spelling.

7. *Never type in all capital letters.* Using all capital letters in an e-mail

message is the digital equivalent of shouting; it is considered rude to type in all capital letters.

8. *Check spelling in your e-mail message before you send it.* Most Web browsers and e-mail clients offer the option to check the spelling in any e-mail message you are composing. You should be sure to take advantage of this to avoid any unnecessary typos that would diminish the professionalism of your communication. You should also make sure that you include proper punctuation to end sentences.

9. *Use attachments sparingly.* Large attachments can quickly fill an e-mail Inbox; typically, when an Inbox is filled, it prevents the account owner from sending mail until the account is under the allowed limit again. This means you should be careful about sending a large attachment, especially when the recipient is not aware it is coming. It is considered a courtesy to send a short e-mail notifying the recipient that a large attachment is on its way and asking if they are ready to receive it.

10. *Use appropriate priorities and avoid overusing words like "urgent" and "important."* Some e-mail clients allow you to set the priority of the message. When doing so, you should not overuse the high priority setting if the actions needed are not actually urgent. Eventually, setting this priority flag to high will lose any meaning if you do it for most of your messages. You should also avoid words like "urgent" or "important" in the subject line. These detract from the overall content of the message and give no real preview of the subject. It is better to allow the content of the message to establish the urgency. In a real emergency situation, a phone call or in-person meeting is a much better option.

CHAPTER SUMMARY

This chapter covered the fundamentals of using e-mail clients. Electronic mail is a convenient and efficient form of professional communication and it has become a standard for transmitting information in the modern business environment. If you do not have an e-mail account, Gmail by Google and Microsoft Windows Live Hotmail are two alternatives for creating a free account to use for your communication needs. There are a variety of personal e-mail clients available for use including those preinstalled on the computer for the operating system it uses. Microsoft Outlook is a professional e-mail client that is part of the Microsoft Office productivity suite of software available on Windows and Macintosh machines. The ribbon interface described in this chapter for Outlook will be seen throughout the rest of this book for the remaining tools in the Microsoft Office suite of software programs. The next section of the book focuses on the most common productivity task in modern organizations: word processing.

CHAPTER EXERCISES

1. Create a list of possible e-mail address local parts that you could use as a personal account to register with a free Web e-mail provider. Choose an e-mail account provider and register one of the addresses from your list. Compose an e-mail containing the possible local parts in your list and explain why you chose the particular address you did and the particular service. Send the e-mail to your new account and save it to a local file using an e-mail client. Make sure the message conforms to e-mail etiquette practices, including the subject line.

2. Use the calendar available in either your e-mail client or your Web mail client to set an appointment to read the next chapter. Include any additional e-mail accounts you use in the list of recipients. Include a description, location, and resources for the event. If you are using this book as part of a course, include your professor in the invitation list. Set a reminder for the event (if your e-mail client supports them) for 15 minutes prior to your appointment.

CHAPTER KNOWLEDGE CHECK

1 The following are all examples of an e-mail client except:

○ **A.** Windows Live ID

○ **B.** Microsoft Outlook

○ **C.** Macintosh Mail

○ **D.** Mozilla Thunderbird

2 A valid e-mail address can contain all of the following characters:

○ **A.** Uppercase letters

○ **B.** Lowercase letters

○ **C.** Numerical digits from zero to nine

○ **D.** The underscore character

○ **E.** All of the above

○ **F.** None of the above

3 A valid e-mail address can contain multiple full stop (or dot or period) characters.

○ True

○ False

4 A valid e-mail address must contain at least one @ symbol and can contain more.

○ True

○ False

5 Most e-mail clients provide the user with a built-in e-mail account so there is no need to create a new account when you install an e-mail client.

○ True

○ False

6 The following is a violation of the established rules for e-mail etiquette:

○ **A.** Using a descriptive and short subject line

○ **B.** Using BCC for a large group e-mail

○ **C.** Typing a message or subject in all capital letters for emphasis

○ **D.** Using Reply instead of Reply All for a large group e-mail

○ **E.** All of the above

○ **F.** None of the above

7 The calendar system in Microsoft Outlook does not allow you to hide appointments, so you must only enter details you wish to make public.

- ○ True
- ○ False

8 The following event type should be used in Microsoft Outlook for having coffee with a friend:

- ○ Meeting
- ○ Appointment

9 Most e-mail clients allow e-mail messages in the following formats:

- ○ **A.** Plain text
- ○ **B.** Rich text (text with some formatting)
- ○ **C.** HTML
- ○ **D.** All of the above
- ○ **E.** None of the above

10 The following is a valid e-mail address for Microsoft Windows Live Hotmail:

- ○ **A.** mY_great_e-mail@gmail.com
- ○ **B.** hey!e-mail-me!@hotmail.com
- ○ **C.** my.great.e-mail@live.com
- ○ **D.** All of the above
- ○ **E.** None of the above

Introduction to • *Word and Word Processing*

This chapter presents an overview of productivity software and an exploration of word processing, the most common productivity application used in today's business environment. You will create your own word processing documents as you learn about the software, formatting text, and utilizing templates. As an example project, you will also learn to create a resume and cover letter, which are fundamental tools for any job search. Once you complete the chapter, you will be able to:

- Locate and use the File menu for most applications

- Access the help files for an application

- Construct a word processing document from a blank document or a template

- Format and manipulate text in a document

- Save and manage files within productivity software

INTRODUCTION TO PRODUCTIVITY SOFTWARE

Microsoft Office is an example of a software suite that is used for productivity. A *software suite* is a collection of individual programs that are used to perform related tasks; in the case of Office, this is the management of documents for word processing, presentations, spreadsheets, and e-mail. You were introduced to Outlook in the previous chapter; Outlook is one of the software packages included in the Office suite, which itself is considered productivity software.

PRODUCTIVITY SOFTWARE *is a program that assists you in performing tasks that are necessary for you to accomplish at home or in the workplace. Productivity is a measurement of how much you can accomplish in a given period of time.*

Office includes the following set of programs: Outlook (covered in Chapter 4, "Microsoft Outlook and E-mail Clients") for e-mail and calendar management, Word (Chapters 5 – 7) for word processing tasks, PowerPoint (Chapters 8 – 10) for professional presentations, and Excel® (Chapters 11 – 13) for spreadsheet creation and data management. Office has different versions depending on which operating system you have on your computer. Office 2010 is the most current version for a Windows machine, and Office 2011 is the most current version for a Macintosh. Both versions allow for the completion of nearly identical tasks. However, Office 2010 also includes

Microsoft Access® (Chapters 14 – 16) for creating databases and Microsoft One-Note® (Appendix A, "Additional Productivity Software") for compiling information into a digital notebook; these programs are not available in Office 2011.

If you do not already have Office installed on your machine, you can get a trial version of the 2010 software for Windows from the Office home page at *www.office.com* (select the *Products* link at the top of the page to get to the Office download). For the 2011 version of the Office software for Macintosh, go to *www.microsoft.com/mac.*

Companies like JourneyEd (*www.journeyed.com*) offer discounted professional software to students. If you are using another site to get a discount on your software, remember that whenever you purchase software from a source other than the official vendor, you should make sure the site is legitimate before you attempt to make a purchase or enter any personal information. This is part of being a responsible Web user.

For the most part, there is little difference in functionality between the Office 2010 and Office 2011 versions of the programs. The differences are mainly in the placement of commands between the two versions, and these will be pointed out in the text as you follow along with the examples, just as they were for Outlook in the previous chapter. You access the programs that are part of Office on a Windows machine by selecting the *Start* menu, choosing *All Programs*, and then choosing *Microsoft Office*; you will then see a listing of programs from which to choose. For this chapter, choose *Microsoft Word.*

To access Office 2011 on the Macintosh, you may be able to click the icons installed on the Dock (when you installed the software, you probably had the option to place the shortcut icons there). If you do not have the icons on your Dock, you can access the programs in the Office 2011 suite by selecting *Macintosh HD* (or whatever name you have given your machine) from the desktop, opening the *Applications* folder, and then opening the *Microsoft Office 2011* folder. Select *Microsoft Word* from the available programs.

There is a free alternative to Office that was developed as part of the open source software initiative. OpenOffice.org has counterpart programs for most of the Office suite, including word processing software, presentation software, spreadsheet software, and database software. These alternatives will be explained along with the equivalent Office program in each chapter; you will be given the instructions to complete all of the chapter tasks with OpenOffice.org wherever it is possible to do so. If you are using OpenOffice.org to complete the exercises in the book, you will still benefit greatly from reading the text outlining the tasks and operations given for the Office program. In most cases, the difference in functionality may be a simple placement issue, and thus

Whenever you activate one of the Office programs on a Macintosh, you will first be presented with a gallery of options for selecting templates or existing documents. You can simply select *Cancel* on this screen to get to the standard interface.

the majority of the overview and topic coverage may be found in the sections of the chapter devoted to Office. The OpenOffice.org equivalent to Word is OpenOffice.org Writer.

You can download the full version of OpenOffice.org from *www.openoffice.org*. This site services all operating systems for which the software is available. You can also download the source code if you want to compile it yourself, but that is an advanced topic beyond the scope of this text.

The File Menu

5.1.1

The *File* menu and the help files should be the first items you locate in any new software system. The File menu exists in almost all software applications written today and enables you to perform the essential tasks of creating a new file, opening an existing file, saving a file, printing a file, and exiting the program. While there may be additional options available in the File menu, these basic tasks warrant further investigation. The File menu is typically located at the left side of the software interface. Figure 5.1 shows the File menu for Word. In Word 2010, the File menu (which is also called the Backstage view in the Office 2010 suite) is found to the far left on the ribbon interface. In Word 2011, it is located beside the Apple menu at the top of the computer screen.

There are several essential commands found within the File menu with which you should become familiar:

- *New*—The New command is used to create a new file of the type associated with the program. In the case of Word, this file is a word processing

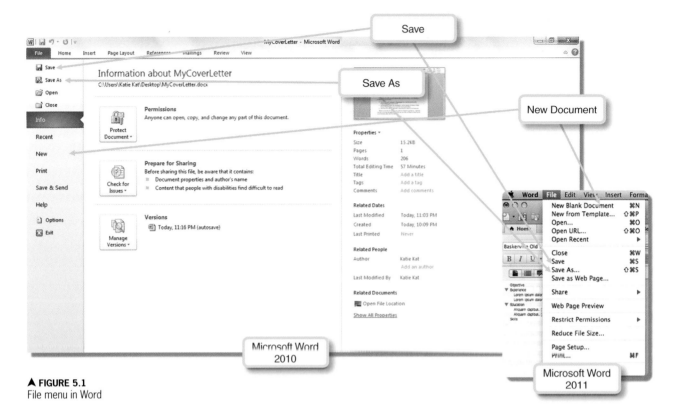

▲ FIGURE 5.1
File menu in Word

document. The New command may present you with several alternatives if the program supports different document types or document creation options.

- *Save As*—This command opens a dialog box to allow you to select the name, file type, and location to which you would like your file stored; this operates on the file that is currently active in the program. If you have already saved your document and want to save a copy or save it with a different name, you can do so with this option. For Word, the default file type is *Word Document (.docx)*, but there are several alternative file types available when saving a document including *Portable Document Format (.pdf)*. It is important to use Save As to save a new file you have created so your work will not be lost if there is a problem with the software system or you close it by accident. The Save

As dialog box for Word is shown in Figure 5.2.

- *Save*—The Save command allows you to save the file that you currently have open within the software application; this is useful for making sure your recent changes are retained in the document. The first time you save the document after it is created, this command will typically function like the Save As command.

- *Open*—The Open command is used to reopen existing documents. Selecting this command opens a dialog box that is similar to the one used to save documents and allows you to select a document from the current folder on the righthand side of the dialog box. You can also type the name of the file you want to open in the File Name field, and any files that are a match to the partial string you have typed will appear in a box as options to select.

- *Print*—This command allows you to send the current file to an installed printer. Printing requires additional hardware and a driver installation for that hardware to work. In Office 2010, you are given a software-based print option of *Send to OneNote 2010* as a possible printer regardless of what other printers you have installed. If you have installed Adobe Acrobat® Professional, you will also get the software-based option of printing to a *Portable Document Format (.pdf)* file. Both of these printing options are discussed further in Appendix A.

- *Exit*—Selecting this command will close the program. On a Macintosh, closing the windows of the program will not exit the program entirely; you must select the *File* menu and choose *Exit* to fully close the program.

Document Management

Whenever you are working on a project, it is important to manage the files associated with that project. You have already learned about using folders in previous chapters. Throughout the rest of this text, you will be creating projects in every chapter. You should be sure to keep your work organized—not just for the purposes of learning but also for the general management of productivity. If you already have a designated folder for your projects, you should create a new folder within it and title the folder *Documents*. You can similarly create other folders for the rest of the productivity software packages and title them *Presentations*, *Spreadsheets*, and *Databases*. It is a

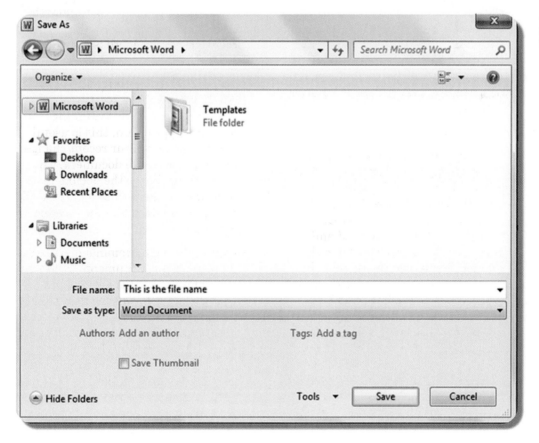

◄ **FIGURE 5.2**
Save As dialog box in Word

good idea to create folders to manage your different responsibilities so you can find items when you need them; the same rules that apply to filing and sorting paper documents also apply to organizing electronic documents.

5.1.3

Help Files

Help files are almost always included in a software system. These files allow you to get definitions of elements in the software system and obtain help in performing common tasks and troubleshooting. On a Windows machine, pressing the *F1* key will activate the Help interface for whatever program you currently have selected (if you are using the operating system when you press *F1*, you will open the help interface for the operating system). On a Macintosh, the Help interface is available by selecting the *Help* menu at the top of the screen; this will be context-sensitive for the program you have active. The Word Help interface is shown in Figure 5.3. Most help files, including those in Office, allow you to search for entries using a keyword search.

Productivity Shortcuts

5.1.4

Productivity shortcuts are keyboard commands that can be entered quickly to save you the time of having to open a menu or ribbon to find the command you wish to use. These exist for the most common actions you perform in a software system and are common to most software programs that utilize individual documents or files to store and organize information.

You activate a shortcut command by holding down the *Ctrl* key on a Windows machine and typing the letter corresponding to the shortcut while the *Ctrl* key is held down. These shortcuts work on a Macintosh machine as well, except the *Command* key is used to activate the shortcut instead of the *Ctrl* key. The most common shortcuts

▲ FIGURE 5.3
Word Help interface in Word

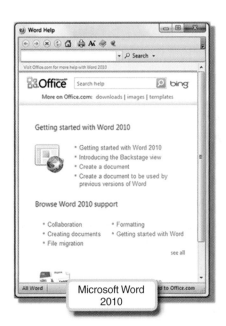

Microsoft Word 2010

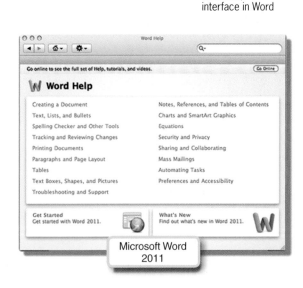

Microsoft Word 2011

with which you should be familiar are as follows:

- *New Document* (*Ctrl-N* on Windows machines or *Command-N* on Macintosh machines)—This command opens a new blank document in the active program.

- *Open Document* (*Ctrl-O* or *Command-O*)—This is used to open an existing file. It will open a dialog box that allows you to choose the file you wish to open.

- *Save Document* (*Ctrl-S* or *Command-S*)—This is the same as selecting the *Save* command; it will save any progress in an open document that has already been saved. If the document has not yet been saved, it will act like the *Save As* command.

- *Print Document* (*Ctrl-P* or *Command-P*)—This command initiates the printing process. If the software allows you to set options before you print, it will open a dialog box; otherwise, it will attempt to use the default printer to initiate a print command.

- *Undo Last Action* (*Ctrl-Z* or *Command-Z*)—This will attempt to undo the last action you performed in the open document; not all actions can be undone with this command. Some programs maintain a buffer of actions, allowing you to undo multiple changes that you made to the document.

- *Redo Last Action* (*Ctrl-Y* or *Command-Y*)—This will reverse the effects of the Undo command; not all actions that are undone can be reversed by the Redo command. Again, there are some programs that will maintain a buffer of commands and changes, allowing you to redo multiple actions that were reversed by the Undo command.

- *Select All Content* (*Ctrl-A* or *Command-A*)—This command will select all of the content in the current document or document element (like a table cell) that is allowed to be selected. This is a useful command if you want to perform actions like applying formatting to everything in your document.

- *Quit* (*Ctrl-Q* or *Command-Q*)—This command will attempt to exit the currently active program.

There are additional shortcuts that are used often to utilize the system clipboard for transferring information quickly and easily from one document or location to another. These are valuable to learn and will save you a considerable amount of time when you are typing. There are also shortcuts to common formatting changes that will be discussed later in this chapter as you start your first project in word processing. Additionally, specific programs may have a unique set of shortcut commands in addition to or instead of the ones covered here.

The System Clipboard

5.1.5

The system clipboard is temporary storage for anything you copy from a document or folder that allows you to use it again elsewhere. When you copy an object or a grouping of text to the clipboard, all of its formatting and content are retained. The copied material can then be pasted in another location in any of the productivity software programs. For instance, you can copy formatted text from Word and paste it into PowerPoint and it will retain any formatting that was applied to it. Similarly, you can copy a chart from Excel and paste it into a Word document. This interoperability and the ease of use of the clipboard make it a valuable tool for productivity.

The three commands that apply to the clipboard are:

- *Copy*—The Copy command is used to make a duplicate of selected text or objects in a document. Copy will leave the original source of the material intact in the document and make a duplicate on the clipboard. The Copy icon looks like two sheets of paper overlapping each other. The shortcut for the Copy command is *Ctrl-C* on a Windows machine and *Command-C* on a Macintosh machine.

- *Cut*—The Cut command functions like Copy except it removes the original source material from the document (whether it is text or an object) and places it on the clipboard. The Cut icon is traditionally a pair of scissors; the shortcut for the Cut command is *Ctrl-X* on a Windows machine and *Command-X* on a Macintosh machine.

- *Paste*—The Paste command is used to place the contents of the clipboard at the active cursor location within a selected document. Whether the contents are then removed from the clipboard depends on the specific program; in Word, they are not removed and can be pasted multiple times. The Paste icon looks like either a clipboard or a bottle of rubber cement (which was traditionally used to place clippings of documents in other documents). The shortcut for Paste is *Ctrl-V* on Windows and *Command-V* on Macintosh.

In Word, you are given a choice of options when you paste something from the clipboard. This appears as a clipboard icon, which opens to a menu when you place an object from the clipboard, as shown in Figure 5.4. Typically, these options are whether you want to keep the formatting from the source, whether you want to match the formatting to that of the document where you are placing the text (called *Merge Formatting* in Word 2010), or whether you want to retain the text without the formatting. These options vary from program to program. Try this functionality yourself by typing a simple sentence in your open

If you copy formatted text from one document and paste it into a document location that does not allow formatting, such as Notepad on a Windows machine, the text will be pasted and the formatting will be removed. The spacing of the letters (such as blank space characters created using the spacebar or tab indents from the Tab key) will be retained to match the way the keys and spacing are defined in the target document. This can actually be helpful for removing unwanted formatting from Web documents or PDF files.

document, selecting it, cutting it from the document, and pasting it back into the document. If you open the clipboard icon, you will see the available paste options.

INTRODUCTION TO WORD PROCESSING SOFTWARE

Word processing is the most common task in any modern business environment. Word processing software is the digital equivalent of letter writing. Word processors have their origin in typesetting and the manual typewriter, which used an ink ribbon and a striking wheel to pound individual letters from the wheel onto the ribbon, imprinting the letter on the paper.

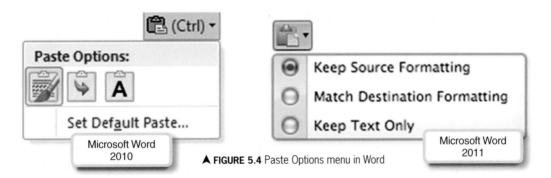

▲ **FIGURE 5.4** Paste Options menu in Word

If any mistakes were made, you had to either use a strikethrough character to alert the reader or use correction fluid to cover up the error.

Early electronic word processors allowed a user to enter a line of text and, when the user hit the return carriage key (the equivalent of the Enter key), would mechanically type the letters one by one onto the paper using the striking wheel; this allowed the user to avoid most typos with a quick read through of the line before hitting the return carriage. Now word processing is almost universally done on a computer, allowing an enormous level of convenience and collaboration for creating and utilizing documents.

5.3 ANATOMY OF MICROSOFT WORD

Word is one of the more popular software applications for word processing. Whenever

WORD PROCESSING *in modern terms is the use of a computer system to create, manipulate, and share text. The traditional means of word processing is through the use of the keyboard and mouse, though modern speech recognition programs allow you to create text from audio input.*

you open Word from either a desktop icon or the Start menu of a Windows machine, it will open with a new blank document (which defaults to the name *Document1*). You can save this document with a name of your choosing using the *Save As* command in the *File* menu (the File menu is shown in Figure 5.1).

When you select the *Save As* command, it will open a Save As dialog box, as shown in Figure 5.2. This allows you to select the location where you want to store your file. You can select the folder you want to use from the right hand Navigation pane. The contents of the active folder are shown at the left side of the Navigation pane. Select the *New Folder* icon to create a new folder to use inside the current folder. Finally, you can type a name for your file and select the file type you want for your document. The default file type for Microsoft Word is *Word Document* (*.docx*). Save your document in the Documents folder you created earlier with the filename *MyCoverLetter*.

Whenever you are working on a document, you should save it often. Your software could quit because of a machine error or a glitch and any unsaved progress on your work could be lost. You could also accidentally delete a portion of your work or make a change that the Undo command cannot correct; if you have saved your document before these changes, you can close the current document and open the saved version to get back to where you were.

To open an existing document in Word, select the *File* menu and then choose *Open*. This will display an Open dialog box, as shown in Figure 5.5. The left-side Navigation pane is similar to the Save As dialog box where you can navigate to the folder you want to open. The right side of the dialog box lists the contents of the current folder. You can select any of the files with file types that can be opened in Word; the name of the file will display in the *File*

Name field and you can click the *Open* button (or simply double-click the name of the file).

You can also start typing the name of the file you want to open in the File Name field of the Open dialog box. A drop-down menu will appear from the File Name field, displaying all of the filenames within the active folder that match the partial string of characters you have typed. You can then select an item from the list instead of typing the entire filename or manually sorting through all of the contents of the active folder. Word 2010 for Windows and Word 2011 for Macintosh allow you to perform the same functions to create a document; however, the interface for these two applications is different. You can jump to the section

▶ FIGURE 5.5
Open dialog box
in Word

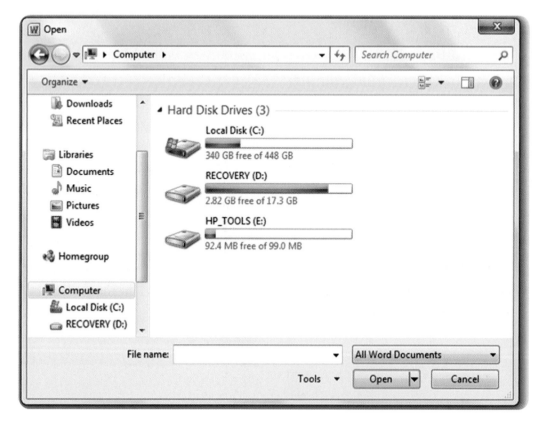

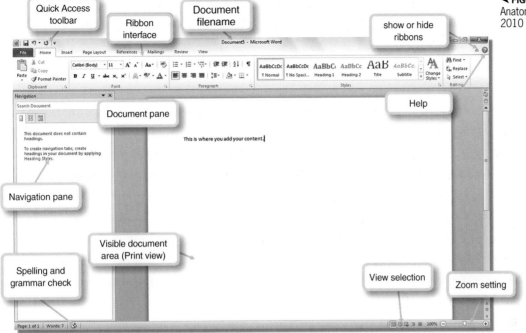

Quick Access toolbar

Ribbon interface

Document filename

show or hide ribbons

Help

Document pane

Navigation pane

Spelling and grammar check

Visible document area (Print view)

View selection

Zoom setting

of the text that applies to the version you have.

5.3.1

Microsoft Word 2010

Figure 5.6 shows an example of the standard interface for Word 2010. Across the top of the window for each open document is the Quick Access toolbar, which contains shortcuts to commonly used commands. By default, Save, Undo, and Redo are included as direct links. The arrow beside the Undo command contains a buffer list of prior actions that can be undone; all of the actions after the one selected will be undone if this list is used. The Microsoft Word icon in the far-left corner contains commands for moving and resizing the

window. The far right of the interface contains icons to minimize the window (which removes the document from the screen while keeping it open), maximize the window (to take up the full available space of the computer screen), or close the document and the window.

The ribbon interface for Word 2010 is beneath the toolbar. The File menu can be found to the left of the ribbons that are available. The Home ribbon is the first ribbon you will see. This ribbon, shown in Figure 5.7, contains common formatting commands for your document. You can also manage styles from this ribbon, which you will learn about in the next chapter. The other commands here to note are the

▼ FIGURE 5.7
Home ribbon in
Word 2010

Find, Replace, Copy, Cut, and Paste icons. You will use these extensively in creating documents.

The Insert ribbon, shown in Figure 5.8, is used to add special content to your document; this includes tables, images, drawing objects, and clip art. There are special document elements available in this ribbon as well, particularly the Header, Footer, Cover Page, Blank Page, and Page Break (which immediately pushes subsequent content to the next page regardless of whether there is room left on the current page). Other formatting options include Drop Cap, Symbols, and Hyperlinks. You can add a hyperlink to an external document or Web page, or link to a section within the current document (defined as a bookmark).

The Page Layout ribbon is the next one in line. This ribbon allows you to control the size of the document, document orientation for printing, indents, spacing, and alignment. This ribbon is discussed in Chapter 6, "Developing and Editing Documents." The References ribbon is used for documents that require citations, endnotes, and footnotes; this ribbon is also covered in the next chapter. The Mailings ribbon is used to construct documents such as envelopes and labels and individualize mailing documents for letters to multiple recipients. This is one of the more advanced features of Microsoft Word.

The next ribbon of interest is the Review ribbon, shown in Figure 5.9. This ribbon contains the icon for Spelling and Grammar, which should be used to review any document prior to submitting it; clicking this icon will start parsing your document for known spelling and grammar errors and prompt you to correct them. Additional research tools like the Thesaurus and Word Count are also located here, as well as the ability to turn on Track Changes and add and remove comments, which are useful when working on a collaborative document.

The View Ribbon is the last standard ribbon and is shown in Figure 5.10. You can change the view of the document in this ribbon. Unlike some of the other programs in the Office suite, there is not usually a reason to deviate from the Print Layout for most documents; this view shows the text broken up into pages where the editable regions are bright white and anything not on the printed page is shown as a gray background. The Full Screen Reading view shows the document with the maximum amount of screen space devoted to the content. Web Layout shows the contents of the page as they would look if the page were converted to an HTML document. Outline view shows the levels of the document and is similar to an outline of content; you can promote or demote content using this view and select how many levels of headings you want to see. Draft view works like Print Layout view

▼ FIGURE 5.8
Insert ribbon in
Word 2010

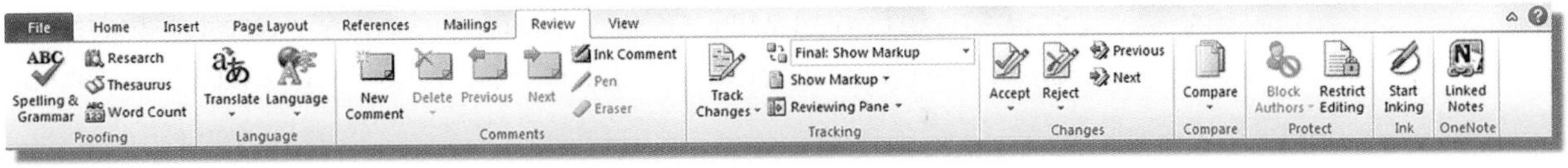

but without showing the text as it would appear on the printed page. One item to note here is the *Navigation Pane* checkbox; this will show or hide the Navigation pane, which provides you with an outline or pre-view of your document in a separate, mobile pop-up window. Make sure this checkbox is selected.

The Navigation pane has three tabs. The first tab (which looks like a small docu-ment with outline format) is a display of the document outline by heading; you can adjust the number of levels of the document outline to display by right-clicking on a heading and choosing *Show Heading Levels* and the level you want to show. The Browse tab displays a thumbnail view of the pages of your document so you can jump quickly to a page by clicking its thumbnail. Finally, the Browse Results tab shows the results of a keyword search of the document using any keywords entered in the text box above the tabs.

The bottom of the standard interface contains page information, word count, a proofing error indicator, and View and Zoom settings. You can see the current page in which you are working and the total number of pages in the document. The word count defaults to the total number of words in the document; if you have some text selected, the words in that selection are displayed as a fraction of the total word count. The View settings are shortcuts to the different views available. To change the zoom percentage, you can use the slider or the + and – but-tons. The zoom percentage is how much the document is magnified from standard print/screen size. A zoom of 100% is the actual size of the document.

Microsoft Word 2011

The main difference you may notice between Word 2010 and Word 2011 is the inclusion of the menu bar in Word 2011. The menu bar is standard with any Macintosh software application, and it contains a lot of the functionality of the ribbon interface plus some convenient shortcuts that are not eas-ily accessible from the ribbon. The menu bar is located beside the Apple menu at the top of the computer screen; the menu choices begin with the Word menu and include the File menu and Help menu. In the document window itself (shown in Figure 5.11) are the icons to close the document, minimize it, or maximize it on the screen. Beneath those are the Quick Access toolbar icons. By default, there are more of these icons in Word 2011 than there are in Word 2010;

▲ **FIGURE 5.9**
Review ribbon in Word 2010

5.3.2

▼ **FIGURE 5.10**
View ribbon in Word 2010

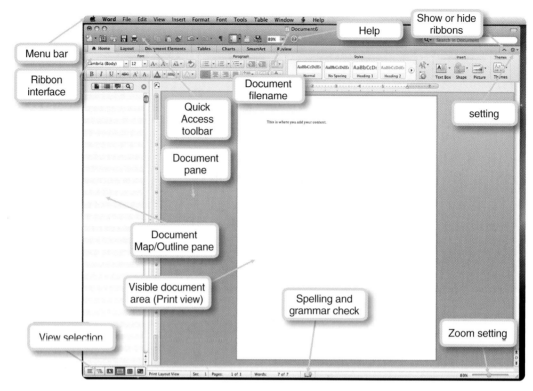

▲ **FIGURE 5.11** Anatomy of Word 2011

► **FIGURE 5.12**
Home ribbon in
Word 2011

these include shortcuts to the standard File menu commands (such as New, Open, Save, and Print), along with Cut, Copy, Paste, Undo, Redo, and Format Painter.

The Quick Access toolbar also contains an icon to open the Help interface; this appears as a circle with a question mark inside of it. Beside the Quick Access toolbar is a text box for searching the document; you simply type a keyword into the box and press *Enter* or click on the magnifying glass icon to perform the search. The ribbon interface is beneath this toolbar.

The Home ribbon for Word 2011, shown in Figure 5.12, contains the tools you will

need to format your text. This includes the Font and Paragraph panels for altering various settings that affect how your text will display. You also have access to the available styles in this ribbon, which are covered in the next chapter. In Word 2011, you can also insert pictures and shapes from the Home ribbon.

The Layout ribbon, shown in Figure 5.13, contains all of the tools for setting up the pages of your document. These include setting whether you want your document layout to be *Portrait* (the standard printed page with the longer side having the vertical measurement) or *Landscape*

(where the shorter side is the vertical measurement). You can also set your margins from this ribbon. The margin is the amount of white space between the edge of the printed page and the beginning of your content; these typically default to 1" on each side. This ribbon allows you to add page breaks, set the number of columns in your document, and use advanced functionality, such as adding a watermark to the document or changing the background color of the page.

The Document Elements ribbon, shown in Figure 5.14, allows you to add common items to your page. These include a cover page, a blank page, and various types of page breaks. You can add a Table of Contents, Header, and Footer to your document from this ribbon using the predefined formats. This ribbon also includes tools for using references and citations; this is covered in the next chapter.

The Tables, Charts, and SmartArt ribbons are used to add advanced features to your document. These ribbons are covered in later sections of this book. You are welcome to click on them to see what they contain, but they are not used in this chapter. The Review ribbon is used primarily for editing collaborative documents for which you want to track changes and for sharing documents

with others. Some of the features in this ribbon are discussed later in this chapter.

The Document Map pane lets you see an outline of your document, similar to the Navigation pane in Word 2010. To do this, select the *View* menu, choose *Sidebar*, and then choose *Document Pane*. The four tabs across the top of the Document pane correspond to Thumbnails, Document Map, Reviewing, and Find and Replace. The Thumbnail pane shows a miniature version of the pages of your document as they appear when printed. The Document Map pane shows the outline of the document arranged according to the document headers. The Reviewing pane identifies comments and tracked document changes. The Find and Replace pane will locate instances of the text you enter in the Find text box and allow you to select options for replacing that text with what you enter in the Replace text box. The Document pane is useful for jumping quickly through your document and seeing an outline of the text you are constructing.

The bottom of the interface includes shortcuts for changing the view of the document. The views included here are Draft, Outline, Publishing, Print, Notebook, and Full Screen. Draft view shows your document without the page formatting. Outline

view shows the contents of your document arranged as an outline where you can see higher level headings for text farther to the left. Full Screen view is a special mode that shows your document on the full screen without any desktop interface, as shown in Figure 5.15; when you are in this view, you have access to just a subset of the normal formatting commands. Select *Exit* to return to the standard Print view. Publishing view and Notebook view are special formats for text documents that require your document to be created or converted to the format for use; Notebook Layout view is similar to Office OneNote 2010 and is covered in Appendix A.

In addition to the view selection, the bottom of the interface has several other convenient data points. You will see the page number you are currently on out of the total page count. You will also see your current word count; if some text is selected, you will see the word count of the selected text out of the total word count. There is also an indicator for spelling and grammar errors; a green check mark means there are currently no mistakes in the document and a red *X* indicates that there are errors according to the spelling and grammar rules of Word 2011. Finally, at the far right of the bottom interface is the current zoom percentage (this is a percentage of actual document size, which is 100%); you can adjust the slider setting to change the zoom.

DIVING INTO WORD PROCESSING

A resume and a cover letter are two documents that everyone needs to

➤ **FIGURE 5.15**
Full Screen view
in Word 2011

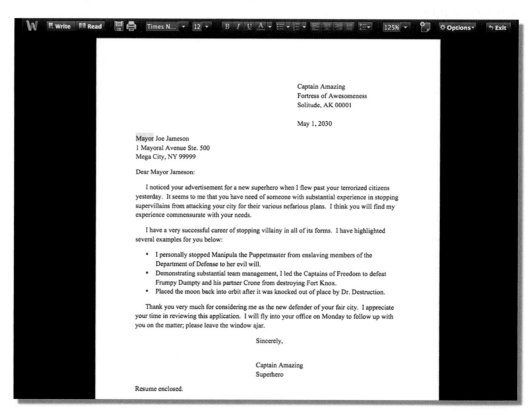

prepare when applying for jobs in the professional world. These documents are designed to showcase your abilities and experience. Since these two documents are almost universally necessary, they are used as a first step into the world of word processing. Even if you are not currently looking for a job, it is always beneficial to remain proficient in the skills used to create these documents. You will be creating two documents for this project, one from a blank document and one from a template. You can use the blank document you already created to start your cover letter. Be sure to clear out any contents of the document you may have entered while exploring the program by using the shortcut to select all (*Ctrl-A* or *Command-A* depending on the operating system) and pressing the *Delete* key. Save the file as *CoverLetter*.

Writing a Cover Letter

A *cover letter* is a type of formal business letter that typically accompanies a resume in response to a job posting. While the resume is a bullet-point account of education, experience, and skills, the cover letter is a paragraph account of the significant points on the resume that apply to the specific job for which you are applying. One way to look at a cover letter is to think of it as a tour guide of the resume for a particular job. A cover letter should be short and tailored to the specific job, highlighting the relevant skills and experience that make you a suitable candidate for that position.

To get started, research a job on Monster (*www.monster.com*) that you would like to have; this will be the job for which you customize your resume and cover letter for the project in this chapter. Because this is a formal business letter, there is a specific format that should be followed. These formatting instructions and the required number of blank lines between each section are shown in Figure 5.16. You should include all of the information on this outline that you can and prepare to write the text of your letter.

A cover letter should consist of three paragraphs of text with a total word count of 150 to 250 words. The first paragraph should describe how you found the job posting, why you are

Your Name
Return Address Line 1
Return Address Line 2 (Optional)
City, State ZIP

Date

Addressee Name
Sending Address Line 1
Sending Address Line 2 (Optional)
City, State ZIP

Salutation Addressee Name:

Letter paragraph one with indentation. Continuing lines will not indent.
Letter paragraph two. More paragraphs may be necessary for content of message.
This is where you thank the reader and include any follow-up items.

Complimentary Closing,

Name
Title

Amendments or Post Scripts (Optional)

▲ **FIGURE 5.16** Example formatting for a cover letter

qualified for the job, and why you are seeking the job (this is especially important if you currently have a job).

The second paragraph should highlight your qualifications. You should have three to four relevant accomplishments or demonstrable skills (with some sort of supporting documentation or recommendation to back up the claim) that you want to highlight in the second paragraph of the letter. The final section of the letter should indicate follow-up actions like when you will contact the potential employer for any next steps on your end.

The company Palladian International, LLC, conducted a study called "Cover Letter Best Practices" that outlined how managers actually use cover letters in the hiring process. The following are their recommendations for creating a more successful cover letter:

- Personalize the cover letter to the specific position.
- Give a reason why you should be hired.
- Identify why you are seeking the position.
- Keep your letter brief.
- Make it easy for the viewer to see the relevant points.

Several other important steps to take are to proofread your document before you submit it and to make sure your document is in the correct format the organization wants for submission. You should also avoid cliché opening lines in your letter; these may get you disregarded entirely so it is better to open with accomplishments relevant to the available position. A completed example of a cover letter is shown in Figure 5.17. This is the model you should follow in constructing your letter (though you will need to add your own text that is specific for the position you selected).

After you have entered your text (as plain text entry), you will need to format your letter. You should have your return address, the recipient address, greeting, first paragraph, bullet-point accomplishments, third paragraph, salutation, and name entered in plain text (formatted from the default text entry settings of the program) at this point. Because the text of your document will vary greatly from position to position, the remainder of the project will concentrate on formatting, reviewing, and managing the document.

Formatting Text

5.4.2

Text entry can be done in simpler programs like Notepad, as the real benefit of word processing software is the ability to format and change the appearance of text. The ability to design the appearance of your text, add additional media to your documents, and share your documents in multiple formats is where word processing stands out against simple text editors. Word has all of these features available to turn the

You can see the word count of your document in the lower-left corner of the interface beside the page number in Word 2010; it is located more to the center of the bottom of the interface in Word 2011. This is indicated by the word *Words:* next to the value.

Captain Amazing
Fortress of Awesomeness
Solitude, AK 00001

May 1, 2030

Mayor Joe Jameson
1 Mayoral Avenue Ste. 500
Mega City, NY 99999

Dear Mayor Jameson:

I noticed your advertisement for a new superhero when I flew past your terrorized citizens yesterday. It seems to me that you have need of someone with substantial experience in stopping supervillains from attacking your city for their various nefarious plans. I thik you will find my experience commensurate with your needs.

I have a very successful career of stopping villainy in all of its forms. I have highlighted several examples for you below:

- I personally stopped Manipula the Puppetmaster from enslaving members of the Department of Defense to her evil will.
- Demonstrating substantial team management, I led the Captains of Freedom to defeat Frumpy Dumpty and his partner Crone from destroying Fort Knox.
- Placed the moon back into orbit after it was knocked out of place by Dr. Destruction.

Thank you very much for considering me as the new defender of your fair city. I appreciate your time in reviewing this application. I will fly into your office on Monday to follow up with you on the matter; please leave the window ajar.

Sincerely,

Captain Amazing
Superhero

Resume enclosed.

plain text you added to your document into a professional-looking cover letter.

5.4.2.1 The Font Panel

The Font panel is common to most of the Office programs. This panel, located on the Home ribbon, contains the formatting commands for changing the font, size, style, and color of your text. The default font for a new document is Calibri (Body) on Windows and Cambria (Body) on the Macintosh.

Select all of the text in your letter by using the *Select All* shortcut (*Ctrl-A* on Windows and *Command-A* on the Macintosh) and select *Times New Roman*.

The Font panel is shown in Figure 5.18. Remember that changes to the Font panel

A **FONT** *is a complete set of keyboard characters in one particular style (the style is the name of the font). Most fonts support standard sizes as well as bold and italic variants.*

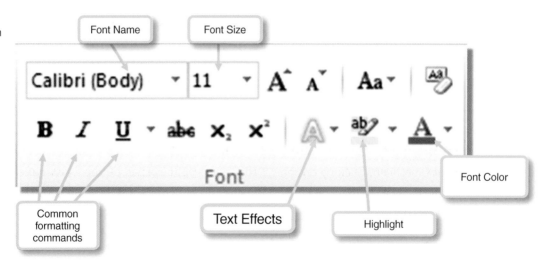

> **FIGURE 5.18**
> Word Font panel in the Home ribbon

settings apply only to text that is selected when the changes are made. If no text is selected, the settings will be changed for text that is added at the current cursor location until another section of formatted text is encountered. By default, the format of new text that you enter will be consistent with the text immediately before it in the document.

You can change the size of your text (called the font size) in a number of ways: by selecting a preset value from the drop-down Font Size field, typing a number manually in the Font Size field, or using the Grow Font and Shrink Font icons to increment or decrement the size of the font. Select all of your text and change the font size to *12*. Font sizes are set in point values; a *point* is the smallest unit of measure in typography. There are 72 points per inch. An intermediate value called a *pica* is the equivalent of 12 points (so there are 6 picas per inch).

You should not add text effects to a cover letter. Readability and clarity are essential for this type of document. However, you

should take note of the styles that you can apply to your text in the Font panel. Bold, Italic, and Underline are all means of adding emphasis to your text. Bold will make the text thicker and darker, Italic will slant the text, and Underline will add a line under the text. Strikethrough retains the text but crosses it out; this is used to show completed tasks in a list of tasks. The strikethrough used to be an indicator of an error correction in typewritten documents, but there is no need for this use in modern word processing software except in tracking changes for collaboration.

You can use the Text Highlight Color option to highlight your text; this is similar to using a highlighter marker on paper. The text will remain visible, but it will be emphasized so it can be quickly found

> There are several keyboard shortcuts for the common formatting enhancements. To bold text, use *Ctrl-B* (or *Command-B* on the Mac); to italicize text, use *Ctrl-I* (or *Command-I*); and to underline text, use *Ctrl-U* (or *Command-U*). These act as a toggle, so repeating the command will turn off the effect.

later. The color of the highlighter can be changed, allowing you to color-code text. To get rid of an existing highlight, select the highlighted text, click the drop-down arrow under the *Text Highlight Color* icon, and choose *No Color*.

To change the color of the text itself, you use the Font Color icon. Clicking on the drop-down arrow opens a menu from which you can select any of the colors of the current theme setting and standard colors. You can also utilize custom colors or a gradient

by selecting these options from the menu. Finally, using the Clear Formatting icon (which looks like an eraser) will remove any changes you have made to the formatting of the selected text and reset it to the default font settings for the document.

In Word 2010, the expansion icon in the lower-right corner of the Font panel opens the Font dialog box. In Word 2011, you open the Font dialog box by selecting the *Format* menu and choosing *Font*. The Font dialog box is shown in Figure 5.19.

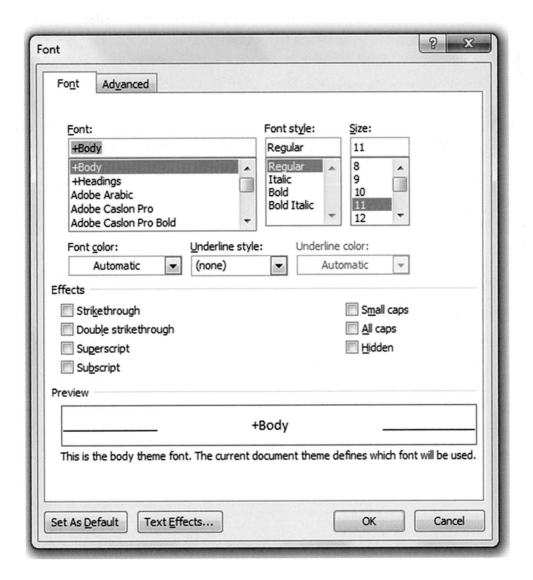

◀ **FIGURE 5.19**
Font dialog box in Word

This dialog box allows you to configure the font, size, effects, and enhancements for your text in a single interface. Of particular note is the ability to change the underline style of your text from the default thin solid line to a preset number of selections included a dotted line, broken line, wavy line, and double line.

5.4.2.2 *The Paragraph Panel*

The Paragraph panel is located beside the Font panel on the Home ribbon and is shown in Figure 5.20. This panel provides options for bullets and numbering, outline formatting, text indent (to increase or decrease indent), text alignment, and spacing between lines. Text alignment will be a bigger concern when you start adding complex visual elements to your word processing documents (and presentation documents). For now, though, use the Align Text Right icon to align the date and return address to the right margin of your cover letter (the margins should be set at the default letter size for now, meaning your text will be 1

inch from the right edge of the paper when printed). To do this, select the date and return address (your address) within the document and click *Align Text Right*. You will notice that the default setting is for text to be aligned to the left.

The Line Spacing icon allows you to select the number of lines of space given for each line of text (by default, this is set at 1.15 lines of space per line in the menu); this spacing is based on the font size of the text, so double spacing (two lines of space per line of text) for a 12 pt font will be equal to 24 pts of space, but for an 18 pt font will be 36 pts of space. There are also a few options for paragraph spacing. The Paragraph dialog box offers a more detailed selection of options for line spacing.

In Word 2010, click the expansion icon in the lower-right corner of the Paragraph panel to open the Paragraph dialog box. In Word 2011, you activate the Paragraph dialog box by selecting the *Format* menu and choosing *Paragraph*. When you open

> **FIGURE 5.20**
Word Paragraph panel in the Home ribbon

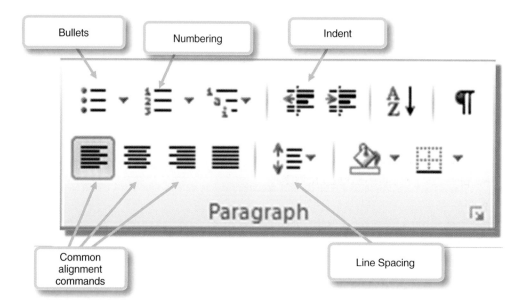

the dialog box, it should default to the *Indents and Spacing* tab, which is where you change the settings for the line spacing.

In the *Spacing* area, select *At Least* under the *Line Spacing* entry, and in the *At* field, enter *16 pt*. This will add some additional space to each line and make your text more readable without wasting too much space. The preset *Single* and *Double* values are also commonly used for formatting, using either one or two times the font size of the line as the vertical space between lines of text.

5.4.2.3 *Format Painter*

It is important to give any document you create a consistent look and feel. You will learn about managing styles in the coming chapters, but one way to provide consistency is to use format painting. This process takes the formatting modifications from the currently selected text and applies them to any text that is highlighted after you click the Format Painter icon. This icon, which looks like a paintbrush, is located in the Home ribbon in Word 2010 and in the Quick Access toolbar in Word 2011.

5.4.3 Bullets and Numbering

It is time to add bullet points to the three or four key items that you highlighted in your cover letter. Select the lines of text for your primary points and then click the *Bullets* icon in the *Paragraph panel* of the *Home ribbon*. This will automatically convert your items to an unordered list of elements. You can change the style of the bullet point by selecting from among the available

options in the drop-down arrow menu for the Bullets icon, shown in Figure 5.21. You can also define a custom bullet style by selecting *Define New Bullet*. This will open a dialog box allowing you to select a symbol, image, or letter from a particular font (like *Wingdings* or *Webdings*) for your bullet point.

Though you are not using it for this project, there are similar options available from the Numbering icon's drop-down arrow menu (shown in Figure 5.22). The significant difference between numbering and bullets is the inclusion of ordering in a numbered list. The numbering options available include letters, numerals, and Roman numerals (a system that uses specific letters to represent numeric values such as *I* for one and *V* for five); you can choose from the predefined set or you can choose *Define New Number Format* to create custom styles.

▼ **FIGURE 5.21** Bullet Library in Word

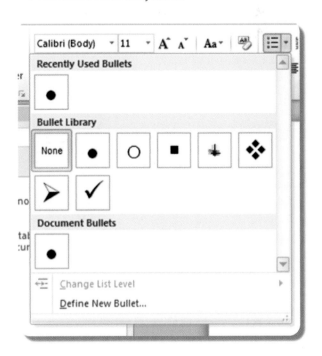

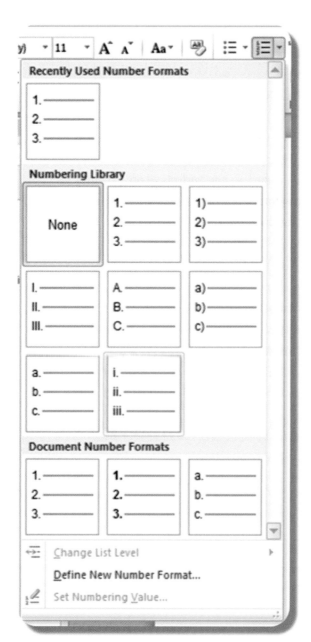

typing the word "an" when you mean to type "and" may not register as a grammatical error and will not be flagged as a spelling error as it is a correctly spelled word. Because of this, it is a good idea to have someone else review your cover letter and resume before you submit them.

In addition to the manual tools for checking spelling and grammar, Word has several AutoCorrect features that will attempt to replace words as you type to correct common misspellings and to replace certain text entries with symbols.

You can configure the AutoCorrect options if you want to add any additional rules or turn off any existing rules. To reach the AutoCorrect preferences in Word 2010, select the *File* menu and then choose *Options*. This will open the Word Options dialog box. From here, click *Proofing* in the menu on the left and select the *AutoCorrect Options* button. In Word 2011, select the *Tools* menu and *AutoCorrect*. The existing rules are displayed in a list at the bottom of the dialog box; you can add a rule by typing the misspelled word in the *Replace* field followed by the correct word in the *With* field and choosing *Add*. These dialog boxes are shown in Figure 5.23.

5.4.4 Document Review

One of the biggest mistakes you can make with a cover letter, resume, or any other professional document is not checking the spelling and grammar of the work before you submit it. Word has some excellent tools for checking spelling and grammar, but there are errors that it will not catch; for instance,

Spelling and Grammar 5.4.4.1

The spelling and grammar check will locate and alert you to any issues that it finds within your document. Clicking the *Spelling and Grammar* icon initiates an automated review of your document. In Word 2010, it is located in the Review ribbon.

In Word 2011, select the *Tools* menu and then choose *Spelling and Grammar*. You will be prompted with any correction issues that the software locates.

An example correction prompt is shown in Figure 5.24. Any suggested alternatives are listed beneath the text field identifying the surrounding text in the document where the error was found. You can choose *Ignore* to retain what Word perceives as an error, *Ignore All* to ignore all equivalent perceived errors, and, if it is a spelling issue, *Add to Dictionary* to force Word to accept the word as a correct spelling now and in the future. If you wish to follow the suggestions for changing the perceived error, you can select *Change* to correct the highlighted instance and *Change*

All of the Office programs have a spelling check option. It is always a good idea to use the *Spelling* or *Spelling and Grammar* option to review your work before you submit it or share it.

All to change all instances of the same type in the document.

Word is not perfect when it comes to document proofreading and corrections. It may highlight items that are actually correct (called a false positive) and it will miss items that are grammatically correct and spelled correctly even if the word usage is wrong (called a false negative). You should always use the automated tool for proofing your document in case you do have easy corrections to make that you may not catch just by reading it, but you also need to make sure

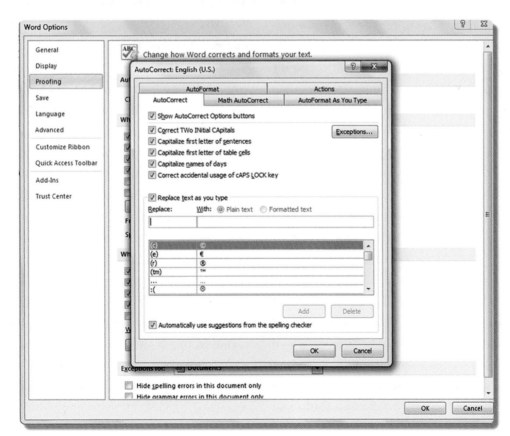

◀ FIGURE 5.23
AutoCorrect options in Word 2010

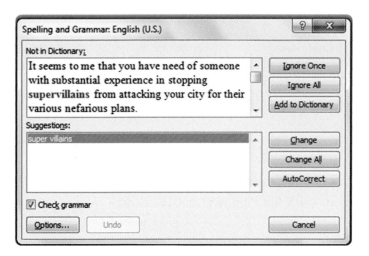

Spelling and Grammar: English (U.S.)

Not in Dictionary:

It seems to me that you have need of someone with substantial experience in stopping supervillains from attacking your city for their various nefarious plans.

Suggestions:

super villains

Ignore Once
Ignore All
Add to Dictionary

Change
Change All
AutoCorrect

☑ Check grammar

Options...   Undo

Cancel

▲ **FIGURE 5.24** Spelling and Grammar check example in Word 2010

5.4.4.2 *Thesaurus*

A thesaurus is a tool for finding words with a similar meaning (called synonyms) as a word you want to replace. This is a useful tool if you find you are using a word too much in your writing and want to vary it throughout. If you find that you have used the same term too often in your cover letter, you probably need to find an alternative word to keep your audience from getting bored of the repetition; if this happens, the audience may start to skim your writing instead of reading every word of it.

You can access the Thesaurus in Word 2010 by opening the *Review ribbon* and choosing *Thesaurus*. In Word 2011, select the *Tools* menu and choose *Thesaurus*. This will open a Research pane to the right side of your document. Type the word for which you want synonyms in the *Search for* field and select the correct Thesaurus from the drop-down menu. Hitting the *Enter* key

(or pressing the *Start searching* icon) will populate the text area beneath it with potential replacement terms. An example is shown in Figure 5.25.

If you are unsure of the exact meaning of the word you are substituting into your document, it is always a good idea to look it up and make sure you are using it correctly. You can use online dictionaries like Dictionary.com (*www.dictionary.com*) to do this or you can use any built-in dictionaries like the one accessible in Word 2011 (by selecting the *Tools* menu and choosing *Dictionary*). In Word 2010, you can also search for the term using the Bing search engine by selecting *Bing* as the source from the drop-down list in the Research pane where you previously selected the thesaurus you wanted to use.

Find and Replace 5.4.4.3

An additional tool that can help you with searching for repetitive terms or finding a particular word in your document is the Find command. This allows you to perform a simple keyword search of your document. In Word 2010, the Find icon is located on the Home ribbon; you can also access the Find command on a Windows machine using the shortcut *Ctrl-F*. In Word 2011, there is an existing search box in the top-right corner of the open document window that will allow you to enter text for a keyword search of your document; you can highlight this search box using the shortcut *Command-F*. This will highlight all instances of the keyword (or words) in your document.

To replace the keyword with which you searched the document with another term, you use the Replace command. In Word 2010, this is located on the Home ribbon; when activated, it will open a Find and Replace dialog box where you can navigate instance by instance through the document (with the Find Next button) or simply replace every instance of the keyword with the text you enter in the Replace field. The Find and Replace dialog box is shown in Figure 5.26. In Word 2010, you can activate the Replace command using the shortcut *Ctrl-H*. To open this same dialog box in Word 2011, select the *Edit* menu, select *Find*, and then choose *Advanced Find and Replace*.

In Word 2011, you can also use the Search pane to perform the Find and Replace functionality. To activate the Search pane, select the *View* menu, choose *Sidebar*, and then choose *Search Pane*. This will open the side navigation pane if it is not already open; you can then utilize the Find functionality by itself or in conjunction with the Replace functionality. The Search pane is shown in Figure 5.27.

Using Document Templates

5.4.5

The next document you will create is a resume. Unlike cover letters, there is no standard formatting for a resume. Fortunately, you can get an idea of how to format a resume using the templates available in Word. A *template* is a preformatted placeholder document for your

content; you can build your own instance of the document using the predefined areas where you can add objects and text, knowing what it will look like when you are finished. It is possible to modify templates just like any other document (you can even create custom templates), but templates save you work in formatting the

document yourself or formatting the same document again. Document templates are a great way to get started with formatting if you are unsure of what your document should look like.

In Word 2010, you can create a new document from a template by selecting the *File* menu and choosing *New*. Beneath the blank document types that you can select are the template selections. In this case, you will select *Resumes and CVs* and *Basic resumes* and then choose one of the options from the window shown in Figure 5.28. Remember that an effective resume is clear and simple.

▶ **FIGURE** 5.27
Search pane in
Word 2011

In Word 2011, you can create a new document from a template either by selecting the *File* menu and choosing *New from Template* or by clicking the *New from Template* icon in the Quick Access toolbar. This will open the Word Document Gallery shown in Figure 5.29. From this interface, select *Resumes* and choose one of the templates. You can select whichever one you want, but the Blocks Resume is a versatile option.

Your new document will open in a new window of Word. Save the document as

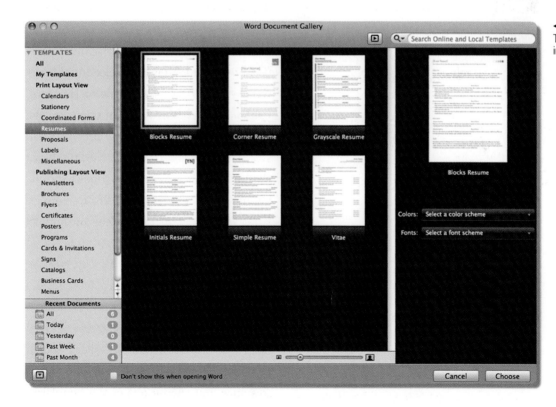

ResumeTemplate in the folder you created for your documents earlier. Note that all of the stylistic elements and categories of information that are necessary for a resume are included in the template. It is important to remember, though, that not all of these may apply to every job to which you may be applying.

5.4.6 Writing a Resume

A resume is an advertisement of you and your skills. The ultimate purpose of a resume is to get you an interview where you can showcase your skills on the phone or in person. It is difficult for a written document to accurately portray the abilities and experience you have to offer, so you have to be careful in constructing it. Your resume should be personalized to the job to which you are applying. You can maintain a comprehensive document for your own reference, but you should pick and choose which elements you want to include in the resume you actually submit. The resume you submit with your cover letter should not be a complete history of your entire life and experience but a showcase of what you have done that is most relevant to the job for which you are applying.

The general guideline is that your resume should fit on a single page; you should only use a second page if you have more than 10 years of experience or an advanced degree in the relevant field.

You can use the format of the template as an example, but be aware that many companies use scanners that perform optical recognition of words and characters; this means that your template-driven resume will not scan as well as one that is written with simplified headings, bullet points, and spacing. This actually makes the document easier to construct in terms of formatting; it just becomes a matter of knowing what to include. Since the document is being scanned for keywords, you should try to use the job posting to identify as many of the keywords as possible that the employer wants to see and use them where they are applicable in describing yourself and your accomplishments.

Your resume should have all of your current contact information at the top of the document. Any outdated information should be removed (such as an e-mail account you rarely check); if the potential employer chooses to use any of the information at the top of the resume to contact you, they should be able to reach you quickly.

You should include an objective statement that addresses in brief what you want from the potential employer and what you can offer them in return; you should not include a specific title in this statement unless the title is relevant and clearly stated in the job description. According to JobStar Central, if you cannot deliver your objective statement in a single sentence, it is too vague for you to use in your resume.

The body of the resume will generally consist of any relevant positions you have held, the degrees or certifications you have completed, and the awards or recognition you have received that are relevant to the position. It should be a showcase of your talents and abilities instead of just a list of what you have done. For any job you have listed, be sure to lead the bulleted list of accomplishments with the most impressive achievement or responsibility that you had in that position. Your bullet points should be brief and easy to scan. They should also be formatted to demonstrate a problem that existed, your actions, and the outcome that resulted. According to Resume-Help.org, you should be sure to include numbers, percentages, and currency figures wherever possible. An example of a resume using these suggestions is shown in Figure 5.30.

An employer spends on average between 10 and 30 seconds looking at a resume, so you need to make sure your text is concise and the person reviewing it can grasp the main topics in that amount of time; if they become interested in that time frame, they are likely to read more of it.

There are a lot of resources available on the Web if you search for "resume tips" or "resume help"; these tips can assist you in modifying the language of your resume to fit what the employer wants to see. For example, Resume-Help. org (*www.resume-help.org*) has a number of sample resumes for different positions and suggested wording and tips for creating professional resumes. Remember that you want to perform some research on the company or organization to which you are applying so that you cantailor your resume to match what they are seeking.

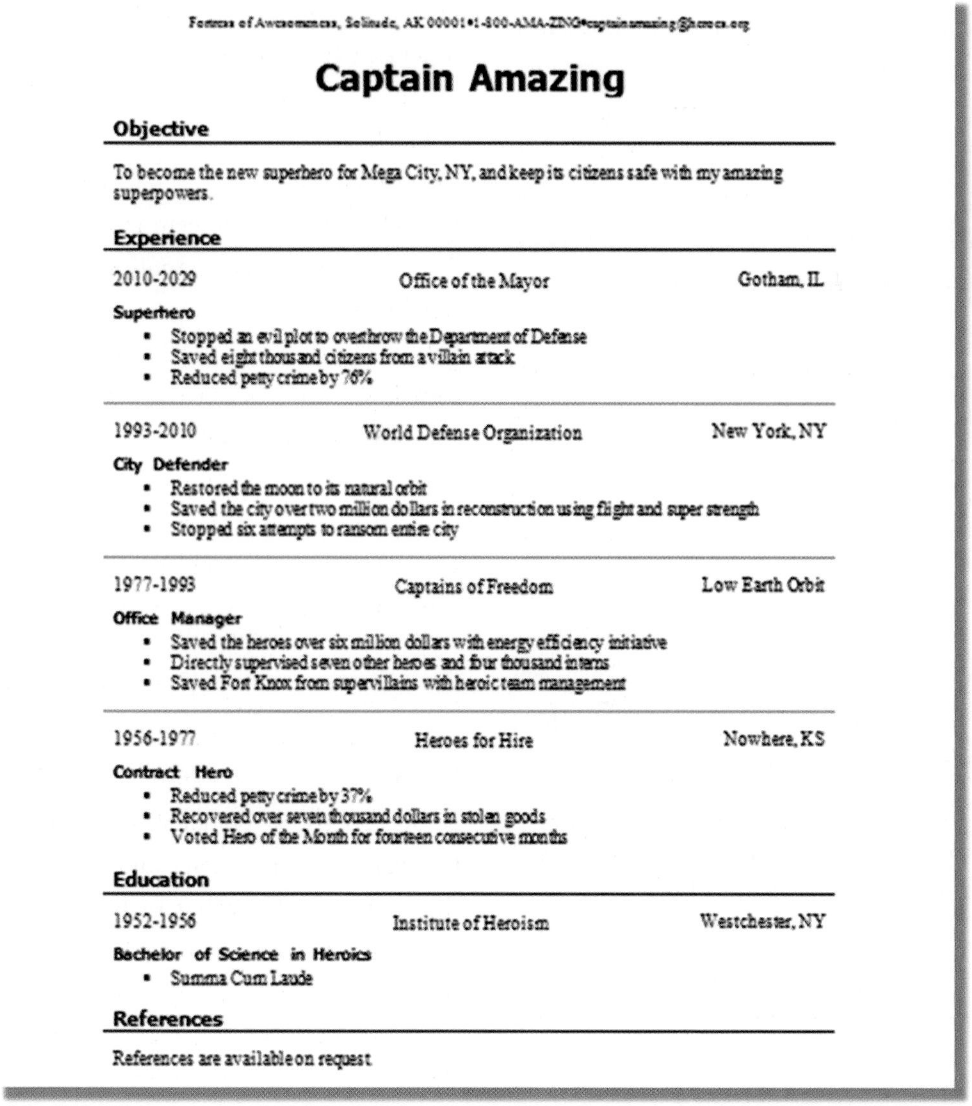

Fortress of Awesomeness, Solitude, AK 00001•1-800-AMA-ZING•captainamazing@heroes.org

Captain Amazing

Objective

To become the new superhero for Mega City, NY, and keep its citizens safe with my amazing superpowers.

Experience

| 2010-2029 | Office of the Mayor | Gotham, IL |

Superhero
- Stopped an evil plot to overthrow the Department of Defense
- Saved eight thousand citizens from a villain attack
- Reduced petty crime by 76%

| 1993-2010 | World Defense Organization | New York, NY |

City Defender
- Restored the moon to its natural orbit
- Saved the city over two million dollars in reconstruction using flight and super strength
- Stopped six attempts to ransom entire city

| 1977-1993 | Captains of Freedom | Low Earth Orbit |

Office Manager
- Saved the heroes over six million dollars with energy efficiency initiative
- Directly supervised seven other heroes and four thousand interns
- Saved Fort Knox from supervillains with heroic team management

| 1956-1977 | Heroes for Hire | Nowhere, KS |

Contract Hero
- Reduced petty crime by 37%
- Recovered over seven thousand dollars in stolen goods
- Voted Hero of the Month for fourteen consecutive months

Education

| 1952-1956 | Institute of Heroism | Westchester, NY |

Bachelor of Science in Heroics
- Summa Cum Laude

References

References are available on request

◀ FIGURE 5.30
Resume example

Whether or not you are actually going to apply for the job you found earlier for this project it is good practice to tailor your resume to the specifics of that job. Enter your information and practice using the Font panel and Paragraph panel to format your text appropriately. When you are finished, be sure to use the automated tools to check spelling and grammar. Always remember to save your work.

5.4.7 Using Headers and Footers

Headers and footers are often used in word processing documents. These allow you to maintain consistent elements on all pages of your document. A header, for example, may contain the title of the document. The footer may contain the page number or copyright information. For the purpose of the resume, you will use the header to enter your name and contact information. This is not a requirement, but it will allow you to format the body of your resume more consistently while keeping your contact information fixed.

You can activate the header of a document by double-clicking at the top of the visible document page. Similarly, you can double-click the bottom of the visible document page to activate the footer. When you do, you will get a context-sensitive Header & Footer Tools ribbon, as shown in Figure 5.31. From here, you can add common elements like the page number. You can also select predefined headers and footers from the respective *Header* and *Footer* icons. In Word 2010, these icons are also available in the Insert ribbon. In Word 2011, these are located in the Document Elements ribbon; you can also use the *View* menu and select *Header and Footer* to activate the header and footer for the document.

For your resume, make sure you include your name prominently, your e-mail address, and your phone number. Additional information is at your discretion. You want to make sure a potential employer has the right information to contact you quickly. There is usually no need for a footer on a resume; even the header is optional (as long as your contact information is included elsewhere).

Document Types

There are several options for saving your files. You should pay close attention to the format in which the potential employer wants the document submitted and comply with that. Some employers may want the document in the native Word format. However, if there is no specification, a safe alternative is to use a PDF. A PDF file is constructed from printing commands and it produces a static document that cannot be edited or reformatted without specialized software. Unlike the native Word format, which can change depending on the software version and installed fonts, there is no variance in the display of a PDF file. This means it will display for the viewer exactly as you intend it to be seen. You can create a PDF file of your Word document by selecting *PDF* as the file type in the Save As dialog box in both Word 2010 and Word 2011.

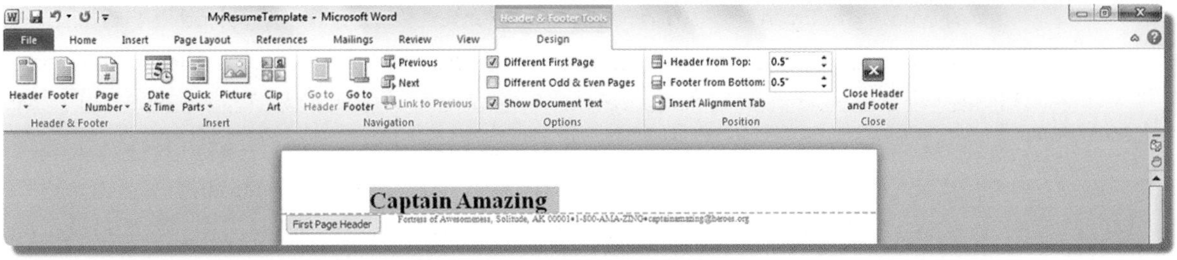

▲ FIGURE 5.31
Header & Footer
Tools ribbon and
example in Word

5.5 OPENOFFICE.ORG WRITER

If you are using OpenOffice.org as an alternative productivity software suite, Writer is the program that is used for word processing. Once you have downloaded and installed OpenOffice.org, it will be available in the Start menu on a Windows machine or from the Applications folder on a Macintosh. Unlike the new versions of Word, Writer uses the more traditional menu and toolbar interface. The approach taken in this text is to include the major content and the description of the project in the section detailing the Office product. For the introduction chapter, a separate section like this one is included to detail the interface and operation of OpenOffice.org for completing the project; in the more advanced chapters for a software application, notes are provided where the instructions differ for the OpenOffice.org program compared to the Office equivalent.

5.5.1 Anatomy of Writer

Go ahead and open a new document in Writer if you have not already done so. You should see the blank document interface shown in Figure 5.32. There is a list of menus across the top of the interface, along with toolbars that provide a shortcut to some of the more common commands available in the menus. Open the *File* menu as a first stop.

The File menu is shown in Figure 5.33. As with most File menus for software applications, this is where you can access commands to manage your files, including New, Save, Save As, Open, and Print. You should note that unlike Office, you can open a new file from any of the applications in the OpenOffice.org suite by selecting the *File* menu and *New*. The Help menu gives you access to the OpenOffice.org help interface. On a Windows machine, you can press the *F1* key to access the help interface for OpenOffice.org if it is the currently active application.

▲ FIGURE 5.31
Header & Footer
Tools ribbon and
example in Word

Sometimes a potential employer will request that you send your resume via e-mail. If you are including it as an attachment, you are safe using a PDF file. If you are including it only as text, you should strip out the formatting and use only standard text with bold and italic emphasis only (if these do not go through, your formatting will not suffer). One important aspect of this type of formatting is to replace any bullet points with the asterisk (*) character and change numbered lists to manually typed numbers; the formatting for bullets and numbering varies depending on the e-mail program used and you want to retain as much control as possible over the display of your document.

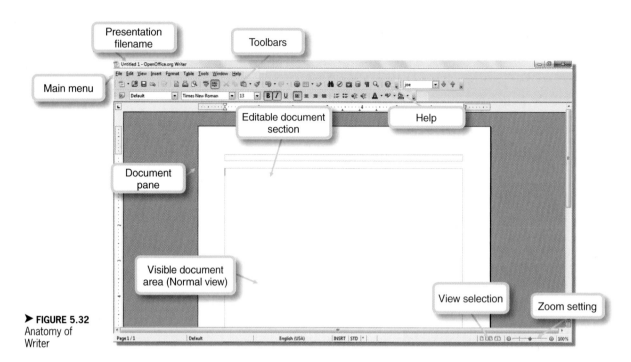

Presentation filename

Toolbars

Main menu

Editable document section

Help

Document pane

Visible document area (Normal view)

View selection

Zoom setting

▶ FIGURE 5.32
Anatomy of Writer

There are a number of toolbars available that will provide shortcuts to common commands. By default, the Standard toolbar, Find toolbar, and Format toolbar are enabled. The Standard toolbar gives you access to file commands (like New, Open, Save, and Print), along with Cut, Copy, Paste, Undo, Redo, and Help. This toolbar also contains several commands that you will use for the projects in this chapter like the Format Paintbrush, the Spelling and Grammar check, and the Navigator.

The Find toolbar allows you to perform a keyword search and move through the results that are found. The Format toolbar is where you will find shortcuts for formatting commands like Bold, Italic, and Underline; this is also where you can change the text size and font selection. The bottom of the interface beneath the document contains the current page number out of the total number of pages, the language in use,

the page layout (which can be changed by selecting the icon you want to use), and the current Zoom setting (remember that 100% is the actual size of the document).

The native file type for a word processing document in Writer is ODF Text Document (.odt). It is possible to save the word processing document in the native Office format but only up to the Word format used in the 1997 to 2003 editions of the software using the .doc extension. This document will still open in newer versions of Word without any difficulty. There is an icon in the Standard toolbar labeled *Export Directly to PDF*, which will allow you to save your document in the platform- and software independent Portable Document Format (.pdf).

Completing the Cover Letter in Writer

5.5.2

You should first save your open blank document as *MyCoverLetter*. Enter the

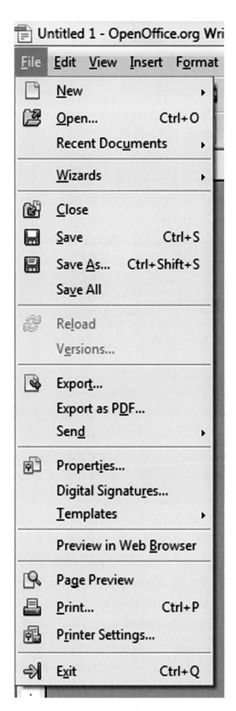

▲ FIGURE 5.33 File menu in Writer

or the *Command-A* shortcut on Mac) and choose the *Font Name* drop-down menu; select *Times New Roman* if it is not already selected. Beside the Font Name drop-down menu, you will see the *Font Size* drop-down menu; use the drop-down box to choose a common size or enter a numeric value in this box. Set your text size to *12*. Beside this menu box, you will see the icons for Bold, Italic, and Underline; these commands can also be activated by the shortcut keys for each command that were described for Word. You can also select the *Format* menu and choose *Character* to set font effects in a single dialog box. For a cover letter, however, you should keep the plain formatting for your text.

To set the line spacing for your document, select the *Format* menu and choose *Paragraph*. The Indents and Spacing tab should be active by default. This is where you will find the Line Spacing values. Select *At Least* for the Line Spacing selection from the menu and type *16pt* as the value in the number entry box. If you click in another box, you will see that the *16pt* value converts to *0.22″* for the final spacing value. Click *OK* when you are finished.

To apply bullet points to the accomplishments you want to highlight in your cover letter, select the text you want to convert to bullet points and then click the *Bullets On/Off* icon on the Format toolbar. This will open the context-sensitive Bullets

You will also find the icon to highlight text in the Format toolbar; you can use the drop-down arrow beside the icon to select the highlight color.

text you want to include as described in the example project in Section 5.4.1. To change the font in Writer, select all of the text (using the *Ctrl-A* shortcut on Windows

and Numbering toolbar shown at the top of Figure 5.34.

To select the bullet style you want to use, click the *Bullets and Numbering* icon at the far right of the toolbar to open the Bullets and Numbering dialog box (also shown in Figure 5.34). This toolbar is also used for numbered lists, and you can use the icons on the toolbar to switch between bullets and numbers. From here, you can promote and demote items in the list to create a more complex outline; for the cover letter, you just want a single level of bullets.

When you have finished entering and formatting text for your document, you should use the automated spelling and grammar check within Writer to detect any errors that the system recognizes as common. Again, this is no substitute for having someone else check your document before you submit it to a potential employer.

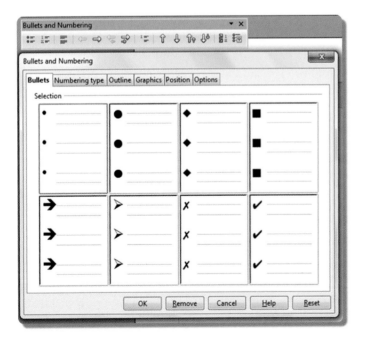

The *Spelling and Grammar* icon used to initiate the scan of your document is located in the Standard toolbar.

The icon beside it is the *AutoSpellcheck* icon; this is a toggle that turns the automatic corrections on or off. To change any of the AutoCorrect rules in the OpenOffice.org suite, choose the *Tools* menu and select *AutoCorrect Options*. This will open the AutoCorrect dialog box where you can remove existing rules or add new ones by completing the *Replace* and *With* fields and selecting the *New* button.

You can also use the Thesaurus by highlighting the word you want to replace, choosing the *Tools* menu, selecting *Language*, and then choosing *Thesaurus*. To perform a search on a keyword from the Find toolbar, enter the keyword in the *Find Text* field, press *Enter*, and use the arrows to move through the results in your document. To perform a find and replace operation on the document, click the icon that looks like a pair of binoculars in the Standard toolbar; this will open the Find and Replace dialog box. From here you can set the keyword you want to find and the text with which you want to replace it; you can select the appropriate buttons to find the next instance, replace the current instance, or replace all instances in the current document.

Completing the Resume in Writer

5.5.3

The next document you will create is a resume; you can review the instructions

Pressing the Enter key inside a list adds a new item to the list at the same outline level. Pressing the Enter key a second time within the blank list item will move to the next layer up (to the left) in the outline; if there are no layers up, it will exit the list formatting and return to the standard text.

for creating a resume in Section 5.4.6. Writer does not come preloaded with a large amount of templates; however, there are a significant number of them available online. To create a document from a template in Writer, select the *File* menu, select *New*, and choose *Templates and Documents*. This will open a dialog box that allows you to navigate to the template you wish to use. The Templates and Documents dialog box is shown in Figure 5.35. If you cannot find a template you want, click on the *Get more templates online* link.

This will open a new browser window (for whichever browser you have set as the default) and bring up the template browser online. You can search for a resume template using the keyword search; when you find the one you want to use, click the *Use It* icon to open an instance of that document locally. Save your file as *MyResume-Template*.

To add a header or footer to your document, select *Header* or *Footer* from the *Insert* menu. *Default* is the only available choice from the pop-up menu on these selections.

The Format Paintbrush icon in Writer works just like its counterpart in Word. To apply the formatting, highlight the text with the formatting you want to copy, click the icon, and highlight the text you want to be formatted. When the Format Paintbrush is active, your cursor will look like a paint bucket.

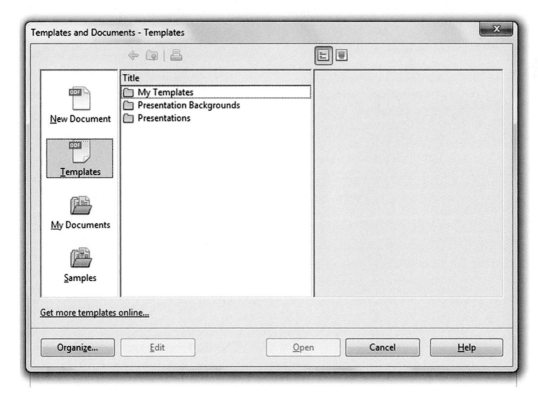

◀ FIGURE 5.35
Templates and Documents dialog box in Writer

You can also insert these elements from the Navigator (which you can open from the Standard toolbar). If you choose a header a new document section will be added to your file at the top of the page; this allows you to enter your own text, and the size will expand to fit the contents. You can adjust properties for the header (or the footer) by selecting the *Format* menu and choosing *Page*. You can then select the tab for *Header* to get additional formatting options; the footer works the same way. Review your document just as you did with the cover letter; you can use the same formatting tools and commands to add more emphasis to your resume than you had for the cover letter.

CHAPTER SUMMARY

This chapter introduced you to the fundamental concepts and operations for creating simple word processing documents. This is the most common productivity application in businesses and organizations. In addition, this chapter covered the use of common File menu commands for most software applications, keyboard productivity shortcuts, and file and file type management. The next chapter expands on the use of word processing software to create more advanced documents and give you exposure to the more complex formatting available in document creation. The menus and tasks introduced in this chapter will carry forward into the other productivity tools covered in this text.

CHAPTER EXERCISES

1. Select an additional job to which you would like to apply that has significantly different qualifications than the one you used for the example project. Revamp your resume and compose a new cover letter for this specific position. Reflect on the key changes you made and which elements of your qualifications applied to both jobs.

2. Compose a simple word processing document describing you in about 200 words. Format the document using text effects, bullet points, and different font sizes for emphasis. Use a header for your name.

3. Compose a formal business letter to a company of your choice. This can be a letter asking for information or a letter to customer service to express a compliment or complaint. Make sure the formatting is correct and the tone is professional. You should include the reason you are writing and any outcome you desire from the letter.

CHAPTER KNOWLEDGE CHECK

1 All of the following are operations that can typically be performed from the File menu in an application except:

- ○ **A.** Opening a file
- ○ **B.** Creating a new file
- ○ **C.** Undoing the last command
- ○ **D.** Saving a file

2 The following are all examples of productivity software except:

- ○ **A.** Word processing
- ○ **B.** Spreadsheet software
- ○ **C.** E-mail management software
- ○ **D.** Presentation software
- ○ **E.** All of the above
- ○ **F.** None of the above

3 The following are valid formatting shortcuts for a Windows machine except:

- ○ **A.** Ctrl-B
- ○ **B.** Ctrl-I
- ○ **C.** Ctrl-S
- ○ **D.** Ctrl-U
- ○ **E.** All of the above
- ○ **F.** None of the above

4 The following operation is used to create a duplicate of selected text or objects on the system clipboard and remove the original:

- ○ **A.** Copy
- ○ **B.** Paste
- ○ **C.** Format Painter
- ○ **D.** Cut

5 Automated spelling and grammar checks will catch every spelling mistake possible in the language that is selected.

- ○ True
- ○ False

6 The following is not a characteristic of a bulleted list:

- ○ **A.** You can select different symbols to display as the bullet point.
- ○ **B.** The order of the items in the list is significant.
- ○ **C.** You can have multiple levels of bullet points in an outline format.
- ○ **D.** All of the above
- ○ **E.** None of the above

7 A resume and cover letter should be individualized for the job to which the applicant is applying.

- ○ True
- ○ False

8 The following document type is designed to display the same regardless of operating system or software application:

- ○ **A.** Word Document
- ○ **B.** ODF Text Document
- ○ **C.** PDF Document
- ○ **D.** Document Template

9 The system clipboard retains any formatting for text that is selected and copied to it.

- ○ True
- ○ False

10 Spelling and grammar checks should be performed for every document you create.

- ○ True
- ○ False

Developing and Editing Documents

This chapter covers the construction of more involved and complex word processing documents. The example for this chapter is a research article, which introduces the concepts of style management, document elements like a table of contents and cover page, and the inclusion of graphic elements. You will also learn to use and manage references and external sources in your work. At the completion of this chapter, you will be able to:

- Apply, manage, and edit styles in your document

- Manage references and sources and insert document citations

- Customize the page layout

- Insert images and adjust their placement in your document

- Add document elements such as a bibliography, table of contents, and page breaks

6.1 WRITING A RESEARCH ARTICLE

Word processing has a myriad of uses from constructing research reports to writing rules and regulations. The primary purpose of word processing software is to create the digital equivalent of a print medium. Whatever the purpose you may have in mind for your individual software, whether it is writing a novel or using it in the context of a business, the tools available are the same, and they provide a robust interface for creating professional documents.

For the purpose of this chapter, the process of creating a research report is used to explore common word processing tasks. If you are using your software for a report, whether for a class or for an organization, there are several considerations you should keep in mind:

- *Remember your point and do not deviate too far from it.* Your audience is reading your document to get information on one particular topic, so be sure you keep that topic in mind when you construct your document and make it as easy as possible for them to get that information. It is difficult for the human mind to maintain too many concurrent points when committing information to memory, so allowing your reader to identify a single overall message and then adding information to that message will maximize the impact of your document.

- *Adhere to any page or word limits.* Having a page or word limit conveys an expectation from the person who receives your work. You should try to get as close as possible to that value. Word allows you to easily view your word and page count at the bottom of the interface so you can remain on track. If you have a lower and upper bound for your document, you should not go below the lower limit or above the upper limit without a definitive need or the permission of the person to whom you are submitting the work. If you are not given a page limit, try to remain thorough but concise with your document; saying more in less space is almost always a better approach.

- *Communicate your ideas clearly and efficiently.* Even if you are not a professional writer, you should strive to communicate clearly in your written work. Part of this is making sure what you write conveys what you want it to convey. You can enlist help from a friend or colleague if necessary to make sure your document is clear. No amount of fancy formatting will make up for a lack of clarity in the work. You should also try not to spend too long elaborating a single point of data or fact; your communication should continue to move forward from one point to another.

- *Set the necessary tone for the document.* The way in which your document will be used should be considered in your language choice. Informal elements like contractions should be omitted from professional documents. Use of any slang should also be restricted in a business setting. A document lacks personal interaction so there is no ability to explain yourself if your document is misunderstood. This also applies to making sure you distinguish fact from opinion in your text; your text can contain opinions, but they should be presented clearly as such.

When you are conducting any kind of research or using sources other than yourself, it is imperative to also observe the following to assist you in managing copyrighted material effectively.

- *Keep track of your sources and evaluate material.* It is important that you have access to your reference material and know where certain information was found so you can access it later and properly create citations. You should also try to make sure you use credible sources for your information, such as published text in books or articles. When you are using information from the Web, you should evaluate the authorship and how reliable the information is.

- *Reference any material that is not your own.* If you are using someone else's idea or work, you need to include that in the list of references for your document. Claiming any material as your own that you did not create or develop may be a violation of copyright laws. It is better to take a cautious approach and make sure that you reference any sources you used to construct the document. Any significant facts that you present that you had to research should have a citation to accompany them.

- *Check the availability for use of images that you did not create.* Using images can be a great way to convey information, but the use of images is also subject to copyright law. You cannot use an image you did not create without written permission from the author allowing you to use it; this permission can be stated in terms on a Web site (where it may specify use or identify the image as royalty free) or via e-mail from the author. This rule applies to all media, but its most common use in a printed document is for images.

Copyright law is a very serious matter. Violations can get you fined or expelled from academic institutions. Copying someone else's work and claiming it as your own is never permissible. In order to use someone else's work, you must always give the original author credit; other elements such as royalties on profits may also come into play depending on the use. Copyright laws of the United States can be reviewed at *www.copyright.gov/title17*.

Outlining the Document

6.1.1

Every document you create will have some purpose, even if it is just for your own reference or use. Before writing your document, it is important to know what you want to convey with the text. You should be able to summarize the document in one to two sentences; the rest of the document should just be an explanation and expansion of that. If you cannot summarize your document, you may need to narrow your focus or consult with the person to whom you are submitting the document. Even technical guidelines have an overall purpose, no matter how long they are. The summary goal for the example in this chapter is *to convey background information and instruction on the use of productivity software to increase the productivity and proficiency of the reader*. The rest of the text is a fulfillment of that purpose.

Once you have established your document's purpose, you will expand on it with particular topics to include. This is a process called *outlining*; it is the establishment of the major topics of the document. The example project in this chapter is a short report on a historical figure: Jean Lafitte, a renowned pirate and hero of the Battle of New Orleans in the War of 1812 between the United States and Great Britain. The report is limited to 1.5 pages in length, so there will not be a large number of topics to discuss. The two elements chosen were the beginning of Lafitte's piracy operation in Barataria Bay and the Battle of New Orleans. Therefore, an introduction, these two topics, and a conclusion are included in the outline for the text.

You are free to choose your own historical figure to follow along with the instructions. Once you have decided on your topic and what you want to convey, you should start gathering reference material for your subject. Remember that you need to evaluate the credibility of your sources before you use them; an important question to ask is "How do I know I can trust what this author has to say?" Make sure you are answering that question with a reason more substantial than its existence on the Internet.

6.1.2 Using and Managing Styles

Once you have established your outline, you need to add titles to each of your sections. For the example, the titles are *The Legend of Jean Lafitte*, *The King of Barataria Bay*, *The Hero of the Battle of New Orleans*, and *Later Years and Legacy*. Begin creating your document by opening

A **STYLE** *is a collection of formatting effects and enhancements used to modify text in a consistent manner. Applying a style to a selection of text will add all of the defined formatting effects and enhancements of that style without the need to individually recreate them.*

a new document and saving it as *MyReport*. Type the headers you will use into the word processing document. To assist in the outlining process, you can also apply styles to the text.

For these titles, you will use the style *Heading 1* from the Styles panel of the Home ribbon. Notice that there are six heading styles already defined for you to use; each of these will appear in the document outline when used. Heading 1 is the highest level and Heading 6 is the lowest level above plain text. You can add additional heading levels to create a more complex outline of your document.

The default style for any Word document is *Normal*. This is a predefined style that defaults to whatever setting is established at installation. You can edit the Normal style just as you can any other style, and all of the text that has Normal as a style will update to reflect the changes. The ability to update all of the text formatted with a style at once is one of the benefits of using styles in a document.

In Word 2010, you can select the Change Styles icon and select a predefined document style from the list that you would like to use. The example for this chapter uses the *Style Set* choice *Distinctive* under the *Change Styles* icon. In Word 2011, the equivalent to change the style settings for the document is the *Change Quick Styles settings* icon, from which you can also choose the *Distinctive* option.

Click the expansion icon of the Styles panel to open the Styles pane in Word 2010. This is accessible in Word 2011 by selecting the *Manage styles* icon. The Styles pane is a listing of the current styles available in the document. An example of the Styles pane is shown in Figure 6.1.

Select a style to apply it to selected text or use the drop-down arrow for the style and select *Modify* to adjust individual elements of the style, similar to how you used the Font dialog box in the previous chapter. You can create a new style using the *New Style* icon.

To duplicate styles from another document in Word 2010, click on the *Manage Styles* icon of the Styles pane. This will open the Manage Styles dialog box; click on the *Import/Export* button at the bottom of this dialog. To access this in Word 2011, select

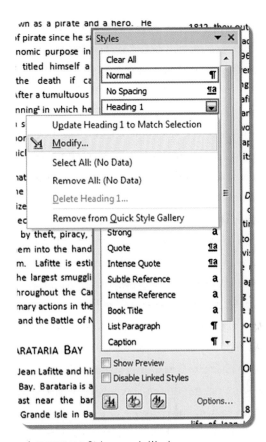

▲ FIGURE 6.1 Styles pane in Word

the *Format* menu and choose *Style*. When the dialog box opens, click the *Organize* button.

You will now see style listings for two files. The file you are developing is on the left and by default the global template *Normal.dotm* is on the right. You can close the Normal.dotm file (using the *Close File* button) and select the file whose styles you want to duplicate using the *Open File* button. Once you have the document open, you can use the mouse to select the styles you want to add to your current document and then use the *Copy* button (which will have a directional arrow showing you where the copies will be placed) to move them over to the current file.

OPEN OFFICE These notes will be used throughout the text to highlight how to perform the same activities described in Office using the OpenOffice.org equivalent. In this case, you will learn how to apply and manage styles in Writer. The predefined styles are available to apply to selected text from the Formatting toolbar using the *Apply Style* menu. Select the icon to the left of the style selection called *Styles and Formatting* to open the Styles and Formatting pane, which lists the available styles; you can also open this pane by pressing the *F11* key.

The Styles and Formatting pane is used to apply styles; right-clicking on a style and selecting *Modify* allows you to make adjustments to it. You can also add new styles to the list by using the right-click menu and choosing *New*. The *New Style from Selection* option in the upper-right corner of the pane allows you to create a new style from the formatting of the selected text in the document. The heading options will be used to construct the table of contents for the document just as it is in Word.

Using the Navigation Pane and Document Map Pane

The Navigation pane in Word 2010 and the Document Map pane in Word 2011 allow you to see the evolving outline of your document as you add headings and subheadings to it. Activate the Navigation pane in Word 2010 by selecting the *View ribbon* and checking the box beside *Navigation Pane*. You should see it appear on the left side of the interface; it will contain the headings you added to your document. An example is shown in Figure 6.2.

The default view in the Navigation pane is the headings for your document. You can set the level of headings you wish to appear by right-clicking any of the headings, selecting

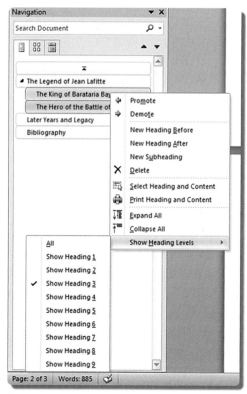

▲ **FIGURE 6.2** Navigation pane in Word 2010 with Show Heading Levels active

Show Heading Levels, and choosing the lowest level of heading you want to appear. You can navigate quickly through your document by clicking on any of the headings that appear; this will jump your position in the document to the location where the heading appears. The second tab in the Navigation pane is a page-by-page preview of your document; you can once again navigate quickly through it by clicking on the thumbnail preview image of the page. The last tab of the Navigation pane shows the results of any search you have performed.

The equivalent of the Navigation pane in Word 2011 is the Document Map pane. Access the Document Map pane by selecting the *View* menu, choosing *Sidebar*, and selecting *Document Map*. This will open the Document Map pane on the left side of the interface. You will see your headings and subheadings here, and you can navigate to them quickly in your document by clicking on any one of them. You can also right-click on any of the headings to select the lowest heading level you wish to display. An example of the Document Map pane is shown in Figure 6.3.

The Document Map pane is the second tab on the pane. The first tab is the Thumbnail pane, which displays a page-by-page preview of your document as thumbnail images; you can jump to any page by clicking on the thumbnail image representing it. The third tab is the Review pane, which is used in document correction and review. The final tab is the Search pane where you can perform find and replace operations in the document.

OPEN OFFICE In Writer, you access the Navigator pane by pressing the *F5* key on the keyboard or by selecting the *View* menu and choosing *Navigator*. The headings of the document will display in the pane just as they do in Word. You can click on any of the headings to jump to that section of the text. To select the deepest level of heading to display, click on the *Heading Levels Shown* icon and choose a numeric value. Using the *Promote Level* and *Demote Level* icons increases or decreases the heading level of the selected item.

6.2 MANAGING CITATIONS

You should now be adding the content of your report for each of the headings you established. It is very important to keep track of your citations as you construct your document. A citation should be added whenever you are either using another source to provide information that is not common knowledge or drawing your own conclusions. It is necessary to manage your sources so you can include citations easily.

Word makes this task easier by giving you the ability to add and store references in conjunction with your document. The functionality for this is located in the

*A **CITATION** is a reference to an external source you used to gather information, text, or other content for your work.*

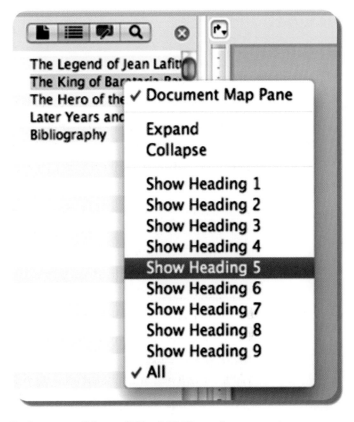

▲ FIGURE 6.3 Document Map pane in Word 2011 with the right-click menu active

References ribbon of Word 2010, as shown in Figure 6.4.

To add new sources or edit existing ones, open the Source Manager (shown in Figure 6.5) by clicking the *Manage Sources* icon. From this dialog box, you can add new citations by clicking *New*. This opens the Create Source dialog box, where you can select the source type from the drop-down list; this will adjust the fields needed to accurately cite the source. You should try to complete as many of these fields as you can to give the most complete citation possible.

▼ **FIGURE 6.4** References ribbon in Word 2010

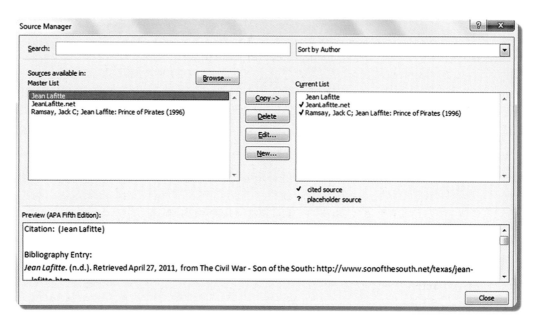

▲ **FIGURE 6.5** Source Manager in Word 2010

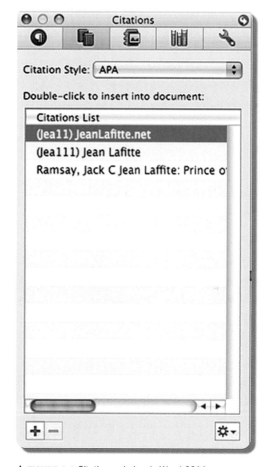

▲ **FIGURE 6.6** Citations window in Word 2011

In Word 2011, you access your sources and add new sources by clicking on the *Manage* icon of the *References panel* on the *Document Elements ribbon*. This will open a new Citations window, as shown in Figure 6.6. To create a new citation entry, select the + icon in the lower-left corner and then select the type of source to adjust the fields necessary for the citation. Clicking on the settings icon in the lower-right corner allows you to edit a citation or open the Citation Source Manager, which is similar in appearance to the Source Manager in Word 2010.

Once you have entered your sources, you can insert in your text a citation to any of the existing sources. These citations are linked to the original citation entry, so editing the source information will update any citations in the document. To add a citation in your document in Word 2010, select the *References ribbon*, choose the style for the citation (APA was used in the example), click the *Insert Citation* icon, and then

It is always important to evaluate the credibility of a source you are using for your work. Textbooks, conference papers, and journals often go through rigorous peer review and technical editing, so they tend to be more trustworthy sources than something published only online. You can find reviews of the textbook, conference, or journal to evaluate whether it meets these criteria. Anything you find on the Web is a different matter; it is easy to create a personal Web site and post any information you want, whether or not it is true. Whenever you encounter an online source, there are some things you should consider when deciding whether you can trust it. Here are a few questions to ask of a potential Web site source before you use it:

- *Who is the author of the site?* If the author is a reputable organization or an individual with expertise in the area, it is more likely to be a credible source.

- *What are the site extension and the domain name of the site?* Once again, a company or organization site is generally more credible than an individual unless that individual is an expert in the field. A professional versus an unprofessional domain name can also indicate the level of trust that should be placed in the source. The site extension is also telling; for example, the site extension of *.gov* indicates a government publication.

- *Does the site use references and cite other sources?* This can indicate whether the author has researched the subject sufficiently. Looking at any references used and evaluating them will help determine if the page is credible.

- *Is the site up to date?* You should be able to check the date it was last updated to determine whether the document is current.

- *Is the site objective with its information or is there another motivation?* You should try to use objective sources in your work and evaluate the reliability of the source; the author may have created the document with a particular motivation in mind to influence the reader.

select the source you want to use. The reference to the source in the correct format for the citation style will be added to your document.

To add a citation to your document in Word 2011, select the citation style (in this case APA) in either the Document Elements ribbon or the Citations window. Then right-click (or double-click) the source you want to reference; the reference will be added to your document at the current location of the text cursor (where the last text was entered in the document). There are three main citation styles that are used in most publications, though other styles do exist. The following is a list of the common styles and a source to get more information on its use for manuscript production:

- American Psychological Association (APA) style—*www.apastyle.org*
- Modern Language Association (MLA) style—*www.mla.org/style*
- The Chicago Manual of Style—*www.chicagomanualofstyle.org*

Footnotes and Endnotes

6.2.1

Footnotes are used to add explanation to an element of a document without

OPEN OFFICE References and sources in OpenOffice.org are all maintained in a global Bibliography Database. You can access this from Writer by selecting the *Tools* menu and choosing *Bibliography Database*; this will open in a new window. To add a source, click on the *Insert* menu and choose *Record*. To add a citation to your text, place the cursor in your document where you want the citation and select the *Insert* menu, choose *Indexes and Tables*, and then choose *Bibliography Entry*.

interrupting the flow of the text. Whether to use footnotes or endnotes is a stylistic choice. The main difference between them is their placement within the text.

A footnote will be placed on the page to which the notation is added; the text will have a superscript number placed beside it and the footnote explanation will be placed in a separate section at the end of the page. To place a footnote in Word 2010, click on the *References ribbon* and choose *Insert Footnote*; your cursor should be placed beside the text you are annotating with the footnote. To add a footnote in Word 2011, select the *Document Elements ribbon* and choose the *Footnote* icon with the cursor in the location you want to annotate.

The current number of the footnote for that page (beginning with the number 1) will be added at the current cursor location and you will be taken to the section at the

bottom-left corner of the page where you can add the footnote text. An example is shown in Figure 6.7. The numbering for the footnotes will be adjusted as text is moved; a link exists within the document connecting the mark in the text and the note.

An endnote is placed at the end of the entire document. By default, endnotes start

> A **FOOTNOTE** is an additional comment aside from the main point of the text that is placed at the bottom of the page and indicated by a reference mark in the main text. This is typically used to clarify a point or provide an explanation that would detract from the content of the document if left in line with the main text. An endnote is the same thing as a footnote except it is placed at the end of the document instead of on the same page with the reference mark.

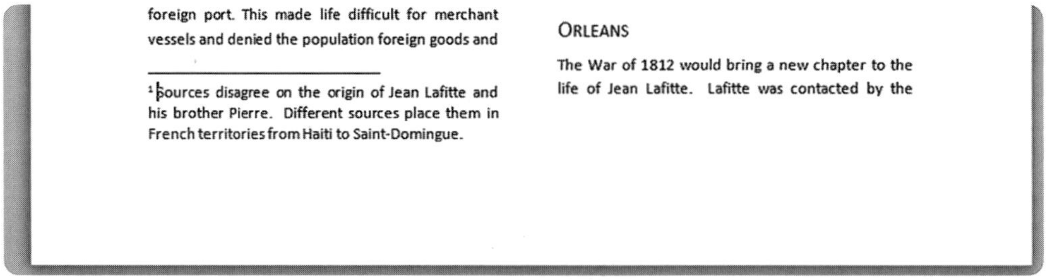

with Roman numerals (beginning with lowercase i) and accumulate throughout the text. Adding an endnote is similar to adding a footnote. The annotation will be placed where the cursor is located in the document and you will be taken to the endnote section to enter the text describing the annotation. To add an endnote in Word 2010, select the *References ribbon* and choose *Insert Endnote*; in Word 2011, you add an endnote by selecting the *Document Elements ribbon* and choosing *Endnote*. While the default properties are sufficient

▶ **FIGURE 6.7**
Footnote placement in Word 2010

foreign port. This made life difficult for merchant vessels and denied the population foreign goods and

---

¹ Sources disagree on the origin of Jean Lafitte and his brother Pierre. Different sources place them in French territories from Haiti to Saint-Domingue.

ORLEANS

The War of 1812 would bring a new chapter to the life of Jean Lafitte. Lafitte was contacted by the for most documents, you can customize characteristics of your footnotes and endnotes in the Footnote and Endnote dialog box shown in Figure 6.8.

To access the advanced properties for footnotes and endnotes shown in Figure 6.8, select the expansion icon on the *Footnotes panel* of the *References ribbon* in Word 2010. This dialog box allows you to change the settings for both footnotes and endnotes, including placement of the notes, the starting value for the annotations, and the numbering format used. To access these advanced properties for inserting custom footnotes and endnotes in Word 2011, select the *Insert* menu and choose *Footnote*.

6.2.2 Creating a Bibliography

In the new versions of Word, adding elements like an index, table of contents, and bibliography is almost a one-click action. If you have prepared your references correctly and added them to the Source Manager correctly, you can click on the *Bibliography* icon in the *References ribbon* in Word 2010 and insert a fully formatted bibliography (with the predefined options of using either Bibliography or Works Cited as the heading). This will add the references formatted according to the citation style you selected in the formatting defined for your document. A completed example and the selection menu are shown in Figure 6.9.

In Word 2011, the Bibliography icon is located in the References panel of the Document Elements ribbon. Clicking on the *Bibliography* icon opens a drop-down menu showing a preview of the

OPEN OFFICE To add a footnote or endnote in Writer, select the location in the text where you want the reference mark to be placed and then choose the *Insert* menu and select *Footnote/Endnote*. This will open a dialog box where you can choose whether you want the entry to be a footnote or endnote and whether you want to continue the automatic numbering or select a unique reference mark from the available symbols.

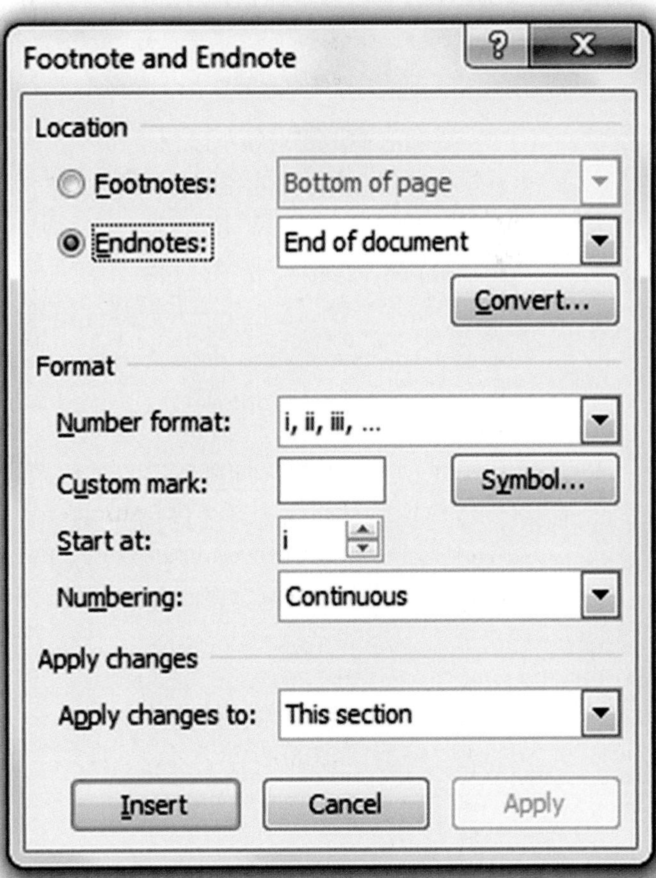

built-in Bibliography and Works Cited options; you can click on either of these to insert the formatted result (arranged in the citation style you selected beside the icon; APA is used in the example) in your document wherever your cursor is placed. For the example project,

▼ **FIGURE 6.8**
Footnote and Endnote dialog box in Word 2010

Footnote and Endnote

Location

○ Footnotes: Bottom of page

● Endnotes: End of document

Convert...

Format

Number format: i, ii, iii, …

Custom mark: _____ Symbol...

Start at: i

Numbering: Continuous

Apply changes

Apply changes to: This section

Insert   Cancel   Apply

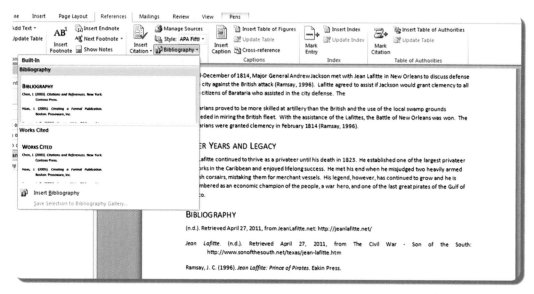

▲ **FIGURE 6.9** Example bibliography and selection menu in Word 2010

tho *Bibliography* entry was chosen and placed at the very end of the document.

6.3 SETTING A PAGE LAYOUT

At this point, you should have all of the text added to your document, so it is time to format the page for a more professional presentation. You have the flexibility in word processing documents to choose the size of your pages. While most home and office printers only accommodate 8 ½" by 11" paper, you can customize the document to whatever dimensions you need up to 22" by 22". There are predefined sizes for envelopes and legal documents as well. Select the page size in Word 2010 by activating the *Page Layout ribbon* and choosing the *Size* icon; this opens a menu for you to select an existing size or customize your own. In Word 2011, the *Size* icon is located in the *Layout ribbon*.

You can change other properties of your document as well. As mentioned previously, you have the ability to change your document from the default Portrait layout to the wide Landscape layout; this is accomplished using the *Orientation* icon in the *Page Layout ribbon* (or the *Layout ribbon* in Word 2011). The *Margins* icon is another useful tool and is found on the same panel with the Orientation and Size icons. Your report should use the *Normal* margin setting of 1" on all sides.

OPEN OFFICE To add a bibliography to your document in Writer, select the *Insert* menu, choose *Indexes and Tables*, and then choose *Indexes and Tables* again. In the Insert Index/Table dialog box that opens, select the *Index/Table* tab and choose *Bibliography* for the Type. You can change the Title to Bibliography or Works Cited as needed. You can also set the bracket type for your citations from this dialog box.

If you want to make a document that is poster sized, PowerPoint is a better software package to use. It is covered in Chapters 8 through 10.

You can see the exact size of your document and the position of elements in your text using the rulers and gridlines built into Word. The ruler gives you the spacing of the text compared to real inches and centimeters on the printed document. This is helpful if you need to place elements within a certain range or in a confined area for printing (such as printing labels or envelopes). Gridlines give you a cross section of the ruler lines so you can position elements more precisely within the document; this is similar to using graph paper for a visual layout. The default gridlines are 1/8" apart.

In Word 2010, you can activate or deactivate these options using the checkboxes next to the *Ruler* and *Gridlines* text entries on the Show panel of the View ribbon. The ruler in Word 2011 can be activated or deactivated by selecting the *View* menu and choosing *Ruler*. In Word 2011, the gridlines options are activated by selecting the *Gridlines* checkbox in the *Layout ribbon*. The gridlines will appear when you select an object that can be repositioned on the document. You can activate these elements for planning your document and then deactivate them later as needed.

6.3.1 Formatting Columns

While the format of the reports you create will vary, the example uses a two-column format for the first page.

To change the number of columns for your document, simply select the text you want to change and choose the *Columns* icon. This is located on the Page Layout ribbon in Word 2010 and the Layout ribbon in Word 2011. You can select from any of the predefined column divisions for the selected text or you can select the *More Columns* option from the drop-down list to access more advanced options (this is labeled simply *Columns* in Word 2011). An example of the advanced menu and the two-column result of the report text are shown in Figure 6.10.

Choose any of the predefined options in the Columns dialog box or create your own columns with customized widths. You can also choose whether you want to apply the column formatting to the entire document or just from that point forward. For the example report, you should estimate the amount of text you want to convert to the two-column first page. The rest of the document (which should amount to about half a page) will be formatted as a single column spanning the whole document width. You can convert the text back and forth as needed by highlighting what you

OPEN OFFICE In Writer, you can format the page size, orientation, and document margins by selecting the *Format* menu and choosing *Page*; this opens the Page Style dialog box from which you should select the *Page* tab to access and change these settings. To activate or deactivate the rulers, click the *View* menu and choose *Ruler* to toggle the setting.

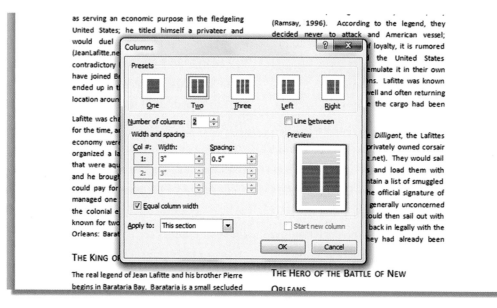

as serving an economic purpose in the fledgeling United States; he titled himself a privateer and would duel (JeanLafitte.ne contradictory have joined B ended up in location aroun

Lafitte was cha for the time, a economy wer organized a la that were aqu and he brough could pay for managed one the colonial e known for two Orleans: Bara

THE KING O

(Ramsay, 1996). According to the legend, they decided never to attack and American vessel; f loyalty, it is rumored the United States emulate it in their own ns. Lafitte was known vell and often returning e the cargo had been

Dilligent, the Lafittes privately owned corsair .net). They would sail s and load them with ntain a list of smuggled he official signature of generally unconcerned could then sail out with back in legally with the ey had already been

The real legend of Jean Lafitte and his brother Pierre begins in Barataria Bay. Barataria is a small secluded

THE HERO OF THE BATTLE OF NEW ORLEANS

▲ **FIGURE 6.10** Advanced column configuration options and two-column formatting of text

want to change and selecting the number of columns from the Columns icon. You will be adding an image to your document, so you will likely have to alter the columns again once the image is in place.

6.3.2 Adding Graphic Elements and Captions

To insert an image into your document, you must first have the image saved on your local machine. Typical image file formats are JPEG (Joint Photographic Experts Group) File Interchange Format, Graphics Interchange Format (GIF), Bitmap, Portable Network Graphic (PNG), and Tag Image

File Format (TIFF); any of these types of files can be inserted into a document. To insert an image into your word processing document in Word 2010, select the *Insert ribbon* and choose *Picture*. This will open the Insert Picture dialog box where you can select the image you want to insert.

In Word 2011, you can insert an image from the *Home ribbon* by choosing the *Picture* icon and then choosing *Picture from File*. As with any content, you must make sure you have adequate permission to use an image file if you have not created it yourself. If you do not have an image to use as an example in your report, you can use the *My Sample Image* file, which is a photograph of Pirates Alley in New Orleans, Louisiana.

You can resize the image using any of the grip points that appear around its edge when it is selected. The midpoint grip points change only one dimension at a time. The corner grip points change the

OPEN OFFICE To change the column formatting in Writer, select the text you want to adjust, choose the *Format* menu, and select *Columns*. In the dialog box that opens, select the number of columns you want to apply to the text selection. For the example, use two columns for the first page.

two sides they connect at once. You can use the context-sensitive Format ribbon for Picture Tools to set the size of the image directly; this ribbon contains a large number of other features that will be more fully explored in Section III, "Presentation Software and Microsoft PowerPoint."

By default, the image will be placed in line with your text, expanding the current line size to fit the image; the image will act like another character in the text of the document in this format. You can click and drag it as you can with any other selected text. You can change how the image behaves by changing its text wrapping properties.

The different text wrap options are *square* (where the image is given a padded rectangle to occupy and the text will surround it), *tight* (which acts like the square setting without the padding on the rectangle), *through* (where the text will come as close as possible to the outline of the shape itself), *top and bottom* (which clears the horizontal space of the entire column of text around the image), *behind text* (which places the image on the layer of the document beneath the text so the text overlaps the image), and *in front of text* (which places the image on a layer of the document above the text, obscuring any text behind the image without displacing it). The use of the *square* setting tends to be the most legible in printed documents; this is the setting used in the example. You can set the text wrap options in Word 2010 by selecting the image, activating the *Page Layout ribbon*, and choosing the *Wrap Text* icon.

TEXT WRAPPING, *or text flow, is the setting in a document or Web page that determines how text behaves around an object. An example of this is how much space is left blank around the perimeter of the object and whether the object is treated as a character in the text or as a separate entity.*

In Word 2011, you can change these settings by activating the context-sensitive *Format Picture ribbon* with the image selected and choosing *Wrap Text*. A completed example is shown in Figure 6.11.

To insert a caption for the image, right-click on the image and choose *Insert Caption* from the menu that appears. This will open the Caption dialog box shown in Figure 6.12. You can add the caption text you want to display and specify how you want it labeled in the document (*Figure* should be the choice for this example). The text added here was "Pirates Alley in New Orleans." You can add a figure number (such as "Figure 1:") to the caption as well; this is recommended if there

▼ FIGURE 6.11
Image in Word with square text wrapping and visible grip points

is more than one image in your document or if it is a more formal submission. It is also helpful to reference your figure by number in the text of the document and identify the enhancement to the text it provides.

There are a number of other formatting options for images in Word. In addition to altering the Word Wrap properties, you can select the positioning of the image at predefined places on the page; when you use this option, it defaults to wrapping the text around the image instead of keeping the image in line with the text. You can use the Align menu to change the alignment of the image to the page or to other elements in the page. You can also send the image forward or backward on the layers of the document (similar to stacking paper clippings where the topmost element is visible in front). This type of image manipulation is covered more extensively in the chapters on presentation software. You can access these advanced image options from the Page Layout ribbon in Word 2010 and from the context-sensitive Format Picture ribbon in Word 2011.

ADDITIONAL DOCUMENT ELEMENTS

There are a number of additional document elements you may need to include. Some of these relate more to larger publications and larger organizations, but it is beneficial to know where to access these items if you need them. These optional document elements include an index, watermarks, borders, cover pages, blank pages, and a table of contents.

Some common elements you may want to use to enhance your document are the following:

- *Watermarks*—A *watermark* is a visual element on the pages of your document to signify either ownership or a certain classification for the document (such as Confidential or Do Not Copy). You can create your own watermark or use an existing logo for an organization or business so that any document created with the watermark will be imprinted with the logo, identifying ownership. To add a watermark to your document in Word 2010, select the *Page Layout ribbon* and choose *Watermark*; from here you can select a predefined watermark or select *Custom Watermark* to build your own. In Word 2011, you can add a watermark by selecting the Insert menu and choosing Watermark.

- *Borders*—Adding a page border may be useful depending on the type of document you are creating. Page borders are most often seen on fliers and personal memos;

they are not generally used in professional publications unless they are highlighting a particular element of text like an abstract for the document. To add a border to your page in Word 2010, select the *Page Layout ribbon* and choose *Page Borders*. This will open a dialog box that allows you to select the type of border you want for your page and choose the width and style for it. To add a page border in Word 2011, select the *Format* menu, choose *Borders and Shading*, and then selecti the *Page Border* tab on the dialog box that opens.

- *Blank Pages*—Sometimes it is necessary to add a blank page to your document; this is commonly found behind the title page of a lengthy report. To create a blank page in Word 2010, selecting the *Insert ribbon* and choose *Blank Page*. In Word 2011, select the *Document Elements ribbon* and choose *Blank* in the *Insert Pages panel*.

- *Page Breaks*—A page break ends the current page regardless of any remaining space on the page and starts a new page. This is useful if you do not want chapters or sections of a document to run together. In Word 2010, you can select *Page Break* from the *Insert ribbon*. In Word 2011, select the *Document Elements ribbon*, choose the *Break* icon, and then select *Page*.

There are a number of additional media elements that can be added to a word processing document to enhance its visual display. These are covered in the next chapter as well as in Section III, which provides more detail on adding and using visual enhancements.

OPEN OFFICE To insert an image in Writer, select the *Insert* menu, choose *Picture*, and then select *From File*. This opens a dialog box from which you can select your image file. You can add a caption to the image either by right-clicking the image and choosing *Caption* or by selecting the image, choosing the *Insert* menu, and then choosing *Caption*. The dialog box that opens lets you adjust the caption properties, including the text. To adjust the text wrap properties, right-click on the image, choose *Wrap*, and select one of the options from the menu that appears.

provides the title and author information for a document. A title page can also provide an abstract for the document; an *abstract* is a short paragraph or a few sentences summarizing the document contents or new ideas presented in the work. There are a variety of predefined cover pages available in Word.

To add a cover page to your report in Word 2010, choose *Cover Page* in the *Insert ribbon*. This will open a menu to select the cover page style you want to use. You can also use this menu to delete the current cover page. In Word 2011, you insert a cover page by selecting *Cover* in the *Document Elements ribbon*. When you add a cover page in Word 2011, a small menu icon is placed on the page to allow you to click and select *Remove Cover Page*. An example cover page with this icon active is shown in Figure 6.13.

Once you have selected the cover page you want to use, you can start entering information in the predefined text boxes. This is similar to completing the resume from a document template

6.4.1 Adding a Cover Page

An optional but commonly used document element is a cover page. A cover page

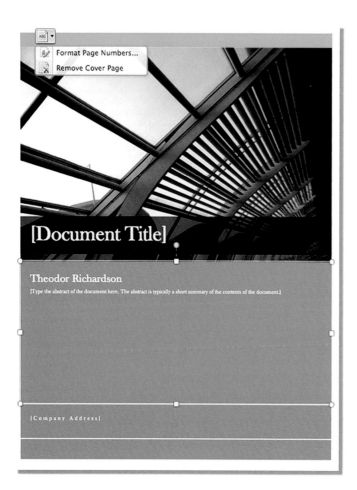

▲ **FIGURE 6.13**
Example cover
page with Word
2011 Cover Page
menu active

not necessary for the short example report, but it is helpful for quick reference in longer documents. The table of contents is created automatically in Word based on the use of the header styles mentioned earlier.

To insert a table of contents into your document, you must first highlight where you want it in your document. A table of contents is typically located before any of the actual document content between the cover page and the first section of the material. In Word 2010, you insert a table of contents by selecting *the References ribbon* and choosing the *Table of Contents* icon. This opens a drop-down menu of predefined options for your table of contents; you can also select *Insert Table of Contents* at the bottom of this menu to access the dialog box shown in Figure 6.14. This dialog box allows you to set up the number of heading levels you want to include and to adjust certain visual elements, such as the character used to link the section heading and the page number. The predefined

in the previous chapter. You should at minimum include a title and the document ownership, whether it is an individual author or the company that owns the document material. Remember that a cover page should only be used when necessary. It is included in the example report as a demonstration, but a short report like the one presented here would be better served with a header on the first page rather than a cover page.

6.4.2 Adding a Table of Contents

Another common element to include in your document is a table of contents. This is

OPEN OFFICE In Writer, you can apply a watermark as a background graphic. To do this, select the *Format* menu and choose *Page*. In the Page Style dialog box that appears, select the *Background* tab and choose *Graphic* as the type (beside the *As* text); you can then browse for the image you want to use. Similarly, the *Border* tab in the Page Style dialog box can be used to add and customize the page border. To insert a page break in the text, choose the *Insert* menu, select *Manual Break*, and then choose *Page Break* in the dialog box that opens. You can use a page break on an empty page with a single line to create a blank page in your document.

options for the table of contents in Word 2011 are available from the Document Elements ribbon or you can click the *Options* icon on the same panel to open the dialog box for customizing your own style. You can also open this dialog box by selecting the *Insert* menu, choosing *Index and Tables*, and then selecting the *Table of Contents* tab in the dialog box that appears.

OPEN OFFICE There is no automatic cover page creation in Writer. You can create a cover page, but you have to format it yourself and arrange the text as you want it to display. You can still use images and borders to establish the same effect as the automatic cover pages in Word.

If you continue to edit or develop your document after you have added the table of contents, you can update it to reflect the current headings included in the text or to adjust the page numbers. In Word 2010, select the *Update Table* icon on the *Table of Contents panel* of the *References ribbon* to perform this task. In Word 2011, select the *Update* icon located on the *Table of Contents panel* of the *Document Elements ribbon*.

In addition to the table of contents, there are three other document elements

A **TABLE OF CONTENTS** *is a list of chapter headings or major content divisions and the page numbers on which they are located. This allows for quick navigation of large documents to find desired elements and sections.*

of note that are similar. All of these are optional and may or may not be necessary for your document:

- *Index*—An *index* is a listing of key terms and concepts and where they are located throughout your document. You add an entry to the index in Word 2010 by selecting the *Mark Entry* icon on the *References* Ribbon. You then click *Insert Index* to access the Index tab of the dialog box in Figure 6.14 to customize the index display in the text. To add an entry to the index in Word 2011, select the *Insert* menu, choose *Index and Tables*, and select the *Index* tab in the open dialog box; you can then click the *Mark Entry* button to enter the index entry information. You can add your index to the document from this same dialog box.

- *Table of Figures*—The table of figures is based on the captions that you add to your document. This works similarly to the table of contents by automatically determining the page number on which the captions reside. To insert a table of figures in Word

▼ FIGURE 6.14
Table of Contents dialog box in Word 2010

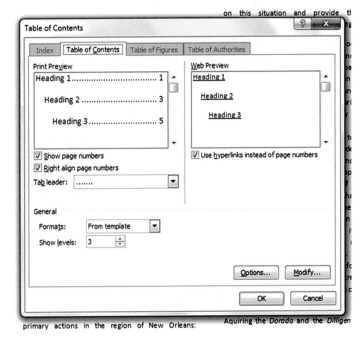

2010, select *Insert Table of Figures* on the *References ribbon*. You can update an existing table of figures by selecting the *Update Table* icon on the *Captions panel* in *the References ribbon*. In Word 2011, you add a table of figures by choosing the *Insert* menu, selecting *Index and Tables*, and choosing the *Table of Figures* tab in the dialog box. The table can be updated if new captions are added by selecting the table, pressing the *Control* key, and choosing the *Update* option.

- *Table of Authorities*—A *table of authorities* is a list of references in a legal document. For most works, you will not need to create one of these, but the option is available in Word.

To add a citation in Word 2010, you can use the *Mark Citation* icon on the *Table of Authorities panel* of the *References ribbon*. To insert the table of authorities, use the *Insert Table of Authorities* icon on the *References ribbon*. The *Update Table* icon in the Table of Authorities panel can be used to update the table later as the document is edited. In Word 2011, select the *Insert* menu, select *Index and Tables*, and then choose the *Table of Authorities* tab in the dialog box. The options to mark a citation and insert the table are in this dialog. You can update the table by selecting the table, pressing the *Control* key, and choosing the *Update* option.

OPEN OFFICE To insert a table of contents in a Writer document, select the *Insert* menu, choose *Indexes and Tables*, and then choose *Indexes and Tables* on the submenu that appears. This will open the Insert Index/Table dialog box. On the Index/Table tab, select *Table of Contents* in the Type category. You can use the remaining tabs to establish the format for the inserted text. This process can also be used to add an alphabetical index of key terms or an illustration index based on the captions inserted in the document; you can rename these as needed in the Title field. To update the automated tables or indexes, select the *Tools* menu, choose *Update*, and then choose *Update All*.

▲ **FIGURE 6.15** Completed example report

CHAPTER SUMMARY

This chapter covered the common use of word processing software for constructing reports and articles. The document elements covered in this chapter are used in a variety of other publications including guidelines, policies, and reports for companies and organizations. You should now be familiar with most of the functions of the word processing software you are using. This includes the use of external references, formatting styles, and the handling of images within your document. The next chapter will cover advanced features of the software and the handling of additional media elements including equations and symbols. An example of the completed report for the chapter is shown in Figure 6.15. You can also view the report by opening the *MyReport* document.

CHAPTER EXERCISES

1. Use word processing software to construct a two- to three-page report on evaluating sources. Make sure you add citations for the sources you use to gather your information and include a bibliography in your document.

2. Construct an outline for a research project of your choice. The document should have at least four level one headings with two to three subheadings each. Add a cover page to the document with a title, a blank page separating the cover from the document content, and a table of contents for the document. Add a page break after the table of contents so the actual content starts on a new page.

CHAPTER KNOWLEDGE CHECK

1 It is only important to evaluate sources from the Web; any printed source can be trusted.

- ○ True
- ○ False

2 Every document you create should have a table of contents.

- ○ True
- ○ False

3 The following document elements support automatic updates of their content to account for document changes in Word except:

- ○ **A.** Table of contents
- ○ **B.** Index
- ○ **C.** Cover page
- ○ **D.** Table of figures
- ○ **E.** All of the above
- ○ **F.** None of the above

4 The only difference between footnotes and endnotes is their placement within the document.

- ○ True
- ○ False

5 The following are common citation styles for a manuscript except:

- ○ **A.** MLA
- ○ **B.** Chicago
- ○ **C.** ABA
- ○ **D.** All of the above
- ○ **E.** None of the above

6 A source should be cited whenever it is used for an idea even if the source is not directly quoted in the text of the document.

- ○ True
- ○ False

7 The following are possible values for text wrapping around an image:

- ○ **A.** In line with text
- ○ **B.** In front of text
- ○ **C.** Behind text
- ○ **D.** All of the above
- ○ **E.** None of the above

8 To add an item to the index of a document, you must manually add it as an entry; the index is not constructed automatically from the text.

- ○ True
- ○ False

9 You can edit existing styles and create new styles for formatting text beyond what is predefined in the word processing program.

- ○ True
- ○ False

10 Headings are used to construct the table of contents for a document and can be used to jump quickly to a section of the document in the Navigation pane.

- ○ True
- ○ False

Advanced • Features of Word Processing

This chapter covers the use of more advanced features of word processing documents. Most of these have specific applications depending upon the nature and format of the document you are constructing, but it is beneficial to understand how they work and where they can be found regardless of your primary use of word processing software. You will learn about advanced features such as Mail Merge, additional document elements, and document editing and review. At the completion of this chapter, you will be able to:

- Complete a mail merge

- Construct equations using the equation editor

- Insert and manage tables in a document

- Add symbols and shapes

- Use the tracking and review options for document editing

MAIL MERGE

One of the tasks for which you will need word processing software is a Mail Merge. In business, you will often encounter the situation in which you want to send personalized copies of the same letter to a large number of recipients. The Mail Merge functionality in word processing allows you to perform this task with just a few steps. You should first create the document you wish to send to your recipients and then organize the list of contacts to which you want the document sent. Mail Merge is capable of constructing documents you can print directly and either printing labels for use on special paper to adhere to envelopes or printing the envelopes themselves. Most word processing applications have a wizard to guide you through this process.

MAIL MERGE *is a function in word processing software that allows you to construct form letters, identical documents that are personalized to individual contacts for fast mass mailing or printing.*

A **WIZARD** *in software is a form of assistant added to a software program to guide you through a complicated process by asking for small elements of input at a time; this typically breaks down larger tasks into manageable step-by-step instructions.*

For this chapter, you will use an existing set of contacts to construct a mail merge inviting potential investors to a big presentation for your new company. The example letter and the list of recipients are shown in Figure 7.1. These two files are included with the companion resources for this text; they are called *MyMergeDocument* and *MyMergeList*, respectively.

◀ **FIGURE 7.1** Example letter and recipient list for Mail Merge

Top Dog Dogs
12 Sausage Place
New York, NY 10027

June 10, 2011

Dear ,

You are invited to a presentation of a dramatic new business opportunity in which you can be a primary investor! We are very excited about the product we have to offer and believe that you will be as excited as we are when we unveil it to you. We know you are very busy, but we hope you will find the time to attend.

The presentation will take place on August 8 at 8:00 PM at Carnegie Hall. We have rented out the entire facility for you and will showcase our sound business strategy while you enjoy a world class environment complete with a performance after the presentation. The Hall will be yours to enjoy until 10:00 PM.

Please contact Samantha to RSVP for the event. Space is not limited, so feel free to bring along as many friends and relatives as you like if they are also able to invest. We do hope you can join us for this monumental event!

Sincerely,

T. Richardson
Entrepreneur

	A	B	C	D	E	F	G
1	Name	Address	City	State or Country	Postal Code	Phone	Email
2	Biggs Banker	1 Big Mansion Drive	New York	NY	10027	212-233-2227	bigbanker@richmail.com
3	Carl Cashman	102 Exchange Street	New York	NY	10027	212-337-5556	cash@ilikemoney.org
4	Martin Moneybags	4 Big Mansion Drive	New York	NY	10027	212-555-6789	moneybags@gmail.com
5	Richie Richardson	7 West Banker Street	New York	NY	10027	212-343-2332	rich@rich.net
6	Erik Euromaker	2 Large Palace Lane	New York	NY	10027	212-556-7778	euro@exchange.co.uk

► FIGURE 7.2
Mailings ribbon
in Word 2010

As a first step in the process, you should open *MyMergeDocument* in your word processing software and change the generic contact information at the top and after the signature line to reflect the business venture you want to advertise. Do not add any contact information for the recipient; this will be done via the list of recipients in the companion spreadsheet. You do not need to open the spreadsheet document; it will automatically be referenced by the wizard used to complete the project. Even though the results are the same, the functionality for performing a mail merge is significantly different in Word 2010, Word 2011, and Writer, so feel free to choose the section that applies to you.

7.1.1 Mail Merge in Microsoft Word 2010

In Word 2010, all of the functionality for performing a mail merge is found in the Mailings ribbon shown in Figure 7.2. This ribbon provides you the ability to create new documents for the mail merge and to select recipients. You can also edit the merge result after the merge is complete. For this example, open the *MyMergeDocument* file, open the Mailings ribbon, select *Start Mail Merge*, and choose *Step by Step Mail Merge Wizard*.

When you activate this command, a Mail Merge pane will appear on the right side of

▼ FIGURE 7.3 Mail Merge pane in Word 2010

your interface as shown in Figure 7.3. There are six steps to the Mail Merge in Word 2010. The first is choosing the document type you want to create; in this case, you want to select *Letters*. You should, however, take note of the other options available. For business mailings, it is common to need both letters and either envelopes or labels to accompany them. When you have made your selection, choose *Next: Starting Document*.

The options for selecting your starting document include the document in which you are currently working (which is the option used here), a new document from a template, or an existing document. You should be working within the *MyMergeDocument* file. Remember to save your changes; then choose *Use the current document* and select *Next: Select Recipients*.

In the next step, you will select recipients for your document. You can create a new list of recipients, choose from your contacts in Outlook, or select recipients from a file or database. In this case, select *Use an existing list* and choose the *Browse* icon to navigate to the *MyMergeList* spreadsheet document. When you have opened this document (and selected the only sheet in the

Notice that you have the option within the wizard to navigate to the next step or the previous one. If you make a mistake, you can always go backward in the wizard to correct it before the final step.

document as the data source), you will see the Mail Merge Recipients dialog box shown in Figure 7.4. You can select the *Name* field and sort them in ascending (A to Z) order; you should retain all of the recipients in the list, but you can uncheck the selection box next to recipients you do not want to include. Select *Next: Write your letter*.

Step 4 of the process is to edit your document by adding the merge fields. You should start by inserting an address block beneath the date entry in your document and place it all the way to the left above the greeting line. You can add an address block by selecting the *Address Block* link, which will open the Insert Address Block dialog box in which you can select how you want your recipient's address to appear. This dialog box is shown in Figure 7.5.

When you have chosen your formatting options, you will see the text *<<AddressBlock>>* in your document; this is a merge field and it will change based on the information obtained from each record in your recipient list. Next, add a greeting line to your document. In Word 2010, the greeting line will replace the entire line, so you should remove the existing "Dear," from your document and place the greeting line entry there.

If you want to add any additional fields to your document from the recipient

▼ FIGURE 7.4
Mail Merge Recipients dialog box in Word 2010

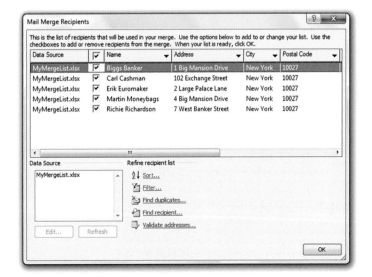

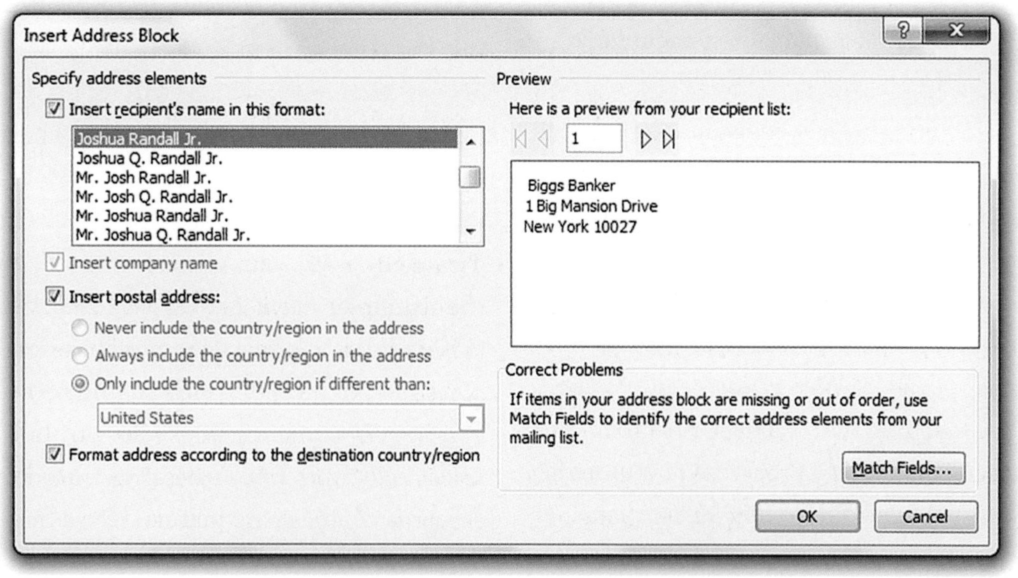

◀ FIGURE 7.5
Insert Address
Block dialog box in
Word 2010

list (such as an account number or e-mail address), you can select them individually by choosing the *More items* link. To add specific fields from your recipient list, use the Insert Merge Field icon from the Mailings ribbon. You can also add electronic postage to your envelopes or labels if you have the proper software and accounts set up from this step in the wizard. When you have finished adding fields to your document, choose the *Next: Preview your letters* link in the Mail Merge pane.

Step 5 provides a preview of your letters. You can use the left and right arrows to see how your results will look for each of the recipients in your list. You can go backward in the process to correct any errors. Formatting changes will apply to the merge fields just as they will to any other document element, so you can adjust the formatting as necessary. Note that the separator between the lines in the address block will always be a paragraph return. When you are satisfied with the results, choose the *Next: Complete the merge* link.

The final step of the Mail Merge wizard, Step 6, allows you to complete the merge and utilize the results. The options provided include the following:

You will need to use the Match Fields button to get your names to display correctly. Select *Name* as the value for the First Name in order to get the automatic completion to work. You will know it is working correctly when you see one of your recipient's names in the preview display on the dialog box.

- *Print*—This prints all of the letters with addresses selected from the data list you created earlier.

- *Edit Individual Letters*—This lets you edit letters. For example, if you wanted to include specific information for one or more of the recipients that was not in the list from which you selected the merge information, you could add it manually in the document and print the result when you are finished.

You can also use this feature to save a copy of the personalized mailings as a record of what exactly was sent.

Electing to edit individual letters will create a new document with the fields completed. The fields will no longer register as merge fields but instead will act as static text. You can still save the document with the merge fields for later use. In this case, save it as *MyMergeDocumentCompleted*. You can use the Mailings ribbon in this document to adjust properties of your merge fields, preview the results for recipients, or output a new merge result. An example of the completed document for the first recipient in the list is shown in Figure 7.6.

7.1.2   Mail Merge in Microsoft Word 2011

In Word 2011, the Mail Merge Manager is the tool you use to complete a Mail Merge. You activate this by selecting the *Tools* menu and choosing *Mail Merge Manager*, which will open the dialog box shown in Figure 7.7. There are six steps to completing a Mail Merge in Word 2011. The first is to select the document type you want to create. In the example, *Form Letters* was selected; this uses the current document as a template for the merge, which should be the *MyMergeDocument* file. You can also select *Labels* or *Envelopes* if you need to create accompanying material for a business mailing.

The second step is to select your recipients. You can create a new list or use an existing document or contact list (such as an Office Address Book or Apple Address Book) as a base for your recipients. Choose *Get List*, select *Open Data Source*, select the file *MyMergeList*, and then choose *Entire Worksheet* to include all of the data it contains.

Unlike Word 2010, the manner of adding merge fields to your document in Word 2011 is to click on the field you want to add and drag it to the desired location in the document. To create the proper address block, drag the fields *Name*, *Address*, *City*, *State_or_Country*, and *Postal_Code* into your document. *Name* and *Address* should each occupy their own line.

◄ **FIGURE 7.6**
Completed Mail
Merge example

Top Dog Dogs

12 Sausage Place

New York, NY 10027

June 10, 2011

Biggs Banker

1 Big Mansion Drive

New York 10027

Dear Biggs Banker,

You are invited to a presentation of a dramatic new business opportunity in which you can be a primary investor! We are very excited about the product we have to offer and belive that you will be as excited as we are when we unveil it to you. We know you are very busy, but we hope will find the time to attend.

The presentation will take place on August 8 at 8:00 PM at Carnegie Hall. We have rented out the entire facility for you and will showcase our sound business strategy while you enjoy a world class environment complete with a performance after the presentation. The Hall will be yours to enjoy until 10:00 PM.

Please contact Samantha to RSVP for the event. Space is not limited, so feel free to bring along as many friends and relatives as you like if they are also able to invest. We do hope you can join us for this monumental event!

example, but this is helpful if you are using a large list from your contacts and wish to specify criteria for who should be included in the mailing. Step 5 is Preview Results. Click the *View Merged Data* icon to toggle whether the current record is shown in the document or the generic merge field references are displayed. You can use the arrows here to scroll through the recipients to preview each of them in the document itself.

Step 6 is Complete Merge. This step allows you to send your results to the printer by using the *Merge to Printer* selection or to create a new document with all of the records appended for individual editing by using the *Merge to New Document* selection. You can choose whether you want to include all of the recipients or define a range of records you wish to use in the result. Defining a range can be helpful if you share printing resources and have hundreds of recipient letters to print.

Mail Merge in OpenOffice.org Writer

7.1.3

There are eight steps in the Mail Merge Wizard for Writer. Begin with the *MyMergeDocument* file open, and then select the *Tools* menu and choose *Mail*

You should then arrange the next line so it contains *City*, a comma, *State_or_Country*, a space, and then *Postal_Code*. Notice that the fields you drag into the document are surrounded by less-than and greater-than signs (such as *<<Name>>*); these indicate the fields are merge fields that will be replaced with the text from the recipient list. You should then drag the *Name* field into the greeting line (to the right of *Dear* but before the comma). When you have finished adding the merge fields to your document, your result should be similar to Figure 7.8.

Step 4 is Filter Recipients, which allows you to define criteria to include or exclude certain recipients in the list. None of the recipients should be excluded in the

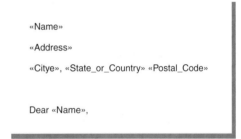

◀ FIGURE 7.8
Merge fields added to document in Word 2011

Merge Wizard. In the first step, select the current document in order to proceed. You can also use an existing document or a document template to complete the Mail Merge. Press the *Next* button to continue. Notice that you have the option to go back to previous steps before completing the final merge, so you can make changes if you wish.

In the second step, you will choose whether to create e-mail messages or letters. For the example, choose *Letter* and click the *Next* button. Step 3 is to choose the recipient list and format the address block. Click the button to select an address list. In the dialog box that opens, click the *Add* button and select the *MyMergeList* document as your source. Click *OK* to return to the wizard. If you want to include an address

block in your document (which you do for this example), keep the checkbox activated. The next step is to click the *Match Fields* button. This will open the dialog box shown in Figure 7.9.

To complete the example Mail Merge, you should equate the following fields: *First Name* in the merge fields should match *Name* in your recipient list, *Address Line 1* should match *Address*, *City* should match *City*, *State* should match *State_or_Country*, and *ZIP* should match *Postal Code*. You can match the values for the phone number and e-mail address as practice, but these are not needed for the example. Click *OK* when you are finished. You cannot proceed to the next step if there are unmatched fields.

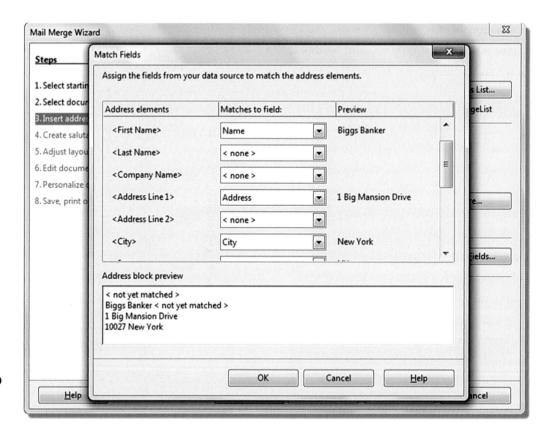

▶ **FIGURE 7.9**
Match Fields
dialog box in
Writer

To complete the example, you will need to use the *More* button next to the entry for the address block format. In the dialog box that opens, add *First Name*, *Address Line 1*, *City*, *State*, and *ZIP*. You should arrange *First Name* and *Address Line 1* on their own lines and the last three fields in sequence on the third line. When you have finished this, click the *OK* button. You can now select *Next* to proceed to the next step in the wizard.

The next step is to add a salutation. You will once again need to match fields for this to work correctly. You can equate *Last Name* with the *Name* value in your recipient list since you customized your own address block. This would ordinarily be a bad idea, though, as ideally you would open the list in a spreadsheet program and separate the names into First Name and Last Name fields; once you master that type of software

later in the text, this would be a worthwhile exercise. When you see the preview panel working correctly for the recipients, select the *Next* button.

The fifth step allows you to adjust the placement of the address block and the salutation line. This placement is based on your margins, but the salutation line should be directly beneath the address block as shown in Figure 7.10. The next step allows you to preview or edit the document. Ideally, you would already have done this, but you can select a record at random and choose *Edit Document*; this will allow you to make any corrections to the document to accommodate the merged fields. When you are ready to return to the wizard to complete the process, select *Return to Mail Merge Wizard* from the floating toolbar that appears.

Step 7 allows you to select and personalize individual documents within the recipient list. You can use the Find functionality to perform a search on your recipients in case you want to add individual customization to a particular letter. The final step in the process, Step 8, allows you to save the original document, save the merged document, send the merged document to the printer,

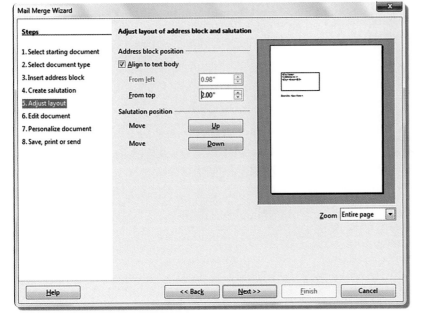

◀ **FIGURE 7.10**
Address block and salutation placement in Writer

or send the merged document as an e-mail. When you select the print option, you can also select the set of records you want to print (if you want to break up a print job into multiple smaller print jobs). If you choose e-mail as your option, you will need a field that matches the e-mail address of the recipients.

7.2 ADDITIONAL DOCUMENT ELEMENTS

Word processing documents can include a number of visual elements beyond the typical text and images. There are several quick enhancements you can add to your document to adjust its visual style or utilize callouts within the main text. These include:

- *Text Boxes*—A text box in Word is a standalone object containing keyboard entered text; it behaves inside the document similarly to the images you previously inserted. You can set the text box to have the same text wrapping properties as an image, which is helpful if you want to add a quote or other note to your text to call it to the attention of your reader; these can enhance the visual style of the document without the use of graphics. Word 2010 has several options for text boxes that are available by choosing the *Text Box* icon on the *Insert ribbon*; you can choose a standard text box and format it yourself or use one of the predefined options available in the list. In Word 2011, you can add either a (horizontal) Text Box or a Vertical Text Box to your document from the *Text Box* icon on the *Home ribbon*. You can apply whatever formatting you like to the resulting text box, but there are no predefined options as there are in Word 2010.

- *Drop Cap*—This is a visual enhancement to a paragraph of text that can apply to the heading or first line of a paragraph. It sets the first letter of the text as an independent text box with a large print size that can be resized and formatted independently of the rest of the text. It is used to call attention to the paragraph and attract the eye of the viewer. This is sometimes used in newspaper or magazine articles as a style choice. To activate this in Word 2010, select the text you want to enhance and choose the *Drop Cap* icon on the *Insert ribbon* and select whether you want it dropped into the paragraph of the text or into the margin. In Word 2011, you add a drop cap by highlighting the text to which you want the effect to apply, selecting the *Format* menu, and choosing *Drop Cap*.

Some of the more advanced examples of visual enhancements are SmartArt in Word and charts. SmartArt is a great way to construct professional-quality graphics quickly using a bulleted list; since this is primarily for a more encapsulated visual medium of presentation, the full description of constructing SmartArt can be found in Section 10.2.4, "SmartArt." Charts are visual presentations of data that must be created from a data source. In Office, the program that manages that data is Excel, so you should reference Section IV, "Spreadsheet Software and Microsoft Excel," for a better understanding of how to construct charts. If you want to see how to create and insert a simple chart, see Section 10.2.3, "Charts."

 **OPEN OFFICE** To add a text box to your document in Writer, you need to activate the Drawing toolbar by selecting the *View* menu, choosing *Toolbars*, and then selecting *Drawing*. From this toolbar, you can select the *Text* icon to draw a text box in the document; you will need to apply formatting so it displays the way you want it to. You can add drop caps to your text by selecting the *Format* menu and choosing *Paragraph*. In the dialog box that appears, select the *Drop Caps* tab and adjust the settings as desired.

There are four remaining areas of visual enhancement for creating effective word processing documents. It is common to include symbols, equations, tables, and drawing objects in your document to vary the visual style and present your information clearly. Each of these topics is described in the sections that follow.

Adding Symbols

Symbols are substitutions for a text character that cannot be found on a regular keyboard. Examples include foreign currency symbols, copyright symbols, and mathematical symbols. To insert a symbol in Word 2010, select the *Insert ribbon* and click the *Symbol* icon. A list of common symbols will appear. You can select the *More Symbols* option to access a dialog box that allows you to select symbols from different languages. An example of this dialog box being used to insert the symbol for British pounds into the report on Jean Lafitte is shown in Figure 7.11.

In addition to currency symbols and letters from other alphabets, there are

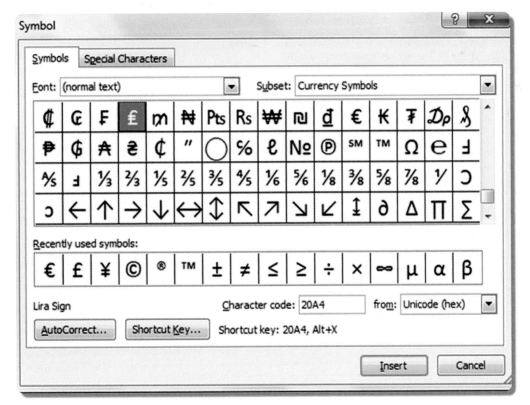

◄ **FIGURE 7.11**
Symbol selection in Word 2010

a few unique fonts that contain symbol libraries instead of text characters. These fonts include Wingdings and Webdings. You can use the Font selection box to choose these symbols to see what is available. You can also select the *Subset* selection box to choose technical symbols or foreign alphabets that do not have representation on your own keyboard. When you have selected the symbol you want, click the *Insert* button to place it in line with your text.

OPEN OFFICE To add symbols to your Writer document, select the *Insert* menu and choose *Special Character*. Adding special characters or symbols in your document in Writer can also be accomplished by the use of specific fonts such as Wingdings or Webdings.

7.2.2 Editing Equations

Word has a library of symbols that allows you to construct equations within your document. To add an equation in Word 2010, select the *Insert ribbon* and choose the *Equation* icon; in Word 2011, select the *Equation* icon in the *Document Elements ribbon*. When you choose the Equation icon, a drop-down list will appear with several common equations that you can insert and modify or you can choose *Insert New Equation* to create your own. For this example, you will construct the equation for finding the root of the quadratic equation; this is commonly called the quadratic formula. When you insert an equation in Word and click within it, a context-sensitive ribbon will appear to help you construct

and edit equations. In Word 2010, this is the Design ribbon for Equation Tools; in Word 2011, it is the Equation Tools ribbon, which chains off of the Document Elements ribbon. An example of the ribbon, the quadratic equation, and the completed solution for adding the quadratic formula is shown in Figure 7.12.

Equations are treated as unique objects in your document just like citations; by default, the equation is given its own line in the document. The context-sensitive ribbon for equations contains all of the common mathematical symbols, which you can simply click to insert. It also contains a variety of structures that can be used to format your equation such as *Fraction*, *Script*, *Radical*, *Integral*, etc.

When you click on any of these icons, a drop-down list will appear from which you can select the elements and formatting you need for your equation. The structures that you can select from these lists contain small boxes surrounded by dotted lines; these are the building blocks of your equation and you can think of the box as containing a set of parentheses in mathematics. Whatever you type inside of the box will become part of the structure. You can also nest structures within each other, which will be demonstrated in the example.

The other feature of the ribbon you should note is the ability to switch your

The equation editor in Word is for formatting and displaying equations only. It cannot be used to compute or solve formulas.

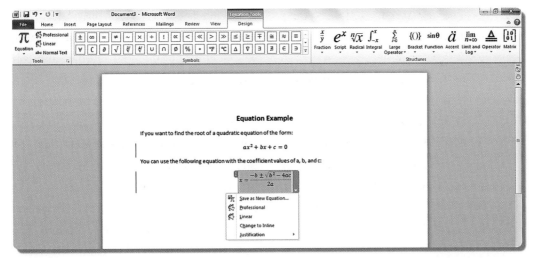

◄ **FIGURE 7.12**
Equation example
in Word 2010

equation from *Professional* to *Linear* format. Professional is the actual arrangement of symbols that you would see in a mathematics textbook; Linear is the arrangement of the symbols and elements in a single line. The Linear format automatically adds parentheses to separate elements of the equation that are implied by the structures in the Professional display. The Linear format for the quadratic formula is shown in Figure 7.13. When you click the outer box around an equation, you will get a drop-down list that allows you to select the formatting.

$$x = (-b \pm \sqrt{(b^2 - 4ac)})/2a$$

▲ **FIGURE 7.13** Linear formatting for quadratic formula

The steps to construct the generic quadratic equation are as follows:

1. Start the linear portion of the equation by typing $a + bx + c = 0$ in the equation editing box.

2. Add the exponent to the a coefficient by placing the cursor beside and to the right of the a and selecting *Script* and then *Superscript*. This will insert two formatting boxes into your equation. Type x in the base box and *2* in the exponent box.

The steps to construct the root solution equation are as follows:

1. After you insert a new equation, type $x =$ in the equation entry box.

2. Choose *Fractions* and select *Stacked Fraction* from the list.

3. Type *2a* in the bottom box of the fraction formatting.

4. Type *–b* in the top of the fraction formatting and insert the stacked +/– symbol from the available symbols.

5. Paste the symbol you inserted, choose *Radical*, and then select *Square Root*.

6. Beneath the radical symbol, type $b - 4ac$ in the formatting box.

7. Use the *Script* option *Superscript* to turn the b coefficient from the previous entry into b squared (this is the same procedure you used in the quadratic equation).

To end equation entry, you must click outside of the equation box. Pressing the Enter key gives you a new equation line in the same formatting box.

 **OPEN OFFICE** In OpenOffice.org, you can insert a formula into your document using a special program called OpenOffice.org Math. It is possible to create a new Math document as well as use its functionality within the other applications in the OpenOffice.org suite. You can add a formula within Writer by selecting the *Insert* menu, choosing *Object*, and then choosing *Formula*. A floating *Elements* toolbar lets you select the pieces to form your formula or equation, and a separate pane in the bottom of the interface will display the formula as you are editing it. Each selection in the top part of the Elements toolbar opens a subset at the bottom of the toolbar from which you can choose the formatting you want to use.

7.2.3 Adding Tables

A table is a great tool to manage information in your document. Tables do not have the computational power of the spreadsheets found in Excel, but they can be effective for presenting a lot of information in a small space. For instance, you can use a table to present a list of values or results, such as the comparison of different currencies shown in Figure 7.14. To insert a similar table in Word 2010, select the *Insert ribbon* and choose the *Table* icon; this will allow you to select the number of rows and columns you want the table to have. You can

also select the *Insert Table* option from the submenu to access a dialog box that allows you to enter the number or rows and columns you wish to include. Word 2011 has a separate Tables ribbon that you use to add tables to your document; click the *New* icon to select the number of rows and columns or select the *Insert Table* option to define the table parameters manually.

When you add a table to your document in Word 2010, two context-sensitive ribbons will help you format your table; these are the Design ribbon and the Layout ribbon for Table Tools shown in Figure 7.15. You can select a style to format your table and choose whether you want to include elements like a header row from the Design ribbon. The Layout ribbon allows you to format the alignment of the text within each cell and add or remove rows. Word 2011 contains most of the formatting options on the existing Tables ribbon; when you add a table to your document, however, the context-sensitive Table Layout ribbon appears, which contains commands for table cell management and alignment.

In the example in Figure 7.14, a header row is included and the table is formatted with the *Light Shading* option.

World Currency Comparison (As of 5/16/2011)

Currency	In Euro (€)	Per Euro (€)
British Pound (£)	1.14	0.87
Australian Dollar ($)	0.75	1.33
US Dollar ($)	0.71	1.41
Chinese Yuan (¥)	0.11	9.21

➤ **FIGURE 7.14**
Example table showing currency comparison

Statistics taken from MSN Money

(*http://moneycentral.msn.com/investor/market/exchangerates.aspx?selRegion=0&selCurrency=9*)

Internal borders have also been added (via the *Borders* icon) to show the delineation between table cells. For an additional example of using tables for visual presentation, see Section 10.2.2, "Tables." The commands for adding borders and shading in Word 2011 are found on the Tables ribbon.

A FIGURE 7.15
Context-sensitive Table ribbons in Word 2010

7.2.4 Adding Shapes

In Word, you can add simple shapes to your document and format them as you would an image. These shapes are treated as objects within your document for which you can set the color and formatting as well as the placement and text wrap properties. To insert a shape in Word 2010, select the *Insert ribbon* and choose the *Shapes* icon. In Word 2011, you add a shape to your document by selecting the *Shape* icon on the *Home ribbon*. The menu that appears is organized into categories rather than displaying all of the options at once. The list of these available shapes is shown in Figure 7.16.

When you insert a shape, a context-sensitive Format ribbon allows you to adjust its format and properties, including the fill, line, and other effects. By default, the shape is set to layer above the text of your document,

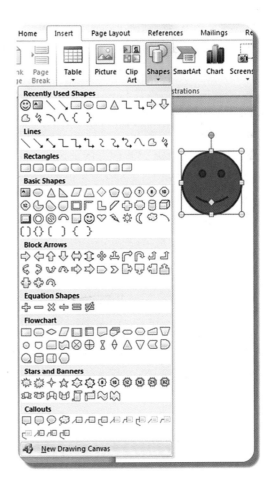

◄ FIGURE 7.16
Shapes menu in Word 2010

OPEN OFFICE In Writer, you add a table to your document by selecting the *Insert* menu and choosing *Table*. From here you can enter the number of rows and columns you want to include. You can also select the *AutoFormat* button to select from a predefined set of table layouts and color schemes similar to the formatting options available in Microsoft Word.

but you can adjust this property as well. Formatting shapes is covered in more detail in Chapter 8. In Word 2010, you can also use the *Shapes* menu to insert a drawing canvas, which is configured as a document object in line with your text where you can place multiple shapes; the entire canvas is treated as a single object.

7.3 EDITING EXISTING DOCUMENTS

As mentioned earlier, you can use the *File* menu to open existing documents. This includes not only the documents you construct but also any documents on your computer that come from someone else. The *Open* command launches a dialog box that allows you to select the document you want to review or edit. Word has some excellent tools in the Review ribbon, shown in Figure 7.17, that are used to edit and review documents. This ribbon exists in both Word 2010 and Word 2011, although the commands available differ slightly.

Word 2010 and Word 2011 have different options for reviewing the formatting that is applied in your document. In Word 2010, you can show or hide formatting marks by clicking the *Show/Hide Paragraph* icon on the *Paragraph panel* of the *Home ribbon*. In Word 2011, you can use the *Reveal Formatting* tool available from the *View* menu to click inside the document and view the formatting that is applied at that location.

Word 2011 also allows you to manage the styles used in the document with the Toolbox available from the Quick Access toolbar; select the *Styles* tab to view the styles used in the current document. You can even color-code where the styles are applied by selecting the *Show Styles Guides* checkbox. You can apply styles directly from this panel or simply review the existing formatting.

Document Comparison 7.3.1

If you have multiple versions of a document that you need to integrate, you can perform a document comparison to view the changes and decide whether you want to keep them. These versions do not have to have the same author so you can perform a comparison after you have sent your document to someone else for editing whether or not they have tracked their changes. As an example, you can use the *MyReport* document and the *MyReportVersion2* document to perform an example comparison.

▼ **FIGURE 7.17**
Review ribbon in Word 2010

OPEN OFFICE You can display the nonprinting characters in Writer by selecting the icon that looks like a paragraph mark in the Standard toolbar called *Nonprinting Characters*. This icon acts as a toggle that will alternately display or hide the hidden characters in the document.

To perform a document comparison in Word 2010, select the *Review ribbon* and choose *Compare*. There are two options available here: *Compare* and *Combine*. Both of these will create a new document that merges the two versions together. Compare is used to show the differences between versions from the same author whereas Combine is intended for documents from multiple authors. In Word 2011, you can perform a document comparison by selecting the *Tools* menu, choosing *Track Changes*, and then choosing *Compare Documents*. The interface for choosing the documents is shown in Figure 7.18. This process will create a new document as a result, so neither of the files needs to be open.

In Word 2010, the result of the comparison will display in a Reviewing pane that includes a top and bottom comparison of the documents beside the new merged document as shown in Figure 7.19. You can toggle the Reviewing pane from the Review ribbon, and you can manually close the version documents in the comparison. If you wish to retain the older versions, save your file with a new document name.

Word 2011 simply creates a new document based off of the original document where the updates in the revised version are tracked as changes. The Sidebar will display the Reviewing pane, which gives you a list of the changes that are included in the document. The differences between the two documents will be tracked as changes that must be either accepted or rejected, no matter which version you use. This is the topic of the next section where you will learn to manage tracked changes in a document.

Track Changes 7.3.2

When you use Track Changes on a document, every change you make will be registered in a different colored (traditionally red) markup. Words or characters that you delete will have a strikethrough effect and new words will be shown in the different color

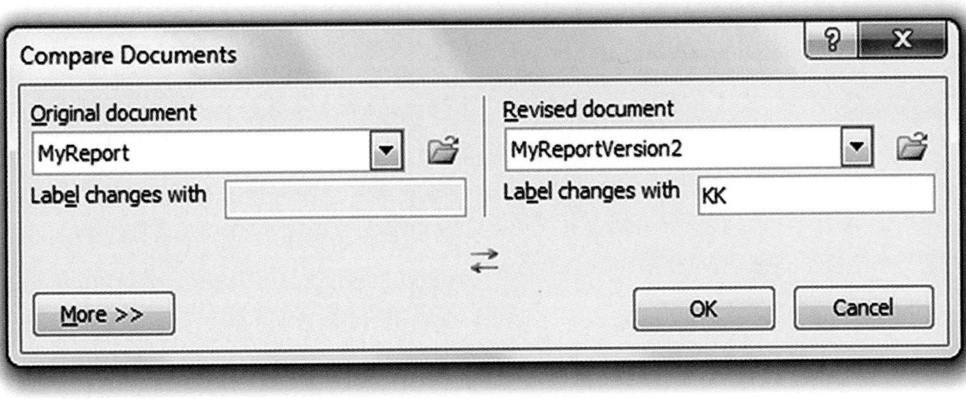

FIGURE 7.18 Compare Documents dialog box in Word 2010

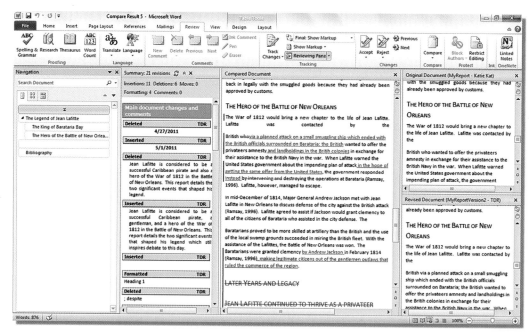

➤ **FIGURE 7.19**
Document comparison in Word 2010

with an underline. This allows you to monitor changes or record them for someone else to review. If you are editing someone else's document, it is a courtesy to track changes so they can identify your edits.

To enable Track Changes in Word 2010, select the *Review ribbon* and choose the *Track Changes* icon; this is a toggle so it is active when it is highlighted. You can use the submenu to customize options for tracking the document changes or edit the name

OPEN OFFICE With the original document open in Writer, you perform a document comparison by selecting the *Edit* menu and choosing *Compare Document*. This will open a dialog box in which you can select the alternate version of the document. The result will be tracked changes of both versions of the document. In Writer, the changes must be accepted or rejected from the list interface that appears when the comparison is complete. The formatting in the document indicating the changes is similar to what is available in Word.

OPEN OFFICE Enabling or disabling Track Changes does not affect any prior changes. If you were tracking changes and turned the function off, you will still need to accept or reject the changes that were tracked. Similarly, if you were not tracking changes, turning the functionality on will not affect prior alterations that were made without Track Changes active.

you wish to use for the change tracking. In Word 2011, you can enable Track Changes on the Review ribbon by moving the slide bar from *OFF* to *ON*. You can slide it back to *OFF* to disable Track Changes.

You can navigate from one tracked change to another using the *Next* and *Previous* icons on the *Changes* panel of the *Review ribbon*. If you want to keep the currently active change, select the *Accept* icon. If you want to remove the change, select the *Reject* icon. These icons also have submenus

OPEN OFFICE You can record changes made to your document in Writer by selecting the *Edit* menu, choosing *Changes*, and then selecting *Record*. This acts as a toggle, so you can repeat the process to turn off the recording of changes. You can tell when these are active when you see the check mark next to the Record selection. Similarly, you can choose whether or not you want to show the changes in your document, giving you the option of recording the changes in the background. When you are ready to finalize your document, you can access the Accept or Reject Changes dialog box by choosing the *Edit* menu, selecting *Changes*, and then selecting *Accept or Reject*. This dialog box presents you with a list of changes that you can resolve by selecting the change and choosing to either accept it or reject it.

attached that will allow you to accept or reject all of the changes in the document without going through them one by one. Word 2011 has these options on the Changes panel of the Review ribbon, along with a toggle icon for displaying the Review pane.

Examine the document that was created from merging the two versions of the report. Practice reviewing changes by navigating through the document and deciding whether you want to accept or reject the changes as appropriate.

You should keep any beneficial change and reject any that are not wanted. Be sure to retain the concluding paragraph in the document.

Comments

7.3.3

Another way to mark a document for potential change when editing is to use comments. A comment in word processing is a note about the document that is written to the author or the editor of a document. You can use comments to identify areas of the document that may need to be changed or clarified. Comments identify the person who created them either by name or by initials, so multiple people can add comments to the same document and you can still identify the source of the comment. Comments are a helpful tool for collaboration and versioning in a document. They appear in the document margin to the right so they do not impede the visibility of the main text. Unlike Track Changes, you do not accept or reject comments; instead you simply add or remove them.

Comments attach to a particular selection of text in the document. You can select the text to which you want the comment to apply, but if you do not select the text, it will attach to the last word before the current cursor location.

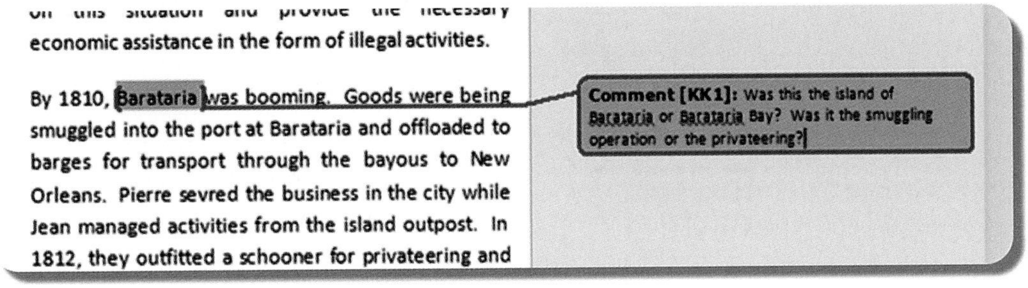

on this situation and provide the necessary economic assistance in the form of illegal activities.

By 1810, Barataria was booming. Goods were being smuggled into the port at Barataria and offloaded to barges for transport through the bayous to New Orleans. Pierre sevred the business in the city while Jean managed activities from the island outpost. In 1812, they outfitted a schooner for privateering and

Comment [KK1]: Was this the island of Barataria or Barataria Bay? Was it the smuggling operation or the privateering?

◀ **FIGURE 7.20**
Example comment in Word 2010

OPEN OFFICE You can add a comment to a document in Writer by selecting the *Insert* menu and choosing *Comment*. This will open a comment attached to the current location of your cursor in the document. A small drop-down menu on the comment gives you the option to delete it or to delete all comments in the document. Choose whether or not you want to view the comments by selecting the *View* menu and either checking or unchecking *Comments*.

In Word 2010 and Word 2011, you add a new comment by selecting the text on which you want to comment, activating the *Review ribbon*, and choosing *New Comment* (or *New* on the Comments panel in Word 2011). The *Next* and *Previous* icons in the Comments panel allow you to move from one comment to another. To delete a comment, click on the comment you want to remove and select the *Delete* icon; the submenu of the Delete icon also allows you to delete all of the comments in the document, which should only be done once they have been reviewed. An example of a comment is shown in Figure 7.20.

You should practice adding comments to and deleting comments from the report document that resulted from the document comparison process. In Word 2010, when you activate the Reviewing pane you can see the comments included in the document. In Word 2011, the comments added to the document will appear in the Review pane whenever it is active.

CHAPTER SUMMARY

This chapter covered some of the more advanced features you can use in word processing documents. Word processing is the primary means of creating print documents in the workplace. Part of the business practice may be to send out periodic mailings for which Mail Merge can provide a tremendous shortcut. There is a lot of overlap between word processing and presentations since both are primarily visual media; however, one of the key differences is the interactive nature of presentations and the static nature of printed documents. Establishing visual appeal and clarity is necessary in both, but generating visual interest and document flow in word processing is much more important since you must convey your ideas solely through what is presented on the page. The next section of the text focuses on constructing presentations; you should notice the common elements between the two productivity applications.

CHAPTER EXERCISES

1. Construct a set of mailing labels or envelopes to accompany the letters you have constructed in this chapter. You can use the MyMergeList file, but you should include both the recipient address and the return address. Make sure your page layout is formatted correctly for the type of document you want to print.

2. Make at least five changes to either the report you constructed in Chapter 6 or the resume you constructed in Chapter 5. Use a document comparison to view the changes. Add at least two comments to the document as well. Save the file with the markup.

CHAPTER KNOWLEDGE CHECK

1 When selecting recipients for a Mail Merge, you must only include the fields for recipient information you will use in your document; any additional fields will cause errors in the merge process.

- ○ True
- ○ False

2 You cannot personalize individual documents in a Mail Merge; the results of the merge can only be sent directly to the printer or to e-mail.

- ○ True
- ○ False

3 Special fonts exist that allow you to substitute symbols for the letters on your keyboard.

- ○ True
- ○ False

4 The following applications are capable of including formulas formatted in traditional mathematic notation:

- ○ **A.** Microsoft Word 2010
- ○ **B.** Microsoft Word 2011
- ○ **C.** OpenOffice.org Writer
- ○ **D.** All of the above
- ○ **E.** Both a and b
- ○ **F.** None of the above

5 Text wrapping can apply to objects other than images.

- ○ True
- ○ False

6 Comments added to a document will not be retained when the document is sent to another recipient; they are strictly for your own use.

- ○ True
- ○ False

7 Changes made to a document while Track Changes (or Record Changes) was not active will not be retained for later acceptance or rejection.

○ True
○ False

8 Activating Track Changes (or Record Changes) will affect all changes made to the document, including changes made before Track Changes was activated.

○ True
○ False

9 The standard options for resolving a tracked or recorded change to a document are as follows:

○ **A.** Accept the change
○ **B.** Reject the change
○ **C.** Move the change to a comment
○ **D.** All of the above
○ **E.** Both a and b
○ **F.** None of the above

10 Symbols (or special characters) are treated as images in your word processing document.

○ True
○ False

Introduction to • *PowerPoint and Presentation Software*

This chapter is an introduction to presentation software and basic elements of constructing a presentation. You will create, edit, and save a simple presentation while learning to use the common tools required for developing professional presentations. Once you have completed the chapter, you will be able to:

- Create and save a new presentation document

- Insert and format text and text boxes in a presentation document

- Insert drawing shapes, clip art, and stored images into a presentation document

- Rearrange slides in a presentation document

- Add slide transitions to a presentation document

INTRODUCTION TO PRESENTATION SOFTWARE

In the past, lecturers, business leaders, researchers, teachers, and anyone wishing to present an idea had to construct their own visual aids on paper or chalkboards to supplement their oral presentations. This was time consuming and generally was not easily transferrable to another venue. Technology like slide projectors and overhead projectors made this process easier, but it still carried a significant development requirement to produce the slides or the overhead sheets. Presentation software is the digital equivalent to these analog technologies and lowers the barrier to creating effective visual supplements to any presentation.

An example of presentation software is Microsoft PowerPoint, which comes with the Microsoft Office suite. The native format for this software is the presentation document, and it takes the form of a slide show. Presentation documents are primarily a visual supplement to an oral presentation, although they can also be used as a stand-alone slide show playing in the background of an event or as a demonstration that can be shared or posted on the Web. A critical thing to remember is that presentation software is not useful for a large volume of written text; that belongs in word processing software. Any text contained in a presentation should be short and to the point (the power point, if you will).

PRESENTATION SOFTWARE *is a computer program that typically runs on a personal computer and allows the user to create visual aids, handouts, and graphics that may include sound and animation.*

ANATOMY OF MICROSOFT POWERPOINT

Whenever you open PowerPoint from a menu or from a desktop icon, a new presentation document (typically named *Presentation1*) will open. Once you have opened PowerPoint, take a look at the *File* menu; this is the orange square at the top-left side of the interface in Office 2010 and the first menu in the list beside the apple symbol and the word *PowerPoint* in Office 2011. The File menu options are shown in Figure 8.1. The detailed options here will be explored later, but for now you should focus on the process of creating and saving a presentation document.

Remember that Microsoft Office 2010 (including PowerPoint 2010) is the latest version available for the Windows operating system. Microsoft Office 2011 (including PowerPoint 2011) is the latest version available for the Macintosh operating system.

To create a new document in PowerPoint 2010, select the *File* menu and then select *New*. A list of document templates from which you can create your presentation will appear. Select *Blank Presentation* and either double-click the icon or click the *Create* button. You can also use the *Ctrl-N* shortcut to create a new presentation with the default settings.

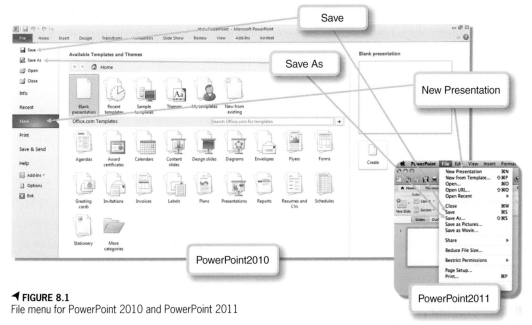

◀ FIGURE 8.1
File menu for PowerPoint 2010 and PowerPoint 2011

In PowerPoint 2011, select the *File* menu and then choose *New Presentation*, or use the shortcut *Command-N*. You can also create a new presentation from an existing template under the File menu, but for now you should just create a new blank presentation.

Whenever you are working on a document, it is imperative to save often. You should always start saving when the document is first created. With your new *Presentation1* (the default file) open, click *File* to open the interface for the file options. On the main list in the open menu, you have the Save and Save As options. Save will attempt to save the document to an existing location, but if you have not yet saved the document, it will act like Save As. Just as in Word, Save As prompts you for a location and filename to store the file. For a refresher on how this works, you can revisit Section 5.1.1, "The File Menu." Go ahead and save your presentation

as *MyPowerPoint*; the native file type is *PowerPoint Presentation* (*.pptx*).

Now you should be at the main slide of your new presentation. PowerPoint has an interface that is very similar to Word. A few of the ribbons contain almost identical tools. PowerPoint is designed for visualization, so the ability to format text and insert media quickly is the essential element that distinguishes PowerPoint from the rest of the Office suite. When you look at the default interface, you will see the initial *title* slide and the available ribbons and commands. A quick tour of the interface is provided first and then you will learn the steps to creating a successful presentation. The interfaces for PowerPoint 2010 and PowerPoint 2011 are slightly different, so feel free to jump to the section that is relevant to you.

Microsoft PowerPoint 2010

Along the top of the PowerPoint 2010 interface (which is shown in Figure 8.2) is a

8.2.1

series of icons that act as quick commands; this is the Quick Access toolbar. The PowerPoint icon itself contains a short list of commands that allow you to move and change the size of your interface window.

Clicking the icon that looks like a floppy disk lets you save your document quickly after you have made changes (it acts like the Save command, but if you have never saved your document it will act as the Save As command).

By default, the Quick Access toolbar also has the Undo command to erase the effects of your last action as though it had never happened; the drop-down arrow beside the icon opens a menu of several prior actions and lets you select how many of them you want to undo. The Redo command allows you to redo what you undid. These two icons allow you to step forward and backward through your changes in case you made a mistake along the way.

On the righthand side at the top of the interface are icons to minimize, maximize, and close your presentation (make sure you save before you click this button). Directly beneath these icons, there is an arrow to show or hide your ribbons and an icon to access the help files. The first ribbon beside the File button is the Home ribbon. From here, you can insert new slides, modify text, insert quick drawing elements, arrange items, and find and replace text in the presentation document.

The main departure from Word you will encounter here is that PowerPoint is arranged into slides and sections instead of pages. To insert a slide, either click the

▼ FIGURE 8.2
Anatomy of
PowerPoint 2010

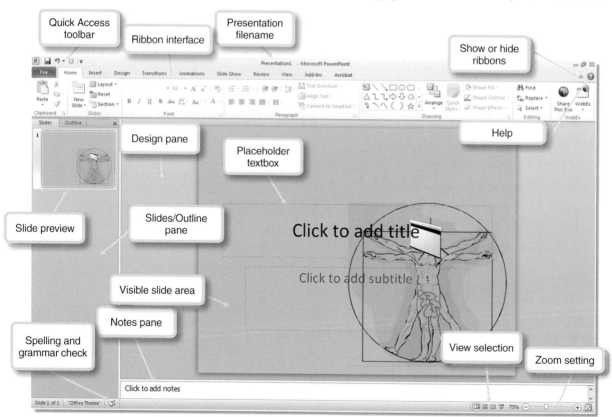

New Slide command on the *Home ribbon* or right-click the *Slides/Outline* pane on the left side of the interface. When you select the *New Slide* command, you can choose the type of layout you want for the slide you are inserting. If you use the right-click option, you will get a new slide with the default layout. Go ahead and add a few slides to familiarize yourself with the process and the available options.

The Insert ribbon, shown in Figure 8.3, is the next one down the line. You will visit this ribbon a lot if you plan to work frequently with media, which is really the main purpose of using PowerPoint! From this ribbon, you can insert just about anything you can imagine, from text boxes and pictures to clip art and equations, not to mention sounds and videos. Try it out by clicking *Shapes* in the *Illustrations* panel. Select a shape you like and place it into your slide. If you select a shape and just click on the slide, a predefined instance of the shape will be stamped into the slide. You can also click and drag to set the size of the shape yourself.

The next ribbon is the Design ribbon, shown in Figure 8.4; this is where you can select how you want your presentation to look. Go ahead and select something from the *Themes* panel. Notice how

doing so reformats your text and recolors any shapes that you did not modify. Each theme has a set color scheme and font choice, but you can change these using the Colors and Fonts menus; each of these has a drop-down list of predefined selections from which you can choose. You can also change the default effects that are applied to shapes within the presentation by clicking on *Effects*. The Background panel lets you change a number of settings, but for now select how you want your background to appear from a preset drop-down list of options under *Background Styles*. These will change based on the overall theme you have selected. Your presentation is starting to look fancy already!

Move on to the Slide Show ribbon, shown in Figure 8.5. (The Transitions ribbon is discussed later in this chapter, and the Animations ribbon is covered in Chapter 10, "Advanced Features of Presentation Software.") The Slide Show ribbon is useful for previewing how your slide show will look when it is presented. On the Start Slide Show panel, you can select either From Beginning or From Current Slide to start your show. Go ahead and select *From Beginning*. (You can also start your slide show from the beginning by pressing *F5* on your keyboard.)

◄ **FIGURE 8.3**
Insert ribbon in PowerPoint 2010

◄ **FIGURE 8.4**
Design ribbon in PowerPoint 2010

Chapter 8 — Introduction to PowerPoint and Presentation Software — **197**

You should now be in the Slide Show view; this is the view you will use whenever you are presenting. It resets your slides to the full size of the screen and hides the design interface of the software. You can move forward in your slides by clicking the mouse, pressing the spacebar, or using the right arrow key. You can move backward through your presentation by using the left arrow key. When you get to the end of your show, moving the presentation forward will display a black screen that says "End of slide show. Click to exit." Moving the presentation forward from this slide will take you out of the presentation mode and back into the Normal view you use for creation. You can also end the slide show at any time by pressing the Escape key.

The Review ribbon, shown in Figure 8.6, is similar to the one found in Word. You can use the Proofing panel to check spelling for your entire presentation, find research references, and use the thesaurus to find alternate words. You can also set your language preferences from this ribbon. Go ahead and click the *Spelling* icon. You should have no errors if you have not yet typed content into the slides! To run a check of spelling at any time, you can press the Spelling and Grammar Check icon at the bottom of the interface; the icon status will indicate if errors are found (a red *X* will appear in this case).

The View ribbon, shown in Figure 8.7, is where you customize the user interface for PowerPoint and format your slides. You can also select your view and arrange your slides from this ribbon and edit the Slide Master for your presentation. The *Slide Master* is a parent of all of the individual slides in your presentation. Formatting changes made to the Slide Master will affect all of the existing and future slides in your presentation. (This tool is covered in Chapter 9, "Creating Effective Presentations.")

There is also an Add-Ins ribbon on your page for any software that interacts with the Office suite. If you have Adobe Acrobat installed on your computer, you may also see a ribbon for that (called the Acrobat ribbon); this is an example of other programs that interoperate with the Office suite.

The largest portion of the interface is devoted to the current slide view. The lefthand side of the interface contains the Slides/Outline pane, which allows you to preview your slides and navigate between them quickly. The bottom of the interface displays the slide count, the currently selected theme, and several valuable quick

► **FIGURE 8.5**
Slide Show ribbon in PowerPoint 2010

► **FIGURE 8.6**
Review ribbon in PowerPoint 2010

links. You can select the view you want by clicking one of the view icons; this includes the Normal view for design, the Slide Sorter view for arranging your slides, and the Slide Show view for watching and presenting your slide show. Finally, you can shift the zoom percentage by moving the slide bar or fit your slide to the current window size by clicking the icon in the far-right corner. Now it's time to go deeper into the software and start creating your first presentation.

8.2.2 Microsoft PowerPoint 2011

PowerPoint 2011 has a concise interface, shown in Figure 8.8, that is very similar to its PowerPoint 2010 counterpart. Aside from some placement differences for certain tools, almost all of the functionality of PowerPoint 2010 is mirrored in PowerPoint 2011 and vice versa. The main menu of the software contains the File menu and a series of additional menus that provide shortcuts to commonly used tools, such as the Insert menu and the Arrange menu. The ribbons contain these functions as well, so it is up to you to decide your preferred method of accessing them.

The common icons to close, minimize, or maximize the presentation are directly beneath the main menu at the top of the free-floating window containing your presentation. As in all Mac software, clicking the close icon will exit your current presentation, but it will not quit the software; to

do this, you must select the *PowerPoint* menu and then select *Quit PowerPoint*.

The Quick Access toolbar for PowerPoint 2011 contains icons to allow you to save your work quickly, print your presentation, create a new presentation, open a presentation, and access help. There is also the Undo icon to allow you to undo any actions you made and the Redo icon to put back any changes you made with Undo. At the far righthand side of the interface is a text box to search your presentation for any keywords you enter.

A **SLIDE** *was originally a small color transparency that was intended to be projected to a larger surface to assist in visualization. This term has been carried over to digital presentation software as the unit of the presentation, similar to a page in a text document.*

The ribbon interface is directly beneath the Quick Access toolbar. The default ribbon is the Home ribbon, which contains tools to modify text, change fonts, and insert new elements into your slides. PowerPoint 2011 combines most of the functionality of the Home ribbon and the Insert ribbon from PowerPoint 2010 into its Home ribbon. The New Slide icon is at the far left of the Home ribbon; this is used to add slides to your presentation. The Home ribbon also contains the Arrange icon, which is used to arrange elements in your presentation; this will be

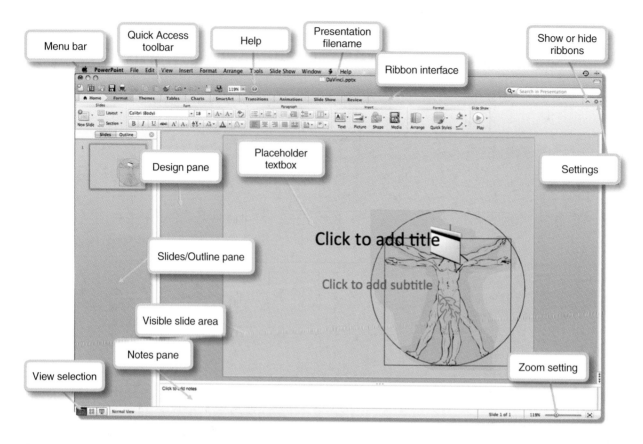

Menu bar | Quick Access toolbar | Help | Presentation filename | Ribbon interface | Show or hide ribbons

Design pane | Placeholder textbox | Settings

Slides/Outline pane

Visible slide area

Notes pane

View selection

Zoom setting

▲ **FIGURE 8.8**
Anatomy of
PowerPoint 2011

visited often in the course of developing your presentation.

The next ribbon of interest is the Themes ribbon, shown in Figure 8.9. This is where you set the look and feel of your presentation. There are a number of preset options from which you can select. Go ahead and choose one that you like and click on your selection to apply it to the presentation. The new theme will set defaults for the color, font, and background settings of your slides. You can make changes to these defaults at any time using the Colors, Fonts, and Background icons. There is a large selection of preset color

schemes and font styles available; you can also use these menus to define your own.

The next several ribbons are used for more advanced functionality, so skip to the Slide Show ribbon, shown in Figure 8.10. This is used to set up your presentation views and timing for when you are presenting your slide show. Go ahead and click the *From Start* icon. This will put you into the Slide Show view, which is the view you will use to present your document to an audience. You can move your presentation forward by using the spacebar or the right arrow key and backward by using the left arrow key. To get out of Slide Show view

▼ **FIGURE 8.9**
Themes ribbon in
PowerPoint 2011

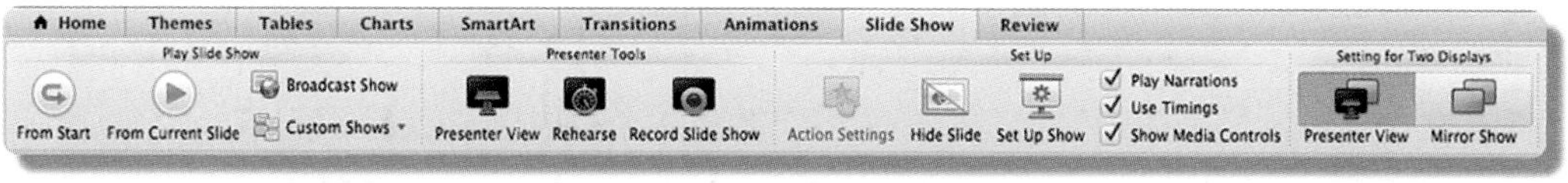

◀ **FIGURE 8.10**
Slide Show ribbon
in PowerPoint 2011

◀ **FIGURE 8.11**
Review ribbon in
PowerPoint 2011

and back to the Normal view used to design your slides, press the *Escape* key.

The Review ribbon, shown in Figure 8.11, contains the functionality to compare versions of your presentation. It also allows you to add and delete comments in your slides and to set permissions for the presentation. Beneath the ribbon interface to the left is the Slides/Outline pane, which allows you to preview and quickly navigate to your slides by clicking on them. The main pane of the interface window is the slide Design pane. This contains the editable copy of your slide.

At the bottom of the interface, you can select your view via quick links; these include the Normal view for editing, the Slide Sorter view for arranging your slides, and the Slide Show view for watching or presenting your slide show. You can also adjust the zoom of your slides by changing the slide bar at the lower-right corner. Now that you have taken the tour of the software interface, you can start using the tools to construct your first presentation!

8.3 DIVING INTO PRESENTATIONS

For your first foray into PowerPoint, you will construct a presentation on a very familiar subject: you! On the first slide, the *title slide*, you will see two *placeholder text boxes*. These text boxes contain text such as "Click to add …" that will disappear the instant you start typing in one of them. An example of the title slide is shown in Figure 8.12. Go ahead and type your name in the title placeholder.

Text Formatting

8.3.1

After you have entered your name, you will add some text formatting to make it look spectacular. PowerPoint offers most of the same text effects as Word. The differences are that there is no highlighting in PowerPoint and the Text Effects feature in PowerPoint 2010 is located on a separate, context-sensitive Format ribbon. Right-clicking on a text box activates a

▼ **FIGURE 8.12**
Example title slide

formatting menu with common links for text modification. You can see both of these in Figure 8.13.

Change the font of the text to something suitable and stylish and change the text to bold by clicking the *Bold* icon or pressing the *Ctrl-B* keys at the same time. Increase the font size by a single increment using the *Increase Font Size* icon. Note that you must select either the box surrounding the text or all of the text to apply your font changes to everything in the box; otherwise the changes will affect only the word in which the cursor is placed. You can change the size to a specific value with the drop-down box; this will accept a number (with or without a decimal point) as input, so you can define a size that is not part of the predefined selection options. Increase the font until the text covers most of the slide. Now your name has some presence!

If you have a long name, it may split into two lines. To keep your first name and last name on the same line, you can widen the placeholder box by clicking on one of the square selection points around the perimeter of the text box, as shown in Figure 8.14. The left square selection point will only move the left edge of the box, and the right square selection point will only move the right edge of the box. Picking one of the round corner selection points lets you change both the width and height at the same time.

Switch the text alignment to the left by selecting the *Align Text Left* icon (or by pressing *Ctrl-L*) or to the right by selecting the *Align Text Right* icon (*Ctrl-R*). This is helpful to remember when you need to line up headings and text with one edge or the other. Titles, however, look better centered,

If you are using a Mac, the Control (Ctrl) key shortcuts all work the same way, but they use the Command (or Apple) key instead of the Control key.

▶ **FIGURE 8.13**
Format ribbon and right-click menu for text boxes

▲ **FIGURE 8.14** Selection points on a text box

so put your name back where it was by clicking the *Align Text Center* icon (*Ctrl-E*).

Now your name is starting to show some pizzazz, but you should give it more flair by adding text effects. The various text effects are in the Format ribbon, which is context sensitive and appears whenever you click in a text box. Text effects are another type of formatting that adds elements like shadow, glow, reflection, and outlines to the letters in the text box. To apply an effect, you must select the text to which you want the effect to apply. To apply the effect to all of the text in the box, you can select the box surrounding the text. Some text effects. like 3-D Rotation and Transform. apply to the entire content of the text box and cannot be applied to individual letters or words.

You can select a predefined overall style from the Word Art Styles panel of the context-sensitive Format ribbon or you can change elements individually. Give your name some depth by adding a shadow. To do so, click the *Text Effects* icon, select *Shadow* from the drop-down list, and then select the one you want. You can also set the perspective of the shadow (the angle of the implied light source) by selecting one of the options at the end of the drop-down menu.

PowerPoint 2011 places a Text Effects icon on the lower-right corner of the Font panel of the Home ribbon.

Clicking *Shadow Options* will allow you to fine-tune the parameters to get your shadow effect just right. The *Distance* parameter, for example, will determine how far away the shadow is from your object.

If you would like to use a reflection instead, cancel the shadow by selecting *Text Effects*, then *Shadow*, and *No Shadow*. Too many text effects at once can ruin the appeal of your display. Now that you are back to plain text, select *Text Effects*, then *Reflection*, and choose a reflection variation you like. Keep the reflection effect for this project, but to cancel it, select the *No Reflection* option in the drop-down menu. You can also fine-tune the reflection by selecting *Reflection Options* just as you did for the shadow effect.

Click on the *subtitle* placeholder. Rather than enter text here, click on the outer perimeter of the subtitle placeholder box and get rid of it by pressing the *Delete* key or the *Backspace* key. You can do this to remove any placeholders that you do not want or to remove any objects you have added that you no longer like. You should now see a slide similar to Figure 8.15 except with your name in the box and the background style that you chose earlier.

Inserting and Formatting Shapes

8.3.2

Now you are going to show everyone what a superstar you are. If you are using PowerPoint 2010, switch over to the *Insert ribbon* and select the *Shapes* icon; if you are using PowerPoint 2011, the *Shape* icon is on the *Home ribbon*. Pick a star from the drop-down list and click inside the slide.

▲ FIGURE 8.15
Completed example

This should stamp an instance of the shape wherever you click.

You can format the star by using the right-click menu or the familiar Format ribbon that appears whenever you click on a shape. This time it will be the *Shape Styles* panel in which you will find what you need. With the shape selected, right-clicking and selecting *Format Shape* will open a dialog box that lets you alter the properties of your star (this is the same dialog box that you get by selecting the expansion icon on the Shape Styles panel in PowerPoint 2010). The Format Shape dialog box is shown in Figure 8.16.

First, change the star's outline to something thick. Select *Line Style* in PowerPoint 2010; select *Line*, then *Weights & Arrows*, then *Style* in PowerPoint 2011. Increase the *Width* to *3 pt*. This should make the outline nice and bold. The *Dash Type* (or *Dashed*) setting determines how the line appears, whether you want a solid line or a dotted line that implies the shape.

In PowerPoint 2010, click on the *Line Color* item in the menu. You have a choice of No Line, Solid Line, or Gradient Line. Having no line would defeat the purpose of making it thicker, so opt for *Solid Line*. In PowerPoint 2011, select either the *Solid* or *Gradient* tab of the *Line* menu to change these settings; select *Solid* and you should see the *Color* setting. Next, you need to choose a color that will work with your background but make the star stand out all the same; choose whatever color you like.

On the *Fill* menu, shown in Figure 8.17, you are going to make your star stand out by selecting a *Gradient* option. This menu will allow you to select from a set number of different gradients; if you are using PowerPoint 2010, you can pick one of the predefined gradients from the Preset Colors list.

You can set Type to *Linear* if you want the gradient to go from left to right or top to bottom or to *Radial* if you want it to start in the center and work its way around a curve. The stops of the gradient are shown on the bar beneath these settings. You can add or delete stops, but the program will interpolate the color from one stop to the next. Click on any of the stops to change the color yourself. The Rotate with shape option determines whether the gradient is created based on the orientation of the slide or the orientation of the shape itself.

Shortcuts to the Line and Fill menu options are available on the Format ribbon.

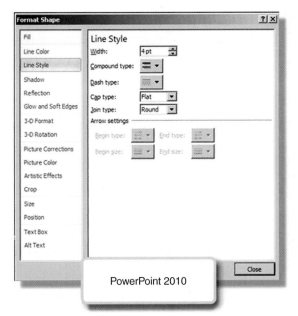

PowerPoint 2010

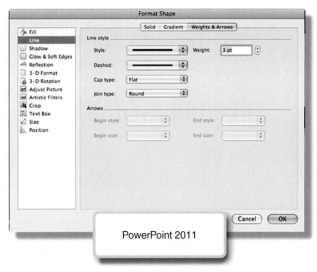

PowerPoint 2011

▼ **FIGURE 8.16** Format Shape dialog box for line settings

When you are done setting the color, click *Close* (or *OK*) to exit the dialog box. You can now resize the star based on just how big of a superstar you are. Use either the round corner grab points or the square midpoint grab points to change the size of the shape. The green circle can be used to rotate the shape. Simply click and hold the green circle and give your shape a spin. You may see one or more small yellow

diamonds inside your shape. These control internal parameters of the shape; for instance, this will set how fat or skinny the triangular legs of your star become.

Finally, make that star shine. Click on the star and select the *Format ribbon*. Click the *Shape Effects* icon, select *Glow*, and pick a glow that fits your star. You can also set the color of the glow by selecting *More Glow Colors* (or *Glow Options*

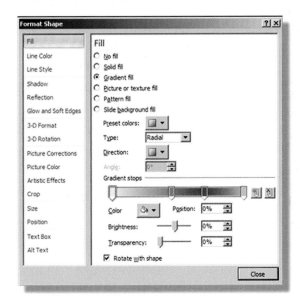

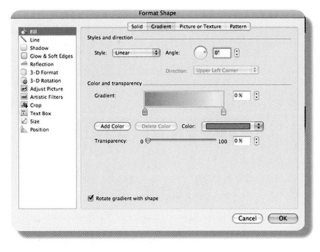

▼ **FIGURE 8.17**
Format Shape dialog box for gradient fill settings

similarly to using the predefined styles for text formatting on the *Format ribbon*. In PowerPoint 2010, choose a style from the menu that appears.

This action will create a text box in your slide. Change the text inside to *Super* and position it where you want it on the slide. This works just like any other text box with some of the settings completed for you. You can still change the font and the size, along with any other properties.

Click on your new text box and go to the *Format ribbon* that appears. Select the *Text Effects* icon and then select *Transform*. Pick a transformation for your text. Now go back to the *Home ribbon* and change the font color or the font. The transformation and overall formatting that was defined should remain intact. Small pink diamonds in your text box will control properties like the angle of the text slant when you click on them and slide them in one direction or another.

in PowerPoint 2011) from the menu. This will open a color picker from which you can cahoose the color you want your star to shine. When you are done, you should have a shining star beneath your name as in Figure 8.18.

Now you need to add the "Super" to your star. To do this in PowerPoint 2010, select the *Insert ribbon* and pick the *WordArt* icon; in PowerPoint 2011, select *WordArt* from the drop-down list under *Text* on the *Home ribbon*. This works

Maybe you are more of a rockstar than a superstar. It is easy enough to change the text to represent that. Just double-click the text box to select it and all of its contents. Now type *Rock* in the box. There you go! Now you have instant "Rockstar" status, and you are just getting started! Compare your rockstar results to Figure 8.19, which shows the elements you should have when you are finished.

Inserting, Manipulating, and Cropping Images

It is time to show your smiling face to the world. Go to the second slide in your presentation. If you have not added a second

slide yet, simply right-click in the *Slides/Outline* pane and select *New Slide*. This second slide should have the default layout for a slide, which consists of a slide title placeholder text box and a single box for content, as shown in Figure 8.20. You are going to add a picture here, so you may want to pick a nice image of yourself. For those of you who are camera shy, you can use an image of a monkey making a silly face instead.

Before you start typing in the content box, which will eliminate the quick links, select the *Insert Picture from File* icon on the slide. This is the same as selecting *Picture* on the *Insert ribbon* (*Picture* is on the *Home ribbon* in PowerPoint 2011); it just saves you a few clicks of the mouse. Using the quick link allows you to select the image and then insert and center it under the title of the slide. Notice that this will replace the placeholder text box entirely. Go ahead and give your slide a title and make sure it is appropriate for what the slide contains, like A Silly Monkey or something. Quickly practice your text modification techniques and create a style to make your title stand out from the background.

Now click back on the image you just inserted. You will see a new ribbon along

▲ FIGURE 8.20
New slide with the default layout

the top of the interface. This is the *Format ribbon for Picture Tools* (the *Format Picture ribbon* in PowerPoint 2011). As you can see from Figure 8.21, this ribbon contains a lot of tools for making your picture look superb.

On the *Picture Styles* panel, select one of the predefined styles that will make the image look like an old printout from a handheld instant camera. Something with a nice thick white border will be perfect. That looks more professional already! On the *Adjust* panel, select the *Corrections* icon; this allows you to increase or decrease the brightness, contrast, and sharpness of the image. The original image will appear in the center of the options, and you can adjust it by clicking one of the options

▼ FIGURE 8.21
Format ribbon for Picture Tools in PowerPoint 2010 and Format Picture ribbon in PowerPoint 2011

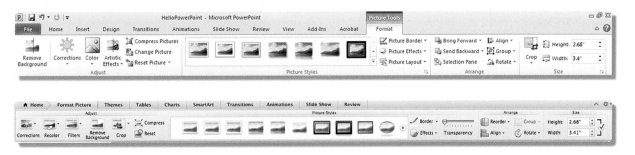

There are a number of settings that can be used to correct a picture that is inserted into PowerPoint. There is a preview visualization of the effect whenever a transformation is selected, but the following list will help you understand these transformation terms:

- **COLOR SATURATION**—This is the term for how pure the color is; the higher the saturation, the purer the color. The primary colors red, blue, and green are the purest (and most saturated) colors.

- **COLOR TONE**—The color tone is how light or dark the color is. Each color can produce a spectrum of tones. The tone value is relative, so the surrounding colors will affect the perception of the tone.

- **SHARPEN AND SOFTEN**—This setting will vary how clear the differentiation is between neighboring pixels of the image. Sharpen will increase the differentiation by more strongly defining boundaries in the image. Soften will decrease the differentiation by blending together the colors of the image.

- **BRIGHTNESS AND CONTRAST**—Brightness is the threshold for the color level that registers as black; higher brightness means there are more colors allowed between pure white and pure black. Contrast is a measure of the spectrum of colors between pure white and pure black; higher contrast will generally show more granular detail of the image.

around it. Increase the contrast slightly to give your photo a richer tone.

Now turn your photo to grayscale. You can do this by selecting the *Color* icon in the *Adjust* panel (this is called *Recolor* in PowerPoint 2011). This gives you options to select the color saturation, color tone, and recolor options. Under *Recolor*, select *Grayscale*. The Adjust panel has some other useful items as well. Along the right side of the Adjust panel are the following options:

- *Compress Picture* will reduce the file size of the PowerPoint file by sampling the picture to the necessary resolution for the screen.

- *Reset Picture* will undo all of the formatting you added since inserting the image at the beginning.

The next thing you need to do is crop the image so that it focuses better on the subject. Cropping allows you to remove parts from the top, bottom, left, or right of the image that you do not want to display. Click on the image and then select *Crop* on the *(Picture) Format ribbon*. Now you can use any of the grab points on the image and move them in toward the center to cut off portions of the image you do not want instead of just resizing the image in place. This process is shown in Figure 8.22.

> **CROPPING** *is the act of cutting off outer portions of an image or object. This is the digital equivalent of using scissors to cut off pieces of an image on paper.*

The *Crop* icon has some other useful options. For instance, you can crop your image to a drawing shape. Selecting any of these options will override your manual cropping. There are two more predefined options that you may find useful:

- *Crop to Fill* causes the entire image to be forced to the area defined by

▲ **FIGURE 8.22** Cropping an image

cropping. This will fill the cropped space with as much of the image as possible, cutting off only what is necessary to preserve the defined space.

- *Crop to Fit* causes the image to be forced in its entirety to the defined space. This may cause gaps in the display if no image information is available to match the space defined.

You can click and drag the image you have inserted to resize it just like any other drawing or graphic object inserted into your slides. The one thing you must remember with pictures is that you should always maintain the original aspect ratio of the image. Otherwise, faces and bodies will look stretched or pinched when you distort the image. This not only looks bad, but it will also grab the attention of your audience in a negative way because their eyes will be drawn to the distortion instead of what you want them to see.

ASPECT RATIO *is the longer dimension of an object divided by the shorter dimension. This is the ratio that should be preserved whenever any changes are made to an object to avoid distortion. The aspect ratio of a standard 5 x 3 photograph is 5:3.*

8.3.4 Arranging, Linking, and Grouping Elements

The old saying is that a picture is worth a thousand words. Well, you are going to add a few more for your picture. Before you get to that, though, you need to move the image back into alignment after it has been cropped. The image was originally centered in the placeholder, but the changes made to it have altered its position on the slide.

The alignment commands are under the Arrange icon in the Home ribbon. Click on *Arrange* and scroll down to *Align*; you should see all of the options for orienting your picture around the screen. The full path is shown in Figure 8.23. These alignment commands work on any element you insert into your presentation. You can also find a shortcut to the alignment options (as an Align icon) on the context-sensitive Format ribbons that appear.

ALIGNMENT *in terms of layout is the relative placement of an object with respect to the overall environment, which in this case is the slide.*

Make sure the *Align to Slide* box has a check mark beside it. This will make all of your alignment adjustments relative to the slide itself. If this is not checked, the elements will align relative to each other. Click the *Align Center* item in the menu to line up your photo to the center of the slide. Click on the photo and press the up or down arrow keys to move it to the center of the lower portion of the slide beneath the title. You can hold down the *Control* (Ctrl) key on your keyboard and press the arrows to move it a smaller distance for each arrow press.

Now you are going to revisit the *Shapes* icon and select a rectangle. You can just pick one and click in your slide to stamp it down, or you can make your selection and click and drag on the slide to set the size yourself. Click on your new rectangle and copy it. You can do this by right-clicking on the object and selecting *Copy* or you can press *Ctrl-C*

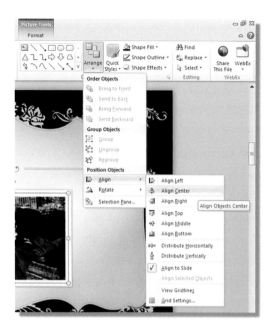

on the keyboard with the object selected. Now paste two more rectangles into your slide.

In PowerPoint 2010, you can do this by right-clicking where you want the rectangle to appear and selecting *Picture* under the *Paste Options*. You can also do this by pressing *Ctrl-V* on the keyboard, which will give you the default paste settings. In PowerPoint 2011, selecting *Paste* from the right-click menu or pressing the shortcut keys to paste will result in a copy placed on top of the original but slightly to the right and down.

Click on one of the rectangles and start typing. Type a descriptive word for the image, such as *Charming*, and notice how the shape automatically accepts the text. Now add two more descriptive words to the other rectangles; you could try *Witty* and *Slobbery*, for instance. Almost all of the drawing shapes allow you to directly insert text into them; the area of the shape

allocated for text will vary, so the length of text may be limited depending on the shape you choose. You can format these shapes just as you did the star in the previous example, and you can format the text inside the shapes as well.

There is a special kind of shape that can connect two elements in your slide. These are found under the *Line* (or *Lines and Connectors*) heading in the *Shapes* menu. Click on an arrow that you like and your cursor will change to a crosshair. Whenever you roll your mouse over an element, you will see small red squares appear; these are linking points for the shape. You can connect a line from one of these linking points to another or draw a line without linking it. For this

In PowerPoint 2010, you can hold down the *Alt* key to allow you to freely move the line's endpoint when you are dragging an arrow; otherwise, the endpoint will align to the closest internal grid point available.

example, you will place one end of the line on the rectangles containing the descriptive words and link the other end to the picture.

If you connect an endpoint of your line to an element, the line will stay connected even if that element is moved. An unconnected end will not stay where it is placed when an object to which it is connected is moved; it will move around with the rest of the object to which it is connected. If neither end is connected, the object will have to be moved manually just like any other object.

To format the ends of your arrows and change how they are displayed, you can use both the usual tools for formatting and the *Format Shape* dialog box, which contains the arrow settings in the panel under *Line Styles* (you need to select *Line* and then *Weights & Arrows* in PowerPoint 2011). Here you can change the Begin Type (Begin Style) or End Type (Begin Style) for the arrow (which affects either the initial or final point of the arrow, respectively) and set the size you want for each; this is shown in Figure 8.24.

Link the rest of your rectangles to your photo with arrows. Format the arrows so they are clearly visible on the slide. You may notice that the arrows you place are on top of the rectangles; this is because any new element added to your slide automatically gets placed in the highest layer available. You will want to put your rectangles on top of the arrows to make the slide look more presentable. To do this, you will need to change the layer on which these elements reside. Think of these items like sheets of paper in a stack. To move an element to the top of the stack, you need to bring it forward. To move it to the bottom of the stack, you need to send it back. You can think of the slide background as the table on which this stack is sitting; nothing can be sent behind the slide itself.

There are two ways to change the layer of an element. You can right-click the element and choose either *Bring to Front* or *Send to Back* (to put it on the very top or bottom, respectively) or use *Bring Forward* or *Send Backward* to change the layer by one position at a time. You can also select the element and click the *Arrange* icon. In PowerPoint 2010, *Order Objects* is the first

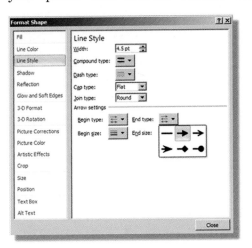

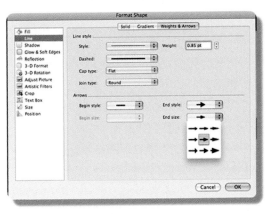

◄ FIGURE 8.24
Arrow settings

PowerPoint 2011 has a great feature to visualize the layers on the slide and allow you to rearrange them. Under the *Arrange* icon, you can select *Reorder Objects* or *Reorder Overlapping Objects*. This launches a visual display of the layers in your slide that you can click and drag to reorder as shown in Figure 8.25. This is also a great visualization of the layers to determine what is visible to the viewer.

▲ FIGURE 8.26 Completed example with grouping

> ➤ **FIGURE 8.25**
> Visualizing layers in
> PowerPoint 2011

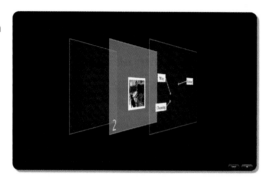

heading you will see on this menu, and it contains all of your options for adjusting the layer. Select each rectangle and choose *Bring to Front*.

Now that you have a nice arrangement for your elements (you should have all of the same elements as in Figure 8.26), you do not want anyone to accidentally move something around if they edit your presentation. A good solution to this is to create a *group* for these objects so they all act like a single element in the slide.

To create a group, click outside of the group and hold down the mouse button while you drag your cursor over all of the items you want to group. Then you can either right-click within the group and select *Group* or you can go to the *Home ribbon*, select the *Arrange* icon, and select *Group*. You can also hold

down the *Shift* key while clicking on each object you want to group and then follow the steps to create the group.

You can still select individual objects from the group by clicking on any one of them (as in Figure 8.26). If you decide these objects need to be separated, click on the whole group, right-click, and select *Ungroup* (this is also available as an option under the *Arrange* icon on the *Home ribbon*). If they need to be put back together, select *Regroup* and the old group will be back together again.

> Note that if an object is inserted into a placeholder, it cannot be included in a group. To get around this, copy the element, paste the copy, and delete the original and the placeholder. The copy can then be included in the group.

Adding Text and Hyperlinks

8.3.5

Now it is time to start adding text to the PowerPoint presentation. Before you use PowerPoint to write that novel you have been planning, there are some things you should know about what PowerPoint should and should not be. First of all, there are two main reasons to construct a PowerPoint document: to create a visual supplement to a presentation and to create a small multimedia presentation for sharing on a computer. PowerPoint text should be brief and easy to read, no matter what purpose the presentation has. You should always keep your bullet points short and meaningful. Presentation software is excellent at showcasing information when it is used in this manner. If you are giving your PowerPoint presentation to an audience, you have to keep readability in mind. Small fonts and changing styles on the same slide are difficult to read.

Add a third slide for your presentation about yourself. Here you are going to explore some of the tools for adding and modifying text in a PowerPoint slide. You can choose here whether you want to include a list of foods you like to eat or a list of hobbies you enjoy; both of these would help describe you and are a good fit for a casual presentation like this. Whichever you choose, go ahead and type a title for your slide. Practice your formatting skills by making sure it matches the appearance of the title text on the slide with your photo on it.

Now choose four or five items to support your title. The example in Figure 8.27 shows five things to eat that begin with the letter *P*. Click in the placeholder text box of the slide (with a default layout) and type your items in a similar manner. You should notice that these are formatted as a list; this is the default format and it makes it easy to distinguish your points. In a

▲ FIGURE 8.27
Bulleted list in the default slide arrangement

presentation, the text does not have to be in complete sentences; the essential thing is to get your points across in as clear and concise a manner as possible.

You should also notice how you have a lot of space left over on this slide. You can either add subtext to each bullet or increase the font size to take up more space. If this is being used for a visual presentation on a projector or screen behind you, make sure you change the font to a sans serif font (such as Arial or Calibri). All those text decorations (the serifs) make the text more difficult to read on a projection. If the presentation is being shared by computer, serif fonts are fine because it is closer to print media format.

Expand your list a little bit by choosing a topic for which you want to add subtext. Note that you should only add subtext if you have at least two things to say about a topic. A single element of subtext looks messy and unorganized; it is also a violation of the rules of outlining. Click on the line for which you want to add text; place your cursor at the end of the text and hit the *Enter* key.

You should see a new line beneath your text with a new bullet beside it that looks grayed out as if it is not completely there. If you start typing now, you will enter text at the same level (level 1) as the original item, so press the *Tab* key to turn this line into subtext for the line above it. Now you should see the bullet type change and the text cursor indent farther into the page to the right. Your text will now be smaller and it will be formatted as the next level down (level 2) in terms of your outline. You can see this in action in Figure 8.28.

You can modify your text using the *Paragraph* panel of the *Home ribbon*. This is where you can change the bullet styles for your slide or even change them to numbers if you need your list to be in a specific order. Unless you make the change in the *Slide Master*, this only changes the bullet style for the current slide in which you are working and only for the bullet points that you have highlighted when you click the icon.

▼ FIGURE 8.28
Two-level bullet list

In PowerPoint 2010, if you type too much text for one slide, a little box will pop up to give you options on what to do. You can choose to change your slide layout or split the content of the text box between two slides. You should always take note when this box appears because it means your slide is starting to get too crowded.

You can set a number of other useful properties with the Paragraph panel, including changing the direction of your text, the number of columns, or the text alignment inside the text box. You can adjust the line spacing and indentation of the text as well.

Now create a new slide (this should be the fourth slide of your presentation); this is where you are going to add some contact information so all of your fans can reach you once they see how great you are. For the title of the slide, add the text *How to Reach Me* and make sure you format it to match the titles of the rest of your slides. This is good practice and it keeps your slides from looking out of place when you click from one to the next.

Consider carefully what you want to add to this page. You probably do not want to give out your home address or personal phone number on a slide that can be seen by anyone. If you have a Facebook or Myspace according to official Web site page or an e-mail address that you don't mind being seen (and used) by the public, you can add those here. When you type any text into PowerPoint that matches the format for a Web site or e-mail address, PowerPoint will automatically convert the text into a

hyperlink. Just like a hyperlink on the Web, when you click on this text, it will either take you to the location specified or open your e-mail account so you can send a message to this address.

Unless you have multiple links or addresses, you probably do not need a bullet point for this slide. To get rid of bullet points on this or any slide, just click at the beginning of the text and press the *Backspace* key (or the *Delete* key for PowerPoint 2011). The bullet point will disappear and your text will no longer be in outline format. With just one item on the page, there is a lot of empty space that can make your slide look bad, even if you increase the font size dramatically.

To correct this, move your link to the horizontal center of the slide by selecting the *Center* icon to center the text (which you can find under the *Paragraph* panel of the *Home ribbon*). You can also move your text to the vertical center of the text box by selecting the *Middle* item in the *Align Text* menu that opens; this icon is in the same panel as the horizontal text alignment options. Your text should now be centered within the text box; note that this does not center it on the slide or center the text box itself.

Now you can use the font tools to increase the size of the link so it takes up more space. Remember that readability is crucial for a presentation, so you may want to stretch your text box so you can increase the size of the hyperlink beyond the original box size to make it easier to see. If you change the width of the text box, make sure you use the selections in the *Arrange* icon

to align it back to the horizontal center of your slide. You can change the font, text effects, and style just like you would any other text in your presentation. The exception to this is the color of the hyperlink text.

To give the color of the link a higher level of contrast to the background, you must set the Hyperlink color in the theme color settings. In PowerPoint 2010, you access this setting in the *Design ribbon* by selecting the *Colors* icon of the *Themes* panel and selecting *Create New Theme Colors*. In PowerPoint 2011, you access this setting by selecting the *Themes ribbon*, selecting *Colors*, and then selecting *Create Theme Colors*. A dialog box like the one in Figure 8.29 will open and you can select the color you want for your link by using the color picker for *Hyperlink*.

Once you click *Save* (or *Apply to All* in PowerPoint 2011) in this dialog box, all of the hyperlinks in your presentation will be updated to the new color. PowerPoint treats your hyperlink colors as all or nothing, so you should be sure that the color you choose works on all of your slides. Note that you can give a name to your custom color scheme in this dialog box as well if you want to use it later. If you do not, it will still appear with the default name *Custom1* in this presentation because it is now in use.

If you want your text to display something other than an e-mail address or the URL to which you are linking, you can use the *Hyperlink* icon. In PowerPoint 2010, you will find this under the *Links* panel of the *Insert ribbon*; in PowerPoint 2011, you will find the *Hyperlink* icon as an entry in the

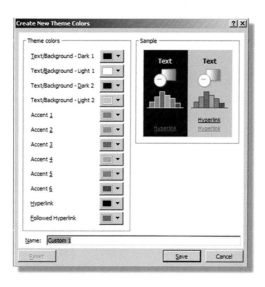

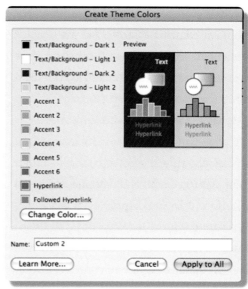

Text icon menu on the *Home ribbon*. Clicking this icon will open a dialog box in which you can select another document, enter a URL for a Web site, or enter an e-mail address. You can change the text that will be visible on the document for the link in the *Text to display* (or *Display*) box. You can also click on the *ScreenTip* button to enter text that will appear if the mouse hovers over the link. If you are not using the address of the link itself, you may want to add the address to the ScreenTip text so a user will know where they are headed when they click the hyperlink. The ScreenTip will only display in the Slide Show view, as shown in Figure 8.30. It will not appear in the Normal view as you are editing the document.

If you add a hyperlink that you later decide you do not want, you can select any part of the text that contains the hyperlink,

right-click, and select *Remove Hyperlink* in PowerPoint 2010 or you can click on the *Hyperlink* icon and click *Remove Link* on the open Edit Hyperlink dialog box. In PowerPoint 2011, right-click the link, select *Hyperlink*, then *Edit Hyperlink*, and then click *Remove Hyperlink* on the dialog box that opens. Another way to remove the link in either version is to place your cursor just past the last letter of the hyperlink. Click *Backspace* (or *Delete* in PowerPoint 2011) on the keyboard and you should see the underline disappear; now your link is gone.

> If you have typed a URL or e-mail address, pressing the spacebar after the address will create an automatic link, no matter how many times you have removed it!

Clip Art and Screenshots   8.3.6

You may be thinking that these last two slides you have made are not very visually interesting. Since presentation software is a visual medium for expression,

it makes sense to add some visual elements. The most common of these elements by far is clip art. Microsoft maintains an enormous repository of clip art images for you to use to enhance your documents. Select the slide with the list of items you created. If you have been following along, this should be Slide 3. You are going to add an element of clip art to this page to enhance your presentation. The handling of clip art is significantly different in PowerPoint 2010 and PowerPoint 2011, so separate sections have been provided to guide you on how to get the same results in either program.

8.3.6.1 Clip Art in Office 2010

Adding clip art is fully integrated into the PowerPoint 2010 and Word 2010 environments. Go to the *Images* panel in the *Insert ribbon* and select *Clip Art*. The Clip Art panel, shown in Figure 8.31, will appear on the side of your interface. This contains the search box and results of your quest for clip art.

Enter a term in the *Search for* box and then select where you would like PowerPoint to search for the artwork. If you have just installed the program, you probably do not have too many options in your local folders, so you should include Office.com content in your searches whenever possible. Using this option requires you to be connected to the Internet. When you click on one of the results, you will see a menu of options.

The first choice is to insert the image into the current slide. You can also copy it to the clipboard so you can paste it into any location that accepts image data (inside the application or elsewhere) or

you can select *Make Available Offline* to add it to your local media collection. If you choose this option from the list, you will be prompted to identify where you want to store the file.

Clip Art in Office 2011 8.3.6.2

PowerPoint 2011 has two options for directly inserting clip art into your presentation. The first is called the Clip Art Browser (which is shown in Figure 8.32); you can access this by clicking on the

➤ **FIGURE 8.32**
Clip Art Browser in
PowerPoint 2011

Picture icon on the *Home ribbon* to open
the menu where you can select *Clip Art
Browser*. This will open a panel of locally
stored and indexed clip art images. If you

want to place one of these images in
the slide, just click on the image and
drag it to the slide. You will see a small
green plus sign on the image when you
are over an area where it can be placed.

The second option is to select *Clip Art
Gallery*, which is also found on the menu
under *Picture* in the *Home ribbon*. This
option will launch a standalone application called Microsoft Clip Gallery, shown
in Figure 8.33. Here you can search for
a specific item you want or select categories. You can also configure your clip
art categories, image classifications, and
image tags and add new media to your
collection using the Import button. To
add one of the clip art items to your slide,
select the graphic you want and click the
Insert button.

➤ **FIGURE 8.33**
Microsoft Clip Art
Gallery

8.3.6.3 Getting Clip Art from Office.com

Whether you are using PowerPoint or the OpenOffice.org alternative software, you can download clips from Office.com (*www.office.com*) to add to your presentation or document. Simply go to the Office.com site and select the *Images* tab. You will then be able to select a category and perform a search on existing clip art within the Office.com repository. If you do not find what you want in that category, you can use the navigation pane on the lefthand side to change the category or find results from all categories. If you visit the site using Microsoft Internet Explorer, the ActiveX® tools allow you to copy the image directly from the site to your system clipboard, as shown in Figure 8.34. You can then simply use the Paste function (or Ctrl-P) to paste the item into your slides.

If you visit Office.com with an Internet Browser other than Internet Explorer, you can still use the clip art that is offered, but you have to download it to a local folder on your machine to make use of it. You do this by clicking on the clip art graphic you want and selecting *Download*, as shown in Figure 8.35. You can add this image into your clip art repository by importing it into your media manager for your version of the Office suite.

Handling Clip Art 8.3.6.4

Once you have inserted the clip art image you want into your slide, you can manipulate it just like any other image, including recoloring it, adding shadows and effects, or reorienting it to suit your needs. You can open the *Rotate* (or *Rotate and Flip*) menu item in the *Arrange* icon menu to select common adjustments like *Flip Horizontal*.

You should take note that visual elements added to your page will make it more visually interesting, but they will distract the viewer from the text itself. The eye will focus on the location with the most visual information, which will typically be the image; this means your audience will see a picture before they see the text that goes with it. Too much of a good thing can turn bad when it comes to clip art. Limit your slides to a single

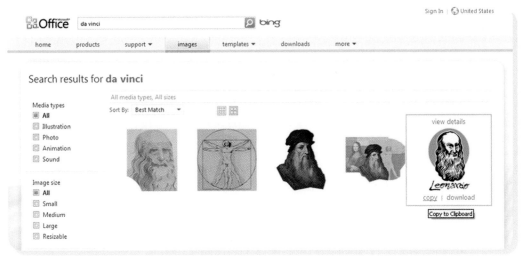

◀ FIGURE 8.34
Clip Art options from Office.com using Internet Explorer

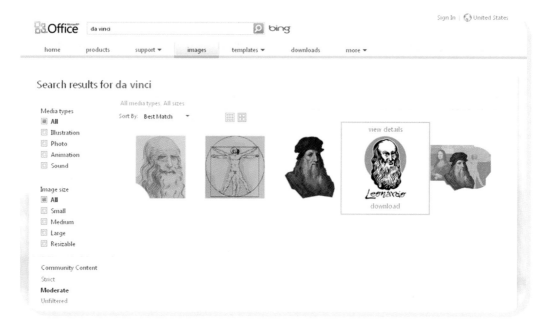

clip art image unless you have a specific point that you are making with the visual component.

Now it is time to make the same enhancements to the contact page. Select a clip art graphic that signifies an e-mail. This is typically an envelope, sometimes with an @ symbol on top of it. You can use the keyword "e-mail" to find clip art appropriate for your page. Select an image you like that fits with the style of your presentation, and add this to the slide with the e-mail contact address. Resize it to appear beneath your e-mail address as shown in Figure 8.37.

You will probably find that there is not enough space at the bottom of your slide for both of these elements. You can move your e-mail address up in this instance without changing its alignment by adding blank lines to the text. To do this, just place your cursor past the last letter of the e-mail address. Hit the *Enter* key until the text is above the image. Align your clip art image to the center of your slide.

Now you are going to add an action to the clip art so that clicking on the envelope opens an e-mail client with the address you have listed as the recipient. This is essentially the same behavior as the hyperlink itself, but it allows the image to act as a button. Select the clip art image and click on the *Action* icon of the *Links* panel in the *Insert ribbon*.

Adding an action to an object in your presentation allows you to do all sorts of advanced things on your PowerPoint slides. In PowerPoint 2010, you can find the *Action* icon on the *Insert ribbon*. In PowerPoint 2011, *Action Settings* is part of the right-click menu; it can also be found as an icon on the *Slide Show ribbon*. It is not the best tool to use if you are giving a linear presentation to an audience, but if you are sharing the presentation on a computer, this allows you to link up different slides and

Adding an action will automatically add a ScreenTip containing the address to which it is connected.

presentations and lets you run programs from within PowerPoint.

For now, you are going to select the *Hyperlink to:* radio button and choose *URL.* This will prompt you for an address that you want to activate with the action. If you are using an e-mail address, add *mailto:* before your address in the text box. This alerts PowerPoint that it needs to launch the mail client on the system showing the presentation and create an e-mail to the address that follows "mailto:" as the intended recipient. You can see an example of these action settings in Figure 8.36.

You can edit this action at any time by selecting the image and using the *Action* (or *Action Settings*) icon that you used to start the process. Just like the hyperlink you added earlier, the action will not occur in

Normal view. It will only work in the Slide Show view, which is shown in Figure 8.37.

Sorting Slides

8.3.7

As a final slide for your presentation on yourself, you are going to show everyone what it looks like when you are hard at work. Insert a new slide after the contact slide. You will want your contact information to be at the very end, so you will have to reorganize your slides to move the new slide you just created to position it before the contact slide. You can do this in one of two ways:

- Click on the *Slide Sorter View* icon at the bottom of the interface. Once this view is open, all of your slides will display on a grid as shown in Figure 8.38. You can simply click and hold your mouse on the last slide and drag it to where you want it to appear (in this case, immediately before the contact slide). Click on the *Normal View* icon in the same location to get back to your slide design in Normal view. You can also double-click on a

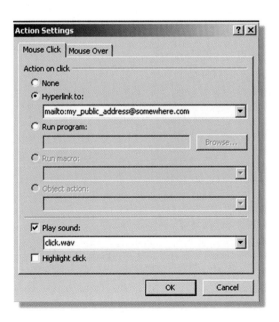

◀ **FIGURE 8.36**
Action Settings dialog box

▲ **FIGURE 8.37**
Contact slide with action enabled clip art

slide in the Slide Sorter view to open the Normal view on that particular slide.

• You can also reorder slides in the lefthand Slides/Outline pane. To do this, just click and hold the slide you want to move and drag it to the position you want it to occupy.

8.3.8 Inserting Screenshots

Once you have your newest slide in the proper place, click in the title placeholder

and type *This Is What My Work Looks Like* and format the text appropriately to match the rest of your slides. You may need to widen the placeholder to keep all of this text on a single line. Remember to align the placeholder to the center of the slide if you change its width so it is not off-center from the rest of your slide titles. Aligning the text box is separate from aligning the text. You are going to show everyone what your computer looks like when you are hard at work. Make sure you have a program open that you use all the time when you are at work.

Now click the placeholder in the lower part of the slide. If you are using PowerPoint 2010, you can just go to the *Insert ribbon* and select *Screenshot* from the *Images* panel. This is an easy way to capture what is happening in a live application on your machine. The menu that appears will show each open application (other than PowerPoint) and allow you

▶ **FIGURE 8.38**
Slide Sorter view

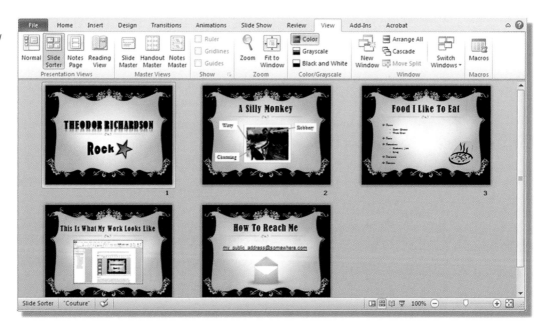

to insert an image capture of that program into your slide. You can also select the *Screen Clipping* option from this menu and select an area of the screen you want to copy into an image. This is an incredibly useful tool for describing and displaying applications or showing an example Web site in a presentation without having to leave PowerPoint.

If you are using PowerPoint 2011, this option is not available to you, but you can create a screen capture by holding down *Shift-Command-3*. This will place an image of your current computer screen on your computer desktop. You will hear a camera clicking sound if you do this correctly. You can now insert this image into your presentation just as you would any other image stored on your computer. Holding down *Shift-Command-4* lets you select an area of the screen to capture using the mouse. If you hold down the *Control* key along with either sequence (such as *Control-Shift-Command-3*), you will copy the image to your system clipboard so you can paste it directly into your slides.

You can generally save a screenshot on a Windows machine using keyboard shortcuts. This is typically done by pressing the *Print Screen* button, typically abbreviated *Prt Scn* or *Prt Sc*. This procedure will vary from computer to computer based on the keyboard layout, so you may have to look up how to do this on your individual machine if you do not have a single button for this. This procedure will copy your current desktop image to the clipboard of the system as a graphic.

Whenever you are using a screen capture tool, make sure you are not exposing private or confidential information from you or your organization. It is your responsibility to make sure whatever is included in that screenshot, regardless of its size or readability, is allowed to be used and shared publicly.

Once the screenshot is inserted, you can work with it just like any other image you have included in your slides. You can add effects to it or crop it to suit your needs. Just remember that it is likely that the content of the inserted image will be difficult for an audience to read, so once again you should be sure that the point you are trying to make is apparent and that you are not giving your audience an eye exam by forcing them to read text that is too small to see. An example of the completed slide can be seen in Figure 8.39.

Transitions

8.3.9

To complete your masterpiece, you should add transitions to your slides. By default, the slides will just change without any transition animation whatsoever.

▼ FIGURE 8.39
Completed example with inserted screenshot

This may be suitable for a business presentation, but you may find instances in which you want a little style in your slide transitions. PowerPoint does not lack for transition options, which range from simple wipe effects to full-fledged animations of your slide being dissolved into a honeycomb and reassembled as the next slide. When adding transitions, make sure the animation does not overshadow the purpose of your presentation. Your audience did not come to see the animations you have constructed for your slide transitions.

With that said, you can use this presentation to experiment with elaborate transitions. You will find them all on the *Transitions ribbon*, shown in Figure 8.40. The Transition to This Slide panel has a selection of animations from which you can choose. The Effect Options icon will change depending on the transition that you select. For the introduction slide, something simple like a fade should be used. Click the *Apply to All* (or *Apply to All Slides* in PowerPoint 2011) icon on the *Transition ribbon* to apply the effect you have configured to every one of your slides. Once you have selected a transition for a slide, you will notice that a small icon appears next to your slide in the Slides/Outline pane on the left side of the interface. Click this icon to preview the attached animation.

The Duration setting determines how long the transition takes. If you are using your slide show as a visual supplement for a live presentation, you probably want short transitions, if you want any at all. You can also add sound to your transition by selecting one of the preset sound effects from the Sound menu. Sound that is used to excess is very annoying to an audience, and it can be very distracting if you have it playing over narration.

In this case, though, give yourself some applause on your introduction slide. You've earned it! To do this, select the drop-down list next to the word *Sound* and select *Applause*. Press *F5* to play your slide show in Slide Show view. Take a bow because you have just completed your first PowerPoint presentation!

OPENOFFICE.ORG IMPRESS

8.4

OpenOffice.org has its own presentation software, called Impress. The interface for Impress looks quite different from the new versions of Microsoft Office Power-Point. If you have experience with older versions of PowerPoint, Impress is vaguely reminiscent of the Office 97 version.

When you open up Impress, the Presentation Wizard appears. For this example, select *Empty presentation*. Now the

▶ FIGURE 8.40
Transitions ribbon

wizard will prompt you to select a slide design from the list of options. A preview of what this will look like displays in the panel on the right side. Finally, the wizard will ask you to select a slide transition for each slide. You can alter each of these properties later, so just select *No Effect* for now. Now you are ready to click *Create*. The steps of this process are shown in Figure 8.41.

Anatomy of OpenOffice.org Impress

8.4.1

The interface for Impress can be seen in Figure 8.42. The main menu across the top has most of the tools you will need. The toolbar beneath it has the common functions to create your presentation, and a context-sensitive toolbar beneath that will change depending on the element you have selected. The left pane of the main window has the slide preview and organization information, just like PowerPoint.

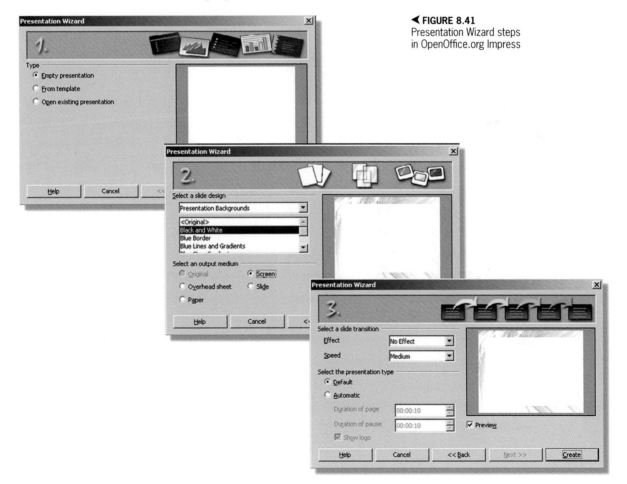

◄ **FIGURE 8.41**
Presentation Wizard steps in OpenOffice.org Impress

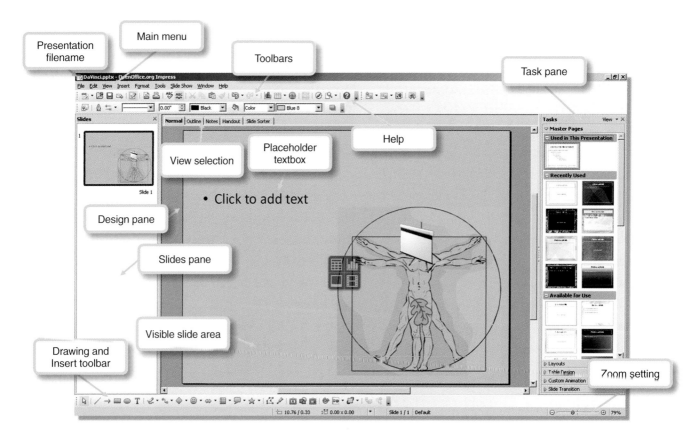

Presentation filename

Main menu

Toolbars

Task pane

Help

View selection

Placeholder textbox

Design pane

Slides pane

Visible slide area

Drawing and Insert toolbar

Zoom setting

• Click to add text

▲ **FIGURE 8.42**
Anatomy of Impress

The middle pane is a display of the current slide that you can edit. The right pane contains a lot of functionality that PowerPoint places in the ribbon interface across the top. This is where you can access the Slide Master pages, change your layouts, and set your slide transitions.

To create a new Impress document, select the *File* menu in OpenOffice.org and select *New* and then *Presentation*. Whenever you create a new document in Impress, the Presentation Wizard is launched. You can skip the steps of the wizard by clicking the *Create* button at any time. This will bring you to the Normal view for your presentation.

Your first step should always be to save your file. You can do this by selecting

the *File* menu and then choosing *Save* or *Save As* or by clicking the icon that looks like a floppy disk. This will open the *Save As* dialog box. The native format for Impress documents is ODF Presentation (.odp). You will notice that Impress can save documents in the Microsoft Office PowerPoint format, but only the 97 version; you can still open these documents in PowerPoint 2010/2011 without any difficulty. Name your presentation *MyImpress* and save it using the default format of *ODF Presentation*.

You can insert new slides in Impress by right-clicking in the *Slides* pane and selecting *New Slide*. You can also insert new slides from the *Slide* icon in the main toolbar at the top. The drop-down list that appears allows you to select the specific layout you want for your new slide. Add a few slides to get started.

Now click on the *Master Pages* tab on the right pane. This is where you will select and apply the style you want for your presentation. Select one of the options that you like and click on your selection. This will update all of the slides in your presentation with the new layout and style of the Master Slide that you have selected.

Press the *F5* key to enter Slide Show view or select the *View* menu and then choose *Slide Show*. From here, you can move your presentation forward using the spacebar or right arrow key and move your presentation backward using the left arrow key. You can exit Slide Show view by pressing the *Escape* key.

8.4.2 ## Completing the Project in Impress

The placeholder text boxes in Impress work just like they do in PowerPoint. To create your first slide, enter your name in the slide title placeholder. You can change the font using the context-sensitive font toolbar that appears beneath the main toolbar whenever you click on a text box. Add a shadow and change your font to something impressive. Click on the remaining placeholder and delete it by clicking on the *Delete* key since you will not be adding a subtitle.

Use your mouse to move the text box containing your name lower in the page and use the *Alignment* icon on the toolbar at the bottom of the interface to align the text box to the horizontal center of

the slide. You can see the Alignment icon menu in Figure 8.43; this menu has only icons to represent the different alignment options you have, but these are supplemented by tooltips that appear when you place your mouse over them.

◄ FIGURE 8.43
Alignment menu in Impress

The shapes for drawing are all located along the toolbar at the bottom of the interface. Select a star shape you like and insert it into your slide; you can do this by selecting the shape menu for the star and picking a specific star you like. Unlike PowerPoint, you cannot just click to stamp shapes; instead, you must click and drag to set the size of your shape in the slide.

Use the context-sensitive drawing toolbar to set your fill and line color. You can also add a shadow effect. Most of the fine-tuning for a drawing object in Impress is done via the Graphic Styles dialog box. You access this by right-clicking on the drawing object and selecting *Edit Style*. Here you can select and edit the properties for your shape's line, fill, shadow, transparency, and text effects for any text entered into the shape. Add transparency to the shadow of the star (50% should be a good setting) and use a gradient fill to make it stand out against the background.

The Fontwork Gallery is the Impress equivalent of WordArt. Select the *Fontwork Gallery* icon on the toolbar at the bottom of the interface and you will be prompted to select a style for your Fontwork. This will stamp a placeholder for the Fontwork in your slide, as shown in Figure 8.44.

You can then double-click the placeholder and enter the text you want. Type *Rock* in the text box and click outside of the text box. You can edit your text later by double-clicking inside the object. Clicking on the Fontwork object opens a pop-up toolbar specific to Fontwork settings and another toolbar that lets you alter the 3D properties of the Fontwork display. You can also set the gradient and line for the Fontwork object using the text formatting toolbar that appears.

Hold the *Shift* key and select both the Fontwork object and the star. Group these objects together by right-clicking on them while they are selected and choosing *Group* from the menu. You can now use the alignment tool from the bottom toolbar to align this group to the horizontal center of the slide.

Note that you cannot add placeholder text boxes to a group, just as in PowerPoint.

Add a new slide to your presentation by either right-clicking in the slide panel on the left side and choosing *New Slide* or by clicking the *Slide* icon in the main toolbar across the top. You are going to add your picture to this slide, so type a suitable caption for the image in the slide title placeholder. Make sure you format your text to match the formatting for your name on the title slide. Consistency is essential for a successful presentation.

Select the *From File* icon on the toolbar at the bottom of the screen. This will open a dialog box for you to select an image that is stored on your computer. Once you have selected an image, it should display in the middle of your slide. The context-sensitive picture editing toolbar will also appear. You can apply a number of effects and filters to your image using this toolbar. Set your image to *Grayscale* using the drop-down menu. You can also crop your image using the Crop tool the same way you would in PowerPoint.

Insert three rectangles using the toolbar across the bottom and click and drag in the slide to define the shape. If you want to draw one rectangle and copy and paste it for the other two, the command is the same as in any other program on a PC: *Ctrl-C* copies the object and *Ctrl-V* pastes the copy. (The Macintosh equivalent of these simply substitutes the Command (or Apple) key for the Control (Ctrl) key.) In Impress, pasting an object places it directly over the original item, so you have to click and drag the copy away to access the original. You can select all of the rectangles and format them at the same time using the drawing object toolbar or you can format each of them separately.

You can type directly into these rectangles by simply clicking on the shape and typing with the keyboard. Add one adjective to each rectangle. You are now going to use the linking objects to add arrows from the rectangles to your picture. Selecti the *Connector* icon from the toolbar at the bottom of the interface and choose which connector you want. These connectors are not as flexible as those in PowerPoint, so you cannot use them to point inside of an object; they will either point to empty space around the slide or they will link directly to one of the connection points of an object. The adjectives you add should therefore describe the picture in general. Format the connectors using the standard line properties. The result is shown in Figure 8.45.

Add your next slide. This is going to be either a slide listing your hobbies or one listing things you like to eat. Format the title for this slide to match the rest of your presentation. The text entry process in Impress is similar to PowerPoint: You simply click inside the text box to type. The context-sensitive outlining toolbar lets you change the indentation of items and move them up and down in the list by clicking on the arrow icons. You can also change the bullet style using the Bullets and Numbering dialog box.

Impress does not offer a clip art library, so if you want any extra images to spice up your presentation, you will have to pick from what is already on your computer or get them from Office.com. Impress accepts the clip art file type, so you can use the Office.com copy feature and paste images directly in your slide. Visit Office.com and select a piece of clip art that works with your list. You can review the steps for getting clip art images from Office.com earlier in this chapter in Section 8.3.6.3.

Add a new slide with the title *This Is Me Working*; this is where you will add a screenshot to your presentation. There is no icon or shortcut for placing a screenshot into Impress. You will have to take the screenshot manually; this process is described in Section 8.3.8. You can either insert this screenshot as an image or paste it into your Impress document on the current slide. You can crop your screenshot just like any other image.

Holding down the *Control* (Ctrl) key while cropping in Impress helps you get a more precise result.

Remember that if your slides get out of order or you want to rearrange them, you can do so by clicking and dragging the slide you want to move in the lefthand *Slides* pane. You can also click on the *Slide Sorter* tab across the top of the design pane to see thumbnails of each of your slides that you can click and drag to move as needed. Just click the *Normal* tab when you are finished to get back to your design view.

▼ FIGURE 8.45
Completed example with connectors in Impress

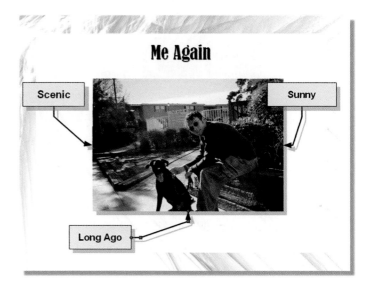

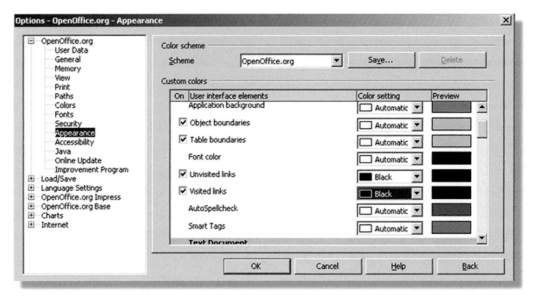

The last slide of your presentation will be the contact slide. If you type a Web site address or e-mail address, Impress will automatically convert it to a hyperlink. You can also add a hyperlink manually by selecting the *Hyperlink* icon in the main toolbar. This will open a dialog box allowing you to enter the destination to which you want to link and the text you want to display.

To change the color of your hyperlink from the default blue, you have to set it as a global setting for your document. To do this, click on the *Tools* menu and select *Options* to open the Options dialog box. Select *OpenOffice.org*, then *Appearance*. You should now see a list of default colors used in your document. Change the color of both the *Unvisited Links* and *Visited Links* to format your hyperlink color correctly. These are found in the *Appearance* category of the menu that appears as shown in Figure 8.46.

Add clip art to enhance your contact slide at the end of your presentation. Now you just need to polish your presentation by adding transitions. You can add these by selecting the *Slide Transition* tab on the righthand pane of the interface. Whenever you select an option in this menu, you are applying it only to the currently selected slide. You can also click the *Apply to All Slides* button to make the transition part of every slide you have. Select *Fade Smoothly* from the choices and apply it to all of the slides.

Now go back to the title slide to add a sound effect to your transition. Remember that sounds can be irritating to an audience, so they should be used with caution. Select *applause* from the *Sound* menu under *Apply Transition* in the *Slide Transition* panel. Save your work (as you should do often), and press *F5* to play your presentation. Listen to that applause; you've earned it!

CHAPTER SUMMARY

This chapter provided an introduction to presentation software. As the world of business becomes more technology-based, the ability to use presentation software proficiently will become more of a necessity to communicate ideas clearly and effectively. It is therefore essential that you understand how to construct a presentation document to share your ideas and contributions. This chapter gave you an overview of the fundamental tools you need to build exciting and engaging presentations, but these are just the beginning when it comes to making your presentations work. The next chapter focuses on how to create and present your presentation effectively. You will get an idea of how to format your presentation to suit your purpose and audience, as well as gain an understanding of the most efficient and effective ways to showcase your ideas.

CHAPTER EXERCISES

1. Begin by thinking about a hobby you enjoy where construction of some sort is involved. Using the Web, find additional research supporting facts about your hobby and then prepare a 10-slide presentation describing the steps you would take to build or assemble some aspect concerning your hobby. For example, you might like building model cars or assembling gift baskets. If you are not able to think of a personal hobby, then use the Web to develop step-by-step instructions on building or installing an object of your choice.

2. Using the Web, research a current legal issue affecting your community. For example, you might research a new law that is difficult to understand. Use your research to develop a 10-slide presentation to clarify what the law means. Make sure you add transitions, images, and hyperlinks to the presentation.

3. Using the presentation software of your choice, develop an outline that explains the steps used to cite sources in either the writing style of your choice or one used at your educational institution. Examples of these styles include APA and MLA format.

4. Develop a presentation that incorporates transitions and photographs to create a digital photo album. The focus of this exercise is to use the formatting ribbons and menus to edit, crop, and format photographs of your choice. Develop a minimum of five slides for this presentation.

CHAPTER KNOWLEDGE CHECK

1 What is the purpose for using the PowerPoint application?

- ○ **A.** Create a visual supplement
- ○ **B.** Create a multimedia presentation
- ○ **C.** Create short video clips
- ○ **D.** Both a and b

2 The View ribbon is where you customize the user interface for PowerPoint and format your slides.

- ○ True
- ○ False

3 If you want to change the bullet styles for your slide or even change them to numbers, you would select the _____ panel on the Home ribbon.

- ○ **A.** Ribbon
- ○ **B.** Insert
- ○ **C.** Review
- ○ **D.** Paragraph

4 The _____ resets your slides to the full size of the screen and hides the design interface of the software. You can move forward in your slides by clicking the mouse, pressing the spacebar, or using the right arrow key.

- ○ **A.** Slide Show view
- ○ **B.** Panel view
- ○ **C.** Normal view
- ○ **D.** None of the above

5 The Print Screen button on a PC, typically abbreviated *Prt Scn* or *Prt Scr*, can be used to copy your current desktop image to the clipboard of the system as a graphic.

○ True
○ False

6 Selecting the _____ in PowerPoint 2011 launches a visual display of the layers in your slide, which you can click and drag to reorder.

○ **A.** Review ribbon
○ **B.** Layer icon
○ **C.** Animations ribbon
○ **D.** Reorder Objects menu item

7 OpenOffice.org includes presentation software called _____.

○ **A.** Impress
○ **B.** Base
○ **C.** Colors
○ **D.** Presentation

8 The native format for OpenOffice.org presentation documents is:

○ **A.** ODF presentation (.odp)
○ **B.** PowerPoint Presentation (.pptx)
○ **C.** OST presentation (.ost)
○ **D.** Both a and c

9 You can add a link to an e-mail address or URL manually by selecting the _____.

○ **A.** Format icon
○ **B.** Hyperlink icon
○ **C.** Color icon
○ **D.** None of the above

10 The keyboard shortcut on a Windows PC that copies an object on the screen is _____, and _____ can be used to paste the copied object.

○ **A.** *Ctrl-C, Ctrl-V*
○ **B.** *Ctrl-V, Ctrl-X*
○ **C.** *Ctrl-X, Ctrl-C*
○ **D.** Both a and b

Creating Effective Presentations

Now that you have some familiarity with the tools available in presentation software, this chapter focuses on teaching you to use those tools effectively to create a meaningful presentation that can truly make a lasting impression on your audience. You will design, format, and share an example presentation to demonstrate these best practices. Once you complete the chapter, you will be able to:

- Format the Slide Master for your presentation to assign a theme, color scheme, and font set

- Outline an effective presentation using the Notes section of your presentation

- Structure your slides in a logical and complete manner to support the topic on which you are presenting

- Present or share your completed presentation document

WRITING YOUR VALUE PROPOSITION

Almost every presentation document in existence is a form of sales pitch. Whether it is a research presentation, a marketing proposal, or a presentation about yourself like the one you constructed in the previous chapter, there is some fundamental point that you are trying to convey and you want your audience to agree with what you are saying or at least understand your perspective. The key to constructing a successful presentation is to remember your value proposition or value statement.

Your value proposition is what you have to offer to whoever is viewing your slides or listening to your presentation. This should guide what you include in every slide you create. In fact, you can even state your value proposition in the first slide after the title slide for everyone to see. It should be concise and clear (two sentences at most) so you can easily evaluate each subsequent slide for relevance to that overall message. The difference between an effective presentation and an ineffective presentation is typically determined by the clarity of the message and the quality of the visual display.

A **VALUE PROPOSITION** *is a concise statement (most commonly associated with business) of the benefits offered by the product or idea under discussion.*

ESTABLISHING A VISUAL STYLE

Part of making your presentation effective is presenting a clear visual style to which the audience can quickly become accustomed; this will allow the audience to recognize the style as you proceed and focus on the content instead of the background. This means choosing an effective style and adhering to that style throughout the presentation. Changing color schemes and backgrounds is distracting; it draws attention to the change instead of what you are trying to highlight. This chapter will guide you through the creation of an effective presentation, no matter what your underlying purpose is. One way to keep your presentation consistent is to use the Slide Master to format your presentation.

A **SLIDE MASTER** *is a template for all slides within a presentation document. Changes made to a Slide Master will affect all of the slides in the presentation built from that master. Any slide constructed from a Slide Master is considered a child slide to the Slide Master.*

Any changes made to the Slide Master will affect all of the slides in the presentation. Using the Slide Master to define your theme, fonts, and colors will give your presentation consistency throughout and will allow you to focus your time and attention on presenting the information rather than on formatting it.

Once you become more familiar with Power-Point, you may want to stop using the Slide Master and change the theme, font, and color scheme directly in the presentation. Even if you end up using it only occasionally, an understanding of the techniques for working with the Slide Master is useful in constructing an effective presentation.

9.2.1 ## Modifying the Slide Master

The great thing about using the Slide Master is that it allows you to set up your initial presentation style once and forget about it. All of the other slides that you create within your presentation will be copies of the Slide Master. Create a new presentation in PowerPoint and save it as *MySalesPitch.pptx*. To access the Slide Master in PowerPoint 2010, go to the *View* ribbon and click on *Slide Master* under the *Master Views* panel. In PowerPoint 2011, select the *View* menu and choose *Master*; then choose *Slide Master* on the menu that appears.

This opens a new context-sensitive Slide Master ribbon, shown in Figure 9.1. The design pane will show a parent slide for all of the different layout options you can choose. Changing the Slide Master will change all of the layout slide masters, which are the children you see in the Slides/Outline pane (one for each layout available). Changing any of the layout slide masters changes each individual slide in your presentation with that particular layout.

You will see several placeholder text boxes along the bottom of your Slide Master that typically do not appear in a new slide. These include predefined places to add the date, footer text, and the slide

OPEN OFFICE If you are using OpenOffice.org Impress, you can edit the slide master by opening the *Master Pages* tab in the pane on the right side of the interface, right-clicking on the slide master you wish to use, and selecting *Edit Master*. This will open a small toolbar for use with the instance of the slide master that you have opened. You cannot change the theme of this slide master once you have selected it, and there are no one-click options for fonts and colors. You have the option to rename the master that you have changed for later use by using the *Rename Master* icon in the toolbar. When you are finished editing this slide master instance, click *Close Master View* to return to the Normal view for your presentation. If you later wish to change the theme for your presentation, you can select *Master Pages* and choose a new layout and theme by clicking on one of the slide masters, but any changes you made to the previous slide master will not carry over to the new slide master.

▼ **FIGURE 9.1** Slide Master ribbon

number. Note that in PowerPoint 2010, when the Slide Master ribbon is open, the Design ribbon disappears; this is because most of the design options that you can apply on a slide-by-slide basis from the Design ribbon can be selected and applied on the Slide Master ribbon. In Power-Point 2011, these options are all available on the Themes ribbon, which will remain visible whether or not the Slide Master is open.

9.2.2 Planning Your Design

Start your presentation with your overall idea and value proposition in mind. The visual style you present in your document will have a big impact on the perception of your idea. You should choose a visual style that supports the message you are delivering and is appropriate for the audience to whom you are presenting. For example, a casual, flashy style with a lot of superfluous animation is not suited to a research presentation because it will give your audience the impression that your graphics are more important than what you have to say. Conversely, a presentation designed for children needs to contain a lot of bright colors or they will quickly become bored and lose interest in what you have to say.

The example project in this chapter is a professional sales pitch. For this type of presentation, you should have a basic idea that you want to convey, which should be supported by all of the slides you add. In this example, the message is simple: "Hot dogs should be the next gourmet food fad." Once you have established the overall message for

The visual design of a presentation has a large impact on the perceived credibility of the content of the design. In a study about Web sites conducted at Stanford University to determine the factors that affect consumer trust, visual appeal was the most often cited reason for whether a site was considered reputable and trusted. The visual clarity of your slides and the visual appeal of the information you present will impact whether your audience trusts what you have to say.

the presentation, you need to establish the audience for the presentation.

You should take your audience into consideration when planning both your design style and your overall purpose. Putting your ideas in a context that is suited to your audience will help them understand the message you are trying to convey. The background, culture, and experience of your audience will affect their perception of your presentation. Identifying as much information about your audience as possible is critical to successfully delivering your intended message.

The setting in which the audience will experience the presentation will also impact their receptiveness to it. If the occasion is formal, you do not want to select a theme that is juvenile. If it is a casual setting, you do not want your theme to be too rigid and formal. Consider who will be viewing your slides, as well as the message you want to convey. As an example of this, Figure 9.2 shows two versions of the same slide; these have the same content but different styles attached to them. The first would be suited to a more formal occasion but the second would not.

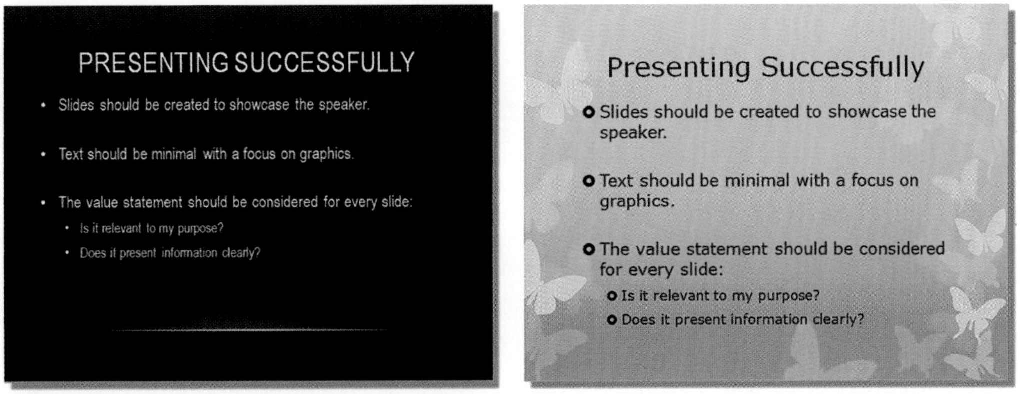

▲ FIGURE 9.2 Alternate designs for the same content

9.2.3 Assigning a Theme

The first step of formatting your master slide is selecting a theme. In PowerPoint, the Theme setting determines the default Font, Color, and Effects settings. In PowerPoint 2010, you select an appropriate theme by clicking the *Themes* icon in the *Edit Theme* panel of the *Slide Master* ribbon and then clicking on one of the preview icons that is displayed. In PowerPoint 2011, these settings are all on the *Themes* ribbon, where you can define the Colors and Fonts settings; there is no equivalent Effects setting.

SELECTING THE RIGHT THEME FOR THE VENUE

When you are choosing a color scheme for your presentation, you need to consider how the presentation will be viewed. If you are showing it on a large screen to an audience, you should consider a color scheme that puts light-colored text over a darker background. A bright background with dark text works well in print, but it can be too harsh to view in a dim room. Similarly, if your presentation is going to be viewed on an individual computer monitor, you should choose a theme that is more akin to text publications. This will also affect your font choices and color scheme, but in PowerPoint these are derived initially from the theme.

For the example presentation, you want a style that is going to fit the topic appropriately, so it needs to be something modern that will fit with the business element you are trying to convince to invest in your proposal; it should also not be too formal or it will detract from the spirit of the idea. When you click on a theme, you will see each of the slide templates in the Slides/Outline pane reset to the theme you have chosen, as shown in Figure 9.3. If you do not like the result, you can simply choose another theme.

Colors, Fonts, and Effects 9.2.4

The next step after choosing a theme is to pick your color scheme. PowerPoint has a significant number of preset color schemes from which you can choose; once you choose a theme, this setting will default to the color scheme that matches that theme. In PowerPoint 2010, you can select any of the preset options from the *Colors* icon (next to the *Themes* icon) in the *Edit Theme* panel of the *Slide Master* ribbon. The *Colors* menu for PowerPoint 2011 is located in the *Themes* ribbon on the *Theme Options* panel.

You can set the Theme, Color, Font, and Effects settings on the Design ribbon if you are not using the Slide Master to format your presentation.

You can also define a custom color scheme by selecting *Create New Theme Colors* at the bottom of the list. This process will start with the colors that you have already chosen and allow you to modify them individually; you should be familiar with this menu if you changed the hyperlink color in your presentation in the previous chapter. You can give your new color scheme a name if you want to use it later or save it with the default name (which begins with *Custom 1*). Any custom color schemes you define will appear at the top of the list in the drop-down *Color* menu. You can edit or delete them by right-clicking on the name of the custom color scheme.

You should also choose a font set that is suitable for your presentation; you select a font by clicking on the *Font* icon and selecting one of the options presented. As a general rule, you should never use more than two fonts on a presentation: one for the title to grab attention and one for the rest of the text in the body of your slides. The two fonts should complement each other well, meaning they should not visually clash in style. Readability should be the highest consideration when you are choosing which fonts to use, followed by aesthetic coherence with the overall presentation. Just like with the themes and colors, there are a variety of predefined sets of fonts from which to choose. You can also define your own font set and save it for later use, just as you can with the color scheme.

Not everyone has the talent to be a professional graphic designer, but there are a few steps you can take to make sure your color scheme works for a presentation. A general guideline is to have two main colors and an accent color. You can use different shades of the main colors, and the two main colors should blend well together. The accent color should be used sparingly and should provide enough contrast to be readable over both of the main colors. You can see a map of complementary and analogous colors on the color wheel in Figure 9.4.

There are an almost endless number of usable color combinations, but using two analogous colors and a complementary (or split complementary) color is usually a safe way to construct your palette. Make sure that any text you include is readable above all else and that the tension between the colors does not draw attention away from the content; you can lighten or darken any of the colors to increase or decrease the contrast presented. Remember, the more contrast you have between your text and the background, the clearer your text will be. One color you should avoid is pure red; it is incredibly difficult for a person to look at pure red on a computer or projector screen for any sustained period of time.

The fonts in your slides have to be comfortable for people at the back of a room to read if you are going to do a live presentation. A live presentation also means you should stay away from serif fonts. The extra text decorations make it more difficult to read what is on the screen. However, if your presentation is destined for sharing on an individual computer screen, a serif font will work just fine. You can present more stylized text in a presentation for an individual computer screen, but you should never sacrifice clarity and readability.

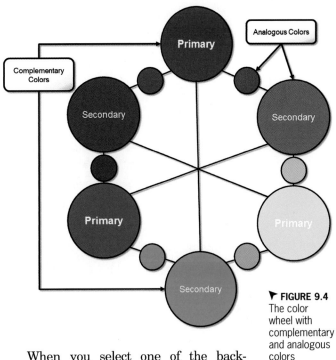

▼ FIGURE 9.4
The color wheel with complementary and analogous colors

When you select one of the background styles from the menu on the *Background* panel of the *Slide Master* ribbon while you have the default Slide Master (Slide 1) selected, the background choice will be applied to each of the layout slide masters that are linked to it. Most of the layouts will have different elements in the slide than the default blank layout, so it is typically better to select the setting for the background styles in each of the different layout slide masters if you wish to make changes to the default. Each theme will have its own background styles menu choices available. If there is a slide layout for which you do not want the background effects to appear, simply check the box next

In PowerPoint 2010, you can set the default style for any graphics added to your presentation using the *Effects* icon on the *Theme* panel as well.

to *Hide Background Graphics* (or *Hide Graphics* in PowerPoint 2011).

Bullets and Numbering

Despite the ease of use for bulleted lists in presentation software, bullet points must be used with care. According to Richard Mayer, a leading researcher in educational psychology, the improper use of bullet points can actually cause learning to cease; bullet points can overload the cognitive systems of the brain that normally allow a person to perceive the information with which they are being presented. Since bullet points have no inherent order by definition, the human brain can get lost in them and stop mapping the information. There is no definitive answer on the maximum number of bullet points that should be used in a slide, but the consensus of the research is that three bullet points on a slide does not inhibit understanding if they present clear information.

If you are going to use bulleted or numbered lists in any of your slides, you should set the styles for those in the Slide Master and use them throughout your presentation. Click on the placeholder text box on the Slide Master containing the sample outline text. The styles for the various outline levels will be preset from the theme you selected. You can select whether they should be ordered (using numbers or letters) or unordered (using bullet points) for each level of organization by clicking either the *Numbering* or *Bullets* icon, respectively. You can choose the style for each layer by highlighting the text at the level you want to change and selecting the style for that level.

To open the *Bullets and Numbering dialog box* (shown in Figure 9.5) to make more specific changes, select *Bullets and Numbering* on the right-click menu or select the customization option from the drop-down menu of either the *Bullets* icon or the *Numbering* icon. Here you can change the size relative to the text, the color of the bullets, and the style of the bullets under the *Bulleted* (or *Bullets*) tab. You can also add a picture of your choosing from a file (or from the built-in set of images) as your bullet point by selecting the *Picture* button or you can use one of the special

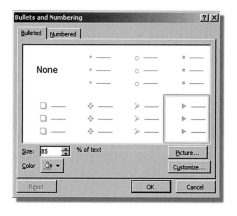
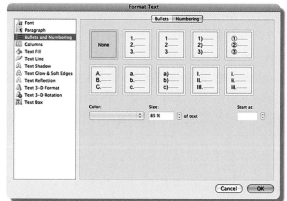

character symbols by clicking the *Customize* button; these options are both under the *Custom bullet* drop-down menu in PowerPoint 2011. On the *Numbered* (or *Numbering*) tab, you can select the outline style you want for the text level and set the starting number or letter by selecting it from the *Starts at* box.

When you are defining the style of your outline for your presentation, you should always keep it as simple and clear as possible. For an unordered list, the text indents should be enough to distinguish the different levels, so you should never need more than one type of bullet. In fact, if you have more than two levels in an unordered list on your slide, the text will become difficult to read. Selecting an image as your bullet point may be novel, but you should only do so if it is not too distracting and it fits with the color scheme and style of the overall presentation. Keep your bullets or numbers the same color within each slide and throughout the entire presentation; changing styles or colors in the same slide just leads to confusion.

9.2.6 Adding and Formatting Slide Footers

Unlike word processing documents, presentations do not contain true headers. The visual impact needs to start at the upper-lefthand corner of the slide. This is where the eye begins viewing the image, so you cannot waste that prime visual space with slide numbers and copyright information. In fact, the only safe place to add this type of information to a slide without causing it to distract the viewer is at the very bottom. The footer is the only area of the slide for which you do not have to worry as much about readability. This is mostly information for the presenter and for later distribution. In fact, any text that is not assisting the presenter (by displaying the slide number, for instance) or needed for copyright information or references should be omitted.

If no information is added to the footer placeholders, they will appear as placeholder text boxes in the regular slide design view for your presentation. You can edit the footer information on each slide by clicking on the text just like any other text box.

To make sure no one takes your presentation and uses it as their own, you can add a small copyright notice to your footer. To do this, just type *(c)* into the box; notice that it automatically converts to the copyright symbol (©). Follow this with your name and format the text however you would like it to appear. Remember that this is part of the footer, so it should be small but clear. A font size of 10 to 12 pt is sufficient for the footer but would be otherwise unreadable on a slide; your audience probably will not be able to discern this text.

Add the slide number to the place-holder on the righthand side of the slide for your reference while you are presenting. You may already have a text box with the # symbol; this is the allocated space for the slide number. In PowerPoint 2010, you can insert the slide number manually if it is not already present by placing the cursor in a text box and clicking on the *Insert* ribbon; you will find the *Slide Number* icon on the *Text* panel. You can now format the slide number text to appear the same as the rest of your footer text. The actual number in this placeholder will not be visible until you are in Normal view for your presentation; on the Slide Master, it will appear as <#>.

In PowerPoint 2011, you can add any of the footer elements that you may have removed by selecting the *Insert* menu, clicking on *Master Placeholders*, and choosing the item you want to add. Only the items that are not already included will be available to select. Changing these text boxes does not set the footer on the slides to be visible in your presentation.

To make the footer visible in PowerPoint 2010, you must select the *Header & Footer*

OPEN OFFICE When using Impress, you can edit the footer text on the slide master just as you would in PowerPoint. To activate any of the footer options for your slide show, select the *View* menu and then *Headers and Footers*. In this dialog box, you can enable or disable all of the options that you can use in PowerPoint, including omitting the footer from the first/ title slide.

icon on the *Text* panel of the *Insert* ribbon. Select the checkboxes that you wish to enable in the *Header and Footer dialog box* that appears, as shown in Figure 9.6. If you want to hide the footer on the title slide of your presentation, check the box next to *Don't show on title slide*. You can reach the Header and Footer dialog box in PowerPoint 2011 by selecting the *View* menu and click-ing on *Header and Footer*.

Formatting Text on the Slide Master

9.2.7

Any text formatting done to the Master Slide placeholder text boxes will be carried over to the rest of your presentation. For-matting text now in the Master Slide will

▶ **FIGURE 9.6**
Header and Footer dialog boxes

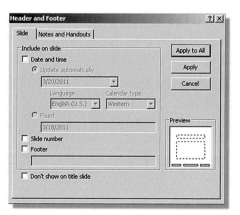

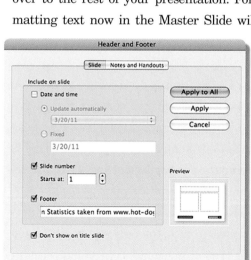

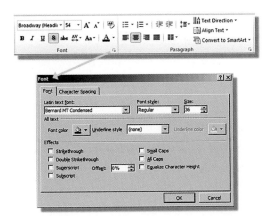

save you the effort of repeatedly formatting the same elements later when you are writing your presentation content. This not only saves you effort, it also allows you to focus on the content of each slide rather than on formatting.

Center your title and add a shadow to it on the main Slide Master. You should see your changes propagate all the way through the rest of the layout slide masters. To configure the text shadow, select *Shadow Options* from the menu beneath the preset options. This allows you to set how dramatic the shadow effect is. The *Distance* element sets how far away the shadow is from the text, which determines the perceived height of the text over the background.

PowerPoint offers a few text options that are similar to what is available in Word but with a different layout; you can view these in Figure 9.7. One of these options is the *Change Case* icon; this allows you to capitalize the first letter of each word (which is very useful for a title), toggle the case of each letter, or convert all of the letters to either upper- or lower-case. Another tool available here is the *Text Shadow* icon, which lets you add a shadow from the *Font*

panel of the *Home* ribbon instead of using the *Text Effects* icon in the *Format* ribbon. There is no icon for superscript or subscript in PowerPoint 2010 as there is in Word. For these effects, you must open the Font dialog box by clicking the expansion icon in the lower-righthand corner of the Font panel.

PowerPoint 2011 gives you a larger selection of options in the Font panel of the Home ribbon. These include all of the options available in PowerPoint 2010, along with a few additions. You can add or edit all of the available text effects from the Home ribbon, including superscript, subscript, and strikethrough text.

Once you have made the changes to the Slide Master, you should go through each of the layout slides that you are going to use and make any formatting modifications to those that are specific to the layout you need. Unlike the Slide Master parent, anything that you change in a layout slide master will change only the slides built from that layout. This means that changing the format of text in a layout slide master will not make the change in the other layout slide masters. For this reason, it is best to keep any significant text and font style changes to the main

Slide Master from which the layout slide masters are created.

Branding Your Slides

If you have a logo for your company or organization, you may want to add it to your slides. You do not want to have to do this for every slide you create, however, and it is best if, once placed, the logo does not change location from slide to slide. Consistency is important to a good presentation, so you should minimize the amount of visual change and misalignment from slide to slide. Slide transitions may mask these changes, but that is not an effective solution to the problem.

You may already have a logo in mind for your presentation, but for the sake of becoming more proficient with the presentation software, you will create one for this project. While the process of creating a logo usually involves hiring an outside expert or going to your organization's graphic designer, here you will use clip art and text boxes to create a sample logo. For a review of

▼ **FIGURE 9.8**
Example logo

how to insert clip art into your slides, refer to Chapter 8.3.6. Pick a graphic that you like and insert it into the Slide Master parent (Slide 1). You will notice that it propagates all the way through the rest of the layout slides as well. Any elements you add to this slide will appear in every slide of your presentation.

You can now format the graphic with whatever effects you like. Try adding an inner shadow so that the graphic appears to be cut out from the slide background itself. Add a new text box in PowerPoint 2010 by clicking on the *Text Box* icon on the *Text* panel of the *Insert* ribbon. In PowerPoint 2011, you add a text box by selecting the *Text* icon on the *Home* ribbon and choosing *Text Box*. You will need to click and drag your cursor to set the size of this or the active selection will default to the nearest placeholder text box or your newly inserted graphic.

Add whatever name you want for your proposed company. The example here uses "Good Dog Dogs." You can now apply text transformations to make your new company name look more stylized. Try wrapping it in a circle or arching it from one end to the other. Once you have the text looking the way you want, click and drag to select both the clip art image and the text and create a group of these two objects. A completed example is shown in Figure 9.8.

Unfortunately, you cannot just leave your logo sitting in the middle of the slide; it will attract too much of the audience's attention and detract from the content you are going to add. You need to fade it into the background so that it can still be seen but everything else on your slide gets more of the attention. Keep a copy of the full-color logo for your title slide; that is one location where it should be allowed to attract attention. If your logo is new, like the one you just created, this gives your presentation a new identity or branding. If your logo already exists in an organization, you are associating your presentation content with the culture of that organization.

Copy and paste your full-color logo to the Title Slide layout slide master. Once you have your color copy in place, go back to the Slide Master parent and click on the clip art graphic of your logo. Select the *Format* ribbon (or the *Format Picture* ribbon in PowerPoint 2011). Go to the *Color* (or *Recolor*) icon on the *Adjust* panel and select a color adjustment that sufficiently blends the image into your background. You can see an example of the completed blending in Figure 9.9. If you are using multiple background colors on the layouts for your presentation, you may wish to do this on each of the layout slide masters instead of the Slide Master parent. Just remember to keep the logo in the same

If you want a more advanced logo, you can add multiple layers to it using different pieces of clip art. You can even select certain pieces and use the picture formatting tools to remove the background of the image to make it align with the color of the background beneath it. You can also add drawing elements to your logo, such as the smiley face added to the logo in the example. Whenever you add drawing elements, you must set the color options manually; for instance, there is no single filter that you can apply for a grayscale version.

▲ FIGURE 9.9
Blended logo

location on each slide so it does not change locations as you click through your slides.

Now you need to alter the text of your logo to fade it into the background along with your graphic. You make these changes using either the *Font* panel of the *Home* ribbon or the options available from the *Format* ribbon. Change any part of your text that is too distracting from the background color to something more appropriate. Anything that creates too much contrast with the background will draw too much attention. You can use the defined colors for your color scheme to help fade the text more effectively. You can generally use the same offset color that you used for the graphic to fade your text. The color names are located along the top row in the Theme Colors area on the drop-down menu of either the Font Color icon or the Text Fill icon; you can select the fade intensity from the column beneath the color name, as shown in Figure 9.10.

Resize your logo to a reasonable size and adjust the font size of the text to maintain the look that you established

▲ **FIGURE 9.10**
Using theme
colors to blend
text

when you initially created the logo. One possible location for your logo is at the upper-lefthand corner of the slide; this is where it will receive the most

If your logo contains too much contrast to filter out using a fade effect, you can add a drawing object rectangle to the slide and set its color and transparency to match the slide background and place it on a layer above the logo but behind the slide content. This will lower the contrast produced by the logo without disrupting the look of the slide. You can see the effect of this in Figure 9.11, which shows the logo with and without the rectangle in place.

attention, but it also means you will be distracting your audience from the content that is on the slide. Having a sufficiently faded logo in the center of the slide is another possibility, but you have to make sure it does not take away the attention that belongs on the content of the individual slide.

Now select the entirety of your logo (the group you made), line it up where you want it on the slide, and send it to the back layer of the slide (*Send to Back*) using the *Arrange* icon. You can also do this using the right-click menu. You should see the placeholder text in front of your faded logo. If you have done this correctly, as shown in Figure 9.12. Readers' eyes are naturally drawn to the area of highest contrast in an image, so make sure the text in your text boxes is formatted so it stands out over the logo.

Next you will need to go through each layout of your presentation and choose where the logo belongs and where it does not; this is a yes or no decision since your only option in each of these slides is to select or deselect the *Hide Background Graphics* checkbox (this is found under the *Background* menu

➤ **FIGURE 9.11**
Effects of a
transparent
rectangle
(shown in the
right image)
on reducing
contrast

in the *Themes* ribbon for PowerPoint 2011). The first stop is the Title Slide layout slide master. Since you should now have both a full-color logo and a faded logo on this slide, you will want to remove the faded copy. To do this, just check the box next to *Hide Background Graphics* (or *Hide Graphics*) on the *Slide Master* ribbon; your faded logo should disappear.

Click the *Save* icon to save your work if you have not already done so. Then click the *Close Master View* icon to get back to the regular design view. Now you are ready to start creating your presentation!

If you have put sufficient effort into the formatting of your Slide Master and you wish to use your design later, you can save your presentation as a template file. To do so, click on the *File* menu just as if you were saving the presentation normally. Name your file *MySalesPitch-Template* and choose *PowerPoint Template* as the document type. Whenever you open a template file such as this one, a new presentation will open based on this style. Give it a try if you like, and then open your *MySalesPitch* presentation file again.

 **OPEN OFFICE** If you are using Impress, your image manipulation options for creating a logo from scratch are more limited. You can still use Office.com to acquire clip art, but you will have to manually alter the image properties unless you use a specific filter like the Grayscale option.

▲ **FIGURE 9.12** Completed slide branding

You can remove background graphics in the regular design view for your presentation as well, so you will always have the opportunity to remove your logo from the background if it is too distracting; this option is found in the *Design* ribbon for PowerPoint 2010 when you are not viewing the Slide Master. However, this will also remove the added slide decorations that are added by default to the theme. In PowerPoint 2011, this option is found on the *Themes* ribbon under the *Background* icon.

CONSTRUCTING AN EFFECTIVE PRESENTATION

9.3

Remember the value proposition you constructed earlier in the chapter? Now it is time to put it into action! You will create your title slide now and then build your presentation from there.

If you have been following along with the example, your title slide should now contain your new logo. Notice that you cannot edit it from here; it is fixed in place from the Slide Master so you have to change it there if you need to alter its placement. Add a suitable title to your presentation; note that this is not your value statement. The title slide should be a quick placeholder to display as a short introduction to what you have to say, with your name or your organization name as a possible subtitle. The title of your presentation should draw interest as the audience gathers if you are using this for a live presentation; it should give some idea about the topic of the presentation, but it should do so succinctly. Whether or not you have a subtitle is up to you.

9.3.1

Outlining

You should always create an outline for your presentation before you start adding your content. PowerPoint is flexible enough to allow you to move slides and add slides as needed, but you need to make sure your message is delivered successfully throughout your presentation. Your goal in any presentation should be cognitive guidance rather than just information presentation. Without this higher level of information presentation, your audience is unlikely to retain for very long anything that you have shown them.

Create a rough draft of your outline on paper. You should focus more on the main topics that you want to present as opposed to the specific slides that you are going to

COGNITIVE GUIDANCE *is the presentation of information in a manner that does not over-burden the cognitive load (or mental processing capacity) of the viewer or recipient while pre-serving the meaning of the information; this is a preferable way to share information, as it leads to increased retention and understanding.*

include. You may have only a short time to present, so make sure you list out the main topics you absolutely must cover first. These topics should all contribute to the overall purpose of the presentation or they should be removed.

Repeat this process with secondary topics and so forth until you have all of the material listed that you are going to cover. Each time you add a new topic, you should evaluate the relevance to your overall purpose and contribution. If it is not essential or meaningful to your presentation as a whole, it should be removed. You can now use this topic list to structure your presentation by constructing a meaningful map of these topics.

Adding Slide Notes 9.3.1.1

You can start to map your presentation from the rough outline that you have just constructed. Add a slide for each topic that you need to cover. You are not going to construct the actual slides at this point; you will save that for the second pass through your presentation. Instead, you are going to use the Notes pane that is visible across the bottom of the interface in Normal view to add an outline for what you want to cover in each slide. This is the one area where you can use as many bullet points as needed. You can use the tools available in the Font and Paragraph panels of the Home ribbon to format the text in this area, but you cannot add graphic elements like clip art. PowerPoint does not allow you to change the font color here or use text effects, either.

your computer; keep that in mind when you outline your topics.

Best Practices for Outlining 9.3.1.2

There are a few guidelines you should always observe in constructing an outline or a map of your presentation. First, you should always get the attention of the audience with the first slide you present; this will be the second slide of your overall presentation. This slide is where the audience will determine how important your topic is to them and whether they will give you their full attention.

You should use the Notes pane for each slide and make an outline of what you want to present. You should not write out everything you are going to say word for word. These should be notes to guide you through your content instead of a set script to follow. If you notice your content for one slide getting too long, you should add a second slide for the topic and split the content between the two. Remember that while your notes will not be visible to the audience when you present, others will be able to view what you have written here when you share the presentation on

Your title slide should just be a placeholder before you begin; you can think of it as the curtain that rises before a theater performance. The second slide in your presentation is actually the first slide that you should showcase.

To help you outline and organize your presentation, PowerPoint 2010 allows you to add section names to your slides to organize them into logical groups. This allows you to make changes to a specific set of slides for one part of your presentation. Your audience cannot see these section names and they do not appear in your outline, so this tool is strictly for your convenience and organization. You can add a section by using the right-click menu or by selecting the *Section* icon on the *Home* ribbon. You can use either the right-click menu or the *Section* icon to change or remove these sections later. In PowerPoint 2011, use the right-click menu or select the *Insert* menu and then choose *Section*.

Your first slide should capture the attention of the audience and interest them in what you have to say. It should be relevant to your presentation, but it should not give away everything you have to say. Give your audience a quick preview of what you are going to show them with your presentation, but do not give them a step-by-step breakdown; you want to emphasize the end goal with this slide. You need to present your main point to the audience three times; this repetition will increase the probability of cognitive recognition in the audience, which will insert the idea into memory. The first occurrence should be at the beginning of your presentation. The second should be as you walk the audience through the problem or opportunity on which your contribution is built. The last iteration of the main idea should be as a summary statement at the end of your presentation.

You need to guide your audience to an understanding of your perspective and show them the value of your main contribution. What you have to say is already important to you, but you need to frame it in such a way that the audience feels it is important to them as well. For example, in a research presentation, you should provide the background on the research problem for which you are presenting a solution; this will allow the audience to see the significance of the research that you have done.

Once you have given the audience your perspective, you should spend the majority of your time presenting what you have to offer. This should be done in a clear manner that the audience can follow from one step or slide to the next. Remember that they are building a cognitive map of this information as you present it, so jumping unexpectedly from a particular topic to something that is unrelated or inconsistent will disrupt that mapping process. Consider the level of prior understanding of your audience to help determine how much information you need to present to them to make it as coherent as possible.

THE 10-MINUTE MARK
Humans have a short attention span. Steve Jobs suggests that 10 minutes into your presentation, you need to do something different to focus attention back on yourself and what you have to say. You can provide handouts at this point, show a video, or otherwise get the audience to react to you and reengage.

When you have demonstrated the main contribution of your presentation, you should emphasize your main point. After all, this is what you came to say, so you need to make sure your audience realizes it. Once you have given your main contribution, you should add any action items that you want the audience to take with them. If they are responsible for some outcome from your presentation, you should deliver your charge to them at this point in your presentation.

Finally, you will add your summary and conclusion. Your summary should be brief and it should state your main contribution for the third time. A single slide should typically be sufficient for a summary; the audience has just experienced your entire presentation, so you should keep the summary short. If you have time for questions, you can add a slide to prompt the audience. A better practice, though, is to transition to a slide with your contact information or the contact information for your organization so people can follow up on their own and then simply ask if they have any questions.

Grabbing Attention in Your First Slide

9.3.2

The first slide of your actual presentation is where you need to grab the audience's attention. If this is a sales pitch and you fail to capture them at the beginning, the likelihood that they will tune in later is slim. There are a lot of different ways to accomplish this. If this is a research presentation, you can build a mystery with an image or a result that the audience wants to see unfolded. With a sales pitch like the

Video can be a great tool to assist a presentation, but it needs to be short and relevant. If you are nervous presenting in front of a crowd, you can include a short video in your first slide to allow you time to calm yourself before you have to start presenting in earnest. You can insert a video in PowerPoint from a file or from a Web site. To add a video in PowerPoint 2010, click the *Video* icon in the *Insert* ribbon and select the option you want; in PowerPoint 2011, select the *Media* icon on the *Home* ribbon. The next chapter will give you more specific guidance on including videos in your presentation and formatting and editing them appropriately. If you are constructing a sales pitch, a short video of interviews showing the market need or demonstrating your product is a great way to grab attention at the outset of your presentation.

one in this chapter, a clear value statement is one way to begin effectively. You should refrain from adding fancy graphics to a text statement here since you do not want to give the impression that you are trying to distract the audience from your main idea.

On the design side, you should evaluate whether your statement stands out well enough with the color scheme you have chosen. If the contrast is not sufficient to showcase your text, you can change the background style to correct the issue. On any slide in Normal view, you can select the *Background Styles* icon on the *Background* panel of the *Design* ribbon to change your options based on the theme you have selected; this is found under the *Background* icon in the *Themes* ribbon in PowerPoint 2011. Unlike a change in the layout slide masters, a change here

will change all of the background styles for the entire presentation. If you need to make this adjustment, you may want to open your Slide Master view and make the design change there instead. Make sure your footer appears correctly on this slide as well. You can see an example of an opening slide in Figure 9.13.

Build the Need for Your Presentation

9.3.3

No matter what type of presentation you are developing, the next step is to give the audience the background of why they should care about the problem or opportunity you are attempting to solve or exploit with your presentation. This is true of research presentations, marketing presentations, and simple information presentations. You cannot fully deliver the value of what you are offering if your audience does not share a similar perspective on the situation to which your solution or contribution operates. You have to build the problem statement for them in language

▼ FIGURE 9.13
Example
opening slide

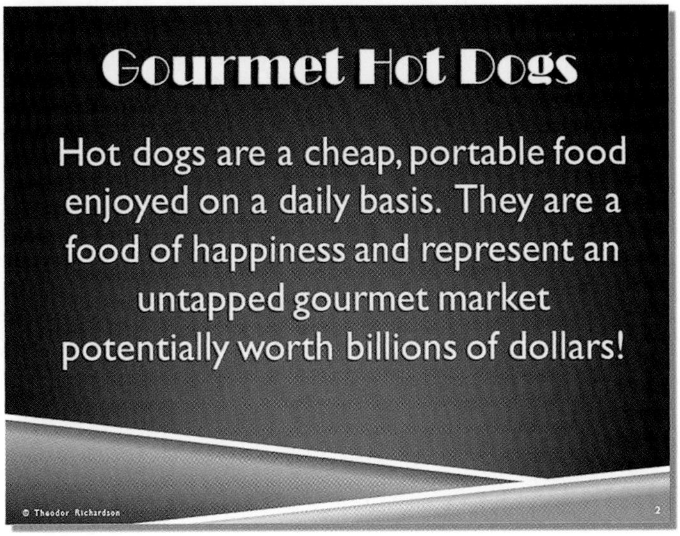

Gourmet Hot Dogs

Hot dogs are a cheap, portable food enjoyed on a daily basis. They are a food of happiness and represent an untapped gourmet market potentially worth billions of dollars!

© Theodor Richardson

they understand so they will at least have enough buy-in to listen to your proposed solution or product.

Always remember who your audience is. Do not waste their time or yours telling them what they already know. Similarly, do not give them a reading assignment with all of the text on your slides, especially if you are presenting in person. The problem formulation should be succinct but clear. The level of detail you add should be determined by the expected audience.

For the example presentation here, it is necessary to build the case for the existence of a market for a new product. Some quick research using the Internet

will assist with this, though as always you must evaluate the legitimacy and credibility of any source on the Web. For this example, the Web site of the National Hot Dog & Sausage Council (*www.hot-dog.org*) provides statistics regarding the average annual consumption of hot dogs and the locations where they are most consumed to support the establishment of a market for the product being offered. To turn this into a meaningful part of the presentation, you need to pull some impressive data from this and engage the audience with some fun facts. The text of your slides should be easy to read and interesting for your audience, even if they do not have the slightest interest in hot dogs!

Your text size should never fall below 24 pt font for anything your audience is expected to read. When you have a few key facts to present but they all have a significant amount of text, you can choose a two-column layout to keep the font size high and keep the text on one slide, as shown in Figure 9.14. You can change the layout of the slide by clicking on the *Layout* icon on the *Slides* panel of the *Home* ribbon. In general, you should not use more than two columns for any presentation because it becomes too difficult for the audience to read when there is too much visual information to absorb at once.

Guidelines vary, but the general consensus seems to be a target of three and a limit of five facts or bullet points per slide for a live presentation. Some professional designers,

▼ **FIGURE 9.14**
Example of two-column slide layout

such as Trine Falbe, even argue that each slide should have its own point and more slides are better than cluttered slides; she argues against the use of any bullet points at all. More than numerical restrictions, the clarity and readability of the slide are the most essential qualities. Keep it clear and keep it concise. Your audience needs to be able to digest any text that you have on your slide while listening to what you have to say.

You can be more liberal with the amount of text you include in a standalone presentation, but you must remember that slides are not pages of text. Focus on how to effectively frame the problem that you want to solve or the opportunity you want to exploit. In the example, you want to show that there is a substantial market for your product. You should try to quickly build suspense with the audience so they are interested in the solution and your contribution. Too much background will overshadow what you have to offer and will usually cause the audience to disengage from what you are presenting.

9.3.4 Present Your Main Contribution

The bulk of your presentation should focus on what you have to offer. It should again be clear and concise. It should showcase how you plan to solve the problem at hand or capitalize on the opportunity you just presented. Your audience can usually tell when you are stretching content or wasting time, just as you can tell when someone else is doing it to you, which means you need to keep them engaged while you present what you have to offer.

 OPEN OFFICE You can change the layout of your slides in Impress using the *Slide Layout* menu icon of the main toolbar. The slide master in Impress does not have direct children for the different layouts that you can alter as you can in PowerPoint, so if you make any design changes to a particular layout, you should copy the altered slide to use for any other slides using the same layout within your presentation.

Keep your slides visually interesting by switching between the different layout options periodically without overwhelming your audience with the change. You can change the layout of the current slide by clicking the *Layout* icon on the *Home* ribbon and selecting one of the options. If you have constructed your Slide Master well at the beginning, you should only need to make minimal changes to the existing layout slides, which will go a long way toward providing consistency and identity to your presentation.

In this example, additional slides have been added to showcase the planned idea and business model. This type of content should be the bulk of your presentation and should be clear to the audience. Experiment with the different layouts to find what works best for your business case.

Effective Visualization   9.3.4.1

Research has shown that the most effective way for people to retain an idea is for them to experience it visually while it is explained to them. This process is termed *dual-channels*. A person has two separate concurrent brain processes that take in information during a presentation: one is the verbal component and the other is the visual component. This same research has concluded that the visual component is superior (termed the *picture superiority effect*), but the best retention comes from the visual component supporting the verbal component. What this means for your presentation is that you need to make sure your visuals supplement what you are saying instead of substituting for it. In essence, your words will be attached to the image you present in the mind of your viewer. Bullet points and lengthy text do not form a concise image in the mind, meaning this retention will not occur if you oversaturate your slides.

The Notes section can contain as much text as you like, but each slide should present only what is absolutely essential. If you can present the same idea with an image or graph, it is better to do so. You should not use the text on your slides as a crutch for your presentation; you should rehearse your presentation well enough that you recognize the points you have to make based on the visual information of the slide. Find the layout that supports the information you are presenting and tie all of the information on the slide together into a single message as much as possible. If you cannot pull all of the information in your slide into a single coherent thought, you need to split the information into multiple slides.

Modifying Layouts 9.3.4.2

You can change the layout of your slide to any of the preset options by selecting the *Layout* icon on the *Home* ribbon and then selecting which option you want to use. How the information is presented is as important as what information is presented; you can see an example of this in Figure 9.15 where the same information is presented in two different ways. Chapter 10 contains more advanced analysis and instructions for including some additional visual elements in your presentation to make it more exciting and interesting.

Tips for Success 9.3.4.3

Keep the following tips for a successful presentation in mind:

- Make your font large enough to read. When in doubt, walk six feet away from your screen and try to read your slide.

▶ **FIGURE 9.15**
The same content in two formats

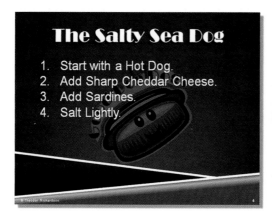

- Use bold formatting or an increase in word size to emphasize words and terms in your presentation, but use these sparingly. Italics typically make the text harder to read from a distance, so it should be avoided.

- Never change the font color for emphasis. Too many colors distract the audience and keep the eye from focusing on any one area, making it difficult for the viewer to read the text cohesively.

- If you have different colors of text (such as a hyperlink), keep them within the color scheme chosen for the overall theme.

- Keep your content brief and to the point. You are creating your presentation to engage the audience.

- Create a presentation you would want to see. If it looks bad to you, it will probably look bad to your audience!

9.3.5 Summarize and Conclude

Your summary and conclusion should reemphasize your value statement and your contribution without repeating it word for word. It should be the final bit of information that you leave with your audience for them to consider. One or two slides should be the maximum for your summary and conclusion; you should not be introducing new information here and you do not want to repeat the entire presentation since the audience has just experienced it. The main purpose of the summary and conclusion section is to provide a third repetition of the main point you want to convey.

Your final slide should contain your contact information for anyone who wishes to follow up with you. If you are part of a team, you should include the contact information for all the team members and the areas for which each person is responsible. Make sure your contact information is displayed long enough for anyone in the audience to copy it down if they wish to follow up on your presentation.

There are some great SmartArt graphics that allow you to format contact information for multiple contacts clearly and effectively. The topic of inserting and formatting SmartArt is covered in Chapter 10.

It is common to include a slide seeking questions from the audience. Your venue should dictate whether this is allowed or feasible. If you decide to include such a slide, you may want it as a precursor to your contact information or concurrently with your contact information. The slide containing your contact information is the one that should linger on the screen for a live presentation while you field questions because it will allow audience members to copy down your information if they do not wish to ask questions in public or if there is not enough time to get to them.

Now that you have completed your presentation, you should view it to make sure it is coherent and presents the message you want with the clarity it needs. You also need to check the alignment of your images and drawings to make sure they are

If you are sharing a presentation document as a supplement after you have presented it, you should adjust the slide for questions to direct the viewer to the person who can answer them. For instance, you would want to change the text "Questions?" to something like "If you have questions, you can contact…" This small change will increase the professionalism of the result.

correct. Misalignment can be distracting to your audience and can ruin the impact your graphic would have otherwise had; an example of the effect alignment has on a graphic is shown in Figure 9.16. Your design work may be complete, but there are several things you still need to do before your new masterpiece is ready for public consumption. If you are giving a live presentation, you will need to prepare your timings and rehearse. If you are sharing your presentation via the Web or another mechanism to present on an individual computer, you can either record your narration or set up your presentation so it plays automatically with the timings that you have defined.

9.4 PRESENTING YOUR MASTERPIECE

Your presentation is a performance piece. Like any theater performance, you need to make sure you rehearse what you have to say so you can present it coherently and with authority. This applies whether you are in front of a live audience or recording your narration. You should never find yourself in a situation where you are reading the slide contents to the audience; doing so will cause them to disengage from what

you have to say and will give you the appearance of being unprepared. Whether or not you like being in front of an audience, you should just be yourself. You do not need to pretend to be more serious than you are.

You, not the slides you are presenting, will engage the audience. You should not be afraid to make them smile and you do not have to be perfect; in fact, the audience will accept you better if you come to them prepared but present as yourself. Most presentation software gives you a variety of options for practicing your slide timing, and PowerPoint gives you the option of directly recording narration for your slides. You can also broadcast your presentation live and even save it as a video to share if you are using PowerPoint.

Live Presentations

You should go through your notes enough times to be familiar with the content you are presenting. This is true whether you have created the presentation or you are just presenting it on someone else's behalf. Your audience will disengage if you start reading the slides to them, so you should have an idea of what you are saying without using the written text on the slide as a script.

> **FIGURE 9.16**
> The effect of alignment on a graphic

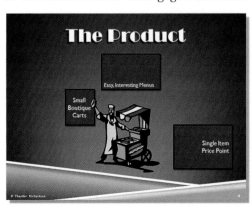

You should know your presentation well enough that you recognize the topics you need to cover on a particular slide based on the slide graphics alone.

You can practice your slide timing using the *Rehearse Timings* icon on the *Slide Show* ribbon. This will start your presentation in Slide Show view with a clock and a small interface for moving your slide show forward or repeating the current slide, as shown in Figure 9.17. PowerPoint 2011 gives you a larger interface called Presenter view (also shown in Figure 9.17), where you can see your notes as well. This will tell you how long you are spending on each of your slides, which is helpful information if you need to present within a fixed time limit. When you are finished with your rehearsal, you will be prompted to save your slide timings. If you choose this option, your slide show will stay on each of the slides for the set amount of time that you took to cover the material and will switch to the next slide automatically when that amount of time has passed.

If you have multiple monitors attached to your computer, such as the regular display monitor and a digital projector, you can select *Use Presenter View* on the *Slide Show* ribbon when

OPEN OFFICE You cannot save slide timings directly in Impress, but you can use this tool to rehearse by selecting the *Slide Show* menu and then selecting *Rehearse Timings*. A clock in the corner of the Slide Show view display will let you know how long you have spent on each slide. You can then use the *Slide Transition* tab in the window pane on the right of the interface in Normal view to set how long you want the slide to remain on the screen using the *Advance Slide* panel and the *Automatically after* setting.

you wish to present. This option allows you to select which monitor will display the show in Slide Show view and which monitor will show the special Presenter view, which contains the slide show and your Notes section for the current slide. Using the Presenter view can be helpful when you are making your presentation, especially if you encounter a particularly difficult topic and want to make sure you present the correct details. However, you should not rely on the Notes section of your presentation to speak to your audience. It is always better if you know your presentation well enough to talk to the audience without continually referring to your notes or your slides.

◀ **FIGURE 9.17**
Rehearse Timings interface

When you are in Slide Show view (or the local Reading view equivalent) in Power-Point 2010, you can use your mouse as a laser pointer on the slide to highlight information. The default behavior of the mouse in this view is to advance the slide just like the spacebar or the right arrow key; however, when you hold down the *Control (Ctrl)* key and left-click the mouse, the cursor will appear as a laser point on the screen for as long as you hold the left button down. You can record this mouse movement during the default recording process that is explained in the next section. The color of the laser pointer cursor can be set in the dialog box that appears when you click the *Set Up Slide Show* icon in the *Slide Show* ribbon. Figure 9.18 shows the dialog box and the pointer in action.

If you need to mark up your slides to highlight information, both PowerPoint 2010 and PowerPoint 2011 give you the option to change your mouse cursor to a pen. To access this, simply right-click on your slides in Slide Show view and select the *Pen* option. This will change your mouse to a pen for the current slide. You will have

to advance the slide using the spacebar or arrow key. but the default mouse behavior will be restored on the next slide.

Recording Narration

If you are sharing your presentation on an individual computer screen, you may find it beneficial to record narration instead of just sharing the slides themselves. In fact, if you have constructed the slides successfully, you will need narration to support them. In PowerPoint, you can easily record narration using the *Record Slideshow* icon. This will prompt you for preferences and allow you to select whether you want to record your narration from the beginning of the presentation or from the current slide. After you have set your options, you will be presented with an interface that looks just like the rehearsal interface except it includes an icon to pause and resume the recording.

In order to record sound on your machine, you must have a sound card and a microphone connected to the audio input line of your computer. Most computers have a default internal microphone that you can use automatically, but not all of them do!

> **FIGURE 9.18**
Using the mouse as a laser pointer

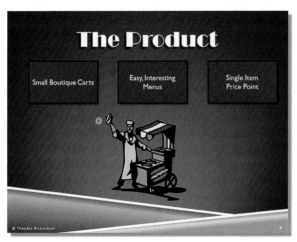

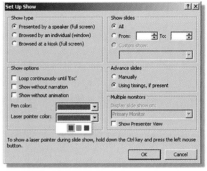

When you have completed your recording, you can review the narration by selecting the Slide Show view (you can do this quickly by pressing *F5*). The narration will play just like the animation and transitions in the preview mode. The individual narrations will appear as a small audio icon in the lower-right corner of the slide and they will play by default when the slide is reached in Slide Show view. If you do not want to keep a particular narration in PowerPoint 2010, select *Clear* from the drop-down options under the *Record Slide Show* icon. In PowerPoint 2011, you can record the presentation again to save over the previous narration.

9.4.3 Sharing Your Presentation

You can share your presentation document just like any other file. It can be e-mailed or placed on transferrable media to share. Be aware, however, that you must include any linked media along with the native presentation document or the media will not be transferred.

In PowerPoint, you have the option to save your presentation document as a PowerPoint Show. To do this, use the *Save As* function and select the document type *PowerPoint Show* (*.ppsx*). If you save your document in this manner, it will open in

> **LINKED MEDIA** *is any file that has been added to the presentation by reference that is not embedded into the presentation document itself. An example of this is a file that opens as a result of an action being activated.*

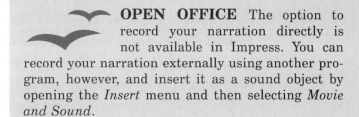

OPEN OFFICE The option to record your narration directly is not available in Impress. You can record your narration externally using another program, however, and insert it as a sound object by opening the *Insert* menu and then selecting *Movie and Sound*.

Slide Show view whenever a user clicks on its icon. The presentation cannot be modified in this format, but the viewer does not have to have PowerPoint installed to view the show; the presentation uses the Microsoft PowerPoint Viewer software instead. This document type is a good choice if you do not want anyone to see the notes you have attached and you want the viewer to experience the presentation as you have scripted it. The drawback of this format is that included elements like video are dependent on the properties of the host machine the viewer is using and may not work as you intended.

The latest versions of PowerPoint have overcome this limitation by providing the ability to save your presentation as a video. In PowerPoint 2010, you can save your presentation as a video by clicking on the *File* menu and selecting *Save and Send* and then *Create a Video*. This will open a new menu of options where you can select the video resolution you want, whether you want to use recorded narration and timings, and if you want to spend only a set amount of time on each slide. Once you have selected your options, click the *Create Video* icon beneath the settings, as shown in Figure 9.19. This will open the Save As dialog box where you can

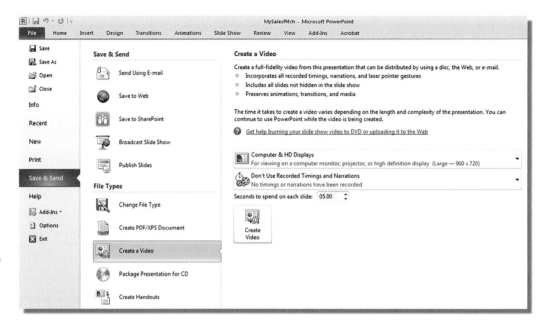

▶ **FIGURE 9.19**
Save As Video
option in
PowerPoint
2010

save the presentation as a *Windows Media Video* (*.wmv*). This format will include all of your content in the video except Apple QuickTime movies and elements that require third-party software to display. You must also update linked media from any Office 2007 (or prior) content that is still included in the presentation for it to be included in the video.

PowerPoint 2011 offers you the ability to save your presentation as a *Movie* (*.mov*) through the regular Save As function. You can adjust the settings for your movie by clicking the *Options* icon on the Save As dialog box with *Movie* selected in the *Format* box.

PowerPoint also offers you the option of broadcasting your presentation in a live synchronous environment. This service is available for all PowerPoint 2010 and PowerPoint 2011 users, but it does require you to have a Windows ID. Clicking the *Broadcast Slide Show* icon on the *Slide Show* ribbon will prompt you to log in using your Windows ID and password. The software will then generate a public link you can share that can be used by up to 50 viewers to access your presentation live over the Internet whether or not they have PowerPoint installed. This will play your presentation in a special Broadcast view, which allows you to control your presentation as you would in a live setting. Once you have finished your presentation, click *End Broadcast*; this will terminate any viewer connections to your presentation and the link will no longer be valid. You should note that the only audio that will be shared in this format is what is recorded within the presentation.

OPEN OFFICE Impress does not have the capabilities for sharing your presentation as a video or live broadcast. However, you can save your presentation as a Web-enabled Flash (.swf) file. This will play all of the transitions, animations, and sounds that you have included in your presentation document and retain the slide timing that you have set up. You can then embed the file in a Web page as another way to share it. To perform this task, select the *File* menu and then the *Export* option. In the dialog box that opens, select the document type *Flash (.swf)*.

▲ **FIGURE 9.20** Completed chapter example slides

CHAPTER SUMMARY

This chapter focused on the effective use of presentation software to impact your audience and assist you in presenting what you have to say in the best possible manner. Using a Slide Master and predefined formatting options, you can quickly create the design of your presentation to allow you to focus on the content, which is by far the most important aspect of any presentation. You should also now have an understanding of how to share and present your new slide show. You can see the completed slides for the chapter example in Figure 9.20. This should give you a comparison for the structure and presentation of your own work. The next chapter will focus on additional graphic enhancements and media you can add to enliven your presentation even more.

CHAPTER EXERCISES

1. Using the skills learned in this chapter, develop a 10-slide presentation on a topic of your choice using all three of the important considerations provided: the idea, value proposition, and consistency. Use the Slide Master to develop a consistent presentation by using a built-in theme and choosing formatting and colors that provide aesthetic coherence.

2. Develop a 10-slide presentation that explains a fictional business plan for an idea that you have for a new venture. Imagine that you are presenting to a group of potential investors who may finance your business idea. The investors have contacted you and advised that they are unable to visit you onsite and have requested that you share the presentation with them using narration. Integrate voice narration and timing into your presentation and prepare the file for sharing as explained in this chapter.

CHAPTER KNOWLEDGE CHECK

1

A _____ is what you have to offer to whoever is viewing your slides or listening to your presentation.

- ○ **A.** Value proposition
- ○ **B.** Brief summary
- ○ **C.** Value add
- ○ **D.** Proposal

2

The _____ is the option that allows you to set up your initial presentation style.

- ○ **A.** Slide list
- ○ **B.** Content
- ○ **C.** Slide Master
- ○ **D.** Theme menu

3

Readability should be the highest consideration when you are choosing which fonts to use in your presentation, followed by aesthetic coherence with the overall presentation.

- ○ True
- ○ False

4

PowerPoint has a number of preset color schemes from which you can choose; once you choose a theme, this setting will default to the color scheme that matches that theme.

- ○ True
- ○ False

5

You should start your presentation with your overall _____ and your _____ proposition in mind.

- ○ **A.** Idea, value
- ○ **B.** Value, business intelligence
- ○ **C.** Idea, proposal
- ○ **D.** Idea, simple

6

To configure a text shadow, select _____ from the menu beneath the preset options.

- ○ **A.** Design
- ○ **B.** Transitions
- ○ **C.** Shadow Options
- ○ **D.** Slide Orientation

7 Three points to keep in mind toward the development of a successful presentation are the following:

- ○ **A.** Idea, value proposition, consistency
- ○ **B.** Proposal value, idea, consideration
- ○ **C.** Idea, value, reliability
- ○ **D.** None of the above

8 Creating too much contrast with the background will draw too much visual attention.

- ○ True
- ○ False

9 On the Master Slide view, you can select the Background Styles icon on the Background panel of the Design ribbon to change your options based on the theme you have selected.

- ○ True
- ○ False

10 You can practice your slide timing using the _____ icon on the Slide Show ribbon.

- ○ **A.** Rehearse Timings
- ○ **B.** Animation Timing
- ○ **C.** Duration
- ○ **D.** Advanced Slide Timing

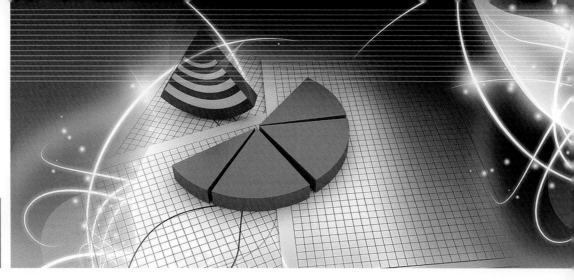

Advanced Features of Presentation Software

Now that you are familiar with the concepts of creating presentation documents, you can improve the impact you have on your audience with the use of advanced media. This chapter covers how to add more complex media elements into your slides and where and how to use them effectively. You will also learn how to create handouts to support your presentation and configure more advanced elements of your presentation content. When you have completed the chapter, you will be able to:

- Format and create handout pages to accompany your presentation

- Add advanced media to your presentation, including sound, video, tables, charts, and graphs

- Create animation within your slides and change the timing and start conditions for your animation effects

- Configure slide properties and define custom sizes and layouts

- Export your slides as image files

CREATING HANDOUTS

When you create a presentation, particularly one that is being presented live, you may want to also create handouts that you can distribute to your audience. You should make sure that any handouts you provide continue the narrative of the presentation in a way that enhances the audience's understanding. You should also be careful not to give out your handouts too soon, especially not before you present or as you begin your presentation. Your audience is always going to be more apt to pay attention to what is in their hands than what they are being shown or told.

There are two main types of handouts commonly distributed with a presentation; these are either miniature versions of the slides themselves as handout pages or a combination of the slide and the accompanying notes in notes pages. You can also print the slides themselves at one slide per page or print just an outline of your presentation, which contains only the text elements of your slides without the theme and background design or formatting and effects. You can preview this outline at any time by selecting the *Outline* tab in the *Slides/Outline* pane. The options for printing any of the handout types are available from the *Print* icon under the *File* menu in PowerPoint 2010, as shown in Figure 10.1. In PowerPoint 2011, you select the type of handout you want to print in the *Print What* entry of the standard Print dialog box (accessed by selecting *Print* from the *File* menu).

▼ FIGURE 10.1
Print options for PowerPoint 2010

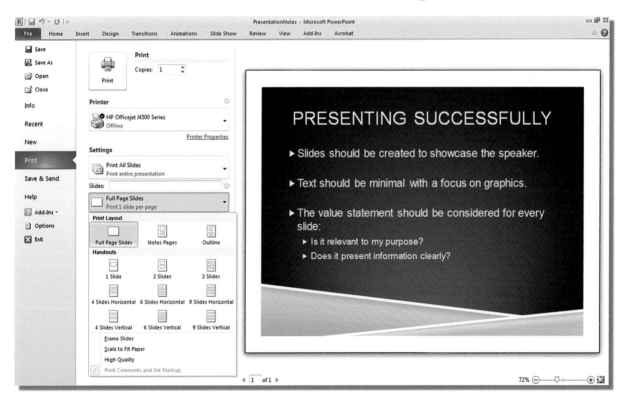

OPEN OFFICE OpenOffice.org Impress offers you the ability to print multiple types of handouts just as you can in PowerPoint. In Impress, this is done by selecting the appropriate setting for the *Document* entry on the Print dialog box, shown in Figure 10.2; your options are Slides, Handouts, Notes, or just an Outline containing the slide text. You can select how many slides you want to appear per page as well. The *OpenOffice.org Impress* tab contains additional options such as the inclusion of hidden slides and the ability to set the color output, and the *Page Layout* tab is where you can customize the slide order.

10.1.1 Modifying the Handout Master

The Handout Master will be used as a template automatically in PowerPoint whenever you are printing multiple slides per page. In PowerPoint 2010, you can customize the Handout Master by selecting the *View* ribbon and selecting *Handout Master*. This will open a context-sensitive Handout Master ribbon, shown

in Figure 10.3. The Design ribbon will once again disappear until you close the Handout Master by clicking the *Close Master View* icon. To access the Handout Master in PowerPoint 2011, select the *Themes* ribbon, choose *Edit Master*, and then select *Handout Master*.

The options in the Handout Master ribbon allow you to make any of the four text boxes in the header and footer of the document visible or invisible. You can edit the contents of these text boxes in the preview document where you ordinarily see the slide you are creating. The default number of slides per page can be set in this ribbon, but you can alter that setting when you print the document. You will not see a preview of your slides on this page, and you cannot edit the slide contents while the Handout Master is open.

The text boxes in this master can accept text effects just like text boxes in any other slide. This means you can change the font, add effects, and change the font color and

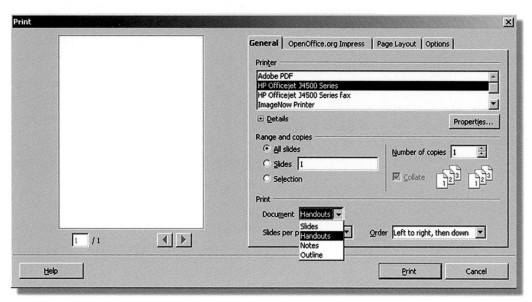

◀ FIGURE 10.2
Print options for Impress

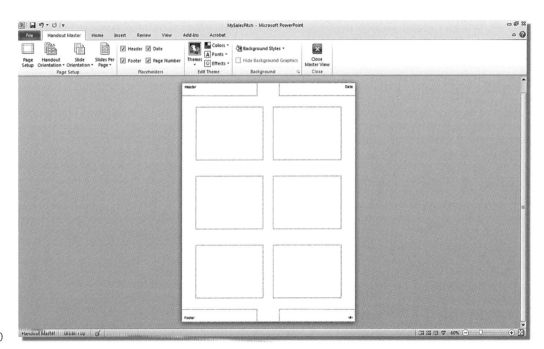

▶ **FIGURE 10.3**
Handout Master
interface in
PowerPoint 2010

size. It is usually a good idea to at least change the font to match the rest of the presentation. When you are creating handouts, you are changing your presentation from a primarily visual medium to a printed one, so you need to keep the consistency of the entire package in mind. The font and color selections for the Handout Master affect this page only (and the printed pages that are based on it) and will not alter the design of the slides themselves.

OPEN OFFICE In Impress, the *Handout* tab works almost exactly like the Handout Master. You have four text boxes with predefined information that you can edit, move, or delete. You can select a layout with different slide arrangements in the *Task* pane on the righthand side of the interface under the *Layouts* tab. To exit the handout master in Impress, select the *Normal* tab in the main design pane.

Modifying the Notes Master

10.1.2

If you followed along with the example project in Chapter 9, you should have substantial outline notes in your sales pitch presentation. If that is the case, you can simply open your *MySalesPitch* file and work from it. If you want to use an existing example to see how the Notes function works, you can open the *MySalesPitchNotes* presentation from the companion resources.

With your presentation open in Power-Point 2010, click on the *View* ribbon and select *Notes Master*. This will open the Notes Master view, which has its own context-sensitive Notes Master ribbon, as shown in Figure 10.4. To access the Notes Master in PowerPoint 2011, select the *Themes* ribbon, choose *Edit Master*, and then select *Notes Master*.

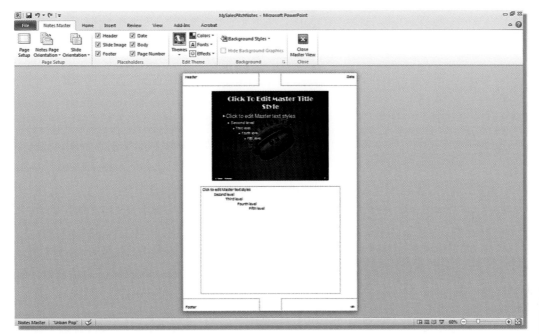

You can format any of the header and footer placeholders in this view using text effects and the font and paragraph settings. You also have the option of setting a background style for the pages, but remember that the text elements need to be legible in print and any background you add will increase ink consumption. Be sure to also consider the quality of the handouts you will be printing when choosing to alter the color scheme of the text; if you are printing in grayscale, using a lot of color in the text boxes or for the background is not a good idea.

While background options are not included in the main ribbon interface, you can format the background in PowerPoint 2011 by using the right-click menu. Just right-click inside of the page and select *Format Background*; this will allow you to alter the background as you would any other object.

The notes that have been written in the slides themselves will be formatted using the options you set in the placeholder text box for the notes in this view; this is where you can add effects such as shadows and reflections to your notes. However, you should make sure the effects fit with the theme of the presentation and the notes are readable in print format. You do not have the restrictions of screen projection to consider with the notes formatting, but the notes should be treated the same as any printed document. The outline levels in the notes text box of the Notes Master view can be formatted the same way as the outline levels of the Slide Master in the Slide Master view. You can alter the position of any of the text boxes on this screen as well, but the default layout is optimal for printing. Double-clicking the

preview of the slide will open the Slide Master view and allow you to edit the Slide Master.

10.2 ADDING ADVANCED MEDIA

A plethora of media options can be embedded into presentation software beyond the images and clip art that have been discussed so far. The key to using media effectively in your presentations is to make sure you are using it with the purpose and audience in mind. It is easy to overdo the amount of media in presentations, so you should restrict the media elements on each slide. For instance, if you add a video to your slide, the video should stand alone. If you have a table, it will be difficult enough for your audience to read, so you can add slight graphic enhancements to emphasize your point, but you should stay away from clip art on the same slide. Keep visibility and focus in mind for your audience.

If you are distributing your presentation on the Web or presenting it on a machine that is not your own, you want to keep the file size of the presentation document in mind as well. Large files will not download as quickly and cannot be as easily shared; your audience may not have the patience to download a large file from a Web site if they are only casually interested in a subject, which means they will not even give your presentation a chance if it is too big. By default, video and sound take up more file space than images and static text. Text and drawing objects do not require a lot of memory to store. Make sure the media you add is necessary or serves a purpose; otherwise, it should be removed. There is no absolute maximum size, but you should take care not to go too far over 2 MB for a casual presentation shared on the Internet. Most Internet connections can handle that amount of information in a short enough time that the user will not become frustrated while the presentation downloads.

Sound and Video

10.2.1

PowerPoint offers a lot of options for inserting sound and video into your presentation. Any sound that you add should be minimal, however. Harsh sound is disrupting to a viewer, especially when fade-in effects are not used. Other than narrating the slides in a saved presentation, you should use sound only when it makes a strong point that a visual element cannot make. To add audio to your presentation in PowerPoint 2010, click the *Insert* ribbon and then the *Audio* icon; to add audio in PowerPoint 2011, click the *Media* icon on the *Home* ribbon and select *Audio from File*. You can choose an audio file either from a file on your local machine or from the clip art collection.

A *fanfare* is a single-use audio file for a slide with a big reveal, such as the venue for your first business location. You should only use it once to get the attention of your audience and it should be short. This only works in a more casual setting; you should not use an audio interruption in a formal setting. You can find a suitable audio clip using the Clip Art panel in PowerPoint 2010 and entering the keyword *fanfare* in the *Search for* box. Once you have selected your sound, you will see an icon that looks like a speaker appear in your slide. This is the action icon for the sound. When you select the action icon for an audio file in PowerPoint 2010, two context-sensitive Audio Tools ribbons appear, as shown in Figure 10.5. The two ribbons are the Format ribbon (which contains the familiar formatting tools you have seen used for images) and the Playback ribbon. PowerPoint 2011 has only the Audio Format ribbon, which combines the formatting options with a small number of additional features from the equivalent Playback ribbon in PowerPoint 2010; the audio editing options in PowerPoint 2010

are not available in PowerPoint 2011. When you select the action icon for the audio file in your slide, a pop-up interface appears that lets you preview the file using the play button and set the volume.

The Playback ribbon (which is only available in PowerPoint 2010) has a number of useful features. The Set Bookmark feature lets you set where you want to start the audio clip or where you want to stop it if it should play from the beginning. You can then use the *Trim Audio* icon to access the Trim Audio dialog box, shown in Figure 10.6, in which you can cut off excess parts of the sound file that you do not want to play.

You can click and drag the green start slider and the red end slider to whatever section of the audio you want to keep. Having the bookmark in place will simply let you slide directly to that mark. You can also preview the audio in the Trim Audio dialog box, so it is

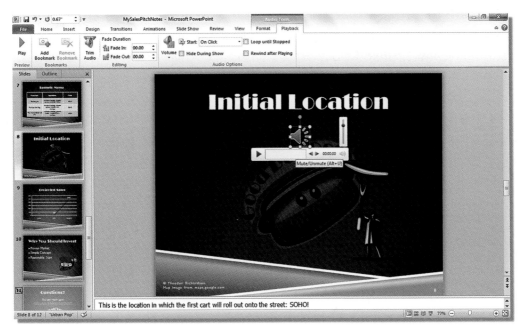

◀ FIGURE 10.5
Audio icon and Audio Tools Playback ribbon in PowerPoint 2010

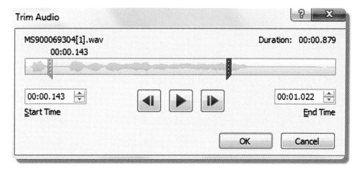

▲ FIGURE 10.6
Trim Audio dialog box in PowerPoint 2010

possible to complete the same task without using bookmarks as you gain more experience. Click *OK* when you are finished to apply the trim. This process does not remove the trimmed ends from the file, so you can go back into the Trim Audio dialog box to make changes later.

You use the Playback ribbon in PowerPoint 2010 to set the start trigger, or what causes the audio to begin; this can be when the slide appears or it can be triggered manually. Setting the Start option to *Play across slides* means the audio will continue even after the slide on which it was started is changed in Slide Show view. You can also set a duration for the Fade In and Fade Out options, which determines how long it takes the sound to start playing from zero volume to its set level or from its set level to zero volume, respectively. PowerPoint 2011 allows you to set the start trigger in the Audio Format ribbon by setting a value in the *Start* field.

You can alter the volume setting for the clip, but be aware that this will be a relative value to the overall volume setting of the machine on which the slide show is being presented.

Now it is time to add a video to the presentation. The video is going to be on the attention-grabbing first slide even before the value statement that you constructed. As this presentation is your first introduction to the audience, it should be something that gets their attention and introduces the subject of the presentation. Insert a new slide after the title slide with the default layout; this is where you will insert your video.

PowerPoint offers the ability to insert a movie from the embed code of a Web site in HTML format. Doing so does not give you the full options for video editing and will instead import the player that is used on the Web site to display the content. It is usually a better choice to use a downloaded video in PowerPoint because you have more control over how it looks and how it plays. There are also a lot of copyright issues you need to consider with the use of any media file taken from the Web.

To insert a video in PowerPoint 2010, select the *Insert* ribbon and then choose the *Video* icon. You can also insert a video from a file using the *Insert Media Clip* quick link in a placeholder text box for content. The Clip Art library has some options available, but they probably are not worth using in the first 30 seconds of your presentation. You should ideally have a specific video in mind for this first slide. For this example, use the file *MySalesPitchVideo*. Once you have chosen your file, you will see the two context-sensitive Video Tools ribbons shown in Figure 10.7. The two ribbons include a Format ribbon, which is

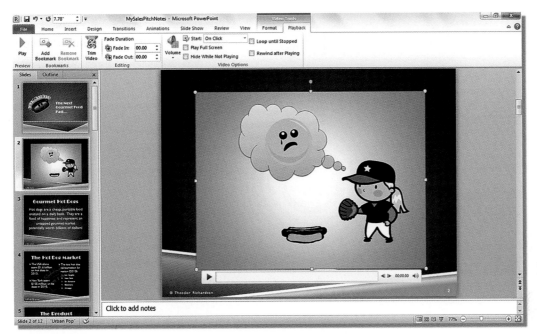

◀ FIGURE 10.7
Video Tools
Playback ribbon
and pop-up
Video menu in
PowerPoint 2010

the same for audio and images, and a Playback ribbon that is almost identical to the audio equivalent. PowerPoint 2011 allows you to add a video from the Media menu in the Home ribbon; this provides you with the context-sensitive Format Movie ribbon, which has all of the formatting commands and a subset of the Playback ribbon options in PowerPoint 2010. When you select a video image in PowerPoint, you will see a small pop-up menu that allows you to play the file, adjust the audio, and move among any chapters that exist in the file.

Most of the configuration options for video are the same as they are for audio. PowerPoint 2010 allows you to configure Fade In and Fade Out effects. Whenever you use a Fade In effect, though, the video screen will fade from solid black and zero volume; similarly, a Fade Out effect will fade to a solid black screen and zero volume. The Trim Video interface (again available only in PowerPoint 2010) has the same functionality as the Trim Audio interface, but it includes a preview of the video as well as the sound.

Whenever you are showing a video, it should take up as much of the screen as it reasonably can within your theming. You can remove the placeholder text box for a title to increase the screen size of the video and make the slide more visually interesting by selecting a unique look for the player. An example of this is shown in Figure 10.8.

 OPEN OFFICE Impress has the ability to import audio and video just like PowerPoint. To add a video or audio element to an Impress presentation, click the *Insert* menu and then choose the *Movie and Sound* icon. The tools for editing these files are more limited than they are in PowerPoint. You can preview the file, set it to repeat, and adjust the volume setting for the sound of the file using the Movie and Sound toolbar that appears, but any file trimming needs to be done externally before the media file is added to the presentation.

▲ FIGURE 10.8
Formatted example of a video within a slide

Tables

Just as in word processing software, tables are a great way to provide visual organization for information. The difference between the use of tables in word processing documents and in presentations is the readability of the information in a table. In a written document, it is easy for the viewer to absorb the information and identify the relevant elements. This is not the case with a presentation. Anytime you use a table, you should either limit the text so the audience can read the entire table quickly or highlight a certain element of the table with additional visual notation so the audience knows where to look. Adding too many rows and columns turns the table into an eye chart for the audience at the back of the room. Remember that when an audience is reading, they are not listening to the speaker.

The next element to add to the sales pitch presentation is a short version of the menu. Add a new slide to your presentation after the slide that shows a graphic of a sample product. There are several ways to insert tables into a slide. The first is to use the quick links from one of the content placeholder text boxes. When you click the table icon, a small Insert Table dialog box appears, as shown in Figure 10.9, in which you can select the number of rows and columns you want for your table. When you have set these values, click *OK*.

Another alternative in PowerPoint 2010 is to use the *Insert* ribbon and click the *Table* icon. This opens a pop-up menu that allows you to highlight the number of rows and columns you want your table to have, as shown in Figure 10.10. You can access the same Insert Table dialog box from this menu that you could from the quick links on the placeholder text box. In PowerPoint 2011, you can add a table from the quick links or by selecting the *Table* ribbon and choosing the *New* icon; this will open the same pop-up menu where

▼ FIGURE 10.9 Insert Table dialog box from quick links in PowerPoint 2010

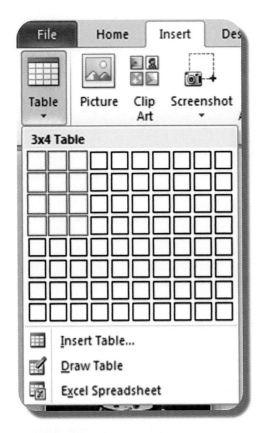

▲ FIGURE 10.10 Table menu from the Insert ribbon in PowerPoint 2010

you can choose the number of rows and columns for your table.

The table in this example has four rows and three columns. Once you have selected the number of rows and columns for the table, you can start to format the table itself.

Clicking and dragging any of the corner grab points or the midpoint grab points resizes the entire table. Clicking and dragging any of the vertical or horizontal lines within the table resizes the table cells. When you select a table in PowerPoint 2010, two context-sensitive Table Tools ribbons appear, as shown in Figure 10.11. The Tables ribbon is always present in PowerPoint 2011, but when you select a table, the Table Layout ribbon appears.

The Design ribbon for the Table Tools in PowerPoint 2010 allows you to set up how your overall table will look; these options are found on the standard Tables ribbon in PowerPoint 2011. Checkboxes let you specify whether you want particular rows highlighted in a different color than the rest. The example uses the *Header Row* and *Banded Rows* options to increase the distinction between the elements of the table. You can select any of the predefined styles from the Table Styles panel, and you can also set the *Shading* color, *Borders*, and *Effects* options for the cell you currently have selected. The Draw Borders panel lets you define the thickness

◀ FIGURE 10.11
Table Tools ribbons in PowerPoint

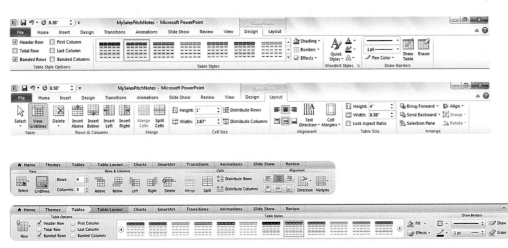

and color of the borders for the currently selected cell (or cells).

The Layout ribbon for the Table Tools (or the Table Layout ribbon in PowerPoint 2011) allows you to modify the size of the selected cells, the size of the overall table, and the placement of text within the cells, as well as add or remove rows and columns. You can also use Merge Cells to merge multiple neighboring cells into a single cell of the table or Split Cells to split a single cell into multiple cells. The Distribute Rows and Distribute Columns icons will attempt to give each of the cells in your table an equal division of the height or width of the table, respectively. A completed example for the menu table is shown in Figure 10.12.

Remember that your table needs to be readable above all else, so if there is a particular cell or result you want

to highlight, you can modify the look of that cell so it draws more attention. You can also add a drawing object like a circle to emphasize to your audience that they should pay attention to that particular element of the table. Long tables can interrupt the flow of a presentation just like a long list of bullet points, so make sure you use tables sparingly.

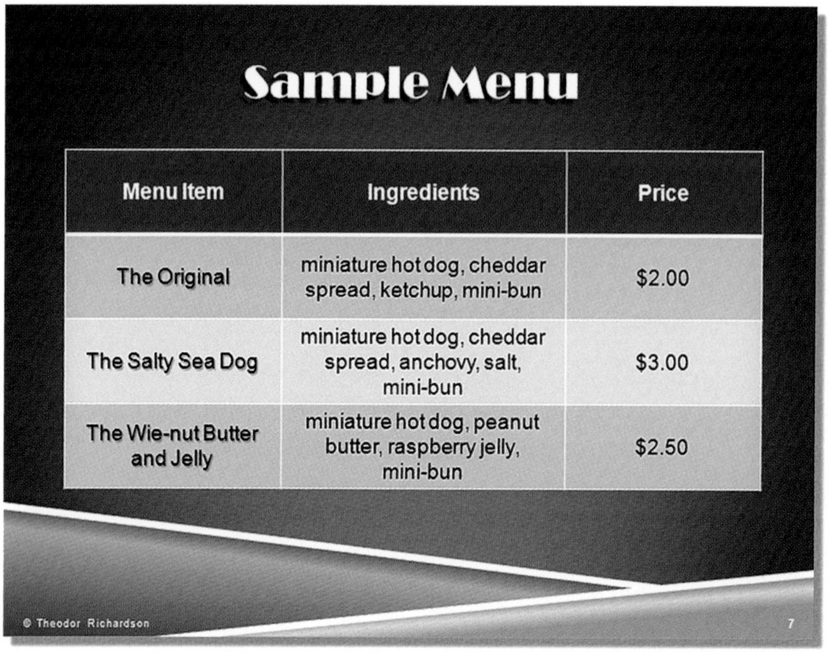

Charts

10.2.3

Charts are another great way to present data quickly. A chart can display a lot of complex data in a single visualization that may take a significant amount of text to explain. In PowerPoint, charts are built from Excel spreadsheet documents. Do not be intimidated if

▼ FIGURE 10.12
Completed table example

Menu Item	Ingredients	Price
The Original	miniature hot dog, cheddar spread, ketchup, mini-bun	$2.00
The Salty Sea Dog	miniature hot dog, cheddar spread, anchovy, salt, mini-bun	$3.00
The Wie-nut Butter and Jelly	miniature hot dog, peanut butter, raspberry jelly, mini-bun	$2.50

Sample Menu

© Theodor Richardson

7

you have never used Excel before, as the example here just uses basic information. (You will learn about Excel in Section IV, "Spreadsheet Software and Microsoft Excel.") To insert a chart in PowerPoint 2010, use the *Insert* ribbon and select *Chart*. In PowerPoint 2011, select the *Charts* ribbon and choose the type of chart you want to insert. You can also add a chart from the quick links *Insert Chart* icon from any content placeholder text box. This opens the Insert Chart dialog box for PowerPoint 2010, shown in Figure 10.13; in PowerPoint 2011, this just activates the Charts ribbon. (You will learn more about creating charts in Chapters 11–13.)

For now, select a simple Line Chart from the list and click *OK*. This will open Excel side by side with Power-Point, as shown in Figure 10.14.

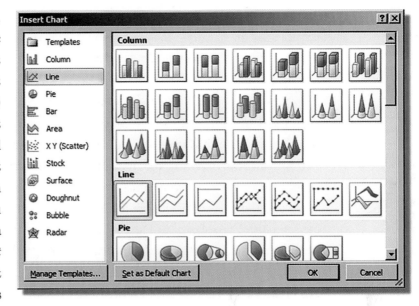

▲ FIGURE 10.13
Insert Chart dialog box in PowerPoint 2010

The data that will be used to construct your line graph is displayed in the spreadsheet in Excel. This example will show a simple line indicating projected sales for the first three months of operation. You can resize the data used in the chart by dragging the blue indicator in Excel that encloses the data used by the chart.

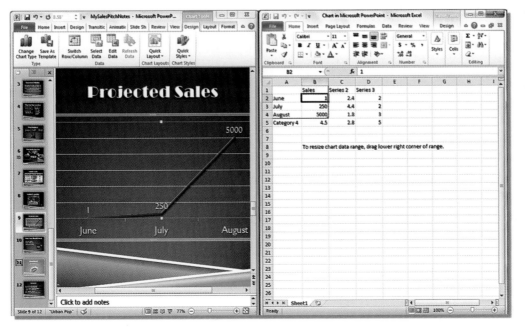

◄ FIGURE 10.14
Completed chart data entry

Since the summer months see the largest sales for hot dogs, the business will launch in June. Therefore, enter *June*, *July*, and *August* for the Category names in Column A of the spreadsheet. Then add the word *Sales* in place of "Series 1." For the data values, June will have 1 sale (cell B:2), July will have 250 (cell B:3), and August will have 5000 (cell B:4). The completed data entry and the proper position for the blue indicator point are shown in Figure 10.14. Once you have completed the data entry, close Excel.

PowerPoint should now return to its former window size and you can see the three context-sensitive Chart Tools ribbons that appear as shown in Figure 10.15. The Format ribbon that appears here should be familiar to you by

now; this allows you to set the text effects and shape effects of the different chart elements. For instance, you can add a shadow to the sales line you have created or add text effects to the chart information, but you should not sacrifice clarity and readability to add effects.

The Design ribbon for Chart Tools (the standard Charts ribbon in Power-Point 2011) allows you to set the look and feel of the chart. There are a number of preset layouts and styles that you can select to display your data from the Chart Layouts panel and the Chart Styles panel. You can also use the *Edit Data* icon (*Edit* in PowerPoint 2011) on the Data panel to open the Excel spreadsheet to make any changes to the data on which the chart is based.

◄ **FIGURE 10.15**
Context-sensitive Chart Tools ribbons

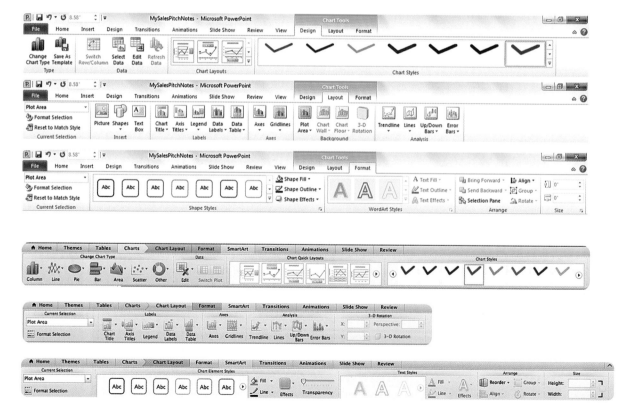

The Layout ribbon for Chart Tools (or the Chart Layout ribbon in PowerPoint 2011) allows you to change the display elements of the chart. You can primarily change how much visual information is displayed on the chart using this ribbon. For the example, select the *Data Labels* icon and choose *Above*. You should now see the projected sales figures for each data point of the chart corresponding to the months. Select the *Legend* icon and choose *None* to remove the series name from the chart; this is not necessary when you have only one variable that you are tracking as in this example. Since there is a slide title, you can also remove the chart title by selecting *Chart Title* and choosing *None*. The completed chart is shown in Figure 10.16.

You can alter the font size for any of the text elements of the chart using the Home ribbon. You can also change the size of the chart manually by dragging the grip points on the corners and midpoints just as you can for any other object in Power-Point. When you use a chart, it should take up the majority of the slide or it will likely not be readable to the audience. If you have specific points you want to make about the chart, you can add drawing objects to highlight particular data points rather than adding any text comments.

10.2.4 SmartArt

SmartArt is a tool that is available in most of the Office applications; it converts bulleted text (typically with two outline levels) into a professional-looking graphic image. The styles and format for SmartArt are all predefined, but you

▲ FIGURE 10.16
Completed chart example

can alter the color scheme to match your presentation and change certain style attributes.

One possible use of SmartArt is to create a graphic for contact information that can include text and images for multiple people, such as if there is more than one author of the presentation or if multiple people or groups should be listed for possible follow-up after the presentation. For the sales pitch example, you are going to use SmartArt to replace the

OPEN OFFICE There is a single icon in the toolbar to add a chart to a slide in Impress. When you have added the default chart, you can edit the chart data by right-clicking the chart and selecting *Chart Data Table*; you can also select this icon from the context-sensitive Chart toolbar. A small window will open with the chart data displayed. You can rename and format the values in the spreadsheet here. When you close window, you can use the Chart toolbar to format the elements of the chart using the drop-down list of items and the available formatting commands. Click the *Chart Type* icon to open a dialog box that allows you to select the type of chart you want to include.

existing contact information slide (which was created in the example project in Chapter 9).

Create a new slide at the end of the presentation with the default layout and add a title (you can use *Questions?* just like you did on your previous contact page). To insert a SmartArt graphic in PowerPoint 2010, select the *Insert* ribbon and choose *SmartArt*; you can also use the SmartArt quick link within the content placeholder text box. This will open the Choose a SmartArt Graphic dialog box shown in Figure 10.17. From here, you can select the type of graphic you want to create. In PowerPoint 2011, you can open the *SmartArt* ribbon and choose the graphic type you want to use. For the example, choose *Vertical Curved List* from the List category. When you insert and select a SmartArt graphic, a small window appears in which you type the text of

your graphic in bulleted outline form. The outline level of the text determines where it is placed on the graphic.

When you select the SmartArt graphic, you will also see two context-sensitive SmartArt tools ribbons; these are the Design ribbon and the Format ribbon. The Format ribbon is similar to the other formatting ribbons you have already seen; you can change the style of the drawing object within the SmartArt graphic selected and you can change the text formatting for any selected text. An example of the active Design ribbon is shown in Figure 10.18 (along with the SmartArt text entry box for the example).

The Design ribbon in PowerPoint 2010 contains several tools specific to SmartArt. The Create Graphic panel provides you with tools to add to your graphic or rearrange elements. The Add Shape icon allows you to insert new graphic objects for your SmartArt and select their placement (relative to

▼ FIGURE 10.17
Choose a
SmartArt Graphic
dialog box in
PowerPoint 2010

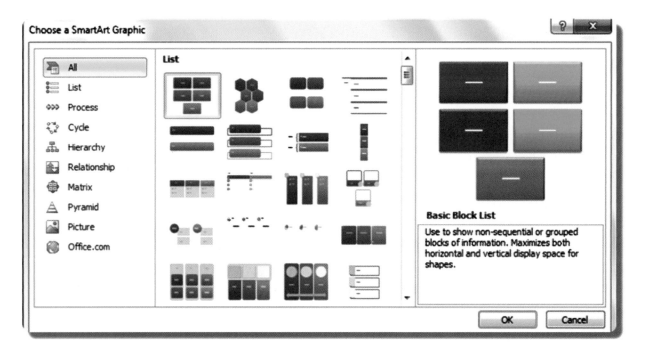

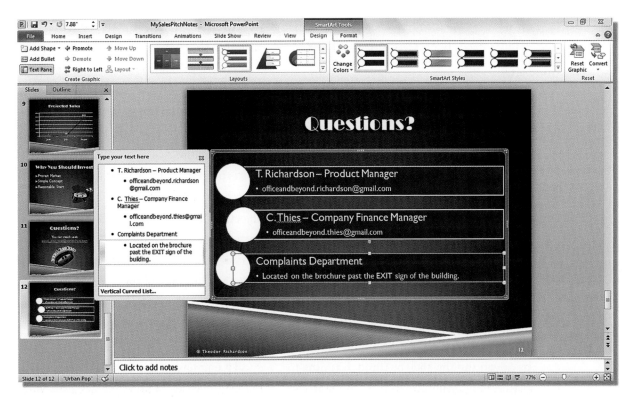

▲ FIGURE 10.18
Example SmartArt
text entry box and
SmartArt Tools
Design ribbon in
PowerPoint 2010

the currently active bullet point or object). You can also show or hide the Text pane using the Text Pane icon. The Promote and Demote icons allow you to change the outline level of the selected bulleted text, and Move Up and Move Down allow you to adjust the order of the objects (you can use these within the Text pane as well). In the Layouts panel, you can change the SmartArt graphic within the same style as the current graphic; if you need to change the entire category, you must create a new SmartArt graphic.

The Colors icon lets you adjust the color scheme of the graphic, and the SmartArt Styles panel allows you to make changes to the look and feel of the entire graphic at once. Reset Graphic sets the style back to the default settings. Finally, the Convert icon allows you to change the SmartArt graphic into regular drawing objects and text. The new slide with the SmartArt graphic will be used as your new contact slide, but do not delete the old contact slide yet; you will use it in a later section of this chapter.

These functions are all available in PowerPoint 2011, but their locations are split between the SmartArt ribbon and the Text pane. The promotion, demotion, and ordering icons are on the Text pane, while the formatting and style options remain on the SmartArt ribbon, where you can change the layout of your graphic as well. The Text

Some SmartArt graphics will have placeholder elements to add a picture. To add pictures, click the picture icon in the graphic or the picture icon next to the text in the Text pane. You can edit the image and its properties with the same Picture Tools Format ribbon that you use for any other image.

pane will appear as a small clickable icon beside the graphic when it is hidden so you can reactivate it from there.

10.2.5 Animations

Animations are one way to call attention to a particular object or group in PowerPoint. These can be triggered either by advancing the slide or through timing to play automatically. Animations can help you emphasize a point or call out a particular visual element, but they can also be easily overused. The animations that you add to your presentation should be short and relevant. All of the settings for animations are housed in the Animations ribbon, shown in Figure 10.19.

To illustrate the concepts and mechanics of animation, you will add animation to the product demonstration slide in the *MySalesPitchNotes* project. The general categories of animation effects are Entrance, Emphasis, Exit, and Motion. Entrance effects are used to start an object

(or group) off of the visible slide and transition it into its placement location; the animation will end with the element in the location where it was initially placed before any animation effects. Emphasis animations start and end with the object in the same location in which it started; this is used to highlight an object for attention. Exit animations are used to remove objects from the slide; these will begin with the object in its original place and end with the object no longer visible on the slide. Motion effects move an object from one position to another; the path for this motion and the beginning and end points can be changed.

To emphasize the hot dog character in the example, apply an emphasis effect like *Teeter* to it. To fly in the second step of creating the product, set the text box to *Fly In*. The arrow should simply fade into existence once the text box is in place, so a Fade effect is appropriate. You can customize any effects using the Effect Options icon; this will change to give you the options available for the current animation you have applied. It is possible to apply multiple animation effects to a single object as long as they do not conflict in motion (so you can use an emphasis effect with an entrance effect but not an entrance effect with an exit effect). You can preview your animation sequence

▼ FIGURE 10.19
Animations ribbons in PowerPoint

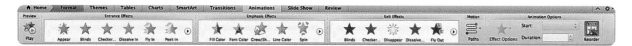

from the Animations ribbon by clicking the *Preview* icon in PowerPoint 2010 and the *Play* icon in PowerPoint 2011. A completed example in Normal view is shown in Figure 10.20. This demonstrates the numbering shown for each sequence to let you know in which order the effects will play; numbers that are the same are part of the same sequence.

After you have added your animations, you can adjust their start condition, triggers, sequencing, and timing. If you added the animation effects in the order you want them to display, you do not need to rearrange them. However, if you want to change the order, open the *Animation Pane* by clicking its icon from the Animations ribbon in PowerPoint 2010; to open the equivalent Custom Animation Pane in PowerPoint 2011, click the *Reorder* icon in the Animations ribbon. With the Animation Pane open, use the Move Earlier and Move Later icons on the Animations ribbon in PowerPoint 2010 (or the up and down arrows at the bottom of the Animation Pane in either PowerPoint 2010 or PowerPoint 2011) to reorder your animation sequence. You can also click and drag an item within the Animation Pane to change its position within the animation order.

The *Start* condition is the action that starts the animation sequence. By default, this is set to *On Click*, which is the same as a slide advance operationally. If you do not want to have to click for each animation to begin, you can change the trigger to *With Previous* or *After Previous*. Setting the animation to *With Previous* starts the selected animation as soon as the previous animation begins; setting the animation

▼ **FIGURE 10.20**
Complex animation sequence in Normal view in PowerPoint 2010

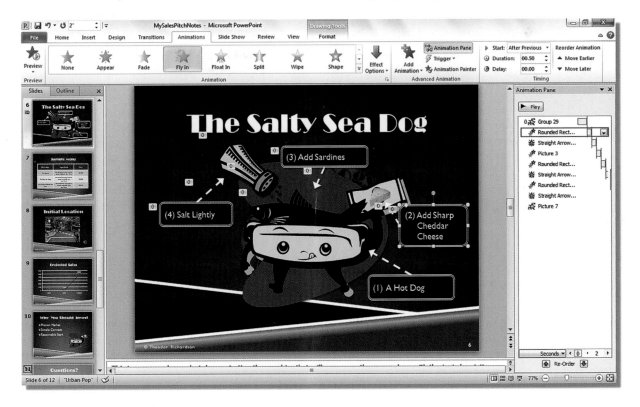

to *After Previous* will start the animation sequence after the previous animation sequence has completed. You can change this setting in the Animations ribbon or the Animation Pane for the currently selected animation.

When you are sharing your presentation for viewing on a personal computer, you should avoid using the *On Click* start condition for animation. It is annoying to a viewer to have to repeatedly click just to get access to the information a slide has to offer. The *On Click* start condition may assist you in presenting, but you should change it to *After Previous* before you share your slides for individual use later.

The Timing panel contains the duration and delay settings for each animation sequence. The Timing panel is part of the Animations ribbon in PowerPoint 2010 but is located on the Custom Animation Pane in PowerPoint 2011. The duration is how long the animation sequence takes to complete; most animations should occur quickly so they do not waste any significant time in the presentation (the preset selections for timing have a minimum of 0.5 seconds and a maximum of 5 seconds). The delay is how long the sequence will

If you do not want your animation to play as part of the normal slide progression in PowerPoint 2010, you can change the *Trigger* attribute. The trigger attribute is what causes the animation to start; by default it is set to take input from the presentation timing and standard presentation advances. However, you can change the trigger to a click of any object within the current slide; this will function like an action setting to start the animation sequence.

pause before starting when the start condition is reached; you should use delays sparingly and only when necessary for presenting the content.

You can optionally add sounds to your animation sequences from the Animation Pane (or Custom Animation Pane) using the *Effect Options* selection. You can access *Effect Options* from the drop-down menu for the sequence entry in PowerPoint 2010; this is a foldout panel for the animation sequence in PowerPoint 2011. You can also set how you want your text animated, either by word or by letter, and the delay between text sequences in the animation. The text settings can be changed using *Effect Options* in PowerPoint 2010 and the separate foldout *Text Animations* panel in PowerPoint 2011.

 OPEN OFFICE In Impress, the animations are all controlled by the Custom Animation tab in the Tasks pane on the righthand side of the interface. To add an animation, just click on the object or group and select the *Add* button. This gives you a choice of effects similar to those offered in PowerPoint, including Entrance, Emphasis, Exit, and Motion effects. You can alter the settings for Start, Direction, and Speed once you have added the effect. All of the animations for the slide are added to the text area beneath the settings options. You can click any of these to change the settings or use the arrow icons beneath the list to move them up or down in the order of display. The Play button will preview the animation, and the Slide Show button will display the current slide in Slide Show view to preview the animation as it will appear during a presentation.

10.3 EDITING PRESENTATIONS

You may not always be working on a presentation document that you create yourself. You also may not be able to create the entire project at once, so it is important to be able to open and edit existing presentation documents. You can change most of the properties of a PowerPoint presentation while it is open, regardless of when it was created or by whom.

If you download a presentation or open it from an e-mail message, Power-Point will restrict the editing options of the document, allowing you to read it without running any additional scripts attached to the document (called macros) and without activating any of the ribbons to alter the content. Once you click the *Enable Editing* button on the warning that appears, you will be able to manipulate and edit the document as usual.

10.3.1 Opening and Editing Existing Presentations

You can open presentations from the *File* menu by selecting the *Open* option; use this to open the *MyBrokenRobot* file from the companion resources for this text. This file has only one slide with a robot whose arms have fallen off of its body. It is your task to reposition and reattach them. Notice that when you open a presentation document, any presentation documents that are already open will remain open in separate windows.

Use your mouse cursor to select each arm and position it on the slide where it can reasonably connect to the shoulder socket of the robot; do not overlap the shapes because you are going to use connector lines to attach the arms. Now use the rotation option to rotate the arm back into position. Add a drawing object connector line from the arm to the shoulder socket.

> Any animation applied to objects that are connected by a connecting line will not animate the connecting line itself. Instead, the line will remain in the initial fixed position for both objects, ignoring any animation movements unless they are part of a group to which animation is applied. If both objects are not part of the same group, the connecting line will ignore the object that is not part of the group in terms of positioning and movement.

Repeat the steps for the other arm. Change the robot's frown to a smile using the yellow diamond controller for the mouth setting. Finally, change the title of the presentation: Use the strikethrough formatting on the word "Broken" and add the word "Fixed" beside it. Remember to send the connector lines you added to the back of the slide layering so they do not appear above the animation of the robot. A completed example is shown in Figure 10.21.

You can also change the theme and the colors of this presentation to better suit your preferences. The colors will automatically adapt when you change the theme in PowerPoint, but you can change your color preference after selecting the theme. Save the completed project as *MyFixedRobot*.

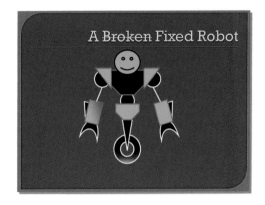

10.3.2   Slide Setup and Slide Orientation

You can set the size of your slides and the slide orientation. If you are presenting your slides on a normal screen or standard projector, you do not need to change the slide size from the default. The default aspect ratio is the best option for standard use. (Although PowerPoint can be used to create brochures and other publications, this is not its primary use.) For this example, select a slide size that is equivalent to standard paper printouts. To change the slide size, click the *Page Setup* icon on the *Design* ribbon in PowerPoint 2010. This will open the Page Setup dialog box shown in Figure 10.22. In PowerPoint 2011, you can change the slide size by selecting *Slide Size* from the *Themes*

ribbon or by selecting the *File* menu and choosing *Page Setup*.

In this dialog box, you can set your slide size to any of the predefined standard sizes or a custom size. It is possible to use PowerPoint to create a poster image (such as those needed for professional research conference presentations), but the maximum size setting of a slide for either the height or the width is 56 inches. That means the largest poster you can create is 56″ by 56″. If your planned project fits within that size limitation, your only concern is how to get it printed. Once you export your poster image from PowerPoint to a Portable Document Format (PDF) file, most professional print shops will accept that format.

> Changing the aspect ratio with content in your slide will change the aspect ratio of the content as well, which may distort images and drawing objects already in your presentation. Therefore, you should try to set the slide size before you start creating the content for your presentation.

The Page Setup dialog box also allows you to set your slide orientation; that is, whether you want it to display in landscape layout (the default where the width is greater than the height) or portrait layout (the standard layout for text documents and printing). You can change this setting for the slides and any printed handout separately. In PowerPoint 2010, you can set the starting number of the slides in this dialog box; it defaults to starting at one for the first slide of the presentation.

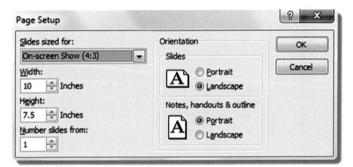

OPEN OFFICE You can edit the slide size in Impress by selecting the *Format* menu and then choosing *Page*. On the Page tab of the Page Setup dialog box, you can set the height and width values for your slide, as well as the page orientation.

10.3.3 Creating a Custom Layout

If you find that you need slides with a particular arrangement of elements that is not provided in any of the default layouts, you can create a custom layout in PowerPoint. To do this, open the Slide Master view and find the *Insert Layout* icon (or *New Layout* icon in PowerPoint 2011) on the *Slide Master* ribbon. Clicking this icon creates a new child layout slide from the main Slide Master. This new slide will initially contain only a

title and footer placeholders. You can add additional placeholders to the new layout slide by clicking the *Insert Placeholder* icon to open the menu that allows you to choose the content type for the placeholder. The default Content placeholder includes quick links to all of the available media elements, while the other options allow specific media and text. The Insert Placeholder drop-down menu is shown in Figure 10.23.

When you have finished creating your new layout, click the *Rename* icon to name your new layout for use in the presentation. When you save the presentation and close the Slide Master view, the new layout you created will be available as a selection in the Layout icon menu of the Home ribbon. The name that displays for the layout will reflect what you renamed it;

▼ **FIGURE 10.23**
Custom layout creation and Insert Placeholder menu in PowerPoint 2010

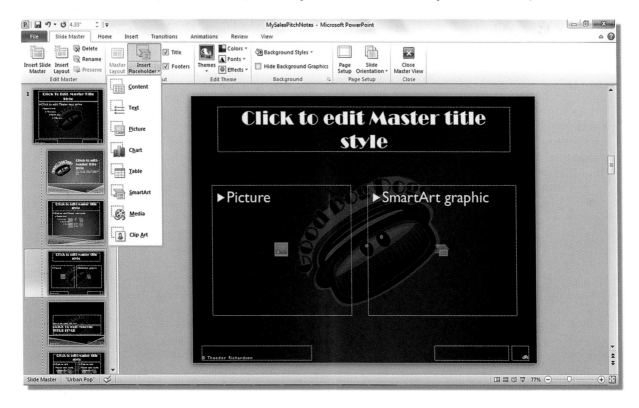

if you did not perform this step, the name will default to "Custom Layout." This custom layout will exist only in the presentation in which you created it; it will not be available for use in other presentation documents.

 OPEN OFFICE Impress does not allow you to define a custom layout, but you can define a custom slide master with your own layout variation. You can apply the slide master by selecting the slide you want to change and clicking the slide master icon you want to use in the Master Pages tab of the Tasks pane.

10.3.4 ## Hiding and Showing Slides

If you need to shorten your presentation to fit a specific time slot or you need to slightly tailor the same presentation for different audiences, you may have some slides that you do not need but that you do not want to delete. For instance, you may have a slide with background information that is not necessary for the general audience, but you may need it if someone asks a particular question. To keep a slide in your presentation without including it in the normal Slide Show view, you can utilize the option to hide the slide.

To hide a slide, select the slide you want hidden and open the *Slide Show* ribbon. Click the *Hide Slide* icon. This will gray out the slide in the Slides/Outline pane to indicate it is hidden. You can still continue to edit the slide, but it will not display during your presentation.

If you need to access a hidden slide during your presentation, select the slide manually by right-clicking within the presentation while Slide Show view is active, choosing *Go to Slide*, and then selecting the slide number and title you want to display. You can also create an action object to point directly to the hidden slide; if you need to view the slide during the presentation, click the action object and the slide will display.

The Hide Slide icon is a toggle. When it is highlighted, the slide is hidden. When you click the icon again, the slide will be visible in the presentation. A hidden slide retains its slide number, so if you have slide numbers visible, the presentation will skip the number of the hidden slide.

To practice this, go to the *MySalesPitch-Notes* project and hide the slide for questions that displayed only a single contact e-mail address (this was replaced by a SmartArt version in Section 10.2.4). Select one of the objects within the SmartArt graphic to link to the previous contact slide. add an action to the object, choose *Slide* as the *Link to* value, and select the hidden slide. Save and test your presentation to make sure it works.

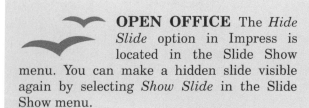 **OPEN OFFICE** The *Hide Slide* option in Impress is located in the Slide Show menu. You can make a hidden slide visible again by selecting *Show Slide* in the Slide Show menu.

Optimizing and Exporting Images from Slides

Adding a large amount of media to your presentation may cause some issues with the file size of the document. If you are emailing the document or presenting it on another machine, you have to consider how easy it is to transfer it from one location to another. Depending on how you are using the document, you can perform some tasks to compress the file size of your presentation while retaining all of the media you have added. If the presentation document is just for use on a computer screen, compressing the images will reduce the file size without sacrificing the media quality. If you are printing your slides on a high-quality printer, compressing them may not be the best choice.

To compress your images, select an image in your presentation and open the *Format* ribbon for Picture Tools. Select the *Compress Pictures* icon (or *Compress* in PowerPoint 2011). This will open the Compress Pictures dialog box shown in Figure 10.24. From here, you can select the resolution you want for your image. You can also set whether you want the cropped areas of the image removed and whether you want to apply these settings to all of the images in the document or just the one you have selected (deselecting the *Apply only to this picture* checkbox in PowerPoint 2010 will apply the setting to all images in the presentation document).

Your presentation slides can be exported as images from PowerPoint. To do this, simply open the *File* menu and

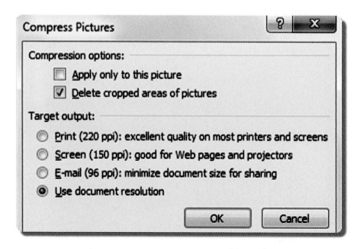

▲ FIGURE 10.24
Compress Pictures dialog box in PowerPoint 2010

choose *Save As*. The common formats for images are GIF (Graphics Interchange Format), JPEG (Joint Photographic Experts Group), TIFF (Tag Image File Format), PNG (Portable Network Graphics Format), and DIB (Device Independent Bitmap). Select the format in which you wish to save your slides; you will be asked whether you want to save the current slide only or every slide in the chosen format. With PowerPoint 2011, it is better to use the *Save as Pictures* command from the *File* menu; this allows you to open an Options dialog box in which you can specify more detailed image options for the format.

OPEN OFFICE Impress offers more export options for images than PowerPoint. These include Encapsulated PostScript (EPS) and Scalable Vector Graphics (SVG) formats, which are used in the professional text editor TeX. Impress also has a native PDF writer that converts a document to the compressed and sharable Adobe Portable Document Format (PDF). These options are available in the Export dialog box, which is accessed by choosing the *File* menu and then selecting *Export*.

CHAPTER SUMMARY

This chapter covered the more advanced media elements that you can include in your slide show presentations. You must always keep your audience and the method of delivery in mind when creating your slides so that they deliver the maximum impact to your audience instead of just providing information. Presentation software can also allow you to create customized images at different sizes, which is a useful feature if you need to create graphics quickly and do not have an advanced graphics editing program available. The next section of the text covers spreadsheet software, which is an excellent tool for managing large amounts of data and performing advanced calculations.

CHAPTER EXERCISES

1. Research a complex topic in computing and create a 10-slide presentation explaining the topic. Include at least three of the media types discussed in this chapter to assist in your explanation. In a separate word processing document of at least 200 words, evaluate whether or not the media elements made it easier to describe a concept and why this was the case.

2. Using the *MyFixedRobot* project you created in this chapter, change the slide size to a poster size of 24″ by 36″ and add captions and a logo to the slide so it looks like an advertisement poster. Save your document as *HugeFixedRobot* and export it as an image file using both the GIF and JPEG formats. In a separate word processing document of at least 200 words, compare the two images that were produced in terms of image quality, text quality, color, and file size.

CHAPTER KNOWLEDGE CHECK

1 Once you have added animation effects to a slide, you cannot change the order in which they occur.

- ○ True
- ○ False

2 You cannot add multiple animations to the same group or object in a slide.

- ○ True
- ○ False

3 Hidden slides are not assigned a number in the slide show. When they are shown again, they change the numbering of the slides that follow them in the presentation.

- ○ True
- ○ False

4 The following type of media requires support from a spreadsheet to calculate the display:

- ○ **A.** Table
- ○ **B.** Chart
- ○ **C.** Animation
- ○ **D.** All of the above
- ○ **E.** None of the above

5 The following type of animation begins with the object or group on the visible slide and ends with it removed from sight:

- ○ **A.** Entrance effect
- ○ **B.** Emphasis effect
- ○ **C.** Exit effect
- ○ **D.** Explosion effect

6 In general, audio and video increase the file size of a presentation more drastically than other media elements.

○ True
○ False

7 Using multiple forms of complex media in the same slide is a good way to present information clearly.

○ True
○ False

8 Tables are a good form of media to use when presenting a large volume of information (at least 10 rows by 6 columns) because they are clear to the audience at the back of the room.

○ True
○ False

9 SmartArt is a tool that allows for quick creation of professional-looking graphics, but SmartArt graphics can be adequately created using drawing objects and text boxes.

○ True
○ False

10 The following is an image format that is common for exporting presentation slides:

○ **A.** GIF
○ **B.** TIFF
○ **C.** JPEG
○ **D.** All of the above
○ **E.** None of the above

Introduction to Excel and Spreadsheet Software

This chapter presents an introduction to spreadsheet software. Through the creation of a simple budget, features of the software package such as formatting and formulas will be explored. You will also learn to add charts to your document to visualize the information contained in the spreadsheet. Once you have completed the chapter, you will be able to:

- Navigate the spreadsheet software interface

- Add and format text and numerical data in a spreadsheet

- Use cell naming and cell formatting to organize information

- Add simple formulas to a worksheet

- Add charts to a worksheet

INTRODUCTION TO SPREADSHEET SOFTWARE

Spreadsheet software is used to manage and process large amounts of data. A spreadsheet is organized into a grid of rows (indicated by number) and columns (indicated by letter). The intersection of these rows and columns is called a *cell*; a cell is identified by letter and number, so A1 would be the first cell of the spreadsheet. A spreadsheet document is not delimited by printed pages or slides as you have previously seen in other software packages. Instead, it is organized as individual spreadsheets or worksheets (identified by the tabs at the bottom of the interface in the common spreadsheet applications); the entire file is called a *workbook*. A worksheet can contain many printed pages worth of material. In fact, a worksheet can contain thousands of rows or columns that would be infeasible to print; the maximum size of a worksheet in Excel contains rows up to row 1048576 and columns up to column XFD.

Cells are not intended for large amounts of text; you should ideally include one piece of data or information per cell. Spreadsheets are best for organizing data and calculating results. If you want the results to accompany text, you should produce your results in a spreadsheet and export the relevant data to a word processing document. There are an enormous number of applications for spreadsheets across disciplines such as accounting and mathematics. The coming chapters provide an introduction to spreadsheet software and its functionality, but the practical applications of this technology go far beyond the scope of this text. Some general uses that you may find for spreadsheet software are formatting information in large tables, creating charts to display a visualization of data, and performing complex mathematical calculations.

The spreadsheet software application in Microsoft Office is called Excel. The equivalent in OpenOffice.org is called Calc. The first task you will complete using the spreadsheet software program is the creation of a personal budget. First, open the software and use the *File* menu to save your new open document as *MyBudget*. The native file type in Excel is Excel Workbook (.xlsx); in Calc, it is ODF Spreadsheet (.ods).

*A **ROW** in spreadsheet software is the horizontal grouping of data that is divided by columns; rows are signified by numbers.*

*A **COLUMN** in spreadsheet software is the vertical grouping of data that is divided by rows; columns are signified by letters.*

*A **CELL** in spreadsheet software is the intersection of a row and a column, containing a single piece of data, which can be text, a number, a formula, or an object; cells are signified by the letter of the column and the number of the row.*

*A **FORMULA** in spreadsheet software is a mathematical calculation that results in a data value; the value is displayed in the cell in which the formula is typed.*

ANATOMY OF EXCEL

Excel uses the ribbon interface with which you should now be familiar.

Beneath the ribbon interface is the Formula Bar, which is used for naming cells and defining calculations. The main pane of the document window looks very different from the applications you have seen so far; it displays the rows, columns, and cells of the document. The bottom of the interface contains tabs for you to select the worksheet that is active in the document pane. Depending on the version of Excel you are using, the ribbons and shortcuts available will be slightly different. You can jump to the section that is relevant to you.

11.2.1 Microsoft Excel 2010

The interface for Excel 2010 has the same ribbon structure and general layout with which you should be familiar from the other Office applications. You can see an example of the interface for Excel 2010 in Figure 11.1. The Formula Bar, located beneath the ribbon interface, identifies the current cell that you have selected and displays the contents of the cell. When you begin using functions, the Formula Bar will become much more relevant. It allows you to perform a formula lookup and will help identify any possible errors in your formula construction.

You may notice that there is a significant departure in the construction and navigation of the document pane of the interface. The document is divided into cells. You can use the arrow keys to navigate from one cell to the next or you can click on a cell to activate it. The current cell is called the active cell and the row and column in which it resides will also be highlighted for you to identify them quickly. Hold the *Shift* key to select multiple cells. Each cell acts like a text box in which you can type information.

The bottom of the interface has a set of tabs, each of which identifies an individual spreadsheet within the overall

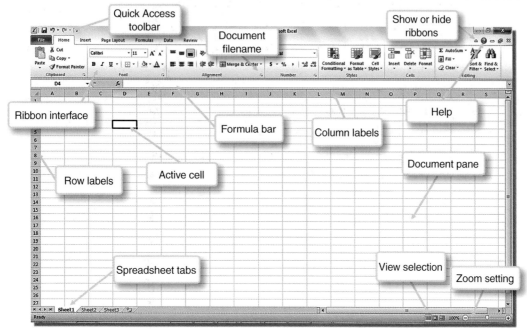

◀ FIGURE 11.1
Anatomy of Excel 2010

workbook (the file itself). You can navigate to these spreadsheets by clicking on the tabs or by using the directional arrows to the right of the tabs. The bottom of the interface also contains the view options, which allow you to see the page breaks in your document in either a Page Layout view or a Page Break Preview; the Normal view tends to be the most helpful for document creation. When you have numeric values selected, the bottom of the interface will also display an automatic calculation of the average of the values, the sum of the values, and the number of values you have selected (omitting white space). This is a nice feature for quickly assessing statistics on a list.

The available ribbons and functions are quite different from the interface for Word and PowerPoint. The Home ribbon contains the Number panel for formatting numeric values (either as direct text input or as the result of formula calculations), as well as commands for style formatting and for adding and deleting cells. Of particular note are the Fill icon, which is used to replicate values or predict entries in a series, and the Sort and Filter icon, which will be used for list management in Chapter 12, "Developing Work-

sheets and Graphic Representations." The Insert ribbon, shown in Figure 11.2, contains several entries of note, particularly the Chart creation functionality, single-cell charts called Sparklines, and the icon to create a PivotTable, which is one of the more advanced features of Excel.

The Page Layout ribbon, shown in Figure 11.3, is used to manage the spreadsheet into printable regions. You can add a background, insert manual page breaks, and set the printable region size for your spreadsheet. If printing is a concern, it may be helpful to preview the print regions to keep your document confined within the desired page delineations.

The Formulas ribbon contains categories of formulas from which you can select to insert into your document. This ribbon also contains the functionality to trace dependencies among cells in your spreadsheet and provides manual links to set calculation options for your spreadsheet; by default, all calculations are updated immediately when a value on which they depend is changed. The Formulas ribbon is shown in Figure 11.4.

The Data ribbon, shown in Figure 11.5, contains several useful commands, including the Remove Duplicates command to

▼ FIGURE 11.2
Insert ribbon in
Excel 2010

➤ FIGURE 11.3
Page Layout
ribbon in Excel
2010

make sure no identical values are repeated in your list and the Text to Columns command to convert continuous text into multiple columns based on a delimiter character. This ribbon also contains commands to manage external sources, perform a What-If Analysis (for goal seeking), validate data, and perform advanced filtering for lists.

The Review ribbon gives you the ability to add comments to your spreadsheet. Unlike Word, Excel places comments in a triangle icon in the upper-right corner of the cell to which they are attached. The Review ribbon also gives you options for protecting your document from changes or sharing your document on a network location for others to edit. You can also select the Start Inking icon to use your mouse as a pen to mark up your document. The Review ribbon is shown in Figure 11.6.

The View ribbon, shown in Figure 11.7, allows you to change the view of the document as usual, but it also allows you to manage your workspace. The views in Excel are primarily the Normal view and views to preview page layouts for printing, such as Page Break Preview. The Page Layout view is not recommended for constructing or working with your document. You can show or hide various document elements from this ribbon as well, such as the gridlines and the Formula Bar. The Freeze Panes functionality allows you to preserve your headings as you scroll through your document. The Split function lets you set up multiple viewing panes of your document so you can view disjoined elements side by side. You can also use the Save Workspace icon to store the configuration of multiple document windows so you can

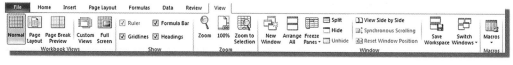

Chapter 11 — Introduction to Excel and Spreadsheet Software — **299**

view different workbooks at the same time on your monitor.

11.2.2 Microsoft Excel 2011

The interface for Excel 2011, shown in Figure 11.8, is very similar to what you have encountered with the other Office applications for Macintosh computers. The interface contains the standard menu and ribbons where most of your functionality is located. In addition, you have a Formula Bar that is used to construct calculations in the spreadsheet and edit information in the cells of the document. The main document is divided into cells, which can be navigated with the arrow keys on the keyboard. The columns are labeled by letters across the top, and the rows are labeled with numbers down the left side. The tabs at the bottom are the individual spreadsheets within the workbook (the overall document).

Clicking with the mouse on a cell in the document makes that cell the active cell; this action outlines the cell in a thick border and highlights the row and column labels for quick reference. The cell reference will also appear on the left side of the Formula Bar. Options in the Quick Access toolbar include a toggle that allows you to show or hide the Formula Bar and links to common functions like SUM (which is discussed later in this chapter). The bottom of the interface contains the view selection where you can alternate between the

▼ **FIGURE 11.8** Anatomy of Excel 2011

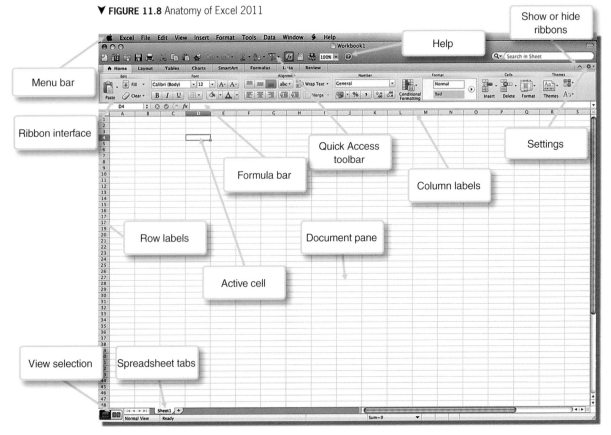

Normal view and a preview of the page breaks in your document for printing.

The Home ribbon contains the standard text formatting options, along with a panel for formatting numeric values. This is necessary for effectively managing and displaying data in the spreadsheets. The Home ribbon also contains icons for inserting and deleting rows and columns and for using special preset formatting options.

The Layout ribbon, shown in Figure 11.9, contains view settings and print options and is primarily used for establishing print regions and previewing the print area. This ribbon can also be used to set up a workspace where you can open multiple workbook documents on the screen for use at the same time.

The Tables ribbon is used to format cells in the document as a table; this is useful for managing and maintaining lists of information. This ribbon also lets you select whether you want to include specific elements in your table formatting, such as a header row. The Charts ribbon is where

you create a visual data representation to include in your spreadsheet. There are a number of chart types available for different types of data and different presentations of information. The SmartArt ribbon is similar to what is found in Word and PowerPoint; you can use this ribbon to add graphics to your document to convey information visually. These three ribbons are shown in Figure 11.10.

The Formulas ribbon is where you can access the available formula library in Excel. This ribbon contains an icon for quick access to formulas for summations and averaging, as well as the Formula Builder icon for creating more advanced calculations. You can also control the recalculation options for your formulas from this ribbon (be default, the recalculation is immediate whenever a value is changed) and trace the cells used in your calculations. The Formulas ribbon is shown in Figure 11.11.

The Data ribbon, shown in Figure 11.12, contains the functionality for

▲ FIGURE 11.9
Layout ribbon in Excel 2011

▼ FIGURE 11.10
Tables, Charts, and SmartArt ribbons in Excel 2011

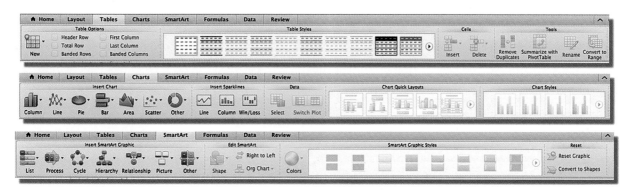

► FIGURE 11.11
Formulas ribbon
in Excel 2011

▲ FIGURE 11.12
Data ribbon in
Excel 2011

managing information in your spread-sheet. You can sort and filter data from this ribbon, manage external data sources, remove duplicate values in a list, and convert the existing text into separate columns. Data validation and grouping is also performed from this ribbon.

The Review ribbon, shown in Figure 11.13, is primarily used for document collaboration and markup. You can add or address comments from this ribbon, and also share your document or set document protection so it cannot be altered.

11.3 DIVING INTO SPREADSHEETS

Now that you are familiar with the interface of the software, the next step is to start creating the budget document used as a project for this chapter. You are going to establish a projected budget and fill in cells with the actual amounts on a month-by-

▼ FIGURE 11.13
Review ribbon in
Excel 2011

month basis. When you have completed this project, you can use the document to assist

with your own financial planning. Select the first tab (labeled *Sheet1*) at the bottom of the interface, right-click on it, and select *Rename* from the menu. Rename the worksheet *Monthly Budget*. Be sure to save your work after you have made changes.

Adding and Formatting Text

11.3.1

Column A will be used to store the line items you are going to account for in your budget. In cell *A1*, type the words *Monthly Budget*; you can format text in Excel just as you can in other Office products using the formatting commands on the Home ribbon. Bold your text to signify its importance as a heading. Since this is not a print document, you can use the sans serif default font for readability. The unformatted text in the cell will appear in the Formula Bar.

Skip over rows 2 and 3 for now; formatting and additional row headings will be added later. Note that skipping rows between major headings is helpful in

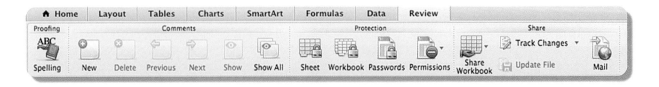

organizing your information. In cell *A4* (where Column A intersects row 4), add the heading *Income*; this is where you will track your monthly income from which you will deduct your expenses using a formula. You should bold category headings and include subheadings in the same column as normal text; in Column A beneath the Income heading, add the following categories:

- Household Expenses
  - Rent/Mortgage
  - Phone
  - Cable
  - Groceries
- Utilities
  - Electric
  - Gas
  - Water
- Car
  - Payment
  - Gas
  - Insurance
- Pets
  - Food
  - Miscellaneous (abbreviated Misc.)
- Recreational
  - Clothing
  - Dining Out
  - Entertainment
- Savings

In the line under Savings, enter the percentage of your monthly income you would like to save each month; for the

You can use the mouse to click the different cells in which you want to enter data, or you can use the *Enter* key to get to the next cell beneath the one currently selected. Press *Enter* twice to add a blank row between categories.

example, this is 10%. The final two categories for Column A are *Total Expense* and *Net Income*. Skip a row above each of these category names. A completed example is

◄ **FIGURE 11.14**
Completed budget headings in Excel 2010

shown in Figure 11.14. You can modify the categories and headings to meet your own needs for budget tracking, or you can follow along exactly with the example to become familiar with the functionality of the application and then later adjust what you have entered as a test of your understanding.

If you need more room in a column for the text you have entered, you can resize its width by selecting the line separating it from the next column and dragging it to expand or shrink the column width; for example, select the line dividing Column A from Column B and drag it to the right to expand Column A. You can also select the cells you want to modify and choose the *Wrap Text* icon to display the text of the cell on multiple lines; this is found in the Alignment panel of the Home ribbon.

Column B will be used to project the monthly estimate of your household income and the cost of each category. In cell *B3*, enter the text *Budgeted Amount*; use the Wrap Text command along with the alignment commands to display the text in the vertical and horizontal center of the cell.

11.3.2 Formatting Values

In Column B, you are going to assign your budgeted values for the respective categories in Column A. Do not add values for the main headings, like Recreational; focus instead on the values for the subheadings, like Clothing and Entertainment. You will use formulas to calculate the values of the overall categories. You may notice as you add numbers to your spreadsheet that they will align to the

> You can apply formatting to an entire row or column by clicking on the row or column label, respectively, and then selecting the formatting commands you wish to apply. If you want to apply the formatting to the entire spreadsheet, select the small unlabeled area to the left of Column A and above row 1 and select the formatting commands.

right of the cell by default; text, on the other hand, aligns to the left. The text formatting commands are all available for use on numeric values as well.

An additional set of formatting commands is available for numbers in the Number panel of the Home ribbon. These commands are shown in Figure 11.15. You can select the formatting you want to use from the predefined list, including Currency, Percentage, and Scientific. You can also choose *More Number Formats* from the Number Format selection box to customize your own number formatting style. This will open the Number tab of the Format Cells dialog box, which is also shown in Figure 11.15. In Excel 2010, you can also open this dialog box by selecting the expansion icon on the Number panel.

The additional commands available from the panel include the Accounting Number Format for currency values; this is a drop-down list of common world currencies. You can also use the Percent Style and Comma Style formats to adjust the cells quickly; apply the *Percent Style* to the number you chose for your monthly savings (in Column A). The Increase Decimal and Decrease Decimal icons are used to increase or decrease the number of significant digits

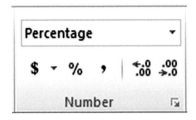

◀ FIGURE 11.15
Number panel and Format Cells
dialog box in Excel 2010

displayed for the value; this does not affect the value itself that is stored in the cell, just the manner in which that value appears.

Once you have entered your monthly budget values in Column B up to the value for Savings (you will compute Savings, Total Expenses, and Net Income as formulas), select the *Accounting* style for the values (which differs from the Currency format in the placement of the symbol identifying the currency, such as $). Now use the *Decrease Decimal* command to remove the decimal points so the numerical values are displayed as whole currency. A completed example is shown in Figure 11.16. Feel free to use your own values rather than those in the example.

Check the result of the formatting change to Percentage on your values to make sure you have the number you intended; this formatting converts the value *1.00* to *100%*, so you may need to convert the formatting for the cell and retype the percentage you want.

Using Sequences

11.3.3

Excel can use two cells to predict simple series like counting numbers, days of the week, and months of the year. You are going to create a yearly budget plan for this example, so enter *January* in cell C3 and *February* in cell D3. When you select both cells with your cursor, you will see them surrounded by a thick border with a grip point at the lower-right corner of the selection; click and drag this grip point in the direction of the series entry (in this case horizontally) to extend the sequence. Click the grip point and drag it out until you have a complete cycle of months from January to December. The grip point and the completed series are shown in Figure 11.17.

You can use the automatic series generator in Excel to create headings for months, days, or years and to create an index for data values. The series can be extended vertically or horizontally, but the direction depends on the adjacency of the example cells you

B4		*fx*	3300

	A	B	C	D
1	**Monthly Budget**			
2				
3		**Budgeted Amount**		
4	**Income**	$ 3,300		
5				
6	**Household Expenses**			
7	Rent/Mortgage	$ 1,000		
8	Phone	$ 50		
9	Cable	$ 120		
10	Groceries	$ 600		
11				
12	**Utilities**			
13	Electric	$ 70		
14	Gas	$ 70		
15	Water	$ 30		
16				
17	**Car**			
18	Payment	$ 250		
19	Gas	$ 100		
20	Insurance	$ 100		
21				
22	**Pet**			
23	Food	$ 60		
24	Misc.	$ 50		
25				
26	**Recreational**			
27	Clothing	$ 100		
28	Dining Out	$ 100		
29	Entertainment	$ 50		
30				
31	**Savings**			
32	10%			
33				
34	**Total Expenses**			
35				
36	**Net Income**			
37				

select; you can continue the sequence only in that direction. Excel will attempt to predict the sequence as an additive series; you must be sure the pattern you are attempting to have Excel predict is simple and you must verify that the values you get in response are correct. If you have only a single value highlighted, Excel will repeat that value in the adjacent cells.

Formatting Cells

11.3.4

Now that you have the headings for the vertical and horizontal entries in your budget, you want to focus on formatting them to make your budget more readable. Start by setting a column width for the monthly entries you have added. To do this, select the column headings from Column C (which should contain your January entry) to Column N (which should contain December). With all of these columns selected, drag the line separating Column C from Column D to set a common width for all of the columns

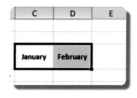

◄ FIGURE 11.17 Series example in Excel 2010

C	D	E	F	G	H	I	J	K	L	M	N	O
January	February	March	April	May	June	July	August	September	October	November	December	

- ○ Copy Cells
- ◉ Fill Series
- ○ Fill Formatting Only
- ○ Fill Without Formatting
- ○ Fill Months

you have highlighted. You should set a width that is sufficient to read the month value for each column. You can also set a specific value for the column width using the *Format* command on the *Home* ribbon with the columns selected; select *Column Width* from the drop-down list that appears and choose *9.5"* as the value for the width.

You can add formatting to the cells by using the Fill Color menu and the Border menu on the Home ribbon. The Fill Color icon gives you the standard selection of theme colors (which can be selected from the Page Layout ribbon in Excel 2010 and from the Home ribbon in Excel 2011) and standard colors. The Border menu allows you to add specific borders (such as a Bottom Border or Outside Borders) from the default selections. You can also select the line styles from this menu in Excel 2010 or choose *More Borders* to access the advanced options for customizing the border; the advanced options are available in Excel 2011 by choosing *Border Options* from the *Border* menu. The selections you make will apply only to the cells that are highlighted when you choose the various options.

To continue building your budget, add the heading *Annual Amount* to cell *O3*. You should use the same formatting as you did

You can access all of these options from the *Format Cells* selection on the right-click menu. You must first select all of the cells to which you want the formatting to apply, right-click, select *Format Cells*, and then choose the tabs for Fill or Border as necessary.

for cell *B3*, including enabling Wrap Text. Select cells *B3* through *O3* and choose a light green fill for the background (you can choose another color if you like as long as the text is still visible) using the *Fill Color* command.

Now select cells *B3* through *O36* (this should be the last cell corresponding to the intersection of the column containing *Annual Amount* and the row containing *Net Income*). Select the More Borders option from the *Borders* menu. In the dialog box that appears, enable the middle vertical border and the right border, as shown in Figure 11.18, and click *OK*.

Next, select the cells in the row where you have the value for your savings amount beginning with Column B and extending through Column O. (If you have followed the example, this will be cells B32 through O32.) Select the *Bottom Border* option from the *Border* menu for these cells; you should notice that the formatting you have already applied to the cells is still active. Finally, select the cells in the row corresponding to the *Net Income* entry from Column B through Column O (this will be cells B36 to O36 if you are following the example). Add a Top Border and Bottom Double Border to the highlighted cells. An example of the completed steps is shown in Figure 11.19.

Freezing Panes

11.3.5

Using the Freeze Panes option allows you to keep your headings visible on the page no matter where you scroll within your spreadsheet. You can choose to

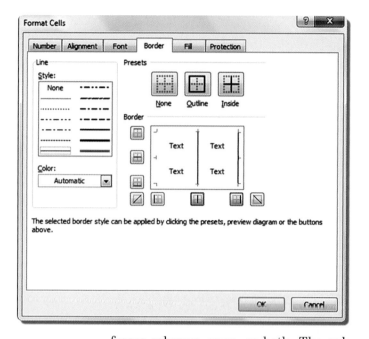

Format Cells

Number | Alignment | Font | **Border** | Fill | Protection

Line

Style:

None

Color:

Automatic

Presets

None | Outline | Inside

Border

Text | Text

Text | Text

The selected border style can be applied by clicking the presets, preview diagram or the buttons above.

OK | Cancel

◀ FIGURE 11.18
Border tab of Format Cells dialog box in Excel 2010

Panes option will define the border of what is frozen; any cells above and to the left of the selection (but not including the selected cell itself) will remain in place as you scroll the document.

In Excel 2010, the Freeze Panes icon is on the View ribbon; in Excel 2011, the Freeze Panes icon is on the Layout ribbon. For the example, click cell *C4* and select *Freeze Panes* to lock your headings and estimated budget in place while allowing the rest of your entries to scroll. The correct cell you need for the example is highlighted in Figure 11.20. Move the scrollbars after this step has been completed to see its effect on your document. To remove the Freeze Pane effect, select the *Freeze Panes* icon again and choose *Unfreeze Panes*.

freeze columns, rows, or both. The only caveat as to what can be frozen is that you must freeze the contents of the upper-left corner of the spreadsheet to the cell you choose for enabling the freeze. The cell you highlight when you choose the Freeze

▼ FIGURE 11.19
Completed cell formatting example

	A	B	C	D	E	F	G	H	I	J	K	L	M	N	O
1	Monthly Budget														
2															
3		Budgeted Amount	January	February	March	April	May	June	July	August	September	October	November	December	Annual Amount
4	Income	$ 3,300													
5															
6	Household Expenses														
7	Rent/Mortgage	$ 1,000													
8	Phone	$ 50													
9	Cable	$ 120													
10	Groceries	$ 600													
11															
12	Utilities														
13	Electric	$ 70													
14	Gas	$ 70													
15	Water	$ 30													
16															
17	Car														
18	Payment	$ 250													
19	Gas	$ 100													
20	Insurance	$ 100													
21															
22	Pet														
23	Food	$ 60													
24	Misc.	$ 50													
25															
26	Recreational														
27	Clothing	$ 100													
28	Dining Out	$ 100													
29	Entertainment	$ 50													
30															
31	Savings														
32	10%														
33															
34	Total Expenses														
35															
36	Net Income														
37															

11.3.6 Adding Basic Formulas

Formulas are an excellent way to perform calculations on the data within your spreadsheet. In fact, a large portion of the power of using spreadsheets is the ability to automate complex calculations. The formulas in your spreadsheet will operate just like equations, with the cells occupying the position of variables. For instance, to calculate the total of the entire Household Expenses category, select the cell in Column B beside the category name and type the equals symbol (=), which signifies a calculation. Next, you can use the cell names as values; for the example, type $B7+B8+B9+B10$. You will see your entry in the Formula Bar along with two new symbols for Enter and Cancel; you can use these to finish your formula or you can press the *Enter* key. When you complete your formula, the value will display in cell B6; you can add any formatting to the cell that you want applied to the value. The example formula is shown in Figure 11.21.

11.3.6.1 *Mathematical Calculations*

You can perform standard mathematical calculations in Excel in addition to entering formulas. The order of operations hierarchy in mathematics is upheld in Excel, where division and multiplication are ranked above addition and subtraction in performance order. Using parentheses will supersede any operation such that whatever is added inside of the parentheses will be performed first in the operation order. Practice creating simple

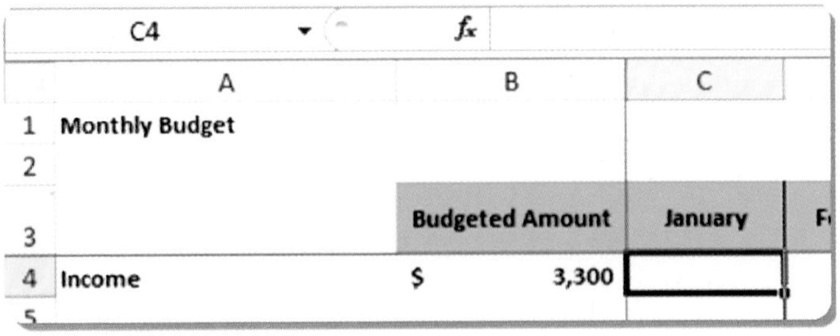

▲ FIGURE 11.20
Example cell selection for Freeze Panes effect

formulas to add the elements of each category up to the Savings category. Apply bold formatting to the category sums (as well as the income entry if you have not done so already).

Once you have the category sums calculated, you are going to enter the equation for Total Expenses; to do this, simply add together the cells containing each category sum. You can see the formula for the example budget in Figure 11.22. If you have followed along with the example, your result should be $2,750. The final equation you will add in this step is for Net Income; this is the income value (cell B4 in the example) minus the Total Expenses value (cell B34 in the example).

▼ FIGURE 11.21
Example formula in Excel 2010

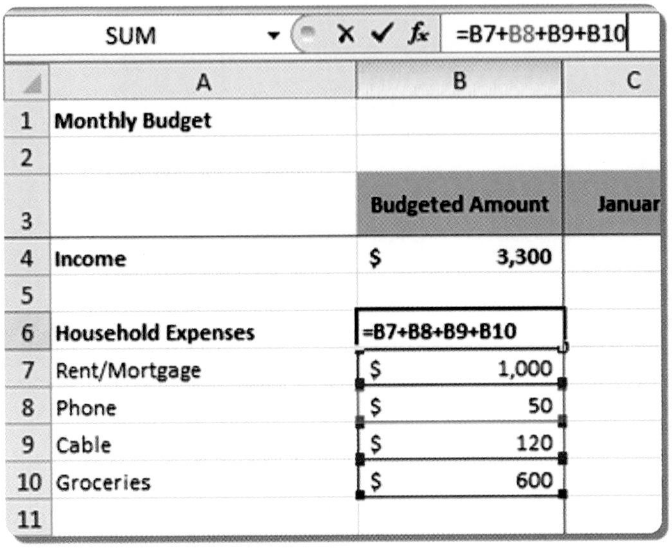

If you have followed the example, the result should be $550.

11.3.6.2 *Freezing Cells in Formulas*

When you copy and paste cells or when you duplicate cells as you will in the next steps for constructing a budget, the cell values will automatically update based on the position of the formula. For instance, if you copy the example formula for Net Income in cell *B36* to cell *C36*, the cell references that previously included cells in Column B (cells *B4* and *B34*) will now refer to the equivalent cells in Column C (cells *C4* and *C34*). To prevent this type of update, use the dollar sign in your formula to fix a certain value.

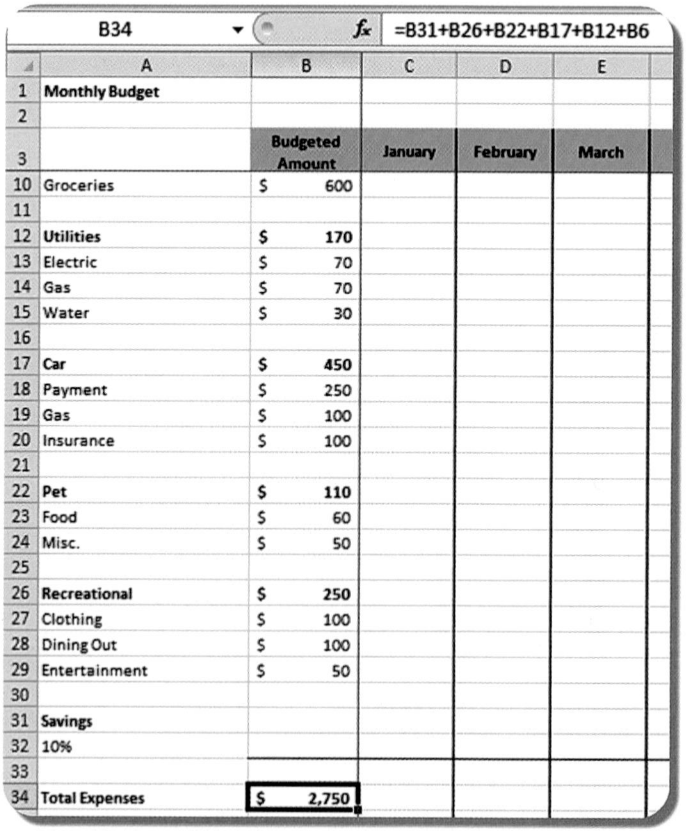

▼ FIGURE 11.22
Example total expenses calculation in Excel 2010

B34			fx	=B31+B26+B22+B17+B12+B6	
	A	**B**	**C**	**D**	**E**
1	Monthly Budget				
2					
3		Budgeted Amount	January	February	March
10	Groceries	$ 600			
11					
12	Utilities	$ 170			
13	Electric	$ 70			
14	Gas	$ 70			
15	Water	$ 30			
16					
17	Car	$ 450			
18	Payment	$ 250			
19	Gas	$ 100			
20	Insurance	$ 100			
21					
22	Pet	$ 110			
23	Food	$ 60			
24	Misc.	$ 50			
25					
26	Recreational	$ 250			
27	Clothing	$ 100			
28	Dining Out	$ 100			
29	Entertainment	$ 50			
30					
31	Savings				
32	10%				
33					
34	Total Expenses	$ 2,750			

As an example of this, consider the following:

- $B4 will preserve the column reference as Column B when copied but will allow the row reference (row 4) to change.

- B$4 will preserve the row reference to row 4 but will allow the column reference, currently Column B, to change.

- $B$4 will preserve the exact reference to Column B and row 4, retaining this fixed value no matter where the formula is copied and placed.

You will use this ability to freeze cell values to construct the formula for the Savings value. To do this, select the cell in Column B beside the percentage value you selected for savings in Column A (for the example, this is cell *B32*). Multiply the percentage value by the income for the budget. When you duplicate this formula, you want it to be based on the monthly income, but you want the percentage to remain the same. Therefore, you will freeze the reference to the percentage by entering =*B4*$A$32* as the cell data; this preserves the reference to cell A32 for the percentage value and updates the income reference wherever the formula is copied. Figure 11.23 shows the example.

The SUM Function 11.3.6.3

In addition to standard mathematical operations, Excel has a library of existing formulas that you can use to perform complex calculations within your spreadsheet. One of the common formulas is SUM, which computes the numeric sum of the cells listed as its argument. An example of using SUM would be to replace the formula for calculating the total Recreational expenses (=B27+B28+B29 from the example) with the SUM formula operating on those cells; the formula would then be =SUM(B27,B28,B29). The term SUM is the name of the formula and the entries in the parentheses are the arguments, or values on which the formula is operating. The result of both of these calculations would be the same.

You can use the colon symbol (:) as a shortcut to include adjacent cells in an argument of a formula. Entering B27:B29 in a formula means all of the cells from cells B27 through B29, inclusive. The SUM function in the example can therefore be rewritten as =SUM(B27:B29) to produce the same result. You can only use the shortcut if you want to include all of the cells in an adjacent range. Practice using the SUM formula by replacing the formulas you constructed for calculating the total expense for each category. An example of this is shown in Figure 11.24.

11.3.7 Using Directional Fill

When you want to duplicate a value or repeat a formula in a spreadsheet, you select the value you want to repeat, highlight the direction in the spreadsheet to which you want to repeat the value, and use the Fill menu to repeat it. The Fill menu, found on the Home ribbon,

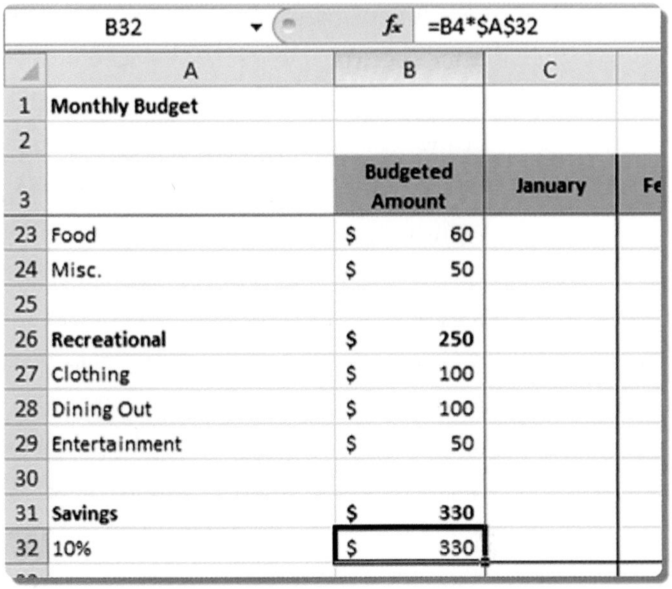

| B32 | ▼ | f_x | =B4*$A$32 |

	A	B	C
1	Monthly Budget		
2			
3		**Budgeted Amount**	**January**	Fe
23	Food	$ 60	
24	Misc.	$ 50	
25			
26	**Recreational**	$ 250	
27	Clothing	$ 100	
28	Dining Out	$ 100	
29	Entertainment	$ 50	
30			
31	**Savings**	$ 330	
32	10%	$ 330	

▲ FIGURE 11.23
Example formula with fixed/frozen cell reference

contains entries for the four primary directions. For example, *Fill Right* will select the leftmost value (which should be the one you want to repeat in the adjacent cells) and copy it to all of the highlighted cells to the right. You are going to practice using the Fill command to duplicate the formulas you constructed for your budget to the cells for the months. Obviously you need to enter the actual monthly values in each of the subcategories and in the cell representing Income, but the calculations will remain the same.

To complete this task for the Household Expenses category, select cell B6 and highlight all of the cells in that row through Column N (which should contain the December heading). With all of these

▼ FIGURE 11.24
Example use of the SUM formula

cells highlighted, select the *Fill* menu from the icon on the *Home* ribbon and choose *Right*. You can perform this same task by clicking the cell you want to duplicate and using the grab point in the lower-right corner to drag the contents to the adjacent cells into which you want to copy the value. Repeat this task from Column B to Column N for all of the rows containing category headings as well as the percentage entry for Savings (which has the reference to the percentage frozen), the row containing Total Expenses, and the row containing Net Income.

The final column for Annual Amounts also needs to be completed before your budget is done. This column is a sum of the yearly expenses and income and a report of the annual differences and net income for the year. Therefore, each of the column entries will be a summation of the respective values from January to December. You can use the Fill command to make short work of compiling this information. In cell *O4* (if you have followed the example), enter the text *=SUM(C4:N4)* to calculate the net income for the year.

Select cell *O4* and highlight the adjacent cells all the way to the row containing the Net Income entry (cell *O36* in the

You may get an error message (which appears as a small green triangle in the upper-left corner of the cell in Excel 2010) when you enter this formula, saying you have omitted adjacent cells in your formula. You should ignore this error since the adjacent cells are the budget value and do not represent the real value of any particular month.

example). Choose the *Fill Down* command to duplicate the formula for every cell in the column. Now format the cells using the *Accounting* style with no digits after the decimal point. Click any filled cells in Column O that correspond to intentionally blank rows and press the *Delete* key to remove the contents. When you are finished, you will have a functional budget sheet to track your annual expenses. Your result should be similar to what is shown in Figure 11.25.

Navigating the Spreadsheet

11.3.8

There are several shortcut commands on the keyboard that will allow you to move through your spreadsheet quickly. The arrow keys can be used to move one step for each keypress in any of the cardinal directions. You can also hold down the Shift key to select the cells between your starting location and where you end (if you move your cursor in two directions, it will select the rectangular set of cells between the starting location and the ending location just as it does when you click and drag the cursor).

The shortcut commands on the keyboard that are coupled with the Control (Ctrl) key can be used for quick navigation as follows (the Command key on a Macintosh is substituted in these examples for the Control key on a Windows machine):

- *Ctrl-a directional arrow*—This will jump the cursor to the last entry in the direction of the arrow key before a blank space in the current selection;

	Budgeted Amount	February	March	April	May	June	July	August	September	October	November	December	Annual Amount
Monthly Budget													
Income	$ 3,300												$ -
Household Expenses	$ 1,770	$ -	$ -	$ -	$ -	$ -	$ -	$ -	$ -	$ -	$ -	$ -	$ -
Rent/Mortgage	$ 1,000												$ -
Phone	$ 50												$ -
Cable	$ 120												$ -
Groceries	$ 600												$ -
Utilities	$ 170	$ -	$ -	$ -	$ -	$ -	$ -	$ -	$ -	$ -	$ -	$ -	$ -
Electric	$ 70												$ -
Gas	$ 70												$ -
Water	$ 30												$ -
Car	$ 450	$ -	$ -	$ -	$ -	$ -	$ -	$ -	$ -	$ -	$ -	$ -	$ -
Payment	$ 250												$ -
Gas	$ 100												$ -
Insurance	$ 100												$ -
Pet	$ 110	$ -	$ -	$ -	$ -	$ -	$ -	$ -	$ -	$ -	$ -	$ -	$ -
Food	$ 60												$ -
Misc.	$ 50												$ -
Recreational	$ 250	$ -	$ -	$ -	$ -	$ -	$ -	$ -	$ -	$ -	$ -	$ -	$ -
Clothing	$ 100												$ -
Dining Out	$ 100												$ -
Entertainment	$ 50												$ -
Savings	$ 330	$ -	$ -	$ -	$ -	$ -	$ -	$ -	$ -	$ -	$ -	$ -	$ -
10%	$ 330	$ -	$ -	$ -	$ -	$ -	$ -	$ -	$ -	$ -	$ -	$ -	$ -
Total Expenses	$ 3,080	$ -	$ -	$ -	$ -	$ -	$ -	$ -	$ -	$ -	$ -	$ -	$ -
Net Income	$ 220.00	$ -	$ -	$ -	$ -	$ -	$ -	$ -	$ -	$ -	$ -	$ -	$ -

▲ FIGURE 11.25
Completed budget example

if the cursor is already at a blank space, it will jump to the next location in line with content or, if there is no content, the cursor will jump to the end of the spreadsheet.

- *Ctrl-Shift-a directional arrow*— This has the same effect of moving the cursor as the shortcut command for Ctrl-a directional arrow, but it also highlights/selects the cells between the starting and ending location.

- *Ctrl-Home*—This returns the cursor to cell A1 regardless of the current cursor location.

- *Ctrl-End*—This sends the cursor to the farthest cell to the right and down on the spreadsheet where content has been added.

- *Ctrl-Page Down (Pg Dn)*—This command advances to the next worksheet in the workbook (just like clicking the tab to the right of the current worksheet).

- *Ctrl-Page Up (Pg Up)*—This command opens the previous worksheet in the workbook (just like clicking the tab to the left of the current worksheet).

- *Ctrl-A*—The Select All command in Excel will select only the cells that contain information that are adjacent to the current cell. Pressing *Ctrl-A* again with the adjacent information selected will select the entire worksheet.

ADDING CHARTS 11.4

Charts are great tools for visualizing information. Because human beings are generally able to process visual information more quickly than text, charts are a great way to express the overall idea or trend of data in a single image rather than either a lengthy text explanation or large amounts of data that must be read. If you have followed along with the text so far, you should have some idea of how charts work by inserting them into your PowerPoint presentations; Excel is the program that actually manages chart data whenever you add a chart to any Office document. For this example, you are going to create a line graph to view your monthly income and your overall monthly expenses.

11.4.1 Chart Data

To create a chart in Excel, select the data range you want to include in the chart. In this case, you will select the row containing Income (row 4 in the example) from Column A (where the heading is located) to Column N (representing the December entry). With these cells selected, choose the chart type you want to insert. In Excel 2010, you can add a chart to your document by selecting the type of chart on the Insert ribbon; in this case, select the *Line* icon and choose *Line* beneath the *2-D Line* heading. In Excel 2011, you can find this option in the Charts ribbon. A chart will be added to your document. Enter values for your income over the months to see the effect it has on the chart display. To preserve your blank chart for your own use, you can save this workbook as *MyBudgetChart* so you can enter information needed for the chart to display correctly.

You may notice that your chart includes the column for your budget estimate, which you want to remove to get a clear picture of your income over the year. To do this, you need to edit the chart data. In Excel 2010, you can find the *Select Data* icon in the context-sensitive Design ribbon for Chart Tools; in Excel 2011, the *Select* icon is located on the Charts ribbon. When you click this icon, a dialog box will appear from which you can edit the cell locations that determine the chart. In Excel 2010, click on the *Income* series and choose *Edit* to open a dialog box where you can select your data. In Excel 2011, simply click on the *Income* series and the fields will display on the right side of the pane. The series name is correct, but the series values should begin at cell C4 and run through cell N4 if you have followed along with the example. You can either enter the information as you would for a formula or click the data selection icon and use your mouse to highlight the correct cells in the document (press the *Enter* key when you have selected the correct cells). The result of this data selection change is shown in Figure 11.26.

The next step is to add a new series to track the total expenses for each month as a comparison against the Income series you already have in the chart. To do this, activate the data selection dialog box just as you did to edit the Income series. This time, choose the *Add* button to create a new series. The correct data selection is shown in Figure 11.27.

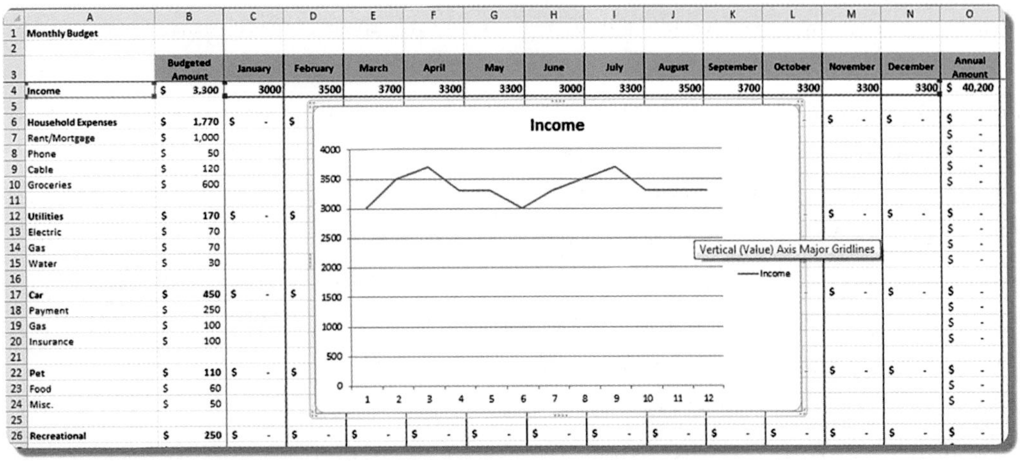

▲ FIGURE 11.26
Example line chart for income

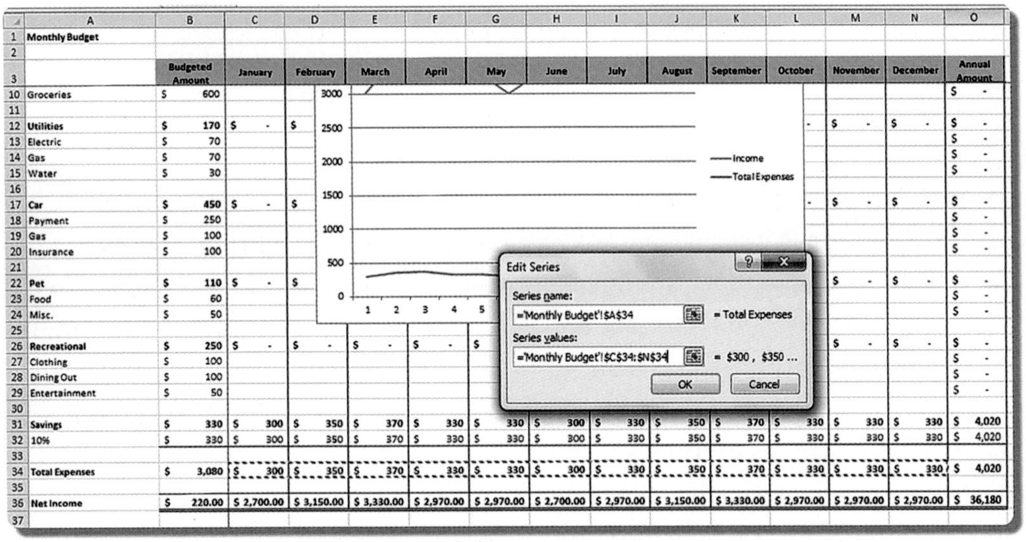

	A	B	C	D	E	F	G	H	I	J	K	L	M	N	O
1	Monthly Budget														
3		Budgeted Amount	January	February	March	April	May	June	July	August	September	October	November	December	Annual Amount
4	Income	$ 3,300	3000	3500	3700	3300	3300	3000	3300	3500	3700	3300	3300	3300	$ 40,200
6	Household Expenses	$ 1,770													
7	Rent/Mortgage	$ 1,000													
8	Phone	$ 50													
9	Cable	$ 120													
10	Groceries	$ 600													
12	Utilities	$ 170													
13	Electric	$ 70													
14	Gas	$ 70													
15	Water	$ 30													
17	Car	$ 450													
18	Payment	$ 250													
19	Gas	$ 100													
20	Insurance	$ 100													
22	Pet	$ 110													
23	Food	$ 60													
24	Misc.	$ 50													
26	Recreational	$ 250													

▲ FIGURE 11.27
Chart data selection for Total Expenses

	A	B	C	D	E	F	G	H	I	J	K	L	M	N	O
1	Monthly Budget														
3		Budgeted Amount	January	February	March	April	May	June	July	August	September	October	November	December	Annual Amount
10	Groceries	$ 600													$ -
12	Utilities	$ 170													$ -
13	Electric	$ 70													$ -
14	Gas	$ 70													$ -
15	Water	$ 30													$ -
17	Car	$ 450													$ -
18	Payment	$ 250													$ -
19	Gas	$ 100													$ -
20	Insurance	$ 100													$ -
22	Pet	$ 110													$ -
23	Food	$ 60													$ -
24	Misc.	$ 50													$ -
26	Recreational	$ 250													$ -
27	Clothing	$ 100													$ -
28	Dining Out	$ 100													$ -
29	Entertainment	$ 50													$ -
31	Savings	$ 330	300	350	370	330	330	300	330	350	370	330	330	330	$ 4,020
32	10%	$ 330	300	350	370	330	330	300	330	350	370	330	330	330	$ 4,020
34	Total Expenses	$ 3,080	300	350	370	330	330	300	330	350	370	330	330	330	$ 4,020
36	Net Income	$ 220.00	$ 2,700.00	$ 3,150.00	$ 3,330.00	$ 2,970.00	$ 2,970.00	$ 2,700.00	$ 2,970.00	$ 3,150.00	$ 3,330.00	$ 2,970.00	$ 2,970.00	$ 2,970.00	$ 36,180

Edit Series

Series name:
='Monthly Budget'!$A$34   = Total Expenses

Series values:
='Monthly Budget'!$C$34:$N$34   = $300 , $350 …

OK   Cancel

The series name should be the cell containing the text "Total Expenses," which is cell A34. The series values should be the cells corresponding to January through December in the row for Total Expenses (row 34).

As a final step for the chart creation, move your chart to another worksheet in your workbook. Click on the tab titled *Sheet 2* and rename it *Budget Chart*; click the chart you created, cut it from the document, select the new *Budget Chart* tab, and paste the chart into the worksheet. Delete any additional worksheets and save your workbook.

Formatting Charts

11.4.2

The next step is to format the chart so it is more readable and representative of its contents. You can start this process by adding a chart title. In Excel 2010, select the *Chart Title* icon on the *Layout* ribbon for Chart Tools and select *Above Chart*. In Excel 2011, select the *Chart Title* icon on the context-sensitive *Chart Layout* ribbon. Clicking the icon will add a default chart title that you can rename by clicking inside the text box and typing; for the example, enter *Income Analysis*.

Next, you will add a forecast trend line to predict both your income and your expenses. In Excel 2010, the trend line commands are located in the Layout ribbon for Chart Tools; in Excel 2011, these are found on the Chart Layout ribbon. To add a trend line, select the *Trendline* icon and choose *Linear Forecast Trendline*. In the dialog box that opens, select *Income* as the series to predict the income trend past the current cycle. Repeat the process to predict the expenses past the current cycle. This will show you if your expenses are approaching your income level, which is an undesirable situation that should guide you to reevaluate your budget.

As a final formatting step, adjust the labels of your horizontal axis to read the months of the year. To do this, activate the data selection dialog box for your chart. In Excel 2010, select the *Edit* button beneath *Horizontal (Category) Axis Labels*; in Excel 2011, the series data for this is called *Category (x) axis labels*, which allows you to type a direct reference or use the selection icon to choose the cells you want to use. Now that your chart is on a new spreadsheet, you will need to click the Monthly Budget tab to get back to the correct data; select the cells containing the names of the month from January to December. Compare your result with the completed chart in Figure 11.28.

OPENOFFICE. ORG CALC

The OpenOffice.org alternative to Excel is a program called Calc. As with the other OpenOffice.org programs, Calc is part of the larger OpenOffice.org program and does not act as a standalone application. You can create a Calc document from the File menu of any of the OpenOffice.org programs in the suite. The native document type for Calc is ODF Spreadsheet (.ods). The interface of Calc should be familiar if you have been using the other OpenOffice.org programs. The primary difference is in the document pane where the information is organized into rows and columns that intersect in cells. Each tab in the document pane represents a single spreadsheet in the overall workbook.

Anatomy of OpenOffice.org Calc

The interface for Calc, shown in Figure 11.29, is similar to the interface for Writer. By default you will see the Formatting toolbar and the Find toolbar beneath the menu selection area. Several of the menu options for Calc are different from the standard menus in the rest of the OpenOffice.org suite. Calc has a new set of formatting options for numeric data values in the Format menu and a new Data menu; these two menus will be used for the majority of your cell and data-specific commands. The File menu contains the same standard functionality common to most applications. The new

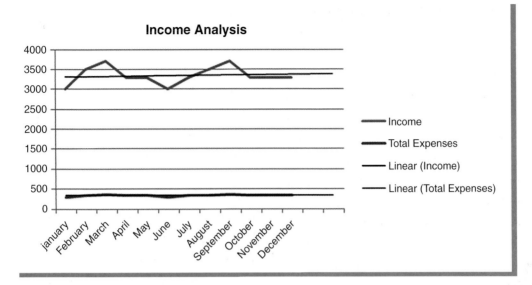

Income Analysis

Formatting toolbar for Calc has several number formatting commands and an icon menu for adding cell borders.

The biggest departure from any of the other OpenOffice.org applications you have encountered so far is the arrangement of the main document pane. The document pane is divided into columns (denoted by letter) and rows (denoted by number). The intersection of these rows and columns is called a cell, and these cells are where you enter data. The highlighted cell is called the active cell, and the respective row and column header will also be highlighted. The bottom of the interface contains tabs for the individual spreadsheets used within the overall document. You can use the arrows in the lower-right corner to switch between spreadsheets or click directly on the tabs.

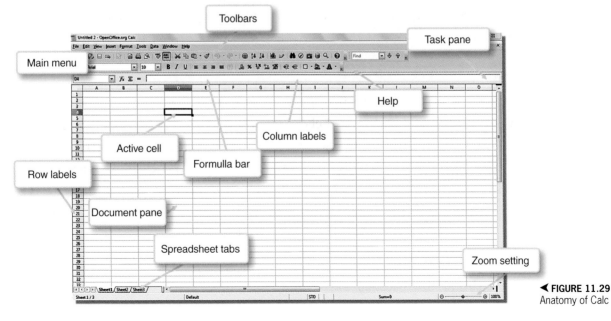

◀ FIGURE 11.29
Anatomy of Calc

You can add, delete, and rename the tabs using the right-click menu. The bottom of the interface also contains an automatic sum calculation for the currently selected cells and a slide bar for the zoom settings.

Inside the actual spreadsheet, you can navigate through the various cells using the directional arrow keys on the keyboard. Holding the Shift key along with a directional arrow allows you to select multiple cells, whether you are using the directional arrows or the mouse. You can also highlight an entire column or row by clicking the header for it; this allows you to format or change data for an entire row or column at the same time.

11.5.2 Creating a Budget in Calc

To use Calc to create the budget document described in Section 11.3, begin by entering your row headings into Column A. You will be using the same information and configuration described for Excel, but the tools are not necessarily located in the same place. When you have finished, though, there should be no difference between your resulting budget document and the one created using Excel. You should also add your desired savings percentage beneath the Savings category heading; the Percent (%) number format you need to apply to this cell is available as a shortcut icon on the Formatting toolbar. As you enter text or values into your cells, you can adjust the column width or row height by clicking and dragging the separator line between the column

or row headings; you can also manually enter values for the column width or row height by selecting the *Format* menu and choosing either *Column* and *Width* or *Row* and *Height*, respectively.

You can use the Formatting toolbar in Calc to bold the category headings and the "Income" label. Add your budget values in Column B. Cell *B3* should contain the text "Budget Amount." Enter your values up to the Savings category, including your projected monthly income. Leave the cells next to the category headings blank since you will use a formula to calculate these sums. Select all of the values from cell B4 down to the cell beside the "Net Income" label; apply currency formatting and then remove the decimal places.

You can customize the format for cells that contain formulas or numbers by using the right-click menu on the selected cell or cells and choosing *Format Cells* (or by selecting the *Format* menu and choosing *Cells*). The Format Cells dialog box can be seen in Figure 11.30. The different tabs in this dialog box allow you to set the background fill and borders of the cells.

Calc can predict simple series entries the same way as Excel, so you can use it to automatically fill in the

Calc has no direct equivalent to the Accounting format in Excel. However, you can apply your own unique formatting code to recreate the style using the Format Cells dialog box. The code for this style (which you can also see in Figure 11.30) is as follows: _("$"* #,##0_);_ ("$"* \(#,##0\);_("$"* "-"??_);_(@_)

months of the year; to do this, type *January* in cell *C3* and *February* in cell *D3*, select both, and drag the grip point on the lower-right corner of cell D3 to the right to complete the series all the way through *December* in row 3. You can also access the series prediction parameters by highlighting the cells you want to use to predict the series and the cells you want to fill, clicking on the *Edit* menu, selecting *Fill*, and then selecting *Series*. Finally, add the heading *Annual Amount* to cell *O3*.

Use the Format Cells dialog box to add a background color (such as the pale green used in the example) to the column headings from cells *B3* to *O3*; this option is accessible on the *Background* tab of the dialog box. You can also use this tool to format the text alignment within the cells by selecting the desired alignment style for *Horizontal* and *Vertical* in the *Alignment* tab of the Format Cells dialog box. The Alignment tab also contains the *Wrap text automatically* checkbox for whether you want your text to wrap to multiple lines. Select all of the cells from cell B3 to the cell at the intersection of Column O and the row containing the "Net Income" label for your budget. Activate the Format Cells dialog box and select

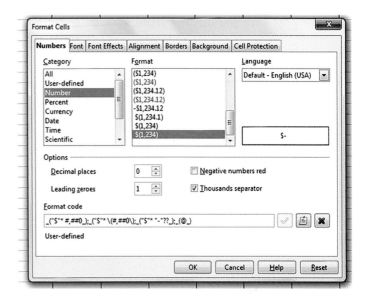

▲ FIGURE 11.30 Format Cells dialog box in Calc

the *Borders* tab; apply a thin border to the left, right, and center of the cells, as shown in Figure 11.31. You can do this by clicking on the diagram at the left until the border you wish to apply is shown; you can adjust the parameters for the border you have selected

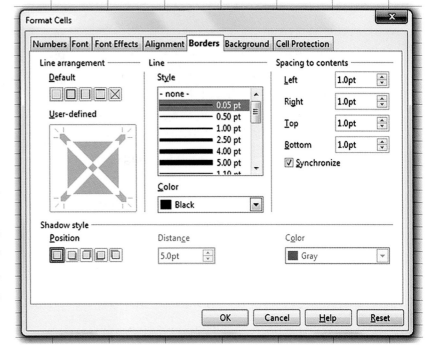

▶ FIGURE 11.31 Borders tab of Format Cells dialog box in Calc

(it should be surrounded by the dotted line) on the right. In this example, you will just apply a thin, single line.

Repeat these steps to apply a bottom border to the row of cells containing the values for the savings percentage each month. Finally, apply a double-line bottom border to the row of cells containing the values labeled "Net Income." You can freeze cells in Calc to preserve your column and row headings as you scroll your spreadsheet. To do this, select the first cell you want to scroll (in the example, it is cell *C4*), select the *Window* menu, and choose *Freeze*.

Formula entry works the same way in Calc as it does in Excel, so you can follow the instructions for entering the correct formulas in Section 11.3.6. The instructions for filling cells from Section 11.3.7 also apply in Calc; to fill adjacent cells in Calc, select the cells you want

to copy and the cells you want to fill, click the *Edit* menu, choose *Fill*, and then select the direction you want to fill. You can also fill cells using the grip point of the last selected cell to copy its contents (or the series if multiple cells are selected) in the direction you drag. The navigation shortcuts for Excel also function in Calc. As a final step for this portion of the project, rename your first spreadsheet tab (which contains your budget data) by right-clicking the tab name, selecting *Rename Sheet*, and giving it the name *Monthly Budget*; you should also delete the third spreadsheet tab (which should be labeled *Sheet 3*) by right-clicking on the tab.

Adding Charts in Calc

11.5.3

You should now rename your budget sheet as *MyBudgetChart* and add sample values for the expenses and income for

▼ **FIGURE 11.32**
Chart Wizard
Step 1 in Calc

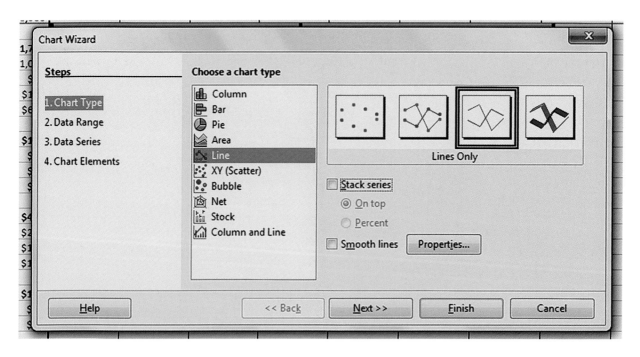

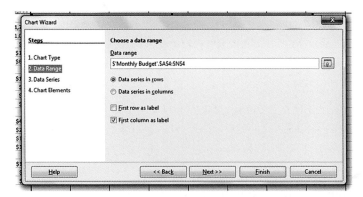

◄ FIGURE 11.33
Chart Wizard Step 2 in Calc

to choose January through December in your spreadsheet (this will hide the original dialog box and show only the cell reference and the spreadsheet data until you hit the *Enter* key to accept the values you have chosen). Next, you should choose *Modify* for the *Y-Values* for the *Income* series to remove the reference to the budget amount in Column B from the actual data. Finally, select *Add* to add a second series to the chart; this time you will select the cell containing the label *Total Expenses* as the Name value and select the entries for January through December as the Y-Values for the series. The completed example is shown in Figure 11.34.

As a final step in the wizard, add your chart title and axis labels. You should display the grid for the Y-axis. The completed example for the final step of the Chart

the year. The Chart icon in the Standard toolbar will launch the Chart Wizard, which is the primary means of constructing a chart in OpenOffice.org. To create the chart of income versus total expenses, select the row containing the Income values from Column A to the column representing the value for December and then click the *Chart* icon. The first step in the wizard that appears is to select the type of chart you want to use. In this case, select *Line* and then choose *Lines Only*, as shown in Figure 11.32.

The next step is to choose the data range. This should already be correct if you have highlighted the relevant cells for income. Check the box next to *First column as label* to use the label in Column A as the series title in the chart, as shown in Figure 11.33.

The next step is to modify the series information and the category labels for the chart. The categories here will be months, so use the *Select data range* icon

▼ FIGURE 11.34
Chart Wizard
Step 3 in Calc

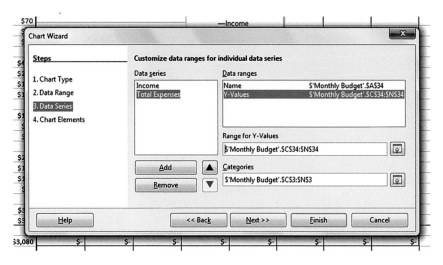

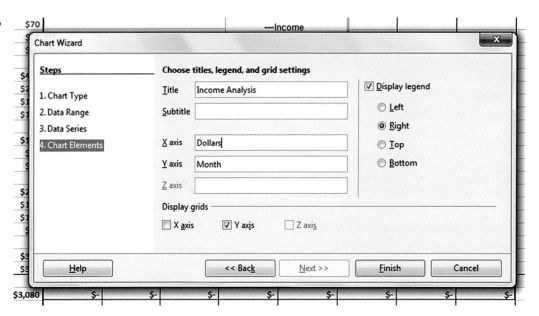

Wizard is shown in Figure 11.35. When you click *Finish*, the chart will be pasted into your current spreadsheet.

Click on the chart elements (such as the legend or one of the axes) to access a special formatting toolbar just for chart elements; this will allow you to change the format of the font, the appearance of the lines, and the tick marks for the axes. Click on the chart, cut it from the current spreadsheet, and move it to the sheet currently labeled "Sheet 2." Rename the spreadsheet *Budget Chart* to complete the project for this chapter.

CHAPTER SUMMARY

This chapter introduced the basic functionality of spreadsheet software. You learned how to add and format data, whether it is text or numeric values, as well as how to utilize that data in basic calculations. Formulas, charts, and organization of information represent the real power and utility of spreadsheets. Now that you have a basic idea of the interface and the navigation of the spreadsheet environment, it is time to turn to the next chapter where you will construct more involved spreadsheets that demonstrate the more powerful aspects of this type of application.

CHAPTER EXERCISES

1. Using the budget example as a basis, create a new spreadsheet page to track your bank account for one week. Categorize the expenses into various categories (you should create a Category column) and add any account credits to the Income category in a separate column from the debits of the account. Use the SUM function and compare the expenses to the credits. You do not have to enter specific information for the purchases, but you should name them so you can recognize what they represent.

2. Using the data from your budget, add a series to the chart for each category of expenses. Format the chart so it is still readable. Is this the correct type of chart to use for this additional information? Do the additional series entries contribute to or detract from the clarity of the visual presentation?

3. Add a new column to your budget document to calculate the average amount per month that is spent on each category and subcategory in your document. You can calculate this value using a direct formula or a calculation from existing data in the document.

4. Construct a budget for a fictional business based on the example you constructed in the chapter. What categories of expenses would you have to add to accommodate the operation of the business? What subcategories would comprise the income?

CHAPTER KNOWLEDGE CHECK

1

The intersection of Column B and row 4 is denoted in a cell reference as:

- ○ **A.** 4B
- ○ **B.** B:4
- ○ **C.** B4
- ○ **D.** None of the above

2

Rows in a spreadsheet are labeled with letters and columns in a spreadsheet are labeled with numbers.

- ○ True
- ○ False

3

Formatting can be applied to cell contents whether it is a fixed value or a formula calculation result.

- ○ True
- ○ False

4

The number of digits to the right of the decimal point that are visually displayed for a value is independent of the accuracy of the value stored in the cell.

- ○ True
- ○ False

5

A formula begins with the symbol:

- ○ **A.** %
- ○ **B.** =
- ○ **C.** $
- ○ **D.** None of the above

6 To fix a reference to the column but not the row of cell A6, the correct cell reference in a formula would be:

- ○ **A.** $A$6
- ○ **B.** $A6
- ○ **C.** A$6
- ○ **D.** A6

7 You can use the Fill command only on numeric values.

- ○ True
- ○ False

8 The SUM function takes cell references as an argument and calculates their total numerical value.

- ○ True
- ○ False

9 The following is the correct use of the SUM function in a cell:

- ○ **A.** =SUM(A4:A6)
- ○ **B.** =SUM(A4, A5, A7)
- ○ **C.** =SUM(A4+A6)
- ○ **D.** Both a and b
- ○ **E.** Both a and c

10 A data series in a chart must be contained in a continuous set of cells (or a single cell) in either the same row or the same column.

- ○ True
- ○ False

Developing Worksheets and Graphic Representations

Now that you have a basic understanding of spreadsheet software and how the data in these documents is arranged, it is time to explore some of the options available for data management and visualization. These include the ability to manipulate cells, format them conditionally, and reference them on other worksheets, as well as selecting the correct type of chart to showcase the information you want to convey. When you have completed this chapter, you will be able to:

- Manipulate cells, rows, and columns for information presentation

- Use Filter and Sort functionality on your spreadsheets

- Reference cells across spreadsheets

- Use formatting as a visual indicator of data in your spreadsheets

- Select the correct type of chart to convey the needed information

CONSTRUCTING A WORKSHEET

There are a variety of applications for spreadsheet software across multiple disciplines from office management to accounting. While spreadsheets are commonly associated with calculations and charts (for which they are excellent tools), they can also be used to manage lists and provide more exact formatting for lists. Regardless of the application for which they are used, understanding how to adjust and manipulate the layout of the spreadsheet is essential. Though spreadsheets are primarily used for calculation, considering how to present the results of your calculations is also important. Open a new spreadsheet document to experiment with these options.

Merging and Splitting Cells

You can merge two or more cells together to act as a single cell in your document. This can be useful if you have a heading that spans more than one column (such as a Name heading over a column containing first names and a column containing last names). You can merge cells in multiple directions, but the result must be a square selection within the document. For example, you cannot merge cells *A1*, *A2*, and *B1* into a single cell without including cell *B2*.

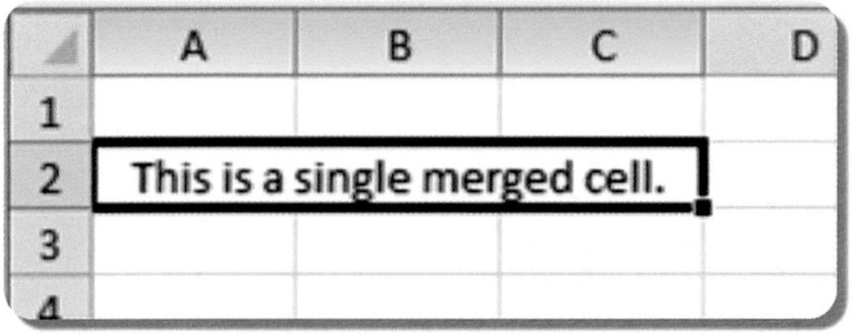

To practice merging cells, select cells *A2* through *C2* in your open document; there should be no content in the spreadsheet currently so this should not disrupt any existing data. In Excel 2010, you can merge cells by selecting the *Home* ribbon and clicking on the *Merge and Center* icon; in Excel 2011, this icon is simply called *Merge*. Selecting *Merge and Center* from the drop-down arrow combines the contents of the cells and centers the result; this is useful for creating headings that span multiple columns in a document. The other available options are Merge Across, which creates merged cells for each row but not across rows; Merge Cells, which combines the cells without adjusting the formatting; and Unmerge Cells, which is used to undo the process of merging the cells. You can see the result of merging cells in Figure 12.1.

>  **OPEN OFFICE** To merge cells in Calc, select the cells you want to combine, click the *Format* menu, and select *Merge Cells*. This acts as a toggle on the menu, so you can undo the merge for cells by selecting them and unchecking *Merge Cells*.

The opposite of merging cells is splitting cells. You can generally only split cells that have already been merged; this process is also called *unmerging* cells. (If you need to add cells to your document, you can add rows or columns in the current location.) The Unmerge Cells option in Excel is located in the same menu you used to merge the cells.

▼ **FIGURE 12.1**
Example of a merged cell

	A	B	C	D
1				
2	This is a single merged cell.			
3				
4				

Adding and Deleting Rows and Columns

You can insert new rows or columns anywhere in the document where you need to add additional information. Keep in mind that inserting a row adds it across the entire document. Similarly, inserting a column adds it all the way from the first row of the document to the last. To add a column in either Excel 2010 or Excel 2011, right-click the column label to the right of where you want to add it (new columns are added to the left) and select *Insert*. Similarly, you can click a row label, use the right-click menu, and select *Insert* to add new rows; these are added above the selected row. You can also add rows and columns via the drop-down menu of the *Insert* icon on the *Home* ribbon.

Existing columns and rows can be removed as well. Doing so will remove the contents of the cells in the column and/ or row and move all of the content in the spreadsheet to the left (for a column deletion) or upward (for a row deletion). The letters and numbers will adjust to accommodate the removal, but the complete alphabetic or numeric ordering will be retained (there will be no gaps in column letters or row numbers, so, for example, removing Column *B* turns the previous Column *C* into the new Column *B*). To remove columns or rows in Excel 2010 or Excel 2011, select the elements you want to remove, right-click, and select *Delete*. You can also perform this action from the *Delete* icon on the *Home* ribbon.

You can empty the contents of a cell by selecting it and pressing the *Delete* key, but you cannot remove an individual cell from

OPEN OFFICE Adding rows or columns in Calc works just as it does in Excel. You click on a column or row label, use either the right-click menu or the Insert menu, and select the option to insert columns or rows as needed. New rows are added above the current location, and new columns are added to the left. You can also select the column or row labels and use the right-click menu to delete the cells, or select the cells you want to remove, click the *Edit* menu, and choose *Delete Cells*; in either case, you will be prompted to resolve the deletion just as you would be in Excel.

a document. When you right-click on a cell, select the *Delete* option; this opens a dialog box that allows you to select how you want to resolve the deletion. The Delete dialog box is shown in Figure 12.2.

When you remove a cell from the document, the rest of the cells around that cell needs to move to accommodate the deletion. You can move all of the contents beneath the cell in the column upward or move all of the cells that are to the right in the row leftward to fill the gap. You can also choose to remove the entire row or column from the document.

◀ FIGURE 12.2
Deletion resolution dialog box

12.1.3 Hiding Rows and Columns

Sometimes you may want to retain data in your spreadsheet without visually referencing it. In these circumstances, you can hide columns or rows in the spreadsheet. The data that is contained in the hidden rows or columns is still present in the document and can be referenced just like any other cell (with a direct reference at least); it is simply hidden from view. You can hide or unhide any columns or rows that you wish. Figure 12.3 shows the result of hiding Column B and Row 3. Notice that if you hide a row or column that is part of a merged cell, the contents will display in the remaining cells.

To hide rows or columns in Excel, simply select the labels for the columns or rows that you want to hide, right-click, and then select *Hide* from the menu. You can also hide rows or columns (or entire spreadsheets) in your Excel 2010 document by selecting what you want to hide (any cell within the sheet will suffice for hiding the spreadsheet itself), selecting the *Format* icon in the *Home* ribbon, and choosing the *Hide & Unhide* option; you can then select

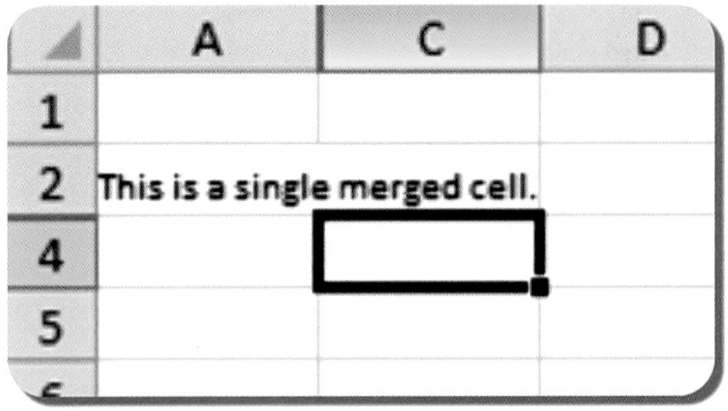

OPEN OFFICE You can hide columns or rows in Calc by selecting the label of the columns or rows, activating the right-click menu, and choosing *Hide*. To display the contents of hidden rows or columns again, select the neighboring rows or columns, right-click, and select *Show*.

the action you would like to perform from the submenu. In Excel 2011, the options to hide and unhide rows and columns are all accessed directly from the *Format* icon in the *Home* ribbon.

If you want to unhide a row or column that you have hidden in Excel 2010 or Excel 2011, select the labels before and after the hidden selection, right-click, and select *Unhide* from the menu. You can also do this from the *Format* icon on the Home ribbon. If you want to unhide everything in the spreadsheet, click the box above *Row 1* and to the left of *Column A* to select the entire worksheet before performing the *Unhide* operation.

12.1.4 Advanced Cell Referencing

You can reference information across spreadsheets in the same workbook; this is a helpful feature if you are using different spreadsheets in the same workbook for complex reporting or information management. It is typically a good approach to reference values rather than retype them. This keeps data consistent across the spreadsheets in your workbook and allows you to perform the necessary update in one location rather than many locations, which helps decrease

▼ FIGURE 12.3
Hidden row and hidden column in a spreadsheet

▲	A	C	D
1			
2	This is a single merged cell.		
4			
5			
6			

the potential for human error in entering the information. If you want to perform a cell reference across spreadsheets, type the name of the spreadsheet you want to reference in single quotes, add an exclamation point, and then type the cell reference. This can be either a fixed, or absolute, reference (using dollar signs to keep the row or column reference constant) or a standard reference.

For example, if you open the *MySupplies* document, you can use the blank Sheet1 to reference a cell on the Supply List spreadsheet. To do this, type *='Supply List'!A4* or *='Supply List'!$A$4*; if you have typed this correctly, you should get the value "Funtime Fishery" in the cell when you press *Enter* to activate the formula. A reference to a cell on another spreadsheet is typically a fixed reference using the dollar sign format, but it will work either way.

OPEN OFFICE Absolute referencing in Calc uses a period (.) instead of an exclamation point after the name of the spreadsheet for a reference across sheets in a document. The example then becomes *='Supply List'.A4*.

12.2 LIST MANAGEMENT

List management is one of the tasks for which spreadsheet software is an excellent tool. This primarily applies when you have a fixed list that you are using to construct derivative data, such as a list of unique values or a sort or filter of that data. Most of the tools for managing data apply to numeric values as well as text. In fact, it is often necessary to give the numeric values context with at least header information, if not further text descriptions. These do not have to be paragraphs of text to be effective; a simple example is a customer and an associated account number. You probably have several accounts of your own where you must maintain some sort of record of your account number and a username.

The example project in this chapter is management of a list of suppliers. Your business proposal from Chapters 9 and 10 went so well that your company has multiple locations, and it is your task to manage the contact information for your suppliers. To begin, open the *MySupplies* document if you do not already have it open, and then open the Supply List spreadsheet on the second tab of the document. Select all of the information on the spreadsheet and copy it to the clipboard.

Excel 2010 offers a variety of options for pasting your data. To see the available options, you can right-click in the top-left cell where you want your data to begin; this will open a menu where you can expand the Paste Options selection. One particular option to note is the Paste Values selections; these allow you to paste the actual calculated contents of any formulas instead of the formulas themselves. The available paste options for Excel 2010 are shown in Figure 12.4. In Excel 2011, you can use the *Paste Special* command in the right-click menu to access the available options for pasting contents into your document, including the Values selection.

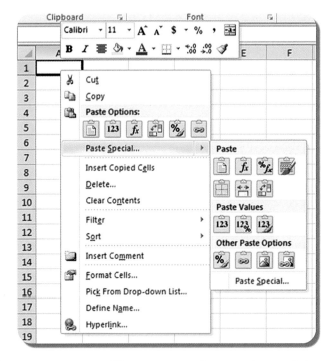

▲ FIGURE 12.4
Paste options in
Excel 2010

The process of sorting can be performed on any column in your spreadsheet. However, each column is treated as independent data, so be aware that if you have an association between columns (such as a name and address), they will be sorted independently if you directly apply the sort functionality. To avoid this circumstance, you can apply a *filter* to the connected data to retain its association. This allows you to set criteria of what you want to view as well as coupling the data in the filtered rows and columns so each row is treated as a line item.

You can apply a filter to any selection of cells in your spreadsheet. When you apply the filter, the software will assume that

> A **FILTER** *is a mechanism in spreadsheet software that allows only list elements that meet defined criteria to be displayed for the selection to which it is applied. This is a way to show only the relevant data from a large list. Filtering also facilitates other functionality such as alphanumeric sorting.*

The contents of an entire worksheet can be pasted only into cell *A1*. However, you will create a new header line in addition to what is already there, so you should paste the cells (the type of paste option you select does not matter since there are currently no calculated values in the spreadsheet) and then insert a new row above the entries you just added. Save your document as *MySuppliers*. Since this is a list of suppliers and not the supplies you purchased, you should delete the contents of the columns containing the Product, Price, and Quantity information and rename the tab for the spreadsheet *Suppliers*.

the first row of the filter contains column headings, so you should include a blank row if you do not have headings entered already. Otherwise, the first data element in your list will be used as heading information and will not be part of the filtered content. Select all of the data that was added to your Suppliers spreadsheet (in this case, cells *A2* to *I27*); this is the data to which you will apply your filter. Note that *Row 2* contains your heading information, so the headings will not present an issue.

OPEN OFFICE You can alter how data is pasted into your document in Calc by right-clicking where you want to paste the content and choosing the *Paste Special* option. The available choices will be displayed in a list from which you can select.

In Excel 2010, you can apply your filter by selecting the *Sort & Filter* icon on the *Home* ribbon and choosing the *Filter* option on the menu. This will add a drop-down arrow to each of the cells containing your heading information. Select the drop-down arrow next to the cell containing the heading "Company" and choose *Sort A to Z*. The result is shown in Figure 12.5. In Excel 2011, the *Filter* icon is located in the Quick Access toolbar and on the Data ribbon; the *Sort* command is located beside the Filter command in both locations.

There are a variety of options available for use in a filter, including the ability to apply individual filters to each column heading to further refine the data. You can select only one column at a time for alphabetic sorting; selecting a new column to sort alphabetically will undo the previous sort. In addition to alphabetic sorting (either ascending or descending), you can filter by color or select the values you want to retain (any item that is checked will display in the filtered list).

OPEN OFFICE To apply a filter in Calc, select the range to which you want the filter applied, open the *Data* menu, choose *Filter*, and then choose *AutoFilter*. This allows you to define the filter criteria in each column or select specific values from the drop-down menu. To apply an alphanumeric sort, select from the lower-right corner of your data to the upper-left corner and then click the *Sort Ascending* icon. The cell that is active will be used as the column to sort. Sorting will remove the existing filter, so you may need to apply the filter again.

The *Text Filters* option on the drop-down menu for the filter performs a keyword search on the elements and selects what you want to display; you can set up the filter so it omits keyword matches, retains keyword matches, keeps elements that begin with the keyword, keeps elements that end with the keyword, or only retains exact matches. You can use the *Custom Filter* option to define your own criteria for what to retain. This is particularly helpful if you are looking for a data range as a subset of the values in the spreadsheet.

	A	B	C	D	E	F	G	H	I
1									
2	Company	Contact	Address	City	State or Country	Postal Code	Phone	Email	Account Number
3	Bun Bakers	Penelope Pastry	11 Shortcake Lane	Candiyland	SC	19219	218-272-6653	pp@bb.com	4665550
4	Bun Bakers	Penelope Pastry	11 Shortcake Lane	Candiyland	SC	19219	218-272-6653	pp@bb.com	4665550
5	Condiment Capital	Carmen Ketchup	3000 Mustard Maker Circle	Washington	DC	20007	112-555-7778	ketchup@mustard.com	4755555
6	Condiment Capital	Carmen Ketchup	3000 Mustard Maker Circle	Washington	DC	20007	112-555-7778	ketchup@mustard.com	4755555
7	Condiment Capital	Carmen Ketchup	3000 Mustard Maker Circle	Washington	DC	20007	112-555-7778	ketchup@mustard.com	4755555
8	Custom Carts	Cal Carter	33 Mechanic Lane	Brooklyn	NJ	19104	553-228-9909	c.carter@carts.com	4775552
9	Daily Dog Delivery	Dan Dogmeister	12 Sausage Way	New York	NY	11101	212-212-2222	ddogmesiter@dailydogdelivery.com	4735556
10	Daily Dog Delivery	Dan Dogmeister	12 Sausage Way	New York	NY	11101	212-212-2222	ddogmesiter@dailydogdelivery.com	4735556
11	Daily Dog Delivery	Dan Dogmeister	12 Sausage Way	New York	NY	11101	212-212-2222	ddogmesiter@dailydogdelivery.com	4735556
12	Force Star Catering	Lea Princess	44 Darth Drive	Yavin	PA	27789	545-343-1441	princess@force_star.com	4775547
13	Force Star Catering	Lea Princess	44 Darth Drive	Yavin	PA	27789	545-343-1441	princess@force_star.com	4775547
14	Force Star Catering	Lea Princess	44 Darth Drive	Yavin	PA	27789	545-343-1441	princess@force_star.com	4775547
15	Force Star Catering	Lea Princess	44 Darth Drive	Yavin	PA	27789	545-343-1441	princess@force_star.com	4775547
16	Funtime Fishery	Steven Bassmaster	202 Ocean Drive	Gulfport	MI	34087	314-435-9770	bass_and_stuff@seabeasties.com	7865554
17	Funtime Fishery	Steven Bassmaster	202 Ocean Drive	Gulfport	MI	34087	314-435-9770	bass_and_stuff@seabeasties.com	7865554
18	Happy Meatery	Clive Cleaver	1 Green Mile	Denver	CO	45607	777-555-4478	cleave@meat.org	4335549
19	Inhuman Resources	Sam Saruman	8 Uruk Hai Crossing	Mordor	VA	91909	447-446-4445	sam.saruman@orcmakers.net	7555546
20	Nutty Nut Farms	Kat Kennedy	1 Crazy Circle	Port Royal	Jamaica	10001	770-664-3355	kk@nuttynuts.edu	7885553
21	Nutty Nut Farms	Kat Kennedy	1 Crazy Circle	Port Royal	Jamaica	10001	770-664-3355	kk@nuttynuts.edu	7885553
22	Nutty Nut Farms	Kat Kennedy	1 Crazy Circle	Port Royal	Jamaica	10001	770-664-3355	kk@nuttynuts.edu	7885553
23	Produce Producers	Matthew Lane	4 Songbird Lane	New York	NY	56647	112-505-5005	m_lane@produce_producers.com	7335548
24	Produce Producers	Matthew Lane	4 Songbird Lane	New York	NY	56647	112-505-5005	m_lane@produce_producers.com	7335548
25	Produce Producers	Matthew Lane	4 Songbird Lane	New York	NY	56647	112-505-5005	m_lane@produce_producers.com	7335548
26	Produce Producers	Matthew Lane	4 Songbird Lane	New York	NY	56647	112-505-5005	m_lane@produce_producers.com	7335548
27	The Umbrella Company	Al Wesker	Research Compound #7	Tokyo	Japan	13121	888-888-8888	ceo@villainy.org	4335551

◀ **FIGURE 12.5**
Filter and sort example in Excel 2010

Suppliers / Supply List

Ready

Removing Duplicates

There are cases where you may need to retain duplicate values in your document, such as when you want to track a count of occurrences. However, it is often beneficial to be able to remove duplicate values. In the example project, you are building a list of supplier contacts, so you want to have a single entry for each supplier. To remove the duplicates, highlight the cells for which you want duplicates removed; in the example, this is cells *A2* through *I27*.

In Excel 2010, open the *Data* ribbon and click on the *Remove Duplicates* icon. You will be prompted to select the columns you want to include in the search and whether your data has headers; leave the header checkbox activated and check all of the columns. Click *OK* to process the removal. The result should resemble Figure 12.6.

In Excel 2011, with the data range selected, you can use the *Remove Duplicates* icon on the *Data* ribbon. Make sure that the items are filtered if you want to treat each row as a single entry in the list. The removal will occur regardless of the number of duplicates present.

OPEN OFFICE To remove duplicate values in Calc, you can apply a *Standard Filter* (from the *Filter* selection under the *Data* menu) and set the criteria to always be true (such as *Column A = -not empty-*), then click the *More* icon, and select the checkbox next to *No duplication*. This will remove the duplicate values from the display, but they will be hidden and not fully deleted. To fully remove the duplicates, copy the visible cells to a new worksheet or somewhere else in the existing worksheet and delete the original list.

Text to Columns

Most spreadsheet software applications allow you to convert delimited text to columns. Delimited text is separated by a specific character such as a comma (called a *delimiter*); when this process is performed, whatever is to the left of the delimiter will be in one column and whatever is to the right will be in another column. The delimiter character itself is typically consumed in the process and will not appear in the results. You can also convert text to columns based on the number of characters you want to include in each column, or you can use whitespace as a delimiter, creating

> ▶ **FIGURE 12.6**
> Result of removing duplicates in Excel 2010

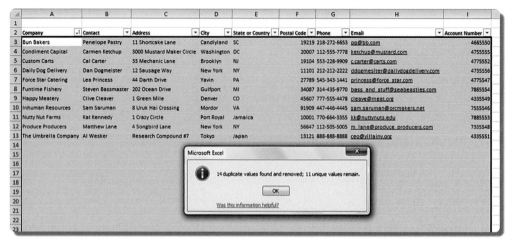

a new column whenever there is a break in the text.

For the example project, you are going to split the first name and the last name of the *Contact* person for the supplier. To begin, insert a blank column to the left of the *Address* label. The prior *Contact* column will become *Contact First Name* and the new blank column will become *Contact Last Name*.

To split the text of the Contact column in Excel, select the values and click the *Text to Columns* icon in the *Data* ribbon. This will open the Convert Text to Columns Wizard, as shown in Figure 12.7. There are three steps to this process; the first is to

A *delimiter* is a character that signifies a break in a continuous value. In spreadsheet software, this is used to define the end of data for one cell and the start of a new cell. Common delimiters are commas, semicolons, and whitespace.

choose whether your text is separated by a delimiter or whether you want to define a fixed width for your new columns. For the example, choose *Delimited* and click the *Next* button.

Step 2 allows you to choose your delimiting character. In the example, select the *Space* character as a delimiter and keep the *Treat consecutive delimiters as one* box selected to keep from creating blank columns. A preview of the new columns the process will create appears at the bottom of the dialog box. You should have a display similar to Figure 12.8. When you are ready, click the *Next* button.

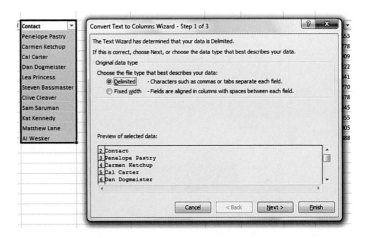

Step 3, shown in Figure 12.9, allows you to select the formatting for each column you will create. You select a column by clicking on it. The format for both of the new columns you are creating should be either *General* or *Text*, which will have the same effect in this case because there is no numeric data in the selection.

When you are finished with your formatting selection, click the *Finish* button to complete the process. You should note that any columns created will overwrite the existing contents that exist in those columns. This is why you created the blank column beside the Address label to accommodate the new column creation. Rename the column headings for the two columns

▲ **FIGURE 12.7**
Convert Text to Columns Wizard Step 1 in Excel 2010

▼ **FIGURE 12.8**
Convert Text to Columns Wizard Step 2 in Excel 2010

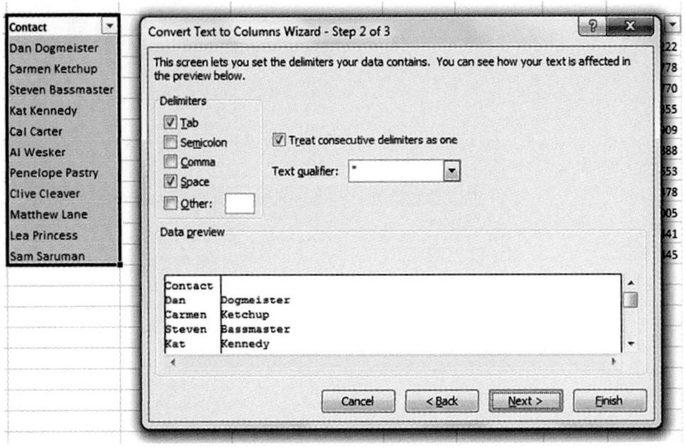

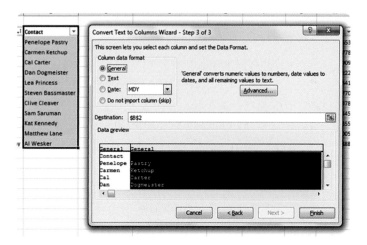

▲ **FIGURE 12.9** Convert Text to Columns Wizard Step 3 in Excel 2010

that were split from the Contact column and save your work.

Table Formatting

You can select a range of cells and format them as a table. This allows you to enhance the visual presentation and organization of your spreadsheet, as well as copy and paste both the cells and formatting to export to other productivity software applications (such as Word and PowerPoint in

OPEN OFFICE You can convert a single column of text to multiple columns in Calc by selecting the column you want to convert and choosing the *Data* menu and *Text to Columns*. You will be prompted to enter the delimiters for separating the columns. For this example, select *Space*. A preview will display at the bottom of the dialog box.

Office). To perform this operation in Excel 2010, select the range of cells you want to format (in the example, this is cells *A2* to *J13*) and select the *Format as Table* icon on the *Home* ribbon. From here, you can choose the style that you want to apply. An example is shown in Figure 12.10. In Excel 2011, the table formatting options are available on the Tables ribbon. Simply select the range of cells to which you want the formatting to apply and choose the style from the available list.

The formatting used for the example is *Table Style Medium 1*. You can also define a custom table style by selecting the *New Table Style* option at the bottom of the drop-down menu. You can format any range of cells as a table no matter where it is located in your document. If a selection is formatted as a table, the formatting will readjust to accommodate any filter settings that are applied. You can see this if you deselect *Custom Carts* from the *Company* filter selection. Select the grab point at the lower=right corner of the table formatting and drag it to extend the formatting over additional rows and columns. In Excel 2010, adding table formatting to your spreadsheet will cause the context-sensitive Design ribbon for Table Tools to appear so you can adjust

► **FIGURE 12.10** Format as Table example in Excel 2010

	A	B	C	D	E	F	G	H	I
1									
2	Company	Contact	Address	City	State or Country	Postal Code	Phone	Email	Account Number
3	Bun Bakers	Penelope Pastry	11 Shortcake Lane	Candlyland	SC	19219	218-272-6653	pp@bb.com	4665550
4	Condiment Capital	Carmen Ketchup	3000 Mustard Maker Circle	Washington	DC	20007	112-555-7778	ketchup@mustard.com	4755555
5	Custom Carts	Cal Carter	33 Mechanic Lane	Brooklyn	NJ	19104	553-228-9909	c.carter@carts.com	4775552
6	Daily Dog Delivery	Dan Dogmeister	12 Sausage Way	New York	NY	11101	212-212-2222	ddogmesiter@dailydogdelivery.com	4735556
7	Force Star Catering	Lea Princess	44 Darth Drive	Yavin	PA	27789	545-343-1441	princess@force_star.com	4775547
8	Funtime Fishery	Steven Bassmaster	202 Ocean Drive	Gulfport	MI	34087	314-435-9770	bass_and_stuff@seabeasties.com	7865554
9	Happy Meatery	Clive Cleaver	1 Green Mile	Denver	CO	45607	777-555-4478	cleave@meat.org	4335549
10	Inhuman Resources	Sam Saruman	8 Uruk Hai Crossing	Mordor	VA	91909	447-446-4445	sam.saruman@orcmakers.net	7555546
11	Nutty Nut Farms	Kat Kennedy	1 Crazy Circle	Port Royal	Jamaica	10001	770-664-3355	kk@nuttynuts.edu	7885553
12	Produce Producers	Matthew Lane	4 Songbird Lane	New York	NY	56647	112-505-5005	m_lane@produce_producers.com	7335548
13	The Umbrella Company	Al Wesker	Research Compound #7	Tokyo	Japan	13121	888-888-8888	ceo@villainy.org	4335551
14									

the formatting you selected and refresh the contents.

12.3 ADDITIONAL FORMATTING ELEMENTS

Visual enhancement is typically the key to a readable spreadsheet. It is beneficial to be able to quickly determine which values in a spreadsheet are important. Borders, shading, and font choices help with this visual distinction, but there are a variety of other formatting options you can use to enhance your spreadsheet. Excel, for instance, comes with a predefined set of cell formatting styles that you can use to add emphasis to a particular piece of information. These are accessible in Excel 2010 by selecting the *Cell Styles* icon on the *Home* ribbon; in Excel 2011, these styles are

displayed as previews in the *Format* panel of the *Home* ribbon.

There are some final finishing touches you should make to the spreadsheet to practice what you have learned about manipulating spreadsheets. First, hide the columns related to the physical address of the company; you do not want to remove this information, but it is not used very often, so it should not impede the vital information on the spreadsheet. You should also merge cells B1 and C1 and enter the heading *Contact* in the new cell; format the heading to match the headings in the rest of the table. Remove the word "Contact" from the headings for the first and last name of the contact person, enter the text *Suppliers* in cell A1, and change the default color of the email addresses to black text. The table within your spreadsheet should look like Figure 12.11.

Conditional Formatting 12.3.1

Sometimes it is helpful to have a visual reference for your information without having to read each entry. For instance, in a financial worksheet you may want any value less than zero to appear red so you can recognize it in a list. To accomplish this, you use conditional formatting. This applies a rule to the contents of the cell to determine how it should appear visually. The display has no effect on the actual data stored in the cell, just on the resulting visualization.

For the example project, the starting value of the account numbers differentiates the type of account. You want to create conditional formatting that will display

	A	B	C	H	I	J
1	**Suppliers**		Contact			
2	Company	First Name	Last Name	Phone	Email	Account Number
3	Bun Bakers	Penelope	Pastry	218-272-6653	pp@bb.com	4665550
4	Condiment Capital	Carmen	Ketchup	112-555-7778	ketchup@mustard.com	4755555
5	Custom Carts	Cal	Carter	553-228-9909	c.carter@carts.com	4775552
6	Daily Dog Delivery	Dan	Dogmeister	212-212-2222	ddogmesiter@dailydogdelivery.com	4735556
7	Force Star Catering	Lea	Princess	545-343-1441	princess@force_star.com	4775547
8	Funtime Fishery	Steven	Bassmaster	314-435-9770	bass_and_stuff@seabeasties.com	7865554
9	Happy Meatery	Clive	Cleaver	777-555-4478	cleave@meat.org	4335549
10	Inhuman Resources	Sam	Saruman	447-446-4445	sam.saruman@orcmakers.net	7555546
11	Nutty Nut Farms	Kat	Kennedy	770-664-3355	kk@nuttynuts.edu	7885553
12	Produce Producers	Matthew	Lane	112-505-5005	m_lane@produce_producers.com	7335548
13	The Umbrella Company	Al	Wesker	888-888-8888	ceo@villainy.org	4335551

the accounts beginning with the number 7 in green and the accounts beginning with the number 4 in red. To do this in Excel, highlight the cells containing the account numbers. Select the *Conditional Formatting* icon on the *Home* ribbon, choose the *Highlight Cell Rules* entry, and then select *Greater Than*. You should see the dialog box in Figure 12.12.

Set the minimum value to *7000000* so all account numbers beginning with 7 will be formatted and set this to green text. You can apply multiple formatting rules to the same set of cells. With the account number cells still selected, choose the *Less Than* option for conditional formatting, enter *4999999*, and set the formatting to red. A completed example is shown in Figure 12.13.

Conditional formatting allows you to select a variety of options such as value ranges, keyword matches, and dates. You can use the formatting options to display

color gradients for the range of values where they get darker as the numbers get smaller or larger, depending on the condition, and apply data bars to track relative values, which is helpful when you are ranking numeric values or currency.

OPEN OFFICE Calc allows for conditional formatting on a selection of cells with up to three conditions. To apply conditional formatting, select the range of cells to which you want the formatting to apply, open the *Format* menu, and choose *Conditional Formatting*; a new dialog box will open where you can define your criteria. For this example, you will need to use two of the conditions to match the account types. You will also need to create new styles for the cells to format them as red or green; when you are defining the new styles, select the font color from the *Font Effects* tab and the background color from the *Background* tab.

Tab Color

12.3.2

Spreadsheet programs allow you to change the tab color that identifies your spreadsheets within the overall workbook. This helps provide a visual reference for either the purpose of different sheets or the department to which the tabs apply. Apply a

Greater Than

Format cells that are GREATER THAN:

7000000   with   Green Fill with Dark Green Text

OK   Cancel

	A	B	C	H	I	J
1	Suppliers		Contact			
2	Company	First Name	Last Name	Phone	Email	Account Number
3	Bun Bakers	Penelope	Pastry	218-272-6653	pp@bb.com	4665550
4	Condiment Capital	Carmen	Ketchup	112-555-7778	ketchup@mustard.com	4755555
5	Custom Carts	Cal	Carter	553-228-9909	c.carter@carts.com	4775552
6	Daily Dog Delivery	Dan	Dogmeister	212-212-2222	ddogmesiter@dailydogdelivery.com	4735556
7	Force Star Catering	Lea	Princess	545-343-1441	princess@force_star.com	4775547
8	Funtime Fishery	Steven	Bassmaster	314-435-9770	bass_and_stuff@seabeasties.com	7865554
9	Happy Meatery	Clive	Cleaver	777-555-4478	cleave@meat.org	4335549
10	Inhuman Resources	Sam	Saruman	447-446-4445	sam.saruman@orcmakers.net	7555546
11	Nutty Nut Farms	Kat	Kennedy	770-664-3355	kk@nuttynuts.edu	7885553
12	Produce Producers	Matthew	Lane	112-505-5005	m_lane@produce_producers.com	7335548
13	The Umbrella Company	Al	Wesker	888-888-8888	ceo@villainy.org	4335551

◀ FIGURE 12.13
Completed example of conditional formatting

green color to the Suppliers tab in your project by right-clicking on the tab and selecting the *Tab Color* option. You can then select a color from the submenu that appears.

12.3.3 Comments

You can add comments to your spreadsheet to identify values that need to be reexamined or to provide descriptions of a particular cell's contents. Comments in spreadsheet software appear as small icons in the upper-left corner of the cell; by default, the comment itself will appear when the cell is selected. For the sample project, add comments for changes to the supplier contact information; for instance, Custom Carts is undergoing a change in leadership as the business is passed from father to son, so it is worth making a comment in your document to remember that this change is coming and to get the new owner's contact information updated as necessary.

OPEN OFFICE In Calc, you can change the color of a tab by selecting the *Format* menu, choosing *Sheet*, and then choosing *Tab Color*. Select whatever color you want and click *OK* to apply it.

To add a comment to your document in Excel 2010, select the cell in which you want the comment to reside, open the *Review* ribbon, and select *New Comment*. This will open the comment text box in which you can enter the information you want to add. Other tools in the Comments panel of the Review ribbon help you navigate through the comments in the document, delete comments, or toggle their display. The completed comment example is shown in Figure 12.14. In Excel 2011, the comment commands are also located on the Review ribbon; to view a comment in the document, however, you have to hover your mouse over the icon representing it.

You can adjust the text as necessary and add other comments to your document as practice. The text of the comment may vary, but you can copy the example shown in Figure 12.14. In Excel 2010, the New Comment icon will change to Edit Comment when you already have a comment added to the cell; you can use this icon to edit the comment contents. In Excel 2011, the New command remains the same, but you can use it to edit an existing comment if the cell that contains it is active.

	A	B	C	H	I	J
1	**Suppliers**		Contact			
2	Company	First Name	Last Name	Phone	Email	Account Number
3	Bun Bakers	Penelope	Pastry	218-272-6653	pp@bb.com	4665550
4	Condiment Capital			112-555-7778	ketchup@mustard.com	4755555
5	Custom Carts			553-228-9909	c.carter@carts.com	4775552
6	Daily Dog Delivery			212-212-2222	ddogmesiter@dailydogdelivery.com	4735556
7	Force Star Catering			545-343-1441	princess@force_star.com	4775547
8	Funtime Fishery	Steven	Bassmaster	314-435-9770	bass_and_stuff@seabeasties.com	7865554
9	Happy Meatery	Clive	Cleaver	777-555-4478	cleave@meat.org	4335549
10	Inhuman Resources	Sam	Saruman	447-446-4445	sam.saruman@orcmakers.net	7555546
11	Nutty Nut Farms	Kat	Kennedy	770-664-3355	kk@nuttynuts.edu	7885553
12	Produce Producers	Matthew	Lane	112-505-5005	m_lane@produce_producers.com	7335548
13	The Umbrella Company	Al	Wesker	888-888-8888	ceo@villainy.org	4335551

T Richardson:
The business is being passed to Cal's son; new contact information will be needed soon.

12.3.4 Text Boxes

A text box in a spreadsheet behaves as an independent object just as it does in word processing software and presentation software. It will occupy the layer above the cells of the spreadsheet by default and will not be affected by resizing elements of the document. Text boxes in spreadsheets can be useful for providing instructions or

OPEN OFFICE You insert a comment in Calc by selecting the cell where you want the comment placed, clicking the *Insert* menu, and selecting *Comment*. The icon for a comment is a small red box in the upper-left corner of the cell; the comment will appear when you hover the mouse over the icon. To delete a comment, right-click inside the cell and choose *Delete Comment* from the menu.

explanations of the document as a whole. You can see an example text box added to the project in Figure 12.15.

To insert a text box in Excel 2010, open the *Insert* ribbon and select *Text Box*. You can resize the text box by using the outer grab points just as you can in the other Office programs. The text box can be moved around the spreadsheet

independently and will cover the cells behind it. Selecting the text box will also activate the context-sensitive Format ribbon for Drawing Tools. In Excel 2011, you can insert a text box by selecting the *Insert* menu and choosing *Text Box*; you can then draw the text box in the location you desire.

CHART TYPES 12.4

Charts can take a wide variety of forms, and different chart types are useful for representing different types of information. The common types of charts you will encounter in spreadsheet software include Column, Line, Pie, Area, and Scatter Charts; all of these types are constructed from underlying data of some form, although not all data can support all

OPEN OFFICE The text box is located on the Drawing toolbar in OpenOffice.org. To add a text box in Calc, select the *View* menu, choose *Toolbars*, and then select *Drawing*; the Drawing toolbar should appear at the bottom of the interface. From here, you can select the *Text* icon and draw the area you want for your text box.

chart types. When choosing a chart type, you need to consider what information you want to present and how you want to present it. There are other forms of charts available for you to construct from your data, but those typically require an area of expertise beyond general use. The following sections provide a further explanation of some common chart types, along with examples of their usage so you can determine which charts are best for your own use.

For this project, open a new spreadsheet document and save it as *MyChart-Examples*. Create a spreadsheet tab for each of the main types of charts discussed here: *Column, Line, Pie, Bar, Area*, and *Scatter Charts*. Use the data provided for each of the following examples and create the charts yourself to investigate the variances in construction of the different chart types. You should be familiar with the process of creating a chart by now, so the details will be omitted unless there is a departure from the standard procedure. For a review of how to insert a chart into your document, you can review Section 11.4.

Column

A column chart is primarily used for comparisons, such as changes over time or a comparison of regions or countries. The best use of a column chart is when the highest column represents the optimal condition. When there are multiple columns coupled together, it is typically to show a comparison of parts of the same overall whole. Figure 12.16 shows an example of a

Sparklines (a term originally proposed by Edward Tufte) are small, highly dense graphs intended to be placed where they make an impact in a document rather than occupying a large amount of space on a separate page or sheet like a traditional chart. These occupy a single cell in Excel. Sparklines can be used to emphasize a particular goal or main point; there is no significant detail or axes in these, but you can easily see a trend or outcome. These can be inserted in Excel 2010 from the Insert ribbon or in Excel 2011 from the Charts ribbon.

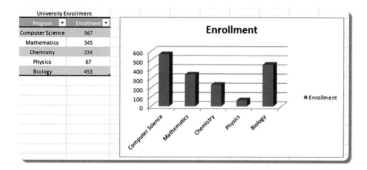

▲ FIGURE 12.16
Column chart
example

column chart and the accompanying data to reproduce it.

12.4.2 ## Line

A line chart is used to track data over set intervals. In most cases, the data in each series has an existing (primarily linear) relationship and the points of data are connected. A line chart is a basic graphing tool that can be used to demonstrate a variety of data in a variety of circumstances; multiple series represent independent sets of observations that may or may not be interrelated. An example of a line chart is shown in Figure 12.17.

▼ FIGURE 12.17
Line chart example

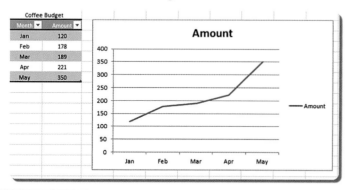

12.4.3 ## Pie

A pie chart is a representation of the elements that comprise a total value. The visual display is a circle comparing the relative values of the components, typically as a percentage of the whole. A pie chart is best used when you want to showcase the

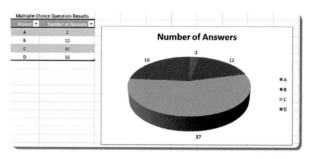

▲ FIGURE 12.18 Pie chart example

proportional contribution of one element of the whole, such as the number of answers selected in a multiple-choice question. Pie charts are best used to illustrate a single item. An example of a pie chart is shown in Figure 12.18.

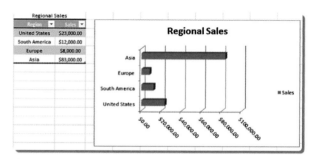

▲ FIGURE 12.19 Bar chart example

Bar
12.4.4

A bar graph shows comparisons among individual items for a single observation. The stacked version of the bar graph compares elements that comprise a whole within each individual item. A representation of sales by region for a single quarter would be appropriate for a bar graph. Figure 12.19 shows an example bar graph and the data used to construct it.

Area
12.4.5

An area chart demonstrates how pieces contribute to a total value through multiple observations. Each piece in each observation should represent a piece of a total value. The area chart should demonstrate relative contributions and trends over time along with the overall trend of the total data measured. You can see an example of an area chart in Figure 12.20.

12.4.6 Scatter

A scatter chart is best used to show data clustering or alignment between multiple series of data; it consists of points plotted on multiple axes without connections (or with nonlinear connections) between either the series or the consecutive points in the series. It assumes there is no defined relationship between points in the data series or at least significant enough variation that a linear connection would be inaccurate. An example of this type of chart would be a map of predictions versus observations in an area where the relationship is not linear, such as observed temperatures. An example of a scatter chart is shown in Figure 12.21.

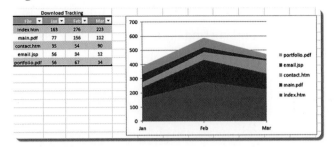

▲ **FIGURE 12.20** Area chart example

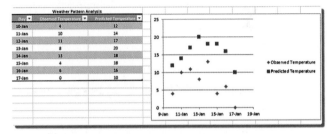

▲ **FIGURE 12.21** Scatter chart example

CHAPTER SUMMARY

This chapter presented more advanced concepts for navigating, formatting, and manipulating cells in a spreadsheet document. One of the common functions of a spreadsheet is to manage a list of information, which includes filtering and sorting data; the necessary procedures for these tasks were covered here. Additional formatting tools like table formatting and tab coloring for easy identification were also described. Finally, various common types of charts that can be produced were explained with examples. The next chapter focuses on the advanced use of formulas for calculation in spreadsheets and describes some of the tools for automatically associating and calculating results; these include the use of data tracing, subtotals, and PivotTables.

CHAPTER EXERCISES

1. Using the *MySuppliers* example you constructed in this chapter, provide more complete management of the Supply List data. Since data should not be repeated in multiple lists, remove the values in the Supply List sheet other than the company and account number that do not pertain to the order. Add a column to calculate the cost of the order using a formula (Cost = Price * Quantity). Filter and sort the list so all of the orders from a particular company are listed together. Format the list as a table and change the tab color. Apply conditional formatting to show the most expensive orders in the list. Use data bars to assist in the visualization if your software application supports them.

2. Add an additional data series to each of the chart examples you constructed and save your work as a new file. How does this affect the display? Which charts should allow additional data series and which should not? Add a text box to your spreadsheet to answer these questions.

CHAPTER KNOWLEDGE CHECK

1

You can sort multiple columns in the same filter at the same time.

○ True
○ False

2

You can apply multiple conditional formatting rules to the same cell at the same time.

○ True
○ False

3

You can unmerge cells that have not been merged to add columns or rows to your spreadsheet.

○ True
○ False

4

Hiding one of the columns of a merged cell also hides the contents of the merged cell.

○ True
○ False

5

The Values selection of the Paste Special option removes formulas from the copied cells and retains only the data calculated by the formulas.

○ True
○ False

6

The following is a valid cell reference for a workbook containing Sheet1 and Sheet2.

○ **A.** 'Sheet2'!6B
○ **B.** Sheet2.B4
○ **C.** 'Sheet2'A3
○ **D.** All of the above
○ **E.** Both a and b
○ **F.** None of the above

7

The following type of chart assumes no clear relationship between the entries in a series:

○ **A.** Column
○ **B.** Line
○ **C.** Scatter
○ **D.** All of the above
○ **E.** None of the above

8 A pie chart is primarily useful for displaying:

○ **A.** Changes over time

○ **B.** Contributions to a total value

○ **C.** Nonlinear relationships

○ **D.** All of the above

○ **E.** None of the above

9 The following is an option for converting text to columns:

○ **A.** Adding a column break where there is whitespace

○ **B.** Using a delimiter such as a comma or semicolon

○ **C.** Establishing a fixed width for each column

○ **D.** All of the above

○ **E.** None of the above

10 Hidden values cannot be used in formula calculations.

○ True

○ False

Advanced Features of Spreadsheet Software

Spreadsheet software is a great tool for managing lists and visualizing information, but it is most commonly used for the advanced analysis and management of data. To that extent, this chapter focuses on the advanced tools of spreadsheet software such as the use of complex formulas, data validation, and variable tracing to equip you to use your spreadsheet software for financial, business, or personal data management. Additional features, including pivot tables, subtotals, variable tracing, and external data management, are also covered to give you a better understanding of the power of this type of software application. At the completion of this chapter, you will be able to:

- Use common functions in your spreadsheet document

- Use IF statements to conditionally evaluate data

- Trace variables through a complex spreadsheet application

- Construct pivot tables and subtotals as additional evaluation methods

- Perform goal seeking and evaluate what if scenarios on numeric data

BUSINESS APPLICATIONS

Spreadsheet software has a variety of uses, but it is most prevalent in accounting and other business applications. For the example project in this chapter, you will manage the financial information for the company that was proposed back in Chapters 9 and 10. The business has gone exceedingly well while you were reading the intervening chapters and your first monthly financial analysis has come due. While this is decidedly business oriented (and primarily financial), as that is the general setting in which most people encounter spreadsheets, you should note that there are a variety of formula types to accommodate complex mathematics, statistics, and engineering applications. Data analysis and calculation belongs almost exclusively to spreadsheet software in terms of the productivity applications in common use.

The project file you will use in this chapter is *MyBusinessWorkbook*, which is available as part of the companion resources for this text. The workbook contains a number of spreadsheets within it that you will utilize and manipulate. Since you are working on the financial information for January and you want to keep the original file as a clean copy in case you need to correct anything, you should save the file as *MyJanuaryRevenue*.

The first sheet in the workbook is *January Commissions*; this is a blank worksheet where you will calculate the

SPREADSHEETS VERSUS DATABASES

Spreadsheet software and database software both excel at managing information. The major difference between the two is the relational aspect of the database, which minimizes data duplication errors, and the calculation abilities of the spreadsheet software. The choice of which to use should ultimately be driven by the purpose of the document you are constructing and the reuse of the information in that document.

For instance, you can manage a list in a spreadsheet with ease, and as long as you do not have multiple copies of the list in existence, the data should be consistent; using a database ensures the list is consistent, but it would probably be a more involved process to initially create the list and to maintain and access it. Similarly, databases can manage information well, but they are not useful for calculation; to perform analysis on the data beyond filters and reports, you will likely need the power of a spreadsheet application. Fortunately, part of the functionality of a spreadsheet program is to connect with a database; this means if you are willing to expend the effort to construct and manage the database, you can use it to store your information and use the spreadsheet to access it and perform the necessary analysis.

While there is no complete list of criteria for this decision, a database is probably necessary for storing your information if any of the following are true in the particular circumstance:

- The data is subject to numerous changes by multiple people.

- Changing information in one spreadsheet requires updating multiple other spreadsheets.

- The information has permanence to the organization and cannot afford to be lost.

- The amount of data makes it unmanageable in a single spreadsheet document.

commissions for your sales team as the chapter progresses. The second sheet is *January Sales*, which is a list of the total sales numbers for the month for all of the companies purchasing your products for use in their venue; some of these are franchises of your original business and others are external companies. The third sheet is called *January Supply List*; this is a record of the supplies that were ordered to fulfill your customers' orders for the month. You should recognize the companies and products from the construction of the supplier list in the previous chapter. The fourth tab is for the *Customer List* spreadsheet. This sheet is a mapping between the customers and the sales representative handling the account. Fifth in the list is the chart of *Sales Representatives*; this details the sales personnel, their commission rate on sales, the threshold for them to qualify for a bonus, and the bonus amount they are awarded if they meet their goals. The final tab is for the *Suppliers*; this should be almost identical to the results you have from the project in the previous chapter.

13.2 ## USING FUNCTIONS

One of the most powerful components of spreadsheet software is the ability to evaluate complex mathematical formulas and trace numeric data through multiple iterations of calculation. There are an enormous number of functions available for use in spreadsheet calculations; this chapter will cover the fundamentals and common functions you will likely encounter and give you guidance on where to look up information on the rest of the

OPEN OFFICE There is only a slight variation in the syntax of formulas in Calc. Instead of an exclamation point being used to reference cells on other spreadsheets, a period (.) is used. Also, to separate the arguments (or parameters) of a function, you must use a semicolon (;) instead of the comma that is used in Excel. Copying contents from Excel to Calc will perform these syntax translations for you, so your formulas can be transported between the two applications.

functions that exist if you need to utilize them. You were introduced to the SUM function in Chapter 11; this is one of many common functions that you will encounter with even basic analysis in a spreadsheet document.

Common Functions

13.2.1

As you may already know, all of the common mathematical operations of addition (+), subtraction (−), multiplication (*), and division (/) can be used in the construction of formulas in spreadsheet software. Whenever mathematical operations are used, they will follow the defined order of operations, calculating whatever is inside parentheses first, then completing formulas, and finally performing division, multiplication, subtraction, and addition. The cell references act as the variables in the calculations, but the actual data in the cell is used as the value wherever the cell is referenced. For the most part, functions operate on numeric values; there are some functions, though, that perform operations on text as well.

You can identify a range of values by separating the cell references with a colon (:), so the reference value *A1:A4* would indicate cells *A1* to *A4* inclusive of the cells between them. When using a range of cells as input, you can use a comma to skip values, so the reference value for the familiar SUM function of *SUM(A1:A4,A6)* would include cells *A1* through *A4*, skip cell *A5*, and include cell *A6*. The comma can be used to skip any number of cells horizontally or vertically; you can view this as separating the sequence of input. You should be aware that not all formulas will allow interrupted input.

Some of the common functions you will encountor in addition to the SUM function (which simply adds the value of every cell given as input) are AVERAGE, COUNT, MAX, MIN, and ROUND. The parentheses after the function name hold the arguments (or parameters) of the function; these are the values on which the function operates. Some functions use a specific set of values and others allow any input (represented here by an ellipsis). The details of these functions are as follows:

- *AVERAGE* calculates the total value divided by the number of inputs given for the formula. The format is AVERAGE(…) and it will accept any number of cells either in range format or individually separated by comma. You will use this to calculate the average sales value for a customer in the list for January on the *January Sales* sheet. To calculate this value, enter *=AVERAGE(B2:B13)* in cell *B15*. If you have done this correctly, you should get the value *8,614* as the whole number component (the digits to the right of the decimal point will vary based on the number of decimal digits your formatting is set to display).

- *COUNT* returns the number of entries in a list of cells; the format is COUNT(…), and it will accept cells, cell ranges, and comma-separated entries. Add an entry for the count of the total number of sales for the month using the formula *=COUNT(B2:B13)* in the same *January Sales* sheet. You should get the value *12*.

- *MAX* returns the single maximum value from the set of cells given as input arguments; it takes the form MAX(…) and accepts any list of cells or cell ranges with or without comma separators. Use the formula *=MAX(B2:B13)* to determine the highest single value for sales in January; this should be *24,000*.

- *MIN* returns a single minimum value from the set of cells given as input arguments; it takes the form MIN(…) and accepts all lists of cells or cell ranges with or without comma separators. The formula to return the minimum single value for sales in January is *=MIN(B2:B13)* on the *January Sales* sheet. The value returned should be *400*.

- *ROUND* takes two arguments, a value on which to operate and a whole number representing the number of digits to the right of the decimal point to include; this takes the form ROUND(*A single numeric value, Integer number of significant digits*). Unlike changes that simply modify the display, using the ROUND function will actually alter the value in the cell itself. Apply the ROUND function to the AVERAGE calculation you used earlier and use two decimal places for the cents component of the currency. The adjusted formula for the average should be *=ROUND(AVERAGE(B2:B13),2)* and the return value should be *8614.17*.

Notice the nesting of functions in the last example. Nesting functions is common in spreadsheet software to calculate complex values; whatever is located in the innermost parentheses or functions will be calculated first. In this case, the AVERAGE is computed and used as the input value in the ROUND function, which is calculated to two significant digits. Take this opportunity to further practice applying formatting to your spreadsheet by formatting all of the numeric values as currency except for the total number of sales in column *B*. A completed example of the formatted spreadsheet is shown in Figure 13.1.

	A	B
1	Client Company	Revenue
2	Dog Eat Doggery	$14,600.00
3	Top Dog Dogs NY	$24,000.00
4	Top Dog Dogs LA	$2,800.00
5	Tokyo Dogs	$23,700.00
6	Singapore Dogs	$4,600.00
7	Dubai Dogs	$910.00
8	Top Dog Dogs DC	$8,800.00
9	Top Dog Dogs ATL	$400.00
10	Top Dog Dogs BWI	$3,570.00
11	Doggy Dogs	$10,800.00
12	Dog Factory	$3,490.00
13	Dig Dogs	$5,700.00
14		
15	Average Sales	$8,614.17
16	Number of Sales	12
17	Maximum Sale	$24,000.00
18	Minimum Sale	$400.00

▲ **FIGURE 13.1**
Calculation results for *January Sales* spreadsheet

Text Functions

There are a number of functions that apply to the manipulation of text as opposed to numeric values. For the most part, these are useful for converting text values that are imported from another data source. Some of the most common functions for manipulating text are as follows:

• *CONCATENATE* is used to join the contents of two or more cells containing text into the same text result. CONCATENATE can accept multiple arguments, whether they are individual cells, cell ranges, or cells separated by a comma. The format of the function is CONCATENATE(…), and it returns a text result. An example is CONCATENATE(A2,A3), which would return the text of both cells joined without spaces in the order specified.

• *LEFT* takes the form LEFT(*A single cell containing text, A whole number value of characters*) and returns the specified number of leftmost characters of its first argument. An example is LEFT(*A4*, 2), which would return the two leftmost characters of cell *A4*. This can be helpful when you need a subset of information to display, such as a piece of an account number. You can use LEFT inside of other functions; it returns a text result but can be applied to numbers or text cell contents.

• *RIGHT* works in exactly the same way as LEFT except it takes the number of rightmost characters specified in the second argument. An example is RIGHT(*B4*, 2), which would return the two rightmost characters in cell *B4*.

• *UPPER* converts its argument to all uppercase text; this can allow for more accurate searching if casing is an issue. It can also help to display entities of importance if coupled with an IF condition, as discussed later in this chapter. An example use of UPPER is UPPER(*A3*), which would return the text of cell *A3* in uppercase.

- *LOWER* converts its argument to all lowercase text; this works in the same manner as UPPER and has the same format. An example use of LOWER is LOWER(*A4*), which would return the contents of cell *A4* in all lowercase letters.

- *VALUE* evaluates the text in the cell entered as an argument into a numeric value; this is particularly helpful if the data is from an external source such as a text file or database that lacks the capacity to convert it to a number implicitly. The VALUE function takes the form VALUE(*A single cell containing a text representation of a number*) with only one argument referencing a cell containing text. An example of the use of VALUE is VALUE(*B4*), which would return the numeric value equivalent of the text contents of cell *B4*. The result can be used in other formulas. This can often help to correct data reading errors if they are present when the formula is otherwise correct, particularly when the data being used is imported.

If you are importing text and you are not getting the correct results in your formulas, you can use the *Text to Columns* conversion to format the text into the format expected by your spreadsheet software. You can do this without constructing multiple columns by choosing the delimited option and selecting a character that does not appear in the text as the delimiter. The preview at the bottom of the dialog box should let you know if you have set it up correctly because it should display only a single column.

You can represent a literal text string by surrounding it in double quotation marks (""). This can be used to include a keyword in a search formula you are constructing or to simply represent a display condition such as "Yes" or "No" in a cell based on an IF condition (as covered in a later section of this chapter). The text concatenation operator is the ampersand (&); this is a shorthand way to invoke the same result as the CONCATENATE function. The results of "=CONCATENATE(A2,A3)" are the same as "=A2&A3" in terms of return value and display. One use of both concatenation and literal strings is adding a space between first and last names; if they were contained in columns *A* and *B*, respectively, the formula would be *A3&" "&B3* to return the contents of cell *A3*, a space, and the contents of cell *B3* as a single text result. While they should not be a part of your final document, Figure 13.2 shows the results of the example functions described earlier as applied to the *January Sales* spreadsheet.

Value Lookup

13.2.3

The ability to look up data in one spreadsheet or section from another is vital in most complicated projects. Using the lookup features also reduces the manual duplication of values, which will help reduce the overall errors in the spreadsheet document. There are two primary functions that can be used to perform a value lookup in your workbook: VLOOKUP and HLOOKUP.

VLOOKUP is a function for performing a vertical lookup of information in a spreadsheet. The format is VLOOKUP(*Item to*

◢	A	B	C	D	E
1	Client Company ▼	Revenue ▼			
2	Dog Eat Doggery	$14,600.00		Formula ▼	Result ▼
3	Top Dog Dogs NY	$24,000.00		CONCATENATE	Dog Eat DoggeryTop Dog Dogs NY
4	Top Dog Dogs LA	$2,800.00		LEFT	To
5	Tokyo Dogs	$23,700.00		RIGHT	00
6	Singapore Dogs	$4,600.00		UPPER	TOP DOG DOGS NY
7	Dubai Dogs	$910.00		LOWER	top dog dogs la
8	Top Dog Dogs DC	$8,800.00		VALUE	2800
9	Top Dog Dogs ATL	$400.00		&	Dog Eat DoggeryTop Dog Dogs NY
10	Top Dog Dogs BWI	$3,570.00			
11	Doggy Dogs	$10,800.00			
12	Dog Factory	$3,490.00			
13	Dig Dogs	$5,700.00			
14					
15	Average Sales	$8,614.17			
16	Number of Sales	12			
17	Maximum Sale	$24,000.00			
18	Minimum Sale	$400.00			

◄ **FIGURE 13.2**
Text functions applied to the *January Sales* spreadsheet

find, Range of cells in which to look, Offset value of column to return, Exact match or approximate match). While it may seem complicated, as you become familiar with the function you will gain an understanding of the arguments. The first argument is simply the text to locate; this can take the form of a literal text string (enclosed in double quotation marks) or a cell reference. The second argument is the list of cells in which to look for the text; the VLOOKUP function will search the first column identified in the range for the value specified in the first argument. The third argument is the offset value of the column of information you want to return if a match is found; the column in which the information is found is considered *Column 1*, so a value of *2* in this argument would indicate the column immediately to the right of the

> **OPEN OFFICE** Representations of true and false in Calc are actually formulas instead of literal values, so to get a true result, you would use *TRUE()*, and to get a false result, you would use *FALSE()*.

column being searched. The final argument is a TRUE or FALSE value; these are literal values representing a condition case of true or false, which can also be equated to *yes* or *no* and *1* or *0* for binary values. In this case, FALSE represents the case where you want the search to return an exact match for the item for which you are searching and TRUE represents the allowance of partial matching for identifying a value to return.

To use this function in practice, you will place the sales representative for the customer in your *January Sales* sheet in *Column C*. The column heading should be

Sales Representative and the formula in cell C2 should be =VLOOKUP(A2,'Customer List'!$A$1:$B$14,2,FALSE), where A2 is the cell whose contents you want to find in the Customer List spreadsheet in the range of cells A1 to B14; these cell references need to be absolute (using the dollar sign for both the row and column) in order to repeat this function for the rest of the column without changing your search range. For this function to work properly, you should make sure the value you are trying to find will occur exactly once in the cell range you are searching. The third argument specifies that the return value is the content of the cell immediately to the right of the matched item, where the search column is considered column 1 and the return value would be the 2 value specified. The FALSE argument indicates only an exact match should be considered. This function works only for returning values to the right of the matched column, so you may need to rearrange your data if your search column is to the right of the value you want to return. A completed example of this lookup is shown in Figure 13.3; use this to compare your results.

There is an equivalent horizontal lookup function called HLOOKUP that searches the first row of the cell range instead of the first column. It assumes the return data is located in the same column but in a row beneath the one being searched. The parameters and usage are otherwise identical.

If you are using a specific cell range to search for values repeatedly, you can actually name the range of cells and use the name to reference the range instead of

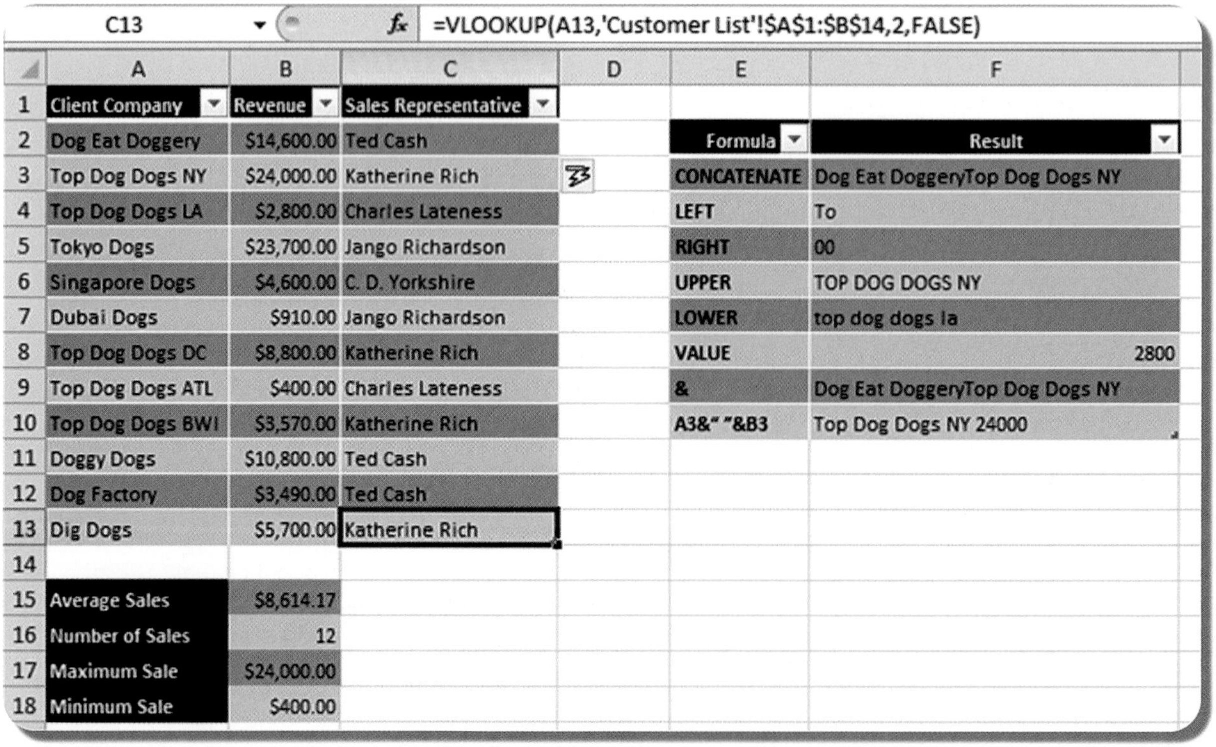

▼ FIGURE 13.3
VLOOKUP example results

C13		f_x	=VLOOKUP(A13,'Customer List'!$A$1:$B$14,2,FALSE)			
	A	B	C	D	E	F
1	Client Company	Revenue	Sales Representative			
2	Dog Eat Doggery	$14,600.00	Ted Cash		Formula	Result
3	Top Dog Dogs NY	$24,000.00	Katherine Rich	B	CONCATENATE	Dog Eat DoggeryTop Dog Dogs NY
4	Top Dog Dogs LA	$2,800.00	Charles Lateness		LEFT	To
5	Tokyo Dogs	$23,700.00	Jango Richardson		RIGHT	00
6	Singapore Dogs	$4,600.00	C. D. Yorkshire		UPPER	TOP DOG DOGS NY
7	Dubai Dogs	$910.00	Jango Richardson		LOWER	top dog dogs la
8	Top Dog Dogs DC	$8,800.00	Katherine Rich		VALUE	2800
9	Top Dog Dogs ATL	$400.00	Charles Lateness		&	Dog Eat DoggeryTop Dog Dogs NY
10	Top Dog Dogs BWI	$3,570.00	Katherine Rich		A3&" "&B3	Top Dog Dogs NY 24000
11	Doggy Dogs	$10,800.00	Ted Cash			
12	Dog Factory	$3,490.00	Ted Cash			
13	Dig Dogs	$5,700.00	Katherine Rich			
14						
15	Average Sales	$8,614.17				
16	Number of Sales	12				
17	Maximum Sale	$24,000.00				
18	Minimum Sale	$400.00				

retyping the reference. You can add a name to a range of cells using the name box to the left of the Formula Bar on the spreadsheet application where the cell reference typically appears. For instance, select the range of cells for the customers and the assigned representatives in the *Customer List* sheet and name it *CustomerReps* as shown in Figure 13.4. You can now substitute the name tag *CustomerReps* to reference these cells on any of the spreadsheets within your workbook. You use the *Name Manager* icon on the Formulas ribbon in Excel 2010 to add or edit the labels for these selected cell ranges; in Excel 2011, use the *Insert Name* icon on the Formulas ribbon to add defined names.

◄ FIGURE 13.4
Naming a cell range

13.2.4 ## IF Statements and Logic

The *IF* function evaluates a condition to either true or false and then returns a different value based on the outcome. The format is IF(*Condition, Result if TRUE, Result if FALSE*). The result of the condition needs to be either the literal TRUE or the literal FALSE; you must make sure the proper logic is applied to return one of these conditions.

To do this, you typically need to use logical operators. Logical operators evaluate the relative value of the arguments on both sides and return whether the condition is true. For example, in the conditional statement *B2>B3*, if the value of cell *B2* is larger than the value of cell *B3*, the result will be TRUE; otherwise it will be FALSE. There are six logical operators you can use: less than (<), less than or equal to (<=), equal (=), not equal (<>), greater than (>), and greater than or equal to.

There are also three functions that can assist in developing a logical evaluation — NOT, OR, and AND.

- The *NOT* function simply negates its argument, returning TRUE if the argument is FALSE and vice versa. For example, NOT(F8) would return FALSE if F8 is TRUE; NOT will only accept as input logical values that will return TRUE or FALSE.

- The *OR* function accepts any number of inputs as long as they return logical values of TRUE or FALSE; it will return TRUE if any individual argument it is given is TRUE and will return FALSE only if all of the arguments given are FALSE. An example is OR(*F5,F6*) where *F5* and *F6* are cells containing either TRUE or FALSE values.

- The *AND* function takes input arguments in the same format as OR. The main difference is that AND will return TRUE only if all of the input arguments are TRUE and will return FALSE if any of the input arguments are FALSE. An example is AND(*F6,F7*) where *F6* and *F7* are cells containing logical values.

You should include an IF statement in *Column D* of your *January Sales* spreadsheet to evaluate whether the sales for that customer are greater than the average value; this may be superfluous at this point, but it would help to identify the largest customers for a business. The formula for cell *D2* should be *IF(B2>=$B$15,"Yes","No")*; this will be the basis for the column, so make sure you use an absolute reference to cell *B15*, which contains the average value you calculated for the monthly sales. This formula will display the text "Yes" if the value of the individual sale is greater than or equal to the average sale value or "No" if it is less than the average sale value. Fill the column with this formula. The results of this calculation along with the logic examples provided earlier are shown in Figure 13.5.

Function Wizard

There are a large number of functions available for use in spreadsheet calculation. Those introduced so far are common functions and operators that you will likely encounter with even casual use of the software. You can look up the functions yourself if you want to use them or you can use the Function Wizard to help you identify and construct the function you want. The Function Wizard is available in both Excel and Calc; you can activate it from the *Function Wizard* icon on the Formula Bar.

The Function Wizard first prompts you to look up the formula or function you want to include in your calculation. When you have selected it, you can then add each argument separately in the dialog box that opens.

In Excel 2011, the Function Wizard is called the Formula Builder; it has the same functionality, but it appears in a toolbox outside of the main interface.

▶ FIGURE 13.5
Logical function evaluations

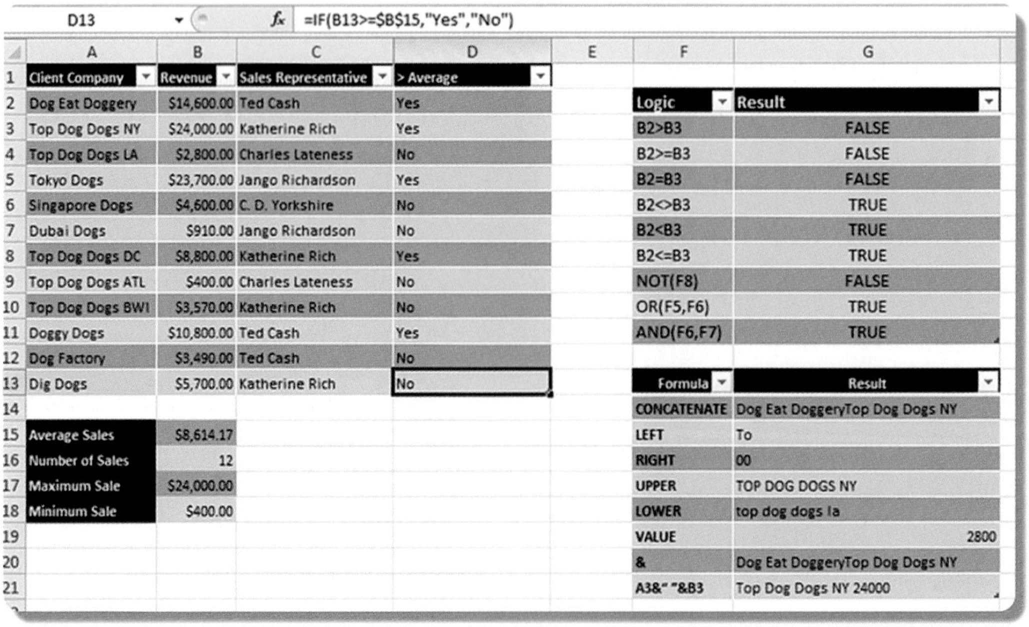

	D13	▼	*fx*	=IF(B13>=$B$15,"Yes","No")			
	A	B	C	D	E	F	G
1	Client Company ▼	Revenue ▼	Sales Representative ▼	> Average ▼			
2	Dog Eat Doggery	$14,600.00	Ted Cash	Yes		Logic ▼	Result ▼
3	Top Dog Dogs NY	$24,000.00	Katherine Rich	Yes		B2>B3	FALSE
4	Top Dog Dogs LA	$2,800.00	Charles Lateness	No		B2>=B3	FALSE
5	Tokyo Dogs	$23,700.00	Jango Richardson	Yes		B2=B3	FALSE
6	Singapore Dogs	$4,600.00	C. D. Yorkshire	No		B2<>B3	TRUE
7	Dubai Dogs	$910.00	Jango Richardson	No		B2<B3	TRUE
8	Top Dog Dogs DC	$8,800.00	Katherine Rich	Yes		B2<=B3	TRUE
9	Top Dog Dogs ATL	$400.00	Charles Lateness	No		NOT(F8)	FALSE
10	Top Dog Dogs BWI	$3,570.00	Katherine Rich	No		OR(F5,F6)	TRUE
11	Doggy Dogs	$10,800.00	Ted Cash	Yes		AND(F6,F7)	TRUE
12	Dog Factory	$3,490.00	Ted Cash	No			
13	Dig Dogs	$5,700.00	Katherine Rich	No		Formula ▼	Result ▼
14						CONCATENATE	Dog Eat DoggeryTop Dog Dogs NY
15	Average Sales	$8,614.17				LEFT	To
16	Number of Sales	12				RIGHT	00
17	Maximum Sale	$24,000.00				UPPER	TOP DOG DOGS NY
18	Minimum Sale	$400.00				LOWER	top dog dogs la
19						VALUE	2800
20						&	Dog Eat DoggeryTop Dog Dogs NY
21						A3&" "&B3	Top Dog Dogs NY 24000

You can see examples of the Function Wizard for Excel 2010 and Calc in Figure 13.6.

In Excel, the Function Wizard (or Formula Builder) allows you to type keywords associated with the function to help you look up the correct function or formula you want to use. In Calc, you must select the function or formula from a list sorted by category. However, the Calc wizard has an additional tab called Structure that shows you the evaluation structure of the formula you are creating.

13.2.6

Calculation Options

You can force a manual recalculation of your workbook by pressing the *F9* key on the keyboard. By default, all calculations are updated as soon as one of the cells that affects a formula result is changed. You can control this behavior, however, if you want to delay the update operation. If you choose to change this setting in Excel 2010, select the *Formulas* ribbon and change the *Calculation Options* menu settings from *Automatic* to *Manual*. You can then use either of the icons to the side; *Calculate Now* will manually recalculate the entire workbook and *Calculate Sheet* will calculate only the

OPEN OFFICE Calc also allows you to change the automatic calculation setting for your worksheets. To change whether the spreadsheet is calculated automatically or manually, check or uncheck the *AutoCalculate* item in the *Tools* menu under *Cell Contents*. You can force a manual recalculation by either pressing the *F9* key or navigating back to the *Tools* menu under *Cell Contents* and choosing *Recalculate*.

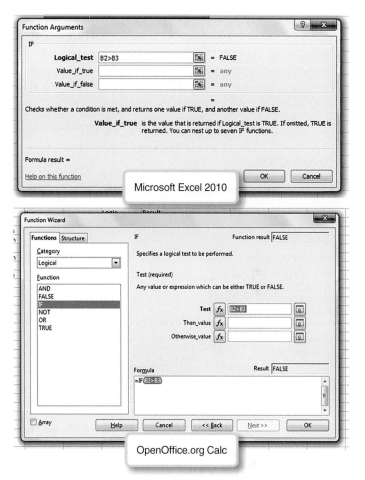

▲ **FIGURE 13.6**
Function Wizard examples

current spreadsheet. In Excel 2011, the settings for manual and automatic calculation are found under the *Settings* icon on the *Calculation* panel of the *Formula* ribbon; this ribbon also has icons to *Recalculate All* and *Recalculate Sheet* manually.

Tracing Variables

13.2.7

You can visually trace the variables used in the construction of your formulas in spreadsheet software; this can be a helpful when you are updating data and want to see how the update will affect your work. You can trace both the dependents and the precedents of your formula; these operations are only valid on formula data. *Dependents* show the connections to cells that are affected by

Formulas ribbon, and clicking the *Trace Dependents* icon. An example of the visual result for performing this action on cell *B15* is shown in Figure 13.7.

You can also activate the visual arrows for precedents of a formula. It is possible to have both of these traces active at the same time. To activate the tracing for precedents in Excel, select the cell containing the formula you want to trace, activate the *Formulas* ribbon, and click the *Trace Precedents* icon. An example of tracing precedents on cell D13 is shown in Figure 13.8.

To remove the traces in Excel, select the *Remove Arrows* icon with the cell selected; this is also located in the Formulas ribbon. In Excel 2010, the panel that contains this functionality also allows you to toggle between the display of calculated values and the formulas themselves by using the *Show Formulas* icon. You can also select the *Evaluate* icon to open a dialog box that will progress through the formula step by step to allow you to examine the results at each stage. In Excel 2011, you can display the formulas instead of the calculated results by checking the *Show Formulas* option under the *Show* icon on the *Formulas* ribbon.

▲ FIGURE 13.7
Trace Dependents example

	B15	fx =ROUND(AVERAGE(B2:B13),2)	
	A	B	C	D
1	Client Company	Revenue	Sales Representative	> Average
2	Dog Eat Doggery	$14,600.00	Ted Cash	Yes
3	Top Dog Dogs NY	$24,000.00	Katherine Rich	Yes
4	Top Dog Dogs LA	$2,800.00	Charles Lateness	No
5	Tokyo Dogs	$23,700.00	Jango Richardson	Yes
6	Singapore Dogs	$4,600.00	C. D. Yorkshire	No
7	Dubai Dogs	$910.00	Jango Richardson	No
8	Top Dog Dogs DC	$8,800.00	Katherine Rich	Yes
9	Top Dog Dogs ATL	$400.00	Charles Lateness	No
10	Top Dog Dogs BWI	$3,570.00	Katherine Rich	No
11	Doggy Dogs	$10,800.00	Ted Cash	Yes
12	Dog Factory	$3,490.00	Ted Cash	No
13	Dig Dogs	$5,700.00	Katherine Rich	No
14				
15	Average Sales	8,614.17		
16	Number of Sales	12		
17	Maximum Sale	$24,000.00		
18	Minimum Sale	$400.00		

a change to the selected formula. *Precedents* show the cells that contribute values to the current formula, such as cells referenced by the formula for calculation.

In Excel 2010 and Excel 2011, you can activate the arrows displaying the dependents of a cell by activating a cell containing a formula calculation, selecting the

▼ FIGURE 13.8
Trace Precedents example

	D13	fx =IF(B13>=$B$15,"Yes","No")	
	A	B	C	D
1	Client Company	Revenue	Sales Representative	> Average
2	Dog Eat Doggery	$14,600.00	Ted Cash	Yes
3	Top Dog Dogs NY	$24,000.00	Katherine Rich	Yes
4	Top Dog Dogs LA	$2,800.00	Charles Lateness	No
5	Tokyo Dogs	$23,700.00	Jango Richardson	Yes
6	Singapore Dogs	$4,600.00	C. D. Yorkshire	No
7	Dubai Dogs	$910.00	Jango Richardson	No
8	Top Dog Dogs DC	$8,800.00	Katherine Rich	Yes
9	Top Dog Dogs ATL	$400.00	Charles Lateness	No
10	Top Dog Dogs BWI	$3,570.00	Katherine Rich	No
11	Doggy Dogs	$10,800.00	Ted Cash	Yes
12	Dog Factory	$3,490.00	Ted Cash	No
13	Dig Dogs	$5,700.00	Katherine Rich	No
14				
15	Average Sales	8,614.17		
16	Number of Sales	12		
17	Maximum Sale	$24,000.00		
18	Minimum Sale	$400.00		

OPEN OFFICE In Calc, you can view the dependents and precedents of a formula using the Detective tool. You activate these items by selecting the *Tools* menu, choosing *Detective*, and then selecting either *Trace Dependents* or *Trace Precedents*. These traces can be removed using the same submenu by electing to remove the dependents, precedents, or both with *Remove All Traces*.

Data Validation

Data validation can be used to monitor specific cells for a range of valid input. This is useful if you are using complex formulas that accept only certain data types or values. For instance, you can apply data validation to the cells containing sales amounts in *Column B* of the *January Sales* spreadsheet so they will only accept positive decimal values. To apply data validation in Excel, select the cell or cells to which you want the data validation to apply, open the *Data* ribbon, and select *Data Validation*. The Data Validation dialog box that appears is shown in Figure 13.9.

You can set the criteria from the various drop-down lists. In the example, set the allowed type to *Decimal* and configure the allowed data so it only accepts values greater than zero. You can use the *Input Message* tab to give your users a text prompt about the allowed values. You can also use the *Error Alert* tab to

OPEN OFFICE You can add data validation in Calc as well. To do this, select the data on which you want to enforce validation rules, select the *Data* menu, and choose *Validity*. This will open a dialog box where you can enter the data type and rules for your cell or cells. You can also use the *Input Help* tab to display the criteria or range to a user when the cell is selected and use the *Error Alert* tab to define the error message that appears if the established rules are violated.

define what will occur when invalid data is entered.

SUBTOTALS

Subtotals are a tool in spreadsheet software that allows you to select the granularity with which you want to view the elements that contribute to an overall summation. Using subtotals is one application of grouping in a spreadsheet. Grouping cells in a spreadsheet couples the display of the cells so either all are showing or none are showing; you can group cells by rows or by columns.

▼ **FIGURE 13.9**
Data validation example

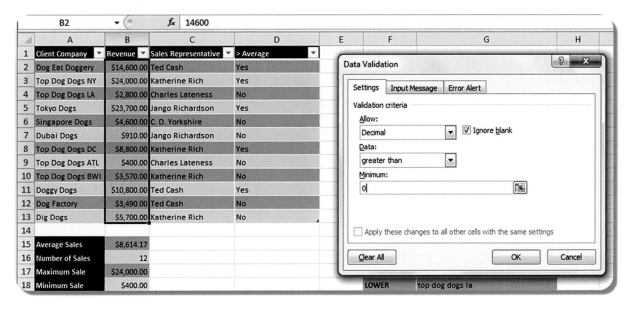

Grouping Cells

When you group cells in a spreadsheet, they can be hidden or shown as a group with the use of a toggle icon. To group a set of rows or a set of columns in Excel, select the row or column labels you want to include and select the *Group* icon from the *Data* ribbon. An example of grouping rows on the *January Supply List* spreadsheet is shown in Figure 13.10.

When you have grouped the rows or columns, you will see an additional space to the left of the row labels or above the column labels. This shows you where your groups are and the current status of their display; when a group is displayed, you will see a line bounding the range of cells included in the group and an icon for a minus sign (–). Clicking this icon will hide the group and turn the icon into a plus sign (+), which can be used to show the hidden group. This is helpful if you have information that you do not always want displayed but is necessary to keep. This is also an alternative to hiding individual rows and columns.

OPEN OFFICE You can group rows and columns in Calc by highlighting the selection you want to group, clicking on the *Data* menu, choosing *Group and Outline*, and then selecting *Group*. The groups in Calc function just as they do in Excel; you can use the plus or minus icons in the margin to show or hide grouped elements. You can also show or hide grouped elements from the *Group and Outline* submenu of the *Data* menu; this is also where the *Ungroup* command is located for removing existing groups.

Grouping items at multiple levels allows the formation of subgroups. You remove a group in Excel by selecting the group and clicking on the *Ungroup* icon on the *Data* ribbon. You can also use the *Show Detail* and *Hide Detail* icons to show or hide the group without using the plus or minus icons in the margin. For the example, remove the grouping since this data set will be used for the construction of a subtotal example.

Constructing Subtotals

Subtotals are an offshoot of the grouping functionality in spreadsheets that allow

▶ **FIGURE 13.10**
Group example

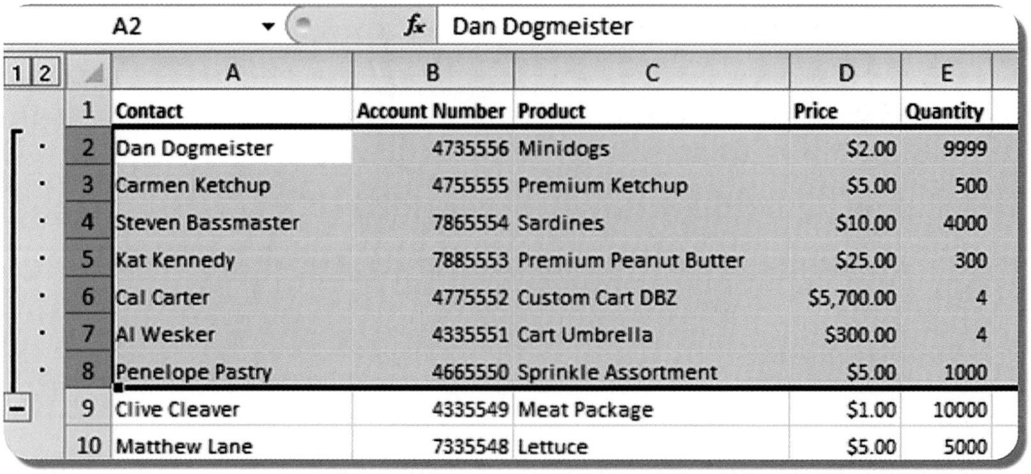

		A	B	C	D	E
	1	Contact	Account Number	Product	Price	Quantity
	2	Dan Dogmeister	4735556	Minidogs	$2.00	9999
	3	Carmen Ketchup	4755555	Premium Ketchup	$5.00	500
	4	Steven Bassmaster	7865554	Sardines	$10.00	4000
	5	Kat Kennedy	7885553	Premium Peanut Butter	$25.00	300
	6	Cal Carter	4775552	Custom Cart DBZ	$5,700.00	4
	7	Al Wesker	4335551	Cart Umbrella	$300.00	4
	8	Penelope Pastry	4665550	Sprinkle Assortment	$5.00	1000
	9	Clive Cleaver	4335549	Meat Package	$1.00	10000
	10	Matthew Lane	7335548	Lettuce	$5.00	5000

A2   *fx*   Dan Dogmeister

for the inclusion of incremental totaling for groupings of similar content. To construct a subtotal example on the *January Supply List* spreadsheet, add a column after the existing data for calculating the cost (which should be the price times the quantity). Subtotals work on filtered data for automatically coupling information into subgroups, so you should filter the data and sort it by *Account Number*. This will place all of the orders from the specific accounts in the same location. You should remove any formatting and filters since the Subtotal command will only operate on regular cells.

To construct this example in Excel 2010, select all of the rows in the *January Supply List* spreadsheet (after you have filtered and sorted the data) and then select the *Subtotal* icon on the *Data* ribbon. In Excel 2011, this option is available by selecting the *Data* menu and choosing *Subtotals*. This will open a dialog box where you can select the settings for your subtotal results. In the example, you should subtotal at changes in *Account Number*, use the *SUM* function, and add totals to the *Cost* value. Make sure the *Summary below data* option is checked. The Subtotal dialog box and results are shown in Figure 13.11.

When you have finished, you can format the result as a table; you are free to show and hide individual elements by grouping. This allows you to view the details of the orders or just the total cost of the order per account. You can also hide all

OPEN OFFICE In Calc, you can create subtotals by selecting the data you wish to use, opening the *Data* menu, and selecting *Subtotals*. This will open a dialog box where you can select up to three grouping levels by column heading and function. You should select *Account Number* and *SUM* for the first group. You can also select the *Options* tab on the dialog box to identify any other modifications you wish to make.

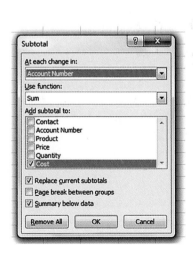

► **FIGURE 13.11**
Subtotal dialog box and results

	Contact	Account Number	Product	Price	Quantity	Cost
1	Contact	Account Number	Product	Price	Quantity	Cost
3		4335549 Total				$10,000
5		4335551 Total				$1,200
6	Penelope Pastry	4665550	Sprinkle Assortment	$5.00	1000	$5,000
7	Penelope Pastry	4665550	Miniature Hot Dog Buns	$4.00	7777	$31,108
8		4665550 Total				$36,108
12		4735556 Total				$23,002
16		4755555 Total				$6,000
17	Lea Princess	4775547	Napkins	$50.00	2000	$100,000
18	Lea Princess	4775547	Plastic Silver Forks	$25.00	2000	$50,000
19	Lea Princess	4775547	Plastic Silver Knives	$25.00	2000	$50,000
20	Lea Princess	4775547	Plastic Silver Sporks	$25.00	2000	$50,000
21		4775547 Total				$250,000
23		4775552 Total				$22,800
28		7335548 Total				$100,000
30		7555546 Total				$120,000
33		7865554 Total				$190,000
34	Kat Kennedy	7885553	Premium Peanut Butter	$25.00	300	$7,500
35	Kat Kennedy	7885553	Premium Walnut Butter	$25.00	300	$7,500
36	Kat Kennedy	7885553	Second Hand Peanut Parts	$5.00	1000	$5,000
37		7885553 Total				$20,000
38		Grand Total				$779,110

F38 =SUBTOTAL(9,F2:F36)

of the information except for the final total cost of all orders.

13.4 PIVOT TABLES

A *pivot table* is a tool for visualizing complex data that allows you to select the granularity with which you want to see the information presented. These can also perform limited automatic data calculation such as averages, summations, and counts. Pivot tables can be used as a supplement to spreadsheet information, and you can even reference the automatic calculations for your own use in other areas of your document.

13.4.1 Constructing a Pivot Table

To construct a pivot table in Excel, first select the data range you want to incorporate into the table and then click the *PivotTable* icon on the *Insert* ribbon in Excel 2010; in Excel 2011, the *PivotTable* command is an option under the *Data* menu. In the example, the data range is the sales information in the *January Sales* spreadsheet. When you click the PivotTable icon, the Create Pivot-Table dialog box, shown in Figure 13.12, will appear. You will be prompted to select the range of cells you want to include and where you want your table located; for the example, choose cell *I2* (the intervening columns containing the formula examples have been hidden).

When you click *OK*, the PivotTable Field List will appear as a pane on the side of the interface (this is the PivotTable Builder window in Excel 2011) along with a placeholder in your document that the resulting pivot table will occupy. Notice there are four categories in the lower portion of the PivotTable Field List; you can drag and drop the category information into each of these areas to arrange your pivot table information, as shown in Figure 13.13.

Each heading can only occupy a single field. The options for selection are *Row Labels*, *Column Labels*, *Values*, and *Report Filter*. The row and column labels provide organization to the table; you can stack multiple values in these categories to create subgroups of data. In this case, add *Sales Representative* as the first row label entry and *Client Company* as the second row label

▶ **FIGURE 13.12**
Create PivotTable
dialog box

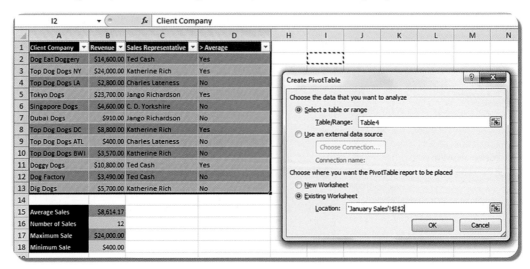

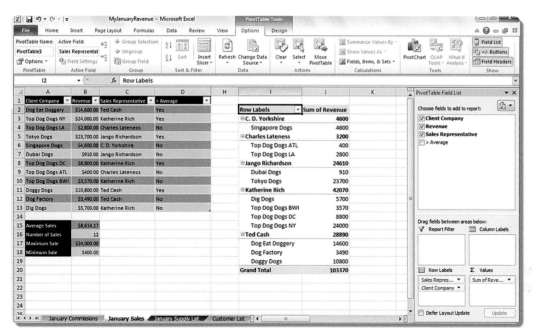

entry; this arranges the data by representative and creates a subgroup of companies beneath the representative's name. Drag *Revenue* to *Values* to create an automatic column header for *Sum of Revenue*. You can change the formula used for computing values by selecting the *Value Field* settings on the menu of options for the *Sum of Revenue* entry (this is the *i* icon beside the field name in Excel 2011); this will open a dialog box where you can alter your choices for reporting information as necessary. There is a much larger range of functions that can be performed with pivot tables, but these are beyond the scope of this text.

13.4.2 Using Pivot Table Values in Formulas

Now you can calculate the commissions for the sales team and determine the overall net profit or loss for the month of January. To do this, you will first need to set up your

 OPEN OFFICE The Calc equivalent of a pivot table is called a *DataPilot*. You can create a DataPilot by selecting the range of values you want to use (in this case, the sales information in the *January Sales* sheet) and choosing the *Data* menu, selecting *DataPilot*, and then selecting *Start*. This will open a dialog box in which you can select the source for your information; this should be the current selection. Next, a window will appear in which you can select the *Page Fields* (which allows a selection of results to use similar to a filter), *Row Fields*, *Column Fields*, and *Data Fields*. These are roughly equivalent to the field options for Excel. Drag the *Sales Representative* box to *Row Fields* and then drag *Revenue* to *Value Fields*, which will convert it to a summation. You should then select the *More* button and change the destination of the DataPilot so it does not overwrite your source information. The *Options* button allows you to change the automatic calculation formula. When you are finished, click *OK* to place the DataPilot in the spreadsheet. You can utilize the subcategory of *Client Company*, but this will make it much more difficult to look up values from the DataPilot for a later step.

spreadsheet on the *January Commissions* tab. The categories for this spreadsheet should be *Sales Representative, Revenue, Commission Rate, Commission, Qualify for Bonus, Bonus Amount,* and *Total Payout.* Copy and paste the names of the sales representatives into the first column. You should then use VLOOKUP and IF statements to construct everything but the *Revenue* amount. The formulas for the first entry in each of these are as follows:

- *Commission Rate* for the first sales representative in cell *A2* is *VLOOKUP(A2,'Sales Representatives'! $A$1:$D$7,2,FALSE).*

- *Commission* for the first sales representatve is *B2*C2.*

- *Qualify for Bonus* for the first sales representative is *IF(B2>=VLOOKUP(A2,'Sales Repre sentatives'!$A$1:$D$7,3,FALSE),"Yes ","No"),*

- *Bonus Amount* for the first sales representative is *IF(E2="Yes", VLOOKUP(A2,'Sales Representatives'! $A$1:$D$7,4,FALSE),0).*

- *Total Payout* for the first sales representative is *D2+F2.*

These formulas are just more complex examples of what you have already practiced. By using VLOOKUP, you can base everything off of the sales representative

OPEN OFFICE The GET-PIVOTDATA function works in Calc as well; you just have to provide the starting value of the DataPilot where the pivot table reference begins. The rest of the formulas and references should be the same for both applications.

name and avoid unnecessary duplication. Once you have all of these values in place and functional, use the fill down command to duplicate them to the cells below.

The function you will use to access the pivot table data is *GETPIVOTDATA.* It has the format GETPIVOTDATA(*Return value category, Pivot Table location, Search category, Search value*). In the example, you want to look up the revenue value for the sales representative, so the formula for looking up the first sales representative would be *GETPIVOTDATA("Revenue",'January Sales'!$I$2,"Sales Representative",A2).* If you have followed along with the example, your result should look like Figure 13.14.

You should now calculate the total payout for commissions. You will use this and the total payout for supplies to compare against the total income from sales. This will give you an idea of your net revenue for the month of January.

▶ **FIGURE 13.14**
Commission calculation example

	B2			*fx*	=GETPIVOTDATA("Revenue",'January Sales'!$I$2,"Sales Representative",A2)		
	A	B	C	D	E	F	G
1	Sales Representatvie	Revenue	Commission Rate	Commission	Qualify for Bonus	Bonus Amt	Total Payout
2	C. D. Yorkshire	4600	18%	$828	No	$0	$828
3	Charles Lateness	3200	12%	$384	No	$0	$384
4	Jango Richardson	24610	20%	$4,922	Yes	$500	$5,422
5	Katherine Rich	42070	22%	$9,255	Yes	$750	$10,005
6	Ted Cash	28890	20%	$5,778	Yes	$750	$6,528
7							
8							
9	Total Payout	$23,167					
10							

WHAT IF ANALYSIS

The tools for conducting a "what if" type of analysis in spreadsheet software include the ability to perform goal seeking on a value in a formula. Goal Seek will solve a formula to find a single optimum value by varying one of the input arguments.

To prepare the final financial information for January, you should import the cost of supplies and the cost of payouts to your sales team and subtract them from the sales revenue. This will give you your net profit or loss for the month. Since you have a substantial loss when you compute this value, you will need to calculate the payoff of a business loan to cover the amount. If you have completed the example correctly, the amount to be borrowed should be $698,907.

Prepare a new section of your spreadsheet to calculate the monthly payment to pay off this loan in 24 months. You will use Goal Seek to determine the interest rate you need to negotiate to make that happen. The values you will need are the total loan amount (which should be the negative of the loss amount for the month), the interest rate (you can start with 5 percent), the number of months to pay off the debt (24), and the payment amount per month; use the PMT function to calculate the monthly payment based on the other entries. This function has the format PMT (*Interest rate, Months to pay, Amount to pay*) and it returns the expected monthly payment. Divide your interest rate by 12 since it is an annual interest rate and you want a monthly payment result. You can now use

OPEN OFFICE To activate Goal Seek in Calc, select the *Tools* menu and select *Goal Seek*. This works the same as it does in Excel.

Goal Seek to determine the ideal interest rate you will need to match your expected payoff.

Goal Seek takes three values: a formula to optimize, the formula result desired, and a parameter to tune to achieve the desired result. To activate Goal Seek in Excel, open the *Data* ribbon, and choose *What-If Analysis* and then *Goal Seek*. You will be prompted with a dialog box as shown in Figure 13.15.

For this example, use the formula for the monthly payment as the formula to optimize. You should set the ideal value to *–50,000*; this is negative because it represents a payment and not a gain. Set the interest rate as the parameter to tune. When you click *OK*, the formula will be optimized to show the maximum interest rate you can have to pay off the loan in the specified amount of time with a monthly payment of 50,000. This should result in an allowed interest calculation of 58%.

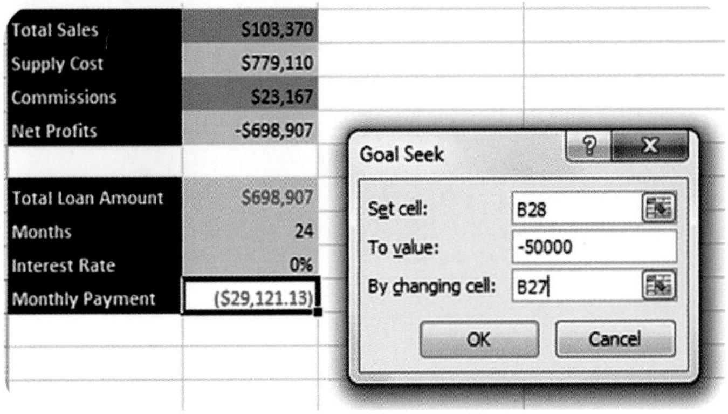

▼ **FIGURE 13.15**
Goal Seek dialog box

Total Sales	$103,370
Supply Cost	$779,110
Commissions	$23,167
Net Profits	-$698,907
Total Loan Amount	$698,907
Months	24
Interest Rate	0%
Monthly Payment	($29,121.13)

Goal Seek

Set cell: B28

To value: -50000

By changing cell: B27

OK   Cancel

13.6 EXTERNAL DATA MANAGEMENT

Spreadsheet software has the ability to import and export data for use across multiple applications. This is especially useful if you want to analyze information from a database source or convert exported text to a spreadsheet for analysis. The common format for a text document that can be opened in spreadsheet software is a *comma-separated values* (CSV) file, which simply uses commas as delimiters for the text and treats each new line as a new row. You can import or export this type of information.

13.6.1 External Data Sources

You can import data into your spreadsheet from a variety of external sources. In business, it is most likely the data is from a database, which you will learn about in Section V, "Database Software and Microsoft Access." You can connect to several data sources from your

▼ FIGURE 13.16
Text Import Wizard

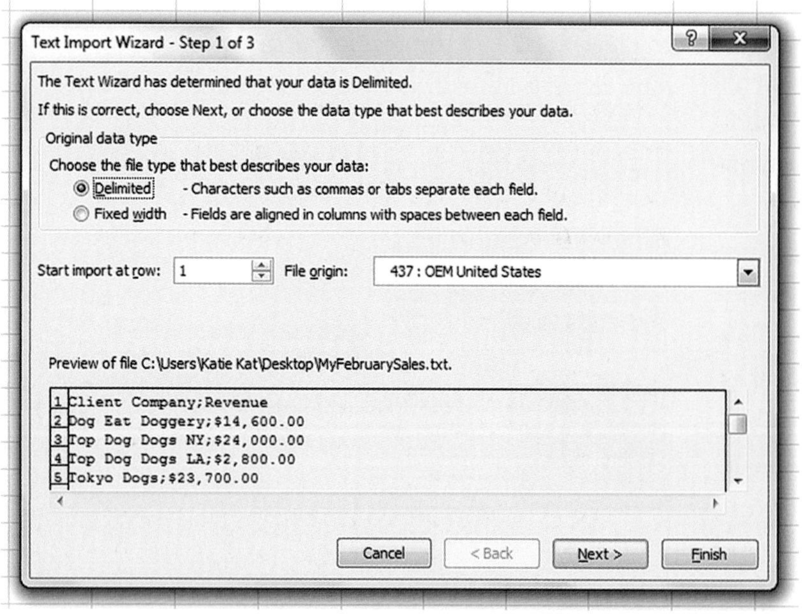

At the time of writing, there are issues in the implementation of the external data import functionality in Calc that have not yet been resolved. You can use the *Insert* menu, select *Link to External Data*, and choose the data you want to include. This can be a local HTML file, a URL, or another spreadsheet; the dialog box will allow you to select the information and format it, but you may not be able to complete the final data insertion. A workaround for this may be forthcoming or may be available now. You should check the OpenOffice.org support Web site to find out more details on the status of this issue. You can still copy and paste data from any supported source or open supported documents from within Calc, but doing so will not preserve the link to the original source.

spreadsheet software including delimited text files, database connections, and other spreadsheet documents. As an example, you can create a new spreadsheet in your workbook and name it *February Sales* and then import the *MyFebruarySales* text file into the spreadsheet as an example. To do this in Excel, select the *From Text* icon (simply called *Text* in Excel 2011) on the *Data* ribbon and follow the prompts for formatting your text; this is similar to the Text to Columns functionality. An example dialog box for this formatting option is shown in Figure 13.16. Since the data includes commas in this case, the delimiter used is a semicolon (;).

You can also connect your spreadsheet to a database, Web location (via URL), or text file.

Text Import Wizard - Step 1 of 3

The Text Wizard has determined that your data is Delimited.

If this is correct, choose Next, or choose the data type that best describes your data.

Original data type

Choose the file type that best describes your data:
- ● Delimited   - Characters such as commas or tabs separate each field.
- ○ Fixed width - Fields are aligned in columns with spaces between each field.

Start import at row: 1   File origin: 437 : OEM United States

Preview of file C:\Users\Katie Kat\Desktop\MyFebruarySales.txt.

```
1 Client Company;Revenue
2 Dog Eat Doggery;$14,600.00
3 Top Dog Dogs NY;$24,000.00
4 Top Dog Dogs LA;$2,800.00
5 Tokyo Dogs;$23,700.00
```

Cancel   < Back   Next >   Finish

The database connection options include SQL Server and the alternate connections include XML data. You can also click the *Existing Connections* icon to manage the connected data and use the *Refresh* icon to access options to update the data in your spreadsheet to match the most current information from the data source.

13.6.2 Exporting Data

Spreadsheet software has a variety of export options available from the Save As command. The most common exports for spreadsheet data are XML, HTML, and text. XML (eXtensible Markup Language) is a special kind of markup language similar in origin to HTML that provides a defined formatting style command based on the tag information provided. XML is commonly used for data formatting and is increasingly used to pass data from one database to another. The XML option allows databases to easily pick up the spreadsheet data. HTML is the common language of the Web and it contains predefined tags for table elements; you can export data from spreadsheet software directly to HTML where it can be used online or interpreted by other programs. Text export is another option; the two common varieties of text export are tab-delimited and comma-delimited text information, where each line in the text document equates to a row. The columns are determined by the delimiter character.

13.7 ARRANGING THE WORKSPACE

Excel gives you a number of options for managing your workspace. These options

OPEN OFFICE You can actually use Calc to define a database in the Base program that is also part of the OpenOffice.org suite.

are located on the View ribbon in Excel 2010 and on the Layout ribbon in Excel 2011. You can select the *New Window* icon (which is just labeled *New* on the *Window* panel in Excel 2011) to open a new window with a view of the current document; this allows you to view multiple spreadsheets in the same document simultaneously. You can then arrange the windows in a manner that lets you manipulate your spreadsheet best. Commands like Cascade and Side by Side allow you to place your Excel windows in a practical arrangement. You can also use the *Save Workspace* command (called *Save Layout* in Excel 2011) to retain this arrangement for future use.

If you want to view multiple areas of the same spreadsheet, you can use the *Split* command on the current view of your document. This separates your document pane into four separate panes with scrollbars to manipulate pieces of them independently and allows you to view different areas of a complex sheet at the same time. This icon acts as a toggle, so you can deactivate it to return to the standard view.

OPEN OFFICE In Calc, you can perform the Split operation on the current view of your document by selecting the *Window* menu and choosing *Split*. This acts as a toggle, so you can uncheck it to return to the standard view.

CHAPTER SUMMARY

Spreadsheet software provides powerful tools for data management, analysis, and visualization. It is capable of effectively managing lists and organizing information. You can create complex formulas that span multiple spreadsheets of data and multiple subformulas. The disadvantage of spreadsheet software is the need to maintain the consistency of data and the potential for errors in duplicating values in multiple locations. You can control this to an extent if you use lookups to keep your spreadsheets as consistent as possible with a piece of data existing in only one location, but the potential for error, especially in collaborative efforts, is high. You can address this disadvantage with the use of database software, which is the focus of the next section of this text. Database software allows you to manage information via relationships so data is gathered by lookup of a value and by reference, minimizing the potential for unwanted duplication and reducing consistency errors. Spreadsheet software also possesses the ability to access external data from database connections, so you can use both tools to manage your data for consistency and perform the analysis you need.

CHAPTER EXERCISES

1. Using the data from the *MyFebruarySales* file and the completed example you produced in the chapter for January, construct sheets in your business document for *February Sales*, *February Supplies*, and *February Commissions*. The sales figures should be derived from the *MyFebruarySales* document and you can assume a reorder of all of the supplies from January except the one-time items associated with the business startup; these are any items in the supply list that have 4 as the total number ordered. Perform all of the steps on the February data that you did for completing the tasks for January. You should also use formulas to determine whether sales are improving or declining for each of the customers. Analyze which products from the supply list are too costly to continue to use based on the sales amounts and whether the business can remain viable if the sales trends and supply costs continue. You can provide your analysis on a separate *Outcome* spreadsheet using text boxes with support from the numbers within the spreadsheet.

CHAPTER KNOWLEDGE CHECK

1 The VALUE function will return a numeric equivalent to text even if the text on which it is operating is not a number.

○ True
○ False

2 *CONCATENATE* is used to join the contents of two or more cells containing text into the same text result.

○ True
○ False

3 The following function would be the most likely to require the use of ROUND to limit the digits following the decimal point:

○ **A.** MIN
○ **B.** LEFT
○ **C.** AVERAGE
○ **D.** SUM

4 The AND function will accept any number of logical input arguments and return TRUE if any of the arguments are TRUE.

○ True
○ False

5 You can nest functions within each other to calculate a complex result.

○ True
○ False

6 The following is true of VLOOKUP:

○ **A.** It searches a column for values that match the search criteria.
○ **B.** It allows for exact matches or partial matches.
○ **C.** It can return values only to the right of the search column.
○ **D.** All of the above.
○ **E.** None of the above.

7 Goal Seek can optimize values for only a single parameter.

○ True
○ False

8 You can name a range of cells and use the name to identify the range in a formula.

○ True
○ False

9 The Split function separates your view window into different sections so you can view different spreadsheets at the same time in a single window.

○ True
○ False

10 You can create subgroups of rows or columns that will be hidden or shown as a single element.

○ True
○ False

11 The Goal Seek function can optimize up to two parameters at the same time.

○ True
○ False

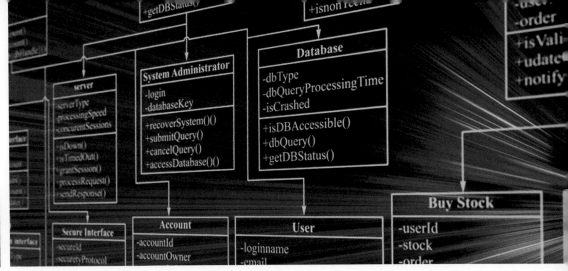

Introduction to Access and Database Software

IN THIS CHAPTER

This chapter covers database development and management using the Microsoft Access data management platform. You will learn basic database concepts and how to gather business requirements to develop a functional database. You will also learn how to navigate the Access interface and develop strong database management practices that promote security and data integrity.

The OpenOffice.org Base platform will also be covered as an alternative. At the completion of this chapter, you will be able to:

- Navigate the Access and Base user interfaces

- Create and save a database

- Create a table using database software

- Develop good database design practices

- Create a database backup

INTRODUCTION TO ACCESS

The Access database application is a Relational Database Management System (RDBMS) that is primarily designed to meet the data management needs of small to medium businesses. Access can store all types of data to include text, numbers, and pictures. You can even import Excel data that can then be queried to produce useful information. Access 2010 also has the ability to be used as a single desktop instance or be shared within an organization's network. One of the nicest enhancements is the ability to upgrade a database to the industrial-strength Microsoft SQL Server® platform. You can also use Access as the front end to an SQL Server engine, which means you can develop the user interface using Access 2010 and have SQL Server on the back end.

You might be wondering what exactly an RDBMS is. A relational database management system is a database management platform based on the relational theory formulated by E.F. Codd in the 1970s. E.F. Codd established the theoretical foundation of developing relationships between tables in a database using algebraic set theory. A *database* is simply a collection of data structures that are organized to serve the particular needs of an organization or person. The RDBMS can have more than one database instance open at once. For example, you might have an inventory database and a customer contacts database that use the

same RDBMS. One of the first questions a student might ask in an Access course is "What is the difference between Access and the Excel application?" This question is a common one because Excel also stores and organizes records.

Imagine you work at a local police department that has a serious problem with evidence management. In the department's early years, there were fewer crimes and a small amount of items in the evidence room. The evidence room is the location where police agencies store items used in a crime for later use in prosecution. Evidence rooms might also store items that have been found and are awaiting recovery by their rightful owner. Matthew, the administrative officer, is quite handy at working with Microsoft applications and decides to use Excel to manage the inventory in the evidence room.

Matthew knows that Access is a superior application for this task but at the time did not have Access available. As the years go by, the evidence list log continues to grow, and Matthew begins to struggle to keep up with the log he maintains in the Excel file. Every time officers add new items, he must make changes to the file, which can be a tedious process. The other compounding problem is that much of the evidence must leave the evidence room temporarily at times to be sent to the crime lab or court and accurate records of each of these transactions must be kept. Using the Excel spreadsheet requires a manual search using filtering to search through the records. This is why many refer to

Excel as a flat file database system. The disadvantage to using Excel for a project such as managing inventory is that there are no relationships between data and no ability to query the data.

In Matthew's case, on the most recent check the evidence inventory had grown to more than 10,000 items and he was beginning to think that maybe he truly needed a database management system. A relational database management system would give Matthew a more user-friendly interface in which to enter and remove pieces of evidence from the system and the ability to pull detailed reports on evidence availability and inventory levels. It is also possible to query the dataset on specific criteria, such as a case number, and produce within seconds the exact location of the item, important dates, names of individuals handling the evidence, and detailed item descriptions.

14.2 WORKING WITH THE INTERFACE

The Access 2010 user interface is quite user friendly; even though it is packed with many options, you can easily master the application with patience and practice. To start Access, you must first make sure you have the correct version of Microsoft Office Suite. There are six editions of Office 2010, but only three of them include Access; these are:

- Microsoft Office Professional 2010
- Microsoft Office Professional Plus 2010
- Microsoft Office Professional Academic 2010

Note that Access is not available in the Office 2011 suite for the Macintosh operating system.

Starting Access is as easy as clicking the *Start* menu button and selecting *All Programs*. Once you have made this selection, you will notice a program menu with a listing of all applications available for use. Find and click *Microsoft Office*; all of the programs available appear as shown in Figure 14.1.

Now simply click on *Microsoft Access 2010* to open the user interface, shown in Figure 14.2.

The Access interface opens to the File menu, which is also called the Backstage

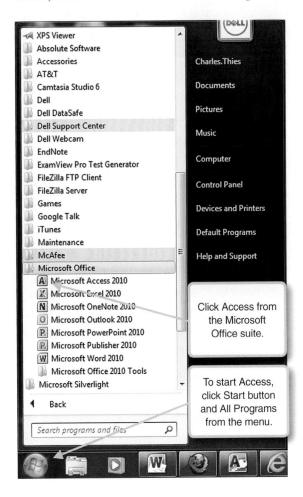

▼ FIGURE 14.1
Starting the
Access application

Click Access from the Microsoft Office suite.

To start Access, click Start button and All Programs from the menu.

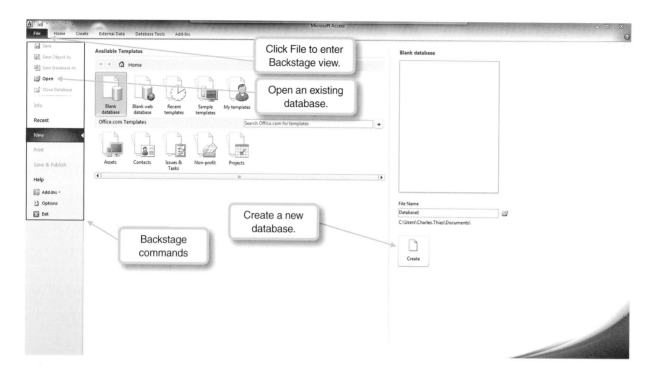

Callout labels in figure:
Click File to enter Backstage view.

Open an existing database.

Create a new database.

Backstage commands

Blank database

Available Templates

Office.com Templates

Assets Contacts Issues & Tasks Non-profit Projects

File Name
Database1
C:\Users\Charles.Thies\Documents\

Create

▲ FIGURE 14.2
Access interface on startup

view and is designed as a place to handle all of your background processes. From the Backstage view, you can complete a series of tasks that include opening a database, creating a database, changing settings, publishing your database to a SharePoint® server or the Web, repairing your database, and even encrypting your database. You can create a series of databases and they will all be listed in the Backstage view. You can open a database file and simply click *File* to return to the Backstage view at any time.

The ribbon, shown in Figure 14.3, is the easily recognizable toolbar used in all Office applications. This ribbon has different options that you will become familiar with as you continue to work through the Access chapters of this text. There are several ribbon tabs, some of which are visible only at certain times. The four main ribbons

you will see when you first open a database are the following:

- *Home*—Provides similar functionality to what you might be used to seeing in other Office applications; used to check spelling and format text.

- *Create*—Creates database objects in your database environment.

- *External Data*—Imports data from other sources, such as an Excel file that has data you want to use in your database.

- *Database Tools*—Provides tools to help migrate your Access database to SQL Server and to analyze your database.

Creating a Database

14.2.1

There are many details to implementing a good database design. Planning your new business database offers many benefits, but there are unfortunately many bad outcomes from bad design. One of the

Ribbon tabs

▲ FIGURE 14.3
Access ribbon

most important concepts to grasp is the gathering of business rules. *Business rules* are the rules that govern an organization and are engrained in daily processes. All business rules must be documented to be implemented into the database design. It is important to develop the conceptual design before building any type of database. Before getting too much further into the design process, however, you need to learn how to create your first database and then you can move toward the development of a fully functional database design. If you have been following along, you probably already have Access open on your screen and you can see the Backstage view. If not, follow the procedures outlined at the beginning of the chapter and start Access.

From the Backstage view, select *New* and then *Blank database*, as shown in Figure 14.4. You must then select a name for your new database; for this example, enter the name *JPDEvidenceInvenDB*. The final step is to click on the *Create* button on the lower-right side of the screen. Once the new database is created, Access creates your database file in the location you selected and a datasheet appears where you can begin developing your first table. Notice at the center of the window in Figure 14.4 that there is a series of templates you can use to create a database. Many templates are available online, but be sure that any templates you download are coming from a trusted source. Recall from earlier chapters that accepting any

▼ FIGURE 14.4
Creating a new database

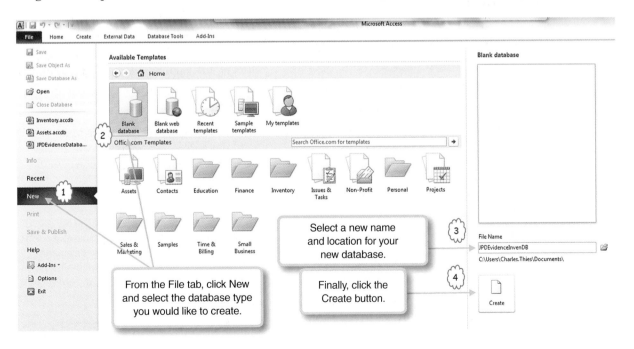

file from an unknown source should be carefully deliberated.

Creating a Database Table

So you might be asking, what exactly is a table? A *table* is an object within a database used to store individual sets of related data. For example, you might start off with an employee table that stores employee records for the inventory database. Each table has fields to store related pieces of data, so for the employee table you might have fields that describe the employee's name, address, and phone number.

If you still have your database open with the database you created, then you are at the Datasheet view with an empty table ready to be developed. If not, reopen the database, select the *Create* tab, and then select the *Table* button. You should know that developing a database table is a structured process. The first step is to build the fields you will use in your first table. Every database table field has what is known as a data type. There are some schools of thought that would start by simply creating a table, populating the table with data, and working backward by adding the data types later. That is not the process used here.

You will notice in the Datasheet view in Figure 14.5 that there are four fields: ID, F_NAME, L_NAME, and a field that is being built. Before you can add any data into a field, you must specify the type of data the field will hold. There are a couple of ways to add or modify a data type while building your table. One way to do so is from the Datasheet view. You can see in Figure 14.5 that the fourth field has a drop-down menu, called Data Type Parts.

As you build your table from the Datasheet view, you can use the Data Type Parts to correctly configure and name your fields. For more data type choices, select the *More Fields* icon in the *Fields* ribbon, and choose from among the data type options in the drop-down menu, shown in Figure 14.6. Note that the

> ▶ **FIGURE 14.5**
> Database instance
> in Datasheet view

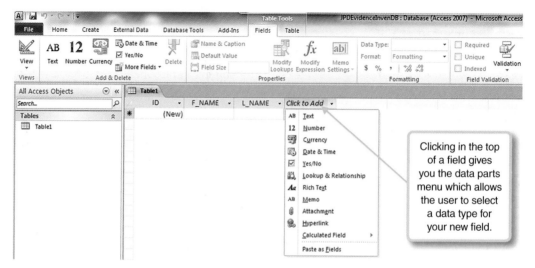

Clicking in the top of a field gives you the data parts menu which allows the user to select a data type for your new field.

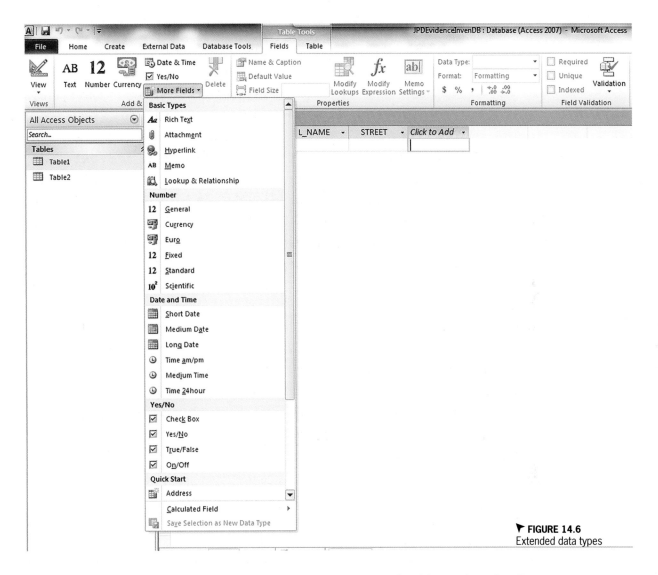

▶ FIGURE 14.6
Extended data types

Fields ribbon is active when you are editing a field within your table.

An alternative way to build database objects is to use Application Parts, as shown in Figure 14.7. You can simply close the table that opened up when you started the new database, select the *Create* ribbon, and then select *Application Parts*. Application Parts provides the following five common objects found in databases that you can implement to develop your own database:

> **APPLICATION PARTS** *is a feature within Access that provides a complete set of common tables that can be customized to suit your needs. Data Type Parts are a feature designed to help you quickly develop tables and field data types.*

- *Comments*—Tracks comments on an issue along with dates. For example, you might be developing a database that tracks comments on papers submitted to a database by students.

- *Contacts*—Tracks contact information for your customers.

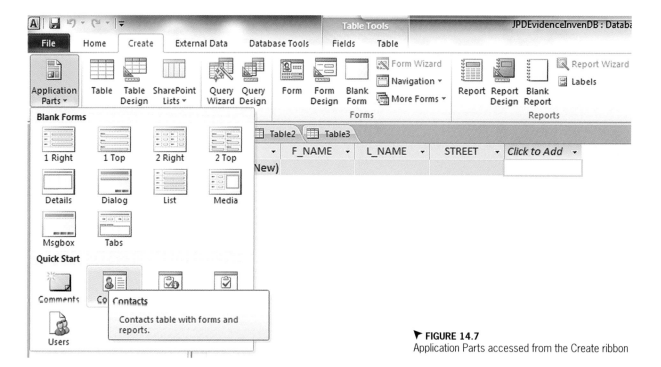

▼ FIGURE 14.7
Application Parts accessed from the Create ribbon

- *Issues*—Tracks issues in an organization. For example, you might be developing a database that tracks work orders at a help desk.

- *Tasks*—Tracks projects in an organization.

- *Users*—Tracks users for your database. The tables and forms can be used to hold basic user information.

When you click on one of the Application Parts, you can add all objects and table structures associated with the chosen Application Part. What happens if the table fields do not quite match what you need? This is no problem at all, as you can modify these objects and tables to meet your needs.

14.2.3 Working with Design View

Building tables using Data Type Parts and Application Parts might work for some projects, but true professionals develop their tables using Design view. You could probably round up enough parts from Application Parts to build the JPDEvidenceInvenDB database discussed earlier with some modification, but you can also develop the tables from scratch. The nice thing about Application Parts is that you have forms, reports, and tables already available.

With Design view, you have to develop all of the objects on your own, preferably by following a plan you created before beginning the project.

Notice in Figure 14.8 that there are three columns to enter a name, data type, and description for each field. Because you are building the table from scratch, you will need to develop all of the fields. As this is a table of employees, make the first field *EMPLOYEE ID*. This number should be unique for every employee, as this

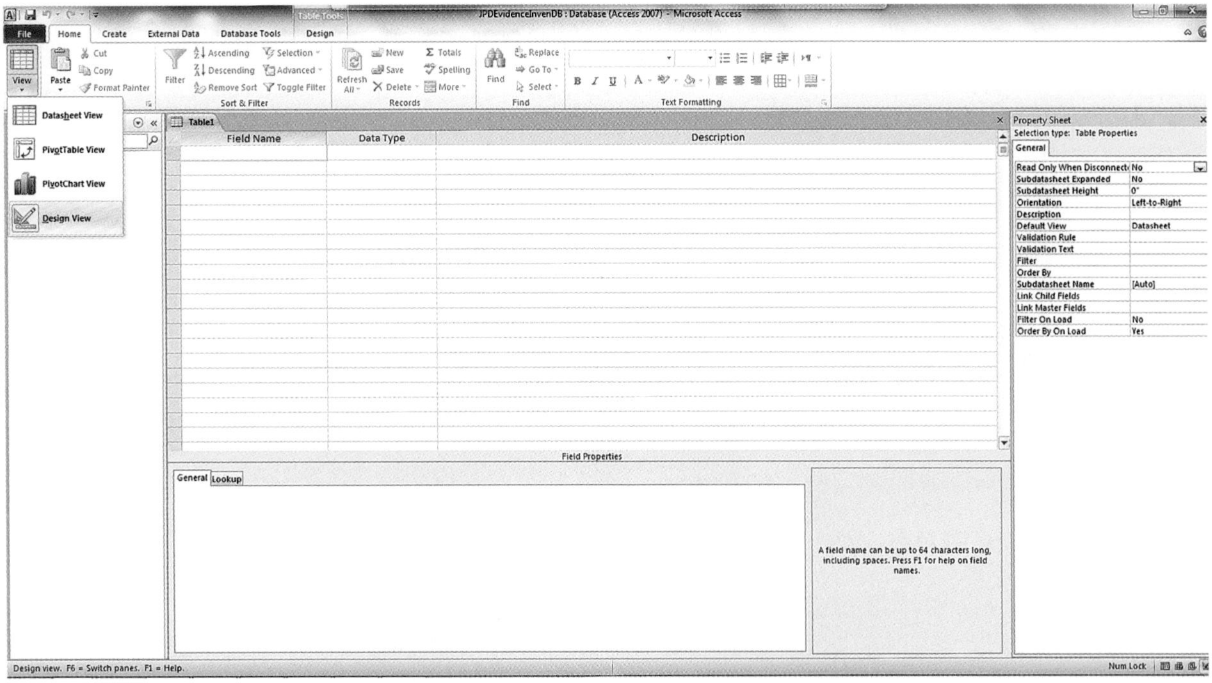

▲ FIGURE 14.8
Design view in
Access

identifier will be used to identify the employee not just in this table but throughout the entire database. This will be the *primary key* for the employee table, and every table you develop should have one.

14.2.4 Primary Keys

A *primary key* is a unique identifier that is used to identify each table in your overall database schema design. Each of your tables will have a primary key that will help to make each record unique; this feature will help prevent the duplication of records in your database. A primary key can be composed of one field or a combination of multiple fields. Notice in Figure 14.9 that the first field in the database has been created and named *EMPLOYEE ID*.

Note that the first field in every table will be the primary key in this example.

Now that you have named the first field, you have two options for creating the unique identifier for the primary key: create a unique ID for the employees that will be different each time a record is entered or have Access develop unique identifiers by selecting *AutoNumber* from the dropdown menu in the Data Type column. It is important to keep in mind that there are other numbers that are unique and widely available, such as a driver's license number or a social security number, although you should keep in mind that some information, such as social security numbers, is subject to privacy laws, and proper security measures must be taken.

Highlight the *EMPLOYEE ID* field and select the *Primary Key* button on the left side of the Design ribbon to make this field the primary key for the table. Notice in Figure 14.10 the icon to the left of the

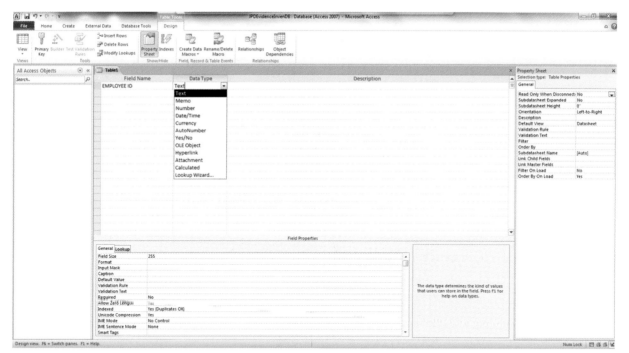

▲ FIGURE 14.9
Creating a field in
Design view

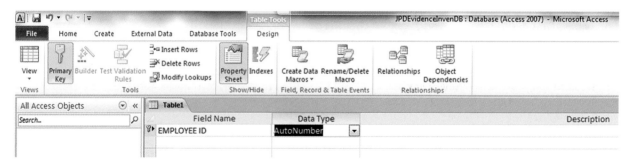

▲ FIGURE 14.10
Selecting the
primary key

EMPLOYEE ID field; this indicates the field is the primary key. After making this change, it is a good idea to save the table.

You can save your table in one of two ways. First, select the *File* menu, then select *Save Object As*; when the Save As dialog box appears, name your object, fill in the *As* box with *Table*, as this is a table, and click *OK*; this process is shown in Figure 14.11.

A quicker method to save a table is to right-click on the *Table1* tab within the Design view and select *Save*, as shown in

Figure 14.12. A dialog box will appear that gives you the option to name the table prior to executing a save.

More on Data Types

14.2.5

A data type lets Access know what type of data you will store in a field. Setting specific data types from within Design view allows you to adjust the field properties to set not only the type of data but also the number of characters you will allow in a given field. In a

small database, the number of characters might not make a difference, but as the database grows, you want all of your transactions to run optimally. It is important to plan out your design so that performance is optimal. Access has several different data types available; the more commonly used ones are the following:

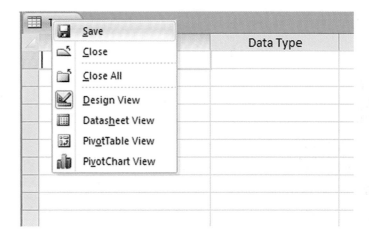

- *Text*—Lets you enter numbers, letters, and symbols up to 255 characters.

- *Memo*—Similar to Text but lets you store much more unformatted text. This is a good data type for possibly long reports in a database.

- *Number*—Used for all sorts of numbers.

- *Currency*—Similar to Number but used specifically for monetary values.

- *Date/Time*—Used specifically for calendar dates.

- *Yes/No*—These are similar to true and false values.

- *Hyperlinks*—Used for fields that store URLs.

- *Attachment*—Used to store a variety of files in the database.

- *AutoNumber*—Generates automatic unique identifier.

- *Calculated*—Generates values based on particular expressions the user supplies.

▲ FIGURE 14.12
Saving a table
from Design view

Some things you should remember about data types include the importance of choosing the correct data type when developing your database. If you must change a data type, you can do so from Design view. This is a risky step as sometimes problems can occur. If you have already populated your tables with data, making a change can sometimes result in data being lost during the conversion process. Thus, it is best to change a data type when the table is empty.

Once you have your new field and data type implemented, you must adjust

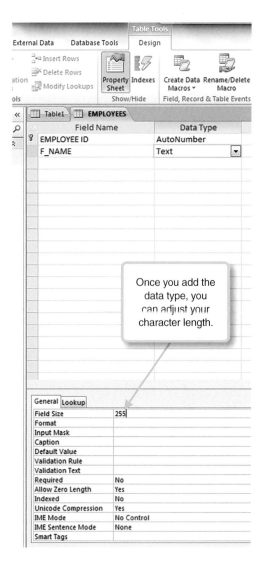

Once you add the data type, you can adjust your character length.

require a General Date format (shown in the Field Properties window at the bottom of Figure 14.14). It is extremely important for both performance and ease of operation that you make sure all fields are given the exact name you need as well as the appropriate data type and character length to ensure you do not have any problems.

14.3

DATA INTEGRITY, VALIDATION, AND GOOD DESIGN PRACTICES

Now that you are beginning to understand how to build tables using Design view, it is important that you understand that one of the benefits of developing a database is to assure data integrity. *Data integrity* is ensuring that the information in a database is correct and has not become corrupted; this is achieved in a variety of ways. The important point to remember to help assure your data is correct is to have a primary key with a unique number. If you develop an ID field in every table you create and use the AutoNumber data type and make it the primary key field, you have already started the process of assuring data integrity. Developing tables with primary keys and later establishing relationships will assure that every record in your database is unique. You will learn more about database relationships in Chapter 15, "Developing Relationships, Queries, and Reports."

Validation in your database is important as well. Allowing all sorts of date

the character length for your field. The default setting is 255 for the Text data type. When setting up the F_NAME field, you might want to reserve 255 characters so that you have enough space for longer names, as shown in Figure 14.13.

You can select a custom date and time format if you have to create a custom date field such as a date of birth (DOB) field, as shown in Figure 14.14. You might a situation where you have a table that tracks comments and times; this would

Field Name	Data Type	Description
EMPLOYEE ID	AutoNumber	
F_NAME	Text	
L_NAME	Text	
DOB	Date/Time	

Field Properties

General | Lookup

Format		
Input Mask	General Date	6/19/2007 5:34:23 PM
Caption	Long Date	Tuesday, June 19, 2007
Default Value	Medium Date	19-Jun-07
Validation Rule	Short Date	6/19/2007
Validation Text	Long Time	5:34:23 PM
Required	Medium Time	5:34 PM
Indexed	Short Time	17:34
IME Mode	No Control	

◄ **FIGURE 14.14**
Custom date formats

and time formats in your fields gives your database a lack of consistency. Access makes it easy to implement field validation with the Input Mask Wizard, shown in Figure 14.15. In this case, the wizard is being applied to the field titled DOB. To store the date of birth of every active employee, you might select *Short Date*.

Say you want to create a field to track the employee's social security number and you want this field to be a required field. In Design view, simply highlight the *SOCIAL SECURITY* field, select the drop-down menu to the right of the Required option in the Field Properties window, and select *Yes*, as shown in Figure 14.16. You should understand that Access has blank fields and empty text. A blank field or null value means there no information was entered. An empty field means a value was supplied, but it is an empty value. An example of an empty value would be pressing the spacebar a couple of times in the field; this is technically a value but an empty one. Both conditions can be prevented if you want to make sure a user enters data into the field.

In Figure 14.18, notice the Allow Zero Length value in the Field Properties window. To avoid empty values, simply select *No* for this value from the drop-down menu at the right side of the window. Selecting Yes to the Required field and selecting No to the Allow Zero Length field resolves the issue by requiring the user to enter a valid value into the field.

Indexing is another form of data integrity used in the database to prevent data duplication and speed up transactions. Without an index, Access must search an entire table for required data

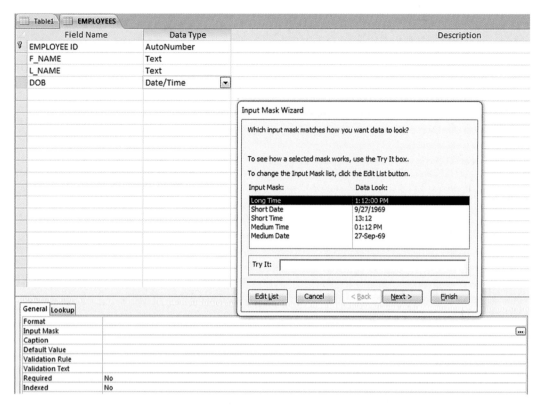

in a query, but with an index, you can quickly find the specific records you are looking for. Say you want to make the SOCIAL SECURITY field an indexed field. Notice there is a selection for Indexed in the Field Properties window of Figure 14.18. Select the drop-down menu to the right side of the window and select *Yes*. If you have already entered data into your table at the time you create an index and duplicate data exists, you will receive an error at the time of implementation.

All of these basic skills require good database design planning. The importance of conceptualizing your initial design cannot be emphasized enough. It will take time and practice for you to be able to develop a perfect database , but quality will come with testing and developing multiple databases over time. Keep the following in mind when designing a database:

• Gather your business rules—Your business rules are all the standards and practices that drive your organization. For example, every sales transaction must be logged by the salesperson. This would be a process you might want to see as part of a database.

• Normalize your database— Normalizing a database is an advanced topic, but at this level you should focus on assuring you develop the data sets you will use in your database while avoiding the collection of duplicate data.

• Avoid redundancy—Redundant information that shows up in other tables. Be sure to break down your tables to ensure you are not acquiring redundant data in your database.

- Create a primary key—Every table must have a primary key, which provides the ability to connect your tables using relationships and offers a mode of data integrity.

Database Backups

You have already learned how to manually save your objects as you complete your work either from the File menu or from the table tab by right-clicking on it and selecting Save. Saving records actually occurs automatically in Access 2010. Anytime you are working with your files and entering or modifying records, the database engine saves all of your work.

Notice in Figure 14.17 that the File menu offers two save options. The Save Object As option is used to save objects with which you are working; you have already used this option. The Save Database As option is used to save a copy of the database. Make sure you save a copy of your database frequently so you do not lose your data. It makes sense to keep a copy of your database at an alternate safe location if you are using the data for an organization and loss of data might cause work stoppages or slowdowns. A backup copy of your database will ensure you can quickly recover and resume database usage. To create a database backup, select *Save Database As*. Keep in mind that Access will close the database and save all objects. Once all objects and the database are closed, a copy is created in the location you chose to store the file.

Compressing and Repairing the Database

The Compact & Repair Database feature available in Access helps you improve database performance. At some point after you have created your database and are using it, you may notice that it is slowing down.

▼ FIGURE 14.17
Saving the database

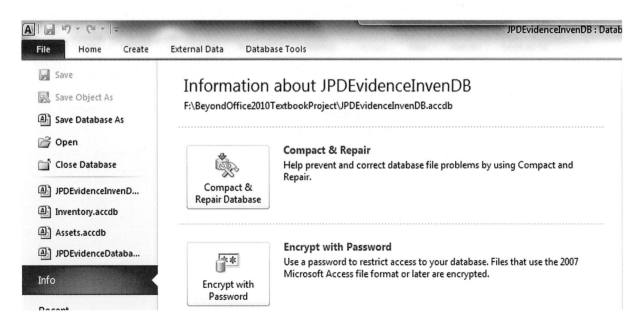

To compress or repair a database, simply select the *File* menu, as shown in Figure 14.17. Select *Info* and then click the *Compact & Repair Database* button. In a new database with few records, the process to compact the database is rather quick. In a larger database, this will take more time; the benefits are well worth the wait, however, as the overall size of the database will decrease.

14.4 BUILDING TABLES IN OPENOFFICE. ORG BASE

OpenOffice.org has a database program called Base. Note that developing a database in Base is significantly different than the process in Access. The steps that remain the same are the conceptual design of the database, including gathering business requirements and deciding what types of data to collect. This section will help you take what you have learned in the previous sections and use it to develop in the Base platform.

You open Base by clicking on the *Start* button, selecting *OpenOffice.org* from the All Programs menu, and selecting *Base*. Once Base starts up, the Database Wizard opens in the center of the screen, as shown in Figure 14.19. You can select either Create a new database

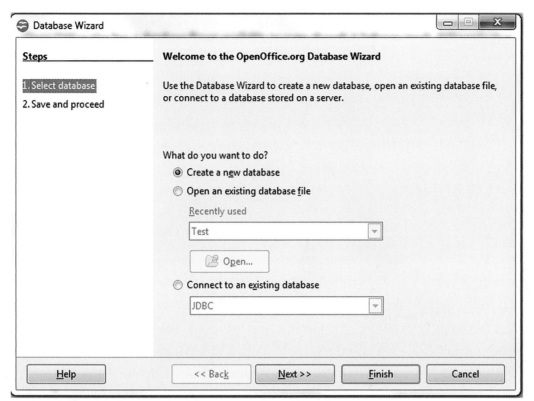

◄ FIGURE 14.19
Database Wizard
startup screen in
Base

or Open an existing database file to get started. For this example, select *Create a new database* and click *Next* to move on to the next step in developing your Base database file.

Once you have created your new database, the user interface appears, as shown in Figure 14.20. You will immediately notice the interface is not quite as busy as Access, although you should also be aware that Access is far more capable as a database platform. Take a look at the interface; you will notice that the left pane of the Base interface window has Tables, Queries, Forms, and Reports icons for creating these objects. In the upper portion of the screen, you have options to enter Design view and develop your tables using a wizard.

Figure 14.21 shows the EMPLOYEE table created earlier using Access. Note that the first field is named EMPLOYEE ID and the data type is set to Integer. There is no formal AutoNumber data type in Base; instead, you must select Integer and then in the Field Properties window at the bottom of the interface, you should select *Yes* for AutoValue, which will generate values automatically. To designate a primary key, simply highlight the field you would like to make the primary key, right-click, and select *Primary Key*.

Notice in Figure 14.22 that a SOCIAL SECURITY field has been created as a required field. You want to specify a data type that allows you to modify the

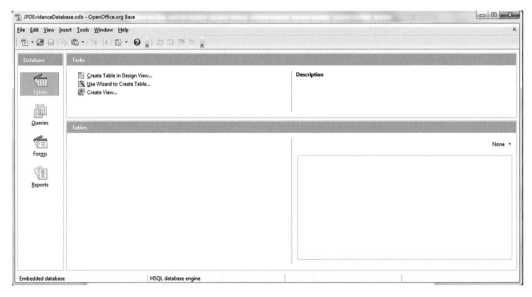

► **FIGURE 14.20**
User interface in
Base

characters to just the number needed for social security numbers, so select the *Number* data type and change the Length field in the Field Properties window to *9*. Make sure the Entry required field is set to *Yes* so that users must enter a nine-digit number every time a new record is entered into the system.

▼ **FIGURE 14.21**
Design view in
Base

An easier way to create tables in Base is by using the Table Wizard. To open the Table Wizard, select *Use Wizard to Create Table* from the Tasks window at the top of the user interface, as shown in Figure 14.23. Once you select the wizard, the Table Wizard dialog box appears and helps you develop your table in a four-step

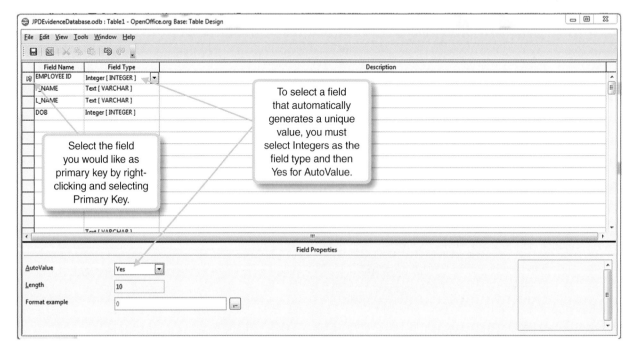

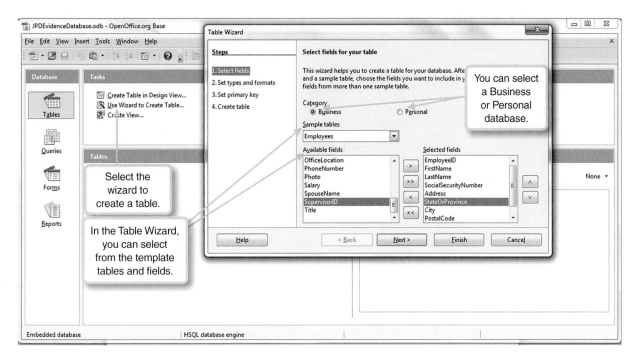

	Field Name	Field Type	
🔑	EMPLOYEE ID	Integer [INTEGER]	
	F_NAME	Text [VARCHAR]	
	L_NAME	Text [VARCHAR]	
	DOB	Integer [INTEGER]	
▷	SOCIAL SECURITY	Number [NUMERIC]	▼

Entry required — Yes ▼

Length — 9

Decimal places — 0

Default value —

▲ FIGURE 14.22 Creating a required social security number field

process. The first step requires that you develop your fields. The nice part about Base is that the application includes a series of table templates you can use to develop your database, based on whether you are creating a business database or a personal database. Select the *Employees* template to begin developing your database.

Once you have selected the Employee table template, you can select fields to develop the table.

The second step is to select the field types (or data types in Access). The first field is EmployeeID; this field will be used later as the primary key. Notice in Figure 14.24 that the selected field type for

▼ FIGURE 14.23
Using a wizard to develop a table

Select the wizard to create a table.

In the Table Wizard, you can select from the template tables and fields.

You can select a Business or Personal database.

Table Wizard

Steps
1. Select fields
2. Set types and formats
3. Set primary key
4. Create table

Select fields for your table

This wizard helps you to create a table for your database. After and a sample table, choose the fields you want to include in y fields from more than one sample table.

Category: ⦿ Business   ○ Personal

Sample tables: Employees ▼

Available fields: OfficeLocation, PhoneNumber, Photo, Salary, SpouseName, SupervisorID, Title

Selected fields: EmployeeID, FirstName, LastName, SocialSecurityNumber, Address, StateOrProvince, City, PostalCode

Help   < Back   Next >   Finish   Cancel

Embedded database   HSQL database engine

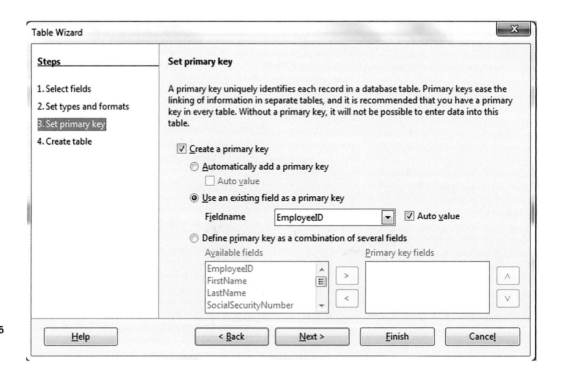

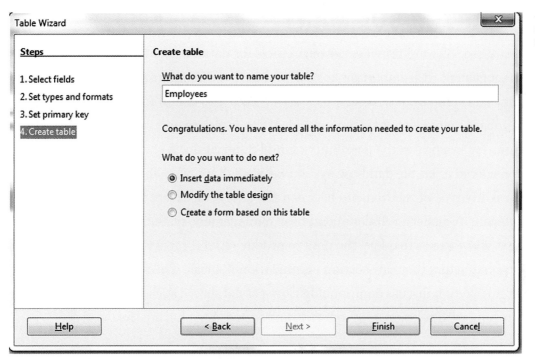

► FIGURE 14.26
Saving a table
using the wizard

Remember that every relational database system, no matter what brand, requires a primary key for every table.

EmployeeID is *Integer* and AutoValue is set to *Yes*, just as you did when you developed the table in Design view.

In Figure 14.25, you will notice that step three of the Table Wizard is to set the primary key. You can set a primary key using either one field or two fields. The *Create a primary key* checkbox at the top of the window should be checked. Select the field name you would like to use, as well as the *Auto value* checkbox, so that the EmployeeIDs are selected automatically and uniquely for your database.

The final step is to save your table using a name you choose and then decide

what you would like to do after you finish using the wizard. Select the *Insert data immediately* option, as shown in

Always remember to set your field character lengths while developing your table. Trying to change these after the database is developed can be time consuming. Also be careful not to delete any fields once you have populated the database with data, as this will delete all of the data in the deleted field.

Figure 14.26. Since you have already created the table based on the specifications you developed during the conceptual design process, you should not have to modify the table design. Form development is covered in Chapter 16, "Developing the User Interface and Sharing Your Database," so the final option here is not discussed at this time.

CHAPTER SUMMARY

Database software provides powerful tools for data manipulation and management. It is important to realize that modern organizations excel when they add value by successfully converting data into useful information. A database management system provides data integrity and, when developed properly, eradicates the possibility of data duplication. A spreadsheet is considered a flat file database system because there is no ability to query data or form any type of relationship between the data sets, except through sorting and filtering. A modern relational database management system uses relationships that allow a user to query the data to produce useful reports on trends and other market factors that can help an organization flourish. The remaining chapters in this section discuss additional features of databases such as creating and working with relationships, queries, and forms, and sharing the database.

CHAPTER EXERCISES

1. Think of a fictional business and formulate the data needs for the organization. The business should be small enough that you are able to manage it properly. (If it gets too big, you might struggle to complete the assignment.) Develop the data requirements and reporting requirements for the business. Write out the business concept on paper and prepare to discuss.

2. Using the database platform of your choice, develop one complete table that includes a primary key, data types, field names, and all validation requirements such as required fields and input masks. Use Design view to complete the assignment.

CHAPTER KNOWLEDGE CHECK

1

The Access database application is a Relational Database Management System (RDBMS) that is primarily designed to meet the data management needs of small to medium businesses.

○ True
○ False

2

From the Backstage view, you can complete a series of tasks that include opening a database, creating a database, changing settings, publishing your database to a SharePoint server or the Web, repairing your database, and even encrypting your database.

○ True
○ False

3

A database is simply a _____ of data structures that are organized to serve the particular needs of an organization or person.

○ **A.** Collection
○ **B.** Menu
○ **C.** Algorithm
○ **D.** Flat file system

4

An organization's _____ are the rules that govern an organization and are engrained in daily processes.

○ **A.** Theft problems
○ **B.** Session rules
○ **C.** Business rules
○ **D.** None of the above

5

Every database table field must have what is known as a data type.

○ True
○ False

6

Indexing is another form of _____ used in the database to prevent data duplication and speed up transactions.

○ **A.** Data cleansing
○ **B.** Data scrubbing
○ **C.** Data integrity
○ **D.** None of the above

7 A _____ of your database will ensure you can quickly recover and resume database usage.

- ○ **A.** Duplicate data
- ○ **B.** Backup copy
- ○ **C.** Outsourcing contract
- ○ **D.** None of the above

8 Data Type Parts are a feature designed to help you quickly develop tables and field data types.

- ○ True
- ○ False

9 Developing a database in Base follows virtually the same process as developing a database using Access.

- ○ True
- ○ False

10 Data integrity is assuring that the information in a database is _____ and has not become _____.

- ○ **A.** Correct, corrupted
- ○ **B.** Deleted, mirrored
- ○ **C.** Correct, copied
- ○ **D.** None of the above

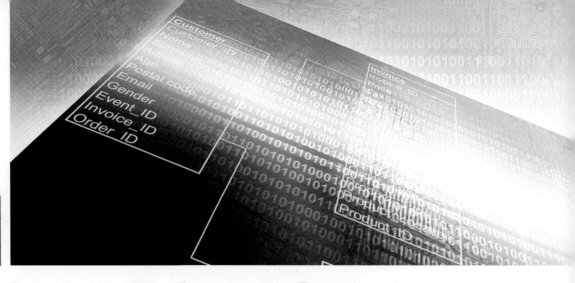

Developing Relationships, Queries, and Reports

In the previous chapter, you learned how to develop tables within the Access database management system. The real power of a relational database system comes with its ability to link tables using relationships, which is a great tool for querying and reporting based on related data within your database schema that will lead to the production of useful information. When you have completed this chapter, you will be able to:

- Develop and link related tables of data

- Edit relationships

- Develop consistency through referential integrity

- Develop a simple query with the Query Wizard

- Work with SQL view

- Create and print reports

WORKING WITH RELATIONSHIPS IN MICROSOFT ACCESS

Recall that in the previous chapter you developed single tables that had all of the elements needed to populate them with data. You created a table that contained a primary key, field names, and character lengths, along with required fields. You also learned that primary keys help develop relationships and that every primary key should have a unique identifier.

In this chapter, you will begin to learn about the real power of an RDDMS. You will find out how to establish a relationship and determine which types of relationships to develop and how to develop them. An example of the database in which you will create these relationships is shown in Figure 15.1.

Notice that the *JPDEvidenceInvenDB* file that you created in the previous chapter now has three tables. If you would like to follow along, you can use your own project from the last chapter or use the database file titled *JPDEvidenceInvenDB.accdb* available on the companion DVD.

The Show Table dialog box appears automatically the first time you open the

Relationships window and can be used to establish relationships between your database tables.

There are three tables for the database named EMPLOYEE, EVIDENCE_INVENTORY, and EVIDENCE_TRANSACTIONS. You will develop relationships between all three of these tables. There are three types of relationships that are available:

- One-to-one
- One-to-many
- Many-to-many

A one-to-one relationship is rarely used because all of the information in the relationship would be in one table. A unique circumstance where you have to divide a table with too many columns might be a circumstance in which you would use such a relationship. In any case, it is not considered good development practice to use this type of relationship.

The one-to-many relationship is the most common relationship. This relationship allows a row to be related to many rows in another table. For the example, you need to establish the relationships involved in the *JPDEvidenceInvenDB* file. You have

▼ FIGURE 15.1
JPDEvidenceInven DB database tables

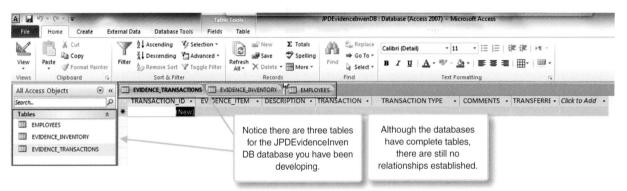

Notice there are three tables for the JPDEvidenceInven DB database you have been developing.

Although the databases have complete tables, there are still no relationships established.

three tables: EMPLOYEE, EVIDENCE_ TRANSACTIONS, and EVIDENCE_ INVENTORY. EMPLOYEE could contain the information for an evidence technician, a police officer, or another person authorized to check out evidence. An authorized person in the EMPLOYEES table could conduct many evidence transactions, but you could not have multiple employees involved in duplicate transactions concerning the same evidence item in question. Creating a one-to-many relationship here assures that tight controls are kept on evidence transactions. In legal matters, there is a term called "chain of custody." A person could easily make a mistake while keeping track of a chain of custody log in which every transaction is maintained manually. Using the database and establishing the correct relationships decrease the chances of losing chain of custody. Establishing this relationship will assure that only one person processes a single evidence transaction at a time but allows many items to be processed during the single transaction, as shown in Figure 15.2.

The many-to-many relationship is the most complex relationship available in Access. New users sometimes struggle to develop these relationships, but this is important to understand because such a relationship must be developed so that the *JDPEvidenceInvenDB* database works as designed.

A many-to-many relationship occurs when many rows are related between any two tables A and B so that neither provides a unique record in the other

One-to-many relationship.

table when associated. In the *JPDEvidenceInvenDB*, you have already established the one-to-many relationship between the EMPLOYEE and EVIDENCE_TRANSACTIONS tables. The issue to resolve, however, is the type of relationship that must exist between the EVIDENCE _INVENTORY and EMPLOYEE tables.

Recall that you started with three tables. In order to establish a many-to-many relationship in Access, you must use what Microsoft calls a junction table. A *junction table* is a table made up of a combination of the primary keys of both of the tables involved in the relationship. Figure 15.3 shows how the many-to-many relationship is established between the EVIDENCE_ INVENTORY and EMPLOYEE tables. This is because many employees can handle

CHAIN OF CUSTODY *is keeping tight control of who handles evidence collected at a crime scene each and every time it is handled without losing track of who had it last.*

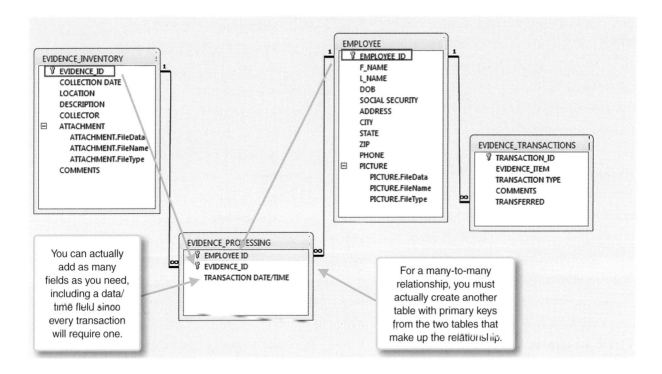

You can actually add as many fields as you need, including a data/time field since every transaction will require one.

For a many-to-many relationship, you must actually create another table with primary keys from the two tables that make up the relationship.

▲ FIGURE 15.3
Creating a many-to-many relationship

many inventory items and vice versa. For example, you might have to pull a report that details how many employees handled an evidence item in inventory. The same inventory item might have been handled by several different employees. You might also have several employees handle several different inventory items. This complex situation affects both tables, which is why a many-to-many relationship is needed.

Using the diagram in Figure 15.3, you can see that the junction table is called EVIDENCE_PROCESSING. This table will act as a junction point where a one-to-many relationship exists and uses the primary key from each table.

15.1.1 Defining Relationships

Now that you have learned about relationships and why they are used, you will learn how to build them in Access.

To begin building your relationships for the *JPDEvidenceInvenDB* file, open the database file named *JPDEvidenceInvenDB* from Chapter 14, available on the companion DVD. This is the base database with the EMPLOYEE, EVIDENCE_INVENTORY, and EVIDENCE_TRANSACTIONS tables. As you learned in the previous section, you need to establish a one-to-many relationship and a many-to-many relationship. Begin with the many-to-many relationship because you will need to create a new table as the junction point for this relationship. To create the fourth table that will link the EMPLOYEE and EVIDENCE_INVENTORY tables, open Design view and create a table named *EVIDENCE_PROCESSING*. Use the primary keys from the two tables combined; these will act as the primary key for the new junction table. You can also simply create a

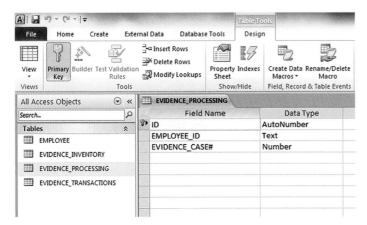

▲ FIGURE 15.4
Junction table for many-to-many relationship

field titled *ID* and identify it as the primary key, as shown in Figure 15.4.

You should develop two fields in the new table that have matching data types identical to the data types used in the primary key fields from the tables you are trying to link. The data types should be set to Number for the EVIDENCE_CASE# field since AutoNumber is already set in the primary tables. The EMPLOYEE_ID field is manually generated, so you would just match this field to the one that already exists in the EMPLOYEE table. If you decide to create a combined primary key, make both of the fields a combined primary key. You convert these by holding down the *Control* key and clicking on the row selector for both fields. You can then leave the table as is or you can add as many fields as needed. In this case, this table will just be used as a junction table with no other fields. You can create a third field titled *TRANSACTION DATE/TIME* and select a data type of *DATE/TIME*; this will produce a timestamp every time you submit a new record into the database. It is important that you also apply appropriate

settings to your field properties. The TRANSACTION DATE/TIME field should be a required field, as shown in Figure 15.5. This is actually a business rule because an evidence chain of custody log requires that dates and times be kept for every transaction. Although the database can work without the date/time settings for test purposes, you can adjust the field properties so that the database automatically produces a date/time stamp by taking the following steps:

1. Select the time format from the Format settings.

2. Enter *NOW()* as the Default Value.

3. Select *Never* from the Show Date Picker.

The date/time stamp field has been inserted into the EVIDENCE_PROCESSING table. The next step is to open the Relationships tool, which is located in the Database Tools ribbon, by pressing the Relationships button, shown in Figure 15.6. This tool will open a new window that will

▼ FIGURE 15.5
Setting field properties for TRANSACTION DATE/TIME

General	Lookup	
Format	General Date	Select the date/time format you would like to use.
Input Mask		
Caption		
Default Value	Now()	
Validation Rule		Typing Now() automatically provides a date/time stamp.
Validation Text		
Required	Yes	
Indexed	No	
IME Mode	No Control	
IME Sentence Mode	None	
Smart Tags		
Text Align	General	Select Never.
Show Date Picker	Never	

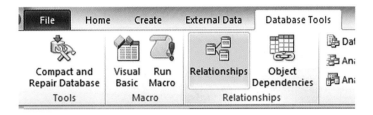

▲ FIGURE 15.6
Accessing the
Relationships tool

help you lay out all of the tables and visually assist you in establishing all of the required relationships discussed so far in this chapter.

Once you have selected the Relationships tool, the Show Table dialog box appears over your Relationships window work area. Here you are able to add the tables you want to link with relationships, as shown in Figure 15.7. You want to add all four tables in this case because you will be linking all of them to establish the one-to-many relationships and many-to-many relationships discussed in this chapter.

▼ FIGURE 15.7
Show Table dialog
box used to add
tables

Once you have added the tables to your workspace you, can hold and drag the tables to arrange them in a way that will best depict the relationships you intend to build. You can also hold your pointer on the edge of the table windows to widen or enlarge them to show all of the fields that are within each table. Begin by establishing the many-to-many relationships between the EVIDENCE_INVENTORY and EMPLOYEE tables using the junction table called EVIDENCE_PROCESSING, as shown in Figure 15.8.

Remember that the many-to-many relationship will be developed by creating two one-to-many relationships between the primary keys in the EVIDENCE_INVENTORY and EMPLOYEE tables. You will notice the three tables have been

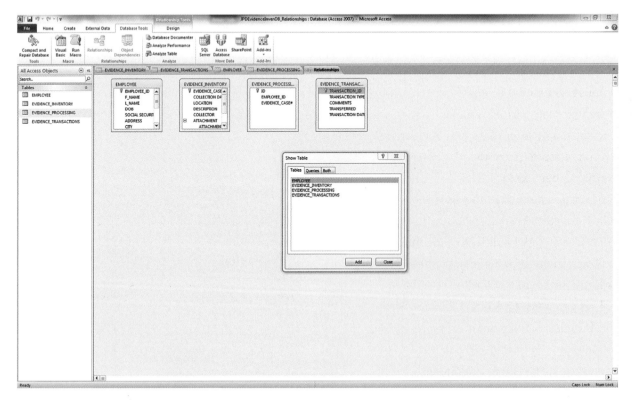

In the Edit Relationships dialog box, you can check the Cascade Update or Cascade Delete box to perform cascade updates or cascade deletes. If you were to use AutoNumber fields in the many-to-many relationship, you would not be able to use the Cascade Update setting because you cannot change AutoNumber fields.

arranged to make it easier for others to understand the relationships that are being prepared.

The first thing to do is to drag the primary key field from EVIDENCE_ INVENTORY to the EVIDENCE_PRO-CESSING/EVIDENCE_CASE# field. In essence, you are matching the same fields from both tables using a one-to-many relationship. When you do this, the Edit Relationships dialog box opens as seen in Figure 15.8.

Check the *Enforce Referential Integrity* box, but do not check either of the cascading options because some of the relationships use AutoNumber data types and you cannot update or modify AutoNumber fields. Do the same thing for the EMPLOYEE and EVI-DENCE_PROCESSING tables. Once you have taken these steps, you will notice you have one more relationship to establish

since you are now finished with the many-to-many relationships.

The final step is to establish the one-to-many relationship using the EMPLOYEE_ ID and TRANSFERRED fields from the EMPLOYEE and EVIDENCE_TRANS-ACTIONS tables, respectively, as shown in Figure 15.9. The TRANSFERRED field is related to EMPLOYEE_ID because this field tracks who made the transaction.

REFERENTIAL INTEGRITY *is designed to validate data in your database and to assure you do not delete or modify data in records that are established in the relationship. Selecting Cascade Updates means that all related records are updated when changes are made. Choosing Cascade Deletes means that all related records are deleted when changes are made. These two options help maintain referential integrity.*

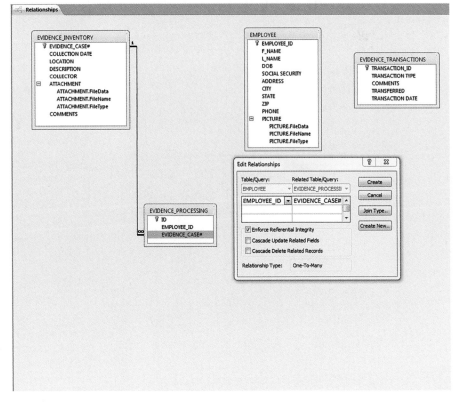

▶ **FIGURE 15.8**
Edit Relationships dialog box

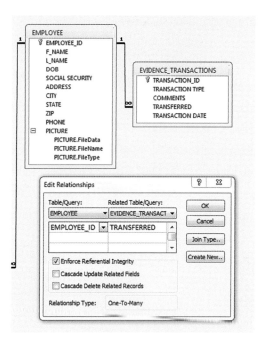

FIGURE 15.9 Setting a one-to-many relationship

TRANSACTIONS table has a field named TRANSFERRED. This field's sole purpose is to keep track of employees who were named in a particular transaction.

You can use the Lookup Wizard, shown in Figure 15.11, to create a list from existing values in a table field. In this example, you would have a drop-down menu that allows you to pick an employee from a list of employees authorized to make transactions. Select *Lookup Wizard* as the data type for the Transferred field to create a lookup field. The lookup field can be either a list you create or a list extracted from another table or query. Remember that choosing a field from another table automatically creates a relationship.

If you develop your own list, you do not have to worry about any additional relationships between tables. You must make an adjustment to ensure you can add new values to your list. In Figure 15.12, you can see the Field Properties window with the Lookup tab properties visible.

Field Name	Data Type
TRANSACTION_ID	AutoNumber
TRANSACTION TYPE	Text
COMMENTS	Memo
TRANSFERRED	Text
TRANSACTION DATE	

Text
Memo
Number
Date/Time
Currency
AutoNumber
Yes/No
OLE Object
Hyperlink
Attachment
Calculated
Lookup Wizard...

▲ **FIGURE 15.10** Selecting the Lookup Wizard

You will enforce referential integrity, but you will not use any of the cascading functions due to the data types used. Once you have established these relationships, the back end of your new evidence inventory database is ready to be populated with data that will be used for conducting queries and reports.

There are a few points to remember about a feature called the Lookup Wizard. For example, say you were looking to query data with a particular officer's name, but due to data entry errors you discovered it had been spelled several different ways in the database. It might be easy to discover this problem early on, but if a few years go by and there are several thousand transactions stored in the database, it would be really difficult to detect inconsistent data and thus your reports based on queries would ultimately be inaccurate. Notice in Figure 15.10 that the EVIDENCE_

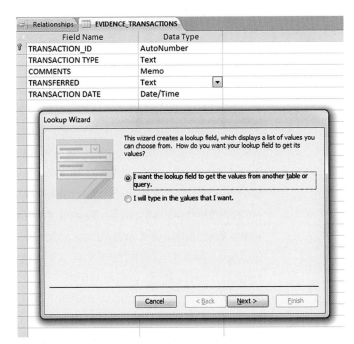

◀ **FIGURE 15.11** Creating a lookup field based on values you create

Set Allow Value List Edits to *Yes* so that you can modify any list you develop for any of your tables. A lookup list helps the database maintain consistent data.

Notice the cutaway section of what a lookup list will look like in the Data-sheet view. The small icon below the list appears every time you activate the list to search for a value. This icon allows you to change or add

▼ **FIGURE 15.12** Lookup Wizard and completed list snippet

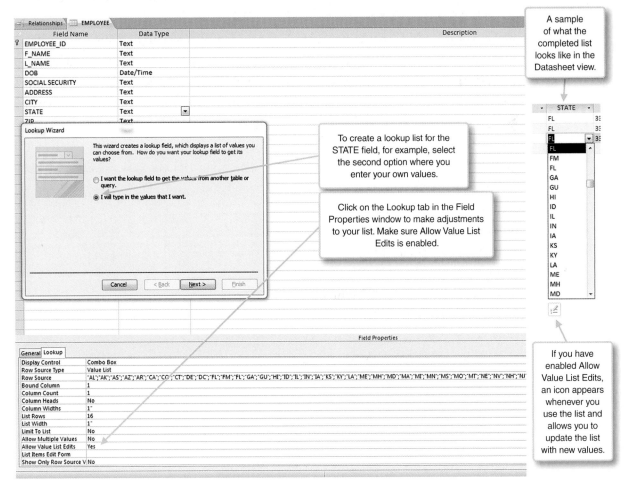

A sample of what the completed list looks like in the Datasheet view.

To create a lookup list for the STATE field, for example, select the second option where you enter your own values.

Click on the Lookup tab in the Field Properties window to make adjustments to your list. Make sure Allow Value List Edits is enabled.

If you have enabled Allow Value List Edits, an icon appears whenever you use the list and allows you to update the list with new values.

values to your list, but keep in mind that you must have the *Allow Value List Edits* option in the Lookup field properties set to *Yes*.

DATA MANIPULATION USING QUERIES

The ability to conduct queries in an Access database provides a wonderful way to manipulate data to produce useful information. Take the *JPDEvidenceInvenDB* database you have been working with in this chapter; imagine being the officer that runs the evidence room and has to use a manual sign-out log or an Excel spreadsheet to keep track of inventory and location throughout the facility.

Using the database you have been working on, you can now conduct queries that will help you find specific items located in specified locations throughout your warehouse; better yet, you can have a date/time stamp with a record of every transaction made related to evidence. You can certainly develop attractive forms that provide a beautiful user interface at this point, only to find that you can only display information contained in the tables. In order to manipulate and display data from more than one table, you have to develop queries.

Basic Queries

The following three methods can be used to conduct queries in the Access database management system:

- Query Wizard—The easiest way to create a basic query, although it has some limitations.

▶ FIGURE 15.13
Query Wizard

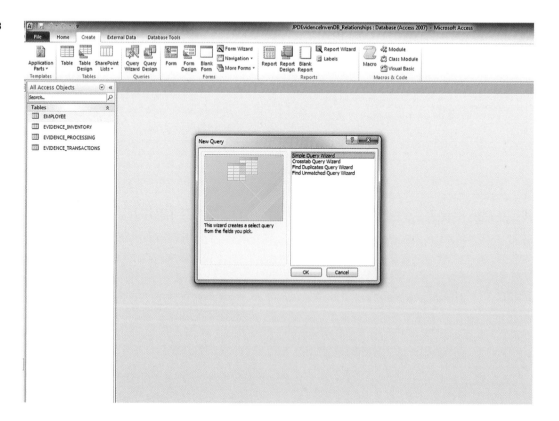

- Design view—Allows you to graphically develop queries and gives you more control over the data than when using the Query Wizard.

- SQL view—Lets you create queries using the SQL language.

The basic query can be created using the Query Wizard, although it usually will need some tuning in Query Design view to arrive at the best outcome for successful data manipulation. To begin using the Query Wizard, which is shown in Figure 15.13, select the *Create* ribbon and click the *Query Wizard* button to begin building a very basic query. The wizard will guide you through a series of questions to arrive at a basic query. You can then use Query Design view to tune your end result.

Using Query Design to Develop Queries

The preferred way to begin building your queries is with the Query Design view rather than the wizard since you will be using this option anyway. Before running any queries, populate each of the tables in the *JPDEvidenceInvenDB* file with a few records so that you actually have a return on your queries. You do not need to populate the junction table EVIDENCE_PROCESSING with any data. Once you have entered a few records, remember to save all of the tables even though the database automatically does this for you.

The next step is to start the Query Design view from the *Create* ribbon.

15.2.2

▼ FIGURE 15.14
Query Design view

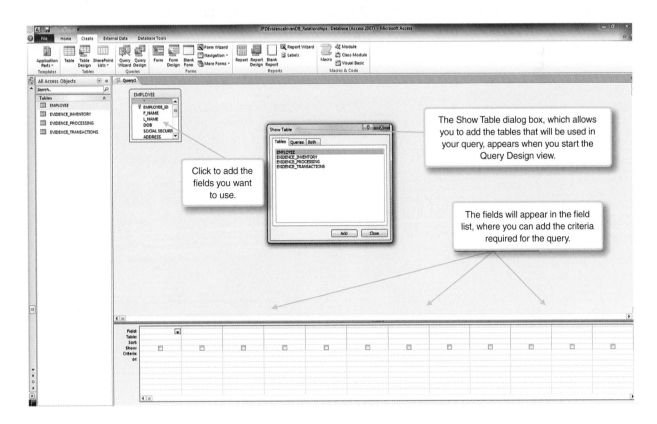

Starting the Query Design view brings up the Show Table dialog box, which allows you to select the tables you want to produce data based on the fields you choose. Once you select the table that you need from the Show Table dialog box, you must select the fields that you want to appear in the results of the query. This process is shown in Figure 15.14.

Once you have selected your fields, click the *Run* button to execute the query and view the results. If you are satisfied with the results, save your query by right-clicking on the *Query1* tab and selecting a name for your new query; saving the query adds it to the left pane of your database window. At the bottom of the interface in Figure 15.15,

▶ **FIGURE 15.15**
Executing
Completed Query

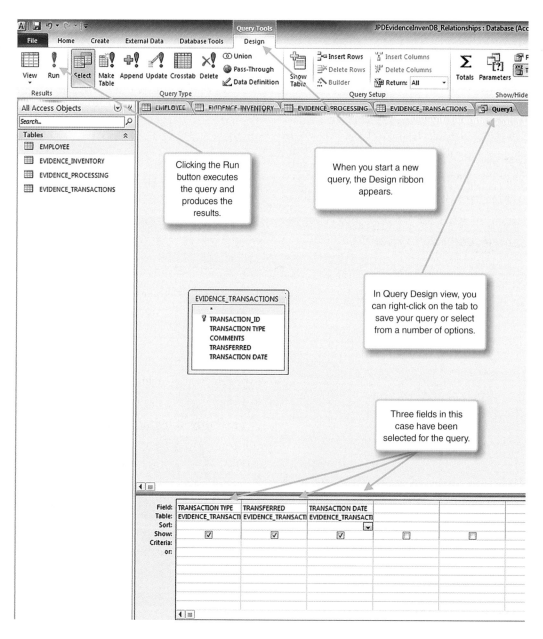

you will notice that there are additional options to refine your query results, including sorting in either an ascending or descending order. You can also hide one or more of the tables and add additional criteria.

Imagine you have 30 records in the database and you need to view just the records relating to transactions submitted by an employee with ID number 104. You might use the Expression Builder to request the records relating to 104, which would produce only the records from a specific employee.

By right-clicking on the criteria and selecting the *Build* option as shown in Figure 15.16, you can customize the query to give you specific results. If you wanted to find all records written by an employee with ID 104, you could simply enter *=104* in the criteria to produce just

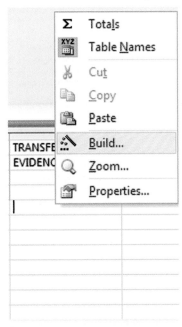

▲ **FIGURE 15.16** Accessing Expression Builder

those records. The final step is to save your query by right-clicking the *Query1* tab, entering a name for your query, and then selecting *Save*.

Working with SQL View

15.2.3

If you are wondering what is happening in the background of your query, then SQL view is the place to look. Structured Query Language (SQL) runs in the background of every relational database management system. Every professional database administrator knows this language and uses it to build databases and develop queries of all kinds. Since this is an introductory text, SQL language is not discussed in detail, but you should understand what it does. You can access the SQL View anytime by simply right-clicking on the Query tab and selecting *SQL View* or by selecting *SQL View* from the *Views* panel of the *Home* ribbon.

Implementing Inner and Outer Joins

15.2.4

Conducting a query from a single table really is of little value to you or an organization. Developing inner and outer joins gives you the power to harness the true ability of using a relational database system. An *inner join* is a join in which there are two linked tables (an existing relationship) that are used to join specific fields within the two tables to produce the desired results. If you do not have a relationship established, Access automatically helps you develop this relationship.

Figure 15.17 shows two linked tables composed of the EMPLOYEE and EVIDENCE_TRANSACTION tables. The figure also provides a snippet of the results that appear after you press the *Run* button on the ribbon. You should note that only the fields needed to produce the desired results are selected.

An *outer join* is one in which you have two directly unrelated tables. You learned previously that an inner join basically joins related tables. The inner join shows only records that are contained in both linked tables.

The outer join can be configured to show everything you would pull from an inner join, along with any unlinked records. Outer joins can help you locate unmatched records. Figure 15.18 shows all of the unmatching records in the database. Notice that there is an important filter added to the criteria as "Is Null,"

If you want to link the unmatched records, you could actually do so using SQL, which is beyond the scope of an introductory text. You could use the EMPLOYEE parent table and create a larger child table that would be the EVIDENCE_INVENTORY table. This would take a small adjustment with your relationships and the eradication of one table, but it could be done this way. Once you have learned more about SQL, you could come back and use the same schema modifying the UNION statement to link the transactions to the EVIDENCE_INVENTORY table.

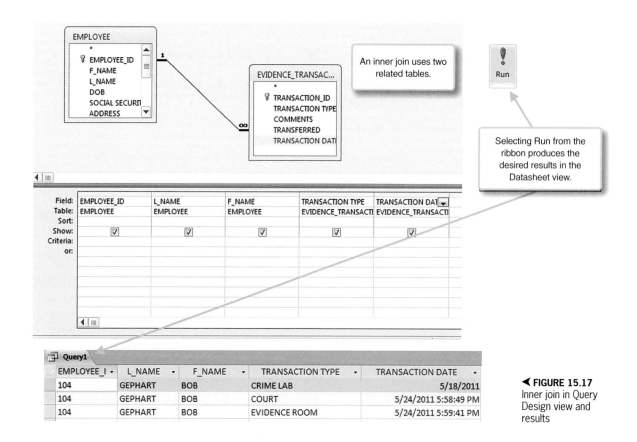

◄ **FIGURE 15.17**
Inner join in Query Design view and results

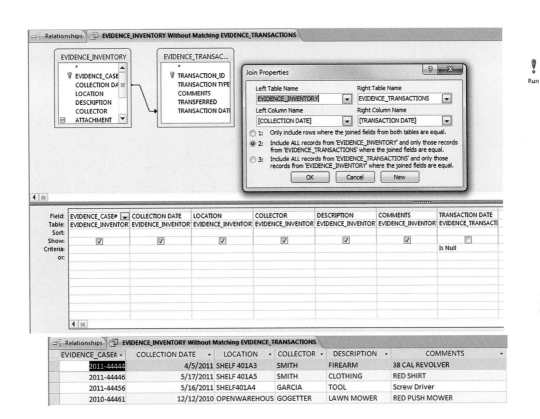

◀ FIGURE 15.18
Outer join using Query Design view to show unmatched records

Run

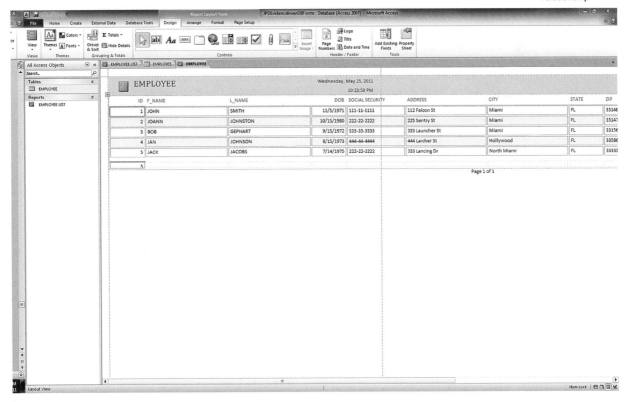

▼ FIGURE 15.19
Outer join using a many-to-many relationship

which forces the table to produce the transaction dates that are not linked.

There are also multiple joins that you can use when more than one table is involved. Remember the many-to-many relationships using a junction table. The database schema has been modified to show how you can conduct a multiple join. In Figure 15.19, the modified schema describes how you might conduct a multiple join when there is a many-to-many relationship.

LEARNING TO DEVELOP REPORTS

You have learned how to work with and develop tables, relationships, and queries. Simply looking at your information in Datasheet view is not very feasible for sharing. If you are planning on providing a copy of your data to the executive staff at your organization, you might want your data to look a little more presentable. You could print the data from your tables, but this does not look very professional. Developing a simple report can be done easily using one of the wizards or the Layout view. If you are following along with the example, open the *JPDEvidence-DBFORMS* file.

One of the easiest ways to create a report is from the Create tab within the Access ribbon. Simply select the *Create* tab and click the *Report* button. Figure 15.20 shows a very basic form that this action produces. Developing a report in this manner selects all the fields, and as you can see it does not provide an attractive report. Notice at the top of the figure you can see some options titled Report Layout Tools. These options let you change the layout to make it more aesthetically pleasing.

▶ **FIGURE 15.20**
Report Layout Tools

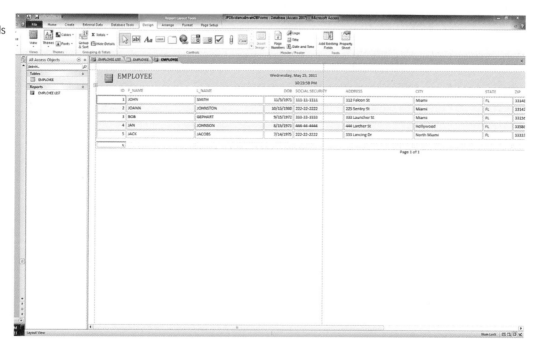

The Report Wizard is another easy way for beginners to create a simple report. The nice thing about the Report Wizard is that you simply answer the initial questions the application runs you through and it creates a basic report with just the fields that you require. Once the report is developed, you can modify and adjust the overall look in Design view.

Once your basic form is complete, you can see what the document will look like before printing to paper by selecting the *File* button, and selecting *Print*. A menu will appear that gives you the option to preview your form; select *Print Preview* to see your document, as shown in Figure 15.21. If you are satisfied, you can simply press the *Print* button on the far-left side of the ribbon.

This is just an introduction to Access reports; there are a significant amount of features available that allow the user and Access database developer to modify reports, include tables and fields from other tables, and change the overall appearance of the database.

UNDERSTANDING OPENOFFICE. ORG BASE RELATIONSHIPS

15.4

In this section, you will learn how Base handles relationships. Be aware that Base does not have the full functionality of Access. In the previous chapter, you created the *JPDEvidenceInvenDB* file for your tables. Just as in Access, you must develop relationships between tables in order to be able to conduct queries and manipulate data within the database management system. Begin by constructing the relationships shown in Figure 15.22.

Recall that you developed a similar relationship with Access earlier in the chapter. To access the Relation Design window, select *Tools* from the menu bar in the main window and click *Relationships*. When you open the Relations dialog box, shown in Figure 15.23, you will see

▼ **FIGURE 15.21**
Viewing a report in Print Preview

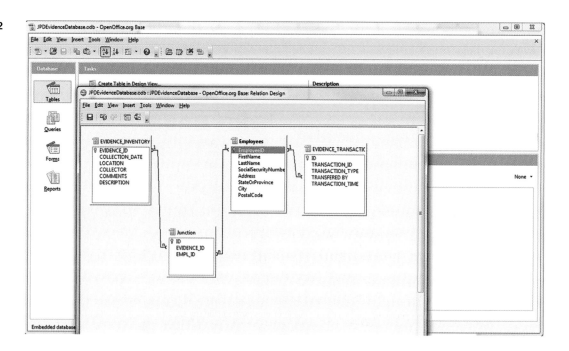

► FIGURE 15.22
Relation Design
window in Base

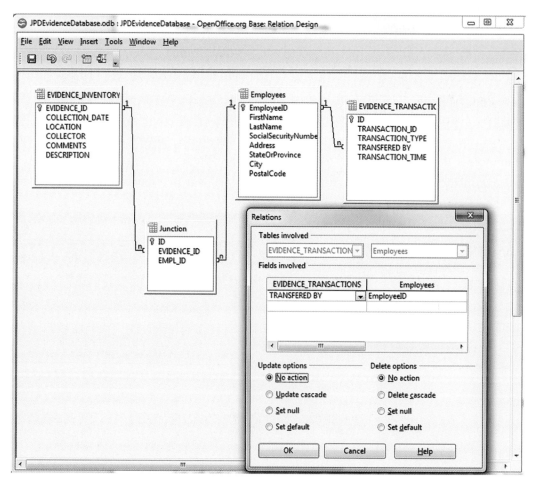

► FIGURE 15.23
Setting database
relationship
Update and Delete
options in Base

an environment similar to that in the Access application.

15.4.1 Developing Queries in Base

Queries are simple in Base in large part because there are fewer options available than there are in Access. As you have already learned, queries are used to manipulate and modify data in the database. One of the easiest ways to create a query in Base is to use the Query Wizard, as shown in Figure 15.24. Just as you did in Access, you can select fields from multiple tables to populate your database.

It is important to realize that with Design view you can create custom queries in Base to address your information needs. For example, you might have the need to conduct an advanced query that requires multiple queries.

15.4.2 Developing Reports in Base

The Report Wizard in Base is a bit less functional than what you might be accustomed to working with in Access. The Report Wizard does give you some functionality to conduct other operations that are beyond the scope of this text, but you should know that you can customize labels, grouping and sorting, and layouts. An example of the Report Wizard's output is shown in Figure 15.25.

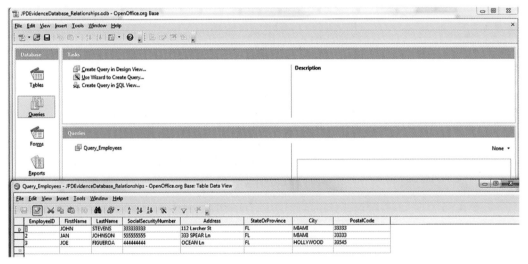

FIGURE 15.24 Using the Query Wizard in Base

Title:
Author: Charles Thies
Date: 5/26/11

EVIDENECE ID	COLLECTION DATE	LOCATION	COLLECTOR
0	40532	12 FORREST LN	JONES
1	40522	23 YACHT LN	MICHALES
2	40558	34 HILL DR	GARCIA

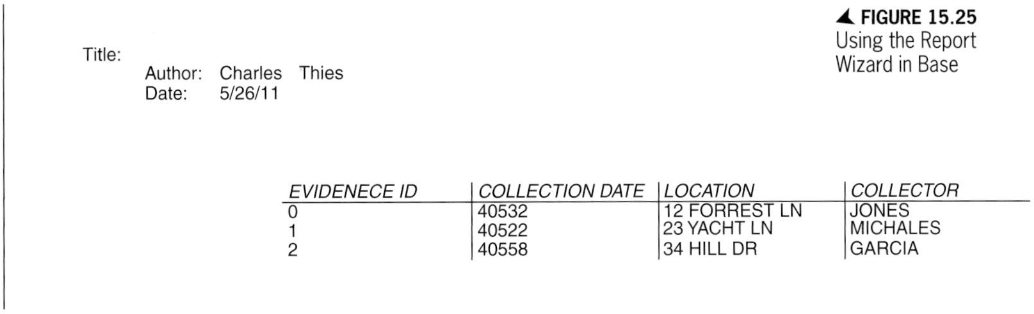

FIGURE 15.25 Using the Report Wizard in Base

CHAPTER SUMMARY

This chapter has addressed the development of both Access and Base reports and queries. There are numerous options and features available in both programs. This chapter was designed to give the new computer user a jump start on developing relationships, queries, and reports in both Access and Base. You have learned that you can complete each task related to queries and reports using different methods, depending on your level of training and how much time and effort you would like to contribute to a project. In Chapter 16, you will learn about developing the user interface and how a database can be shared with other users.

CHAPTER EXERCISES

1. Open either the Base or Access database file that already has the relationships built using the Design view and develop basic reports to meet what you feel are the needs of the organization.

2. Using Access or Base, develop three queries based on the tables in the *JPDEvidenceInvenDB* file that you feel would meet the needs of the organization. One of your queries should involve an outer join used to locate unmatched fields. Remember to populate your database with a few files to help you see the results of your database system.

3. Using the business case scenario you developed in the Chapter 14 exercises, develop the required database tables along with three queries and three reports.

CHAPTER KNOWLEDGE CHECK

1

What are the three types of relationships used in database work?

- ○ **A.** One-to-one, many-to-many, one-to-many
- ○ **B.** One-to-one, many-to-one, one-to-three
- ○ **C.** Many-to-one, one-to-one, three-to-one
- ○ **D.** One-to-one, many-to-many, many-to-none

2

Chain of custody is keeping a tight control of who handles evidence collected at a crime scene each and every time without losing track of who handled it last.

- ○ True
- ○ False

3

A one-to-one relationship is rarely used because all of the information in the relationship would be in one table.

- ○ True
- ○ False

4

A junction table in Access is an additional table that links two tables and is used to establish a many-to-many relationship using the primary key fields from both tables.

- ○ True
- ○ False

5

Outer joins can help you locate unmatched records.

- ○ True
- ○ False

6

The _____allows you to graphically develop queries and gives you more control over the data than when using the Query Wizard. Design view

- ○ **A.** Simple view
- ○ **B.** Query view
- ○ **C.** None of the above

7   _____ is designed to validate data in your database and to assure you do not delete or modify data in records that are established in the relationship. Table relationship

- ○ **A.** Data integrity
- ○ **B.** Referential integrity
- ○ **C.** None of the above

8   The Report Wizard is an easy way for beginners to create a simple report.

- ○ True
- ○ False

9   Developing a simple report can be done easily using one of the wizards or the Database Backup view.

- ○ True
- ○ False

10   An inner join is a join in which there are two linked tables (an existing relationship) that are used to join specific fields within the two tables to produce the desired results.

- ○ True
- ○ False

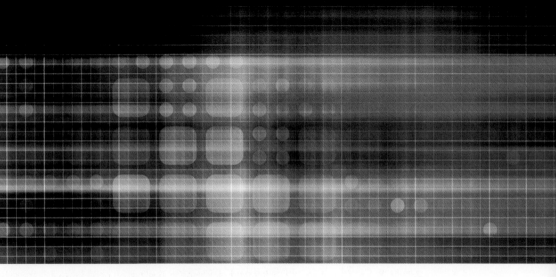

Developing the User •
Interface and Sharing
Your Database

In the previous chapter, you learned how to develop relationships between tables, and build queries and reports. Access is actually a self-contained program for complete development because you can create a complete application from the ground up. In this chapter, you will learn about building forms that provide the user with an appealing frontend to enter and review data within their database in place of having to enter data into the Datasheet view. Once you have completed this chapter, you will be able to:

- Develop simple forms

- Use forms to modify records

- Share your database with others

- Secure your database

- Use Base forms

16.1 DEVELOPING A SIMPLE FORM

Once you have completed your database, you will need to maintain, update, and occasionally modify data for a variety of reasons. Imagine having to open up the database backend each and every time to enter data into each individual datasheet. You can easily update and add records into one location using a custom form in an attractive user interface. Using forms also makes it easier for other users, such as employees or customers, to access the database in a format that is consistent with the organization's business rules.

A form has many advantages over working within the Datasheet view. Imagine having to update two or three tables in an inventory database. You can develop a single form that easily allows entering data into all three tables with total transparency to the user. If you were entering the data from Datasheet view, you would have to work with three different tables, which can become confusing and cumbersome for inexperienced users.

Access forms also support controls such as drop-down menu selections, customized buttons, lists, and checkboxes. Say an organization requires the ability to print out an employee's contact information and photograph. You can easily customize a control to bring up a custom form with the employee's data and photograph and quickly send the information to a printer. The form in Figure 16.1 was created using just one table; it displays text boxes, a checkbox, and record numbers and can be used to enter additional new records.

Creating a simple form is an easy process that can be accomplished using either the Layout view or the Form Wizard. You can use a table or a query to generate the desired results. Follow these steps to create a simple form in Layout view:

1. Highlight the table or query you would like to use for your form from the navigation pane on the left side of the Access window and select the *Create* ribbon.

2. In the *Create* ribbon, select *Form*. A new form will appear in Layout view, as shown in Figure 16.1. Notice that all of the fields in the table you select appear on the new form in the same order in which you selected them. Your fields might also appear large or small, depending on the field size you established when you developed the table.

3. From the Layout view, you can rearrange your fields in any manner you desire. If you have too many fields showing, you can simply select the underlying table (MATERIALS in this case) from the Datasheet view tab as shown in Figure 16.2 and right-click on the unneeded column to choose the option to hide it.

4. It is important to remember that there are two separate field size adjustments. You can modify your field size from the table's properties or you can

▼ **FIGURE 16.1**
Example Form view

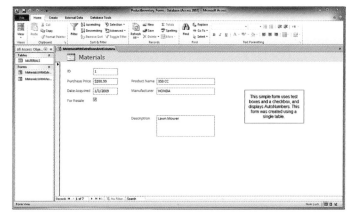

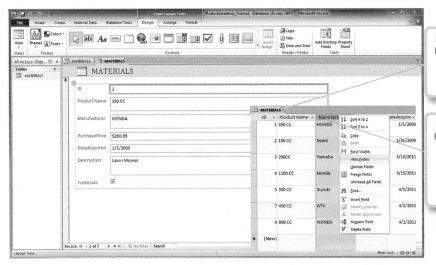

Notice that you can see the form in Layout view and a cutout overlay of the MATERIALS tab, which gives you a view of the MATERIALS table in Datasheet view.

If your text fields are too small or large or there are too many fields showing, you can modify the fields or hide them by selecting the column, right-clicking, and choosing the desired option from the Datasheet view.

▼ **FIGURE 16.2**
Using the MATERIALS table to develop a new form

manually adjust your field size within the form. Remember that you built tables and set properties that included data types and the number of characters allowed per field in Chapter 15. When you build your forms using this method, your text boxes may appear too large. To correct this issue, you can adjust the width in Layout view by highlighting the text field you want to change and adjusting the width or height by grabbing the edge of the text box and pulling it in the needed direction, as shown in Figure 16.3.

5. Finally, you can adjust your field names on the form by double-clicking on them and changing the text to your desired title. You can also adjust colors by using the options available in the Format ribbon. Once you are satisfied with the overall look and feel of your form, save the form by selecting *File* and then *Save*. If you forget to do this, you can be assured that the application will ask you to save before closing.

lets the user design the form with live data. Design view offers more tools to work with your form design, allowing you to apply more precise modification and power over controls on your forms, but has no access to live data. Form view lets you use your new form to modify, add, or delete records. Begin by searching for records using the Form view.

Take a look at the Materials form. Because the form manages items for a store, it is constantly changing. Sold products are removed from the database and new ones are added almost daily. Therefore, much time will be spent updating and searching for records each week.

▼ **FIGURE 16.3**
Adjusting width and height of textboxes

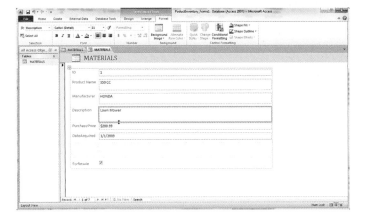

16.1.1

Using Forms to Add, Delete, and Print Records

You have learned how to develop a simple form using the Layout view, which

There are several ways to search for records. You might have a record that needs to be modified or you might need to acquire information about a specific record in the database. If you have just a few records in the database, you can use the control arrows in the lower-left corner of the form window; these are highlighted in Figure 16.4. If you have many files, you can conduct a search using the Search box at the bottom or, if you know the exact record you need, you can enter the number of the record, such as record 23 of 150.

Another option is to use the filter function to search for records. In Figure 16.5, a filter is being applied to the Product Name text box. Click inside the text box to which you would like to apply the filter and press the *Filter* button in the *Home* ribbon. Performing this action produces a drop-down box that gives you a list of product options available in the database. Each time you enter a new record into the database with a new product, this list will reflect the changes. For example, if you added "2500cc" for a new product record, the next time you ran the filter you would see "2500cc" in the list of filters.

▼ **FIGURE 16.4**
Searching for records

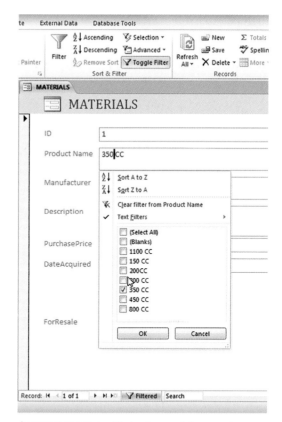

▲ **FIGURE 16.5** Using filtering to search for records

After locating a record, you can use the form to modify the record. You can delete text and add new data. You might remember from the previous chapter that you implement business rules into your database by applying constraints to the database tables. Additionally, you might have nulls implemented into your fields. If either of these applies to your table, you will receive errors while updating or modifying your records. If you realize you have made a mistake after updating a record, you can use the Undo button located on the upper-right side of your application window. This will undo your last change; you can click the Undo button as many times as necessary to undo previous changes.

Entering a new record can be done in one of two ways. You can click the *New*

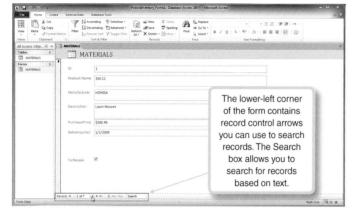

The lower-left corner of the form contains record control arrows you can use to search records. The Search box allows you to search for records based on text.

(blank) record button on the lower-left side of your form, shown in Figure 16.6, or you can press either of the left arrows to move to the next blank record.

To delete a record, click on the *Home* ribbon and from the *Records* panel select the drop-down menu next to the grayed-out *Delete* button; this will give you the option to delete your record. Another way to delete a record is to click the left margin of your form and press the *Delete* key on your keyboard. In both cases, the Access application will always ask you to confirm the deletion, as shown in Figure 16.7. When you confirm to delete the record, that record will be permanently removed from the database. There is no option that allows you to recover the deleted record once the entire process has been executed.

You can print the data on a form by clicking *File* and selecting the *Print* option from the menu. If you press Print selection in the Print dialog box that appears, Access will print every record in the database. If you have only a few records, as in the MATERIALS table, this might not be a problem, but if you have several hundred records you could be using up expensive toner on extra records you might not need to print. The best option is to print only the records you need. Choose the *Selected Record(s)* option in the Print dialog box as shown in Figure 16.8 and enter just the records you would like to print.

One more important tool at your disposal is the filter and sorting function within the Access database management system. Filtering and sorting can help you

To enter a new record, simply press the New (blank) record button.

▲ **FIGURE 16.6** Entering a new record

retrieve just the records that you need. For example, perhaps you want to select a specific type of product. In the Materials database, you could sort through the records to produce the records for items under a certain price or, since the table mostly contains motorcycles, you could search for one in a specific color.

A **FILTER BY FORM** *is a search that converts a preselected form into a search tool by adding a drop-down menu and tabs that can be used to add "or" criteria to produce precise search results.*

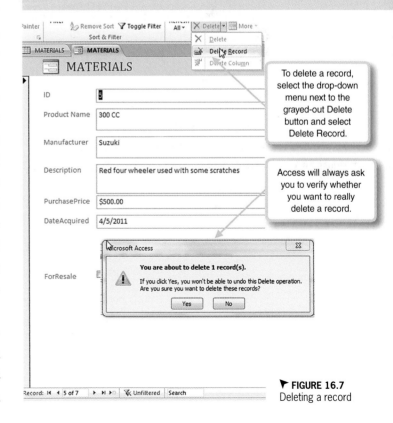

To delete a record, select the drop-down menu next to the grayed-out Delete button and select Delete Record.

Access will always ask you to verify whether you want to really delete a record.

▼ **FIGURE 16.7** Deleting a record

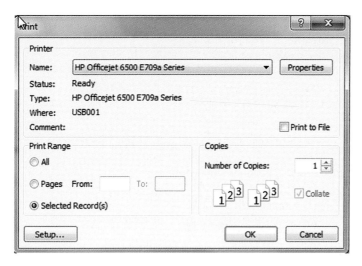

▲ FIGURE 16.8
Printing records

▼ FIGURE 16.9
Filter By Form

To begin using the filter options, you should use the Filter By Form feature. This is one of the advantages over sorting in Excel. The Excel application gives you the ability to sort and filter through data that is primarily flat in nature with no relationships between data; with Access, you have the additional power of relationships and the ability to query specific elements within the database. Adding the functionality to filter and sort gives the user the ability to produce precise results based on the data that has been entered into the database. There are three types of filters you can apply in Access:

- Filter by condition—Setting a condition produces results based on specific criteria within your data elements. You can produce records based on a filter condition that can include either numbers or text.

- Filter by selection—You use this filter when you conduct a query using existing data elements. For example, you might conduct a query that lists all motorcycles with a 350 cc engine.

- Quick Filter—This type of filter can be applied to one or more columns using a particular element or multiple elements.

The Filter By Form feature lets you convert one of your forms into a very powerful search tool, as shown in Figure 16.9. You apply a Filter By Form by opening the form where you would like to add search criteria, selecting the *Home* ribbon, clicking the *Advanced* button within the *Sort & Filter* panel, and then selecting *Filter By Form*.

A drop-down menu arrow will appear in the form along with three tabs at the lower-left corner of the form. The Look for tab is the original search form and the two Or tabs are used to add additional search criteria.

Once you have created a filter, you might wonder whether you need to recreate your filters each and every time you want to use

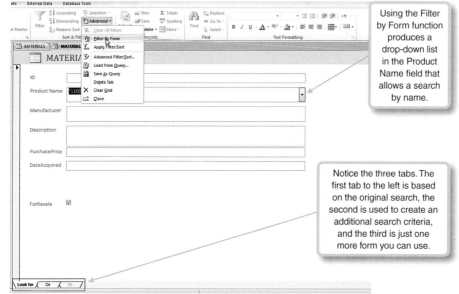

Using the Filter by Form function produces a drop-down list in the Product Name field that allows a search by name.

Notice the three tabs. The first tab to the left is based on the original search, the second is used to create an additional search criteria, and the third is just one more form you can use.

one. The answer to this is absolutely not; you can quickly and easily save a filter as a query. By clicking on the *Advanced* button in the *Sort and Filter* panel of the *Home* ribbon, you can select the *Save As Query* option shown in Figure 16.10. Once this selection is made, the Save as Query window will appear. Select a name that clearly indicates the type of filter you are using to help you and your users determine what the available redeveloped filter does.

You can add further functionality to the Materials form you have been using, as shown in Figure 16.11. A split form gives the user a multidimensional view of the data by displaying the original form with a one-record-at-a-time view of the data along with a split view containing a list of other records. This lets you compare records listed in the table. You will notice in Figure 16.11 that record 1 is highlighted in the top view and also displayed in the form below.

If you want to scroll through your records in the top portion, you can easily highlight other records to have them appear in the form in the lower portion of the screen. Follow these steps to acquire a split view of your data:

1. Using the Materials form, select the Design view.

2. In the Property drop-down list, select *Form*.

If you are trying to create a split form and you do not see your property sheet, you must select *Form Design Tools* while displaying your form in Design view, select the *Design* ribbon, and then press the *Property Sheet* button.

3. Finally, select the default view and choose the *Split Form* option; you will notice the form splits when you change your view back to Form view.

You can easily customize your form from Design view by using the Arrange tab within the Form Design Tools. The Arrange tab gives you the ability to rearrange rows and columns or merge and split cells. Figure 16.12 illustrates the use of merging and splitting to bring the Product Name field and Manufacturer field closer together to make the form look more aesthetically pleasing.

As a final thought on Access forms, note that this chapter simply touches on forms at an introductory level; there are significantly advanced features available that are beyond the scope of what is covered here. You can create subforms, apply macros, and even use programming code to add additional functionality to your forms.

▲ FIGURE 16.10
Saving a filter as a query

USING OPENOFFICE. ORG BASE FORMS

16.2

In the previous chapter, you learned about developing databases using the OpenOffice.org version of Access called Base. If you read through the entire chapter, then you already know that forms in a database not only make it aesthetically pleasing to view data, but also help you to efficiently manage how data is entered into the database. It is quite cumbersome to enter data using Base, especially what adding related data into individual tables. There is no

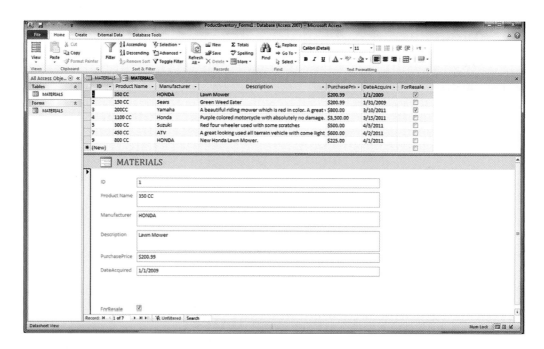

► FIGURE 16.12
Splitting and
merging cells to
customize a form

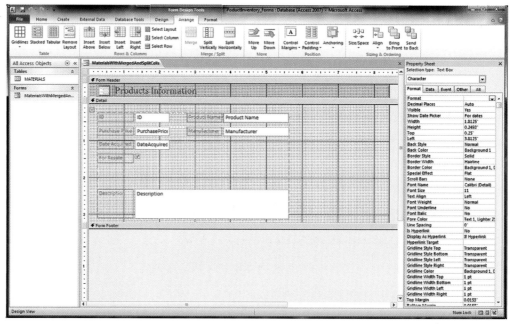

Datasheet view in Base; even in Access, the Datasheet view is too cumbersome to be able to rely on it for managing data entry and modification. In Base, you must open the individual tables to view or enter data, so developing custom forms to aid in the data management effort is quite helpful.

To develop forms in Base, you can use either Design view or the Form Wizard. As you may have already noticed as you have worked your way through the chapters, Base operates on a completely different scale from Access, and the two applications have few similarities.

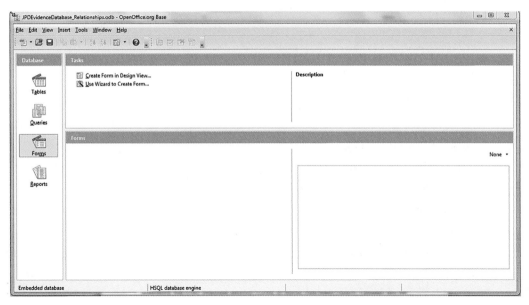

Base appears differently and works completely differently.

In Figure 16.13, you can see that the Base interface is divided into three areas: the Database options on the left-side pane, the Tasks area at the top of the window, and the Forms area, which is currently empty. You will first create a simple form with the Form Wizard using the Employees table you created in Chapter 14. If you wanted to add form controls, it might be better to use Design view, but for this instance just begin with the wizard. Highlight *Forms* in the left pane and then select *Use Wizard to Create Form* to begin developing the new form.

Once you have selected the wizard option, the Form Wizard appears, as shown in Figure 16.14. The Form Wizard provides several options. The most important

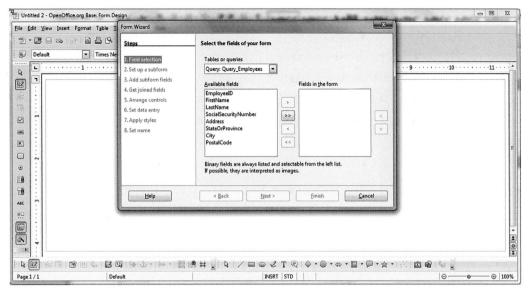

▶ **FIGURE 16.15**
Using the Form
Wizard to arrange
controls

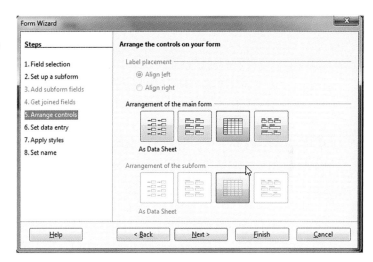

name option and saving your new form.

Figure 16.16 shows the completed form design.

You can use the Form Wizard and go through the same eight steps to create a form that uses a sub-form. In order to create a subform, you must have a relationship between the tables being used. Since there is a pre-established relationship between the Employees table and the EVIDENCE INVENTORY table, you can develop a subform using these two tables. Figure 16.17 shows the new form that contains a subform based on the EVIDENCE_INVENTORY table.

When working with forms in Base, your options are extremely limited in comparison to what is available in the Access platform. Although Base is capable of producing very simple projects, you will notice as you work with the application that your form's graphical capabilities are limited, though sufficient to complete the assignments in this chapter.

decision here is to choose which table or tables to use to develop a custom form. If you have pre-established relationships, you can use fields from multiple tables.

Since the form you are developing is a very simple form, use a single table called Employees.

Notice in Figure 16.15 that the left pane has a total of eight steps to complete the form. Since you are creating a simple form, do not select to add a subform or joined fields. The steps include using the Arrange controls option to determine the layout of your form, The Set data entry step tells the application how you want users to enter or modify data in the database. The Apply styles option lets you define the presentation and look of your form through the application of color and style. The final step should be to name the form by selecting the *Set*

▶ **FIGURE 16.16**
Completed simple form

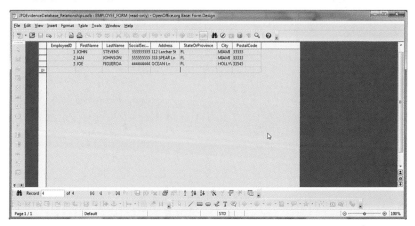

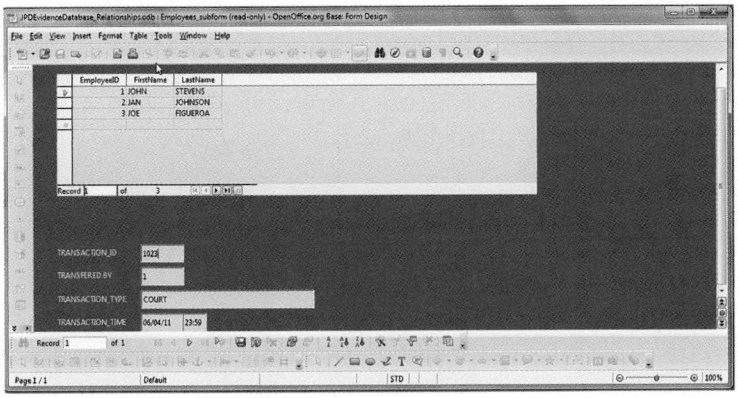

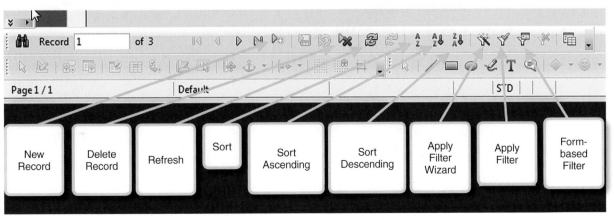

◀ FIGURE 16.17 Completed form with subform

advanced form controls that can be used by advanced users to complete projects. You can add form controls by developing your form in Design view. To enter Design View, simply close your form and reopen it by first clicking on the *Forms* button in the left pane of the Base interface and then right-clicking on the desired form. Figure 16.19 shows the EMPLOYEE_ FORM file in Design view.

Always remember when developing forms that contain subforms to make sure that the corresponding fields in each table also have matching field data types. Keep the following three guidelines in mind when developing a subform:

- Fields in subforms cannot be a primary key from the chosen table.

- Each pair of fields used must have matching field types.

- One of the fields from the parent table must be the primary key.

Sorting in Base is a significantly different process than it is in the Access application. Figure 16.18 shows the controls at the lower-left side of your form that you can use to execute various sorting and filtering tasks. Among these are performing ascending and descending sorts and applying form-based filters. The far-left side of this form control provides the ability to add a new record or delete a record. Keep in mind that when you hit the Delete button, Base will always ask for verification to ensure you really want to delete a record, so pressing the Delete button does not automatically erase a record.

Assume you want to test your skills and further customize your Base forms using Design view. Base also has some

▼ FIGURE 16.18 Sorting and filtering controls for forms in Base

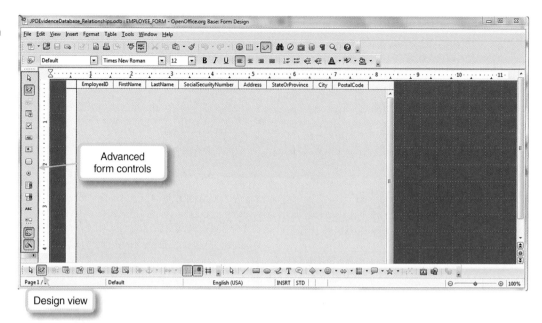

Advanced
form controls

Design view

16.3 SHARING YOUR ACCESS DATABASE WITH OTHERS

Access 2010 has enormous Web capability to share your database with others that is beyond the scope of this chapter. You can use SharePoint to share your Access database application with others in your organization.

SharePoint is also a massive topic and is beyond the scope of what you are learning here. However, you should be familiar with the fact that you can share your Access database by publishing your application to a SharePoint server. In addition to SharePoint, you can place your database in a shared location, such as the shared network drive of your organization's server, where up to 40 people can access the database at any one time. If your user base is much more than that, it is time to upgrade your Access database to Microsoft SQL Server, which is an industrial-strength platform that allows many more users to access your application. Like SharePoint, SQL Server is an advanced topic, and using it can be a difficult task if you lack significant experience; note that there are courses that focus solely on SQL Server.

One of the most common ways for a beginner to share an Access database is when it is hosted from a central location on a network-based asset such as a network drive or using a UNC.

It is important to realize that although 40 people can be in the database simultaneously, only 15 can modify records at a time. There are Access gurus who claim to have increased these numbers significantly, but these experts are coding and tuning the

SharePoint is a Microsoft enterprise product used to provide organizations with a Web-based repository where users can collaborate on documents and share all types of information.

database to a point where it operates in an extremely efficient manner.

There are some steps you have to take to share your database on your organization's network. First, you will need to prepare the database by splitting it into two parts. Use the Materials database for this example. In the *Database Tools* ribbon, select *Access Database* from the *Move Data* panel, as shown in Figure 16.20. Prior to splitting the database, you will need to make a backup of the database. Once you have split the database into two files, you will have a file that contains all of your forms, queries, and reports as the frontend and a secondary file with all your data. If you have password protected your database, you will need to add a password to the backend file after the split. Once the split occurs, you can store the backend in a central network location and have every authorized user install the frontend of the database on their computer or have an icon that links them to the frontend at a central location.

You also need to consider security; assume you now have the frontend, but you realize that just about anyone can make changes to the forms, reports, and queries you have developed. Adding a level of security is actually a pretty easy step and it should be done after you split the database. You can simply create what is known as an .accde file by opening your frontend file

A Universal Naming Convention (UNC) is an industry-wide way of identifying resources on the network rather than using drive letters to map resources. Using a UNC is far more efficient since drive letters can appear differently to users in different parts of the organizations. A UNC might look something like \\ PersonnelServer\Training\TrainingDB.

after you have completed the split, choosing the *File* menu, selecting *Save and* Publish and clicking *Make ACCDE*, as shown in Figure 16.21.

Completing your ACCDE file secures your database by keeping unauthorized users from modifying your objects. You can now store your backend file in a central location and distribute the frontend file to the users of your choice.

OPEN OFFICE The Base database application is quite limited in its security capabilities, lacking the ability to add passwords or split database files. This is one of the biggest flaws with Base.

There are several options available to secure your database. As a beginner, one of the easiest options for you is to apply Windows security to your database. Simply right-click on the backend file you created during your split and access the properties. Once the properties window is open, select the Securities tab and decide which users can make changes to the database

◀ FIGURE 16.20
Accessing the Database Splitter Wizard

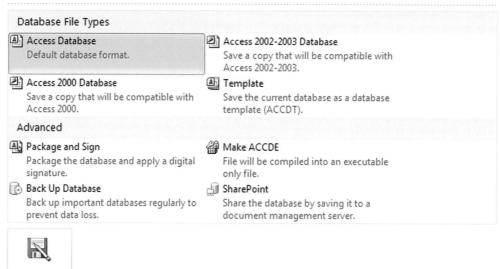

▲ FIGURE 16.21
Save Database As options in Access

▲ FIGURE 16.22
Accessing the Compact and Repair Database tool

or should be denied Access to the database altogether. It is important to realize that if you work in a larger organization, you may have to consult with your system administrator before you make any of these types of changes.

Finally, maintenance is a critical component to your database and should be performed frequently. As the database grows, it stands the chance of suffering from corruption, so it is important that you take some steps to keep your database from becoming inoperable due to improper maintenance. The Compact and Repair Database feature should be used regularly on the backend file you created when you split your database. As the backend file grows with data, you should perform this task frequently. Depending on the size, you may perform this task a couple of times per month to a few times per week.

You can access the Compact and Repair Database feature by opening your backend file, clicking on the *Database Tools* ribbon, and clicking the *Compact and Repair Database* button within the *Tools* panel, as shown in Figure 16.22. This process can take some time. Be sure to have a current backup of all of your data prior to making any adjustments and as part of your overall maintenance plan.

CHAPTER SUMMARY

This chapter covered developing forms in both the Access 2010 and Base environments. You should now be able to plan, design, and develop very basic database applications. Your next step to learn more might be to take an intermediate or advanced course on Access or OpenOffice. You probably have also learned that the Base portion of the OpenOffice.org suite is quite limited in the area of security and sharing. Hopefully these areas will improve in future editions. For now, any advanced application development you pursue should probably focus on Access. Congratulations on completing this text! You should now have the skills you need to manage your productivity at home or at the office.

CHAPTER EXERCISES

1. Using the small database for the fictional business you created in Chapter 15, further develop it by adding any needed relationships, and build simple forms to support each table within the database. After you have completed the forms, develop 10 fictional records to populate your database tables and create 3 reports that are useful to your business.

2. Using the database assignment from the previous exercise, split your database and prepare it for sharing as a network resource by locking down the frontend as described in this chapter and use Windows security to lock down the backend file. Note that this assignment will not work on the Base platform due to its limitations.

CHAPTER KNOWLEDGE CHECK

1 Access forms support advanced controls such as drop-down menu selections, customized buttons, lists, and checkboxes.

- ○ True
- ○ False

2 Design view actually allows you to apply more precise modification and power over controls on your forms.

- ○ True
- ○ False

3 If you have just a few records in the database, you can use the _____ in the lower-left corner of the form to search for records.

- ○ **A.** Arrow finder
- ○ **B.** Control arrows
- ○ **C.** Network resource
- ○ **D.** Flat file

4 One option to delete a record is to click the _____ of your form and press the Delete key on your keyboard.

- ○ **A.** Left margin
- ○ **B.** Right margin
- ○ **C.** Top edge of the window
- ○ **D.** None of the above

5 Filtering and sorting can help you retrieve just the records that you need.

- ○ True
- ○ False

6 Base will always ask for _____ to ensure you really want to delete a record, so pressing the Delete button will not automatically erase a record.

- ○ **A.** Data
- ○ **B.** Verification
- ○ **C.** Integrity
- ○ **D.** None of the above

7

A simple form in Base consists of several fields selected by using _____ or _____.

- ○ **A.** Design view, Form Wizard
- ○ **B.** Form controls, font color
- ○ **C.** Sorting, filtering
- ○ **D.** None of the above

8

SharePoint is a Microsoft enterprise product used to provide organizations with a Web-based repository where users can collaborate on documents and share all types of information.

- ○ True
- ○ False

9

A Universal Naming Convention (UNC) is an industry-wide way of identifying network resources on the network rather than using drive letters to map resources.

- ○ True
- ○ False

10

Completing your ACCDE file secures your database by keeping unauthorized users from modifying your objects.

- ○ True
- ○ False

Additional Productivity Software

ADOBE® READER®

While a number of common productivity tools have been covered in this text, there are a few additional resources that are helpful for office and personal productivity. Adobe Reader is a free application available for both Windows and Macintosh that reads Portable Document Format (PDF) files; in fact, it was Adobe that invented the format. There are a number of other utilities that can perform this task, such as the native Preview application that comes preinstalled on Macintosh computers. However, Adobe Reader has a number of useful tools that make it worthwhile to have installed even if you primarily use another application to read PDF documents.

The latest version of Adobe Reader can be downloaded from *www.adobe.com/downloads* regardless of the operating system you have. Once you have it installed, open it and take a look at the different tools and utilities available. The Adobe Reader interface for Windows is shown in Figure A.1.

There are additional services and tasks that can be performed with the paid versions of Adobe Acrobat. The commercial version of Acrobat installs plug-ins for the Microsoft Office applications to create customized PDF files in addition to the standard PDF export that is included. You can also use Adobe PDF as a print option for any application when you have the commercial version of Acrobat installed; this works similarly to printing to Microsoft Office OneNote, which is covered later in this appendix. You can also subscribe to paid services at *www.acrobat.com* to create and share PDF files online. These online services are accessible from within Adobe Reader if you have an account. The account creation process for the Adobe Web site (*www.adobe.com*) and Adobe Acrobat Web site (*www.acrobat.com*) is free.

Portable Document Format (PDF)

The Portable Document Format was invented by Adobe Systems in 1993; it is an open standard (ISO32000) for use in capturing

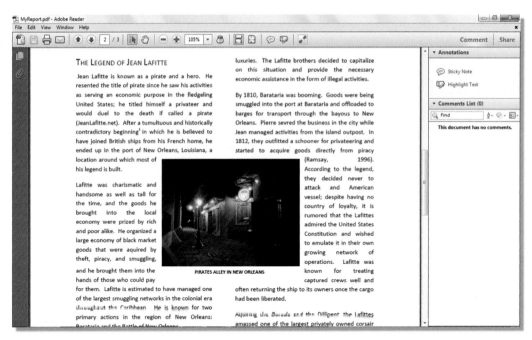

rich media in an application-independent, exchangeable file format. This allows it to be used on any operating system and version without altering the document's appearance. The standard now also incorporates support for live hyperlinks within the document, making PDF one of the preferred formats for distributing documents on the Web. The ability to control the final layout and format of the media in the production of a PDF has been one of the factors influencing its adoption.

If you are going to use the Internet to gather information or conduct research, you are likely to encounter PDF files. They are also a good format for transmitting files to recipients with unknown software and operating systems, such as sending a resume when the potential employer does not specify a document type for submission. PDF is common enough that you can send the document with relative assurance that anyone can read it. Make sure that you have

some means of reading this document type as well, whether or not you use the official reader from Adobe.

PDF files can also be used as forms with predefined areas that are editable. Creating these forms requires the commercial version of the software, but you may encounter PDF forms for work or personal use. To complete a PDF form (which can be done in any current version of the software), simply click into the editable area and type as you normally would on the keyboard; the text will appear in a predetermined font and size and will appear only in the areas that are specified for completion. When you are done, use the *Save As* (or *Save a Copy*) function and select *PDF* as the file type. You cannot save certain modifications or enhancements without the commercial version of the software.

Adobe Reader Tools   A.1.2

In addition to linking to the services of *www.acrobat.com*, the current versions of Adobe Reader have a number of useful tools for viewing PDF documents. You can easily set your zoom percentage to display the document at the size you want. Jumping from page to page is also an easy task using the standard toolbar at the top of the interface. There are differences in functionality between the two versions that are available, so you should select the section that is applicable to you.

A.1.2.1 *Adobe Reader X for Windows*

The Windows version of Adobe Reader allows you to add highlights and comments to the document. The benefit of marking up a PDF file is that the markup does not affect the original document, so it can be added to and removed from the file easily without concern for formatting or causing changes to the document. It should be noted that these marks are typically not suitable for printing, so they would just be for the sake of document review, personal notes, and collaboration. You can also save your document as unformatted text using the *File* menu and choosing *Save As* and then *Text*.

In Adobe Reader X for Windows, the Highlight tool for marking text is located in the standard toolbar across the top of the interface, as is the Comment tool. To make a comment, click where you want to place the comment within the document, and a smaller window will appear for you to add your text. Close this window when you are finished; you can open it again by double-clicking the icon for the comment within the document. Clicking on the icon once and dragging it lets you move the comment. To perform a standard keyword search on the document, select the *Edit* menu and choose *Find*. You can also select the *View* menu, then *Read Out Loud* and *Activate Read Out Loud* to have an automated reader speak the line of text on which you click. This requires the default selection tool to be active. To deactivate this feature, select the *View* menu, choose *Read Out Loud*, and then choose *Deactivate Read Out Loud*.

Adobe Reader X has some other tools that are helpful. In the *Edit* menu, you can select *Copy File to Clipboard* to copy the entire file contents to the system clipboard. You can also select *Take a Snapshot* from the *Edit* menu; this allows you to click and drag across an area of the document that you want to copy and save it to the system clipboard as an image. If you simply click in the document, any area that is visible will be copied to the clipboard as an image. You must select another tool to disable the Snapshot tool once it is active.

To add additional tools to the standard toolbar, choose the *View* menu, select *Show/Hide*, and then select *Toolbar Items*. This submenu has several options for tools that you may find useful. The default tool that is active is the *Select* tool, which is available under the *Select and Zoom* submenu. This tool allows you to select text and copy it to the system clipboard. Under the *Rotate View* submenu, you will find the *Clockwise* and *Counterclockwise* commands; these can be used to rotate a page that is not oriented properly on your screen. Under the *Select and Zoom* submenu, the *Hand* tool is useful for scrolling the document quickly on the visible window;

clicking selects the document and moving the mouse repositions the document within the window. Also under the *Select and Zoom* submenu is the *Loupe* tool; this tool creates a new window that enhances the magnification of a small selection of the document wherever the mouse is clicked, allowing you to magnify a portion of the document for closer examination. This is particularly useful for examining images.

A.1.2.2 Adobe Reader 9 for Macintosh

The functionality and tools available for Adobe Reader on the Macintosh are very similar to those found in the Windows equivalent. An example of the interface of Adobe Reader 9 for Macintosh is shown in Figure A.2. Unlike its counterpart in

▼ FIGURE A.2
Adobe Reader 9 for Macintosh interface

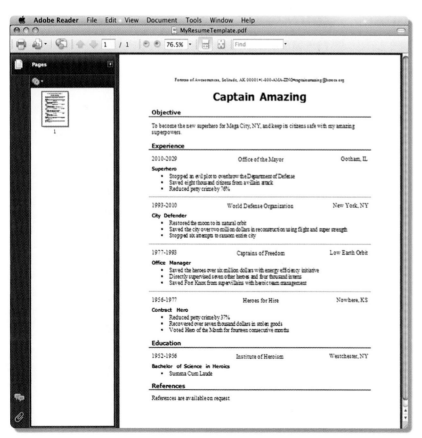

Windows, Adobe Reader 9 does not allow you to add comments or highlights to the text. You can still take advantage of several of the unique tools that Adobe Reader has to offer and can use Adobe Reader to export the text of your document (without any formatting) by selecting the *File* menu and choosing *Save as Text*.

From the *View* menu, you can select *Read Out Loud* and then *Activate Read Out Loud* to enable the automated reader to speak the selected line of text. The default selection tool for the cursor must be active for this to work correctly. You can turn off the automated reader by selecting the *View* menu, *Read Out Loud*, and then *Deactivate Read Out Loud*.

The Tools menu contains several tools of interest located in the Select and Zoom submenu. The *Select* tool is active by default; it operates like any cursor and allows you to click and drag to select text from the document that you can copy to the system clipboard. The *Hand* tool allows you to click on a portion of the document and drag it around the window interface to quickly position it as you want it. The *Loupe* tool lets you click on a portion of the document to open a window with that selection zoomed in to a much larger magnification; this is particularly useful for examining images. You can use the *Snapshot* tool to copy a selection of the document to the clipboard as an image; to create a snapshot once the tool is selected, just click and drag within the document to select the area you want to copy. Clicking once inside the document will copy the entire visible area of the document to the clipboard. You must select another tool to disable the Snapshot tool once it is active.

MICROSOFT ONENOTE FOR WINDOWS

Microsoft OneNote is a Windows-exclusive program that acts like a digital notebook and helps you manage personal and work files in separate notebooks. You can use it to take notes with ease and link notes to other documents. It can also be used as a printer to store any printed information you want to keep and store it on its own page for easy organization.

The drag-and-drop functionality and the ability to dock the program beside another Office application make it a useful note-taking and organization application.

Anatomy of Microsoft OneNote 2010

Figure A.3 shows the interface for OneNote 2010. This displays the Quick Access toolbar, the ribbon interface, and the different levels of organization available in OneNote. Notice that the Quick Access toolbar contains icons called Dock to Desktop and Full Page View. These allow you to switch between the two primary operating modes on OneNote. Dock to Desktop fixes OneNote to the side of your screen and allows you to take Linked Notes, which are described in Section A.2.3. The Full Page View icon is used to return to the standard mode of operation.

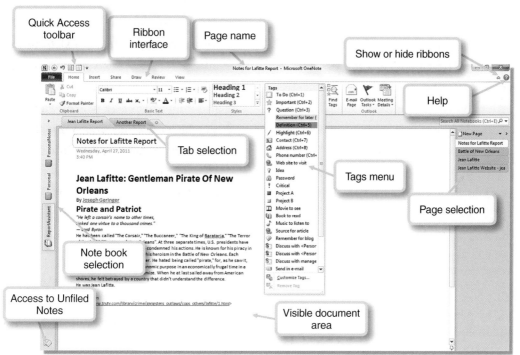

◀ FIGURE A.3
Anatomy of OneNote 2010

There is no traditional Save icon in either the Quick Access toolbar or the File menu because OneNote will automatically save changes to your document.

The Home ribbon (also shown in Figure A.3) contains the formatting commands and styles that can be applied to the text of your notes page. This ribbon also contains the available tags for notes, shown in an expanded list in Figure A.3. Tags are annotations to the content of your document that identify different characteristics for the individual note, such as Question, Contact, and Critical; these tags appear as small icons next to the text or as a highlight color over the text. You can use the *Find Tags* icon to locate all of the tags in the current page of notes. The Home ribbon also contains the links to the functionality integration with Microsoft Outlook, enabling you to email a page from your notebook, set an Outlook task, or interface with your meetings.

The Insert ribbon, shown in Figure A.4, can be used to add additional media content to your notes page, including images, screen clippings, external files, and file printouts. This is also where you can initiate the process to add an audio or video note to your page using the *Record Audio* and *Record Video* icons, respectively.

The Share ribbon contains shortcut links for adding your notebook to your SkyDrive on Windows Live or to a Microsoft SharePoint site. You can also create a new shared notebook from this ribbon or search notes by author. The Draw ribbon, shown in Figure A.5, contains the functionality for using your mouse as a pen on the document. This is particularly helpful with a tablet PC that uses a stylus. You can also use the automated functions to convert your ink markup to text or equations.

The Review ribbon includes spelling and grammar checks as well as research and translation options. The View ribbon, shown in Figure A.6, allows you to change the modality of operation; these options are Dock to Desktop, Full Page View, and Normal View. You can also customize the appearance of your notebook and create

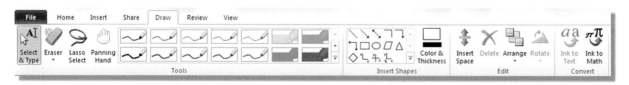

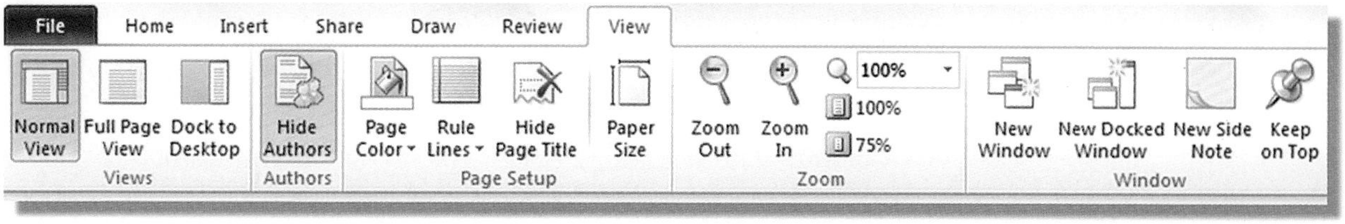

▲ FIGURE A.6
View ribbon in
OneNote 2010

a side note, which acts like a managed version of a sticky note.

A.2.2

Adding and Organizing Media and Notes

OneNote supports a variety of note-taking options. You can click anywhere on the page and start typing to create a new note. You can also add any form of media, including images, video, and audio; in fact, you can easily record audio and video notes if your computer is equipped with a microphone or Webcam. Selecting the Draw ribbon enables you to turn your mouse cursor into a pen tip or highlighter to write text into your notebook; you can even use automated text recognition inside OneNote to convert your written notes into typed text or equations. OneNote has a number of context-sensitive ribbons to support modification of the media elements within the document, including the Playback ribbon for Audio & Video from which you can review your recordings or media elements and record new audio and video notes.

The OneNote file can contain multiple individual notebooks, each divided into sections located in the tab names across the top of the document window for the open notebook. Each of the sections has associated pages located on the left side of the open document; you can add a new page by selecting *New Page*. You can click and drag to rearrange the order of any of these elements, including the notebooks. This level of organization allows you to manage your notes effectively. If you have any notes that are not filed, you can find them and arrange them using the *Unfiled Notes* icon at the lower-left corner of the interface.

Linked Notes

A.2.3

OneNote can be used to take what are called Linked Notes. These are context-sensitive notes that include a link to the active document in any other Office product beside which OneNote is docked. Linked Notes are standard text notes or snippets of content that include a link to the document on which you were working when the note was created. For instance, if you copy or cut content from a document in any other Office product, you can paste it into OneNote to retain it, and OneNote will automatically create a link to the original document. You can also click in the open docked notebook for OneNote and start typing a note; this activates a document link that will appear beside the content. To access the source of the clipping or open the document to which the note applies, double-click the icon representing the linked program.

If you copy content or notes from a Web site, OneNote will automatically add the source to the end of the clipping. This allows you to better maintain any citations you need to add for an article or paper, and it also allows you to easily access the source of the information later. You cannot copy images directly to One-Note from a Web site source; if you try to drag an image into OneNote, you will only get a citation of the source. Images can be added to OneNote from other sources such as other Office documents or through the use of the *Send to OneNote 2010* function-ality, which acts like a standard document printer.

To dock OneNote to the desktop to allow you to take Linked Notes for your other applications, select the *Dock to* *Desktop* icon. This will move your appli-cation to the right side of the screen and open Page view, which contains a special Page ribbon for creating and managing pages and hides the notebook organi-zation. Linked Notes will be active by default. You can turn the linking on and off by using the linked notes menu (which looks like a chain link). To return to Nor-mal view, click the *Normal View* icon in the Quick Access toolbar, press the *F11* key, or click *Normal View* in the *View* ribbon. Figure A.7 shows an example of the docking and Linked Notes.

Printing to OneNote

A.2.4

Installing OneNote on your machine gives you the ability to use a spe-cial printer called Send to OneNote

▼ **FIGURE A.7**
Docked view and Linked Notes in OneNote 2010

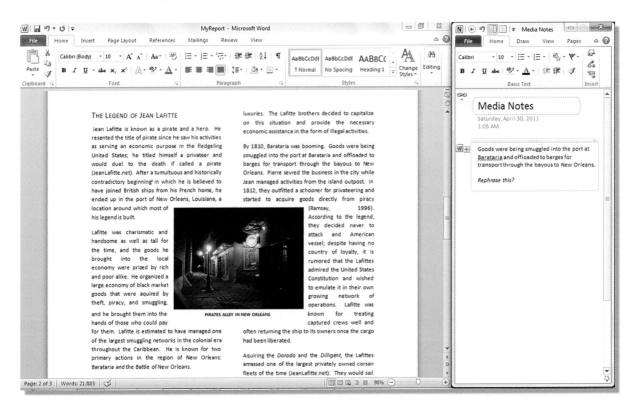

Live ID and is discussed further in Appendix B, "Online Document Creation and Collaboration." Details of constructing a Windows Live ID (whether you use a Windows machine or a Macintosh) are found in Chapter 4.

2010 from any other program on your machine. This works like any other print dialog box. An example of the process is shown in Figure A.8.

Once you have chosen OneNote as the destination, you will be prompted to select a location for your printout within your existing notebooks for OneNote. When you select a destination, a new page called "Untitled Page" will be created in that section with the print results. Entering a title in the area indicated by the dotted line adds that title both in the title section and the righthand navigation area.

A.2.5 Saving and Sharing Notebooks

You can save OneNote notebooks to your SkyDrive using your Windows Live ID. SkyDrive serves as an online storage location that is free to use with a Windows

To share one of your OneNote notebooks, select the *File* menu and choose *Share*. This is a three-step process, as shown in Figure A.9. First select a notebook that you want to share. Next, you must choose whether you want to place the notebook on your SkyDrive or on a network location such as a SharePoint site. Make sure that you are placing it in a location that is secure enough for the information contained within it. If you have any personal information in the notebook, be cautious of saving it to any network resource that can be accessed by others. The SkyDrive is password protected and allows you to select those with whom you want to share the document. Finally, you must provide your credentials for either your SkyDrive or the network location. Once the connection is established, click *Share Notebook*.

Once the upload to the SkyDrive is successful, you will be prompted to share the link to the notebook via email. You can access the link to the notebook

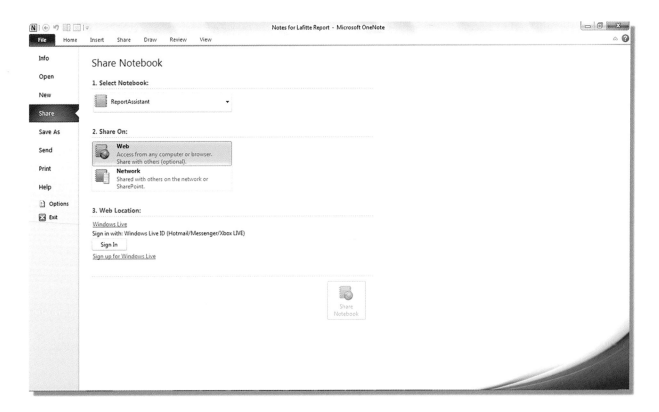

▲ FIGURE A.9
Steps to share
a notebook in
OneNote 2010

at any time by selecting the *File* menu and choosing *Share*. Only people to whom you give permission on your Sky-Drive account can access the file via the online link.

A.3 MICROSOFT WORD NOTEBOOK LAYOUT VIEW FOR MACINTOSH

While the Macintosh version of Office does not include OneNote in the 2011 suite, Word 2011 comes with a special view called Notebook View that offers some of the functionality of OneNote on the Macintosh. This is a tool for taking notes and organizing them into pages and sections. The note-taking functionality is not as extensive as in OneNote, but it does allow for the addition of text notes, using the mouse as a pen in the document, and adding audio notes.

Notebook Layout View

A.3.1

When you click on Notebook Layout View in Word 2011, you will be prompted to create a new document or convert your existing document. This is a special version of a Word document with its own unique properties and interface that allows you to manage notes and add quick audio notes. The interface for the Notebook Layout View for Word 2011 is shown in Figure A.10.

The Home ribbon contains formatting commands for the notes. You can use the note levels to organize your document into an outline and rearrange elements within it. You can also change

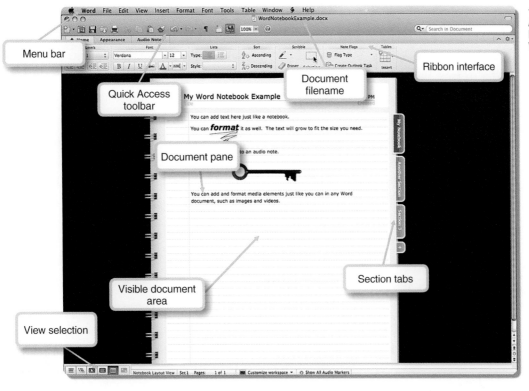

Menu bar

Quick Access
toolbar

Document
filename

Ribbon interface

Document pane

Visible document
area

Section tabs

View selection

the list formatting and list styles. The Scribble panel allows you to use your mouse as a pen tool on the document to add written notes; this is most beneficial when using a tablet computer with a stylus interface. The Note Flags panel can be used to add annotations to your notes, such as text that indicates a priority level or a colored checkbox that can be used to create tasks. You can also insert a table and create an Outlook task from the Home ribbon.

The Appearance ribbon, shown in Figure A.11, allows you to customize the design of your notebook. You can change the background pattern for the notebook, the style of the tabs, and the spacing on the rule lines (or get rid of them), as well as rename the tabs of your notebook, change the tab colors, and remove the tabs.

Adding and Organizing Media and Notes

A.3.2

You can enter notes in your document just as you would in any other Word document. The page is divided into individual lines and you can skip to the line you want to use by clicking inside of it. The active line is

indicated by a small dot in the margin. This is also where the annotations appear for any flags that you have added. You can add any media to your notes that is available from the Media Browser or any other source that works for other Word documents. These will all have the usual context-sensitive ribbons to handle the media as necessary, including text wrapping settings for images and other objects that are available in standard word processing documents.

One additional feature of the Notebook Layout View is the ability to add audio notes to your document. These will appear as an audio icon in the margin of the page. The Audio Notes ribbon, shown in Figure A.12, allows you to record and play back the audio notes. Adding new notes will continue recording where the last note ended if you add them to the same line. You can also export these notes to the MP4 file format.

▼ **FIGURE A.12**
Audio Notes ribbon in Word 2011 Notebook Layout View

APPENDIX

B

Online Document Creation and Collaboration

WINDOWS LIVE SKYDRIVE

A benefit of creating a Microsoft Windows Live ID is gaining access to the SkyDrive. The SkyDrive is a free online storage location that gives you 25 GB of storage with password protection and the ability to share your documents with others. The instructions for creating a Windows Live ID can be found in Section 4.4.4. Once you have created your account, log in at *login. live.com* and choose the *Office* link at the top of the page. The window shown in Figure B.1 will appear.

From this window, you can use the Web app versions of some of the Microsoft Office applications to create new documents online without having to access the full version of the software. This includes Word, PowerPoint, Excel, and OneNote. After you have created the documents, you can share them online or download them to your local machine. To create a document or folder, select *New* and choose the Web app you would like to create. The Web app versions of the software have more limited capabilities than the standalone versions, but they are useful tools for creating quick documents and collaborating with others. When you select a document or folder to create, you will be prompted to give it a name.

Microsoft Word Web App

The Word Web App on SkyDrive has three standard ribbons you can use to create your document. The File menu gives you the ability to save your document and to share it with others. Figure B.2 shows an example of the interface and ribbons for the Word Web App.

The Home ribbon contains the standard formatting commands along with copy and paste shortcuts and the Spelling icon to check spelling in the document. You can utilize styles in this version, but you cannot modify the styles themselves. The Insert ribbon allows you to add

➤ **FIGURE B.1**
Windows Live
SkyDrive access

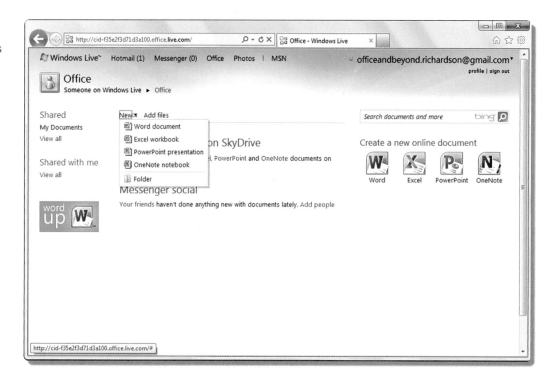

➤ **FIGURE B.2**
Word Web App
interface and
ribbons

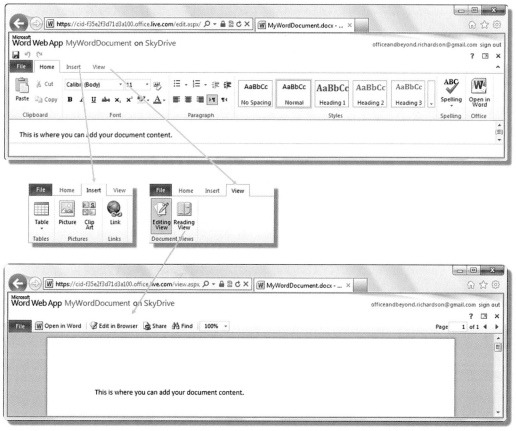

a subset of media, including a table, hyperlink, image, and clip art. The Clip Art icon allows you to search the available clip art at *www.office.com*. The View ribbon lets you select the default Editing view or an optional Reading view that displays the document but does not let you edit it.

B.1.2

Microsoft PowerPoint Web App

When you create a presentation using the PowerPoint Web App, you are prompted to select a presentation style before you can edit the document. To leave the style blank, you can simply click *Cancel*. Once you have selected a style, choose *Apply*. You will be taken to the slide creation interface with a preview of the slides on the left and the current slide that you can edit in the main document pane. Figure B.3 shows an example of the PowerPoint Web App interface and ribbons.

The Home ribbon contains shortcuts for copying and pasting elements into your slides as well as applying font and paragraph formatting; you can copy or hide the slide using this ribbon as well. To insert a slide into your presentation, select *New Slide* from the *Home* ribbon; you will be prompted to select the slide layout from the predefined list. The Insert ribbon gives you the ability to add links, images, clip art, and SmartArt. The SmartArt icon has its own context-sensitive ribbon to select the graphic type and adjust the parameters of the graphic. The View ribbon lets you display the presentation in Slide Show view and switch between the Editing view and Reading view. The final element of the View

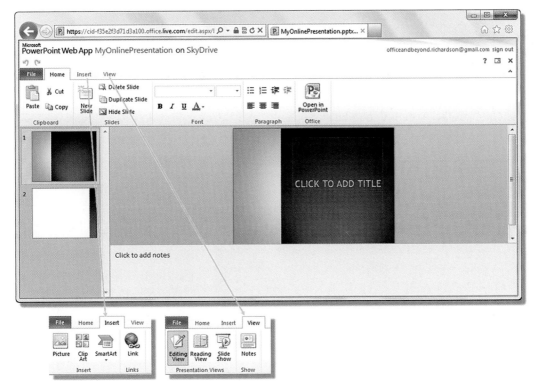

◄ **FIGURE B.3**
PowerPoint Web App interface and ribbons

ribbon is the Notes icon, which toggles the display of the notes pane in the interface so you can add or hide notes.

Microsoft Excel Web App

The Excel Web App allows you to create simple spreadsheets online. The File menu does not contain a Save command because the document saves automatically when you complete an action. The worksheets are located at the bottom of the interface. The Home ribbon contains the formatting options, including the ability to wrap text in the cells, along with limited data options like sorting and filtering. You can add charts to your document from the Insert Ribbon by choosing the data you want to use to create the chart and then selecting the type of chart; this will insert the chart and give you the context-sensitive Design ribbon for Chart Tools. Figure B.4 shows the interface and ribbons for the Excel Web App.

Microsoft OneNote Web App

OneNote is a digital notebook application for the Windows version of Office. It is covered in detail in Appendix A, "Additional Productivity Software." The online version, OneNote Web App, is organized into sections and pages. You can title each page by entering text in the title section, and you can rename sections by right-clicking the section name and choosing *Rename*. The sections and pages are listed on the left side of the interface. To add new notes to your document, click anywhere in the page. The OneNote Web App saves your changes automatically after you complete them, so once again there is no Save command. Figure B.5 shows the interface for the OneNote Web App.

The Home ribbon of the interface contains formatting options, the spell-check functionality, and tags you can use to annotate your notes to assist you in organization. The Insert ribbon allows you to add tables, images, hyperlinks, and clip art, as well as new pages in the current section and new sections in your notebook. The View ribbon contains the Editing View and Reading View icons, and lets you show or hide the author information for the notes added to the page.

Sharing and Saving Documents

In the Office view of your SkyDrive, you can navigate to the folder where your document is located in order to share or download it. When you have located your document, hover the cursor over it to get a menu of options, as shown in Figure B.6. You can download

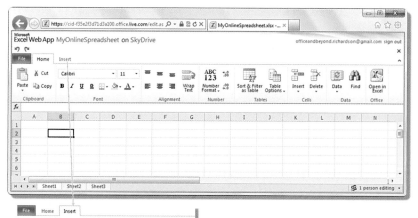

▼ **FIGURE B.4**
Excel Web App interface and ribbons

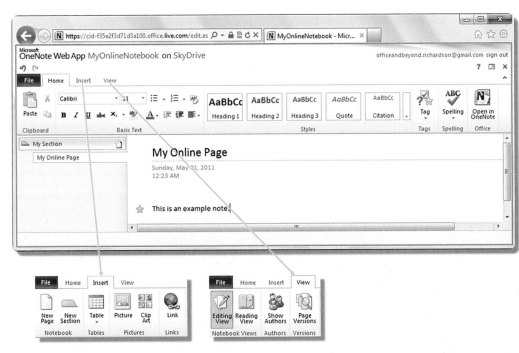

▲ FIGURE B.5
OneNote Web
App interface and
ribbons

the document to your local machine by choosing the *More* menu and then selecting *Download*. You will be prompted with instructions for completing the download based on the Web browser you are using.

To share a document, you must first edit the permissions to indicate who is allowed to view it. To change the permissions to include additional people (who can all edit the document online for collaboration efforts), hover over the document name, select the *More* menu, choose *Share*, and then select *Edit Permissions*. You will be taken to a new page where you can edit the permissions of your document and add email addresses for others who are allowed to access it. Anyone you list must register for a Windows Live ID if they do not already have one associated with the email address you enter.

Once you have edited the permissions for your document, send a link to the document by hovering over the title, selecting the *More* menu, and choosing *Send a Link*. This opens a dialog box where you can select those who will receive a link to the document. Selecting *Get a Link* from the *More* menu will give you a Web address

▼ FIGURE B.6
Downloading
and sharing
documents on the
SkyDrive

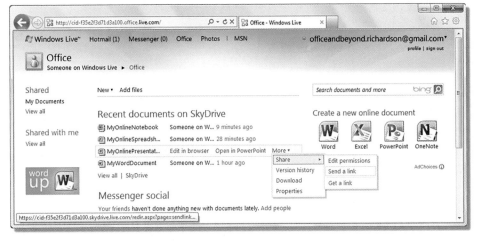

at which the document can be accessed by those with permission. You can also create a public link to the document, which allows it to be accessed by anyone without signing into Windows Live ID; the document can be viewed at the public link but cannot be edited unless it is made public in the permissions for the file. Delete your files by selecting the *Delete* menu icon (which looks like an *X*).

B.1.6

Microsoft Office 2011 Document Connection

Office 2011 for the Macintosh comes with a special application called Document Connection that allows you to access your SkyDrive files (or a SharePoint site) on your local machine without going through a Web browser. You can use this application to read and open documents on your local machine that are saved on your SkyDrive and to upload new documents to your SkyDrive directly from your machine. This includes any documents that have been shared via your Windows Live ID account. You must log in to your Windows Live ID account to access your documents. Figure B.7 shows the interface for Document Connection.

GOOGLE DOCS

B.2

Google Docs is another online application that provides free file storage and online document creation and collaboration. Google Docs allows simultaneous access to a document by multiple authors (each author must be authorized by the original document creator to edit the document). You can register for a Google Docs account the same way you register for Gmail by Google. Note that you do not have to have a Gmail address to access Google Docs. Instructions for creating a Gmail or Google account are in Section 4.4.3. Figure B.8 shows the Google Docs interface. You can access Google Docs by selecting *Documents* on the account interface or by selecting *More* and then *Documents* from the top of the window on the Google home page (*www. google.com*).

From this interface, you have the ability to upload documents and folders to your Google Docs account, which stores them online. Google Docs provides 1 GB of storage space for any files that are not created in the Google Docs format (or converted

▼ **FIGURE B.7**
Office 2011
Document
Connection
interface

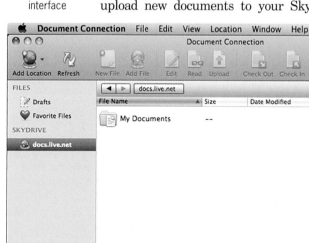

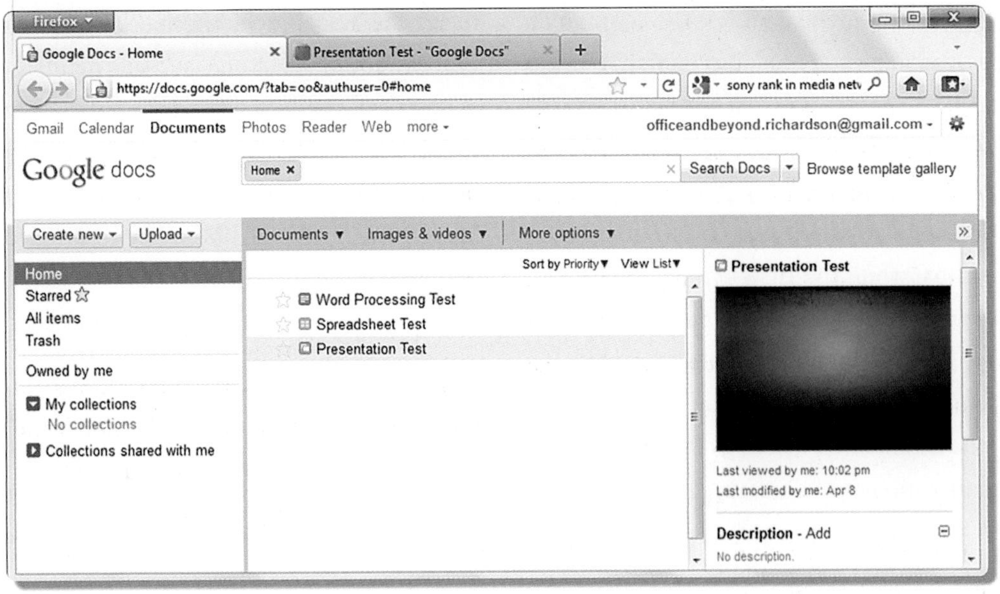

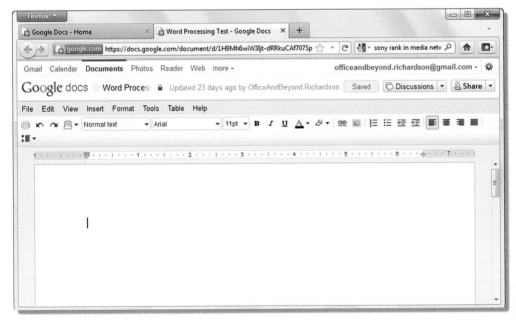

▲ FIGURE B.8
Google Docs
interface

to that format). You can also view your folders and the documents contained within them. To open an existing document, select the filename in the main interface. To create a new document, select the document type from the *Create New* menu.

B.2.1 Document

The document application in Google Docs allows you to perform most of the tasks necessary for word processing. The interface, shown in Figure B.9, is a menu and toolbar interface. The toolbar contains most of the font and paragraph formatting commands. You can use the File menu to save, rename, and close the document, as well as download it to your local machine (using the *Download As* command) as an ODT, Word, PDF, or HTML document.

▲ FIGURE B.9
Document example
in Google Docs

The Edit menu contains the commands for undoing and redoing actions, copying and pasting, and selecting all content, along with the find and replace functionality. The View menu can be used to toggle the display of the rulers and spelling suggestions, while the Insert menu allows you to add hyperlinks, images, headers, footers, page breaks, equations, and symbols to your document. The Format menu has a shortcut to the available formatting effects, the Tools menu contains the command to calculate the word count, and the Table menu is used to manage and insert tables.

Presentation

B.2.2

The presentation application of Google Docs starts you out with a single slide that has no theme or formatting. You can add a theme to your presentation by selecting the *Format* menu and choosing *Presentation settings* and then *Change theme*; this will open a dialog box where you can select a presentation theme. You can add slides by using the + icon near the the slide thumbnail view or by selecting the *Slide* menu and choosing *New Slide*; this opens a dialog box in which you can select the slide layout you want to use. Figure B.10 shows an example of the interface for the presentation application.

You can add speaker notes by selecting the *Speaker Notes* icon to the right of the document pane displaying the slide being edited. To start the presentation as a slide show, select *Start presentation* from the *View* menu. The Insert menu allows you to add various media elements to your slide, including images, videos, tables, and drawing objects. You can rename the file by selecting *Rename* from the *File* menu. The download options (accessed by selecting the *File* menu and choosing *Download As*) are PDF and PowerPoint.

Spreadsheet

B.2.3

The spreadsheet application in Google Docs allows you to manage data in cells just as you can with other spreadsheet software. You can utilize formulas and formatting on the cell entries as well as add new worksheets to the document. The interface, shown in Figure B.11, is a menu and toolbar interface. The formula bar is located beneath the main toolbar. The View menu allows you

▼ FIGURE B.10
Presentation example in Google Docs

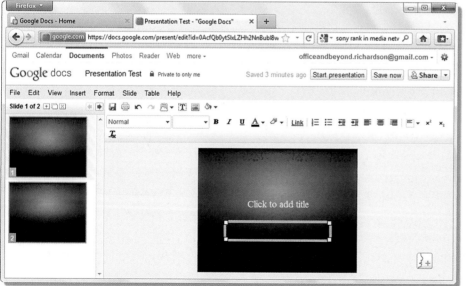

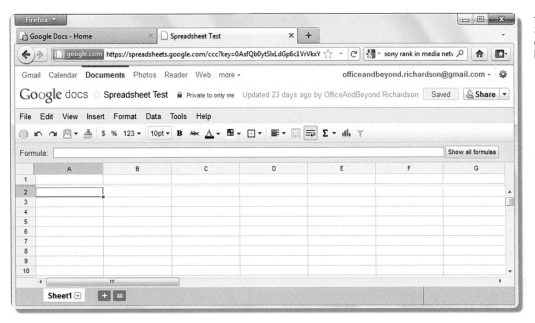

to add rows and columns to your spreadsheet, and the Data menu lets you freeze rows and columns. The rest of the functionality available is linked to the toolbar. The File menu can be used to rename your document and save any changes. You can download your document by selecting *Download As* from the *File* menu; the formats supported include PDF, Excel, OpenOffice.org format, and HTML.

B.2.4
Sharing and Saving Documents

To share a document in Google Docs, you can hover your cursor over the document and select the *Actions* menu; from here, select *Share* and choose *Share settings*. This opens the dialog box shown in Figure B.12, where you can change the permissions on the document by adding email addresses for people who should be granted access to your document. After you have added the email addresses, select the mailing options you want to use. When you

click *Share*, the permissions for the file will be updated and the email notification will be sent according to the specifications you have indicated.

▲ FIGURE B.12
Google Docs
Share Settings
example

You can also select the *Download* option from the *Actions* menu. This allows you to download your online documents to your local machine in the specified format. Office, OpenOffice.org, and PDF are all generally supported for document export. You can click and drag the title of the document to move it to a different folder or drag it to the trash to remove it. Selecting *Move to trash* in the *Actions* menu also will move it to the trash folder. When you click the *Trash* folder, the option to *Empty Trash* will delete all items in the folder.

Excel Functions

The companion DVD for this text contains six files demonstrating various Excel functions that you can modify for your own use and understanding. These can be found in the *Excel-Templates* folder and each of them has multiple spreadsheets utilizing the different functions available. This is not an exhaustive list of all available functions, but these represent the ones most commonly used in the following categories: **Math, Text, Formulas, Conditional Formatting, Logical, and Lookup**. These are part of the text, *Microsoft Excel Functions and Formulas 2/e*; B. Held; 9781936420018, available from Mercury Learning and Information for those interested in advanced study in spreadsheet software functions.

APPENDIX

D

Answers to Odd-Numbered Chapter Knowledge Check Questions

Chapter 1

1. A   3. A   5. C   7. A   9. A

Chapter 2

1. A   3. B   5. True   7. A   9. True

Chapter 3

1. D   3. A   5. True   7. A   9. False

Chapter 4

1. A   3. True   5. False   7. False   9. D

Chapter 5

1. C   3. C   5. False   7. True   9. True

Chapter 6

1. False   3. C   5. C   7. D   9. True

Chapter 7

1. False   3. True   5. True   7. True   9. E

Chapter 8

1. D   3. D   5. True   7. A   9. B

Chapter 9

1. A   3. True   5. A   7. A   9. False

Chapter 10

1. False   3. False   5. C   7. False   9. True

Chapter 11

1. C   3. True   5. B   7. False   9. D

Chapter 12

1. False   3. False   5. True   7. C   9. D

Chapter 13

1. False   3. C   5. True   7. True   9. False

Chapter 14

1. A   3. A   5. A   7. B   9. False

Chapter 15

1. A   3. A   5. A   7. B   9. False

Chapter 16

1. A   3. B   5. True   7. A   9. True

Index

A

Access database application, 372
Access 2010 user interface
    Access ribbon, 374–375
    database creation, 374–375
    database table creation, 376–378
    data types, 380–382
    primary keys, 379–380
    starting Access application, 373
    working with Design view, 378–379
adding shapes, 183–184
adding tables, 182–183
Adobe® Reader®
    version 9 for Macintosh, 438–439
    for Windows version, 437–438
advanced cell referencing, 330–331
alignment, definition, 209
AND function, 355–356
animations, 284–286
Apple Safari, 58–60
application, definition, 3
area chart, 342–343
ARPANET, 46–47
aspect ratio, definition, 209
attachment data, 381
AutoNumber data, 381
AVERAGE function, 350

B

bar chart, 342
Basic Input/Output System (BIOS), 11–12
bibliography, 155–156
blank pages, 161

bookmark, definition, 56
booting process, 12
brightness, definition, 208
bullets and numbering, 125–126, 242–243

C

cable high-speed Internet, 52
calendar, 94–96
cell, definition, 296
central processing unit (CPU), 3
Certificate Authority (CA), 53
chain of custody, 397
charts
    area, 342–343
    bar, 342
    column, 341–342
    data, 314–315
    formatting, 315–316
    line, 342
    in OpenOffice.org Calc, 320–322
    pie, 342
    in PowerPoint presentation,
        278–281
    scatter, 343
citation management
    bibliography creation, 155–156
    definition, 151
    footnotes and endnotes, 153–155
    in Word 2011, 152
clip art, 216–221
cognitive guidance, 250
color saturation, 208
color tone, 208
column chart, 341–342

column, definition, 296

Command Prompt window, 49

comments, 187–188

common functions, 349–351

compress picture, 208

computer
  definition, 2
  hardware, 3–4
  software, 2–3
  working process
    BIOS, 11–12
    data storage, 14–15
    do's and dont's, 15–16
    input hardware devices, 12–13
    output hardware devices, 13–14
  working with files
    Text Edit for Macintosh, 40–41
    WordPad on Windows, 37–40

computer memory, 5

computer system
  elements of, 2
  purchasing, 4–7

CONCATENATE function, 351

conditional formatting, 337–338

connection speed, definition, 52

constructing effective presentation
  building needs, 253–255
  contributions
    effective visualization, 255–256
    modifying layouts, 256
    summarize and conclude, 257–258
    tips for success, 256–257
  grabbing attention in first slide, 252–253
  masterpiece presentation
    live presentations, 258–260
    recording narration, 260–261
    sharing, 261–263
  outlining
    best practices, 251–252
    slide notes, 250–251

contrast, definition, 208

Control Panel, 25–26

Copy command, 110

Copyright law, 147

COUNT function, 350

cover letter
  definition, 119
  OpenOffice.org Writer, 136–138
  Word processing, 119–121

cover page, 161–162

creating a research report
  considerations, 146

Document Map pane, 150
  Navigation pane, 150
  observing and managing, 147
  outlining document, 147–148
  using and managing styles, 148–149

creating effective presentations
  visual style
    adding and formatting slide footers, 243–244
    branding slides, 246–249
    bullets and numbering, 242–243
    colors, fonts, and effects, 239–241
    formatting text on Slide Master, 244–246
    modifying Slide Master, 237–238
    planning design, 238–239
    theme assignment, 239
    writing value proposition, 236

cropping, definition, 208

crop to fit, 209

Ctrl-End command, 313

Ctrl-Home command, 313

currency data, 381

Cut command, 110

D

Dashboard, 31

data
  chart, 314–315
  definition, 46
  types, 381
  validation, 359

database
  backups, 385
  compressing, 385–386
  creating, 374–375
  definition, 372
  designing, 384–385
  repairing, 385–386
  software, 348

database table creation, 376–378

data integrity, 382

data storage, 14–15

Date/Time data, 381

delimiter, 335

desktop, definition, 24

desktop gadgets, 26–27

dialog box, definition, 24

dial-up Internet connection, 52

digital certificates, 53

digital phone service, 51

digital subscriber line (DSL), 52

disk formatting process, 15
document comparison, 184–185
document elements
    blank pages, 161
    borders, 160–161
    cover page, 161–162
    index, 163
    page break, 161
    table of authorities, 164
    table of contents, 162–163
    table of figures, 163–164
    watermarks, 160
document management, 107–108
document templates, 129–131
Download Manager, 54
download speed, definition, 52
Downloads window, 58–59
driver, 12
Drop Cap icon, 178
dynamic password, 9

E
e-commerce, 53
editing documents
    comments, 187–188
    document comparison, 184–185
    track changes, 185–187
editing equations, 180–181
editing presentations
    custom layout, 289–290
    hiding and showing slides, 290
    opening and existing, 287
    optimizing and exporting images, 291
    slide setup and orientation, 288–289
Electronic mail (E-mail)
    address, 70–71
    clients
        Macintosh mail, 85–87
        Microsoft Windows Live Mail,
            84–85
        Mozilla Thunderbird, 87–89
        remote connection, 90
    definition, 68
    etiquette, 97–99
    structure, 68–70
encryption, 53
endnotes, 153–155
Ergonomics, 6
Excel functions, 457
Exit command, 107
Exposé and Spaces, 31–32
extended validation (EV) key, 57

eXtensible Markup Language (XML), 367
external data management
    exporting data, 367
    external data sources, 366–367

F
File menu
    Exit command, 107
    New command, 105–106
    Open command, 106
    OpenOffice.org Writer, 135–137
    Print command, 107
    productivity software, 105–107
    Save As command, 106
    Save command, 106
filter
    definition, 332
    types, 422
filter by condition, 422
filter by form, 421
filter by selection, 422
Flash Player, 62
Font, definition, 121
Font panel, 121–124
footnotes, 153–155
Force Quit option, 32
Format Painter, 125
formatting charts, 315–316
formatting elements
    comments, 339–340
    conditional formatting, 337–338
    tab color, 338–339
    text box, 340
formula
    definition, 296
    freezing cells, 310
    mathematical calculations,
        309–310
    SUM function, 310–311
Freeze Panes, 307–308
function wizard, 356–357

G
Gmail
    account creation, 78–79
    composing, 80–81
    logging out and logging in, 81–82
    navigating and opening, 79–80
Goal Seek, 365
Google Docs
    document application, 453–454
    interface, 452–453
    presentation application, 454

sharing and saving documents, 455–456
spreadsheet application, 454–455
graphical user interface (GUI), 24

H

handout creation
    Handout Master, 269–270
    Notes Master, 270–272
hardware, definition, 3
hardware devices
    input, 12–13
    output, 13–14
    processing, 14
headers and footers, 134–135
Help files, 108
hibernation, 8
HLOOKUP function, 354
Hotmail
    account creation, 72–74
    composing, 76–77
    logging out and logging in, 77–78
    navigating and opening, 74–76
hyperlinks, 381
Hypertext Markup Language (HTML),
  48, 367

I

icon, definition, 24
IF statement, 355
iMac power button, 9
index/indexing, 163, 383–384
information, definition, 46
inner join, 407
input device, 3
input hardware devices, 12–13
Internet
    connecting to, 51–52
    connection types, 52
    definition, 46
Internet Corporation for Assigned Names and
  Numbers (ICANN), 50
Internet Explorer, 52–56
Internet Message Access Protocol (IMAP), 72
Internet Service Providers (ISPs), 51

J

junction table
    definition, 397
    for many-to-many relationship, 399

K

keyboard, 13
keyboard shortcut, 27

L

LEFT function, 351
line chart, 342
linked media, 261
Linked Notes, 441–442
list management
    definition, 331
    removing duplicates, 334
    sorting and filters, 332–333
    table formatting, 336–337
    text to columns, 334–336
live presentations, 258–260
local area network (LAN),
  definition, 50
logical operators evaluation,
  355–356
LOWER function, 352

M

Macintosh computer, 9–11
Macintosh mail, 85–87
Macintosh OS X desktop
    Dashboard, 31
    The Dock, 18, 30–31
    Exposé and Spaces, 31–32
    The Finder, 19, 29–30
    Force Quit option, 32
Mail Merge
    definition, 170
    in OpenOffice.org Writer, 175–178
    in Word 2010, 171–174
    in Word 2011, 174–175
Malware, definition, 61
managing citations
    bibliography creation, 155–156
    footnotes and endnotes, 153–155
    in Word 2011, 152
many-to-many relationship, 397–398
masterpiece presentation
    live presentations, 258–260
    recording narration, 260–261
    sharing, 261–263
MAX function, 350
memo data, 381
menu, definition, 24
microphone, 13
Microsoft Access
    data manipulation using queries
        basic queries, 404–405
        inner and outer joins, 407–410
        query design, 405–407
        SQL view, 407

relationships
    defining, 398–404
    types, 396–398
  report development, 410–411
  sharing database, 428–430
Microsoft Excel 2010
  Data ribbon, 298–299
  Formulas ribbon, 298–299
  Home ribbon, 298
  Insert ribbon, 298
  interface, 297
  Page Layout ribbon, 298
  Review ribbon, 299
  View ribbon, 299
Microsoft Excel 2011
  Data ribbon, 301–302
  Formulas ribbon, 301–302
  Home ribbon, 301
  interface, 300
  Layout ribbon, 301
  Quick Access toolbar, 300–301
  Review ribbon, 302
  Tables ribbon, 301
Microsoft Excel Web App, 450
Microsoft Internet Explorer,
  52–56
Microsoft Office 2011 Document
  Connection, 452
Microsoft OneNote
  adding and organizing media and
    notes, 441
  definition, 439
  Linked Notes, 441–442
  printing, 442–443
  saving and sharing notebooks,
    443–444
Microsoft OneNote 2010
  Home ribbon, 440
  Insert ribbon, 440
  interface, 439
  Quick Access toolbar, 439–440
  Review ribbon, 440
  Share ribbon, 440
  View ribbon, 440–441
Microsoft OneNote Web App, 450
Microsoft Outlook
  calendar, 94–96
  contacts, 96–97
  definition, 90
  managing E-mail, 93–94
  Outlook 2010 version, 91–92
  Outlook 2011 version, 92–93
  tasks and notes, 97

Microsoft PowerPoint 2010
  clip art, 217
  Design ribbon, 197
  File menu, 195
  Home ribbon, 196–197
  Insert ribbon, 197
  Review ribbon, 198
  Slide Show ribbon, 197–198
  View ribbon, 198–199
Microsoft PowerPoint 2011
  clip art, 217–218
  Home ribbon, 199–200
  Quick Access toolbar, 199
  Review ribbon, 201
  Slide Show ribbon, 200–201
  Text Effects icon, 203
  Themes ribbon, 200
Microsoft PowerPoint Web App, 449–450
Microsoft Windows Live Hotmail
  composing, 76–77
  creating account, 72–74
  logging out and logging in, 77–78
  navigating and opening, 74–76
Microsoft Windows Live ID, 82–83
Microsoft Windows Live Mail, 84–85
Microsoft Word 2010
  AutoCorrect options, 127
  bibliography and selection menu, 156
  caption dialog box, 160
  comment, 187
  compare documents dialog box, 185
  context-sensitive table ribbon, 183
  document comparison, 186
  Find and Replace dialog box, 130
  footnote and endnote dialog box, 155
  footnote placement, 154
  Home ribbon, 113
  Insert ribbon, 114
  Navigation pane, 115, 150
  Page Layout ribbon, 114
  References ribbon, 151
  Review ribbon, 114–115, 184
  Shapes menu, 183
  Source Manager, 151
  Spelling and Grammar, 128
  standard interface, 113
  symbol selection, 179
  table of contents dialog box, 163
  Template selection, 131
  View ribbon, 114–115
Microsoft Word 2011
  Citations window, 152
  cover page, 162

Document Elements ribbon, 117
Document Map pane, 117, 150
Full Screen view, 118
Home ribbon, 116
Layout ribbon, 116–117
for Macintosh
    adding and organizing media and
      notes, 445–446
    Notebook Layout View, 444–445
Mail Merge manager, 174–175
Quick Access toolbar, 115–116
Search pane, 130
Template selection, 131
Microsoft Word Web App, 447–449
MIN function, 350
10-minute mark, 252
monitor, 13
mouse, 13
Mozilla Firefox, 56–58
Mozilla Thunderbird, 87–89
My Documents folder, 33–35

N
navigating desktop
  Macintosh os X desktop
    Dashboard, 31
    The Dock, 30–31
    Exposé and Spaces, 31–32
    The Finder, 29–30
    Force Quit option, 32
  Windows 7 desktop
    Control Panel, 25–26
    desktop gadgets, 26–27
    jump lists, 27
    libraries feature, 27–28
    Start menu, 25
    Task Manager, 27
nesting functions, 351
Netscape®, 48
network, definition, 46
New command, 105–106
New document (Ctrl-N), 109
Notes Master, 270–272
NOT function, 355
number data, 381

O
one-to-many relationship, 396–397
one-to-one relationship, 396
online document creation
  Google Docs
    document application, 453–454

interface, 452–453
presentation application, 454
sharing and saving documents,
    455–456
spreadsheet application, 454–455
Skydrive
  Document Connection, 452
  Excel Web App, 450
  OneNote Web App, 450
  PowerPoint Web App, 449–450
  sharing and saving documents,
    450–452
  Word Web App, 447–449
Open command, 106
Open document (Ctrl-O), 109
OpenOffice.org, 105, 149
OpenOffice.org Base
  building tables, 386–391
  relationships
    developing queries, 413
    developing reports, 413
  simple forms
    in Design view, 428
    forms options, 425
    Form Wizard, 425
    sorting and filtering controls, 427
    split forms, 424
OpenOffice.org Calc
  budget creation, 318–320
  charts, 320–322
  interface, 316–318
OpenOffice.org Impress, 224–230
OpenOffice.org Writer
  cover letter, 136–138
  File menu, 135–137
  resume, 138–140
open source, definition, 48
OR function, 355
organizing files and folders
  on Mac, 35–37
  in Windows, 33–35
outer join, 408
outlining
  best practices, 251–252
  slide notes, 250–251
output device, 3
output hardware devices, 13–14

P
page borders, 160–161
page break, 161
Page down command, 313

page layout setting, 156–157
    formatting columns, 157–158
    graphic elements and captions, 158–160
Page up command, 313
pane, definition, 24
Paragraph panel, 124–125
password, 9, 74
Paste command, 110
personal e-mail account
    Gmail
        account creation, 78–79
        composing, 80–81
        logging out and logging in, 81–82
        navigating and opening, 79–80
    Hotmail
        account creation, 72–74
        composing, 76–77
        logging out and logging in, 77–78
        navigating and opening, 74–76
    Microsoft Windows Live ID, 82–83
    types, 70–71
pie chart, 342
pivot table
    constructing, 362–363
    definition, 362
    in formulas, 363–364
Port 25, 72
portable document format (PDF), 134, 435–436
Post Office Protocol version three (POP3), 71
presentation documents
    adding text, 212–215
    arranging, linking, grouping elements, 209–212
    clip art and screenshots, 216–221
    hyperlinks, 215–216
    inserting and formatting shapes, 203–206
    inserting, manipulating, cropping images, 206–209
    inserting screenshots, 222–223
    software, 194
    sorting slides, 221–222
    text formatting, 201–203
    transitions, 223–224
presentation software
    handout creation
        Handout Master, 269–270
        Notes Master, 270–272
    media options
        animations, 284–286
        charts, 278–281
        SmartArt tool, 281–284

        sound and video, 272–276
        tables, 276–278
primary keys, 379–380
Print command, 107
Print document (Ctrl-P), 109
printer, 13–14
productivity shortcuts, 108–109
productivity software
    definition, 104
    document management, 107–108
    File menu, 105–107
    Help files, 108
    shortcut keys, 108–109
    system clipboard, 109–110

Q

Query Wizard, 400
quick filter, 422
Quit command (Ctrl-Q), 109

R

Random-Access Memory (RAM), 5
Read-Only Memory (ROM), 5
Really Simple Syndication (RSS), 26
recording narration, 260–261
Redo Last Action (Ctrl-Y), 109
referential integrity, 401
Relational Database Management System (RDBMS), 372–373
relationship
    defining, 398–404
    many-to-many, 397–398
    one-to-many, 396–397
    one-to-one, 396
report development, 410–411
Report Wizard, 411
resume writing
    OpenOffice.org Writer, 138–140
    Word processing, 132–134
Rich Text Format (RTF), 39–40
RIGHT function, 351
ROUND function, 350
row, definition, 296

S

Save As command, 106
Save command, 106
Save document (Ctrl-S), 109
scatter chart, 343
screen capture tool, 223
screenshots, 216–223

search engine
    definition, 60
    on Web, 60–62
Secure Sockets Layer (SSL), 53
Select All Content (Ctrl-A), 109
sequences, 305–306
SharePoint, 428
sharpen, definition, 208
Shut down menu, 8
simple form
    add, delete, and print records, 419–423
    advantages, 418
    creation in layout view, 418–419
SkyDrive, 447
slide
    definition, 199
    sorting, 221–222
Slide Master
    definition, 236
    formatting text on, 244–246
    modifying, 237–238
SmartArt tool, 178, 281–284
soften, definition, 208
software applications
    client-based program, 3
    Web-based applications, 3
software program, definition, 3
software suite, definition, 104
sorting and filters, 332–333
sound and video, 272–276
sparklines, 341
speaker, 14
spelling and grammar, 126–128
spreadsheet software
    adding and formatting text, 302–304
    adding basic formulas
        freezing cells, 310
        mathematical calculations,
            309–310
        SUM function, 310–311
    business applications, 348–349
    vs. database software, 348
    directional fill, 311–312
    external data management
        exporting data, 367
        external data sources, 366–367
    formatting cells, 306–307
    formatting values, 304–305
    Freeze Panes, 307–308
    Goal Seek, 365
    navigating spreadsheets, 312–313
    nesting functions, 351

pivot table
    constructing, 362–363
    in formulas, 363–364
subtotals
    constructing, 360–361
    grouping Cells, 360
using functions
    calculation options, 357
    common functions, 349–351
    data validation, 359
    function wizard, 356–357
    IF statement, 355
    logical evaluation, 355–356
    text functions, 351–352
    tracing variables, 357–358
    value lookup, 352–355
using sequences, 305–306
Start menu, 25
static password, 9
Structured Query Language (SQL), 407
style, definition, 148
subfolder, definition, 37
subtotals
    constructing, 360–361
    definition, 359
    grouping Cells, 360
SUM function, 310–311
symbols, 179–180
system clipboard, 109–110

T
tab color, 338–339
table formatting, 336–337
table of authorities, 164
table of contents, 162–163
table of figures, 163–164
tables, 276–278
Task Manager, 27
text box, 178, 340
text data, 381
Text Edit, 40–41
text flow, 159
text functions, 351–352
text wrapping, 159
The Dock, 30–31
The Finder menu, 29–30
theme assignment, 239
thesaurus tool, 128
toolbar, definition, 24
tracing variables, 357–358
track changes, 185–187

U

Undo Last Action (Ctrl-U), 109
Uniform Resource Locaters (URLs), 50–51
upload speed, definition, 52
UPPER function, 351–352

V

VALUE function, 352
value proposition, 236
video cameras, 13
visual style presentations
    adding and formatting slide footers, 243–244
    branding slides, 246–249
    bullets and numbering, 242–243
    colors, fonts, and effects, 239–241
    formatting text on Slide Master, 244–246
    modifying Slide Master, 237–238
    planning design, 238–239
    theme assignment, 239
VLOOKUP function, 353

W

watermarks, 160
Web
    background and historical context, 46–48
    connecting to Internet, 51–52
    and fair use, 62–63
    search engines on, 60–62
    working process, 48–51
Web browser
    Apple Safari, 58–60
    definition, 47
    icons for, 48
    Microsoft Internet Explorer, 52–56
    Mozilla Firefox, 56–58
    plug-ins, 62
Web crawler service, 60
Web page, 48
Web server, definition, 47
Website, definition, 47
wide area network (WAN), definition, 50
window, definition, 24
Windows 7 desktop
    Control Panel, 25–26
    desktop gadgets, 26–27
    jump lists, 27
    Start menu, 25
    Task Manager, 27

Windows Live Skydrive
    Microsoft Excel Web App, 450
    Microsoft Office 2011 Document Connection, 452
    Microsoft OneNote Web App, 450
    Microsoft PowerPoint Web App, 449–450
    Microsoft Word Web App, 447–449
    sharing and saving documents, 450–452
Windows operating system, 16–17
Windows personal computer, 7–9
wireless 3G networks, 52
wizard, definition, 170
WordPad, 37–40
Word processing
    bullets and numbering, 125–126
    cover letter writing, 119–121
    definition, 111
    document review
        Find and Replace, 128–129
        spelling and grammar, 126–128
        thesaurus tool, 128
    document templates, 129–131
    document types, 134
    formatting text
        Font panel, 121–124
        Format Painter, 125
        Paragraph panel, 124–125
    headers and footers, 134–135
    resume writing, 132–134
Word processing documents
    adding shapes, 183–184
    adding tables, 182–183
    Drop Cap icon, 178
    editing equations, 180–181
    symbols, 179–180
    text boxes, 178
Word processing software, 110–111
workbook, 296
worksheet
    adding and deleting rows and columns, 329
    advanced cell referencing, 330–331
    hiding rows and columns, 330
    merging and splitting cells, 328
workspace arrangement, 367
World Wide Web, definition, 46

Y

Yes/No data, 381